LearningExpress®'s
CLEP
Test Prep

LearningExpress®'s
CLEP
Test Prep

NEW YORK

Library of Congress Cataloging-in-Publication Data:
LearningExpress's CLEP test prep.—1st ed.
    p. cm.
 ISBN: 978-1-57685-624-6
 1. College-level examinations—Study guides. 2. College Entrance
Examination Board. College-Level Examination Program. I.
LearningExpress (Organization) II. Title: CLEP test prep.
 LB2353.68.L43 2008
 378.1'662—dc22
                    2008022049

Printed in the United States of America

9 8 7 6 5 4 3 2 1

First Edition

ISBN 978-1-57685-624-6

For more information or to place an order, contact LearningExpress at:
LearningExpress
  2 Rector Street
  26th Floor
  New York, NY 10006

Or visit us at:
  www.learnatest.com

Contents

CONTENTS

CONTENTS

LearningExpress®'s
CLEP
Test Prep

Introduction ▶

▶ CLEP Test Overview

In 1965, the College Board and the Educational Testing Services created the College-Level Examination Program (CLEP). Once a person completes a CLEP exam, he or she can do any of the following:

- Continue with higher-level courses in the same discipline.
- Choose to take more electives.
- Avoid taking courses that repeat what he or she already knows.
- Earn college credit.

Individuals who take CLEP demonstrate that they have successfully achieved college-level understanding in specific subject areas. CLEP has proven to be a valuable examination for the following groups:

- people with job-related training and self-study
- students who have been home-schooled
- students who have completed the equivalent AP or advanced courses in high school
- students enrolled in unaccredited postsecondary schools who want credit for courses taken in that setting
- applicants whose potential employers require a standard assessment of skills

CLEP exams are administered at more than 1,400 test centers in colleges and universities across the United States, and approximately 3,000 colleges offer credit for satisfactory scores.

CLEP exams accurately assess candidates' understanding of college-level material. Research demonstrates that students who earn course credit through the CLEP exams perform better than those students who have completed the equivalent college-level introductory courses. Students who score well on CLEP exams can also move quickly into third- and fourth-year college courses. Most importantly, students who score well on CLEP exams often finish their degrees sooner than students who do not take CLEP exams.

▶ The Two Types of CLEP Exams

The College-Level Examination Program is made up of two types of exams—the General Exams and Subject Exams.

The CLEP General Exams measure your knowledge in five basic liberal arts areas:

- English Composition
- Social Sciences and History
- Mathematics
- Natural Sciences
- Humanities

The General Exams are not intended to measure specialized knowledge of a particular discipline; they assess knowledge within the subject areas that are commonly referred to as the liberal education requirement.

Each General Exam is a 90-minute test and, with the exception of English Composition with Essay, consists entirely of multiple-choice questions presented in two separately timed sections.

Breakdown of the CLEP General Exams

English Composition with Essay
   Part I: Includes questions about identifying sentence errors, improving sentences, and revising work
   Part II: Essay

English Composition without Essay
   Includes questions about identifying sentence errors, improving sentences, revising works in progress, restructuring sentences, and analyzing writing

Humanities
   Includes questions about literature (drama, poetry, fiction, and nonfiction) and fine arts (visual arts, music, performing arts, and architecture)

Mathematics
   Includes questions about sets, logic, real number systems, functions and graphs, probability, and statistics

Natural Sciences
   Includes questions about biological science and physical science

Social Sciences and History
   Includes questions about world civilization, U.S. and world history, political science, sociology, economics, psychology, geology, and anthropology

The CLEP Subject Exams test your knowledge of specific college course material and are used to grant exemption from and credit for these courses. Like the General Exams, the Subject Exams are 90 minutes long and consist of multiple-choice questions in two separately timed sections. The Subject Exams in Composition and Literature also include an optional 90-minute essay section. (Check to see if your selected college requires the essay component.)

Some other important things to remember about the CLEP Subject Exams:

- In all of the CLEP subject exams, a percentage of the questions are not scored; they are pretest questions.
- Time spent on tutorials or in providing personal data is in addition to the actual test time.
- Most colleges award either two or four semesters of credit, depending on your CLEP scores.

Composition and Literature

The composition and literature tests measure your understanding of American literature, your ability to analyze and interpret literature, and your ability to create a well-written essay. Read on to learn more about these exams.

American Literature

The American Literature examination includes content that is covered in a two-semester survey course or a similar course at the college level. This examination explores American poetry and prose from colonial times to the present. You will be responsible for an understanding of literary works and their titles, authors, content, and background. You will also need to be familiar with the terminology and concepts used by literary critics and historians. While the examination briefly explores the essay, drama, and autobiography, the majority of the questions highlight fiction and poetry. There are 120 questions in this 90-minute examination.

Analyzing and Interpreting Literature

The Analyzing and Interpreting Literature examination includes material covered in a two-semester first- or second-year course in literature. You will be expected to have critically read a variety of works in poetry, drama, fiction, and nonfiction. You will need to be able to answer questions about various passages from a variety of American and British literature. You are not required to have previous experience with the selected examples of American and British literature, nor do you need to have previous experience with the passages to successfully answer the questions. This 90-minute examination includes about 80 multiple-choice questions.

English Literature

The English Literature examination covers material usually taught in a full-year or two-semester college course (or the equivalent). The examination highlights major authors and literary works. A percentage of the examination includes questions on some minor writers. You will be expected to know commonly used literary terms, such as simile or metaphor, and personification, and certain literary forms, such as the parable, the sonnet, and the epic poem. This examination's questions follow the historically driven survey course in English literature. The questions are prepared for students who appreciate English literature, have read widely in this genre, and understand the literary periods and the history of English literature.

If the university or college you apply to requests a writing sample, an optional essay section is also available. You will be expected to respond to two of three essay topics. You are required to write an essay on the first topic. It is suggested that you spend 35 to 40 minutes on the first topic. You choose one of two topics for your second essay. Plan to spend 50 to 55 minutes on the second essay. University or college faculty will score these essays. The essays are scored locally by faculty. The 90-minute examination includes 95 questions.

Freshman College Composition

The questions in the Freshman College Composition examination assess skills required for first-year college English courses. The examination addresses elements of grammar and language, a variety of formal and informal writing, and brief analyses and interpretations of short excerpts of prose and poetry. Preparation for this exam requires a foundation in the fundamentals of rhetoric and standard written English. You will need to be familiar with the development of a research paper and reference skills.

If the university or college you apply to requests a writing sample, an optional essay section is also available. You will be asked to write clearly and effectively on two essay topics, spending approximately 45 minutes on each essay. This 90-minute examination includes 90 questions.

Foreign Languages

These foreign language exams include content learned in the first two years of college language study. Reading comprehension and listening skills are tested in separately timed sections. Depending on your exam, most universities and colleges award two to four semesters of credit (up to 12 credits).

French Language CLEP Exam

The French Language examination measures knowledge reflecting two to four semesters of college French language study. This 90-minute examination includes 121 questions. Most colleges or universities award the equivalent of two or four semesters of credit, depending on the candidate's score on the French exam.

German Language CLEP Exam

The German Language examination measures knowledge reflecting two to four semesters of college German language study. The exam consists of three separately timed sections.

This 90-minute examination is made up of 120 questions. These three sections are equally weighted, and they contribute equally to the total score. Most colleges or universities award the equivalent of two or four semesters of credit, depending on the candidate's score on the German exam.

Spanish Language CLEP Exam

The Spanish Language examination measures knowledge reflecting two to four semesters of college Spanish language study. This 90-minute examination is made up of 120 questions. Three separately timed sections are weighted so that each question contributes equally to the total score. Time spent on tutorials or in providing personal data is in addition to the actual test time. Two Listening sections and one Reading section have their own timing requirements.

History and Social Sciences

These tests cover material that is wide-ranging, including the American Government, Human Growth and Development, Educational Psychology, Introductory Psychology, Introductory Sociology, Principles of Macroeconomics, and more. Keep reading for details on each test.

American Government

The American Government CLEP examination covers material that is usually taught in a college level, one-semester introductory course in American government and politics. The examination covers material on national government and its history, and development in such areas as the Constitution, federal government and its institutions and policies, civil liberties, political parties, interest groups, and political beliefs and behavior. This 90-minute examination is made up of 100 questions.

Human Growth and Development

The Human Growth and Development CLEP examination (Infancy, Childhood, Adolescence, Adulthood, and Aging) includes material covered in a college-level, one-semester introductory course in developmental psychology or human development. Candidates should have a good grasp of the significant research and major theories related to physical, cognitive, and social development. Candidates will be required to answer 90 questions in 90 minutes.

Introduction to Educational Psychology

The Introduction to Educational Psychology CLEP examination includes material usually covered in a college-level, one-semester undergraduate course. The examination pays close attention to the principles of learning and cognition, teaching methods and classroom management, child growth and development, and evaluation and assessment of learning. Candidates are required to answer 100 questions in 90 minutes.

Introductory Psychology

The Introductory Psychology examination includes material usually covered in a college-level, one-semester undergraduate course in introductory psychology. Some of the topics included in this examination are the biological bases of behavior, sensation and perception, states of consciousness, learning, cognition, motivation and emotion, developmental and social psychology, personality, and psychological disorders. The examination emphasizes basic principles, concepts, and facts in the field. This 90-minute examination is made up of 95 questions.

Introductory Sociology

The Introductory Sociology examination assesses an individual's knowledge of the material typically covered in a college-level, one-semester introductory sociology course. The examination highlights key facts and concepts and accepted theoretical methodology in the field of sociology. Candidates do not need to demonstrate a trained knowledge of the subject or an understanding of the methodology in the field. This 90-minute examination is made up of 100 questions.

Principles of Macroeconomics

The Principles of Macroeconomics examination includes material covered in a college-level, one-semester undergraduate course in introductory macroeconomics. This examination emphasizes principles of economics that include the general price level, output and income, and interrelations among sectors of the economy. Candidates must understand the determinants of aggregate demand and aggregate supply and the monetary and fiscal policy tools used to achieve specific policy objectives. Candidates must also understand measurement concepts such as the gross domestic product, consumption, investment, unemployment, inflation, inflationary gap, and recessionary gap. Candidates are also expected to demonstrate a working knowledge of the Federal Reserve and its monetary policy tools used to stabilize economic fluctuations and promote long-term economic growth and fiscal policy—specifically issues related to income, employment, price level, deficits, and interest rate. Finally, candidates should have a good appreciation of foreign exchange markets, balance of payments, effects of currency, and the impact of the appreciation and depreciation on a country's imports. This 90-minute examination is made up of 80 questions.

Principles of Microeconomics

The Principles of Microeconomics examination covers material that is usually taught in a one-semester undergraduate course in introductory microeconomics. This aspect of economics deals with the principles of economics that apply to the analysis of the behavior of individual consumers and businesses in the economy. Questions on this exam require candidates to apply analytical techniques to both hypothetical and real-world situations and to analyze and evaluate economic decisions. Candidates are expected to demonstrate an understanding of how free markets work and how resources are allocated efficiently. They should understand how individual consumers make economic decisions to maximize utility, and how individual firms make decisions to maximize profits. Candidates must be able to identify the characteristics of the different market structures and analyze the behavior of firms in terms of price and output decisions. They should also be able to evaluate the outcome in each market structure with respect to economic efficiency, identify cases in which private markets fail to allocate resources efficiently, and understand how government intervention fixes or fails to fix the resource allocation problem. Candidates should also understand the determination of wages and other input prices in factor markets, and analyze and evaluate the distribution of income. This 90-minute examination is made up of 80 questions.

History of the United States I: Early Colonization to 1877

The History of the United States I: Early Colonization to 1877 CLEP examination includes material covered in the first semester of a two-semester course in U.S. history. The examination covers the period of U.S. history from early European colonization to the end of Reconstruction, with the majority of the questions on the period of 1790–1877. In the part covering the seventeenth and eighteenth centuries, emphasis is placed on the English colonies. This 90-minute examination is made up of 120 questions.

History of the United States II: 1865 to the Present

The History of the United States II: 1865 to the Present examination covers material that is usually taught in the second semester of what is often a two-semester course in U.S. history. The examination covers the period of U.S. history from the end of the Civil War to the present, with the majority of the questions on the twentieth century. This 90-minute examination is made up of 120 questions.

Western Civilization I: Ancient Near East to 1648

The Western Civilization I: Ancient Near East to 1648 CLEP examination includes material that is usually taught in the first semester of a two-semester course in Western Civilization. The questions in the examination cover the civilizations of ancient Greece, Rome, and the Near East; the Middle Ages; the Renaissance and Reformation; and early modern Europe. As you prepare for this examination, keep in mind that you may be asked to define a historical term, select a particular historical figure based on his or her political beliefs, or identify the significant relationships between two historical factors or an erroneous connection between an individual and an event. You may be asked questions requiring you to interpret, evaluate, or connect a passage, a map, or a picture to other information, or you may need to understand, analyze, and use the data contained in a graph or table. The 90-minute examination is made up of 120 questions.

Western Civilization II: 1648 to the Present

The Western Civilization II: 1648 to the Present examination includes material frequently taught in the second semester of a two-semester course in Western civilization. The examination questions cover European history beginning with the mid-seventeenth century and through the post-Second World War period. This examination also covers such political, economic, and cultural developments as scientific thought, the Enlightenment, the French and Industrial Revolutions, and the First and Second World Wars. As you prepare for this examination, keep in mind that you may be asked to define a historical term, select a particular historical figure based on his or her political beliefs, or identify a significant relationship between two historical factors or an erroneous connection between an individual and an event. You may be asked questions requiring you to interpret, evaluate, or connect a passage, a map, or a picture to other information, or you may need to understand, analyze, and use the data contained in a graph or table. This 90-minute examination is made up of 120 questions.

Science and Mathematics

The science and mathematics exams include Biology, Calculus, Chemistry, College Algebra, and Precalculus. In the following sections, you will find a brief breakdown of the components of each test.

Biology

The Biology examination includes material that is frequently covered in a one-year college general biology course. The subject matter in this examination expects the examinee to be familiar with the broad field of the biological sciences, organized into three major areas: molecular and cellular biology, organismal biology, and populational biology. The examinee will have a basic understanding of biology and its facts, and of the principles and processes of the field. The examinee should also be able to understand how information is collected and interpreted, how hypotheses are formed from available information, and how conclusions and predictions emerge from the data. Finally, the examinee should be able to appreciate that science, a human

activity, has social consequences. This 90-minute examination is made up of 115 questions.

Calculus

The Calculus examination includes skills and concepts usually taught in a one-semester college course in calculus. The CLEP Calculus examination is approximately 60% limits and differential calculus and 40% integral calculus. The exam tests your intuitive understanding of calculus and your experience with its methods and applications. It is assumed that you have skills, training, and knowledge in preparatory mathematics, including algebra, plane and solid geometry, trigonometry, and analytic geometry. You will also demonstrate your skills in algebraic, trigonometric, exponential, logarithmic, and general functions. Students are not permitted to use a calculator during the CLEP Calculus exam. The candidate will be asked to answer 45 questions in 90 minutes.

Chemistry

The Chemistry examination includes material frequently taught in a one-year general chemistry course. A successful score reflects your understanding of the structure and states of matter, reaction types, equations and stoichiometry, equilibrium, kinetics, thermodynamics, and descriptive and experimental chemistry. You will also demonstrate your ability to interpret and apply this material to new and unfamiliar problems. During this examination, the testing software provides a calculator function and a periodic table. This 90-minute examination is made up of 75 questions.

College Algebra

The College Algebra examination includes material frequently covered in a one-semester college course in algebra. About half of the test covers standard problems requiring basic algebraic skills. Candidates must demonstrate an understanding of the concepts in the remaining, less routine problems. The examination questions cover basic algebraic operations; linear and quadratic equations, inequalities, and graphs; algebraic, exponential, and logarithmic functions; and miscellaneous other topics. Candidates should be familiar with algebraic vocabulary, symbols, and notation. Please note that the CLEP College Algebra examination does not test arithmetic calculations, nor does the test include questions that require a calculator. The CLEP software will make an online scientific calculator (non-graphing) available during the examination. This 90-minute examination is made up of 60 questions.

Precalculus

A new CLEP Precalculus exam replaces the CLEP College Algebra-Trigonometry and Trigonometry exams. The Precalculus examination assesses your understanding of the skills and concepts required for a first-semester calculus course. A significant portion of the exam tests your aptitude with functions and their properties. Other questions test your understanding of types of functions: linear, quadratic, absolute value, square root, polynomial, rational, exponential, logarithmic, trigonometric, inverse trigonometric, and piecewise-defined. These functions can be presented symbolically, graphically, verbally, or in tabular form on the examination. You will need to demonstrate a thorough understanding of these categories of functions. These types of functions form the core of all precalculus courses and they are a prerequisite for entry into calculus and other college-level mathematics courses.

This 90-minute examination is made up of 48 questions. Your successful score on the Precalculus examination will enable you to bypass a math proficiency course to earn three college credits.

Business

The business tests cover information from accounting and business law to computer applications, marketing, and management. The following sections detail these tests.

Financial Accounting

The new CLEP Financial Accounting examination, introduced in January 2007, is comparable to a one-semester course. This exam, which replaced the Principles of Accounting exam, covers two semesters of knowledge—financial accounting and managerial accounting. Candidates must demonstrate a thorough understanding and mastery of the skills and concepts necessary for success in a first-semester financial accounting course. Candidates must be familiar with accounting concepts and terminology and understand the details and practice in the preparation, use, and analysis of accounting data and financial reports developed for both internal and external purposes. Candidates must master the computations and the accounting techniques needed in problem-solving situations. Finally, the examinee must have a thorough understanding of the current principles and producers in accounting. This 90-minute examination is made up of 75 questions.

Introductory Business Law

The Introductory Business Law examination includes material covered in an introductory one-semester college course in the subject. The examination emphasizes functions of contracts in American business law. Examination questions cover a variety of topics including the history and sources of American law, legal systems and procedures, agency and employment, and sales. This 90-minute examination is made up of 100 questions.

Information Systems and Computer Applications

The Information Systems and Computer Applications examination includes material frequently taught in an introductory college-level business course. Questions on the examination test not only knowledge, terminology, and basic concepts, but also the candidate's ability to apply that knowledge. The examination contains questions on information systems and computer applications, but the test does not focus on hardware design, language-specific programming techniques, or specific application packages. While the examination may refer toward processing, spreadsheets, and data management, the questions do not assume the candidate's familiarity with a specific product. Rather, the examination tests for a thorough understanding of the application of concepts and techniques to a number of products and environments. This 90-minute examination is made up of 100 questions.

Principles of Management

The Principles of Management examination includes material frequently taught in an introductory course on the fundamentals of management and organization. This course requires an understanding of human resources and the operational and working aspects of management. This 90-minute examination is made of up 100 questions.

Principles of Marketing

The Principles of Marketing examination includes material frequently covered in a one-semester introductory course in marketing. The exam is focused on the role of marketing in culture and society and within a firm. The examination will also include questions about consumer and organizational markets, marketing strategy planning, the marketing mix, and marketing institutions. Other topics in the examination include international marketing, ethics, marketing research, services, and not-for-profit marketing. The candidate should have a working knowledge of various trends intrinsic to marketing, including economic/demographic, social/cultural, political/legal, and technological trends. This 90-minute examination is made up of 100 questions.

▶ Where CLEP Exams Are Given

CLEP exams are given online in more than 1,400 test centers throughout the United States. These centers are usually located on college or university campuses. You can search for the center nearest you at the CLEP website: http://apps.collegeboard.com/cbsearch_clep/searchCLEPTestCenter.jsp.

As an alternative, you can also e-mail for information at clep@info.collegeboard.org, call 800-257-9558, or write to the following address:

CLEP
P.O. Box 6600
Princeton, NJ 08541-6600

If you live more than 150 miles from the nearest test center, you may be able to arrange a special test location that is closer to your home. However, there will be an additional fee and arrangements take about five weeks. If you live outside the United States, you must select three possible test cities at least four months before you wish to be tested.

Please note that some universities and colleges administer the CLEP exams, but restrict participation to their own students.

As you may discover, each test center has its own set of registration instructions. Please make sure that you adhere to the center's policies and registration requirements.

▶ Registration

To obtain information about registering for the CLEP exam, go to www.collegeboard.com/prod_downloads/ student/testing/clep/infocand.pdf to read "Information for Candidates." This guide contains the registration/ admission form and instructions for completing it, as well as other useful information about CLEP.

The first step in registration is to find a testing center near you. Contact your desired center to learn about their registration procedure. They will be able to tell you about their service fees, their testing schedule, and parking/transportation information.

Next, complete the registration/admission form and mail it to the test center address. You may use a credit card, check, or money order to pay for your fees. The majority of colleges and universities around the country also charge a nonrefundable administration fee, which may vary among test centers.

Please note that the military funds CLEP exams for its members. If you are a veteran, you can file a claim to be reimbursed for your CLEP exam fee and administration fees under provisions of the Veterans' Benefits Improvement Act of 2004 (Public Law 108-454). Visit the U.S. Department of Veterans Affairs at www.gibill. va.gov/pamphlets/testing.htm to learn if you are eligible for the CLEP benefit and learn how to submit a claim.

Attention Military Personnel

CLEP exams are available to eligible military personnel as a way to save time and money while earning college credit. To assist military personnel in meeting their educational goals, the Defense Activity for Non-Traditional Education Support (DANTES) funds CLEP exams for eligible military service members and eligible civilian employees.

If you are living outside of the United States, and you are interested in taking the CLEP exam but have no testing centers in your area, you might consider taking the CLEP exam when you arrive in the United States. Go to the college or university you have enrolled in and ask the registrar, admissions, or an international student advising department about the college's CLEP policy.

If you have a learning or physical disability that might prevent you from taking the CLEP exam, you may request special accommodations and arrangements for either a regularly scheduled test date or another scheduled administration. For details, and before you register, please contact the CLEP test administrator at the test center where you plan to take the exam.

CLEP can also provide specific accommodations to students with documented hearing, learning, physical, or visual disabilities. If you are not enrolled at the college or university-based testing institution, you must submit an IEP (Individualized Education Plan) from your score-recipient institution, or you must show other documentation to a test-center administrator. Each test center has its own specific guidelines for submitting documentation and approving accommodations. The following are examples of testing accommodations that may be provided to individuals with the appropriate documentation:

- ZoomText (screen magnification)
- modifiable screen colors
- use of a reader or amanuensis or sign language interpreter
- scripts (for language exams)
- extended time
- untimed rest breaks

▶ Computer-Based Testing

Since 2001, all CLEP exams have been given on computers. The computer-based exam has several advantages:

- instant scores
- speedy score reporting
- increased security

With a computer-based exam, it is critical that you follow all instructions prior to and during the exam. It is important to be comfortable with using a computer and with your word processing skills prior to taking a CLEP exam.

If you prefer to take a paper-and-pencil CLEP exam, contact CLEP directly. Paper-and-pencil administrations of the CLEP exams are available in 14 CLEP titles only. The fee for each paper-and-pencil exam is $120. Please note that immediate score reports are not available with paper-and-pencil testing. You will receive your scores two to three weeks after the testing date.

▶ Scoring

Colleges and universities have different policies for awarding credit for the CLEP exam. Each college uses its own system to determine which CLEP exam score will be given credit. In most instances, colleges and universities refer to the guidelines set up by the American Council on Education (ACE) and the recommendations the ACE sets for scores. Teams of professors and subject matter and technical experts work together to determine whether you are eligible for credit based on your CLEP score.

Contact the colleges as you apply for admission and request their guidelines in awarding credit for CLEP scores. In some instances, these awarded credits can be used toward a degree. The college will let you know if you have received credit for the exam and if you are exempt from taking the course in a particular subject area.

Finally, you will need to decide which college should receive your CLEP exam scores. Talk to an academic advisor or college advisor at the college. Ask them the school's policy on accepting CLEP scores. How many credits do they accept? Find out which scores are needed.

Your total score on an exam consists of two calculations. A "raw score" is first calculated, and this score represents the number of correct questions. This raw score increases with each correct answer. Keep in mind that you do not gain or lose points for unanswered questions or incorrect answers. Next, a statistical process called "equating" turns your raw score into a scaled score.

Your scores are given only to you unless you request that the scores be sent to a specific school, college, or other designated site. The exam software allows you to designate where to send the score. You are not billed if you make this request when you register for or take the CLEP exam; however, there is a fee for all transcripts requested after the test.

When you receive your exam score, CLEP gives you a detailed pamphlet explaining how they interpret your score. CLEP keeps your scores on file for 20 years.

After you have completed your CLEP exam, you may decide whether to see your score. If you choose to see your score, it is automatically sent to the college you have indicated. This automatic send cannot be cancelled. You will also receive a copy of your score and, if you have taken the exam at a college to receive the score, the college will keep a copy. If you took the English Composition with Essay exam, your score will be mailed to you between two and three weeks after you take the exam.

If you do not want your scores sent before the exam ends, you can cancel your score—you must make this decision, however, before you see your score. You will not receive a candidate copy and no report will be sent to the receiving institution.

After you cancel an exam, you cannot take the CLEP exam again for six months, and your exam fee will not be refunded to you. In this period, you may review the content or choose to take a course in a college classroom. If you take the same exam within this period, your score will be listed invalid and your fees forfeited.

If you have been in the military and you are a DANTES-funded military examinee, you cannot choose to cancel your score. You will also need to wait 180 days before you can take the test again. At a later time, all test takers may request that their scores be deleted from their transcripts.

Scoring the Essay

English professors from universities and colleges all over the country are selected to grade the essay portion of the English Composition with Essay. Two professors read and grade each essay. The sum of the two scores is combined with the multiple-choice score, and the final scaled report score is between 20 and 80. These professors are trained to review and score CLEP essays.

Four other CLEP Subject Exams offer an elective essay. In some instances, universities and colleges may require that you take the elective essay for the American Literature, Analyzing and Interpreting Literature, English Literature, and/or Freshman College Composition exams. Please contact your university to see if it requires one of these elective essay tests. You will need to pay an additional $10 per test made payable to the test center. These elective essays are completed on paper, and the school or college's faculty grades this essay. If you decide to write an elective, you may wish to know how much weight the essay counts compared to the multiple-choice questions. The school adminis-

tering the test will provide you with guidelines for the essay and the criteria they use to score your test.

If you have taken English Composition with Essay, you will receive a combined score usually three to four weeks after your test date. If you want to send your scores to a college, employer, or certifying agency, you must select this option through the exam software on the day of the exam. This service is free of charge only if you select your score recipient at the time you test. A $20 fee will be charged for each transcript ordered at a later date.

Candidates cannot receive scores by fax or e-mail under any circumstances, and scores are not available online. All scores are sent by first-class mail and scores are kept on file by CLEP for 20 years.

Many colleges award CLEP credit to their enrolled students. There are other stipulations, however, that vary from college to college. Here are some additional questions to keep in mind:

- Do you have to "validate" your CLEP score by successfully completing a more advanced course in the subject?
- Does the college require the optional free-response (essay) section for the examinations in composition and literature as well as the multiple-choice portion of the CLEP exam you're considering?
- Do you need to formally apply for CLEP credit by completing and signing a form?
- Will you be required to pass a departmental test such as an essay, laboratory, or oral exam in addition to the CLEP multiple-choice exam?

Knowing the answers to these questions before you take the CLEP exam will permit you to schedule the optional free-response or departmental exam when you register to take your CLEP exam.

▶ About *CLEP Test Prep*

The College-Level Examination Program (CLEP) was created on the assumption that some individuals enrolling in college have already learned concepts taught in college courses. They have attained this level of education through nontraditional means—through noncredit adult courses, job training, independent study, and advanced high school courses. The individuals registering for CLEP are as diverse a group as any group of students. These test takers can be college bound, in the military or retired military personnel, individuals seeking certification for their work, or individuals simply interested in college-level material.

Whatever your background and reasons for choosing to take CLEP, LearningExpress's *CLEP Test Prep* will help you identify which exams you want to take and successfully prepare for the tests you choose. If you devote time to really studying this book, you will be on the path to scoring well on the CLEP and receiving college credit for your knowledge and hard work. Carefully work through the subject sections, complete each pretest and practice set, and gauge your skills with a battery of practice exams. Then, you'll know what to expect when it comes time to take the CLEP exams.

CLEP Test Prep is intended to help test takers prepare for the five CLEP General Exams—English Composition, Social Sciences and History, College Math, Natural Sciences, and Humanities. The official CLEP focuses on the key concepts of these subjects and this book is strategically designed to help you to address those key concepts.

In *CLEP Test Prep*, you will learn all about the CLEP:

- how to register for the exam
- where and when they are given
- how they are scored
- test-taking tips
- what kind of Subject Exams are available and what they consist of

- how to prepare for the General Exams with hundreds of practice questions and answers typical of those found on the actual tests

Used correctly, this book will show you what to expect and give you a convenient review of the subjects of the five General Exams. Even if your study time is limited, this book will still help you:

- familiarize yourself with the type of exam you can expect
- improve your general test-taking ability
- prepare yourself in the particular fields covered by the CLEP General Exams
- improve your skill and speed in answering test questions

This book outlines what to expect on the five General Exams and gives you plenty of practice with these skills—from a full-length pretest for each General Exam, skill practice questions, and two full-length practice tests per subject. All pretest and practice test questions are accompanied by thorough answer explanations to help you truly understand why you answered a question correctly or incorrectly. By purchasing *CLEP Test Prep*, you will also be given a password to access two additional practice tests for each General Exam subject—ten online tests in total! The combination of CLEP practice will help you identify your weaknesses fast. Once you know your trouble areas, you can best use the time leading up to the day of the test to sharpen your skills. Don't forget that previous official CLEP exams are not made available to you, so these practice tests are invaluable.

Remember, if you have recently graduated from high school, your wealth of knowledge can assist you as you prepare for CLEP. Although it is impossible to study for everything that will be covered on the exam, the subjects you covered in high school will help you identify the subject areas that you excel in or need to further review.

On the other hand, if you graduated from high school a while ago, you will discover that your reading and work life have exposed you to many valuable ideas and concepts, which will help you on the CLEP.

As you move forward in your CLEP study, follow this checklist of questions:

- ▸ Are you familiar with all of the exams?
- ▸ Have you identified which exam or exams you wish to take?
- ▸ What is your plan of action when studying for the CLEP exam?

▶ Test-Taking Tips

As you use this book to help study for the CLEP, you may find the following hints valuable:

- Pace yourself as you take the *CLEP Test Prep* practice tests. Follow the official CLEP time limit for each General Subject practice test. If you adhere to these time restrictions now, you will be comfortable with the actual timed tests.
- Consider your ideal study environment. Do you need quiet? Is the room too warm or too cold? Will the telephone be a distraction? Do you have enough light in the room? Is there room to stretch and spread out your study materials? If you have not had to study in a while, you may have difficulty concentrating at first. Make sure you are comfortable and free from distractions as you prepare.
- Schedule breaks as you study, so that you can absorb, retain, and efficiently use the information you accumulate.
- Consider your schedule and other daily or weekly obligations. Create a weekly chart to identify

blocks of time you can set aside to prepare for CLEP and estimate the number of hours each day or week that you can devote to studying. You may need to rearrange your current schedule and possibly eliminate less pressing obligations and activities. Get in the habit of studying a little bit each day. Daily study gives you the time needed to gradually review material and strengthen your understanding of the concepts, principles, key players, and key events.

- Use aids that work best for you. Study aids can be a great support. Ask yourself, "How do I best remember ideas and concepts?" Create flash cards, outlines, or highlight your reading material with different colored markers to help you distinguish between topics and subtopics.
- Find other materials, resources, and supplementary study aids to help you prepare for your examination. For example, view *National Geographic* or *Nova* videotapes. Use audio language tapes. Ask your college librarian about similar resources on computer software. Watch a PBS series or a film. Read the newspapers, or attend a play or concert. All of these activities can enrich your life and further prepare you for the CLEP exam.

Think you're ready to take the CLEP? Make sure to ask yourself these important questions:

▶ Have you made a contact with the college where you hope to receive college credit?

▶ Have you secured information about the college's policy regarding CLEP?

▶ Have you spoken with your college about requesting credit for your score?

▶ Do you know how many credits you can earn with your successful scores?

▶ Have you contacted your local test center to register for a test date?

▶ Have you requested that the test center send your scores to the college or colleges of your choice?

As you prepare for the CLEP exam, keep in mind that while it's important that you have a good understanding of the content, it is equally important that you fine-tune your test-taking skills. You'll need a good command of the content and experience taking tests. If you feel a bit rusty at taking tests, this is a good time to hone those skills. Here are some tips to remember when you take the CLEP exams:

■ Before you set out to your local test center, eat a light breakfast. You may not be able to concentrate on a growling stomach, and too much food may make you sluggish.

■ Leave early for the test center. You will want to have enough time to find the test center and park.

■ Listen to the administrator's instructions. This is very important. Read over the online instructions carefully. As well, you should feel comfortable asking the test administrators any last-minute questions before you begin your examination.

■ Note the amount of time that you have for the test, and be prepared to work at an appropriate pace. The testing software has a clock that you can use as you answer questions, or you can turn it off. In either case, make sure that you are checking the time. Halfway through a 90-minute examination, you should be about halfway through the test.

■ As you read each section, don't rush to answer the questions until you are certain that you have read the whole question and all of the answer choices that follow. While the first couple of choices may seem plausible, remember, there may be a better answer in that list of choices.

■ Read the questions carefully. Sometimes the question may seem complex, but a good second read will significantly increase your understanding of a question.

■ Some test questions can have key words that offer clues. Words such as *only, never,* or *always* suggest that there are simply no exceptions in the answer you choose. On the other hand, words such as *possibly, rarely, often,* or *generally* suggest that there are possible exceptions to that test answer.

■ Try not to spend too much time on a question. If you are struggling with a question, mark that question using the exam software and come back to it later. Sometimes when you leave a difficult question and go on, you are more prepared to tackle it later.

■ Finally, do not waste your time trying to find trick questions, a pattern in the questions or answers, or faulty wording in the test. The CLEP examination is straightforward and direct, and the questions are not designed to trick the examinee. Remember that CLEP uses subject area experts and college and university faculty to carefully review each question. These individuals carefully study each question and make sure that there is only one correct answer for each test question.

A compulsory essay is part of the CLEP English Composition with Essay exam. The essay portion of the exam is also administered on the computer. Please review your word processing skills before taking the CLEP English Composition with Essay exam, as you must be comfortable with typing in order to finish this section of the exam. CLEP's website offers an online sampler of the essay for you to practice typing an essay online.

The following strategies can be used to strengthen your score in the CLEP essay exams.

- Read the questions for the essay and write down any ideas or thoughts. Create a mind map or outline.
- Focus first on the questions you will find easy to answer. You can come back to the more difficult questions later.
- After you have determined which questions you will answer first, take a moment to assign testing time to each question. Think about how many minutes you will want to give to each answer. If it is possible, try to allot the same amount of time to each question.

On the day that you take the CLEP examination, you are NOT allowed to have any of the following items with you:

- cellular phones/pagers, beepers, walkie-talkies, wireless communication devices
- calculators (the exam software has a calculator function)
- all digital watches, including wristwatch cameras and alarm watches
- any kind of photographic or copying device
- radios, recorders, media players with headphones or earphones
- dictionaries, books, pamphlets, or reference materials
- papers of any kind (scratch paper will be provided by the test center administrator)
- mechanical pencils, pens, or highlighters
- slide rules, protractors, compasses, or rulers
- food, beverages, or tobacco products
- hats (unless worn as a religious requirement)
- any other unauthorized testing aids

About the CLEP English Composition Exam

The English Composition CLEP exam includes content covered in a college freshman composition course. The English Composition exam evaluates your understanding of standard American English, including your use of grammar, punctuation, and usage; your ability to interpret, analyze, present, and support a point of view; and your ability to write an essay. Although the exam does not expect you to know the definition of specific grammar terms, you will be expected to understand the principles and conventions associated with college writing.

Two versions of the test are offered. The English Composition without Essay exam is a 90-question multiple-choice exam. The English Composition with Essay exam has two separately timed sections. Section I contains approximately 50 multiple-choice questions to be answered in 45 minutes. Section II is one essay question to be answered in 45 minutes. This essay section is equal to 50% of the exam. You will be asked to respond to a prompt and write your answer in 45 minutes. On both versions, some of the multiple-choice questions are pretest questions and are not scored.

Both versions of the English Composition exam include the following types of questions:

Identifying Sentence Errors: This includes looking for wording that is not consistent with standard conventions of English. These questions address the following:

- sentence boundaries
- sentence variety
- sentence clarity

- agreement (subject-verb agreement, pronoun reference, shift)
- active versus passive voice
- diction and idiom
- syntax (includes parallelism, dangling modifiers, coordination and subordination)
- sentence variety

Improving Sentences: In this section, you will choose the revised sentence that best conveys the meaning intended in the original sentence.

Restructuring Sentences: These questions appear only in the English Composition without Essay examination. You will be given a sentence to rewrite and to improve its structure and clarity. One of five choices is the correct phrase for the restructured sentence. In some portions of the multiple-choice section and the essay exam, you will need to identify the following:

- the main idea and thesis
- how ideas are organized in a sentence, paragraph, or essay
- if the ideas support the thesis
- the quality of the details added
- how to measure the audience and purpose
- the quality of the argument
- the relationship and/or unity between paragraphs
- the use of tenses and point of view

Revising a Work in Progress: In this portion of the exam, you will be required to review and improve a rough or early draft of writing.

Analyzing Writing: In this section of the English Composition without Essay examination, you will be required to answer questions about the strategies an author uses in two very different passages.

▶ Who Scores the Essay?

CLEP selects college writing instructors to score the essay. Two readers read and assess your essay. The two scores are weighted and combined with your multiple-choice score, resulting in a combined score between 20 and 80. Separate scores are not provided for the multiple-choice and the essay sections.

Readers will assign scores based on the following scoring guide. Remember, the essays must display the following characteristics in response to the assigned task.

A 6 essay demonstrates a high degree of competence and sustained control, although it may have a few minor errors. A typical essay in this category:

- addresses all elements of the writing task effectively and insightfully
- develops ideas thoroughly, supporting them with well-chosen reasons, examples, or details
- is well focused and well organized
- demonstrates superior facility with language, using effective vocabulary and sentence variety
- demonstrates general mastery of the standard conventions of grammar, usage, and mechanics, but may have minor errors

A 5 essay demonstrates a generally high degree of competence, with occasional lapses in quality. A typical essay in this category:

- addresses the writing task effectively
- is well developed, using appropriate reasons, examples, or details to support ideas
- is generally well focused and well organized
- demonstrates facility with language, using appropriate vocabulary and some sentence variety
- demonstrates strong control of the standard conventions of grammar, usage, and mechanics, but may have minor errors

A 4 essay demonstrates clear competence with some errors and lapses in quality. A typical essay in this category:

- addresses the writing task competently
- is adequately developed, using reasons, examples, or details to support ideas
- is adequately focused and organized
- demonstrates competence with language, using adequate vocabulary and minimal sentence variety
- generally demonstrates control of the standard conventions of grammar, usage, and mechanics, but may have some errors

A 3 essay demonstrates limited competence. A typical essay in this category exhibits one or more of the following weaknesses:

- addresses only some parts of the writing task
- is unevenly developed and often provides assertions but few relevant reasons, examples, or details
- is poorly focused and/or poorly organized
- displays frequent problems in the use of language
- demonstrates inconsistent control of grammar, usage, and mechanics

A 2 essay is seriously flawed. A typical essay in this category exhibits one or more of the following weaknesses:

- is unclear or seriously limited in addressing the writing task
- is seriously underdeveloped, providing few reasons, examples, or details
- is unfocused and/or disorganized
- displays frequent serious errors in the use of language that may interfere with meaning
- contains frequent serious errors in grammar, usage, and mechanics that may interfere with meaning

A 1 essay is fundamentally deficient. A typical essay in this category exhibits one or more of the following weaknesses:

- provides little or no evidence of the ability to develop an organized response to the writing task
- is undeveloped
- contains severe writing errors that persistently interfere with meaning

A 0 essay is off topic (i.e., provides no evidence of an attempt to respond to the assigned topic), is written in a language other than English, merely copies the topic, consists only of keystroke characters, or is illegible or nontextual.

Colleges differ in what portion of the CLEP English Composition they accept. Some colleges only accept and offer credit for the version with the essay, while other colleges offer credit for either version. In many instances, colleges grant six semester hours of credit.

English Composition with Essay includes

50% Multiple-Choice Questions

- ◗ Identifying Sentence Errors
- ◗ Improving Sentences
- ◗ Revising Works in Progress

50% Essay

Part I: 45-minute examination with 50 questions

Part II: 45-minute examination with one essay

English Composition without Essay includes

- ◗ Identifying Sentence Errors
- ◗ Restructuring Sentences
- ◗ Improving Sentences
- ◗ Revising Work in Process
- ◗ Analyzing Writing

90-minute exam with 90 questions

CLEP English Composition Pretest

Before reviewing topics that will be covered on the CLEP English Composition exam, test your existing skills by taking this pretest. You will encounter 50 questions that are similar to the type you will find on the CLEP English Composition with Essay exam. The questions are organized into the three content areas:

- Identifying Sentence Errors
- Improving Sentences
- Revising Works in Progress

The exam also includes an essay, similar to the essay you will find on this CLEP pretest.

For now, you should ignore the time restraints of the official CLEP; take as much time as you need to complete each question and the essay.

Answer every question; however, if you are not sure of an answer, put a question mark by the question number to note that you are making a guess. On the official CLEP, you are not penalized for unanswered or incorrect answers, so making a good guess is an important skill to practice.

When you are finished, check the answer key on page 34 carefully to assess your results. Your pretest score will help you determine how much preparation you need and in which areas you need the most careful review and practice.

▶ CLEP English Composition Pretest

1.	ⓐ	ⓑ	ⓒ	ⓓ	ⓔ		**26.**	ⓐ	ⓑ	ⓒ	ⓓ	ⓔ
2.	ⓐ	ⓑ	ⓒ	ⓓ	ⓔ		**27.**	ⓐ	ⓑ	ⓒ	ⓓ	ⓔ
3.	ⓐ	ⓑ	ⓒ	ⓓ	ⓔ		**28.**	ⓐ	ⓑ	ⓒ	ⓓ	ⓔ
4.	ⓐ	ⓑ	ⓒ	ⓓ	ⓔ		**29.**	ⓐ	ⓑ	ⓒ	ⓓ	ⓔ
5.	ⓐ	ⓑ	ⓒ	ⓓ	ⓔ		**30.**	ⓐ	ⓑ	ⓒ	ⓓ	ⓔ
6.	ⓐ	ⓑ	ⓒ	ⓓ	ⓔ		**31.**	ⓐ	ⓑ	ⓒ	ⓓ	ⓔ
7.	ⓐ	ⓑ	ⓒ	ⓓ	ⓔ		**32.**	ⓐ	ⓑ	ⓒ	ⓓ	ⓔ
8.	ⓐ	ⓑ	ⓒ	ⓓ	ⓔ		**33.**	ⓐ	ⓑ	ⓒ	ⓓ	ⓔ
9.	ⓐ	ⓑ	ⓒ	ⓓ	ⓔ		**34.**	ⓐ	ⓑ	ⓒ	ⓓ	ⓔ
10.	ⓐ	ⓑ	ⓒ	ⓓ	ⓔ		**35.**	ⓐ	ⓑ	ⓒ	ⓓ	ⓔ
11.	ⓐ	ⓑ	ⓒ	ⓓ	ⓔ		**36.**	ⓐ	ⓑ	ⓒ	ⓓ	ⓔ
12.	ⓐ	ⓑ	ⓒ	ⓓ	ⓔ		**37.**	ⓐ	ⓑ	ⓒ	ⓓ	ⓔ
13.	ⓐ	ⓑ	ⓒ	ⓓ	ⓔ		**38.**	ⓐ	ⓑ	ⓒ	ⓓ	ⓔ
14.	ⓐ	ⓑ	ⓒ	ⓓ	ⓔ		**39.**	ⓐ	ⓑ	ⓒ	ⓓ	ⓔ
15.	ⓐ	ⓑ	ⓒ	ⓓ	ⓔ		**40.**	ⓐ	ⓑ	ⓒ	ⓓ	ⓔ
16.	ⓐ	ⓑ	ⓒ	ⓓ	ⓔ		**41.**	ⓐ	ⓑ	ⓒ	ⓓ	ⓔ
17.	ⓐ	ⓑ	ⓒ	ⓓ	ⓔ		**42.**	ⓐ	ⓑ	ⓒ	ⓓ	ⓔ
18.	ⓐ	ⓑ	ⓒ	ⓓ	ⓔ		**43.**	ⓐ	ⓑ	ⓒ	ⓓ	ⓔ
19.	ⓐ	ⓑ	ⓒ	ⓓ	ⓔ		**44.**	ⓐ	ⓑ	ⓒ	ⓓ	ⓔ
20.	ⓐ	ⓑ	ⓒ	ⓓ	ⓔ		**45.**	ⓐ	ⓑ	ⓒ	ⓓ	ⓔ
21.	ⓐ	ⓑ	ⓒ	ⓓ	ⓔ		**46.**	ⓐ	ⓑ	ⓒ	ⓓ	ⓔ
22.	ⓐ	ⓑ	ⓒ	ⓓ	ⓔ		**47.**	ⓐ	ⓑ	ⓒ	ⓓ	ⓔ
23.	ⓐ	ⓑ	ⓒ	ⓓ	ⓔ		**48.**	ⓐ	ⓑ	ⓒ	ⓓ	ⓔ
24.	ⓐ	ⓑ	ⓒ	ⓓ	ⓔ		**49.**	ⓐ	ⓑ	ⓒ	ⓓ	ⓔ
25.	ⓐ	ⓑ	ⓒ	ⓓ	ⓔ		**50.**	ⓐ	ⓑ	ⓒ	ⓓ	ⓔ

▶ Part I: Multiple Choice

Identifying Sentence Errors

Directions: The following sentences test your knowledge of grammar, usage, diction (choice of words), and idiom. Some sentences are correct as written. No sentence contains more than one error.

You will find that the error, if there is one, is underlined and lettered. Assume that elements of the sentence that are not underlined are correct and cannot be changed. In choosing answers, follow the requirements of standard written English.

If there is an error, selected the <u>one underlined part</u> that must be changed to make the sentence correct. If there is no error, select choice **e**.

1. The substitute, <u>whom</u> I am sure <u>I have seen working</u> at Ice Cream Café, <u>will be teaching</u> our class
            a   **b**   **c**

   <u>for the rest of the semester</u>. <u>No error.</u>
           d   **e**

2. <u>Susan B. Anthonys speech</u> about the <u>equal rights</u> of women was inspiring not only to women but also to
   a   **b**

   the <u>abolitionists who were</u> fighting to put <u>an official end</u> to slavery. <u>No error.</u>
          c   **d**   **e**

3. Even though <u>neither of us</u> has ever taken a single music lesson, <u>Carmen and myself</u> <u>have managed</u> to put
         a   **b**   **c**

   together a band <u>that has already gotten</u> play time on several of the local radio stations. <u>No error.</u>
                 d   **e**

4. The <u>four most popular movies</u> <u>of the entire year</u> <u>was seen</u> by a total of 5.6 million people <u>in less than</u>
      a   **b**   **c**   **d**

   three months. <u>No error.</u>
         e

5. <u>Each of the children</u> <u>were given</u> three flavors of yogurt to sample, <u>discuss</u>, and then <u>fill out a form</u> as to
   a   **b**   **c**   **d**

   which one they liked the best of all. <u>No error.</u>
                         e

6. Regardless of how <u>it may appear</u>, according to the Entertainment Software Association, the number of female
             a

   <u>gamers are growing</u> at a steady rate with the average <u>woman spending</u> 7.4 hours a <u>week playing</u>. <u>No error.</u>
      b   **c**   **d**   **e**

7. When <u>anyone logs</u> onto the computer to check his or his library card, <u>he or she</u> should always have his or
a
b

her library card at hand to ensure <u>they type</u> the <u>number</u> correctly. <u>No error.</u>
c   d   e

8. Once you finally decide <u>where you want to go</u> on vacation with your family, <u>you will need</u> to plan how much
a
b

money <u>a person</u> should take, making sure that you figure in the <u>constantly rising</u> cost of gas. <u>No error.</u>
c   d   e

9. If the North <u>had not won</u> the Civil War as it did, it <u>might have taken</u> even longer for the <u>Civil Rights</u>
a
b
c

movement <u>to begin</u> bringing equality to the nation. <u>No error.</u>
d
e

10. Christina tried on <u>both</u> the dresses; she just <u>could not figure out</u> <u>which</u> was <u>most flattering</u> to her
a
b   c   d

figure. <u>No error.</u>
e

11. Suddenly, <u>without no warning</u> whatsoever, the car in front of Elizabeth <u>did</u> a U-turn, <u>almost causing</u> an
a
b   c

accident in three different <u>directions</u> at once. <u>No error.</u>
d
e

12. Regardless of what diet Nancy <u>tries</u>, her determination and willpower <u>have virtually</u> <u>no affect</u> on
a
b   c

curbing her appetite or <u>her calories</u>. <u>No error.</u>
d   e

13. It is <u>amazing</u> how many people <u>get addicted</u> to soap operas, <u>tuning in each week</u> to see who is dying, who
a
b
c

is getting divorced, <u>who lies in a coma</u>, and who is telling lies. <u>No error.</u>
d
e

14. Ellen DeGeneres, a comedienne <u>and who has</u> her own daily talk show, <u>has also</u> <u>amused thousands</u> through
a
b   c

her voice as <u>*Finding Nemo*'s character</u> Dorrie, the fish with short-term memory loss. <u>No error.</u>
d
e

15. The author dropped <u>her glasses</u> when the phone rang, <u>reaching down</u> and <u>blindly searching</u> for them

                                a   **b**   **c**

before the caller <u>hung up</u>. <u>No error.</u>
                  d   **e**

16. The Chance of Rain Café <u>is an unusual</u> and unique coffee shop where <u>exotic teas</u> and coffees <u>are offered</u>

                             a   **b**   **c**

by friendly baristas <u>in steaming hot porcelain cups</u>. <u>No error.</u>
                  d   **e**

17. Because of the <u>dramatic increase</u> in foreclosures, many mortgage companies <u>have decide</u> not to lend as

                a   **b**

much money to <u>new homeowners</u> as in <u>the past</u>. <u>No error.</u>
               c   **d**   **e**

18. After getting out all of <u>our notes, textbooks, and pens,</u> <u>we spent</u> the next hour <u>talking about everything</u> in

                           a   **b**   **c**

the world except what we <u>should of been</u> discussing. <u>No error.</u>
                       d   **e**

19. The artist <u>formally known</u> as Prince <u>has been</u> part of the soul and funk music world <u>since</u> the early 1980s

              a   **b**   **c**

and has <u>worked</u> as a producer, composer, arranger, and performer on a variety of songs. <u>No error.</u>
          d   **e**

20. The multiple-choice questions turned out to be <u>simpler, quicker,</u> and <u>better</u> than we had <u>originally anticipated</u>

                                               a   **b**   **c**

when <u>we first looked</u> at the test. <u>No error.</u>
           d   **e**

Improving Sentences

Directions: In each of the following sentences, part of the sentence or the entire sentence is underlined. Beneath each sentence, you will find five versions of the underlined part. Choice **a** repeats the original; the other four are different.

Choose the answer that best expresses the meaning of the original sentence. If you think the original is better than any of the other alternatives, choose **a**; otherwise, choose one of the others. Your choice should produce the most effective sentence—one that is clear and precise, without awkwardness or ambiguity.

21. <u>The reason that I was late was because</u> I had to stop for three trains, I had a flat tire, and five people called me on my cell phone.
   a. The reason that I was late was because
   b. The reason that I am late was because
   c. I was late because
   d. I was late for the reason because
   e. I is late because

22. <u>Whizzing by at a steady pace, I watched the line of cars on the highway.</u>
   a. Whizzing by at a steady pace, I watched the line of cars on the highway.
   b. Whizzing by at a steady pace, the line of cars on the highway I watched.
   c. The line of cars on the highway I watched whizzing by at a steady pace.
   d. I watched the line of cars whizzing by at a steady pace on the highway.
   e. I watched the line of cars on the highway whizzing by at a steady pace.

23. The credits on the movie <u>were rolling already, I did not move</u> because I was still in shock at the incredible plot twist at the end.
   a. were rolling already, I did not move
   b. were rolling already; I did not move
   c. were rolling already: I did not move
   d. were rolling already I did not move
   e. were rolling already since I did not move

24. You can pay off a 30-year mortgage in less than 15 years <u>if one just has the determination</u>, knowledge, and funds to do so.
   a. if one just has the determination
   b. if one just had the determination
   c. if you just has the determination
   d. if he or she just has the determination
   e. if you just have the determination

25. The squirrel was dodging place to place grabbing acorns, stuffing them into its cheeks, <u>and it hurried back to its home</u> to stash its treasures away.
   a. and it hurried back to its home
   b. and it hurries back to its home
   c. and hurrying back to its home
   d. and hurrying back to his home
   e. and it hurried back to the home

26. Hiking the mountains of the Cascade Mountain range with <u>a 70-pound backpack full of supplies are considered</u> one of the toughest elements of search and rescue work.
   a. a 70-pound backpack full of supplies are considered
   b. a 70-pound backpack full of supply is considered
   c. a 70-pound backpack full of supplies are considers
   d. a 70-pound backpack full of supplies is considered
   e. a 70-pound backpack full of supplies is considering

27. <u>Tossing his opponent down on the mat</u> with a primitive grunt that could be heard all the way in the back row of the gymnasium.
   a. Tossing his opponent down on the mat
   b. He tossed his opponent down on the mat
   c. She tossed his opponent down on the mat
   d. Tossed his opponent down on the mat
   e. Tosses his opponent down on the mat

28. <u>Even though he was on his last legs, he kept me on the edge of my seat</u> with his story of how he escaped from the hungry grizzly bear.

   a. Even though he was on his last legs, he kept me on the edge of my seat

   b. Even though he was on his last legs, he kept me riveted

   c. Even though he was exhausted, he kept me on the edge of my seat

   d. Even though he was tired, he kept me interested

   e. Even though he was exhausted, he kept me riveted

29. During the professor's lecture on the works of Dean Koontz and Stephen King, <u>he made a number of illusions</u> to the prolific works of Edgar Allan Poe.

   a. he made a number of illusions

   b. they made a number of illusions

   c. he made a number of allusions

   d. both made a number of allusions

   e. it made a number of illusions

30. In a number of homes in America, instant messaging has taken the place of sending emails, making telephone calls, and <u>even holding face-to-face conversations</u>.

   a. even holding face-to-face conversations

   b. even to hold face-to-face conversations

   c. even having held face-to-face conversations

   d. even held face-to-face conversations

   e. even from having held face-to-face conversations

Revising Works in Progress

Directions: Each of the following passages consists of numbered sentences. Because the passages are part of longer writing samples, they do not necessarily constitute a complete discussion of the issues presented.

Read each passage carefully and answer the questions that follow. The questions test your awareness of a writer's purpose and of characteristics of prose that are important to good writing.

Use the following passage to answer questions 31–35.

(1) There is an old cliché that certain events in life can make time stand still. (2) For the people of London, England, on August 11, 2007, that is exactly what happened. (3) That was the day that Big Ben, the world famous giant clock, comes to a standstill.

(4) Big Ben got its name from the $13\frac{1}{2}$ ton bell that is stationed inside the clock tower. (5) The tower itself, meanwhile, is actually called the Great Bell. (6) The clock has chimed every hour and quarter hour throughout the day and night. (7) It first sang out the time in 1859 and did it ever since. (8) In 2009, the clock will celebrate its 150th birthday. (9) The clock towers over London's Houses of Parliament, which has four faces. (10) It is featured in many travel and history books about London and was always a popular tourist stop.

(11) Big Ben is typically scheduled to be cleaned every five years. (12) It took very courageous workers to do the job, however, because of the tower's height. (13) In August, a brave team of repair workers climbing more than 300 feet up into the air and turned the nine-foot-long hour hand and the 14-foot-long minute hand into the midnight positions. (14) That is when time officially will stop. (15) For weeks, these daring workers clean the clock and all of its parts. (16) Finally, they put the hands back to work. (17) I bet people will be relieved too. (18) Time starts

again—but it will continue silently because next the workers turning to cleaning the huge bells inside the tower.

31. Which of the following is a valid criticism of the passage as a whole?

a. It is inconsistent in its use of tenses.

b. It is not organized in a logical order.

c. It keeps switching from first person to third.

d. It does not provide enough details to support the idea.

e. It does not have any kind of closure to bring it all together.

32. Which of the following is the best way to combine sentences 1 and 2 (reproduced here)?

There is an old cliché that certain events in life can make time stand still. For the people of London, England, on August 11, 2007, that is exactly what happened.

a. There is an old cliché that certain events in life can make time stand still, for the people of London, England, on August 11, 2007, that is exactly what happened.

b. There is an old cliché that certain events in life can make time stand still although for the people of London, England, on August 11, 2007, that is exactly what happened.

c. There is an old cliché that certain events in life can make time stand still: for the people of London, England, on August 11, 2007, that is exactly what happened.

d. There is an old cliché that certain events in life can make time stand still and for the people of London, England, on August 11, 2007, that is exactly what happened.

e. There is an old cliché that certain events in life can make time stand still and in London, in August, that is exactly what happened.

33. Which of the following is a valid criticism of sentence 9?

a. It is too long.

b. It is too wordy.

c. It has a punctuation error.

d. It contains a dangling modifier.

e. It is in the wrong place in the passage.

34. What should be done with sentence 17?

a. It should be left as it is.

b. It should be taken out.

c. It should be moved to the end of the paragraph.

d. It should be moved to the end of the first paragraph.

e. It should be rewritten from first person to third person.

35. What would be the best choice to replace *meanwhile* in the middle of sentence 5?

a. furthermore

b. consequently

c. however

d. therefore

e. moreover

Use the following passage to answer questions 36–40.

(1) Like a lot of other people my age, I think playing video games absolutely rocks! (2) I cannot believe how fast the technology surrounding them changes though. (3) Recently I read about one of the newest pieces of equipment headed for the gaming market. (4) It is for players like me whose hands cramp up from holding controllers and pushing buttons. (5) Instead of relying on our fingers, this invention can almost read a player's thoughts.

(6) For only a few hundred dollars, you can eventually buy a neuroheadset that seems to be almost telepathic. (7) Apparently it is designed to read the gamer's conscious thoughts and expressions as well what the designers call "nonconscious" thoughts. (8) It does this by reading the electrical signals around the brain. (9) Supposedly, the headset can detect emotions like anger, excitement, and tension. (10) It can also understand facial expressions and physical actions like pushing and pulling.

(11) According to what I read, the headset was shown off at the 2008 Game Developers Conference in San Francisco. (12) It will be released along with a specific game to go with it, but, according to the company producing it, the headset can be used with other already existing ones. (13) In addition, users will be able to log on to an online portal where they can play additional games, chat with other players around the world, and download their own content to the portal, including music and photographs. (14) I can't wait until these headsets hit the market!

36. The main problem with the introductory sentence is that
   a. it does not have anything to do with the rest of the passage.
   b. it is in the first person and the rest of the passage is in the third person.
   c. it uses a slang term that some people would not understand.
   d. it does not clearly express the author's opinion of the topic.
   e. it does not relate in any way to the following sentence.

37. The final paragraph would be improved if it
   a. said specifically who is producing the headset.
   b. used more technical terms for the description.
   c. gave a list of the other computer games it works with.
   d. explained the process of how to log on to the Internet.
   e. provided information about when the headset will be available.

38. In context, the best phrase to replace *ones* in sentence 12 would be
   a. headsets.
   b. gamers.
   c. video games.
   d. players.
   e. companies.

39. Which of the following might better replace sentence 14 as a conclusion to the passage?
   a. I can't wait to find out more about these headsets and how I can get one for myself.
   b. I will enjoy watching the technology of this new invention and where it takes gamers.
   c. The headset was a huge hit at the conference and people are already turning in orders.
   d. An invention like this will certainly make it easier on gamers' hands and wrists.
   e. I wonder what other fascinating inventions were shown at this year's convention.

40. The function of sentence 3 is
   a. to act as the essay's topic sentence.
   b. to define what the new headset can do.
   c. to identify how much the equipment costs.
   d. to explain how the headset reads brain signals.
   e. to convince gamers they should go out and get one.

Use the following passage to answer questions 41–45.

(1) Don't touch—it's hot. (2) Look both ways. (3) Wear a jacket. (4) Don't paint on the walls. (5) Most of us have heard statements like this again and again as we were growing up. (6) Artist Timm Etters listened to most of those pieces of advice but ignored the one about painting. (7) As a teenager, he started spray painting on public buildings and city bridges. (8) Clearly, this was a mistake, but at least his art was a huge step above the typical tagging skills. (9) His skillful spray painting always contained positive messages.

(10) One day, he decorated one bridge with a mural dedicated to the veterans of the Vietnam War. (11) He got caught by the police and received an interesting punishment from an understanding officer. (12) Told he had to paint a mural in the school cafeteria. (13) "It wasn't much of a punishment at all," recalls Etters. (14) "I realized how much I loved working on such a large scale, and found what I wanted to do for the rest of my life."

(15) Etters was a determined artist from an early age. (16) When he was in third grade, his doctor told him he was colorblind his interest in painting did not change, however. (17) When he was 16, he was diagnosed with cancer. (18) More than 20 years later, he is still going strong.

(19) Today, Etters spends his time doing two things: painting and talking to kids about art. (20) More than 270 of his incredible murals can be found in schools, businesses, banks, and sports arena throughout the state of Illinois. (21) Etters has visited more than 130 schools warning kids not to paint bridges but instead stick to canvas and paper until they can find the right wall—and permission to paint all over it.

41. From this passage, you can conclude that its author
   a. is skeptical about Etters' type of art.
   b. thinks that Etters is not very talented.
   c. admires what Etters is able to do with murals.
   d. is also a mural artist for many companies.
   e. is a student who has an interest in creating murals.

42. Sentence 12 is an example of
   a. a run-on sentence.
   b. a dangling modifier.
   c. a mistake in verb tense.
   d. a sentence fragment.
   e. an error in punctuation.

43. The quotations in sentences 13 and 14
   a. are completely irrelevant to the rest of the passage.
   b. provide support for the information in sentences 11 and 12.
   c. show the reader that Etters is a real person and not a fictional character.
   d. shift the focus of the passage to how Etter's health conditions affected him.
   e. pinpoint how important art was to Etter and how he would talk to kids about it.

44. The passage concentrates on
   a. how to paint large-scale murals.
   b. how not to get caught painting bridges.
   c. how to cope with being colorblind.
   d. how to turn a passion into a career.
   e. how to become a famous artist.

45. Which of the following is a valid criticism of sentence 16?
- **a.** It is a fragment.
- **b.** It is a run-on sentence.
- **c.** It is irrelevant to the topic.
- **d.** It needs to be omitted from the passage.
- **e.** It needs to be shifted to an earlier paragraph.

Use the following passage to answer questions 46–50.

(1) Anyone who has ever owned a pet knows what comfort it can bring. (2) It loves you, snuggles with you, plays with you, and spends time with you. (3) It can be your best friend. (4) For people living in nursing homes, pets can be a wonderful source of friendship, but many of them are not able to properly take care of an animal anymore.

(5) To test out the theory, Dr. William Banks, a professor of geriatric medicine, studied 38 nursing home residents. (6) They were divided into three groups. (7) One group was visited regularly by a real floppy-eared pup named Sparky. (8) One was visited by AIBO. (9) The third group was not visited at all. (10) After seven weeks, Sparky and AIBO tied for bringing the most comfort and happiness to the residents.

(11) A recent study proved that time spent with a pet cheers people up, even if the pet itself is made out of nothing more than buttons, metal, wires, and plastic, meanwhile known as a robot dog named AIBO or Artificial Intelligence Robot. (12) According to the study, residents are capable of loving and relating to it just as much as a real dog!

46. Which of the following is a valid criticism of the passage as a whole?
- **a.** It does not include any one of authority to verify the idea.
- **b.** It is outdated and too old-fashioned to be of current use.
- **c.** It is not organized in a logical or chronological order.
- **d.** It switches verb tenses so often it is confusing to the reader.
- **e.** It contains too many irrelevant details that it doesn't make sense.

47. From this passage, you can conclude that the author
- **a.** has an inherent dislike of robots.
- **b.** knows someone in a nursing home.
- **c.** appreciates the value of a pet.
- **d.** is a personal friend of Dr. Banks.
- **e.** thinks that this study was not professional.

48. Which of the following is the best way to combine sentences 2 and 3 (reproduced here)?
It loves you, snuggles with you, plays with you, and spends time with you. It can be your best friend.
- **a.** It loves you, snuggles with you, plays with you, and spends time with you and it can be your best friend.
- **b.** It loves you, snuggles with you, plays with you, and spends time with you; it can be your best friend.
- **c.** It loves you, snuggles with you, plays with you, and spends time with you, it can be your best friend.
- **d.** It loves you, snuggles with you, plays with you, and spends time with you although it can be your best friend.
- **e.** It loves you, snuggles with you, plays with you, and spends time with you if it can be your best friend.

49. What would be the best choice to replace *mean-while* in the middle of sentence 11?
   a. unfortunately
   b. furthermore
   c. therefore
   d. consequently
   e. otherwise

50. The function of sentence 5 is
   a. to describe the organization of the study.
   b. to show who was conducting the study.
   c. to quote the person in charge of the study.
   d. to list the results of the overall study.
   e. to provide the statistics from the study.

▶ Answers

1. **a.** *Whom* should be *who*. We use the subjective case because *who* is the subject of the verb *have seen*.
2. **a.** *Anthonys* should be *Anthony's*, because it is possessive and not plural.
3. **b.** *Myself* should be *I*; *I is* the subject of *managed*, while *myself* is a reflexive pronoun.
4. **c.** *Was* should be *were*, because *movies* is plural and the subject and verb need to agree in number.
5. **b.** *Were* should be *was*; the subject (*each*) is singular.
6. **b.** *Are* should be *is*; the subject (*number*) is singular.
7. **c.** *They* should be *he or she* because the antecedent *anyone* is singular.
8. **c.** *A person* should be *you*; the antecedent *you* is second person.
9. **e.** There is no error in this sentence.
10. **d.** *Most* should be *more*.
11. **a.** *No* should be *any*; this is an example of a double negative.
12. **c.** *Affect* should be *effect*.
13. **d.** *Who lies in a coma* should be *who is lying in a coma*.
14. **a.** The sentence parallels a noun with a dependent clause; the correct wording is *who has*, omitting the word *and*.
15. **b.** The participial phrase has no word in the sentence to modify. Who is reaching down? It isn't the phone.
16. **d.** The phrase *in hot steaming porcelain cups* is misplaced. The phrase should appear after *teas and coffees*.
17. **b.** *Have decide* should be *have decided*.
18. **d.** *Should of been* should be *should have been*.
19. **a.** *Formally* should be *formerly*.
20. **e.** This sentence has no error.
21. **c.** This choice keeps the original meaning but eliminates the wordiness. Choice **b** changes the verb tense. Choice **d** is still too wordy, and choice **e** has a subject-verb disagreement.
22. **d.** This choice takes the misplaced modifier and puts it in the proper place. Choice **b** is awkward, while choice **c** still has the modifier in the wrong place. Choice **e** also misplaces the modifier, which is modifying *highway* as written.
23. **b.** This choice links the two complete sentences together with a semicolon. Choice **c** uses a colon, which is not the correct punctuation. Choice **d** removes any punctuation, failing to fix the run-on sentence. Choice **e** adds a coordinating conjunction, which could solve the problem, but it is the wrong word to use and does not make sense with the sentence.
24. **e.** Choice **b** changes the verb tense to an incorrect tense. Choice **c** changes the *one* to *you*, which is correct, but chooses the wrong verb tense. Choice **d** is not correct because *he or she* does not parallel the *you* used in the first part of the sentence.

25. c. Choice **b** does not use the right verb to maintain the parallelism. Choice **d** changes the pronoun to an incorrect form, and choice **e** changes the pronoun to an article, which is also incorrect.

26. d. This choice changes the verb so that it agrees in number with the subject. Choice **b** changes supplies to singular and that does not fit the sentence. Choices **c** and **e** change the verb tense incorrectly.

27. b. The sentence is missing a subject and this choice provides one. Choice **c** also provides a subject but it does not match the pronoun in the other part of the sentence. Choice **d** changes the verb but there is still no subject, which is also true for choice **e**.

28. e. This sentence contains two clichés that have to be replaced with words strong enough to describe them. Choice **b** only replaces one cliché and choice **c** does the same thing. Choice **d** replaces the clichés but with bland words that do not really capture the cliché meanings. Choice **e** does just that.

29. c. This is an example of commonly confused words: *allusion/illusion*. Choice **b** changes the pronoun incorrectly, while choice **d** eliminates the pronoun and replaces it with *both*, which refers to the writers, so it is incorrect. Choice **e** changes the pronoun incorrectly and keeps the wrong word.

30. a. There are no errors in this sentence.

31. a. This passage constantly switches from past to present to future in its verb tenses, confusing the reader as to when things happened.

32. d. Choice **c** uses a colon, which is not proper punctuation, and choice **e** takes out important details.

33. d. The sentence has a dangling modifier, making it appear as if Parliament has four faces instead of the clock tower.

34. b. The sentence does not fit because it is in first person and it expresses a personal opinion that does fit the pattern of the rest of the passage. Shifting it to third person, as in choice **e**, would not fix it either as the statement still does not belong.

35. c. A transition word indicates contrast is needed, and none of the other selections do this.

36. c. This choice uses slang, which makes it too casual and can create misunderstanding. It does relate to the topic, so choice **a** is incorrect; first person, choice **b**, is used throughout the passage; it definitely expresses an opinion, eliminating choice **d**; and it does relate to the second sentence, choice **e**.

37. e. This paragraph makes the reader want to know when this technology will actually be on the market. Choice **a** would not necessarily be relevant, choice **b** would be too specific for the audience, and choice **d** is too simplified to add to the passage.

38. c. The implication of *ones* is referring to how the headset can be used with other video games.

39. b. This ties the excerpt together and refers to a point made in the introduction. Choice **a** is too casual and choice **c** would be out of order as it belongs earlier in the paragraph. Choice **d** expands on what was said in the first paragraph, and choice **e** is also out of place in the organization of the passage.

40. a. This sentence tells you what the rest of the passage is going to be about. It does not touch on any of the other topics in the distracters.

41. c. A number of key words such as *skillful* and *incredible* show that the author thinks Etters' art is impressive.

42. d. The subject is missing in the sentence, making it a fragment. The remaining choices do not apply: The verb tense and punctuation are correct. There are no modifiers or two complete sentences joined together.

43. b. The quotations fill in additional details about being caught by the police and act as a transition to the next two sentences.

44. d. The main idea of this passage is to explore how a young boy turned his passion into an actual career.

45. b. This is an example of two complete sentences joined together without the proper punctuation or conjunction.

46. c. The second and third paragraphs are not in the correct order and need to be switched around. The other choices don't describe the passage accurately. There is an authority in the passage, it is current, it does not switch tenses, and all details are relevant to the topic.

47. c. The way the author describes the importance of a pet makes it clear that he or she appreciates the value of pets.

48. b. Choice **a** creates a run-on; choice **c** creates a comma splice; choice **d** uses the wrong transition word, as does choice **e**.

49. e. All of the other transition words change the meaning of the sentence.

50. b. The statement is made to show who is in charge of the study. It does not describe the organization or the results; it contains no quotes and lists no statistics.

▶ Part II: Essay

Directions: You will have 45 minutes to plan and write an essay on the topic specified. Read the topic carefully. You are expected to spend a few minutes considering the topic and organizing your thoughts before you begin writing. *Do not write on a topic other than the one specified. An essay on a topic of your own choice is not acceptable.*

The essay is intended to give you an opportunity to demonstrate your ability to write effectively. You should therefore take care to express your thoughts on the topic clearly and precisely and to make them interesting to the reader. Be specific, using supporting examples whenever appropriate. Remember that how well you write is more important than how much you write.

Author Stephen Covey once said, "Opposition is a natural part of life. Just as we develop our physical muscles through overcoming opposition—such as lifting weights—we develop our character muscles by overcoming challenges and adversity." How do you think opposition has affected your character muscles?

▶ Answers

Sample Score 6 Response

I have been told a number of times that opposition is a natural part of life and while I accept that as a life truth, I wish that it were not one. The opposition I have experienced so far in life may be building up my character muscles, but I prefer to think it is primarily teaching me valuable life lessons that I can use in the future so I won't have to repeat or experience them again.

The first time I remember having to flex my character muscles was when my best friend moved away. I was nine years old and we had been best friends since kindergarten. I thought that world had come to an end, but over the years, we were actually able to keep in touch with each other. Even today, we email, write, and call each other on a regular basis.

The second time I encountered something that required me to call on those muscles was when my house caught fire. We were not home at the time but we lost a great many of our belongings, including things that were quite important to me. I still miss some of the toys, books, and clothing that were taken.

Finally, just a few weeks ago, my character muscles got their toughest workout of all. I fell down the stairs at my house and broke my ankle. The pain was awful but it was not what made the experience so terrible. What was so awful about it was that it happened two days before I was to compete in the state gymnastics tournament. That was a disappointment that I am still struggling to have strong enough character muscles to carry.

Clearly, opposition and adversity are an essential part of life that people, including myself, have to accept. However, no one has to enjoy it in the process. We just have to remember that without those moments, we would not be able to appreciate the ones where our character muscles can sit back, relax, and take it easy for a while.

Score Explanation: This essay succeeds on all counts. It is completely on topic; it states a clear opinion and then it follows it up with clear and relevant details. In the end, it ties everything up and comes to a clear conclusion supported by the information in the passage.

Sample Score 4 Response

I am sure that my character muscles are actually more developed than my physical ones. Even though I am still a young person, I have gone through quite a bit during my life time. Since my parents are in the military, I move quite often. This has made my life full of challenges.

So far, I have lived in eight different states. Moving from one place to another is

hard. I hate having to pack up all of my belongings so often. It gets old. After a while, I just want to keep everything in boxes and live out of them instead. I also get tired of meeting people and making friends with them, only to have to turn around and leave them months later. It just makes getting friends and keeping them too hard.

I realize that opposition is a natural part of life and that it makes us stronger, but I do not think that means a person has to like it. One who has to deal with a lot of stress and tension must also find ways to relax oneself. Maybe that search is why we develop those character muscles in the first place. I can feel mine growing now.

Score Explanation: This student does a decent job of answering the question. It is on target and she applies the writing prompt to her own life. She then follows up with some personal examples to support her opinion. In the last paragraph, she shifts away from first person, which makes the paragraph read awkwardly. The student has not included enough details to elevate this decent essay to an excellent one.

Sample Score 2 Response

I never thought about having charcter muscles. When I think about muscles, I think about the work out I do. Every week three or four times. I like feeling really strong. It helps me at my job working on cars.

I go up against my brother alot. We don't along all that great. So he gives me a lot of adversity, I'd say. I know he thinks that I am a challenge. Maybe, one day, when I am a lot older, I will find out that all the disagreements we had were actually making me a stronger person. That would be cool.

My muscles are getting stronger inside and out every day, I think. I don't miss more than two days of working out, I run into troubles of some kind, or opposition, I will handle it. Maybe those character muscles are bigger than I thought.

Score Explanation: Although the student does address the right question, he does not really provide any supportive examples. He also makes a number of spelling and grammar errors. There is no clear thesis statement and there is little demarcation between the introduction, middle, and conclusion.

1 ▶ Identifying Sentence Errors

The following chapter will provide you with an understanding of common sentence errors and the kinds of questions you can expect on the CLEP English Composition exam. All writers make similar and common mistakes when constructing well-written sentences and paragraphs. Some of these errors include comma splices, run-ons, sentence fragments, incorrect pronoun use, and dangling modifiers. Writers occasionally spell a word wrong, choose an incorrect verb tense, or choose a plural verb when the subject calls for a singular verb.

The following examples represent some of the common errors writers make, which are also the kinds of questions you will see on the CLEP English Composition exam.

▶ Run-On Sentences and Comma Splices

Make sure you're not combining two sentences in an incorrect way. Sometimes, without realizing it, you may make the mistake of combining two sentences, when they should either be entirely separate sentences or be linked with correct punctuation. This is called a run-on sentence error.

Example

He ordered the laptop over the Internet he will pay for it when the bill comes.

Corrections

He ordered the laptop over the Internet. He will pay for it when the bill comes.
He ordered the laptop over the Internet; he will pay for it when the bill comes.

To fix the error, you could either add a period after *Internet* and capitalize the *h* of *he* to make them separate sentences. You could also use a semicolon to separate these two independent sentences. This form of punctuation shows that the two sentences are related and independent.

It would be incorrect to do this:

He ordered the laptop over the Internet, he will pay for it when the bill comes.

You cannot fix the sentence by simply inserting a comma between the two sentences. This is called a comma splice.

There is another way that you can correct a run-on sentence. You can add a dependent clause, as follows:

He ordered the laptop over the Internet and will pay for it when the bill comes.

A dependent clause is a group of words that has a subject and a predicate but does not express a complete thought.

In general, if you use a comma to connect two independent clauses, it must be accompanied by a conjunction. Examples of these conjunctions include *and, but, for, nor, yet, or, so.*

▶ Sentence Fragments

The most common mistake that people make when forming sentences is leaving out either the subject or the predicate. If either the subject or the predicate is left out of a sentence, it's not complete. It's a sentence fragment. The good news is that once you are easily able to identify subjects and predicates in sentences, you'll be able to check for sentence fragments in your essay.

A sentence must convey a complete idea and include the following:
- a subject (the person or actor in the sentence)
- a predicate (the verb or action in the sentence)
- a complete thought (this means that the thought can stand alone)

Examples

After the rain stops.
If you join me.

Corrections

After the rain stops, we can race across the street to the theater.
If you join me, we can go to the gathering together.

To fix the error, you can complete the thought by adding a subject and predicate. (There are many variations here.)

▶ Pronoun Errors

A **pronoun** is a word that replaces a noun in a sentence. Sometimes knowing which pronoun to use can be complicated, especially when replacing nouns other than proper names. Take a look at this incorrect sentence.

Everyone has *their* favorite food.

Everyone is singular, even though it seems plural. Think of it as *every one person*. *Their* is plural, so the two don't go together. The correct way to write this sentence follows.

Everyone has *his* or *her* favorite food.

Here is a list of some other pronouns that seem like they are plural but are really singular. Each would need to be used with another singular pronoun, such as *his* or *her*.

nobody
everybody
no one
each
somebody
either
anyone

Pronouns take the subjective case (pronoun as subject), objective case (pronoun as object), or possessive case (pronouns that describe ownership).

▶ Pronouns as subjects include *I, you, he, she, it, we, they,* and *who.*

▶ Pronouns as objects include *me, you, him, her, it, us, them,* and *whom.*

▶ Pronouns that show possession include *my* (*mine*), *your* (*yours*), *his, her* (*hers*), *it* (*its*), *our* (*ours*), *their* (*theirs*), and *whose.*

Pronouns can also get confusing when they are paired with *I* or *me.* For instance, the following sentence is incorrect.

Her and me went to the mall.

An easy way to see which pronoun to use in a sentence is to test them individually. See if either *her* or *me* makes sense in the sentence by itself. It would be incorrect to say *Her went to the mall,* and it would also be incorrect to say *Me went to the mall.* So, together, they don't make sense. To be correct, you would say *I went to the mall* or *She went to the mall,* so the sentence should read as follows.

She and I went to the mall.

So, if you're facing a pair of pronouns and are unsure which to use, just read the sentence with only one pronoun at a time to figure it out.

Example
Ray and me want to open up an ice cream shop.

Correction
Ray and I want to open up an ice cream shop.
In this sentence, *I* is part of the subject.

Example
The women, three of who had jobs in engineering, decided to go to graduate school.

Correction
The women, three of whom had jobs in engineering, decided to go to graduate school.
In this sentence, *whom* is correct when talking about three women.

▶ Errors in Word Choice and Diction

In this instance, the writer may choose words or phrases that are unclear or incorrect. Are word choices clear and direct? Are there any repetitive or awkward sentences or phrases? Are there any clichés, pretentious language, or confusing jargon? Does the writer avoid using ambiguous words and phrases?

When editing his or her work, a writer should clean up and clear up words and sentences to make them better convey your intended meaning and easier to understand.

Example

He could of gone to the County Clerk's Office before they closed.

Correction

He could have gone to the County Clerk's Office before they closed.

In this sentence, the preposition *of* should be replaced with the verb *have*.

Example

He was setting outside for at least an hour before the mail arrived.

Correction

He was sitting outside for at least an hour before the mail arrived.

Set means to put or lay something down. In this sentence, the correct word is *sitting*.

Word Choices for Concise Writing	
WORDY:	**REPLACE WITH:**
a lot of	many or much
all of a sudden	suddenly
along the lines of	like, such as
are able to	can
as a matter of fact	in fact or delete
as a person	delete
as a whole	delete
as the case may be	delete
at the present time	currently or now
both of these	both
by and large	delete
by definition	delete
due to the fact that	because
for all intents and purposes	delete
has a tendency to	often or delete
has the ability to	can
in order to	to
in the event that	if
in the near future	soon
is able to	can
it is clear that	delete
last but not least	finally
on a daily basis	daily

on account of the fact that	because
particular	delete
somewhere in the neighborhood of	about, around
take action	act
the fact that	that, or delete
the majority of	most
the reason why	the reason or why
through the use of	through
with regard to	about or regarding
with the exception of	except for

▶ Dangling Modifiers

The dangling modifier is a word or phrase that modifies a word or phrase in a sentence. The error occurs when a phrase or clause is left without a particular word in the sentence to modify.

Example
While setting the table, the doorbell rang.

Correction
While I was setting the table, the doorbell rang.

Who was setting the table—the doorbell? No, so the pronoun *I* needs to be used to explain who is setting the table.

Example
My sister won first place in the beauty pageant that was great.

Correction
It was great that my sister won first place in the beauty pageant.

In the first sentence, it is not clear if the pageant is great or if the sister winning the pageant is great.

▶ Practice Questions

Directions: The following sentences test your knowledge of grammar, usage, diction (choice of words), and idiom. Some sentences are correct. No sentence contains more than one error.

You will find that the error, if there is one, is underlined and lettered. Assume that elements of the sentence that are not underlined are correct and cannot be changed. In choosing answers, follow the requirements of standard written English.

If there is an error, selected the <u>one underlined part</u> that must be changed to make the sentence correct. If there is no error, select choice **e**.

1. The fellow <u>stopped</u> the car, <u>throwing</u> open the door, <u>raced</u> up to the house, <u>and rang</u> the doorbell several

               a   b   c   d

times. <u>No error.</u>

        e

2. The author <u>explain</u> to the students that <u>he spent</u> five years <u>revising</u> his <u>recently published</u> current novel.

               a   b   c   d

<u>No error.</u>

   e

3. The taxi driver <u>hit</u> the <u>brakes</u>, and the passenger <u>jumped out</u> of the car <u>and into</u> the ravine. <u>No error.</u>

                  a   b   c   d   e

4. She <u>studied</u> the two photographs, <u>but she could</u> not decide <u>which</u> was the <u>most</u> beautiful picture. <u>No error.</u>

         a   b   c   d   e

5. Susan <u>works near</u> a <u>deli, every</u> morning she <u>grabs</u> a bagel and coffee before <u>heading to</u> her office. <u>No error.</u>

            a   b   c   d   e

6. <u>Neither</u> <u>of the</u> girls took <u>their</u> backpack to the auditorium for the <u>before-school</u> assembly. <u>No error.</u>

    a   b   c   d   e

▶ Answers

1. b. This sentence lacks parallel construction—that is, a series of words, phrases, or clauses written in a parallel structure. This enables the reader to see the relationship between the words and the intent in the sentence. The first verb, *stopped,* ends in *-ed*. The next verb, *throwing,* is an *-ing* verb, also called a gerund. This form of the word *throw* is not parallel in construction with the word *stopped* or the verb *raced*.

2. a. The correct verb is *explained,* a singular, past-tense verb for the singular subject *author.*

3. e. No error.

4. d. The word *most* should be *more* when you are making a comparison between two things.

5. b. This is an example of a comma splice. There should be the conjunction *and* after the comma and before the word *every.*

6. c. A pronoun will often refer to a noun or serve as a substitute for a particular noun. *Neither* is singular, so the answer would be *her backpack,* not *their backpack.*

Restructuring Sentences

On the CLEP English Composition exam, you will encounter questions that ask you to rework words or phrases in order to deepen clarity and coherence in a sentence. In some instances, you will need to change part of the original sentence. In other instances, you will need to change the whole sentence.

As you rebuild the given sentence, the intent in the original sentence should be reflected in the revision.

Example

Might it not be better for the actors if we rehearse the first act of the play and spend less time on the second act of the play?

End with <u>a period</u> instead of <u>a question mark</u>.

Your new sentence will contain

a. will be better
b. it will be better
c. might be better
d. might not be better
e. will not be better

Your rephrased sentence will probably read: "It might be better for the actors if we rehearse the first act of the play and spend less time on the second act of the play." The new sentence contains the correct answer, choice **c**, *might be better*.

Writers need options when they revise their work. There is often more than one way for an idea or purpose to be expressed. As you read the Restructuring Sentences CLEP questions, you may decide to remove certain words or add words.

▶ Practice Questions

Directions: Revise each of the following sentences according to the directions that follow it. Some directions require you to change only part of the original sentence, while others require you to change the entire sentence. You may need to omit or add words in constructing an acceptable revision, but you should keep the meaning of the revised sentences as close to the meaning of the original sentence as the directions permit. Your new sentences should follow the conventions of standard written English and should be clear and precise.

Look at answer choices **a** through **e** under each question for the exact word or phrase that is included in your revised sentence and choose that answer letter. If you have thought of a revision that does not include any of the words or phrases listed, try to revise the sentence again so that it does include the wording in one of the answer choices.

1. *The reader is given a sense of the difficult but colorful lives of people in Isak Dinesen's stories about Africa.*

   Begin with <u>Isak Dinesen's stories</u>.
   Your new sentence will contain
   a. describe
   b. will provide the reader with
   c. make the reader
   d. tell the reader
   e. would have given

2. *Most of the voters doubt that their candidate will be among the election winners.*

   Begin with <u>Few voters</u>.
   Your new sentence will contain
   a. lack hope
   b. have no hope
   c. have little expectation
   d. expect
   e. expected

3. *According to the American Dietetic Association, babies born to vegetarian moms are on average the same birth weight as babies born to non-vegetarian moms.*

   Begin with <u>An American Dietetic Association report</u>.
   Your new sentence will contain
   a. does not believe
   b. claims that
   c. on average states that
   d. defends babies
   e. worries that babies

4. *In May, the instructor was fired from her job because she refused to learn the computerized grading system used throughout the university.*

Begin with <u>The instructor refused</u>.

Your new sentence will contain

a. ; in May she was fired

b. , but she was fired

c. , yet she was fired

d. , and resulting in,

e. , because she was fired

5. *Stepping off the train, the woman immediately found the new bookstore she had read about in the Sunday paper.*

Begin with <u>The woman stepped</u>.

Your new sentence will contain

a. and immediately

b. and she looked for

c. looking for the

d. immediately and then

e. before she found

▶ **Answers**

1. a. Your rephrased sentence will probably read: "Isak Dinesen's stories *describe* the difficult but colorful lives of people in Africa."

2. d. Your rephrased sentence will probably read: "Few voters *expect* that their candidate will be among the election winners."

3. b. Your rephrased sentence will probably read: "An American Dietetic Association report *claims that* babies born to vegetarian moms are on average of similar weight to babies born to non-vegetarian moms."

4. a. Your rephrased sentence will probably read: "The instructor refused to learn the computerized grading system used throughout the university; *in May she was fired* from her job."

5. a. Your rephrased sentence will probably read: "The woman stepped off the train *and immediately* found the new bookstore she has read about in the Sunday paper."

3 ▶ Improving Sentences

There are several elements of sentence construction that support clear and cohesive writing. Sometimes these elements of good sentence building are missing.

In this chapter, you will see examples of questions that ask you to improve sentences. On the English Composition exam, you are expected to evaluate the quality and structure of a sentence. A good way to conquer these questions is to read the original sentence together with each answer choice in your head. The one that sounds correct, usually is correct.

Example

Our local pizzeria was shut down <u>because the owner sold pizza slices to patrons that were full of mold.</u>

    a. because the owner sold pizza slices to patrons that were full of mold.

    b. because the owner sold pizza slices to moldy patrons.

    c. because the owner sold pizza slices to patrons who were full of mold.

    d. because the owner sold moldy pizza slices to patrons.

    e. because the owner sold pizza slices who were moldy.

Choice **d** would improve this sentence. The owner sold moldy pizza to patrons. The clause *that were full of mold* is placed at the end of the sentence. The original sentence reads as if the patrons are full of mold. A misplaced clause can cause confusion for readers.

Example

Many homeowners are "going green," as more and more Americans are expressing concern over global warming.

 a. As more and more Americans are concerned about global warming, many homeowners are "going green."
 b. Many homeowners are switching to "green" habits, more and more Americans are expressing concern over global warming.
 c. More and more Americans are concerned about global warming, and this trend is best seen in the way homeowners are switching to "green" habits.
 d. More and more Americans are concerned over global warming as many homeowners "go green."
 e. If more and more Americans express concern over global warming, many homeowners will "go green."

Choice **a** would improve this sentence. Choice **a** suggests that there is a growing concern about global warming and many homeowners are practicing "going green."

▶ Practice Questions

Directions: In each of the following sentences, part of the sentence or the entire sentence is underlined. Beneath each sentence, you will find five versions of the underlined part. Choice **a** repeats the original; the other four are different.

Choose the answer that best expresses the meaning of the original sentence. If you think the original is better than any of the other alternatives, choose **a**; otherwise choose one of the others. Your choice should produce the most effective sentence—one that is clear and precise, without awkwardness or ambiguity.

 1. The long-term effects of caffeine on individuals with high blood pressure are more pronounced than they are for people with normal blood pressure.
 a. more pronounced
 b. most pronounced
 c. seriously pronounced
 d. much pronounced
 e. more pronounced it seems

 2. The little girl sat the vase on her grandmother's coffee table and darted outside to play.
 a. The little girl sat the vase
 b. The little girl can set the vase
 c. The little girl set the vase
 d. The little girl is setting the vase
 e. The little girl will set the vase

 3. Reaching the summit of Mt. Washington through Tuckerman's Ravine are truly one of the most exhilarating adventures for the New England traveler.
 a. Mount Washington through Tuckerman's Ravine are truly
 b. Mount Washington on Tuckerman's Ravine are truly
 c. Mount Washington's though Tuckerman's Ravine is truly
 d. Mount Washington through Tuckerman's Ravine is truly
 e. Mount Washington's through Tuckerman's Ravine is truly

4. Also called "flying rodents," researchers have noted that bats play an important role in nature because they pollinate certain species of flowers, and they help in seed dispersal.

   a. Also called "flying rodents," researchers have noted that bats play an important role in nature because they pollinate certain species of flowers, and they help in seed dispersal.

   b. Bats, also called "flying rodents," play an important role in nature because they pollinate certain species of flowers, and they help in seed dispersal researchers have noted.

   c. Unexpectedly called "flying rodents," researchers have discovered that bats play an important role in nature because they pollinate certain species of flowers, and they play an important role in seed dispersal

   d. Researchers have noted that bats, also called "flying rodents," play a critical role in nature because they pollinate certain species of flowers and they help in seed dispersal.

   e. Researchers have noted that bats can and do sometimes play an important role in nature because they pollinate certain species of flowers and they help in seed dispersal

5. Nineteenth-century composer, Eric Satie, known as an eccentric to his friends and other musicians, gave unusual instructions to his performer; the instructions were supposed to be a conversation between the composer and the performer.

   a. Nineteenth-century composer, Eric Satie, known as an eccentric to his friends and other musicians, gave unusual instructions to his performer; the instructions were supposed to be a conversation between the composer and the performer.

   b. Nineteenth-century composer, Eric Satie gave instructions on a conversation between the composer and the performer known as an eccentric to his friends and other musicians.

   c. Nineteenth-century composer, Eric Satie, known as an eccentric to his friends and other musicians gave unusual instructions to the performer, the instructions were supposed to be a conversation between the composer and the performer.

   d. Giving instructions that were supposed to be a conversation between the composer and his friends; Eric Satie, a nineteenth-century composer, also known as an eccentric to his friends and other musicians.

   e. Nineteenth-century composer, Eric Satie, gave instructions to the performer that were like a conversation because he was known as an eccentric among his friends and with other musicians.

▶ Answers

1. **a.** Choice **b** is incorrect; *most pronounced* is incorrectly used for a comparison of two kinds of individuals. Choice **c** is incorrect; *seriously* gives the sentence a new and different meaning than the original sentence. Choice **d** is incorrect; *much pronounced* does not fit the standards of conventional English. Choice **e** is incorrect; *more pronounced it seems* changes the meaning of the sentence.

2. **c.** The word *set* is used when referring to an object. Choice **a** is incorrect; *sat* means to sit (as in a person sitting in a chair). Choice **b** is incorrect; it changes the meaning in the sentence. Choices **d** and **e** change the verb tense of the original sentence.

3. **c.** *Reaching . . . summit* is the singular subject of this particular sentence; *are* should be *is*.

4. **d.** *Flying rodents* refers to the bats, not the researchers.

5. **a.** The original sentence is correct. There are two independent clauses connected together by a semicolon.

CHAPTER

4 ▶ Revising Work in Progress

When you write an essay, it's not really done until you proofread and revise it. It's tempting to stop after you've initially put down the pen—you've worked hard to create a clear piece of writing, with well-thought-out points and well-constructed paragraphs. You'd be amazed, however, at how much your essay can improve with a little revising and editing.

When you revise an essay, you'll be looking at it with a fresh pair of eyes. When you're working on writing your essay and you're in it up to your elbows, it can be difficult to see some of the mistakes that you're making. It's important to take a little time to rejuvenate yourself, and then come back to your writing and fix it up, so that it's the best that it can be.

When revising, you go back over what you've written to make it clearer, more concise, and more organized. The process of revising is simple. Just ask yourself some questions, and while you do that, read over what you have and make sure you're able to answer each question with a definitive *yes*. Here are some questions to ask yourself as you revise.

- Does your introduction draw in the reader?
- Does your essay have a thesis statement?

- Have you addressed the topic?
- Is your writing clear?
- Have you included unnecessary details or information?
- Is your style consistent?
- Is there a good flow from beginning to end?
- Does each paragraph have a topic sentence and supporting ideas?
- Does the conclusion flow logically out of the paragraph before it (or does it seem disjointed)?
- Does your conclusion remind the reader of your thesis and supporting ideas without repeating word for word what you said in your introduction?

When you revise your writing, you're also going to look for errors in grammar, spelling, punctuation, and word usage. To do this, you're going to need to read each sentence very carefully. As you're reading each sentence, look for the following problems:

- inconsistent tense
- grammar errors
- spelling errors
- punctuation errors
- misused words
- overuse of passive voice
- words and phrases that are repeated too often

Some CLEP English Composition questions ask you to revise a rough draft of a student's work in progress. The sentences in the work are numbered to assist you in locating text. In some instances, sentences or portions of the selection will need to be changed.

There are basically seven kinds of Revising Work in Progress questions on the English Composition exam:

- Sentence combining and revising: Which of the following is the best way to revise and combine sentences 1 and 2?
- Adding before or after a sentence: Which of the following sentences, if added after (or before) sentence 1, would best link that sentence to the rest of the paragraph?
- Changing part of a sentence within the context of the paragraph: Which of the following is the best version of the underlined portion of sentence 1?
- Determining the strategies used by the author: All of the following strategies are used by the writer in the passage EXCEPT . . . .
- Replacing part of a sentence with different words or leaving it the same: Which of the following is the best replacement for the last word in the sentence?
- Changing sentences by moving them, combining them, etc.: The writer of the passage could best improve sentences 1 and 2 by . . . .
- Improving a sentence: The writer of the passage could best improve sentence 1 by . . . .

▶ Practice Questions

Directions: Each of the following passages consists of numbered sentences. Because the passages are part of longer writing samples, they do not necessarily constitute a complete discussion of the issues presented.

Read each passage carefully and answer the questions that follow. The questions test your awareness of a writer's purpose and of characteristics of prose that are important to good writing.

Use the following passage to answer questions 1–4.

(1) What is your method or strategy for choosing a topic for an essay? (2) What do you do to choose a topic for an essay? (3) How do you know if your topic is too broad or too narrow? (4) Mind mapping can assist you in identifying your topic and explore the details you may want to include in your essay. (5) And, mind mapping is a more structured strategy than simply jotting down random thoughts in a brainstorming strategy.

(6) The connections or branches that generate from your initial idea. (7) The branches can help you remember the details you wish to explore in your central idea. (8) These branches are a road map of ideas. (9) A visual display of connections. (10) The random recording of a writer's ideas might lead to problems in finding a structure for your essay. (11) Mind maps work because the visual display leads you to constructing good and substantive details for your essay.

1. What should be done with sentence 2?
   a. Leave the sentence as it is.
   b. It should be placed after the last sentence.
   c. It should be placed after sentence 8.
   d. It should be used as the topic sentence in paragraph 2.
   e. The sentence should be removed.

2. Which of the following is the best way to rewrite the underlined portion of sentence 4 (reproduced here)?
   Mind mapping can assist you in identifying your topic and explore the details you may want to include in your essay.
   a. explored the details
   b. once you have explored
   c. finding ways to explore
   d. in exploring the details
   e. in the exploration of

3. Which of the following is the best way to combine and rewrite sentences 6 and 7 (reproduced here)?
   The connections or branches that generate from your initial idea. The branches can help you remember the details you wish to explore in your central idea.
   a. The connections or branches that generate from your initial idea; the branches can help writers remember the details you wish to explore about your central idea.
   b. The connections or branches that generate from your initial idea and the branches can help you remember the details you wish to explore in your central idea.
   c. Use the branches to create your ideas and to explore your ideas
   d. The connections or branches that generate from your initial idea are the same branches that can help you remember the details you wish to explore in your central idea.
   e. The connections or branches that generate from your initial idea can help you remember the details you wish to explore in your central idea.

4. The best words to substitute for the phrase *leads you to constructing* in sentence 11 is
   a. assists you in constructing
   b. mind maps
   c. creates a visual to your constructing
   d. gives you ideas for constructing
   e. constructing

Use the following passage to answer questions 5–8.

(1) Mario Vargas Llosa a novelist and journalist was born in Peru in 1936. (2) As an undergraduate in Peru, he studied literature and law and later he worked on his PhD at a university in Spain. (3) He has written many novels. (4) Many are successful. (5) Vargas Llosa's first highly acclaimed novel, *La Ciudad y los Perros (The City and the Dogs)*, was published in 1963. (6) Having gone to school there, the novel takes place at Leoncio Prado Military Academy in Peru.

(7) In the novel *The Storyteller*, Vargas Llosa writes about the diverse but separate communities in Peru. (8) Peru has many different cultures. (9) Saul Zuratas a novel character tries to rid himself of his western upbringing and traditions and decides to live with a Peruvian tribe, the Machiguengas. (10) But Zuratas cannot separate himself from his past the heritage of what he is. (11) And in fact, the very roots he attempts to shed he imposes on the Machiguengas. (12) This struggle to understand the self is a common theme in Vargas Llosa's novels.

5. Which is the best revision of sentence 1 (reproduced here)?

Mario Vargas Llosa a novelist and journalist was born in Peru in 1936.

a. Mario Vargas Llosa is a novelist and journalist and born in Peru in 1936.

b. Mario Vargas Llosa, a novelist and journalist, was born in Peru in 1936.

c. Mario Vargas Llosa was a novelist and journalist born in Peru in 1936.

d. Mario Vargas Llosa was born in Peru in 1936 a novelist and journalist.

e. Born in Peru in 1936, Mario Vargas Llosa is a novelist and journalist.

6. Which of the following is the best way to rewrite and combine sentences 3 and 4 (reproduced here)?

He has written many novels. Many are successful.

a. A prolific writer, Vargas Llosa written many novels; many are successful.

b. A prolific writer, Vargas Llosa has written many successful novels.

c. He has written many novels he is a prolific writer.

d. He has written many successful novels, and some are successful.

e. He has written many novels and furthermore many of them are successful.

7. What would be the best way to rewrite sentence 6 (reproduced here)?

Having gone to school there, the novel takes place at Leoncio Prado Military Academy in Peru.

a. Having gone to high school there, the novel took place at Leoncio Prado Military Academy in Peru.

b. Having gone to high school there; the novel took place at Leoncio Prado Military Academy in Peru.

c. The novel took place at Leoncio Prado Military Academy in Peru, where Vargas Llosa attended high school.

d. The novel took place at Leoncio Prado Military Academy in Peru and that is where Vargas Llosa attend high school.

e. Vargas Llosa attending high school at the Leoncio Prado Military Academy, where the novel would take place.

8. What should be done with sentence 8?

   a. It should be left as it is.

   b. It should be omitted.

   c. It should be placed before sentence 7.

   d. It should be combined with sentence 9.

   e. It should be used as the topic sentence of the paragraph.

▶ Answers

1. e. Sentence 2 repeats sentence 1.

2. d. The word *exploring* is a construction that is parallel with the word *identifying*.

3. e. Sentence 6 is a fragment. It is not a whole and complete idea. Combining sentence 6 with sentence 7 makes the idea whole. You do not need to repeat *branches* in the second half of the combined sentence.

4. a. The mind map doesn't construct the good details, but it does help or assist the writer in constructing the details.

5. b. Commas are needed to offset a novelist and journalist.

6. b. The dependent clause *a prolific writer* describes Vargas Llosa.

7. c. Choice **c** places the dependant clause correctly.

8. b. Sentence 8 is not needed because it repeats sentence 7.

5 ▶ Analyzing Writing

The CLEP English Composition exam contains Analyzing Writing questions, where test takers are given a set of passages in which the sentences are numbered for easy reference. In most cases, the passages are part of a longer writing sample, but test takers will not get the entire sample. This often requires test takers to infer how the original passage was presented. These questions test the student's ability to analyze a writing sample and determine several key components:

- the main idea or thesis statement
- content
- the writer's style
- the inner organization of the paragraph based on sentence relationship
- functions of specific sentences to the whole piece
- general revising

These questions assess your understanding of the skills needed to write an essay. You will read a brief passage and respond to questions that require you to consider the right steps you need to take in revising, and in some instances redirecting, a passage. You will be asked to answer questions that explore the organization of the essay, sentence structure and sentence combining, and the style and tone of the writing in the essay. You may also be asked to make inferences, identify the theme and tone in the essay, and find the thesis statement as well as the introductory and concluding paragraphs. Finally, you may be asked to respond to questions about the audience.

The English Composition exam includes seven types of Analyzing Writing questions:

- Main Idea: The main idea of the passage is that . . . OR Which of the following most accurately describes what happens in the second paragraph?
- Purpose: The purpose of this passage (or paragraph 1) is primarily to . . . .
- Description of Content: Which of the following pairs of words best describes the speaker's reaction to the experience?
- Style: The descriptive details in sentence 1 (or in sentences 1, 2, and 3) provide a . . . OR The order of presentation provides . . . .
- Relationships: The relationship of sentence 1 to the rest of the paragraph is . . . OR The relationship of the two paragraphs to each other is . . . .
- Functions of Sentences: The function of sentence 1 is primarily to . . . .
- Revising: What treatment of sentence 1 is most needed?

▶ Practice Questions

Directions: The following passage consists of numbered sentences. Because the passage is part of a longer sample, it does not necessarily constitute a complete discussion of the issues presented.

Read the passage carefully and answer the questions that follow it. The questions test your awareness of a writer's purpose and of characteristics of prose that are important to good writing.

Use the following passage to answer questions 1–6.

(1) Friedrich Wilhelm Herschel was born in Hanover (Germany) in 1738. (2) William's father conducted the military band, and his mother watched over him and his brothers and sisters. (3) As a young man, William studied music, but he had an insatiable thirst for knowledge, particularly the night sky. (4) He couldn't learn enough. (5) William knew from early on that he wanted to know more about night sky than astronomers already knew. (6) As a child and a young adult, William spent countless hours with his father and brothers discussing the theories in physics and astronomy.

(7) When William was just 18, he moved to England and settled in the town of Bath. (8) William quickly developed a career as a musician; he played the oboe, conducted the church choir, and composed music. (9) But William could not forget his interest in astronomy. (10) He read James Ferguson's book, *Astronomy,* and other books on optics and on building telescopes. (11) When William built his first telescope, visitors came from all over Europe to view the night sky. (12) No one had ever seen the rings of Saturn as clearly as they could be seen with William's telescope. (13) On March 13, 1781, William Herschel discovered what he initially thought was a comet. (14) His discovery turned out to be a planet that was later named Uranus. (15) A noted astronomer, William Herschel saw more than others before him, and he was a major player in the field of astronomy.

1. Which of the following pairs of words best describes the speaker's description of William Herschel?
   a. disgust and anger
   b. anxiety and fear
   c. respect and admiration
   d. delight and joy
   e. disinterest and detachment

2. What should be done to improve sentence 4?
   a. The sentence should appear at the beginning of the first paragraph.
   b. The sentence should be combined with sentence 3.
   c. The sentence should be removed.
   d. The sentence should appear after sentence 5.
   e. It should be repeated at least twice more in the essay.

3. The details of Herschel's life in sentences 7–15 provide
   a. a view from a competitor's perspective.
   b. a chronicle of a man finding his passion and following his dream.
   c. a narrative of a man's fall into obscurity.
   d. a completely inaccurate description of Herschel.
   e. a sense that all is not good with Herschel.

4. How would you describe the relationship between paragraphs 1 and 2?
   a. Paragraph 1 describes Herschel's early work and paragraph 2 describes his later work.
   b. The second paragraph has nothing to do with the first paragraph.
   c. Paragraph 1 establishes a thesis and paragraph 2 specifically reinforces and supports that thesis.
   d. Paragraph 2 has more details than are needed to support paragraph 1.
   e. Paragraphs 1 and 2 are equally vague.

5. The tone of the paragraph is
   a. informal.
   b. satiric.
   c. very formal.
   d. witty.
   e. convincing.

6. The passage is an example of
   a. argumentative writing.
   b. too much detail.
   c. fiction writing.
   d. comparison/contrast writing.
   e. biographical writing.

▶ Answers

1. c. The author expresses a measured and reverent view of William Herschel.
2. c. The sentence merely repeats sentence 3.
3. b. This section reinforces Hershel's passion, as described in paragraph 1.
4. c. Paragraph 2 explains how Herschel followed his interest in astronomy.
5. e. The thesis statement in sentence 3 explains that he has a goal and a dream. Paragraph 2 explains how he reaches that dream.
6. e. The essay explores the life of William Herschel.

6 ▶ Writing an Essay

This chapter will prepare you to take the essay portion of the English Composition exam. If you choose to take this section of the examination, your exam will not include the Analyzing Writing and Restructuring Sentences sections. In this essay, you are expected to present a point of view in response to a topic and to support it with a logical argument and appropriate evidence. Your essay will be typed on the computer.

The CLEP English Composition essay may be unlike any other kind of writing you've had to do. Although the fundamentals of good writing remain a constant, the approach to this task is radically different. You don't have time to brainstorm, outline, revise, and edit the way you would if the clock wasn't ticking. When you have just 45 minutes, each one counts. The scorers know this, so they're trained to look for "polished rough drafts." Does that mean you can forget about spelling, verb tenses, and idioms? Not exactly. How can you produce a high-scoring essay under pressure? The key is preparation.

Today the concept of the word *essay* is a common form of writing, but the origins of the essay date back to the French influence on Early Modern English. The actual word *essay* comes from the French verb *essai,* which means "to examine, test, or (literally) to drive out." This ancient word remains part of our writing culture today; the academic essay is an opportunity to explore a topic and examine the ideas within that topic.

▶ The Art of Persuasion

The CLEP essay calls for a persuasive essay, one in which you choose an idea and show why it is legitimate or worthy. Your purpose is not to merely to explain your point of view, but to convince your reader that it makes sense. In order to persuade effectively, you must base your argument on reasoning and logic.

If you are unsure or undecided in your stance, your writing will be weak and your score will suffer. However, even a strong opinion is not enough. Like a lawyer before a jury, you must convince your reader with evidence that your opinion is valid. This evidence consists of concrete examples, illustrations, and details. Therefore, the most important strategy for the persuasive essay is to choose the side that has the best, or most, evidence. If you believe in that side, your argument will most likely be even stronger. (Although, as previously mentioned, you don't have to believe in it to write a good essay.)

The essay does not require specific knowledge of literature, history, or current events. However, the topics are broad enough that you will probably be able to use your knowledge from these areas to answer the question. While you can always rely on personal experience, as many high-scoring essays do, it's a good idea to review areas you've studied or are otherwise familiar with to use on test day. (Don't try to learn new material for the essay.) Here are some ideas for what to review:

- **Literature:** poems, novels, plays, and myths with broad themes that can be applied to a number of topics. Orwell's *Animal Farm,* for example, could be used to discuss equality ("some animals are more equal than others"), the class system, or forms of government.
- **History:** events and time periods such as World War II, the Great Depression, treatment of Native Americans, and America's break from British rule. Historical events may be written about from many perspectives, and can be used to make points about a variety of subjects. The Depression, for example, was an economic event that had many factors, including human emotion (such as fear).
- **Science:** technology, space exploration, the concept of absolute zero, acid rain, and other environmental issues. For example, you could discuss global warming in terms of humans' disregard for the planet, or in terms of a positive worldwide response that is bringing together many nations.

Whatever the subjects you've studied, think in terms of flexibility. How many different ways can you look at an event, an invention, or a work of nonfiction? What does it mean to people, how do they respond to it, or how has it changed the world (for better or worse)? Having a few adaptable subjects fresh in your mind may help you respond quickly, specifically, and thoroughly to what will most likely be a very general prompt.

► Anatomy of an Essay

Forty-five minutes is not enough time to come up with an innovative structure for your essay. You need to address the topic in a clear, well-organized fashion, using examples and details to make your point. The best way to accomplish those goals is to stick to a traditional format, the five-paragraph essay. Aim for an introduction, three body paragraphs, and a concluding paragraph. Organized within this format, your ideas will be easily available to your reader (the person scoring your essay), and you will have more time to develop and substantiate them.

Introduction: Thesis Statement and Hook

The introduction presents the reader with your topic and point of view. It is more general than the body paragraphs of the essay, which contain the specific examples and evidence that help you substantiate and develop your topic. The goal of the introduction is to make the reader clearly understand your position, without being trite or boring. To accomplish it, you'll need to write two things: a thesis statement and a hook.

A clear thesis statement is one sentence that refers directly to the topic. It gets right to the point, because the real "meat" of your essay, where you can deliver the greatest impact to the reader, is in the body. Stating your thesis quickly and clearly means avoiding disclaimers such as "I'm not sure, but . . ." and "This may not be right . . . ." Such disclaimers are a waste of time and will lose points with your reader. No matter how strong your argument becomes in later paragraphs, that initial poor impression will stick. Instead, be confident and direct. A clear thesis statement shows the graders that you understand the assignment and have formulated a relevant response to it. It also sets the stage for a well-developed essay supported by specific and interesting examples.

But direct doesn't mean trite. Relying on overused words and phrases to help make your point is the most common way to weaken your introduction. Compare *In today's society, people don't practice good manners often enough* with *Good manners are an essential part of a civil society*. The problem with the first sentence is the first three words. *In today's society* is a clichéd opening, whereas the second sentence makes its point directly, without any overused language.

Once you've narrowed down your topic and have a clear, confident thesis statement, think about how to grab your reader's attention. Imagine you're an essay grader reading hundreds or thousands of CLEP essays. It's late and you're tired. Which of the following first sentences would make you sit up and take notice of the essay?

Imagine a world in which plant life is reduced to a few hardy specimens, drought is commonplace, and the world's coastal regions are under water.

The future effects of global warming will be bad.

The first sentence is a *hook*; it is designed to inspire the reader to want to read the rest of the essay. How can you come up with something so seemingly clever and innovative in a minute or two? It's not as hard as it looks; what at first glance appears clever and innovative is really the product of a learned method. Two types of hooks are quick and easy to create. If you study them and practice writing them from sample prompts, you'll be able to write a hook for your essay.

One type of hook is used in the first example: a dramatic scenario, saying, or statistic. A **scenario** paints a vivid picture with words. A related **statistic**, **proverb**, or other **saying** can boldly introduce your topic, show off your knowledge, and give your writing some heft. Statistics in particular add a tone of seriousness and importance to your writing; they say, "I'm not the only one who thinks this way—there are studies to back me up." Compare the following examples:

Not only is the number of overall incidents of cancer in Americans decreasing, but survival rates are dramatically increasing.

More people survive cancer these days.

The other type of quick hook to study and practice is **questioning**. Pose a specific, relevant question to your reader that will naturally lead into your topic. In the following introductory paragraph, the hook is in bold.

Example

Is the difference between a good neighbor and a bad neighbor simply that one doesn't hit baseballs through your windows, and the other does? It's not that simple. There are many qualities of a good neighbor, and one of the most important is distance. Having your own space, and having your neighbor respect that space, is the key to a good next-door relationship. This is true whether discussing the person whose lawn abuts yours, the students you attend class with, or the nation with which yours shares a border.

In this introductory paragraph, the writer mentions three examples that will be explored in the essay. This is a great way to transition the reader from the introduction to the body of the essay. However, it's not always possible to have those three examples at the ready. What if you have two, but are betting the third will come to you while writing the body? It's still better to give the reader an idea of the direction you're headed before jumping into the "meat" of the essay. This technique shows off your thinking skills and your ability to organize your ideas.

Body

In the body of your essay, you develop and illustrate your ideas on your topic. It is where you add the interesting details and examples that support your thesis and make your essay stand out. The body should be three paragraphs, one for each example or idea.

It's been said already that a few small grammar or mechanics errors will be overlooked. However, you probably noticed when reading the scoring rubric that sentence variety is important to your reader. Don't use too many short, choppy sentences; vary your sentence structure so that your reading is interesting and flows easily.

In addition, word choice is important. A sophisticated vocabulary will make your essay stand out from those with a more basic vocabulary. While nothing can take the place of years of reading challenging material and exposing yourself to a variety of texts, study can help. Keep up your reading in the months before the CLEP. When you encounter new words, notice their context and look up their definitions in the dictionary. Search the Internet with the terms CLEP and vocabulary. You'll find dozens of websites with lists of words that frequently appear on the CLEP. Study those you don't know, aiming to learn at least five new words a day.

The more words you know, the easier it will be to choose specific, interesting ones rather than general, dull words. *Bad* gets the point across, but *detrimental, harmful,* and *injurious* could be better choices. As you write your essay, be conscious of the words you select. Avoid repeating the same words; use a synonym after you use a word twice.

In addition, follow this crucial advice when writing the body:

- Include only information that pertains to your topic (do not go off on tangents).
- Illustrate or explain each point with appropriate details. Some essays may call for personal experiences, while others may require historical examples. Don't simply state that something is true; prove it.
- Organize the body with three paragraphs.
- Maintain coherence by staying on topic; every sentence should relate to your topic.
- Use transition words like *first, next,* and *then.*

- Get creative if necessary. Your reader will never know if you really traveled to Bombay, won a hot-dog eating contest, or attended science camp. The quality of your writing is what is being tested, not the truthfulness of every detail. If you need to get creative and come up with a strong example or piece of evidence, and you can do so convincingly, go ahead.

- Take all the time you can to fully develop your ideas. If you stop writing too soon, it may be because you haven't explained yourself completely, or backed up your assertions with examples.

Transition Words

These are useful when moving from paragraph to paragraph, or point to point. Transition words help the reader follow your thoughts.

after	it follows that
afterward	in addition
after this	moreover
as a result	next though
another	nevertheless
because	on the contrary
consequently	on the other hand
conversely	similarly
despite	simultaneously
finally	subsequently
first, second, third	then
for this reason	therefore
however	yet

Conclusion

Your concluding paragraph can simply restate your thesis and the points you made in the body of your essay, but remember to reword them to keep the conclusion fresh. Don't repeat your introduction, or use phrases such as "I wrote about," or "This essay was about."

If you have time, end with something more interesting. A speculative conclusion refers to a future possibility or prediction, such as "perhaps years from now…." If you wrote about a problem, try a conclusion that offers a solution. If you have a fitting quotation, use it to conclude your essay. The person quoted doesn't have to be famous, but the quote should help you make your point. For example, "My third grade teacher put it best. . . ." These types of conclusions can leave your reader with a better overall impression of your work. (Although be aware that you can't overcome a weak essay with a clever conclusion.)

Conclusion Checklist

✔ do not contradict anything you said earlier in the essay

✔ be clear and concise

✔ do not introduce new information

✔ maintain the tone you used in the rest of your essay

✔ do not repeat your introduction

✔ do not use clichéd sayings or phrases (*You can't judge a book by its cover, In conclusion, As I stated above*)

✔ do not apologize for anything (especially lack of time)

Remember the following points when tackling the essay section:

- Organize your thoughts, and support them with strong facts and details. This is your opportunity to demonstrate your skills as a writer.
- Note that you will be asked to agree or disagree with a statement. Please note that the statement may be controversial—for example, "The No Child Left Behind Act made marked improvements in public schools across the country" or "The rapid development of malls across the country is destroying vast acres of natural land and destroying wildlife." As you review the statement, you will need to quickly decide if you are in support of the statement or against the statement.
- After you have determined whether you intend to support or refute a statement, go to the heart of the problem. The testing center will provide you with scratch paper. Jot down at least four arguments to support your particular position. You will want to make arguments that you can easily support with good examples. After you have completed these tasks, write your thesis sentence.

▶ Practice Question

Directions: You will have 45 minutes to plan and write an essay on the topic specified. Read the topic carefully. You are expected to spend a few minutes considering the topic and organizing your thoughts before you begin writing. *Do not write on a topic other than the one specified. An essay on a topic of your own choice is not acceptable.*

The essay is intended to give you an opportunity to demonstrate your ability to write effectively. You should therefore take care to express your thoughts on the topic clearly and precisely and to make them interesting to the reader. Be specific, using supporting examples whenever appropriate. Remember that how well you write is more important than how much you write.

For several years now, a few senators have proposed a bill in Congress to abolish the production of the penny. Their statistics state that the penny almost costs more to make than it is worth. If this bill is passed, it would change our pricing system, as all prices would be in five-cent increments. Choose to defend one position. Develop your response into a well-written essay.

About the CLEP Social Sciences and History Exam

The Social Sciences and History portion of the CLEP examination is broad in scope and includes content you would expect to study in freshman and sophomore social studies college courses. The examination covers U.S. history, Western civilization, world history and government, political science, geography, sociology, economics, psychology, and anthropology.

A satisfactory score on this examination demonstrates that you have the basic knowledge required of students who have met the necessary general education requirements in the social sciences/history subject areas.

You will have 90 minutes to answer 120 questions. Note that any additional time spent on tutorials or in providing personal data does not count against the exam time.

Candidates registered for the Social Sciences and History examination should be comfortable with key terminology, facts, conventions, methodology, concepts, principles, generalizations, and theories. You should be able to apply your knowledge in this area by demonstrating an ability to interpret and analyze a variety of graphic, pictorial, and written material. In your preparation for this exam, you should plan to review data and demonstrate an ability to construct hypotheses, concepts, theories, and principles based upon specific data.

The Social Sciences and History examination includes material from the following disciplines. The percentages listed next to each topic represent the approximate number of questions on that topic.

- 40% History—the major chronology of events throughout history, including
  - 17% U.S. History
  - 15% Western Civilization
  - 8% World History
- 13% Government and Political Science
- 11% Geography
- 10% Economics
- 10% Psychology
- 10% Sociology
- 6% Anthropology

▶ Choosing Resources to Help You Review

As you prepare for the Social Sciences and History exam, visit your local college bookstore or university library and review their collection of introductory college-level textbooks. Your local college bookstore will help you locate textbooks for courses in history, sociology, Western civilization, and related fields. Review these textbooks and check the table of contents in these texts for the content tested in the Social Sciences and History examination.

If you afford the time, you may wish to review resources suggested for other CLEP exams, including American Government, History of the United States I and II, Principles of Macroeconomics, Principles of Microeconomics, Introductory Sociology, and Western Civilization I and II. The Internet is another resource you could explore; many college professors post a syllabus and a list of textbooks and related resources for a course online.

CLEP Social Sciences and History Pretest

Before reviewing topics common to the CLEP Social Sciences and History exam, test your existing skills by taking this pretest. You will encounter 120 questions that are similar to the type you will find on this exam. The questions are organized by the nine content areas tested by the CLEP Social Sciences and History exam:

- Western Civilization
- World History
- U.S. History
- Government/Political Science
- Geography
- Sociology
- Anthropology
- Psychology
- Economics

On the test day, you will have 90 minutes to complete this exam. For now, ignore the time restraints of the official CLEP and take as much time as you need to complete each question.

Answer every question; on the official CLEP, there is no penalty for incorrect answers. If you are unsure of an answer, try using the process of elimination to improve your chance of selecting the correct answer.

When you are finished, check the answer key on page 92 carefully to assess your results. Your pretest score will help you determine how much preparation you need and in which areas you need the most careful review and practice.

▶ CLEP Social Sciences and History Pretest

1.	ⓐ ⓑ ⓒ ⓓ ⓔ	41.	ⓐ ⓑ ⓒ ⓓ ⓔ	81.	ⓐ ⓑ ⓒ ⓓ ⓔ
2.	ⓐ ⓑ ⓒ ⓓ ⓔ	42.	ⓐ ⓑ ⓒ ⓓ ⓔ	82.	ⓐ ⓑ ⓒ ⓓ ⓔ
3.	ⓐ ⓑ ⓒ ⓓ ⓔ	43.	ⓐ ⓑ ⓒ ⓓ ⓔ	83.	ⓐ ⓑ ⓒ ⓓ ⓔ
4.	ⓐ ⓑ ⓒ ⓓ ⓔ	44.	ⓐ ⓑ ⓒ ⓓ ⓔ	84.	ⓐ ⓑ ⓒ ⓓ ⓔ
5.	ⓐ ⓑ ⓒ ⓓ ⓔ	45.	ⓐ ⓑ ⓒ ⓓ ⓔ	85.	ⓐ ⓑ ⓒ ⓓ ⓔ
6.	ⓐ ⓑ ⓒ ⓓ ⓔ	46.	ⓐ ⓑ ⓒ ⓓ ⓔ	86.	ⓐ ⓑ ⓒ ⓓ ⓔ
7.	ⓐ ⓑ ⓒ ⓓ ⓔ	47.	ⓐ ⓑ ⓒ ⓓ ⓔ	87.	ⓐ ⓑ ⓒ ⓓ ⓔ
8.	ⓐ ⓑ ⓒ ⓓ ⓔ	48.	ⓐ ⓑ ⓒ ⓓ ⓔ	88.	ⓐ ⓑ ⓒ ⓓ ⓔ
9.	ⓐ ⓑ ⓒ ⓓ ⓔ	49.	ⓐ ⓑ ⓒ ⓓ ⓔ	89.	ⓐ ⓑ ⓒ ⓓ ⓔ
10.	ⓐ ⓑ ⓒ ⓓ ⓔ	50.	ⓐ ⓑ ⓒ ⓓ ⓔ	90.	ⓐ ⓑ ⓒ ⓓ ⓔ
11.	ⓐ ⓑ ⓒ ⓓ ⓔ	51.	ⓐ ⓑ ⓒ ⓓ ⓔ	91.	ⓐ ⓑ ⓒ ⓓ ⓔ
12.	ⓐ ⓑ ⓒ ⓓ ⓔ	52.	ⓐ ⓑ ⓒ ⓓ ⓔ	92.	ⓐ ⓑ ⓒ ⓓ ⓔ
13.	ⓐ ⓑ ⓒ ⓓ ⓔ	53.	ⓐ ⓑ ⓒ ⓓ ⓔ	93.	ⓐ ⓑ ⓒ ⓓ ⓔ
14.	ⓐ ⓑ ⓒ ⓓ ⓔ	54.	ⓐ ⓑ ⓒ ⓓ ⓔ	94.	ⓐ ⓑ ⓒ ⓓ ⓔ
15.	ⓐ ⓑ ⓒ ⓓ ⓔ	55.	ⓐ ⓑ ⓒ ⓓ ⓔ	95.	ⓐ ⓑ ⓒ ⓓ ⓔ
16.	ⓐ ⓑ ⓒ ⓓ ⓔ	56.	ⓐ ⓑ ⓒ ⓓ ⓔ	96.	ⓐ ⓑ ⓒ ⓓ ⓔ
17.	ⓐ ⓑ ⓒ ⓓ ⓔ	57.	ⓐ ⓑ ⓒ ⓓ ⓔ	97.	ⓐ ⓑ ⓒ ⓓ ⓔ
18.	ⓐ ⓑ ⓒ ⓓ ⓔ	58.	ⓐ ⓑ ⓒ ⓓ ⓔ	98.	ⓐ ⓑ ⓒ ⓓ ⓔ
19.	ⓐ ⓑ ⓒ ⓓ ⓔ	59.	ⓐ ⓑ ⓒ ⓓ ⓔ	99.	ⓐ ⓑ ⓒ ⓓ ⓔ
20.	ⓐ ⓑ ⓒ ⓓ ⓔ	60.	ⓐ ⓑ ⓒ ⓓ ⓔ	100.	ⓐ ⓑ ⓒ ⓓ ⓔ
21.	ⓐ ⓑ ⓒ ⓓ ⓔ	61.	ⓐ ⓑ ⓒ ⓓ ⓔ	101.	ⓐ ⓑ ⓒ ⓓ ⓔ
22.	ⓐ ⓑ ⓒ ⓓ ⓔ	62.	ⓐ ⓑ ⓒ ⓓ ⓔ	102.	ⓐ ⓑ ⓒ ⓓ ⓔ
23.	ⓐ ⓑ ⓒ ⓓ ⓔ	63.	ⓐ ⓑ ⓒ ⓓ ⓔ	103.	ⓐ ⓑ ⓒ ⓓ ⓔ
24.	ⓐ ⓑ ⓒ ⓓ ⓔ	64.	ⓐ ⓑ ⓒ ⓓ ⓔ	104.	ⓐ ⓑ ⓒ ⓓ ⓔ
25.	ⓐ ⓑ ⓒ ⓓ ⓔ	65.	ⓐ ⓑ ⓒ ⓓ ⓔ	105.	ⓐ ⓑ ⓒ ⓓ ⓔ
26.	ⓐ ⓑ ⓒ ⓓ ⓔ	66.	ⓐ ⓑ ⓒ ⓓ ⓔ	106.	ⓐ ⓑ ⓒ ⓓ ⓔ
27.	ⓐ ⓑ ⓒ ⓓ ⓔ	67.	ⓐ ⓑ ⓒ ⓓ ⓔ	107.	ⓐ ⓑ ⓒ ⓓ ⓔ
28.	ⓐ ⓑ ⓒ ⓓ ⓔ	68.	ⓐ ⓑ ⓒ ⓓ ⓔ	108.	ⓐ ⓑ ⓒ ⓓ ⓔ
29.	ⓐ ⓑ ⓒ ⓓ ⓔ	69.	ⓐ ⓑ ⓒ ⓓ ⓔ	109.	ⓐ ⓑ ⓒ ⓓ ⓔ
30.	ⓐ ⓑ ⓒ ⓓ ⓔ	70.	ⓐ ⓑ ⓒ ⓓ ⓔ	110.	ⓐ ⓑ ⓒ ⓓ ⓔ
31.	ⓐ ⓑ ⓒ ⓓ ⓔ	71.	ⓐ ⓑ ⓒ ⓓ ⓔ	111.	ⓐ ⓑ ⓒ ⓓ ⓔ
32.	ⓐ ⓑ ⓒ ⓓ ⓔ	72.	ⓐ ⓑ ⓒ ⓓ ⓔ	112.	ⓐ ⓑ ⓒ ⓓ ⓔ
33.	ⓐ ⓑ ⓒ ⓓ ⓔ	73.	ⓐ ⓑ ⓒ ⓓ ⓔ	113	ⓐ ⓑ ⓒ ⓓ ⓔ
34.	ⓐ ⓑ ⓒ ⓓ ⓔ	74.	ⓐ ⓑ ⓒ ⓓ ⓔ	114.	ⓐ ⓑ ⓒ ⓓ ⓔ
35.	ⓐ ⓑ ⓒ ⓓ ⓔ	75.	ⓐ ⓑ ⓒ ⓓ ⓔ	115.	ⓐ ⓑ ⓒ ⓓ ⓔ
36.	ⓐ ⓑ ⓒ ⓓ ⓔ	76.	ⓐ ⓑ ⓒ ⓓ ⓔ	116.	ⓐ ⓑ ⓒ ⓓ ⓔ
37.	ⓐ ⓑ ⓒ ⓓ ⓔ	77.	ⓐ ⓑ ⓒ ⓓ ⓔ	117.	ⓐ ⓑ ⓒ ⓓ ⓔ
38.	ⓐ ⓑ ⓒ ⓓ ⓔ	78.	ⓐ ⓑ ⓒ ⓓ ⓔ	118.	ⓐ ⓑ ⓒ ⓓ ⓔ
39.	ⓐ ⓑ ⓒ ⓓ ⓔ	79.	ⓐ ⓑ ⓒ ⓓ ⓔ	119.	ⓐ ⓑ ⓒ ⓓ ⓔ
40.	ⓐ ⓑ ⓒ ⓓ ⓔ	80.	ⓐ ⓑ ⓒ ⓓ ⓔ	120.	ⓐ ⓑ ⓒ ⓓ ⓔ

▶ Pretest Questions

Directions: Each of the questions or incomplete statements below is followed by five suggested answers. Select the best answer for each question.

Western Civilization

1. How did the city of Rome extend its influence before 300 B.C.E.?
   A. annexation of parts of Italy
   B. decreeing the use of Italian
   C. granting citizenship to captured peoples
   D. maintaining a standing army
   a. A, C, D
   b. A, D
   c. B, C, D
   d. B
   e. A, B

2. Which is the only one of the Seven Wonders of the Ancient World to survive today?
   a. statue of Zeus
   b. Egyptian pyramids
   c. Alexandria lighthouse
   d. Colossus of Rhodes
   e. Hanging Gardens of Babylon

3. Which religious belief spread from the Roman Empire through much of the known world in the first century C.E.?
   a. monotheism
   b. polytheism
   c. Hellenism
   d. Judaism
   e. Catholicism

4. What was a hallmark of the Hellenistic philosophy?
   a. the pursuit of happiness
   b. dependency on the state
   c. love of luxuries
   d. encouragement of all pleasures
   e. monotheism

5. What was one accomplishment of the Gupta rulers in India in the 400s?
   a. monotheism
   b. the use of zero and decimals
   c. classical music
   d. establishment of a stock market
   e. worship of the Buddha

6. What distinguished the city of Alexandria from the first to the third centuries?
   a. the study of science and mathematics
   b. development of economics
   c. great architecture
   d. early Olympic Games
   e. advanced transportation

7. Which city became a sophisticated center in the eighth century, when interactions among Jewish, Christian, and Arab intellectuals were encouraged?
   a. Baghdad
   b. Cairo
   c. Islamabad
   d. Teheran
   e. Jerusalem

8. Invasions by which groups of people aided the spread of Islam in the twelfth century?

a. Bantu

b. Mongols

c. Russians

d. Persians

e. Turks

9. Among the affects of the bubonic plague on medieval Europe were

a. higher wages and peasant uprisings.

b. great movements of people.

c. the growth of an agrarian economy.

d. rising populations across Europe.

e. higher marriage rates.

10. What did the increased use of clocks in European cities in the fourteenth century signify?

a. a start of the 24-hour day

b. a business mindset was forming

c. expansion of cities

d. improved transportation

e. rising literacy rates

11. Which invention in 1475 aided European exploration of the New World?

a. tobacco pipes

b. the rifle

c. paper

d. smaller sailing ships

e. chronometer

12. Which sixteenth-century religious leader preached that faith alone leads to salvation?

a. King Henry VIII

b. Pope Paul III

c. John Knox

d. Martin Luther

e. John Calvin

13. Which African nation escaped European colonization?

a. Zanzibar

b. Fulani

c. Ethiopia

d. Liberia

e. South Africa

14. The present-day fascination of many Japanese for things Western is similar to which movements in mid-1800s Japan?

a. Westernization and modernization

b. isolationism and separatism

c. extreme anti-Westernism

d. left-wing rebellions

e. intellectualism

15. Which philosophy did a factory town in Scotland and a communal farm in mid-1800s Massachusetts share?

a. communism

b. conservatism

c. democracy

d. utopian

e. Shaker

16. What was one clue to the imminent collapse of the Ottoman Empire?

a. the Opium War

b. the assassination of a Hungarian archduke

c. Balkan nationalism

d. fear of socialism and communism

e. cross-border transport of arms

17. In which profession might a person have kept very busy in pre-World War I Western Europe?
   a. teaching
   b. investment banking
   c. entertainment
   d. accounting
   e. nursing

18. Which of the following were clues to the eventual breakup of the Soviet Union?
   a. the emergence of oligarchs
   b. protests against the Berlin Wall
   c. widespread elections in the republics
   d. greater travel out of the Soviet Union
   e. reforms and decline of communist power

World History

19. Using land caravans and ships, which Asian nation exchanged the fruits of its golden age for spices from Africa?
   a. Japan
   b. Vietnam
   c. China
   d. Tibet
   e. Nepal

20. Which of the following was the first to win independence in the early nineteenth century?
   a. Mexico
   b. Haiti
   c. Cuba
   d. Chile
   e. Uruguay

21. Which of the following statements is true?
   a. Europeans arriving in Australia helped themselves to land when they did not recognize an Aboriginal political structure.
   b. Aborigines in Australia spoke few languages when Europeans arrived.
   c. The Aborigines of Australia welcomed Europeans and helped them learn how to manage the land.
   d. Aborigines in Australia today celebrate the British settlement at Sidney Cove.
   e. Europeans and Aborigines in Australia celebrated a fellowship.

22. Which of the following helped cause widespread revolutions in Europe in 1848?
   A. demands by the middle class for a greater political role
   B. unemployment
   C. cholera epidemic
   D. poor harvests
   a. A, B
   b. A, B, D
   c. A, D
   d. A, B, C
   e. A, B, C, D

23. When Germany signed a peace treaty with the Bolsheviks of Russia in 1918, which territories did the loser give up?
   a. Ukraine, Poland, and Finland
   b. Hungary, Czechoslovakia, and Austria
   c. Poland, Ukraine, and Czechoslovakia
   d. Finland, Sweden, and Denmark
   e. none

24. In 1938, what did the British prime minister predict after a meeting with Adolf Hitler, which preceded Germany's invasion of Czechoslovakia?

a. Hitler would cede conquered lands.

b. peace and prosperity

c. peace for our time

d. Germany would not declare war.

e. Germany might invade England.

25. Which of the following groups does NOT belong in the same category as the others?

a. Armenian citizens

b. Australian Aborigines

c. Japanese-Americans

d. Irish farmers

e. Native Americans

26. Which is one of the most pervasive problems facing the African continent?

a. decimation of wild animals

b. spread of AIDS

c. emerging rebel groups

d. flooding and tsunamis

e. democracy

27. What has been a common root of violence in parts of Eastern Europe and Africa?

a. apartheid

b. colonialism

c. far-right governments

d. far-left governments

e. ethnic allegiances

28. What was one disagreement between the United States and other NATO members in 2008?

a. the number of soldiers NATO nations agreed to send to Iraq

b. where NATO troops should be headquartered

c. who would lead NATO

d. whether NATO should continue to exist

e. who should belong to NATO

United States History

29. In 1763, the British government banned American colonists from settling further west than a certain point in the Appalachian Mountains to

a. maintain peace between Native American tribes and the colonists.

b. declare the land the king's property.

c. protect Native American tribal lands.

d. protect the mountains.

e. show support for Native American tribes.

30. What major problem did George Washington encounter in mustering a professional Continental army?

a. The soldiers spoke only French.

b. Many of the soldiers served for a short time and then returned home.

c. The soldiers were overqualified.

d. Many soldiers supported the British cause.

e. Washington was a poor administrator.

31. Which law(s) passed by the United States in 1798 suppressed criticism of the government and allowed the deportation of citizens of enemy as well as friendly nations?

a. Alien and Sedition Acts

b. Federal Judiciary Act

c. Naturalization Act

d. Embargo Act

e. Alien Friends Act

32. Which of the following was NOT a main cause of the Civil War?

A. sectionalism

B. secession

C. slavery

D. slave rebellions

E. Lincoln's election

a. A, B

b. C, D

c. A, B, C

d. D, E

e. E

33. How did the election of President Rutherford B. Hayes in 1876 affect Reconstruction and freed slaves in Southern states?

a. Hayes pulled out federal troops, leaving no protection for black people and ending the gains they made during Reconstruction.

b. It encouraged white Southerners to give more rights to black Southerners.

c. It extended Reconstruction and led to the election of more freed slaves as officials of Southern states.

d. Hayes sent more federal troops to enforce the rights of white Southerners, ending Reconstruction.

e. It had no effect.

34. How did the boll weevil and racism in Southern states affect the industrialized Northern states, especially from 1910 to 1930?

a. The North was not affected.

b. Many Northern factories shut down because of lack of workers.

c. The Ku Klux Klan moved its operations north.

d. Northern states began to suffer a lack of housing.

e. Millions of African Americans moved north as part of the Great Migration.

35. An action in 1933 that helped bring about a greater normalization of banking was

a. the declaration of a bank holiday.

b. the addition of Sunday banking hours.

c. setting minimum deposits of $100.

d. disallowing foreign deposits.

e. closing banks on weekends.

36. What labor practice did the Fair Labor Standards Act ban in 1938?

a. male-only staffs in federal offices

b. child labor in companies involved in interstate commerce

c. hiring women for only low-paying jobs

d. not hiring war veterans

e. child labor in companies with more than 50 employees

37. What partially successful program from 1933 to 1939 attempted to end the Great Depression by providing federal help to the business community and the general public?

a. the Great Society

b. Workman's Compensation

c. Social Security

d. the New Deal

e. the WPA

38. In 1940, isolationists responded to the possibility of the United States entering World War II by
  a. forming the group America First.
  b. founding the Ku Klux Klan.
  c. joining the Daughters of the American Revolution.
  d. increasing the number of people enlisting in the army.
  e. vowing allegiance to the Axis.

39. In early 1941, how did the U.S. Congress and President Roosevelt circumvent the Neutrality Act of 1939 to provide help for Britain?
  a. Congress tacked a rider onto a money bill.
  b. Congress passed the Lend-Lease Act to provide war materials without receiving payment.
  c. At Roosevelt's urging, Congress passed the Marshall Plan.
  d. Roosevelt declared war and Congress approved it.
  e. The act was declared unconstitutional.

40. What precipitated a turning point in the U.S. war effort in the Pacific in 1942?
  a. Tired Japanese forces surrendered to U.S. forces.
  b. General Dwight D. Eisenhower took over command of the region.
  c. The head of U.S. naval operations mandated the use of aircraft carriers rather than battleships.
  d. U.S. jets began bombing targets in the Philippines.
  e. The United States pulled out of the Pacific area.

41. In which 1954 landmark case did the U.S. Supreme Court say that the doctrine of "separate but equal" violated the equal protection clause of the Fourteenth Amendment?
  a. *Plessy v. Ferguson*
  b. *Brown v. Board of Education of Topeka*
  c. *Miranda v. Arizona*
  d. *Dred Scott v. Sanford*
  e. the Civil Rights Act

42. During the cold war, what did President Harry Truman's policy of "containment" aim to accomplish?
  a. ship containers to Eastern Europe
  b. limit military uprisings in East Germany
  c. contain the Soviet Union's weapons
  d. stop the spread of communism
  e. stop the spread of capitalism

43. "It is our alarming misfortune that so primitive a science has armed itself with the most modern and terrible weapons, and that in turning them against the insects it has also turned them against the Earth." Whose thinking did this statement express?
  a. Margaret Mead
  b. Ernest Hemingway
  c. Charles Darwin
  d. Albert Einstein
  e. Rachel Carson

44. President Lyndon Johnson's program that included the War on Poverty, Head Start, Medicaid, and three civil rights acts was called
  a. Medicare.
  b. the New Deal.
  c. the Great Society.
  d. Peace Corps.
  e. the New Frontier.

45. Which U.S. president would most likely NOT have agreed with Lyndon Johnson's extensive federal social programs?
   a. Abraham Lincoln
   b. John F. Kennedy
   c. Ronald Reagan
   d. Bill Clinton
   e. John Adams

46. After 1973, what was expected to be a result of changing to an all-volunteer armed force from a compulsory draft?
   a. The United States pulled its forces out of Vietnam.
   b. More people became marines.
   c. Fewer women joined the army.
   d. More women joined the army.
   e. Pay and benefits were supposed to improve.

47. What was one result of the North American Free Trade Agreement (NAFTA) of 1994?
   a. less costly cars for American consumers
   b. better pay for migrant workers in California
   c. elimination of tariffs on food shipped between Canada, the United States, and Argentina
   d. American companies saving money on exporting products to Mexico
   e. better relations with Central American nations

48. The report that called for the restructuring of U.S. intelligence organizations was the
   a. Warren Commission Report.
   b. 9/11 Commission Report.
   c. 2002 State of the Union address.
   d. Mitchell Report.
   e. Report from the National Security Council.

Government/Political Science

49. What system did James Madison allude to when he wrote that each government official has "the necessary institutional means and personal motives" to resist other institutions?
   a. vetoes
   b. federalism
   c. dissent
   d. checks and balances
   e. war powers

50. Why did the Senate select Richard Johnson as the ninth vice president?
   a. He was the beneficiary of payoffs.
   b. He fell one vote short of a majority of the Electoral College.
   c. His state, Kentucky, was influential.
   d. The candidate he ran with had less than half the vote.
   e. He was a popular former senator.

51. Which work could a historian consult for first-hand information about the debates leading to the writing of the U.S. Constitution?
   a. Benjamin Franklin's *Poor Richard's Almanac*
   b. the journals of James Madison
   c. newspapers from New Amsterdam
   d. *The Philadelphia Inquirer*
   e. *The New York Times*

52. Which of the following defined the House of Representatives and the Senate?
   a. the Articles of Confederation
   b. the Declaration of Independence
   c. the Great Compromise
   d. the Missouri Compromise
   e. the Bill of Rights

53. In 1791, Vermont revised a law that said who could vote. What did this change mean to the electorate?

   a. All adult white males, not just property owners, could now vote.

   b. Women who owned property could now vote.

   c. Only adult white males who owned property could vote.

   d. The state declared universal suffrage.

   e. It had little meaning for voters.

54. Who were the Democratic Republicans of the early 1800s?

   a. the forerunners of the Federalist Party

   b. a coalition of opposing political groups

   c. Andrew Johnson and Henry Clay's party

   d. groups of fanatic federalists

   e. isolationist groups

55. What did the elections of George W. Bush and Abraham Lincoln most have in common?

   a. Both won the presidency with less than 50% of the popular vote.

   b. Both won all 50 states.

   c. Both belonged to the Republican Party.

   d. Both won Illinois and Massachusetts.

   e. Both won during a war.

56. What is a basic proposition of constitutional law?

   a. Local interests must come first if the nation is to endure.

   b. The executive branch has ultimate approval of the torture of terror suspects.

   c. Congress has only the powers that are delegated to it by the Constitution, but they can be expanded.

   d. Miscreants in congress must be tried by a joint conference of the two houses.

   e. The president cannot veto congressional acts.

57. Which event influenced John F. Kennedy's election in 1960 and set a precedent for future presidential elections?

   a. Richard Nixon's pledge to visit all 50 states

   b. Kennedy's speech about his religion

   c. a "fireside chat" with the Kennedy family

   d. important endorsements

   e. the first televised debate between Kennedy and Nixon

58. "Whenever the states cannot act, because the need to be met is not one merely of a single locality, then the national government representing all the people, should have complete power to act." President Theodore Roosevelt, who said this, was clearly a believer in which philosophy?

   a. community rights

   b. national power

   c. states' rights

   d. socialism

   e. conservation

59. What qualifications does Article I, Section 3 of the Constitution set for becoming a U.S. senator?

   a. A senator must be 30 years old, a U.S. citizen for nine years, and a resident of the state represented at the time of election.

   b. A senator must be 21 years old, a U.S. citizen for five years, and a resident of the state represented at the time of election.

   c. A senator must be 30 years old, a U.S. citizen for ten years, and a resident of the state represented for two years.

   d. A senator must be 30 years old, a U.S. citizen for nine years, and a resident of the state represented at the time of being sworn in.

   e. A member of the Senate must be born in the United States.

60. A decision about capital punishment during the U.S. Supreme Court's 2004–2005 term most affected offenders who
   a. committed crimes before age 15.
   b. committed crimes before age 18.
   c. reached 21 while on trial.
   d. were mentally disabled.
   e. committed crimes before age 21.

61. What is the order of the impeachment process?
   A. Senate votes for or against conviction
   B. removal from office
   C. House brings charges
   D. Senate holds trial
   E. office holder accused of "high crimes and misdemeanors"
   a. B, A, D, C, E
   b. A, B, C, D, E
   c. E, C, D, A, B
   d. E, A, C, D, B
   e. C, A, D, E, B

62. What is a significant positive role third-party or independent candidates play in presidential elections?
   a. They focus attention on their states.
   b. They draw voters from major party candidates.
   c. They point up the importance of electoral votes.
   d. They greatly increase the number of people voting.
   e. They focus attention on significant but less-publicized issues.

63. In 1998, what was the fate of legislation giving the president a line-item veto?
   a. It was passed by the Senate.
   b. It was passed by the House.
   c. It was rejected by a congressional committee.
   d. It was declared unconstitutional by the Supreme Court.
   e. It was approved and put into practice by the House.

64. After the 2000 presidential election, when the U.S. Supreme Court blocked a recount of votes in Florida, what reason did the majority give for the decision?
   a. Most of the justices were loyal to the Republican candidate.
   b. Differences in the ways various locations recounted their votes violated the equal protection clause of the Fourteenth Amendment.
   c. A recount would have violated Article 1 of the U.S. Constitution.
   d. The justices felt they should not interfere with states' rights.
   e. Florida has its own election rules.

Geography

65. Which factor has most affected cartography in recent years?
   a. global warming
   b. changes in technology and specialized software
   c. discoveries of land masses and bodies of water
   d. a changing political landscape
   e. discoveries of bodies of water

66. To which professionals can geographers—who divide the world into regions—be compared?

    a. librarians and grocers

    b. baseball and basketball players

    c. fine artists and dancers

    d. professors and writers

    e. chefs and poets

67. In which part of the world is Iraq?

    a. the Middle West

    b. the Middle East

    c. Africa

    d. Europe

    e. the southern hemisphere

68. The United States has one-fourth the population of which of the following Asian nations, though they are about the same physical size?

    a. Japan

    b. Cambodia

    c. South Korea

    d. India

    e. China

69. Which water system makes it possible for small shipping vessels to reach the Gulf of Mexico by way of the Illinois Waterway?

    a. the Hudson

    b. the Rio Grande

    c. the Mississippi

    d. the Great Lakes

    e. Prudhoe Bay

Use the following map to answer question 70.

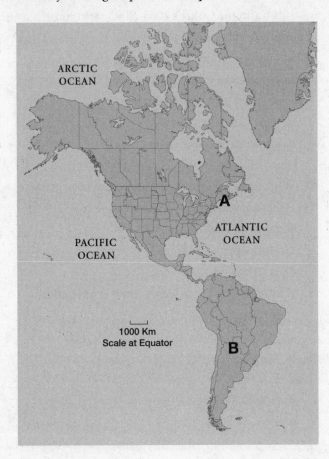

70. For which season must a traveler going from A in the winter to B need to be prepared?

    a. summer

    b. winter

    c. fall

    d. spring

    e. all seasons

71. In studies of U.S. college students, which of the following has been disclosed about their mental maps?

a. Few students preferred to remain in the area in which they grew up. They wanted to escape childhood memories.

b. Most students wanted to move to California or South Dakota even if they had never been in either place.

c. Southerners preferred remaining in the Southeast and Northerners in the Northeast. Their mental maps reflected divisions dating back to the Civil War.

d. Several states were ranked low in mental maps of students who had frequently visited there or grew up there.

e. U.S. college students have a wide knowledge of geography.

72. According to some studies, how do socioeconomic factors affect mental maps?

a. The quality of a college education pinpoints the difference, rather than relative wealth.

b. The mental maps of people in lower socioeconomic groups cover smaller geographic areas than the mental maps of more well-to-do people.

c. The mental maps of people in higher socioeconomic groups cover smaller geographic areas than the mental maps of less well-to-do people.

d. They do not affect them.

e. The wealthier the person, the more eager he or she is to travel.

73. Which of the following would be the least useful to geography students?

a. *World Almanac*

b. *Central Intelligence Agency World Factbook*

c. World Population Data Sheet

d. a world atlas

e. *Guide to Regional Laws*

Use the following table to answer questions 74 and 75.

YOUNG ADULTS (18–24 YEARS OLD) LIVING AT HOME OR IN DORMITORIES		
YEAR	**% OF MALES**	**% OF FEMALES**
1960	52	35
1970	54	41
1980	54	43
1990	58	48
2000	57	47
2004	56	42

Sources: Bureau of the Census, U.S. Dept. of Commerce, the *World Almanac.*

74. What trend seems to be developing among young women in the United States?

a. Young women will be moving in with their parents with increasing frequency.

b. By the time of the next census, the number of young women living at home may go below three out of every ten.

c. The percentage of young adults living at home will have a negative affect on the building of new homes.

d. After decades of decreasing, the percentage of young women living at home seems to be increasing.

e. More young women are getting married.

75. What trend seems to be developing among young men in the United States?

    a. After decades of decreasing, the percentage of young men living at home seems to be rising.

    b. Young men will live with their parents with increasing frequency.

    c. The percentage of young men living at home will have a negative effect on the furniture industry.

    d. More young men are getting married.

    e. By the time of the next census, the number of young men living at home will probably remain steady.

76. Which of the following nations in the western hemisphere have three or more time zones?

    a. Mali, Iraq, Bolivia

    b. Turkey, England, Canada

    c. the United States, Algeria, South Africa

    d. the United States, Brazil, Canada

    e. Bolivia, Brazil, England

77. What is spatial interaction?

    a. the width of Earth's circumference

    b. the transport demand/supply relationship expressed over a geographical space

    c. a kind of mental maps

    d. the international date line

    e. the lines of latitude

Sociology

78. Which of the following is NOT a functional consequence of deviance?

    a. defining right and wrong

    b. encouraging group unity

    c. promoting happiness

    d. encouraging social change

    e. clarifying moral boundaries

79. A generally universal definition of family says it is

    a. our first reference for how we look at the world.

    b. a group of people with a common goal.

    c. a modern way to avoid wars.

    d. a tradition that exists for the group.

    e. a nuclear unit.

80. Which is NOT exclusively an agent of social change?

    a. war

    b. understanding how society works

    c. good or bad weather

    d. the environment

    e. widespread illness

81. Without patterned interactions,

    a. complete unpredictability would ensue.

    b. no one would have instinctive feelings.

    c. norms would always remain the same.

    d. wars would break out.

    e. organization would improve.

82. Being a young student is

    a. role negotiation.

    b. a norm.

    c. a status position.

    d. a predetermined decision.

    e. important in today's society.

83. Social stratification refers to

    a. an individual's religion.

    b. how many men or women live in an area.

    c. varying layers of class in society.

    d. how much wealth a community has.

    e. how much poverty a community has.

84. From a sociological point of view, which are society's three scarce resources?

a. class, prestige, power

b. class, prestige, merit

c. prestige, merit, wealth

d. power, prestige, merit

e. class, prestige, wealth

85. Which sociologists held diametrically opposed views of the results of Russian socialism? One said it would result in mass bureaucracy, the other predicted "the withering away of the state."

a. Emile Durkheim and Karl Marx

b. Karl Marx and Auguste Comte

c. Max Weber and Karl Marx

d. Auguste Comte and Emile Durkheim

e. Max Weber and Emile Durkheim

86. In his studies of suicide, what did Emile Durkheim find?

a. Suicide rates depend on the strength of norms in a society.

b. Sociologists can predict individual suicides.

c. The extent of social deviance does not affect the suicide rate.

d. Individual suicides can be easily explained by sociologists.

e. Suicide is based on the strength of religious ties.

87. Demographics depict

a. birth and mortality rates only.

b. life expectancy only.

c. how religion affects a society's norms.

d. eye and hair color.

e. all characteristics of the human population.

88. What information would be essential to a company before it chooses a teen-oriented TV show on which to advertise?

a. mortality rates in the show's location

b. demographics of the show's audience

c. social behavior information about the audience

d. credit information for adolescents

e. TV rating among those under ten years old

89. The Census Bureau reported that as of 2004, seven out of ten children lived in two-parent homes. To which of the following groups would this information be most useful?

a. TV networks

b. clothing manufacturers

c. book publishers

d. departments of education

e. the Little League

Psychology

90. Erik Erikson's theory of psychosocial development claims that personality

a. depends on multiple intelligences.

b. develops based on a fear of punishment.

c. depends on a need for self-actualization.

d. develops in eight stages.

e. has no quantifiable measure.

91. The ten neuroses Karen Horney identified were said to

a. be necessary for social development.

b. set men and women apart.

c. be hallmarks of deviant behavior.

d. depend on deviancy.

e. be coping mechanisms that are part of normal life.

92. Francis Crick said that the way we feel and act is associated with
 a. our nerve cells and their associated molecules.
 b. how we behaved as adolescents.
 c. our perceptions and sensations.
 d. our height and weight.
 e. our DNA.

93. Which of the following statements is true?
 a. Scientists have failed to establish a connection between human behavior and the nervous system.
 b. A link between the human nervous system and behavior has been found during scientists' study of people whose nervous systems were seriously injured.
 c. A person's level of education plays an important role in the development of his or her nervous system.
 d. Perception of pain determines how people behave.
 e. Thin people are more nervous.

94. In his study of how children mature, Lawrence Kohlberg theorized that there are six stages of
 a. cognitive objectives.
 b. moral development.
 c. psychology.
 d. personality.
 e. compassion.

95. "The most effective way of developing a strong sense of efficacy is through mastery experiences." This statement explains the philosophy of
 a. Sigmund Freud.
 b. Albert Bandura.
 c. Henry Murray.
 d. Abraham Maslow.
 e. Anna Freud.

96. The conduct of the German people during the Holocaust provides psychologists a precise situation in which to study
 a. the results of individual conformity and obedience.
 b. the effects of anecdotal observations.
 c. reactions from the perspective of a broad-based sample.
 d. biological foundations of behavior.
 e. the rise of fascism.

97. In studies of ways to promote cooperation, which of the following qualities were most apparent in cooperative people?
 a. pride and helpfulness
 b. guilt or anger
 c. accountability and concern for reputation
 d. hostility or feelings of inadequacy
 e. type A personalities

98. Psychologists working in the field of abnormal psychology deal with disorders such as
 a. neuroses and migraine headaches.
 b. women's reproductive health.
 c. hepatitis and sexual deviancy.
 d. depression and obsession-compulsion disorder.
 e. sexually transmitted diseases.

99. In a traditional society, which of the following defines socialization?
 a. knowing which clothing is appropriate to a situation
 b. developing resiliency in difficult circumstances
 c. being aware of folk wisdom
 d. adapting to a culture's norms
 e. being part of a conventional family

100. A person seeking a therapist who is compassionate, respectful, and encourages patient participation would want someone who has studied the work of
   a. Elizabeth Loftus.
   b. Jean Piaget.
   c. Albert Ellis.
   d. Carl Rogers.
   e. Karen Horney.

101. In psychology, which principles of perception conclude that things are "more than the sum of their parts"?
   a. subliminal perception
   b. Weber's Law
   c. absolute threshold
   d. Gestalt
   e. recessive perception

Anthropology

102. To which field did Stewart Culin contribute when he wrote *Street Games of Boys in Brooklyn, New York* as well as observations of other games people played in the late 1800s?
   a. paleoanthropology
   b. archaeology
   c. economics
   d. ethnography
   e. urban studies

103. "I have spent most of my life studying the lives of other peoples—faraway peoples—so that Americans might better understand themselves." This quote expresses the thoughts of which anthropologist?
   a. Albert Einstein
   b. Margaret Mead
   c. Charles Darwin
   d. Rachel Carson
   e. Mary Leakey

104. According to Charles Darwin, where did humankind begin?
   a. Tierra del Fuego
   b. Asia
   c. Africa
   d. the Arctic
   e. Eastern Europe

105. Thanks to her groundbreaking find in 1959, which modern science was Mary Leakey credited with starting?
   a. anthropology
   b. ethnography
   c. paleoanthropology
   d. psychology
   e. sociology

106. Our knowledge of human origins has been enhanced most by the discovery of
   a. early human fossils.
   b. footprints in volcanic ash.
   c. ancient seashells.
   d. prehistoric buttons.
   e. skulls.

107. The boundaries of cultural anthropology have been expanding to include fieldwork in
   a. corporations and businesses.
   b. outer space.
   c. local governments.
   d. exotic societies.
   e. beach erosion.

108. An anthropologist who seeks to learn about modern-day Aboriginal peoples would be best advised to
   a. do telephone interviews.
   b. send out surveys.
   c. live among them.
   d. read their writings.
   e. read anthropology texts.

Economics

109. Three statistics that economists have traditionally used to measure the performance of a nation's economy are
   a. the gross state product (GSP), the marginal propensity to consume (MPC), and the efficiency of labor.
   b. the minimum wage, the gold standard, and the gross metropolitan product (GMP).
   c. the gross national product (GNP), consumer price index, and the unemployment rate.
   d. the gross domestic product (GDP), the discount rate, and the interest rate.
   e. the unemployment rate, the consumer price index, and the minimum wage.

110. Economists often predict that recessions are part of business cycles, but recessions are not
   a. erratic or imaginary.
   b. regular or predictable.
   c. long-lasting or damaging.
   d. phenomena that affect all sectors of the economy.
   e. global.

111. In the early 1970s, the Organization of Petroleum Export Countries (OPEC) reduced the available oil supply, which resulted in
   a. stagflation.
   b. a decrease in inflation.
   c. terrorism.
   d. the development of alternative energy sources.
   e. an improved global economy.

112. The rate of unemployment, which is the percentage of the labor force that is unemployed, measures the number of people who are unemployed against the
   a. number of people in the country from ages 8 to 98.
   b. number of people working in blue-collar jobs in the country.
   c. number of people employed by the defense industry of the country.
   d. number of people in the country who have a job or are looking for a job.
   e. number of people in the country who are collecting unemployment insurance.

113. A tax where you pay an extra 25 cents per gallon of gasoline for each gallon used is a
   a. value tax.
   b. quantity tax.
   c. lump-sum tax.
   d. fixed quantity subsidy.
   e. variable-quantity subsidy.

114. Bonds are financial assets because
   a. they have a financial value.
   b. their rates of return eventually reach a plateau.
   c. they are liquid assets.
   d. they are not risky assets.
   e. they provide a flow of money to the bond holder over time.

Use the following diagram to answer question 115.

Player B

Player A		Confess	Deny
	Confess	-3,3	0,-6
	Deny	-6,0	-1,-1

115. This classic example of game theory, which is used to map strategic interaction between businesses, is called
   a. the assurance game.
   b. the prisoner's dilemma.
   c. chicken.
   d. the zero-sum game.
   e. the friendly kidnapper.

116. When two countries rapidly raise their tariffs in response to each other, it often results in
   a. a period of increased protection for infant and adolescent industries.
   b. an increase in bulk imports.
   c. an increase in bulk exports.
   d. a decline in trade.
   e. an increase in trade.

117. If only one company offers a service, that company can charge whatever it wants, creating a
   a. oligopoly.
   b. monopoly.
   c. monopsony.
   d. quango.
   e. oligopsony.

118. Nations can "stretch" the world's gold supply by
   a. devaluing gold at different rates.
   b. inflating the value of the dollar.
   c. devaluing silver.
   d. devaluing gold at equal rates.
   e. creating artificial gold.

119. A "Giffen good" is a good for which the maximum demand decreases when the good's price falls. This term might best describe
   a. a widget.
   b. a consumer staple.
   c. a luxury item.
   d. an aircraft carrier.
   e. a necessary item that the government buys for government agencies.

Use the following diagram to answer question 120.

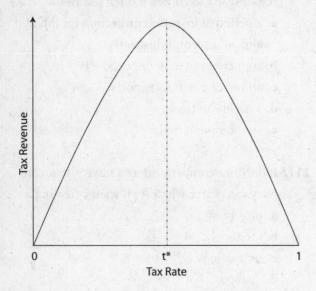

120. This type of curve, which measures the relationship between tax rates and tax revenue, is called the
   a. industry supply curve.
   b. short-run equilibrium.
   c. Laffer curve.
   d. Engel curve.
   e. indifference curve.

▶ Answers

1. **a.** Over 100 years, Rome annexed all of Italy south of the Po River. Latin was spoken by many of the conquered people.

2. **b.** The pyramids can still be seen in Giza, on the west bank of the Nile. Choice **a** was in a sacred grove in Greece; choice **c** towered over Alexandria; choice **d** was a statue of the sun god that overlooked the harbor of Rhodes. Choice **e** was near the Euphrates River, which supplied the water to keep the gardens lush.

3. **b.** People of the Holy Roman Empire worshipped many gods. Choice **a** is the worship of one god; choice **c** is the culture and customs of Greece; choice **d** refers to the Jews who were split into sects in the first century.

4. **a.** During the Hellenistic Era, a Greek-oriented culture spread from Western Europe to India.

5. **b.** The Guptas, enlightened rulers of India, encouraged many cultural and mathematical achievements. India was mainly Hindu, not Buddhist (choice **e**).

6. **a.** Alexandria was the center of science financed by the Ptolemy family, which built a grand library and museum and also encouraged the study of astronomy and medicine.

7. **a.** The civilization that grew here brought a golden age of learning and Arabic as a widespread language to Baghdad.

8. **e.** Coming from Central Asia, the Turks conquered and spread Islam throughout North Africa, the Middle East, and much of Eastern Europe. Their power lasted until the late 1500s. The Bantu (choice **a**) were Muslims in Central Africa. The Mongols (choice **b**) conquered the Russians (choice **c**), who retreated into isolation. The Persians (choice **d**) shared their language and high culture with other lands.

9. **a.** The bubonic plague, also known as the black death, killed half the population of Europe from 1348–1350. This led, among other things, to a scarcity of labor.

10. **b.** Clock towers in cities symbolized the rise of a business and financial mentality. Portable clocks became popular in the fifteenth century and the first watch was invented in 1502.

11. b. Guns permitted explorers and colonizers to subdue native populations. Explorers carried tobacco (choice **a**) home from the New World. Paper (choice **c**) was invented in China and aided in the growth of a bureaucracy. Sailing ships (choice **d**) became larger, not smaller, which helped exploration. The chronometer (choice **e**) was invented in the eighteenth century.

12. d. Martin Luther attacked the leadership of the pope. Henry VIII (choice **a**) broke from the Roman Catholic Church in 1534. John Knox (choice **c**) established a theocracy in Scotland, and John Calvin (choice **e**) did the same in Geneva.

13. c. Ethiopia, by fighting off the Italians, was able to escape colonialism. Choices **a**, **b**, and **e** were colonized by European powers. Zanzibar was founded by slave traders. Liberia was founded by freed American slaves.

14. a. Visits by the American navy to Japan forced it to end its isolation and allowed westernized rules to take control.

15. d. Utopian socialists hoped to establish perfect societies. They were among many people experimenting at the time with a variety of political and philosophical movements, including communism.

16. c. A revolution of young Turks in 1908 forced the corrupt Ottoman government to permit some reforms and to recognize the nationalistic feelings of its people. By 1912, the Ottoman Empire had lost almost all its lands in Europe. The Opium War between Britain and China (choice **a**) lasted from 1859–1942. The assassination of Archduke Franz Ferdinand (choice **b**) was in 1914. A bourgeois fear of socialism and communism (choice **d**) was prevalent in the mid-1800s.

17. b. Foreign capital investments soared in the early 1900s, marking the start of a world economy.

18. e. In the 1980s, reforms and a decline in the power of communism began in the Soviet Union and in most of Eastern Europe. The beginning of the end came when Lithuania, Latvia, and Estonia declared their independence in August 1991. Others soon followed.

19. c. The brilliance of inventions, arts, and medicine during the Tang dynasty (618–906) helped China extend its influence to Africa. Other Asian nations remained isolated.

20. b. Toussaint L'Ouverture led a slave rebellion that resulted in independence from France in 1804. Mexico (choice **a**) declared itself a republic, independent from Spain, in 1823; Spain gave up claims to Cuba (choice **c**) in 1898; Chile (choice **d**) became independent from Spain from 1810 to 1818.

21. a. No matter their level—convicts or government officials—the British brought their colonial way of thinking with them and did not understand the cultural power structure of the native people of Australia.

22. e. Nationalist feelings and the burgeoning strength of the bourgeoisie ran strong in 1848. France, Rome, and Venice declared themselves republics. Hungary declared its independence.

23. a. Finland declared its independence in 1917. After World War I formally ended on November 11, 1918, Poland and Ukraine declared their short-lived independence. As a result, the map of Europe was redrawn.

24. c. Neville Chamberlain returned from a visit to Hitler confident that the German leader would keep his word. When he did not, the British tried a policy of appeasement by promising land to Hitler. Again, Hitler proceeded with his invasion plans. Chamberlain's popularity plummeted, the British entered the war in 1939, and Winston Churchill became prime minister.

25. a. Requests to Turkey to apologize for Armenian genocide have been unsuccessful. Choices **b**, **c**, **d**, and **e** all received apologies for their neglect and/or cruelty, albeit belatedly, from the governments of Australia, the United States, and Britain.

26. b. According to the World Health Organization (WHO), 70% of AIDS cases worldwide are in Africa.

27. e. Ethnic, or tribal, violence has devastated nations around the world for centuries, most recently in the former Yugoslavia, Chechnya, Sudan, Kenya, Ethiopia, and Somalia.

28. a. The war in Iraq has been a divisive issue among the members of the North Atlantic Treaty Organization, which prefers to maintain a united front.

29. a. After the French and Indian War, the British became more involved in colonial affairs. The British felt that keeping Native Americans and colonists apart would maintain peace and simplify their control. But the colonists wanted to be able to expand their holdings.

30. b. The Continental army was made up mainly of part-time soldiers, unlike the British army, which was highly professional. The colonists were poorly trained and poorly equipped. By 1777, General Washington had only 3,000 men under his command. Even for them, he had a hard time raising money and paying for food and housing.

31. a. The Alien and Sedition Acts comprised four laws: the Alien Friends Act, Alien Enemies Act, Sedition Act, and the Naturalization Act. They were passed at the behest of President John Adams, who anticipated war with France and felt that increased security was necessary. Choice **d** was passed in 1807 and forbade exports from American ports.

32. e. Slavery was the main cause of the Civil War. The two other causes dealt with basic cultural rifts between the North and the South and over states' rights. Slave rebellions, while significant, was tied in with the three main causes. One of the biggest slave rebellions was led by Nat Turner, a literate slave, in 1831 in Virginia and led to the end of many of the slaves' rights, including learning to read and write.

33. a. During Reconstruction, former slaves were able to hold elective office and enjoy civil rights, including the right to vote without hindrance. But with the Compromise of 1877 and the subsequent withdrawal of the military, the rights of black Southerners were once again denied and segregation became a way of life.

34. e. The boll weevil destroyed cotton fields, causing black workers to lose their jobs. In a search for a better quality of life and for greater job opportunities, black people boarded trains to the North. There, they still faced de facto racism, which was not as widespread and virulent as it had been in the South.

35. a. President Franklin D. Roosevelt closed all U.S. banks on March 6, 1933 as an emergency measure. During the Great Depression, depositors caused a run on banks as they demanded their money. Banks failed because they did not have enough cash on hand to meet the unexpected demand. Roosevelt's action stemmed this cycle and the banks reopened on April 1.

36. b. The first child labor law was declared unconstitutional in 1918. It was not until 1938 that Congress passed a law that forbade children (some as young as five) from working in interstate industries.

37. d. The New Deal was an overall name given by the Roosevelt administration for social and business programs to aid in recovery from the Great Depression. Choice **a** was President Johnson's domestic program passed in 1966; choices **b** and **c** were important parts of the New Deal.

38. a. America First was a conservative group that lasted about a year until the United States entered World War II. The isolationist tradition existed in the United States going back to colonial times. Choice **b** was founded during Reconstruction to terrorize former slaves and became an anti-Catholic, anti-Semitic, and anti-Black group. The Daughters of the American Revolution was founded as a patriotic group in 1890.

39. b. For Britain, World War II began in 1939, two years before the U.S. entry. Britain was essentially fighting on its own and was ill supplied. President Roosevelt saw defending Britain's security as crucial to the United States.

40. c. Admiral Ernest J. King was a great believer in the importance of fighting from the air at a time when the Japanese were dominating the Pacific area. Choice **b**, Dwight Eisenhower, was commander of Allied Forces.

41. b. In *Brown v. Board of Education of Topeka*, the Supreme Court declared school segregation unconstitutional. The "separate but equal" doctrine had been in place since *Plessy v. Ferguson* in 1896 (choice **a**). Choice **c** from 1966 said that the police must tell suspects about their rights on arrest. Choice **d** denied Congress the right to set territorial boundaries for slavery. Dred Scott was a slave who sued for his freedom.

42. d. A fear of communism and the expansion of the Soviet Union in the late 1940s and 1950s was at the center of American foreign policy.

43. e. The marine biologist Rachel Carson published *Silent Spring* in 1962, in which she called for the end of pesticide use, which was harming the environment. Mead (choice **a**) was an anthropologist; Hemingway (choice **b**) was an American writer; Darwin (choice **c**) was a British naturalist; Einstein (choice **d**) was a German-born American physicist.

44. c. Choice **a** was part of the Great Society, which sought to improve the lives of poor and underserved people. Choice **b** was a Depression-era program set up by President Franklin D. Roosevelt. Choice **d** was an overseas volunteer program that was part of President John F. Kennedy's New Frontier, choice **e**.

45. c. Reagan was a former Democrat who became a Republican and a strong believer in limited interference by the federal government. Lincoln (choice **a**) was a member of a precursor of the Republican Party; Kennedy (choice **b**) and Clinton (choice **d**) were with the Democratic Party. Adams (choice **e**) was a Federalist who was the second president of the United States who might have agreed with Johnson had there been comparable social programs during his lifetime.

46. e. After the Vietnam War ended, so did the draft, which had begun during the Civil War. Improved benefits were promised as a way to stimulate volunteering.

47. d. NAFTA is a trade pact among the United States, Mexico, and Canada. It took effect on January 1, 1974 and its affect on U.S. workers has been controversial ever since.

48. b. The 9/11 Commission looked into the terrorist acts of 2001. Choice **a** was a report about the assassination of John F. Kennedy in 1963; choice **c** was a speech given by President George W. Bush; choice **d** is a report on steroid use by baseball players. Choice **e** was a generic report.

49. d. The system of checks and balances is a way of allowing different parts of the government to share power. A president can veto (choice **a**) laws passed by Congress, and Congress can override the veto, for example. Choice **b** is a form of government in which political power is shared between the national and state governments.

50. b. In 1836, Johnson became the only vice president to be elected by the Senate. Johnson fell one vote short of a majority in the Electoral College. Vice presidential candidates Francis Granger and Johnson had a "run-off" in the Senate under the Twelfth Amendment, where Johnson was elected 33 votes to 17.

51. b. James Madison, one of the 55 men who met in Philadelphia in 1787 to create a new constitution, kept meticulous notes. To prepare himself for the work ahead, Madison read as much as he could about the relationships between rulers and ruled, especially the Magna Carta.

52. c. The Great Compromise resulted in a two-house legislature with the Senate being based on equal representation and the House of Representatives based on population. Choice **a** was the first constitution of the United States. It set up a legislature with each state having one vote. Choice **b** is the document in which the colonies declared independence. Choice **d** set boundaries for slavery in new territories. Choice **e** is the first ten amendments to the Constitution.

53. a. The Vermont law allowed both rich and poor white men to vote. Women (choice **b**) in the territory of Wyoming won the right to vote in 1869 and all women received the right in 1920. Only in 1964 were the voting rights of African Americans assured by law.

54. b. The Democratic Republicans Party was created in opposition to the Federalist Party by James Madison and Thomas Jefferson. Choice **c** concerns early versions of the Democratic and Republican parties.

55. a. Both men's victories proved the power of the Electoral College.

56. **c.** Over the years, the Supreme Court has interpreted the extent of the powers of Congress. The results have sometimes been flexible and reflected the times.

57. **e.** The key word here is *televised.* Kennedy appeared fresh, charismatic, and prepared during this first televised debate. Nixon appeared rumpled and frazzled. The event was a major event in television's growing influence on the political process. Nixon did visit the states (choice **a**), but the journey left him exhausted. Kennedy's Catholic religion (choice **b**) threatened to be an issue at first, but ended up being relatively irrelevant to the election. Fireside chats (choice **c**) were actually held by President Franklin D. Roosevelt.

58. **b.** Roosevelt became president in 1901. He was an advocate of a strong federal government.

59. **a.** The Seventeenth Amendment changed the way senators are chosen. They are elected rather than appointed.

60. **b.** In *Roper v. Simmons,* the court ruled that executing criminals who committed crimes as teenagers was "cruel and unusual punishment."

61. **c.** Impeachment is the first step in removing an accused official from office. Presidents Andrew Johnson and Bill Clinton are the only leaders to be tried, but neither was convicted by the Senate.

62. **e.** Third-party or independent candidates have focused on a variety of issues that they felt were not adequately discussed by the major party candidates. Among these issues have been corporate power, domestic priorities, campaign finance, and states' rights.

63. **c.** The line-item veto law, passed in 1996, gave the president the right to delete specific items in spending bills sent to him by Congress. The Supreme Court ruled that Congress did not have the power to allow the president to do that. The court said that the president must either sign legislation or return it to Congress.

64. **b.** The Constitution sets a timeline for election events, such as when the Electoral College meets. In its 2000 ruling, the court also said that another recount in Florida would not permit constitutional deadlines to be met.

65. **b.** Technological improvements have helped cartographers create even more exact maps. They have also improved the ability to more clearly communicate geographic matters.

66. **a.** Like geographers, librarians and grocers have to establish an order in the way objects are arranged.

67. **b.** Iraq occupies most of what was ancient Mesopotamia. Its neighbors are Jordan, Syria, Turkey, Iran, Kuwait, and Saudi Arabia.

68. **e.** China's population hovers around 1,306,300,800. The U.S. population is close to 281,400,900.

69. **d.** The Great Lakes, the world's largest body of fresh water, have many connected systems for inland water transportation. The Great Lakes are Superior, Michigan, Huron, Erie, and Ontario. The Hudson River (choice **a**) is one of the connected waterways. Choices **b** and **c** are not.

70. **a.** In January, temperatures range from 13 to 31 degrees in the northern states, such as Maine. In South America, temperatures near the equator at the same time are usually in the high 70s and above.

71. c. Based on the surveys, Southerners preferred remaining in the Southeast and Northerners in the Northeast, reflecting divisions from the Civil War.

72. b. Mental maps are personal maps that illustrate how we see the world. They involve perceptions as well as realities.

73. e. Though being aware of local laws is helpful, geographers need to know detailed information about places in the world.

74. b. Though the rise has been undramatic, the number of young women striking out on their own has passed that of young men. Anecdotal evidence points to the increasing independence and increased earning power of women.

75. e. Anecdotal evidence points to more young men returning to their parents' homes after college as a way of saving money.

76. d. Mali, Iraq, Turkey, England, Algeria, and South Africa are not in the western hemisphere.

77. b. Spatial interaction, which describes local supply and demand, follows the flow of products, people, services, or information among places.

78. c. Emile Durkheim defined four functions of deviance: establishing norms of right and wrong, clarifying moral boundaries, promoting social unity, and encouraging social change.

79. a. Family gives us our first sense of socialization. Family is meant to nurture, care, support, and to pass on knowledge, obligations, and values.

80. c. Social changes come about because of a myriad of reasons. These could include the building of a highway through an established neighborhood that displaces dozens or hundreds of people, for example, or a conflict that displaces millions.

81. a. Patterned interactions provide a stable foundation in our lives. Each of us has a unique slant to our routines and organization methods, without which chaos would ensue.

82. c. A status position is the place a person occupies in society. This position creates expectations of behavior. People may expect students, for example, to be young and carefree. This doesn't mean all students are like that. It is simply a way to identify what is expected of them.

83. c. Social stratification plays a large role in our lives, whether or not we are aware of it. It refers to the unequal distribution of measurable resources, such as wealth, education, prestige, and power.

84. a. This controversial theory says that class plays a role in a person's success, which leads to prestige and power. Karl Marx was among those who wrote on this subject.

85. c. Max Weber predicted a society inundated by bureaucracy; Karl Marx foresaw the disappearance of the state. Durkheim (choices **a**, **d**, and **e**) is considered the father of sociology for his studies of religion, suicide, and the mores of society. Comte (choices **b** and **d**) was the founder of positivism.

86. a. Durkheim concluded that a society's suicide rates can be predicted, though most individual suicides cannot.

87. e. Demographics depict just about every aspect of the human population, including birth and mortality rates (choice **a**) and life expectancy (choice **b**). Demographics also provide straightforward statistics about religion, but this does not include its effects.

88. b. Advertisers would need to have statistics about who watches a particular show. Choices **a**, **c**, **d**, and **e** would not be relevant in most cases.

89. d. Departments of education need to make projections many years ahead and having as much information about the families or students they serve is essential. Choices **a**, **b**, **c**, and **e** concern groups that also depend on demographics, but education departments are most dependent on them.

90. d. Each stage involves a conflict that a person must resolve before reaching the next stage.

91. e. Horney pioneered a new way of looking at the causes and affects of neuroses. She blamed them, not of the neglect of patients by their parents during childhood, but of their indifference.

92. a. Crick, better known for his co-discovery of DNA, was speaking of the biological foundations of behavior.

93. b. As they treated patients with damaged nervous systems, scientists found the patients' behavioral patterns were also affected.

94. b. Kohlberg found that everyone starts with a first step, which is self-centered and based on fear of punishment, and goes on to intermediate steps, which deal with concern for others, but rarely reaches the final steps.

95. b. Albert Bandura's specialty is the social cognitive theory and self-efficacy. He believes that people help themselves by being self-organizing and proactive. Freud (choice **a**) was the founder of psychoanalysis; Murray (choice **c**) was a psychologist whose theory said that individual personalities are based on inborn needs; Maslow (choice **d**) devised a hierarchy of human needs. Anna Freud (choice **e**) contributed to the then-new field of psychoanalysis. Compared to her father, Sigmund Freud, her work stressed the importance of the ego and its ability to be trained.

96. a. A mob mentality infused much of the German population as it elected and paid unquestioning allegiance to Hitler.

97. c. People may experience all the feelings in choices **a**, **b**, and **d** and be type A personalities when they are working on a team or in a group. But those who are most successful tend to take responsibility for their actions and care what others think of them.

98. d. Abnormal behavior includes many disorders, from depression to obsession-compulsion to sexual deviation. Migraines (choice **a**), reproduction (choice **b**), hepatitis (choice **c**), and STDs (choice **e**) are physical, rather than mental, health.

99. d. Our degree of socialization is determined by how well we play our roles in society and by how well we behave within its confines.

100. d. Rogers's commonsense approach was based on mental health being part of life's natural progression. He founded client-centered therapy. Loftus (choice **a**) is known for her work with false memory and eyewitness testimony. Piaget (choice **b**) worked with children and determined that they have their own way of reasoning; Ellis (choice **c**), a psychotherapist, supported short-term therapy. Horney (choice **e**) defined neuroses.

101. d. Gestalt is a theory of visual perception. The word, which is German, means "unified whole." Choices **a**, **b**, **c**, and **e** deal with other kinds of perception.

102. d. By writing books describing his observations of groups playing games, Culin was an important contributor to the science of ethnography.

103 b. A pioneering anthropologist, Mead observed the values and gender roles, among other qualities, of tribes in the South Pacific. Her books about them were bestsellers in the United States. Einstein (choice **a**) revolutionized physics and science in general. Darwin (choice **c**) theorized about the foundations of the human race. Carson (choice **d**) was a marine biologist and writer. Leakey (choice **e**) was an anthropologist who worked in Africa.

104. c. Darwin discussed his theories in *Origin of the Species* and in his journals from his three-year voyage on the *HMS Beagle.* Many years later, Louis Leakey worked to prove Darwin correct.

105. c. Studying African prehistory, Leakey wrote about the archaeology of Olduvai Grange in Africa. Her discovery there of the fossil of the earliest human made her and her husband Louis famous and started the modern science of studying human origins.

106. a. Though choices **b**, **c**, and **e** have revealed significant information, fossils have provided the deepest insights into the origins of humankind.

107. a. Studying corporate cultures has yielded important information about how we live and work today.

108. c. As every prominent scientist has shown, firsthand research is always more valuable and usually more reliable than that done from a distance.

109. c. The gross national product (the market value of goods and services produced by a country in one year), the consumer price index (measure of consumer goods and services purchased by a household), and the unemployment rate of a country, all taken together, have traditionally been used to paint a good picture of a nation's economic health.

110. b. Recessions usually do not occur as part of a regular pattern; they can be erratic or imagined, which discounts choice **a**. Choice **c** is incorrect because recessions can be long lasting and damaging. Choice **d** is incorrect because recessions can affect all sectors of the economy. Choice **e** is incorrect because recessions can be global.

111. a. The reduction in the world's oil supply caused a worldwide phenomenon called stagnation, a combination of a stagnant economy and inflation. Choice **b** is incorrect because the reduction of the world's oil supply caused an increase in inflation. Choice **c** is incorrect because the reduction of the world's oil supply did not cause terrorism. Choice **d** is incorrect because the reduction of the world's oil supply did not assist or result in a significant development of alternative energy sources. Choice **e** is incorrect because the reduction of the world's oil supply had a negative effect on the global economy.

112. d. The unemployment rate is found by comparing the number of people who do not have a job with the number of people who have a job or are looking for a job. Choice **a** is incorrect because the number of people who are unemployed are measured only against the sector of the population that is working or wants to work. Children and older adults who are well past an age where they would work should not be included in the number of people that are working or want to work. Choice **b** is incorrect because the unemployment rate is not determined by a comparison of the number of unemployed people against the number of people who work in blue-collar jobs. Choice **c** is incorrect because the number of people who are working in the defense industry in particular is irrelevant in figuring the unemployment rate. Choice **e** is incorrect because the unemployment rate is not realized by comparing the number of people who are not working with the number of people who are collecting unemployment insurance.

113. b. A quantity tax is a tax based on the volume or amount of an item that is sold. This type of tax is also called an excise tax. Choice **a** is incorrect because a value tax is a tax that is based on the total market value of an item. Choice **c** is incorrect because a lump-sum tax is a type of income tax in which each taxpayer is required to pay the same amount, regardless of their income. The tax described in the question is a type of sales tax, and would not strictly fit into the category of an income tax. Choice **d** is incorrect because a fixed-quantity subsidy is a type of grant by the government to the people of the country. In a fixed-quantity tax, the government provides a set amount of an item that is worth value to the people, such as a fixed number of food stamps. Choice **e** is incorrect because a variable-quantity subsidy is also a type of subsidy. In a variable-quantity subsidy, the government pays a certain amount of the price of an item and lets the people pay the rest of the price, depending on how much they want to purchase of the item.

114. e. A financial asset is an asset that pays money returns to the investor as the asset matures. A bond is a good example of a financial asset; a stock is another. Choice **a** is incorrect because a bond is not a financial asset solely because it is worth money. Choice **b** is incorrect because financial assets are not defined as such because they reach plateaus. In addition, bonds are not usually formed so that their value eventually reaches a plateau. Choice **c** is incorrect because a bond is not a financial asset for the reason that it is a liquid asset (an asset that can easily be converted into cash). Choice **d** is incorrect because a bond cannot be a financial asset simply because it is not a risky asset.

115. b. This model shows the possibilities for a game called the prisoner's dilemma. In the prisoner's dilemma, there is only one Nash equilibrium, which occurs when both players defect.

116. d. A tariff war leads to a decline in trade because both countries have made the tariffs on imported goods too high for consumers to want to purchase imported items, which immediately discounts choice **e**. Choice **a** is incorrect because a tariff war has a negative effect on emerging industries. Choice **b** is incorrect because a tariff war causes both countries to reduce exporting items to each other, resulting in a decrease in bulk imports. Choice **c** is incorrect because a tariff war causes both countries to reduce exporting items to each other, resulting in a decrease in bulk exports.

117. b. A monopoly is a situation where a single company controls the production of a particular good or service. Choice **a** is incorrect because an oligopoly is a situation where a small number of companies control the production of a particular good or service. Choice **c** is incorrect because a monopsony is a situation where there is a single buyer of a particular good or service. Choice **d** is incorrect because a quango is a quasi-national government office, not a major producer or consumer in the marketplace. Choice **e** is incorrect because an oligopsony is a situation where a small number of buyers purchase a particular good or service.

118. d. Devaluing gold at equal rates will allow nations to freely trade gold instead of hoarding it or selling it. Choice **a** is incorrect because devaluing gold at different rates will not stretch the world's gold supply. Choice **b** is incorrect because inflating the value of the dollar will not stretch the world's gold supply. Choice **c** is incorrect because devaluing silver will not have a significant and direct effect on the world's gold supply. Choice **e** is incorrect because it is expensive to create artificial gold. The substance cannot be created without nuclear reactors or particle accelerators. The creation of artificial gold, called *gold synthesis,* is not a solution for stretching the world's gold supply.

119. c. A "Giffen good" is an item that people buy because it has a high price. A luxury good fits this classification of item. Choice **a** is incorrect because a widget is a term that economists use to describe a good. A widget could be any good. Because it is not a specific good, it is not clear whether it could fit the qualifications for a "Giffen good." Choice **b** is incorrect because a consumer staple is an item that people need no matter what that item costs. The demand for a consumer staple would not decrease if its price fell. Choice **d** is incorrect because an aircraft carrier is a large piece of defense equipment typically purchased only by the government. The demand for an aircraft carrier would not fall if its price fell. Choice **e** is incorrect because government agencies are required to buy certain necessary items for government agencies. The demand for these items would not decrease if the price for them fell.

120. c. The Laffer curve, which was invented by the economist Arthur Laffer, shows the rate of taxes measured against the revenue collected from taxes. The Laffer curve is significant because it indicates that past a certain point, if tax rates are too high, people will not work hard. Then the government will not be able to collect an increased amount of tax revenue.

7 ▶ Western Civilization I

The CLEP divides the historical and cultural study of Western civilization and its roots into two large sections. The first, "Ancient Near East to 1648," traces the development of Western culture from civilization's beginnings in the modern Middle East to the rise of the colonials and commercial empires of Europe. The second test covers 1648 to the present. This chapter will cover some of the basic concepts that are likely to appear on the Western Civilization I exam. To keep things simple and emphasize cause-and-effect relationships, the topics in this chapter will proceed chronologically. The chapter will end with ten review questions to help you assess your knowledge.

▶ The Ancient Near East: 3200 B.C.E. to 500 B.C.E.

Many of the political and social structures that would reappear in human civilizations throughout history got their start in the ancient kingdoms of the Middle East and Northern Africa. These civilizations both developed in fertile river country. In the Middle East, the Sumerians, Mesopotamians, and other distinct city-states developed along the banks of the Tigris and Euphrates Rivers, near what is now the Persian Gulf. This area was part of a massive swath of rich farmland that stretched from the Persian Gulf to the Mediterranean Sea. This lush area is known as the **Fertile Crescent**, after its crescent shape. In Northern Africa, Egyptian culture developed along the banks of the Nile, where seasonal flooding kept the soil rich and productive.

The Sumerians were not a single culture, but a collection of separate states with some common characteristics. All the city-states of Sumer were organized into hierarchies, with the royal family at the top and various civil groups ranked beneath them. They were polytheistic, worshiping many gods. They invented a writing system called cuniform and are the source of *The Epic of Gilgamesh,* the world's first recorded epic poem. The Sumerians were eventually incorporated into the growing empire of the Mesopotamians. In 2300 B.C.E., Sargon, ruler of the city of Akkad, launched a campaign to conquer and unify Sumer. He would be the first of several conquerors who would replace one empire with another: the Babylonians, the Hittites, and ultimately the Persians. During this time, the empires of the Middle East developed civil and criminal law codes, horse drawn chariots, an early form of a currency economy, and the first written alphabet.

In Africa, two distinct cultures had developed along the Nile: Upper Egypt, which had developed several hundred miles upriver, and Lower Egypt, which developed near the delta of the Nile. In 3100 B.C.E., these regions were united.

Egyptian history is divided into three periods. The **Old Kingdom** (2575 B.C.E.–2130 B.C.E.) encompasses the time period when the political system of the pharaohs developed. The pharaohs were the absolute power in Egypt. A complex governmental bureaucracy of specialists helped the pharaohs run the kingdom. It was during this time the Great Pyramids were built. The **Middle Kingdom** (2040 B.C.E.–1640 B.C.E.) was a period of internal strife and hardship. Massive crop failures, political power struggles, and foreign invasions battered the Egyptian people. The **New Kingdom** (1570 B.C.E.–1070 B.C.E.) was an era of resurgence. Egypt's first female ruler, Hatshepsut, improved trade and strengthened the Egyptian economy. The rulers after her expanded the boundaries of the kingdom through conquest. Egypt would remain the dominant power in North Africa until the 1100 B.C.E., when invaders from Persia would conquer the region.

During the long reign of the pharaohs, Egypt developed hieroglyphics, a writing system that used pictures and symbols to represented concepts and sounds. Egyptians were talented scientists, especially in the field of medicine and astronomy. Their visual and written arts were quite advanced as well.

The final group from the region to make a lasting impact on Western culture was the Israelites, who developed a kingdom of their own in Canaan, modern-day Israel. Perhaps the single most significant thing the Israelites contributed to the modern world was monotheism. The belief in a single divine being would form the basis of the three dominant religions of Western culture: **Judaism**, **Christianity**, and **Islam**.

▶ Ancient Greece (1750 B.C.E.– 133 B.C.E.)

In ancient Greece, seafaring cultures developed into a group of diverse city-states. The most influential of these city-states would be **Athens**. In 700 B.C.E., in response to public discontent, the Athenians began to develop a limited form of democracy. By modern standards, this democracy was extremely limited. However, under the leadership of the statesman Pericles, Athens developed into a direct democracy. Qualified citizens could directly affect government policy, rather than working through elected representatives. This period of direct democracy (460 B.C.E.–429 B.C.E.) was also a period of great financial prosperity and cultural development.

Unfortunately, conflict with other city-states ended Athens's cultural dominance. The prosperity of Athens was oppressive to some of the other Greek city-states. Pro- and anti-Athenian states formed two large alliances. Athens and its allies formed the Delian League. Sparta and other enemies of Athens formed the Peloponnesian League. The war between these two great alliances ultimately ended in defeat for the Athenians. They were stripped of their fleet, which destroyed their economy. The brutality of the war and the loss of Athens as a political anchor sapped Greek culture of its vitality.

Eventually, the Greek city-states were conquered by the Macedonians, who came from the mountainous regions to the north of Greece. The Macedonian leader Phillip II led the invasion. However, this conquest did not extinguish Greek culture. Phillip II was a great admirer of the Greeks and he sought to perpetuate what he thought was best in their arts and sciences. He even went so far as to hire the Greek philosopher Aristotle as the private tutor for his son Alexander. This period of Greek-influenced Macedonian dominance is known as the Hellenistic period.

Under the leadership of the expansionist Alexander, the Macedonian Empire spread across Eastern Europe, the Middle East, and much of Asia. As Alexander conquered new lands, he brought Greek cultural influences with him. Just as Alexander spread Greek ideas, the ideas of the cultures he encountered and conquered influenced Macedonia. The Macedonian capital was moved to Alexandria in Egypt. This capital city boasted architectural marvels, such as a 440-foot-tall lighthouse and a museum that was a library, zoo, and university all in one. Hellenistic culture also expanded the social role of women. Many women were educated and noble women often took leadership positions, such as Cleopatra VII, who ruled after Alexander's death. Hellenistic scholars created the basis of modern geometry, developed the first astronomical theory that stated the Earth revolved around the sun, and discovered many of the basic concepts of modern applied engineering. Hellenistic philosophers developed the philosophy of stoicism that stressed self-control and reason over emotion and prejudice. This philosophy would later influence the Romans and the early Christians.

The lasting impact of Greek and Hellenistic culture on Western culture is hard to overestimate. The concepts of Greek philosophers like Socrates, Plato, and Aristotle are still studied today. Greek architecture styles are considered the classical forms and, even today, continue to inspire architects. Perhaps most importantly, democracy, though not exactly as the Greeks practiced it, would become the dominant political system of the Western world.

▶ Ancient Rome (509 B.C.E.– 476 B.C.E.)

The predecessors of the Romans, the **Latins**, were one of several groups living in what is now modern Italy. It is believed the Latins migrated to the peninsula prior to 800 B.C.E. When the various villages of the Latins formed into a single city-state, Rome, the group became known as the **Romans**. In the early days of Rome, the city was ruled over by the **Etruscans**, a now extinct cultural group that dominated much of central Italy. In 508 B.C.E., the Romans overthrew their Etruscan rulers and founded a republic. A unique political system designed to prevent any one person from accumulating too much power, the Roman republic consisted of a 300-member Senate. These members were selected from the upper classes. The Senate created and passed laws. Each year, the Senate elected two consuls, who carried out the laws that the Senate passed. Those without land could not become senators, but they could vote for tribunes. The tribunes could veto laws made by the Senate. This way the upper classes could not pass laws that would be unfair to the lower classes. Finally, in times of crisis, the Senate could elect a dictator. Dictators had complete control over the government, but the duration of their rule was limited by the Senate.

Rome expanded its borders through a long series of conquests. By 44 B.C.E., the Roman Empire had expanded west through what is now France and Spain, south to cover a long stretch of the northern coast of Africa, and as far east as modern Syria. This imperialist expansion brought great power and wealth to Rome, but social inequalities ensured the drastically uneven distribution of these gains. This caused civil unrest and led to a series of civil wars. When the dust cleared, the Senate was no longer the supreme power in Rome. Instead, powerful leaders transformed the role of dictator in a more permanent position. With power centralized in the role of the emperor and a professional army keeping control over a considerable portion of the known world, the empire entered in a 200-year span of peace and prosperity called the **Pax Romana**, or "Roman Peace."

Unfortunately, once power left the hands of the Senate, the fortunes of Rome rose and fell with the character of its emperors. Some emperors were effective and just rulers, while others were so violent and irrational as to appear psychotic. Political violence became commonplace. Domestic affairs in the massive empire were ineffectively handled. Eventually, the empire was split into two separate political entities: the Western and Eastern Roman Empires. The Western Empire's capital was Rome, while the Eastern Empire was ruled from Constantinople.

It was during this time that Rome legalized Christianity, a breakaway religious sect that had formed in its Jewish colonies. This was significant in that it reflected the growing popularity of the new religion among the Roman upper classes, further divorced traditional Roman political authority from the religious beliefs that justified it, and set the stage for the creation of the powerful Roman Catholic Church.

Although the division of the empire improved conditions for the citizens and resolved many domestic issues, the benefits were temporary. The empire was no longer strong enough to stop foreign invaders and, in 378 C.E., Rome itself was attacked and looted. The economy sagged under heavy taxes. Government leaders proved corrupt or ineffective. Still, there was no spectacular fall for the Roman Empire. Rather, it slowly gave way to the next leaders of the Western world.

▶ Medieval History (500–1500 C.E.)

In the aftermath of the collapse of the Roman Empire, Europe broke up into smaller nation states. Despite this collapse, there remained a common thread that helped Europeans keep a transnational "Western" identity: Christianity. By the time the Roman Empire had completely faded into history, the once outlawed religion had become the dominant faith of Europe. This Christian identity was intensified in the early 700s when Islamic leaders spread their faith throughout the Middle East, Africa, and even into Spain. The existence of these Islamic leaders gave Christian rulers in Europe a shared enemy, and regular religious war against Islamic kingdoms was often the only thing that brought Christian rulers together in common cause.

During this period, two great empires would rise in Europe. In modern-day France, the Emperor Charlemagne would expand the **Kingdom of the Franks** well into what is now Italy and Germany. Charlemagne envisioned himself as the founder of a new Christianized Roman Empire. Along with his military accomplishments, he encouraged the arts and sciences under his rule. This led to a revival of Latin. Through a system of Christian monasteries, scribes would maintain and copy classical texts, becoming the conduit for the intellectual achievements of Greece and Rome. Charlemagne's empire never attained the scope or permanence of

Rome's. After his death in 814, his heirs were unable to maintain the empire and Europe was shattered by repeated invasions and internal conflicts.

The other great European empire of this period was the **Byzantine Empire**. Under Justinian, the Byzantine Empire emerged out of the collapse of Eastern Roman Empire. Justinian rebuilt Constantinople and established an elaborate code of laws that became a model for other European monarchs. By 1360, the Byzantine Empire had expanded as far west as Italy and followed the coast of the Mediterranean as far as the south of Spain.

It was during this time that conflicts between western and eastern Christians reached a breaking point. After a long period of relative unity on points of faith, the differences in opinion had grown so drastic that the church broke into a Western church, which would become the Roman Catholic Church, and an Eastern Church, the Eastern Orthodox Church.

As with Charlemagne, Justinian's heirs were incapable of maintaining the size and strength of the empire. During the Fourth Crusade, Christian knights headed off to fight Muslim forces in the Middle East were convinced by Italian merchants to sack and loot Constantinople. This marked the beginning of the end for the empire. The final blow was delivered by Muslim invaders from modern-day Turkey. The Turks invaded Constantinople in 1453.

After the rise and fall of the second and last great European empire, power devolved to a diverse collection of monarchs who, instead of following imperialistic impulses, tended to focus on building strong nation-states.

Ironically, it was during the rise of local monarchs that the first institutional checks on kings and queens were developed. In England, William the Conqueror, a French-speaking nobleman, gained control. He expanded the king's powers and developed a unified legal code based on the customs of the English people.

Years later, these reforms encouraged lesser nobles to demand limitations of royal authority. In 1215, a group of nobles created and forced King John to sign a document called the Magna Carta. The Magna Carta reserved some rights for the nobles. These rights were later extended to commoners as well. These reforms led to the creation of Parliament, which would later become England's chief legislature. In France, Phillip II set up the Estates General in 1302. Made up of nobles, clergy, and commoners, the Estates General was an advisory body. Though it never gained the official force of the Parliament, it acted as an informal check on royal power.

The medieval era was wracked repeatedly by international warfare. There were four different crusades in which soldiers and citizens from multiple nations would march on the Islamic nations to the east in an effort to liberate Jerusalem. More often than not, these campaigns accomplished little more than the depletion of Europe's resources as men and material left home on these quixotic efforts. Within Europe, rival powers in France and England fought a long series of bloody conflicts that collectively came to be known as the Hundred Years' War. This protracted conflict introduced the longbow, the crossbow, and the cannon to European warfare.

Another destabilizing factor in medieval life was the **Black Death**, a global plague that swept through Europe from 1347 to 1353. The plague originated in China and was brought to Europe on a trading vessel traveling from the Black Sea to Italy. By the end of the epidemic, an estimated 25 million people died in Europe. This was roughly a third of the population of the continent. The plague would vanish for a couple centuries before returning in smaller, but still deadly, waves throughout the 1600s.

Three extra features of medieval life demand special attention. First, as the period progressed, **education** spread to the upper and middle classes. After the collapse of the Roman Empire, education was often limited to small segments of church scholars, many of which lived isolated monastic lives. Before the end of the Middle Ages, universities were set up for the benefit of people outside the church. The second notable feature is the **feudal system**. Under this system, local lords governed their own lands. These lords owed military service to a higher lord, usually the king, but otherwise were free to do as they pleased. Under each lord lived farmers and peasants who would work the lord's land in exchange for protection and very basic services. The feudal system's tendency to tie up opportunities for non-landowners encouraged many to move to cites to seek their fortune. This led to the development of the third notable feature: a new urban and affluent **merchant class**. The interests of this merchant class, especially their need for efficient trade routes, would help drive the creation of modern Europe and the European colonies abroad.

▶ The Renaissance and the Reformation (1300–1560)

The Renaissance is a term used to describe a series of profound intellectual and social revolutions that transformed nearly every aspect of life in Europe. Though it is often described as a distinct period, its slow spread means that it overlaps a significant portion of what was considered the medieval era.

The Renaissance began in Italy. There are several reasons for this. First, the great inspiration for Renaissance thought was classical Greek and Roman scholarship. Resources from the past were abundant in Italy. Another reason was the wealth of Italy's merchant classes. Trade and banking generated an enormous amount of wealth for a handful of Italian families. The most famous of these, such as the Medicis of Florence, became financial and political powerhouses. They were also important patrons of the arts and sciences, using their vast fortunes to fund the careers of thinkers and artists.

As the Renaissance spread across Europe, other factors would contribute to its spread. Perhaps no single contribution was more important that the invention of the printing press with movable type. The new printing press encouraged literacy and made a broad range of knowledge available to large audiences all over Europe.

The overall direction of Renaissance thought has been described as *humanistic*. Inspired by classical models, Renaissance thinkers began to make a careful study of the world around them. In the Middle Ages, supernatural and religious doctrines dominated European thought. In the Renaissance, the study of the human experience began to take center stage. Philosophical studies of pragmatic, rather than spiritual, leadership were produced, such as Machiavelli's *The Prince*. Castiglione's *The Book of the Courtier* instructed nobles to not only master ethical virtues, but also gain knowledge of the arts and sciences. In painting, direct observation became tantamount. Visual artists developed perspective to realistically simulate the world around them. Painters and sculptors made a careful study of the human anatomy, a process that prefigured the scientific method's dedication to observational practices. Finally, the literary arts flourished. Poets revived classical form and innovated new styles. It is a sign of how important the artists of this time are to the modern world that at least two Renaissance-era writers, Dante and Shakespeare, are often considered to be the greatest writers ever produced by their respective nations.

The growth of humanistic thought set the stage for the largest break in the Christian religion since the Eastern Orthodox/Catholic schism. Throughout the medieval era, there had been conflicts between church authorities and various groups. Monarchs frequently strained at the extra-national authority the church wielded. Within the church, followers and local leaders often criticized the church leaders. Charges of corruption and differences in doctrine put a strain on the unity of the faith. During the Renaissance, these issues came to a head. The boom in printed materials meant Bibles could be quickly and cheaply distributed in the native languages of the faithful, rather than the official Latin of the church. This emphasis on the individual led many to question the church's authority over religious matters. In 1517, a German monk named Martin Luther publicly posted a list of 95 arguments against the then-common church practice of granting indulgences, essentially an exchange of blessings and grants of forgiveness for money. This act set off a long series of revolts again church authority. Breakaway groups from the church would be known as Protestant faiths and their revolt would be known as the **Reformation**.

In England, the Reformation took an unusual shape: The religious revolution was driven by the reigning monarch rather than radical segments within the clergy. Henry VIII was desperate for a male heir, but ran afoul of Catholic bans on divorce. Rather than submit, Henry created the Church of England and appointed himself its pope. The Church of England mixed Protestant and Catholic practices, but eliminated the Catholic Church's power over England's monarch.

The Protestant Reformation gave power to reform-minded activists within the Catholic Church. These Catholics started the Catholic or Counter-Reformation. The church held a council in 1545 to end corruption in the church and affirm certain tenants of the faith. Unfortunately, this also led to the strengthening of the Inquisition. Set up in the Middle Ages, the newly empowered church court used coercive and sometimes brutal methods to enforce church orthodoxy.

▶ Early Modern Europe (1492–1648)

Throughout the Renaissance and Reformation, Europe's commercial interests were expanding. The need for imported foreign goods and the desire to create new markets for European goods sent explorers and merchants to Africa, the Middle East, and the Far East. Overland routes were well established, but they were slow, and the dangerous political tensions between Christian Europeans and the Islamic kingdoms of Africa and the Middle East made them unreliable. European explorers had discovered a sea route that passed around the southern tip of Africa. However, this route was not much faster or safer than the land routes.

In 1492, Christopher Columbus, funded by the Spanish crown, attempted to find a sea route to India by going west and circumnavigating the globe. Instead of a trade route to India, he made landfall in the Caribbean. His voyage started a new phase of global imperialism for the European powers. The North and South American continents represented a vast and open commercial opportunity. The development of Atlantic colonies would drive European powers to seek colonies in Africa and Asia as well.

In Africa, Portugal established forts along the eastern coast. The primary goal of these merchant imperialists was gold, but the trade in slaves ultimately became the most profitable enterprise. Some African leaders resisted the slave trade, but the power of the imperialists and the lure of profits led most African rulers to support it.

In Asia, Portugal established colonies in India. The Dutch displaced the Portuguese, using a combination of business and military methods to push them out of the region. The Spanish conquered the Philippines in 1571.

In South America, Spanish conquistadors conquered modern-day Haiti, Santo Domingo, Cuba, and

Puerto Rico. From there, they launched campaigns into South America, Central America, and southwestern regions of North America. The conquest of South and Central America was a disaster for the native inhabitants. Mighty empires fell before the Spanish. The Spanish crown established the system of *encomiendas,* which granted conquistadors the right to demand labor and tribute from the native population. This essentially reduced the entire native population to slavery. Portugal established a colony in modern-day Brazil, but their treatment of the native population was no more humane.

France, England, Spain, and the Dutch all clashed over the eastern coast of North America. French colonies were established in what is now Canada. English colonies stretched down the coast of what is now the United States, with the exception of New York, which was a Dutch colony. Spain claimed what is now Florida.

Although some colonists were motivated by their religious beliefs or political necessity, the main reason for the growth of the colonies was economic. And, back in Europe, the economy was transformed by the wealth pouring in from the colonies. Private business was on the rise, making capitalism the dominant economic model for most Europeans. New bookkeeping methods and newly invented business organizations, such as the joint stock company (in which owners purchased stock, representing shares of ownership, in a company) made business more efficient. Inflation, caused by gold and silver from the new world, pushed prices up and made the merchant class extremely wealthy. This gave rise to the mercantilist theory of wealth. Mercantilists believed that a nation's wealth was measured by the gold and silver stores it possessed. Consequently, European nations tried to stop the outgoing flow of precious metals by limiting what they imported. This led to more colonization, as the only way to gain resources and trading partners was to expand the borders of the country.

One of the most profound impacts of the international expansion of the European empires was the environmental impact. The **Columbian Exchange** describes the process by which European plants and animals made their way to America and vice versa. In America, Europeans introduced wheat, sugar, coffee, horses, pigs, and chicken. Colonies sent corn, potatoes, tomatoes, and cocoa to Europe. Unfortunately, viruses also traveled with the colonists. European colonists introduced smallpox and typhus to the Americas. The native populations had no natural immunities to these diseases, and the results were devastating.

The wealth and conflicts occurring in the so-called **New World** reshaped governments and nations in Europe. The prosperity of Europe translated into approval for European monarchs. Moves to limit the power of monarchs were reversed in several countries. In France and Spain, the national leaders became **absolute monarchs**, or rulers with no checks to their power. England would be one of the few counterexamples to this trend. During this same period, the Parliament would grow in strength. Ultimately, this clash would develop into a full-blown civil war that would start in 1642 and last until 1651.

Spain, fueled by the silver and gold of its new colonies, entered a sustained period of prosperity and political importance. The fearsome Spanish navy, known as the Spanish Armada, defeated many foreign fleets during this period. Ultimately, Spanish designs to build a new European empire were checked when the English navy, under Queen Elizabeth, defeated the Spanish navy in 1588.

▶ Practice Questions

1. Which of the following terms describes the chief minister under the pharaoh in ancient Egypt?
   a. aristocrat
   b. vizier
   c. consul
   d. plebeian
   e. jurist

2. All of these are considered factors in the decline of the Roman Empire EXCEPT
   a. widespread corruption in the government.
   b. strain on the economy caused by high taxes.
   c. attacks from Islamic kingdoms from the east.
   d. increasing commonness of political violence.
   e. inability to fend off Germanic invaders.

3. Which of the following terms describes a feudal landowner who has pledged allegiance to a greater lord?
   a. fief
   b. knight
   c. yeoman
   d. vassal
   e. trebuchet

4. Which of the following describes the role of the tribune in the Roman republic?
   a. power to create new laws
   b. final authority on religious matters
   c. right to determine market prices
   d. authority to conduct war
   e. veto power over the legislature

5. All of the following were effects of the Black Death EXCEPT
   a. inflation from surviving laborers demanding higher wages.
   b. increased tension over who controlled the English Channel.
   c. outbreaks of anti-Semitic violence.
   d. food shortages from crop failures.
   e. migrations away from cities and to rural areas.

6. "To us Jerusalem is as precious as it is to you, because it is the place from where our Prophet made his journey by night to heaven. Do not dream that we will give it up to you." This statement is most likely a reaction to what event?
   a. the Battle of Legano
   b. the fall of Constantinople
   c. the Hundred Years' War
   d. the Reconquista
   e. the Third Crusade

7. "Here the question arises: is it better to be loved than feared, or vice versa? I don't doubt that every prince would like to be both; both since it is hard to accommodate these qualities, if you have to make a choice, to be feared is much safer than to be loved." This was written by which Renaissance philosopher?
   a. Niccolò Machiavelli
   b. Desiderius Erasmus
   c. Thomas Moore
   d. Martin Luther
   e. Jacques Cartier

8. Which of the following rulers established a code of criminal law for the ancient Mesopotamians?
   a. Gilgamesh
   b. Zoroaster
   c. Hammurabi
   d. Nebuchadnezzar
   e. Sargon

9. What was the purpose of the capitalist "putting-out" system of work distribution?
   a. to avoid the price controls of the labor guilds
   b. to concentrate resources in urban areas
   c. to lock unskilled laborers out of the labor market
   d. to protect domestic vendors from foreign competition
   e. to ensure the highest quality of services and goods

10. "During the time men live without a common power to keep them all in awe, they are in that condition which is called war. . . . In such condition there is no place for industry . . . no arts; no letters; no society; and which is worst of all, continual fear and danger of violent death." The political view advanced here is best described as
   a. direct democratic.
   b. republican.
   c. anarchy.
   d. absolutism.
   e. parliamentarianism.

▶ **Answers**

1. b
2. c
3. d
4. e
5. b
6. e
7. a
8. c
9. a
10. d

CHAPTER

8 ▶ Western Civilization II

It is an old cliché that history moves faster the closer it gets to the modern era. True or not, it definitely describes the assumption behind the second CLEP Western Civilization exam. The Western Civilization I exam covered nearly 2,000 years, but divided all that information into just six general eras. In contrast, the Western Civilization II exam covers about 400 years, but the College Board divides this section into 12 distinct periods. Despite the density of this information, it is still possible to get a bird's-eye view of the subject.

This chapter will review the general trends and key concepts of the periods covered by the Western Civilization II exam. The topics will be covered in chronological order. After the review, the chapter will end with ten review questions.

▶ Europe Transformed

In the late 1400s, European governments began an extensive program of overseas colonization. These new colonies provided the European nations with new markets for trade and new sources of revenue. This new prosperity had some drastic effects on the economies and governments of Europe. Some nations turned into absolute monarchies while others began to develop more democratic and liberal modes of government.

During his rule in Spain, King Philip II had spread his influence over several areas in Europe. One of these areas included what is now known as the Netherlands. In the 1560s, riots broke out in the Netherlands against the brutal tactics of the Inquisition, a group Philip II supported. Philip II tried to suppress the rioters. Conflict between Dutch rebels and the Spanish authorities lasted until 1581, when the seven Dutch provinces finally threw off Spanish rule and declared their independence. The Dutch Netherlands were founded as a republic and officially recognized in 1648. Although the government was officially a republic, in practice, nobles were always elected or selected to crucial positions in the government.

In England, political tensions between King Charles I and the Parliament exploded into full-blown civil war. From 1642 to 1651, supporters of the king fought pro-Parliamentary forces. In 1649, King Charles was beheaded. This was the first time a king had ever been executed by his own people. Victorious, the Parliamentary forces founded the English Commonwealth. The Commonwealth was short-lived. In 1660, Parliament voted to install Charles II as king. In 1688, the monarchy was in trouble again. James II, who took the throne after Charles II, was a Catholic. This angered many in the Church of England and they replaced James with the Dutch noble William III in a bloodless coup called the Glorious Revolution. Under William, a governmental system of checks and balances developed in England.

In contrast, the French King Louis XIV used the period of prosperity to consolidate his power. Louis ignored the Estate General, an advisory body made up of representatives from all strata of French society. He developed a complex bureaucracy to help him control all levels of government. He strengthened France's industrial base, helping the economy, but would also persecute non-Catholics, as he viewed Protestants a threat to his power.

Germany, then a collection of smaller states, became entangled in the ruinous Thirty Years' War. Devastated by the cost in gold and blood, the remaining states signed the Treaty of Westphalia. This brought peace, but left Germany divided into hundreds of separate little states. Eventually, two expansionist kingdoms—the Catholic Austrian and the Protestant Prussian empires—would come to dominate the region.

In Russia, the Tsar Peter the Great would undertake a massive project to modernize his nation. Peter took on the powers of an absolute monarch, forcing lesser nobles to accept positions in his government. He brought the church under his control and expanded Russia's borders, stretching the reach of the kingdom all the way to the Pacific Ocean. He built the massive capital city of St. Petersburg and fought naval battles with rival European powers with mixed results.

▶ The Global Empires

The dominant economic policy of the day, mercantilism, held that the wealth of nations could be measured by the amount of gold and silver they held. Colonial expansion was viewed as a way to increase gold stores while creating new markets that would allow you to trade without giving gold to foreign powers. Consequently, the creation of overseas colonies became a crucial goal for European powers.

These new global empires scattered the once confined populations of Europe. No longer geographically confined, the global population increased. The colonies also encouraged political and religious diversification. Religious and ethnic peoples persecuted in Europe found refuge in the colonies.

During this vast expansion of the European empires, the various governments engaged in shifting alliances to keep the others in check. For example, in 1700, Louis XIV's grandson inherited the throne of

Spain. The idea of a single French-Spanish power panicked other European powers. An alliance of English and Dutch forces fought to prevent the unification of the two thrones. In 1713, Louis was forced to sign the Treaty of Utrecht, preventing the unification of the two empires.

▶ The Scientific Revolution

During this time, the sciences underwent a massive shift. Francis Bacon, the English philosopher, is credited with emphasizing the importance of experimentation as a way to advance science. The French philosopher René Descartes emphasized the importance of reason and logic in discovering the truth. Combining these two concepts with the observational methods devised in the Renaissance produced the **scientific method**: a process combining experiments and observations to determine naturalistic explanations for worldly phenomena.

This paradigm shift produced immediate results in the field of medicine. The field of anatomy advanced the human understanding of the body. In 1684, Anton van Leeuwenhoek used a microscope to become the first person to identify red blood cells. William Harvey described the human circulatory system. The chemist Robert Boyle developed the first system of what would become the atomic theory.

In the field of physics, Isaac Newton developed the first functional theory of gravity. He and Gottfried Wilhelm Leibniz simultaneously developed calculus, a set of mathematical tools that scientists and mathematicians still use and refine today.

The advances of science led many to believe that natural political and moral truths could also be discovered. This link is what connects the scientific revolution to the **Enlightenment** that followed.

▶ The Age of Reason

Central to Enlightenment-era thought is the notion of natural rights. Advanced by John Locke and others, this was the notion that some rights are reserved to humans at birth. Locke maintained that humans formed governments to ensure these natural rights. To ensure that governments do not trample on the natural rights they were formed to protect, the philosopher Montesquieu proposed that governing power should be distributed to different branches, guaranteeing no one person or group became too powerful. In England, Mary Wollstonecraft made the case for extending full political rights to women, a group left almost entirely disenfranchised in Europe.

Enlightenment thought affected fields beyond political science. In education, philosophers stressed the importance of encouraging the innate talents of students. In economics, Adam Smith stressed the value of free markets, letting the logic of economic systems operate without economic intervention. In the arts, the new ways of thinking encouraged experimentation and political awareness.

The new ideas of the Enlightenment filtered through society and some monarchs and rulers became relatively liberal and reform-minded. For example, tensions over control of Poland were resolved diplomatically, rather than militarily. In 1772, Russia, Austria, and Prussia divided up Poland.

However, the largest impact of Enlightenment thought would be felt in the coming revolutions that would topple, rather than reform, monarchies.

▶ Age of Revolutions and the French Empire

Fed by the ideals of the Enlightenment, revolution fever spread throughout the colonies of Europe. In 1775, the American colonies began to revolt. Revolutions in

Haiti, Paraguay, Chile, Columbia, Mexico, Peru, Brazil, and Bolivia would follow.

In 1789, the citizens of France caught the fever. Economic inequality, government and clerical corruption, and political stalemates over the creation of a constitution all broke into civil violence when angry Parisians stormed the Bastille, a former fortress repurposed as a prison. Urban and rural revolts forced the National Assembly, the French legislature, to create a constitutional monarchy. The royal family was essentially imprisoned in Paris and the church was put under state rule. In 1791, a new constitution was put in place. Foreign monarchies threatened to intervene to protect the French monarchy, but this did not stop radicals from abolishing the monarchy and executing the king and queen in 1793. Under more radical leadership, the French Revolution entered a brutally fanatical phase known as the Reign of Terror. More than 17,000 people were executed for counter-revolutionary crimes at the hands of the new government. The excesses of the Terror left a more moderate, but corrupt government in charge. Facing civil unrest over the poor state of the economy and official wrongdoing, the new government turned to a well-known war hero, **Napoleon Bonaparte**, to act as a figurehead for the new government.

Napoleon, however, was not content to be a figurehead and quickly took control of the new government. During the Revolution, Napoleon became famous for a series of victories against foreign foes. Capitalizing on that popularity, he declared himself the emperor of France and launched on an imperialistic campaign in Europe. He conquered and annexed portions of Italy, the Netherlands, sections of Germany, and Poland. He overthrew the king of Spain and put his own brother on the throne.

Ultimately, Napoleon's imperial designs were thwarted. His effort to invade Russia was repelled and his territories in Spain and Austria were constantly in revolt.

These failures led to unpopularity at home, and in 1814, Napoleon abdicated briefly. In 1815, he returned to chase Louis XVIII out of France and take on the British military. At the Battle of Waterloo, the British forces and their allies defeated Napoleon. He was exiled and died on the island of St. Helena in 1821.

After Napoleon's defeat, representatives of the European powers met at the Congress of Vienna in hopes of restoring order to Europe. The Congress reestablished the hereditary throne of France and the Concert of Europe, a system of periodic diplomatic meetings between the heads of Europe.

▶ The Industrial Revolution

The relative stability of Europe after the Napoleonic Wars encouraged economic and industrial development. Agriculture was the first sector of the economy to innovate. Cattle breeding, soil and manure experiments, and the development of new mechanized farming practices all contributed to increased yields. Notably, these innovations were the product of farmers themselves and not government reforms.

In industry and transportation, two major technological innovations opened the way for new development: improved steam power and high quality steel. With these improvements in place, the process of **industrialization** began. The process started in England. England had abundant coal sources, which drove the steam engines, and a large skilled workforce. It also had a tradition of business entrepreneurship that drove owners to seek new and more efficient means of production.

The industrial revolution encouraged urban migration as workers moved to be closer to industrial centers. It also created two new social classes: a wealthy class of business owners and a vast class of less wealthy industrial laborers. Life for the laboring class could be hard. Conditions in many factories were brutal and many industrial jobs were dangerous. The positive results of industrialization spurred the growth of philosophies that emphasized limited government regulation, such as utilitarianism. Others were disturbed by the social costs of industrialization and urged reform. One of the most extreme of these reform philosophies was Marxism.

▶ The Rise of Nationalism

In the period after the Congress of Vienna, competing ideas regarding the future of Europe spread across borders and social classes. Concerned about the violence of the French revolution and its role in the rise of Napoleon, conservatives urged a return to monarchal government. Liberals pushed for constitutional governments and stressed democratic processes and free markets. Because of the empire building of the fifteenth and sixteenth centuries, many nation states spread over a vast area and incorporated diverse populations. Nationalists felt that these empires should be broken up and different cultural groups should be able to form their own nations. Finally, socialists believed that governments should exert greater control over their economies, ensuring a more equitable distribution of wealth. More moderate socialists felt that governments could improve the lot of their citizens by nationalizing just a few key industries. The most radical felt that total control of all industry was required to prevent exploitation and inequality. To a degree, all these philosophies would shape the post-Napoleonic era.

Liberal revolts broke out in several nations. In 1830, the French again revolted. Angry Parisians seized the streets and erected barricades. After the king was replaced with a more acceptable ruler, the unrest died down. The peace was, however, short-lived. Economic hardship and government corruption sent Parisians

into the streets again in 1848. The result of this second revolt was the creation of a republican government. It lasted less than a decade. Napoleon III, nephew of the famous emperor, was elected president, and in 1852, he proclaimed himself emperor.

Liberal revolts occurred in several of the German states. Initially it appeared as if these movements would be successful in creating a constitutional monarchy. Fredrick William IV, the Prussian king who ruled the rebellious states, refused the new constitution and the liberal movements collapsed.

In the Austrian empire, Hungarian nationalists revolted in an effort to form an independent government. The Austrian government initially reacted with a series of social reforms, but then the government reversed course and crushed the rebellion.

▶ The Age of Nationalism

In the late 1800s, Otto von Bismark united the fractious German states into a single nation. Elected prime minister in 1862, Bismark used military and diplomatic strategies to create a single German state under Prussia. The new state was a constitutional monarch in which the kaiser, or king, shared legislative power with a two-house legislature.

Italy, like Germany, had long existed as a collection of loosely affiliated states. This fragmentation was exacerbated by the fact that foreign powers—the Austrians, the Prussians, and the French—controlled some of the Italian states. As in Germany, the unification of the nation was largely due to the efforts of a brilliant prime minister: Count Camillo Cavour, the prime minister of the Italian state of Sardinia. Through a series of alliances with major European powers and the help of Italian nationalist rebels, Cavour completed the process of unification in 1870.

Facing pressure from reformers within and military defeats abroad, the Austrian monarchy formed a dual monarchy with the monarch of Hungary in 1867. Under the new system, Austria and Hungary remained two separate states, each with its own constitution and parliament, but Hungarian monarch Francis Joseph ruled over both. The governments of both nations were rendered ineffective by nationalist revolts and social unrest, specifically from Slavic ethnic groups demanding their own nations.

The once-mighty **Ottoman Empire** collapsed as nationalist groups revolted and tossed off foreign rule. While some of these rebellious states, such as Greece, gained their independence, many nationalist breakaway states were quickly assimilated by other European powers. The chaos of the Ottoman collapse left Central Europe with a legacy of conflict that helped spark the First World War.

In Russia, social unrest forced Tsar Alexander II to enact widespread social reforms. The benefits of these reforms were mitigated by the abuses of power that followed. Fearful of losing his power, the tsar created a vast secret police network and engaged in campaigns of ethnic and religious persecution. In 1905, anti-tsarist rebels revolted. Tsar Nicholas II reacted to the revolt by creating a national legislature.

In England, under Queen Victoria, suffrage was greatly expanded. Prior to 1815, less than 5% of the population had the vote. In 1832, reforms gave the vote to a vast majority of the middle class. By the end of the century, most males had the right to vote. Reform campaigns swept through England: anti-slavery campaigns, campaigns to end capital punishment, and campaigns to improve conditions for workers and the poor. Despite the confidence and liberality of the era, nationalist violence and unrest in Ireland proved an intractable problem. The Great Famine struck Ireland in 1845. This disastrous crop failure killed more than one million people. Another million people emigrated from Ireland to escape "the Great Hunger."

Under Napoleon III, France undertook a ruinous war with Prussia. Napoleon was captured during the war, and the French defeat might have been total, had not a citizen army held Paris against Prussian siege in 1870. In 1871, the National Assembly created a new republican government, the third since the French Revolution. That same year the new government violently suppressed a citizens' uprising. Despite this shaky beginning, the Third Republic would act as the French government for more than 70 years.

▶ The Second Imperial Era

Spurred by a mixture of economic, military, and even misguided humanitarian motivations, European powers once again turned their attention to building overseas empires.

European explorers and missionaries had been exploring the continent of Africa for several hundred years. In the early part of the twentieth century, this exploration turned into imperial expansion. Belgium, Britain, France, Germany, Italy, Portugal, and Spain all gained or expanded their colonial holdings. By 1914, the high of imperial expansion in Africa, only two nations remained completely independent: Ethiopia and Liberia.

Throughout the nineteenth century, European powers clashed over control of China. Some nations, like Russia and Britain, actually occupied sections of the country. Most used diplomacy and trade to manipulate local governments, exerting a powerful influence over the Chinese without officially establishing a colony.

By 1850, Britain had control over just over half of India. It also established colonies in Burma. The French established a colony in Indochina (present day Vietnam), and the Dutch colonized Sumatra, Borneo, and part of New Guinea.

Despite this imperial growth, it was during this period that two of Britain's largest colonies achieved self-rule: Canada gained self-rule in 1867, and Australia gained self-rule in 1901.

▶ The First World War

The chaos left behind by the decline of the Ottoman Empire in Central Europe was known as the **Balkan Powder Keg**. In 1914, the powder keg exploded. On June 28, an Austrian noble was assassinated by a Bosnian nationalist in Sarajevo. With the backing of Germany, the Austrian government declared war on Serbia. France and Russia backed Serbia, bringing them in conflict with Germany and Austria. In order to attack France, Germany had to occupy Belgium. Britain, an ally of Belgium, entered the war against Germany and Austria.

Germany and its allies were dubbed the **Central Powers**. Britain, France, and Russia were known as the **Allied Powers**.

As warfare in Europe developed into a bloody stalemate, Europe's overseas colonies were pulled into the conflict. The Ottoman Empire joined Germany and Austria and attacked British colonies in the Middle East and Africa.

In 1917, revolutionary forces overthrew the Russian government. Dominated by communists who felt the war was being fought to perpetuate the oppression of the working class, the new Russian government established peace with Germany and its allies. Russians left the battlefield and began transforming Russia into the core of the **Soviet Union**.

That same year the United States entered the war on the side of France and Britain. Allied troops managed to force German forces out of France and Belgium in 1918. German military leadership began to view the war as a lost cause. Back in Germany, the wartime economy collapsed and angry citizens rioted in the streets. Germany's military leaders convinced William II, the kaiser of Germany, to step down. A new government was formed and immediately peace-brokering efforts began. Germany's allies also sued for peace. On the 11th hour of the 11th day of the 11th month of 1918, the war officially came to an end.

The war had been disastrous for Europe. More than eight million soldiers and another 6–13 million civilians died as a result of the war. Collectively, the nations involved in the war spent more than $200 billion on the war. The economies of Austria-Hungary, France, and Germany were shattered. To make things worse, the 1918 influenza epidemic added to the misery of the conflict. The flu epidemic would claim 20 million lives worldwide.

In 1919, representatives from the warring nations hammered out the Treaty of Versailles. The conditions the Allies placed on the former Central Powers were harsh. The Allies demanded $30 billion in reparations, and sections of the treaty were intended to cripple Germany's economic might. The treaty also stripped Germany, Austria-Hungary, and the Ottoman Empire of their overseas colonies. Austria and Hungary were fully divided into individual countries.

▶ The Great Depression and the Rise of the Soviet Union

In Russia, the 1917 revolution became a civil war between communist "reds" and anti-communist "whites." The communists prevailed and the new government was founded on communist principles. The transition was not easy. Counter-revolutionary elements were brutally suppressed. Differences in political theory were grounds for assassination or deportation or, as in the case of Leon Trotsky, both.

In 1924, Joseph Stalin took control of the Communist Party. He consolidated power under him and became as powerful in Russia as any absolute monarch was in the age of empire.

While the revolution transformed Russia, social upheavals shook European colonies abroad. In India, nationalist leaders, including Mohandas Gandhi, began to protest colonial rule. In China, communist revolutionaries under the leadership of Mao Zedong and nationalist leaders began unifying the country and dismantling the system of local rule that Europeans found so easy to influence.

To complicate things, post-war politics crippled the ability of the western democracy to respond to these developments. In France, political corruption and the rise of new political parties meant that governmental administrations obtained and lost power so quickly that no administration could accomplish anything. England was occupied with domestic trouble. Working-class resentment led to the creation of the Labour Party, which caused a conservative backlash in the form of restrictions on workers' rights. In 1922, the Irish Free State was formed. Unfortunately, the peace between the new country and British-controlled Northern Ireland was short-lived, and terrorism continued. These domestic troubles contributed to the failure of ambitious foreign policy goals, such as the inability to support a strong League of Nations.

As the 1920s came to a close, a series of financial missteps and crashes created a global economic depression. In 1929, the stock market in the United States crashed. Demand for products and services shrank. To prevent overproduction, laborers lost their jobs. The system of war payments and debts set up at the end of World War I meant that the effects of the crash in the United States spread throughout the global economy. In countries like Germany, where the economy was already crippled from the war years, the impact was severe. In other countries, like Britain, it became the backdrop for a struggle between socialist reformers and more traditional liberal free market leaders.

In Italy and Germany, perhaps the most important result of the **Great Depression** was the rise of fascism. Democratic governments, unable to reverse the economic downturn, were voted out of office and replaced with totalitarian governments. In Italy, the Fascist Party led by Benito Mussolini forced King Victor Emmanuel III to form a new government with Mussolini as prime minister. The **Nazi Party** of Germany, under the leadership of **Adolf Hitler**, was voted into power. Once in power, the Nazis quickly dismantled the democratic institutions of Germany.

The rise of totalitarianism, in Stalin's Russia as well as in Germany and Italy, put democracy on the retreat in Europe. In Russia, Italy, and Germany, purges of scapegoats and political rivals were ruthless and deadly. In Germany, Jewish citizens were persecuted. Eventually, this ethnic persecution led to the Holocaust: Germany's genocidal effort to systematically execute any Jews and other "undesirables" living under Nazi control. More than six million died in the Holocaust. In Russia, Stalin sent more than four million citizens to labor camps, or gulags. When farmers refused to go along with Soviet-style collective production, Stalin used his control of the economy to create famine conditions that killed five to eight million people.

▶ The Second World War

The totalitarian governments of the post-war years had imperial ambitions. In 1935, Italy invaded Ethiopia. In 1936, Germany broke the conditions of the Treaty of Versailles and mobilized troops in an area designated as a demilitarized zone. Germany would support Fascist forces in the Spanish Civil War, ensuring their victory. Germany would then invade Austria and Czechoslovakia.

The democratic nations, eager to prevent another global conflict, adopted a policy of appeasement: allowing current aggression in the hopes of preventing future aggression.

Italy, Germany, and Japan, which was building an empire in Asia, formed a pact to fight the spread of communism and not interfere with each other's imperial plans. With this agreement in place, these three countries formed the Axis powers.

In 1939, Germany invaded Poland. France and Britain declared war on Germany. This declaration of war began World War II. Germany's allies, Japan and Italy, joined the conflict. Despite a non-aggression pact, Germany invaded the Soviet Union. This caused the Soviet Union to join the war on the side of the Allies, Britain and France. In 1941, Japan attacked the United States. This ended the United States's policy of neutrality and America entered the conflict on the side of the Allies.

After a long string of victories, the Axis Powers found themselves suddenly stalled. Germany suffered a long and disastrous defeat at Stalingrad and the naval war in the Pacific Ocean turned against the Japanese. By the end of 1944, Allied troops had conquered Italy. Sensing defeat, Italians rebelled and overthrew the Fascist government. In 1945, the Allies advanced into Germany, and victory over Germany was declared. Before the year was over, the United States dropped two atomic weapons on Japan and ended the war in the Pacific.

▶ Contemporary Europe

In the aftermath of the war, Allied forces divided Germany into zones of control. Two governments, one democratic and one communist, were set up in the divided country.

In 1945, eager to prevent future large-scale conflicts, delegates from 50 nations created the charter for the **United Nations** (UN). Originally conceived as a peacekeeping organization, the UN's mandate would grow to include global health monitoring, the management of refugee services, and the regulation of worldwide environmental initiatives.

In contrast to the international spirit of the UN, one of the other significant effects of the war was the **cold war**. Once the common enemy of Fascism was defeated, the Soviet Union and the western democracies entered into a protracted rivalry. It was a matter of communist policy that communism should be spread to other countries, either through diplomatic persuasion or military force. By the same token, western democracies wanted to ensure free markets and democratic governments dominated the globe. In 1949, the Soviet Union developed its first atomic weapon. The threat of nuclear war prevented the western democracies and the Soviet Union from clashing directly. Instead, the cold war was fought by building alliances, supporting proxy states, and attempting to thwart the expansion of the rival ideology. While the cold war was primarily a conflict between the Soviet Union and the United States, most of Europe's democracies joined NATO, the North Atlantic Treaty Organization: a military treaty designed to organize a western response to potential Soviet aggression. The cold war would remain the dominant face of global diplomacy until the 1980s, when Soviet leaders, facing chronic economic troubles, a failed war in Afghanistan, and social unrest in satellite states, began to dismantle communism. By 1991, Germany was reunified and most of the nations absorbed by the Soviet Union after World War II had formed independent nations.

The collapse of the Soviet Union had a dark side. As Soviet power receded, ethnic and religious hostilities that had been forcefully suppressed by communism were unleashed. In Chechnya and the former Yugoslavia, regional conflicts with genocidal aims broke out. The former continues to plague the Russian republic in the form of terror acts, while the latter was resolved only by the UN-led efforts of several member nations.

In a parallel to the decline of communist imperialism, the post-war years marked the decline of imperialism by the western democracies. India and Pakistan both gained their independence in 1947. The Dutch East Indies became free states by 1949. In Africa, once nearly entirely colonized by European powers, every former colony was reconstructed as an independent state by 1990.

As Europe rebuilt, most of the western democracies developed as welfare states: market economies with extensive government intervention in the citizens' social and economic lives. In exchange for generally higher taxes, the citizens in much of Europe had access to universal healthcare and pension programs. Governments also controlled many basic industries, such as power and transportation. This trend toward governmental control would continue until the 1980s, when conservatives in Britain would begin to question the long-term economic impact of the welfare state. Later, citizens in France would also elect politicians who promised less government intervention and more free market capitalism.

In 1956, six nations—West Germany, the Netherlands, Belgium, Luxembourg, France, and Italy—founded the European Community: an organization created to encourage free trade among its member states. The European Community would grow to include new member nations, and eventually it would evolve into the European Union. By the year 2000, most of Western Europe had joined the European Union. In 2002, the European Union introduced the Euro, a single currency used by a majority of its member states. Though the citizens in several member states rejected a European Union constitution, the European Union continues to develop as a crucial unifying bond between the nations of Europe.

▶ Practice Questions

1. All of the following are reasons for the European powers policy of appeasement prior to World War II EXCEPT
   a. Hitler's actions were seen as a reasonable response to the overly harsh Treaty of Versailles.
   b. diplomats assumed even fascist nations would act to avoid a highly destructive global conflict.
   c. widespread economic depression would have made an effective military response difficult.
   d. fascist advances stabilized the region and benefited France and England financially.
   e. German fascism was seen as an important counterbalance to Stalinist communism.

2. "What is the Third Estate? *Everything.*
   What has it been until now in the political order? *Nothing.*
   What does it want to be? *Something.*"
   This quotation describes the political sentiments behind which of the following events?
   a. the French Revolution
   b. the modernization of Russia
   c. the Congress of Vienna
   d. the Glorious Revolution
   e. the Thirty Years' War

3. Which of the following Russian tsars is known for securing a year-round, warm water seaport for Russia?
   a. Alexander II
   b. Peter the Great
   c. Nicholas II
   d. Ivan the Terrible
   e. Catherine the Great

4. Which of the following best describes the motivations of the Paris Commune?

   a. to preserve republican government from monarchists

   b. to destroy the Third Republic coalition government

   c. to support the reforms of Napoleon III

   d. to defend Paris from the assaults of the Austrian army

   e. to promote Zionism in France

5. Which of the following best describes a philosophy that holds that the aim of society should be "the greatest happiness for the greatest number"?

   a. Marxism

   b. utilitarianism

   c. romanticism

   d. social Darwinism

   e. absolutism

6. The British Raj was the term for the colonial government of

   a. Nigeria.

   b. Hong Kong.

   c. Egypt.

   d. India.

   e. Burma.

7. Which three nations formed "the Triple Entente"?

   a. Austria-Hungary, Britain, Russia

   b. France, Russia, Britain

   c. Germany, France, Austria-Hungary

   d. Britain, Japan, Germany

   e. Russia, Germany, Japan

8. Which of the following figures is most associated with the concept of *Realpolitik?*

   a. Vladimir Lenin

   b. Giuseppe Garibaldi

   c. Thomas Paine

   d. Queen Victoria

   e. Otto von Bismark

9. All of the following are characteristics of fascist governments EXCEPT

   a. strict censorship of the media and artists.

   b. a single party political system.

   c. commitment to free market economic policies.

   d. use of political spies and fear to control the population.

   e. a cult of personality surrounding a central leader.

10. Which of the following French philosophers edited the *Encyclopedia?*

   a. Jean-Jacques Rousseau

   b. Voltaire

   c. Denis Diderot

   d. Baron de Montesquieu

   e. Alexis de Tocqueville

▶ Answers

1. d
2. a
3. e
4. a
5. b
6. d
7. b
8. e
9. c
10. c

9 ▶ United States History I and II

The CLEP divides American history into two broad periods. The first period covers the colonization of America to the end of Reconstruction. The second period overlaps slightly with the first: It covers Reconstruction and runs to the present. According to the College Board, the CLEP covers "material that is usually taught in . . . a two-semester course in United States history." That's a considerable amount of material, and no single chapter could possibly review everything that might appear on the test. However, being aware of broad trends in crucial historical periods will provide a helpful context for the items you might encounter. This chapter will include capsule overviews of 15 important historical eras, including a list of key concepts for each period. These overviews and key concepts will give you the basic structure you will need.

▶ The Colonial Period

Throughout the fifteenth and sixteenth centuries, the fate of what would eventually become the United States of America was fiercely contested by European empires, the native cultures of North America, and conflicting groups of colonists.

Spain dominated early exploration of North and South America. The Dutch established the colony of New Amsterdam (later New York). Finally, the French claimed vast stretches of land, but never managed any sustained colonization efforts within the territory that would become the modern United States.

In 1607, England established the first permanent English settlement in North America, the Jamestown colony. The slow-building success of the Jamestown colony inspired the founding of a second colony. In 1620, the Plymouth colony, located in modern Massachusetts, was settled by a combination of Puritans in opposition to the state church of England and economically motivated opportunists. Unlike the disastrous first decades of the Virginian colony, the Plymouth colony was immediately successful. More than 20,000 immigrants, most of them radical Puritans, had arrived in Massachusetts by 1642.

Other colonies soon followed. In 1634, Catholic colonists formed the colony of St. Mary's. This would eventually become the modern state of Maryland. In 1644, Roger Williams, a Puritan who broke with the religious authorities of Massachusetts, established Rhode Island as a haven for unorthodox religious believers. Pennsylvania and Delaware were chartered as colonies in 1681 and 1682. These colonies were home to Quakers and other persecuted religious minorities. The final of the 13 British colonies, Georgia, was founded in 1733 as a utopian experiment.

In 1619, Dutch traders shipped the first slaves to Virginia. As the colonies expanded, the slave trade became an integral part of colonial life. No British colony was free of slavery. In some colonies, such as South Carolina, a majority of the people living in the colony were slaves.

Key Concepts for the Colonial Period

Five civilized tribes: The native inhabitants of what is now the southeastern United States were called "civilized" because they used advanced farming techniques and lived in settled communities. The five tribes comprised the Choctaw, Creek, Chickasaw, Cherokee, and Seminole people.

Massachusetts Bay Company: Established in 1629, the company funded the colony of Plymouth. In 1684, the company's charter expired and Plymouth became a royal colony. Similar companies established most of the American colonies.

Mayflower Compact: Signed in 1620, the compact was an agreement between the colonists that became the foundation of civil government in Plymouth.

Salem Witch Trials: In 1692, political fears and religious intolerance led to the execution of 19 on charges of witchcraft. The trials have become part of the political lexicon: A *witch trial* has become a metaphor for a paranoid, politically motivated persecution.

▶ The American Revolution

As the British colonies grew more prosperous and expanded, violent conflicts arose among these colonies, the native population, and the French colonies. From 1636 to 1763, the colonies found themselves engaged in one bloody conflict after another. These conflicts were devastating to all sides. Some Native American tribes, such as the Yemasee of South Carolina, were completely destroyed. King Philip's War claimed the life of one out of every 16 male colonists of military age.

Although these conflicts left Britain as the uncontested master of colonial North America, they were the beginning of the end of Britain's American rule. The colonists believed these sacrifices entitled them to the status of full legal citizens within the British Empire. This growing dissatisfaction found a philosophical framework in the liberal ideals of Enlightenment thought. Tensions between England and its colonies grew. The anger of the colonists began to focus on a series of taxation measures enacted to help Britain pay for the long series of Native American and French conflicts. Protests in various colonies turned violent, which provoked a more militaristic lockdown on the northern colonies. By the time representatives from the 13 colonies met to devise a unified response, open warfare between colonial militias and British troops had begun. The colonial representatives adopted the Declaration of Independence on July 4, 1776. A year later, the colonial leaders would produce the Articles of Confederation, the initial basis for interstate government among the free colonies.

It was not until early 1777 that the rebels could claim any real victories on the field. These successes convinced the French to support the colonial revolutionaries. French support was soon followed by Spanish support. As Washington rallied in the North, fighting in the South degenerated into desperate guerilla-style warfare. In 1781, a combined colonial and French force laid siege to Yorktown, Virginia, and the British forces surrendered. This marked the end of significant combat in the Revolutionary War. The Treaty of Paris officially ended the war in 1783.

Key Concepts for the American Revolution

Continental Congress: A legislative body created by the colonies, this group acted as the government during the Revolution. This body produced the Declaration of Independence and the Articles of Confederation.

Intolerable Acts: Colonists dubbed the series of laws passed by the British in 1774 the "Intolerable Acts." These laws pushed the colonists further toward rebellion.

Loyalists: Colonists who remained loyal to the British government were also called *Tories*. It is estimated that nearly a third of the colonists were loyalists.

Navigation Acts: These laws, which restricted shipping to and from the colonies, were intended to protect the British economy from foreign competition. They became another source of tension between the colonies and Britain. The colonists saw the acts as restrictive and unfair.

The Stamp Act: Taxation laws like the Stamp Act, which taxed paper goods, were a major source of colonial discontent. The Sugar Act and the Townsend Acts were other unpopular tax laws.

▶ The Early Republic

The Articles of Confederation rapidly proved inadequate to meet the needs of the newly formed nation. In 1787, 55 delegates from every state in the confederation met in Philadelphia to hammer out a new constitution. Three crucial compromises emerged out of the debates:

1. **The Connecticut Compromise.** In order to strike a balance between larger and smaller states, Roger Sherman, a delegate from Connecticut, proposed that the number of state representatives in the House of Representatives would be determined by a state's population, while every state, regardless of size, would get two representatives in the Senate. He also proposed the Electoral College system used to elect the president.

2. **The Three-Fifths Compromise.** In order to boost their representation in the House, delegates from the Southern states proposed that slaves be counted as citizens even though they would have no rights as citizens. Ultimately, it was agreed that a single slave would count as three-fifths of a citizen.

3. **The Bill of Rights.** Concerned that the new Constitution would give oppressive power to a centralized federal government, some delegates demanded the addition of a list of rights guaranteed to individual citizens. This list became the first ten amendments to the Constitution and is known as the Bill of Rights.

The Constitution was officially ratified in 1788. A series of political challenges put the new government to the test. In 1789, the Judiciary Act, which established the power of judicial review, was passed. Later, during the two terms of Andrew Jackson, the political franchise was extended to groups that would have made the founding fathers nervous, such as unpropertied men. Finally, the Nullification Crisis, in which the state government of South Carolina threatened to nullify federal law, set the precedent of the primacy of federal law over state law.

During this period, the nation experienced explosive growth. With the Louisiana Purchase of 1803, the country instantly doubled in size. This expansion gave the country access to resources—notably gold, the discovery of which led to the 1849 Gold Rush—that would fuel American growth to the present day. It also ushered in a long period of frequent and bloody struggles with displaced Native Americans. From the date of the purchase until well into the nineteenth century, so-called Indian Wars would break out in the west.

The United States also faced its first major international crisis: the War of 1812. This two-year conflict with the British was not a triumph for the nation, but the simple fact that the young nation survived the conflict was enough to establish the United States as a strong presence in international affairs.

Key Concepts for the Early Republic

Slavery compromises: Throughout the pre-Civil War years, numerous political compromises were made to attempt to diffuse the issue of slavery. These compromises included the Missouri Compromise and the Compromise of 1850.

Federalists: One of the first political parties in America, Federalists believed in strong central government. *The Federalist Papers* is a series of essays that presents the Federalist view in the debates over the Constitution. Their opponents were known as anti-Federalists.

Manifest Destiny: This term, coined by a journalist in 1845, described the belief that the United States had a special and divine duty to spread over the entire North American continent.

The Texas Revolution: In 1836, expatriate Americans rebelled in Texas and took the territory by force of arms. The Republic of Texas joined the Union in 1845.

▶ The Civil War and Reconstruction

Slavery became an all-consuming obsession for Americans in the early nineteenth century. The looming crisis was delayed by various compromises and political deals, but the tensions between the North and South eventually overwhelmed the federal government's efforts to keep the peace. Although armed conflict had already started in some sections of the nation, it was the election of Abraham Lincoln that proved to be the flashpoint of the war. South Carolina seceded before Lincoln was inaugurated. Mississippi, Florida, Alabama, Georgia, Louisiana, Texas, Virginia, North Carolina, Tennessee, and Arkansas all followed. Calling themselves the Confederate States of America, the rebel states formed a government and began building their military might by seizing United States military installations throughout the South. The explosive situation turned into a shooting war when the soldiers of Fort Sumter refused to surrender to the Confederate forces of South Carolina. Fort Sumter was bombed into submission in 1861 in what most consider the first battle of the Civil War.

The North had superior numbers and was the greater industrial power. Still, ineffective leadership and the lack of will among the Northern populace hampered the war effort. In 1862, Lincoln issued the Emancipation Proclamation, freeing all slaves in the rebel states. The proclamation's effect on the Northern states was to give the war new moral purpose.

General Robert E. Lee surrendered the Army of Northern Virginia to the commander of the Union forces, General Ulysses S. Grant, on April 9, 1865. The remaining Confederate forces surrendered just 15 days later. On April 14, the eve of the Union's triumph, Abraham Lincoln was assassinated.

The conclusion of the war left the nation the massive task of reintegrating the South into the United States. Before his death, Lincoln had proposed generous terms of reconciliation intended to quickly mend the nation. After his assassination, the dominant Republican Congress pushed for a more punitive model of Reconstruction. The political fighting over Reconstruction led to the first presidential impeachment: Andrew Johnson was impeached, but his congressional foes were unable to remove him from office. Reconstruction moved ahead sporadically. Organizations were created to help enfranchise African Ameri-

cans. Unfortunately, state governments and groups like the Ku Klux Klan undermined these efforts and attempted to maintain the status quo. Federal Reconstruction officially ended in 1876 when Republican lawmakers pulled federal troops out of the South in exchange for the Democrats' concession of the contested 1876 presidential election.

Key Concepts for the Civil War and Reconstruction

Abolitionism: This widespread movement to end slavery was especially strong in the years leading up to the Civil War.

Black Codes: Restrictive laws regulating the lives of African Americans passed by Southern states during Reconstruction, they developed into the segregation laws that would last until the 1960s.

Free Soil Party: This anti-slavery party was formed in 1848 and later merged with the fledgling Republican Party.

Fugitive Slave Acts: This series of laws passed from 1787 to 1864 dealt with the treatment of escaped slaves. Enforcing the laws became more and more difficult as the Civil War approached.

Indian Wars: This long series of conflicts with various tribes occurred throughout the nineteenth century. In 1834, the United States set aside territory for Native Americans, but this territory was reduced again and again.

▶ Industrialization

Prior to the Civil War, the United States was undergoing a technology-driven industrial revolution. The cotton gin revolutionized southern agriculture and mass production techniques spurred the growth of northern industry. Networks of train tracks and telegraph lines created transportation and communication networks up and down the East Coast. After the war, capitalist enterprises took on new forms, such as the massive Standard Oil monopoly and the national banking network of J.P. Morgan. This new financial order encouraged technological advances. The Transcontinental Railroad, the telephone, the phonograph, the Brooklyn Bridge, the skyscraper, and the first airplane are all products of this era.

These innovations came at a price. Government regulations often failed to keep pace with business development, leading to unethical practices. Conditions for workers were often abysmal. In some cases, such as the Triangle Shirtwaist Company Fire of 1911, these harsh conditions proved deadly.

Key Concepts of Industrialization

Assembly line: This industrial process involves breaking down a complicated task and having a different worker specialize on a single specific task.

Mass production: Mass production began back in 1798, when standardized parts were first introduced. However, the postwar era saw mass production techniques become a crucial aspect of America's growing industrial economy.

Monopoly: An organization that becomes the sole provider of a product is said to have a monopoly on the product. Monopolies, because they lack competition, can drive up prices without fear of a consumer backlash.

Robber barons: A derogatory term; robber barons were wealthy and morally questionable businesspersons, specifically those with vast banking or industrial empires.

Trust: This legal device is no longer allowed in American business, but it once allowed the creation of monopolies by placing numerous businesses in the control of a single board of trustees.

▶ The Progressive Era

In the decades before World War I, several groups working independently on social reforms managed to make sweeping changes in the practice of democracy, increase the governmental role in social welfare programs, and improve conditions for American workers. Journalists brought unfair labor practices and public corruption to the attention of Americans nationwide. They also reported on conditions in slums, prisons, and asylums, urging readers to press for change. This occasionally led to crucial reforms, such as the Pure Food and Drug Act.

Laborers organized themselves into labor unions. Through collective bargaining and strikes, the unions attempted to improve conditions for the working class. Some of the strikes collapsed, such as the violent Homestead Strike of 1892. Still, it was the work of the labor unions that ultimately helped establish the idea of the eight-hour day and the weekend.

The federal government was another source of progressive reform. Convinced that monopolies impeded beneficial economic competition, Presidents Theodore Roosevelt and Taft began using antitrust laws to break the corporate empires of monopolies like Standard Oil.

Progressives tackled international concerns too. In 1898, the United States went to war with Spain. The short conflict left the United States in control of several former Spanish territories, including Puerto Rico and the Philippines. Progressives saw this as a form of imperialism and campaigned for the independence of both territories. (The Philippines achieved independence in 1946; Puerto Rico is still a territory of the United States.)

Key Concepts of the Progressive Era

The American Federation of Labor and Congress of Industrial Organizations (AFL-CIO): The largest union in America, the AFL-CIO was formed in 1886. Early unions would form around a single occupation; later groups, like the AFL-CIO, would organize laborers from different trades to increase their strength.

The Grange Movement: This political movement, organized by farmers in the Midwest and the South, was aimed at regulating railroad companies. The farmers believed they were the victims of illegal price fixing by the railroad.

The Homestead strike: A blow to the labor movement, this 1892 strike pitted workers against the Carnegie Steel Company. It became a violent conflict, and the state militia was called in against the workers. This was followed by another violent and unsuccessful strike: the 1894 strike between railroad workers and Pullman Palace Car Company.

Muckrakers: President Theodore Roosevelt coined the term *muckrakers* to describe investigative journalists who sought to expose social ills. Famous muckrakers include Jacob Riis, Upton Sinclair, Lincoln Steffens, and Ida M. Tarbell.

▶ The First World War

In 1914, the assassination of an Austrian archduke by a Serbian nationalist sent Europe spiraling into war. A complex web of alliance treaties pulled nation after nation into the conflict. President Wilson, reflecting the majority sentiment of the nation, followed a policy of neutrality. This position grew harder to maintain after German submarines sank the passenger liner RMS *Lusitania,* killing 128 American passengers. It became impossible to maintain after the Zimmerman Telegram, a secret communication from Germany proposing a German-Mexican alliance against the United States, was intercepted. America entered the war in 1917. America would lose more than 100,000 soldiers in the war, a loss that was compounded by a worldwide influenza epidemic that started on the filthy battlefields of Europe and eventually claimed the lives of more than 21 million people around the globe.

America emerged from the war in a unique position. The nation was now considered a global power on the scale of the European nations. Furthermore, with the Atlantic between it and the ravages of the battlefield, America had been spared much of the devastation that wrecked the governments and economies of Europe. Wilson was confident that America could leverage this newly won status as a global power into a more permanent position of international influence. Wilson lobbied to get America involved in the League of Nations, but Americans instead retreated into a more comfortable isolation.

Key Concepts of the First World War

Fourteen Points: President Wilson's 14 principles for peaceful international relations would be worked into the Treaty of Versailles at the end of the war. Unfortunately, the treaty also included punitive measures against Germany that contained the seeds of the Second World War.

Trench warfare: One of the characteristics of World War I was protracted fighting between heavily fortified trenches.

U-boat: One of many technological inventions used in the war, the U-boat, or submarine, was used most famously by Germany to terrorize shipping lanes. Machine guns, bombers, tanks, and chemical weapons were all recent innovations that were used on the battlefields of World War I.

▶ The 1920s

Called the "Roaring Twenties," the decade after the war was marked by an economic boom. Stock market speculation, driven in part by unstable spending practices, fueled stock values and brought Americans who previously relied on other investments into the market.

This prosperity also brought sweeping social changes. After nearly a century of dedicated suffragette agitation, women were finally given the vote in 1920.

Finally, in what is often considered the greatest legislative failure in American history, the creation, importation, sale, and consumption of most alcoholic beverages was outlawed. Violations of the law were rampant and the money to be made in providing illegal bootleg liquor actually encouraged the growth of organized crime. The amendment authorizing Prohibition was repealed in 1933.

This long economic boom came to a sudden halt with the stock market crash of 1929. In one day, stocks lost an average of 40 points. It was the beginning of a long downward spiral.

Key Concepts of the 1920s

Harlem Renaissance: This artistic and intellectual revolution in the African-American community set the stage for the Civil Rights movement to come.

Red Scare: The first of two panics about supposed communist infiltration, this scare led to the deportation of nearly 6,000 people.

Lost Generation: A loose collection of postwar artists and thinkers, the Lost Generation energized the arts by helping introduce modernism to American audiences.

▶ The Great Depression

The exact cause of the global economic depression that caught up America for nearly a decade is still debated. Blame has been assigned to the expansion of the money supply, the contraction of the money supply, a decline in international trade, corruption in big business and banking, and the incompetence of government officials. Whatever the cause, the effect was clear. In the United States, unemployment reached 25%. The incomes of those still employed decreased, sometimes by as much as 50%.

President Franklin Roosevelt launched wave after wave of government reforms. Collectively, these reforms are known as **the New Deal**. Work programs like the Civilian Conservation Corps, the Tennessee Valley Authority, and the Works Progress Administration put millions back to work. New regulatory bodies were created, such as the Securities and Exchange Commission. Price and wage regulations were put in place.

Historians debate the practical effect the New Deal may have had on the severity and duration of the Depression. Regardless, Roosevelt's programs were extremely popular with much of the country, and some of his aid programs remain in place today.

Like so much else about the Depression, what ended the crisis is unclear. Some argue that the economy goes in cycles and the Depression ended naturally, as all downturns must. Others feel that the economic crisis was ended by an increase in government spending at the start of an even greater crisis: World War II.

Key Concepts of the Great Depression

Dust Bowl: Poor land management caused crop failures and massive sandstorms in the midwest. Hard-hit families left their farms and migrated, often to California. Regardless of where they were from, these migrants were often called *Okies*.

Hoovervilles: Large collections of temporary housing created by the legions of homeless during the Great Depression, in the public mind these villages were symbols of government inaction under Hoover (after whom they were named).

Organized crime: The lasting effect of Prohibition was to organize illegal alcohol producers into large syndicates. Soon the syndicates branched out into other illegal activities. The Federal Bureau of Investigation was created in part to battle these crime syndicates.

▶ World War II

The Great Depression spurred the growth of fascist and militaristic governments in Europe. The Spanish government fell to fascism in a coup. Then the fascist governments of Germany and Italy began programs of conquest and colonialism. In Asia, the militaristic government of Japan began its own program of expansion.

As it did at the beginning of the last World War, America proclaimed neutrality. However, this neutrality did not prevent the government from lending financial and material aid to democratic countries like England and France. On December 7, 1941, Japanese forces attacked the American naval base at Pearl Harbor, Hawaii. America entered the war against the Axis powers. Americans fought on two fronts: Europe and the Pacific. Mussolini, the Italian dictator, was overthrown

by his own government in 1943. The Germans, now pushed back to their own capital, surrendered on May 7, 1945. The Japanese surrendered on September 2, 1945, after the United States dropped two atomic bombs, one on the city of Hiroshima and the other on the city of Nagasaki.

Key Concepts of World War II

Internment: By executive order, more than 100,000 Japanese-Americans, especially those living on the West Coast, were relocated to camps called *war relocation centers*. Despite this violation of their rights, many Japanese-American citizens fought for America in World War II.

The Lend-Lease Act: Passed prior to America entering the war, this act authorized shipping war materials to countries whose defense was considered essential to the United States.

The Manhattan Project: The code name of the project to build the first atomic bomb was named after the program's original location on the island of Manhattan in New York City.

The Marshall Plan: Secretary of State George Marshall drew up a massive plan for assisting European reconstruction. More than $13 billion (between $100 and $500 billion at current values) was spent to rebuild Europe.

▶ The 1950s and the Cold War

Just as victory in World War I had led to a period of economic prosperity, the decade after World War II was a boom time. However, America's new status as an international superpower meant that it could not retreat into isolationism. America would provide a home for the new United Nations.

The spread of global communism was considered a dire threat to the United States and other democratic countries. Shortly after the destruction of the Axis Powers, the Soviet Union (Union of Soviet Socialist Republics, or USSR) emerged as a second superpower. The USSR refused to relinquish control over territories it seized while pushing back the Germans and invaded Czechoslovakia in 1945. In 1949, communist revolutionaries took control of China. Communist dictatorships came to power in several Southeast Asian and Latin American countries.

The United States and its democratic allies decided on a policy dubbed *containment*. President Truman declared that the United States would act to prevent the spread of communism wherever it was deemed a threat to democracy.

In 1950, the United Nations decided to take military action in Korea. North Korean communists, aided by the Chinese, had invaded democratic South Korea. Americans soldiers joined an international force that fought against the Chinese and North Koreans until the cease-fire was agreed on in 1953.

The fear of communism abroad took on a virulent form at home. Senator Joe McCarthy began a second Red Scare. He began exposing alleged communist subversives. His charges are now considered dubious at best, but the lengths to which the senator was allowed to pursue alleged subversives reveals how widespread anxieties about "the red menace" were.

Key Concepts of the 1950s

Brinkmanship: First advocated in 1956, this was the policy of pushing issues with the Soviet Union to the brink of a nuclear exchange on the assumption that the USSR would always back down. This policy's greatest test would come later during the Cuban Missile Crisis.

Domino theory: One of the beliefs of American foreign policy leaders was the domino theory. This held that every country that turned communist set up another country to turn communist. This belief fed into the policy of containment.

The iron curtain: Winston Churchill coined the phrase *iron curtain* to describe the barrier of hostility and distrust that existed between democratic and communist countries.

North Atlantic Treaty Organization (NATO): The North Atlantic Treaty Organization is a mutual defense pact that was meant as a democratic power balance to the Soviets. Although NATO has outlived its original purpose, it still exists today.

► The 1960s and 1970s

The 1960s and 1970s were a time of great social upheaval. A combination of international and domestic factors fueled sweeping changes throughout American society.

Pursuing a policy of containment led America into its longest and most controversial conflict: the Vietnam War. Since the Korean War, there had been conflicts with communism, notably in Cuba. But the Vietnam War was unique in both its duration—from 1959 to 1975—and the civil unrest it fueled. Protests and acts of civil disobedience aimed at ending the war had the broader effect of politically galvanizing large sections of society.

The public struggle over Vietnam coincided with the largest push for African-American rights since the Civil War. Protesting lasting political and social inequalities, civil rights activists managed to move their long struggle into the mainstream consciousness of America. This culminated in the passage landmark Civil

Rights Act of 1964. This had an empowering effect on other minority groups, especially women's rights groups and advocates for the rights of Hispanic laborers.

Finally, the faith many Americans had in their government received two rapid blows. The first was the 1963 assassination of President John F. Kennedy. The second was the resignation of President Nixon after the Watergate scandal. As the 1970s came to a close, the economy suffered a recession and an energy crisis—shortages in gas due to supply restrictions from oil producing countries in the Middle East.

Key Concepts of the 1960s and 1970s

Bay of Pigs: An unsuccessful 1961 American-backed invasion of communist Cuba, it was a prelude to the Cuban Missile Crisis of 1962.

Counterculture: An unorganized youth movement with roots in the 1950s and stretching into the 1970s, the counterculture could be understood as an attempt to question, undermine, or provide alternatives to the values of mainstream culture. It was the cultural side of the civil and political unrest of the era.

The Equal Rights Amendment: A proposed amendment that would have stated that equal rights could not be abridged because of sex; the power of the growing feminist movement was enough to get it passed by both houses of Congress. However, it was never ratified by enough state governments and failed to become part of the Constitution.

The Great Society: An ambitious collection of social reform packages passed by President Johnson, these reforms included Medicaid, Medicare, and anti-poverty measures.

▶ The Late Twentieth Century

The financial stagnation of the 1970s continued until rises in stock values and new markets opened up by the boom gave the economy a needed shot in the arm. Unfortunately, because of a stock crash, a series of recessions, scandals regarding corporate governance, and the overvaluation of Internet-based companies, this rise was not steady after the 1980s.

The social and political turmoil of the 1960s and 1970s led to a conservative backlash. The policy of actively containing communism was left behind. Instead, America and the Soviet Union entered into a costly nuclear arms race. Stung by the loss in Vietnam, America limited the exercise of military power to small, short conflicts (such as the invasion of Grenada) or UN-sanctioned multinational campaigns (such as the first Gulf War).

This conservative backlash was partially to blame for the country's slowness to act when acquired immune deficiency syndrome (AIDS) started to claim the lives of Americans. Cuts to social aid programs meant that the first efforts at combating the spread of the disease were left to private groups. As the century came to a close, the global nature of the health crisis became clear.

This conservative turn also gave birth to the so-called New Right. This loose coalition of conservative Christians, traditional Republicans, and former liberal neo-conservatives became the political conservative's answer to progressive organizations and coalitions formed in the 1960s and 1970s.

Ironically, the policy of containment was discarded not long before the European communism began to crumble. By 1991, Germany was reunited and the Soviet Union had transitioned to an uneasy democracy.

With the end of the cold war, America had to face the chaos that was left behind as the Soviet Union collapsed. Racial and ethnic tensions once kept in check by the Soviets surfaced again in Europe. African and Middle Eastern regimes that were once propped up by the United States or the USSR fell into totalitarianism and turned to fighting one another, or (in rare cases) started making the slow move toward democracy. From this more chaotic picture would emerge the chief military threat of the early twenty-first century: conflicts with militant ethnic and religious groups.

Key Concepts of the Late Twentieth Century

Black Monday: Largely considered the end of Reagan's economic turnaround, this 1987 stock crash cost investors $870 billion in a single day.

The Iran Contra scandal: Members of the Reagan administration were caught illegally selling weapons to Iran and using the profits to illegally support anticommunist rebels in Nicaragua. Three conspirators in the scheme were convicted of crimes, but they were all pardoned by Reagan's successor, George H.W. Bush.

Militia movement: Throughout the 1990s, local and federal law enforcement clashed with domestic terrorists associated with various radical ideologies. These incidents included the Oklahoma City bombing, the Ruby Ridge shootings, the serial bombings of the Unabomber, and the disastrous shootout in Waco, Texas.

Militant Islam: Starting with the Iranian Revolution, led by the theocratic Ayatollah Ruhollah Khomeini, this radical form of Islam played an increasingly important role not only in the Middle East, but also in Asia. Before the century closed, radical Islamic governments would appear in Libya, Syria, Afghanistan, and elsewhere.

▶ Practice Questions

1. All of the following were outcomes of the colonial wars of 1636 to 1763 EXCEPT
   a. forming the New England Confederation.
   b. increased financial burdens placed on the colonies by the British government.
   c. displacing the Acadians, later known as Cajuns, from Nova Scotia.
   d. introducing of African-American slaves to the colonies.
   e. destroying the Pequot and Yamasee tribes.

2. Which of the following best describes the founders of Jamestown?
   a. utopian visionaries
   b. financial adventurers
   c. political refugees
   d. religious separatists
   e. military invaders

3. The goal of the policy of containment was to
   a. stop the spread of communism.
   b. protect industries from foreign competition.
   c. restrict immigration.
   d. avoid military commitments abroad.
   e. promote fair trade practices.

4. All of the following contributed to start of the War of 1812 EXCEPT
   a. the impressment of American sailors by the British.
   b. the agitation of congressional War Hawks.
   c. national humiliation following the Virginia Affair.
   d. desired territorial expansion into Florida and Mississippi.
   e. conflicts with British-backed Native American tribes.

5. "The great rule of conduct for us in regard to foreign nations is in extending our commercial relations, to have with them as little political connection as possible. So far as we have already formed engagements, let them be fulfilled with perfect good faith. Here let us stop. Europe has a set of primary interests which to us have none; or a very remote relation. Hence she must be engaged in frequent controversies, the causes of which are essentially foreign to our concerns. Hence, therefore, it must be unwise in us to implicate ourselves by artificial ties in the ordinary vicissitudes of her politics, or the ordinary combinations and collisions of her friendships or enmities." This statement best represents what ideological point of view?
a. jingoism
b. isolationism
c. communism
d. anti-Federalism
e. progressivism

6. In chronological order, which of the following events happened first?
a. The Works Progress Administration is established.
b. Nazi troops enter the demilitarized zone on the Rhineland.
c. Social Security law passes.
d. Prohibition is repealed.
e. The Black Tuesday stock market crashes.

7. Which of the following writers is most identified with the Harlem Renaissance?
a. Toni Morrison
b. W.E.B. DuBois
c. Gertrude Stein
d. F. Scott Fitzgerald
e. Langston Hughes

8. Which of the following domestic economic policies is most equated with President Ronald Reagan?
a. increased spending on social programs
b. aggressive cuts to military spending
c. expanding government budgets
d. reduction of the tax burden on businesses
e. strict regulation of banking institutions

9. Which of the following was a major factor in the Union victory in the Civil War?
a. military and financial aid from foreign governments
b. effective military leadership at the start of the conflict
c. the greater manufacturing capacity of Northern industry
d. popular support for abolition in the border states
e. the technological superiority of Union forces

10. "Television brought the brutality of war into the comfort of the living room. The war was lost in the living rooms of America, not on the battlefields." This statement describes the writer's feelings about what conflict?
a. the Vietnam War
b. World War II
c. the Korean War
d. the Gulf War
e. the Panama Invasion

▶ Answers

1. d
2. b
3. a
4. c
5. b
6. e
7. e
8. d
9. c
10. a

10 ▶ Government and Political Science

The material that appears on the American Government examination is all material that might be taught in an introductory college course on American political structures and behaviors. More than half of the exam covers the institutions of government and the way in which these institutions interact. It focuses almost exclusively on federal and national institutions. Another third of the test covers the ways in which citizens can influence the political system, with an emphasis on election behavior, political parties, and special interest groups. Finally, the exam usually includes some information about the Constitution and the political ideals it expresses.

This chapter will follow roughly the same plan. It will focus mainly on the three branches of the federal government. Then, the chapter will discuss parties, interest groups, the electoral process, and how citizens become political agents. Finally, it will provide a quick overview of the Constitution and the constitutional ideas and controversies that still impact our government.

▶ The Federal Government

The United States is a **representative democracy**. American citizens elect representatives who then govern for their constituents. In the United States, every state has a limited level of sovereignty. Certain powers, however, are reserved for the federal government, which is empowered to act on a national level and is considered the highest level of government in the country. There are three branches of the federal government: the legislative, the executive, and the judicial branch.

The Legislative Branch

The United States Congress is the legislative branch of the government. The Congress is **bicameral**, which means it consists of two different governing bodies: the **House of Representatives** and the **Senate**.

The House of Representatives contains 435 members. Legislators settled on this number in 1911. The Constitution contains no specific instructions on limiting the size of the House. Each member of the House represents a single congressional district within his or her home state. Members do not represent the state as a whole.

Each state in the union gets representation proportional to its population. Currently, California seats the greatest number of representatives, 53. Every ten years, census data is used to adjust the number of representatives allotted to each state. Regardless of population, every state gets at least one representative. As of 2008, seven states had only one representative. Representatives are elected for a two-year term. There are no term limitations on representatives.

To qualify as a representative, the candidate must be at least 25 years old. The candidate must have been a U.S. citizen for at least seven years prior to his or her election. Candidates must also be residents of the states they represent. Some states require that candidates live in the districts they represent, but this is not a federal law.

From the general pool of representatives, the members of the two parties with the greatest representation select officers. The party with the greatest number of representatives picks the **majority leader**, who becomes the ranking member of their party, and the **majority whip**, an officer whose job it is to ensure party loyalty among the party's representatives. The party with the second largest number of representatives selects a parallel set of officers: the minority leader and minority whip. The House also elects a speaker. Because this is an elected position, the speaker usually comes from the majority party. The speaker is the presiding officer of the House, serves as the highest-ranking member of the House, and is second in the line of presidential succession, becoming president in the unlikely event that both the president and vice president cannot fulfill the duties of the office.

Along with the state representatives, the House includes several resident commissioners. These elected officials represent constituencies in federal districts (such as Washington, D.C.), U.S. territories, protectorates, and colonies. Resident commissioners do not have the full participatory rights that representatives have.

As one of the two legislative houses, the House of Representatives shares some legislative powers with the Senate. For example, all bills must pass by both houses of the legislature before being passed along to the president for approval or veto. However, there are some legislative powers that are reserved for the House of Representatives. All taxation legislation must originate in the House. Only the House of Representatives can impeach federal officials. Impeachment is the first of two steps needed to remove a federal official from office. The second step, conviction, is the job of the Senate. Finally, in the case of an electoral election deadlock, the House elects the president.

The Senate is the other house of the legislature. In accordance with the Constitution, every state is represented by two **senators**. These senators represent the entire state rather than the constituents of a single district. The senator who has held office the longest is called the **senior senator**. The other senator is known as the **junior senator**. Senators are elected to a six-year term. There are no term limits on senators.

To qualify for the office, the candidate must be at least 30 years old. The candidate must have been a U.S. citizen for at least nine years prior to his or her election. Finally, the candidate must reside in the state he or she wishes to represent.

The Senate has two unique officer positions. First, the vice president acts as the president of the Senate. The Senate also elects a president *pro tempore* (Latin for "temporary president") who acts as the president of the Senate when the vice president cannot perform the duties of his or her office. As in the House, the party with the most members in the Senate is called the majority party. The party with the next greatest number is the minority party. In cases of a tie, the party affiliation of the vice president determines which party becomes the majority party. Each party elects a party leader, who acts as the chief spokesperson for the party. Each party also elects a whip.

As with the House, some powers are reserved for the Senate. The Senate has the power of "advice and consent" over presidential appointees, meaning the Senate approves or blocks most federal appointees. Only the Senate ratifies treaties with foreign governments. In situations involving a deadlock in the Electoral College, the Senate elects the vice president. Finally, although the House can impeach a federal official, only the Senate may try to convict impeached officials.

The Executive Branch

The president, the vice president, and the majority of the vast bureaucracy of the federal government make up the **executive branch**. It is the single largest branch of the government, employing nearly five million people. It includes the president's cabinet, the members of their departments, the diplomatic corps, the armed services, the park service, the Federal Bureau of Investigation, the postal system, and any part of the federal government that does not work for the legislature or the court system.

In the Constitution, the legislative role of the president is clear. The president may sign and approve or veto and reject legislation passed by Congress. The Constitution clearly identifies the president as commander in chief of the armed forces. It also gives the chief executive the power to appoint judges, including justices of the Supreme Court, and grant pardons and reprieves. Finally, within the limitations of the Senate's powers to "advice and consent" and ratify treaties, the president can appoint federal officers and make treaties with foreign powers.

All of the other powers assumed by the president of the United States come under the relatively ambiguous constitutional mandate that the chief executive "take care that the laws be faithfully executed." As the laws of the nation have expanded, the president's authority and power have increased in direct proportion.

The president is elected indirectly by the **Electoral College**. The Electoral College will be discussed in detail in the section on voting. The president is elected on a slate with a vice president. Presidents are elected to a term of four years. The Constitution limits the president and vice president to two terms in office. The vice president can, however, then run for the office of president and, if successful, serve another two terms as president.

To qualify for the office of president, the candidate must be at least 35 years old. The candidate must be a natural-born citizen of the United States. Finally, the candidate must have been a resident of the United States for at least 14 years prior to the election. No candidate who held the office previously, but was removed by impeachment and conviction, may hold the office again. The candidate for vice president must possess the same qualifications. Finally, under the Constitution, the president and vice president cannot reside in the same state at the time of election.

Judicial Branch

The **judicial branch** is the federal court system. The federal court system is organized in a hierarchy. At the top is the **Supreme Court**. Underneath the Supreme Court are various courts of appeals. Beneath the courts of appeals are numerous district courts. There are 11 federal court districts. Each district may contain several federal courthouses.

At the lower levels, the judicial branch conducts legal proceedings regarding federal laws. Federal courts also hear cases that arise from United States treaties, cases that involve foreign ambassadors in the United States, cases in which the United States government is a defendant, cases involving complaints between the citizens and governments of two different states, and bankruptcy cases.

The highest court in the land, the Supreme Court, deals with interpretations of the Constitution and acts as a check to the other branches through the power of judicial review. The Supreme Court can strike down or nullify a law deemed unconstitutional.

Judges at all levels of the judicial branch are presidential appointees. They are usually lawyers, state judges, or legal scholars, but there is no requirement for the office other than a presidential appointment. As with all presidential appointees, the appointment of all judges is subject to senatorial review under their power to advise and consent. Nine judges currently sit on the Supreme Court. The Constitution does not specify the number of judges that should sit on the court, so the number has been left up to Congress to specify. Once appointed, judges may hold office "during good behavior," an archaic way of saying that they hold the position for life unless removed for criminal actions or an ethical breach.

Though originally conceived as a stop on legislative abuses, the power and importance of the judiciary has steadily grown over the years. With its sweeping power to define federal law combined with the constitutional guarantee of "equal protection under the law," a federal court decision, especially a Supreme Court decision, can have a massive effect on the laws of the country. Throughout the 1960s and 1970s, social reformers made extensive use of the federal court system as an instrument for making social policy. Because it was insulated from political pressure and capable of making declarations that can supersede state laws, activists viewed the court system as a more efficient way to refine the law than the legislative process. However, the political direction of the judiciary can change over time. After a couple of decades of relatively liberal court decisions, several years' worth of conservative appointments has made the judiciary less reform-minded.

▶ Citizen Participation

The following section will discuss the ways in which U.S. citizens can influence their government. The section will cover voting, party participation, and special interest groups.

Voting

The most fundamental way a citizen can influence the American government is through **voting**. In the United States, the job of running elections is left to the states. Citizens 18 years of age or older, who legally reside in any of the 50 states or Washington, D.C., or are legal citizens living abroad have the right to vote. States may make rules regarding the voting rights of convicted felons and the forms of identification that must be presented by voters, but they may not infringe on any citizen's federally protected rights. In most states, voters must register as a member of a political party or as an independent. This affiliation is non-binding, but it does affect voter participation. Depending on the state and the party, a voter's party affiliation determines whether they may participate in party-specific votes, such as primary elections.

In the United States, voting is voluntary. Elections are generally held on November 2, with exceptions for state-specific special circumstance elections and party-specific voting. Voter turnout is usually highest in presidential election years. In 2000, 55% of eligible voters voted in the election. In 2004, 60% of eligible voters participated in the election. In non-presidential election years, voter turnout usually hovers around 40%.

Although presidential elections draw the highest participation levels, they are also subject to one of the most misunderstood political processes: indirect election by the Electoral College. When a U.S. citizen casts a vote for a presidential candidate, what he or she is really doing is voting to send a specific elector to the Electoral College. Then, 41 days after the popular election, these electors gather in Washington or at their individual states' capital buildings to elect the president.

The exact procedures for an electoral election vary from state to state, but all these procedures must get congressional approval to be considered valid. In most states, the electoral vote is **winner-take-all**, meaning that the winner of the electoral voting gets all the electoral votes in the state counted toward his or her total. Only Maine and Nebraska allow their electors to split their state totals between multiple candidates. After the electoral vote is finished, the states send notification to Congress. One month after the popular election, Congress officially declares the winner of the election. The Electoral College currently includes slots for 538 electors. Each state gets a number of electors equal to the number of representatives and senators it has in Congress. Washington, D.C. also gets three electors, the minimum any state can receive. California has the greatest number of electoral votes with a total of 55. To win an election, a presidential candidate needs to receive 270 electoral votes.

Parties can appoint or elect their electors. These electors are pledged to vote for a specific candidate. In many, but not all states, this pledge is binding. In rare cases, an elector from a state where pledges are not binding will not fulfill his or her pledge. For example, in 2004, one elector cast a presidential vote for vice presidential candidate John Edwards. Despite the possibility of electors reneging on their pledges, no presidential election on record has even been decided by the votes of so-called faithless electors.

The reason for the Electoral College and its future are matters of debate. The Electoral College was a product of debates among the framers of the Constitution. In early drafts of the Constitution, the president was elected by the legislature. Many of the framers felt this would leave the process of selecting a president too vulnerable to political dealing and trickery. The proposed solution was to let state legislatures send representatives to elect a president. Some members of the Constitutional Convention proposed election by popular vote, but this idea was not met with enthusiasm. It is unclear why the idea was not pursued further. It may have been that the framers felt popular voting should be restricted to the election of members of Congress. Perhaps the technological limitations of the eighteenth century made the idea impractical. Whatever the reason, a majority of the delegates approved the Electoral College system.

Modern Americans appear to be increasingly dissatisfied with the Electoral College system. Many disapprove of the fact that, under the system, the winner of the popular vote is not necessarily going to be the winner of the electoral vote. Others feel that the uneven distribution of electoral slots means that the relative value of a single vote varies from state to state. Others feel that the winner-take-all system adopted by most states minimizes the impact third-party candidates can make. Unless a third-party candidate can take the entire state, the winner-take-all system effectively eliminates any gains he or she might have made in a region.

Still, the system does have its defenders. Proponents of the electoral model argue that the winner-take-all system tends to minimize turnout difference between the states. All of a state's electoral votes will be cast regardless of any temporary spikes or dips in voter turnout. Advocates also claim that the electoral vote system forces presidential candidates to appeal to a broad support base and empowers minority voters. Under a winner-take-all system, getting a tiny lead in the popular vote could produce big leads in the electoral vote. Consequently, no voting block can be entirely dismissed.

Political Parties

Despite warnings against their pernicious influence from the founding fathers, **political parties** have become a permanent feature of the American political landscape. For most of the nation's history, there have been two dominant parties. The first parties were the Federalists and the Democratic-Republicans. The two parties that currently dominate the political scene are the Democrats and the Republicans. The Democratic Party, one of the oldest political parties in the world, underwent a major political shift in the 1960s and 1970s. It now represents the more liberal of the two parties. The Republican Party, originally formed as a counter-balance to pro-slavery political forces, went through a similar realignment in the 1910s, and again in the 1960s, that made it the conservative party of the United States.

There is a long tradition of third parties in the United States. Some of these minor parties coalesce around a specific issue, such as the Anti-Mason Party or Free Soil Party, while others were created to combine the efforts of broad constituencies that, for some reason or another, do not find a home in the major parties. The Populist Party is an example of this kind of broad-based third party. Third parties tend to do better in local elections than on a national level. While third-party candidates have won House and Senate

seats in the past, none has ever won more than five states in a presidential election.

Party politics in America reflect a few demographic trends, but the correlations are hardly overwhelming. In general, males identify themselves as Republicans and females identify themselves as Democrats. Whites tend to identify with the conservative party, while minorities tend to identify with the liberal party. African Americans tend to strongly identify with the Democratic Party: In the 2004 election, 65% of African-American voters cast their ballot for the Democratic candidate, 29% voted for an independent candidate, and only 6% voted Republican. Religious voters show a slight preference for the Republican Party, with the exception of Jewish voters, who overwhelmingly identify with the Democratic Party. People with an annual income of less than $50,000 tend to identify with the Democratic Party, and people who make more than $50,000 a year tend to belong to the Republican Party. As a general rule, the older the voter, the more likely he or she is to identify with the Republican Party. Education levels may also shape party identification. Voters who did not pursue an education past a high school degree tend to be Democrats. As of the 2004 election, voters with a college education were evenly split between Democrats and Republicans.

Parties have a major impact on the American political system. Parties provide major funding for their candidates. They organize the political efforts of their large and often diverse membership. Although there is no constitutional mandate for a two-party system, the two parties are now such an important feature of American politics that many political institutions have developed traditions around their existence. For example, the positions of the majority and minority party officers in the House and Senate reflect the two-party split. Despite how entrenched the party system is, there are some common criticisms of the party system. Some critics have suggested that a two-party system suppresses original political ideas. Because parties must appeal to a broad base of people, parties tend to emphasize non-radical, middle of the road positions. Furthermore, others have suggested that parties, by promoting party insiders, discourage candidates with nontraditional backgrounds.

Special Interest Groups

The right of Americans to attempt to influence their politicians is protected by the First Amendment of the Constitution. When enough people share the same concerns, they may combine their efforts and form a **special interest group**. A special interest group is any coalition of people that attempts to sway the political process to further its own agenda. Special interest groups can be built around a specific issue, to promote a specific candidate, or advance the interest of an affinity group, such as agricultural industries or senior citizens. **Lobbying** is the term given to the influential efforts in the interest of more than 17,000 professional lobbyists operating in Washington.

One of the important ways special interest groups can influence politicians is by providing financial campaign assistance. There are extensive laws regulating the amounts interest groups may contribute to candidates or political parties. Still, even with these limitations, the amount of money involved is considerable. In a nine-year span, from 1998 to 2007, the special interest groups representing the finance, insurance, and real estate industries contributed nearly $3 billion to various political campaigns. Each year since 2003, lobbyists from across the spectrum have spent more than $2 billion on campaign financing.

Lobbyists also influence lawmakers through education efforts. Lobbyists spend time communicating to lawmakers the concerns and ideas of the special interest groups they represent. In extreme cases, special interest groups and their lobbyists go so far as to actually draft legislation that lawmakers then submit to Congress.

Though lobbyists are regulated and the rights of special interest groups are well established, many have important criticisms of special interest groups and lobbyists. Many critics have suggested that the vast sums of money corporate lobbyists can raise cause politicians to give contributing industries preferential treatment. They charge that these campaign contributions are little more than bribes. Other critics feel that the connections between lobbyists and politicians have grown so close as to create a culture of favor swapping that locks out the politicians' real constituents: the voters. The critics often point to the great number of lawmakers who, on leaving office, find jobs as lobbyists. Finally, after a series of public scandals involving illegal financial contributions and under-the-table gift giving, many have argued that current regulations on lobbyists are not strict enough.

The Formation of Political Beliefs

In the 1960s and 1970s, the question of just how citizens develop their political beliefs became a subject of intense interest to sociologists and political scientists. The results of these studies suggest that the two main factors in the development of political identity are the family and education institutions. Families are important vectors of political ideals. According to one study, parents who identify with the Democratic Party have a 66% chance of producing offspring who identify with the Democratic Party. The same is true of households headed by Republican parents: They are 51% likely to have children who eventually identify themselves with the Republican Party. Even independents pass along a sense of political identity to their offspring. Independent parents have a 53% chance of having children who do not align themselves with either major political party. Along with family members, schools are the second major source of political socialization. Researchers posit that, while family members have a profound influence on ideological outlooks, schools provide citizens with a majority of their practical information regarding American political processes and institutions.

After these two significant sources of political socialization, research suggests that social organizations, like a workplace or church, are the second most significant sources of political socialization. Finally, social context provides a limited but significant source of political socialization. Social scientists also identify three special sources of political socialization: the life-cycle effect, the period effect, and the cohort effect. The life-cycle effect is the term used to describe the seemingly predictable ideological changes that occur as a political agent grows older, such as the general correlation between age and conservatism. The period effect describes the broad political shifts that may occur during historically unique periods, such as times of war or economic depressions. Finally, the cohort effect refers to a political shift, specifically an exception to an overall ideological outlook, that occurs in relation to a person's ethnic or cultural identity.

▶ The Constitutional Basis for Government

A small portion of the CLEP exam is dedicated to crucial political ideals embodied in the U.S. Constitution. There are two important concepts that will almost assuredly appear somewhere on the exam: Federalism and the separation of powers.

Federalism is a political philosophy that holds that the government is formed by a voluntary gathering of people who consent to be ruled over by a constitutionally limited central body. In American politics, the contrasting philosophy is often described as *anti-Federalist* and places an emphasis on the decentralization of power. Typically, Federalists favor a strong national government, while anti-Federalists would prefer the balance of power tip in favor of the states. Historically, the trend in American politics has been one of increasing federal power.

The term **separation of powers** was coined by French philosopher Baron de Montesquieu to describe a model of government where political authority is distributed among many different positions, ensuring that no single official accumulates too much power. In Montesquieu's time, the contrasting system would have been an absolute monarchy: a form of government where all authority resided in the hands of the king or queen. The Constitution's division of the government into three branches reflects the influence of this idea.

Another important aspect of the Constitution's separation of power is the system of checks and balances. The founding fathers sought to limit the potential for abuse of power by making each branch answerable to the other two branches in some way. Congress makes laws, but the president can veto a bill or the Supreme Court can overturn the new law. The president must obey the law as interpreted by the Supreme Court, but also gets to choose who serves on the Supreme Court, with the consent of the Senate. These institutional limits are a crucial aspect of the founding fathers' vision of how the U.S. government could operate as a strong central authority without becoming tyrannical.

▶ **Practice Questions**

1. Which of the following cases established the Supreme Court's power of judicial review?
  a. *Scott v. Sandford*
  b. *Roe v. Wade*
  c. *Mapp v. Ohio*
  d. *Marbury v. Madison*
  e. *Brown v. Board of Education*

2. The Rules Committee of the House of Representatives exists to set
  a. ethical guidelines for representatives.
  b. limits on the debate surrounding bills.
  c. universal standards for weights and measures.
  d. policies for lobbyists and other interest groups.
  e. salaries and benefits for congressional workers.

3. The Eighth Amendment prohibits
  a. peacetime quartering of soldiers in a private home.
  b. possession of sale of alcoholic beverages.
  c. cruel and unusual punishment.
  d. unreasonable search and seizure.
  e. government seizure of private property.

4. Which of the following is an argument against the Electoral College system?
  a. The risk that a faithless elector might significantly alter the results of an election is too high.
  b. Small differences in voter turnout from state to state are magnified by the system to the benefit of larger states.
  c. The tendency of states to use a winner-take-all system effectively locks third-party candidates out of the running.
  d. It promotes sectional differences by limiting the number of votes needed to win an election to just two or three states.
  e. The system gives large financial donors and wealthy interest groups unreasonable access to the candidates.

5. The Senate's power to advise and consent would affect which of the following presidential acts?
  a. choosing a vice president
  b. giving standing orders to military personnel
  c. vetoing a taxation bill
  d. issuing a presidential pardon to a convicted felon
  e. selection of ambassadors

6. All of these are examples of concurrent powers EXCEPT
  a. establishing courts.
  b. enforcing laws.
  c. borrowing money.
  d. declaring war.
  e. collecting taxes.

7. Which clause of the Constitution requires that every state must respect the public acts and judicial rulings of the other 49 states?
   a. the Free Exercise Clause
   b. the Speech or Debate Clause
   c. the Necessary and Proper Clause
   d. the Establishment Clause
   e. the Full Faith and Credit Clause

8. Executive privilege is the term used to describe the executive branch's power to
   a. resist search warrants.
   b. grant pardons.
   c. appoint federal judges.
   d. fire federal officers.
   e. ratify foreign treaties.

9. The president of the United States can affect monetary policy by
   a. submitting a balanced budget to Congress.
   b. appointing a new chair to the Federal Reserve.
   c. authorizing the sale of federal park land.
   d. veto tax cuts passed by Congress.
   e. requiring more efficiency from federal agencies.

10. The Voting Rights Act of 1965 outlawed what voting practice?
   a. literacy tests
   b. the exclusion of female voters
   c. poll taxes
   d. property requirements
   e. loyalty oaths

▶ **Answers**

1. d
2. b
3. c
4. c
5. e
6. d
7. e
8. a
9. b
10. a

11 ▶ Geography

The CLEP does not have a separate geography exam, but it does include geography topics in the Social Sciences and History exam. According to the College Board, just more than 10% of the Social Science and History exam covers the discipline of geography. This chapter will cover cartographic methods, as well as key theorists and issues in cultural and physical geography.

▶ Cartographic Methods

The making of maps is known as cartography. There are three broad types of maps:

Topographic maps: Topographic maps are concerned with the accurate depiction of the surface conditions of an area. Topographic maps adhere to the same size scale, use shading or other graphics to indicate physical features, and include all features and details relevant to the map's scale. Here is a topographic map of San Diego.

Notice that the details are rendered in the same scale. Contour lines indicate elevation changes. Like all topographical maps, this is an effort to render, as realistically as possible, the physical landscape of the area this describes.

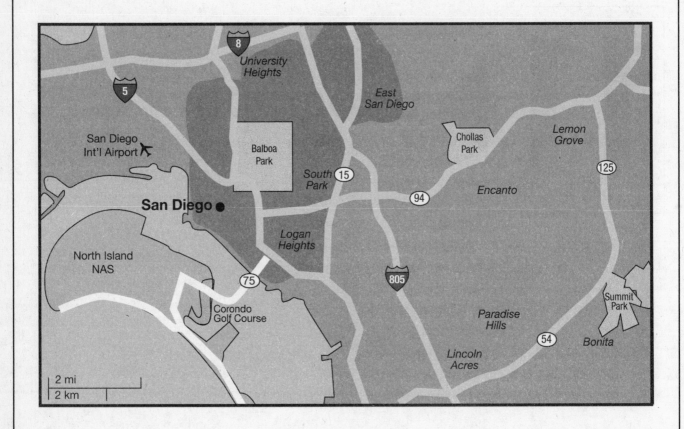

Topological maps: In contrast to topographic maps, topological maps are maps that have been simplified to the point where only a few pieces of key information stand out. Unlike topographical maps, the point of topological maps is to present essential information to a reader as clearly as possible. Here is a topological map of the New York City subway system.

The function of this map is to describe the relative location of subway stops and explain what train lines stop at which stations. To help communicate this clearly, the map ignores all but the most basic physical information. It also eliminates scale. In this map, Manhattan is shown larger than it actually would be if drawn to scale. This is because the density of stops in Manhattan would make the map too difficult to read if it was shown in the proper scale.

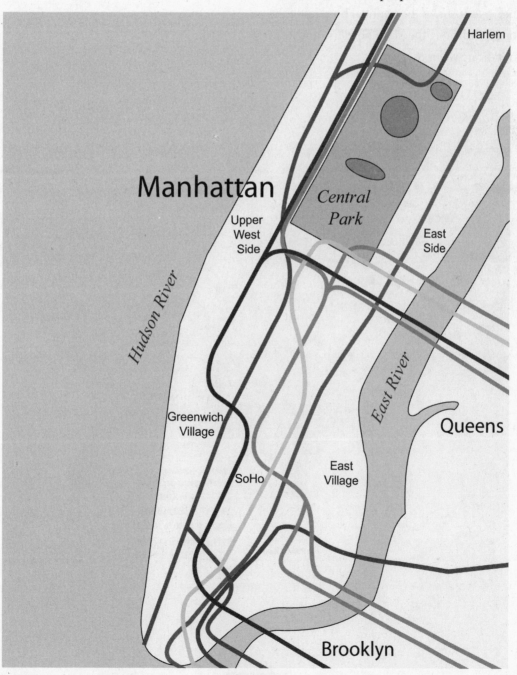

Thematic maps: Like topological maps, thematic maps simplify geographical accuracy in favor of better communicating specific and focused information to the map user. The significant difference between the topological map and thematic map is in the type of information displayed. Thematic maps display social, political, or otherwise nongeographical data in conjunction with geographical information. For example, the following map shows a rough outline of American coasts; otherwise, it shows the national borders of the United States, indicates the state borders, and uses shading to indicate water usage.

Thematic maps are crucial to the study of cultural geography, or the study of how cultural traits and activities (such as language use, ethnic migration, and industrial diversity) are spatially distributed.

Water withdrawals in million gallons per day:
0 to 2,000
2,000 to 5,000
5,000 to 10,000
10,000 to 20,000
20,000 to 52,000

0   250 Miles   500 Miles
0   250 KM   500 KM

▶ Cartographic Terms

Cartographers have developed a handful of traditional devices and techniques to communicate information to map users. They might appear on any of the three major types of maps. This section will detail some of the most common.

Compass Rose

Maps often indicate the cardinal directions—north, south, east, and west—with a compass rose. Here is a compass rose that marks the four cardinal points and several intermediate points.

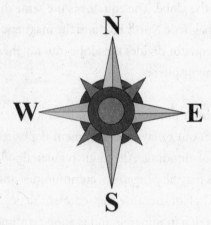

Locator Globe

Many maps include small globes that highlight the area shown in greater detail by the map. The function of these globes is to orient the map user with regard to a global position.

Key

This is also called the legend or the caption. It is a section of the map that explains any representational features, such as symbols or meaningful color usage, to the user. Here is a key for a map of North Korea.

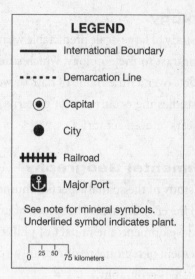

Scale Bar

A scale bar translates the representational differences into their real-world equivalents. Most maps produced in the United States have scale bars that show distances in both metric and traditional units.

Title

Most maps will have a title. With topographical maps, the title will most likely identify the region depicted on the map. The title of topological and thematic maps will usually explain the purpose of the map, giving the user a sense of what information will be presented and what information will be excluded.

▶ Physical Geography

The study of geography is divided into two broad areas of study: physical and human geography. Put simply, one studies the natural features of the Earth, while the other studies how humans spread over and interact with the Earth.

There are several subsets of physical geography, all dealing with different aspects of the Earth's physical features. The CLEP focuses on just a few of these specializations. Following is a list of the fields that are likely to be covered in CLEP.

Climatology

This is the study of large-scale predictable weather patterns. In contrast to meteorology, which studies how weather reacts over a time frame of days or weeks, climatology studies the occurrence of patterns over the course of years or even centuries.

Environmental Geography

This is the study of the spatial aspects of human interaction with the environment. The spread of urban and suburban development, the impact of pollution, and the management of regional resources are all concerns of this branch of geography.

Geomorphology

This branch of geography identifies and describes the processes that shape geographic features.

Glaciology

This is the name given to the study of the formation and action of glaciers. The study of glaciers has become more intense as global trends in climate have caused glaciers to recede.

Hydrology

The study of the motion and distribution of water around the Earth is known as hydrology. Perhaps the greatest contribution of hydrologists to geography has been the description of the hydrologic cycle: a model of how water is recycled through a system of evaporation, precipitation, and motion.

▶ Important Concepts in Physical Geography

The CLEP will also require a familiarity with common geographic terminology. What follows are some of the most essential terms.

Basin: a geographic depression, often filled with water.

Bay: a body of water partially surrounded by land. The land surrounding a bay tends to provide shelter from both harsh weather and military invasion, so bays were historically considered excellent places to establish ports.

Delta: a plain at the mouth of a river, often triangular in shape. Rivers deposit sediment in their deltas, which may make the land especially fertile farmland.

Equator: this is an imaginary line drawn across the middle of the globe. The equator is the same distance from the magnetic North Pole and the magnetic South Pole. The equator divides the globe into northern and southern hemispheres.

Flood plain: a plain on either side of a river. Flood plains form out of layers of sediment deposited over centuries of flooding. Although regular flooding of these areas may be dangerous, communities often settle in flood plains because the sediment deposited by flooding is rich in minerals and is good farming soil.

Frigid zone: the climate zones of the Arctic and Antarctic Circles. The seasonal cycle of the frigid zones lack any warm summers. In the frigid zone, no month has an average temperature greater than 42° Fahrenheit.

Glacier: large, slow-moving mass of snow and ice. The movement of glaciers, which advance and retreat over time, can carve valleys out of a stony landscape and deposit mineral resources over an extensive area. Recent climate changes have caused concerns that the glaciers are shrinking.

Hill: a raised area of land under 2,000 feet in height.

Island: an area of land completely surrounded by water.

Isthmus: a narrow strip of land connecting two larger regions. Historically, isthmuses have been important to trade. The fact that they are so narrow compared to the region made them attractive places to built canals. Even without a canal, overland travel on an isthmus was sometimes cheaper and easier than sea routes.

Mountain: a raised area of land greater than 2,000 feet in height. The area at the bottom of the mountain is referred to as the **base**. The top of the mountain is the **peak**. When the mountain stretches over a distance, the peak is referred to as a **ridge**.

Mountain pass: a gap between mountains. Historically, early travelers depended on passes to travel through mountainous regions. Even today, roads and rail lines are likely to take advantage of natural passes.

Mouth: the point where a river enters a sea or lake.

Peninsula: a region mostly surrounded by water, but still connected to land.

Plateau: a large, flat area raised above the surrounding area. Normally, at least one side of the plateau terminates in a steep slope.

Prime meridian: a line of longitude that, by international agreement, marks 0° longitude. The line passes through Greenwich, England, and divides the globe into eastern and western hemispheres.

Source: the origin point of a river. Water flows from the source to the mouth.

Strait: a narrow body of water between two landmasses.

Temperate latitudes: the climate zones that lie between the tropical latitudes and the polar circles. The northern temperate latitudes exist between the Tropic of Cancer and the Arctic Circle. The southern zone can be found between the Tropic of Capricorn and the Antarctic Circle. The seasonal cycle in the temperate zones includes a distinct spring, summer, fall, and winter.

Tributary: a river or stream that flows into another river. In contrast, a **branch** is a river or stream made when the flow of water leaves a larger river.

Tropic latitudes: the climate zone between the Tropic of Cancer and the Tropic of Capricorn. The seasonal cycle in the tropic includes a hot dry season, a cool dry season, and a rainy season.

Valley: a low stretch of land between raised areas of land. Valleys are formed by the action of rivers cutting paths out of the surrounding land. Most rainfall in an area will drain out through the valley.

▶ Human Geography

A population is any group of individuals that shares some common characteristic. In geography, populations are often defined by geographical proximity and political or ethnic identity. However, numerous traits have been identified, any of which a geographer might use. These include, but are not limited to, birth and mortality rates, age distribution, economic indicators, and public health factors. Population geography is the study of spatial variation within and among populations. Population geographers study the distribution and density of individuals in a population. They study the increase or decrease in the number of individuals within a population. The movement, labor structures, and settlement patterns of a population are of special interest to geographers. Finally, population geographers study how populations react to geographic change.

There are four general schools of population geography. Environmental determinism holds that the definitive reasons populations form specific features can be found in their surrounding natural environments. Regional geography identifies and studies population characteristics that are unique to a certain regional population. Quantitative geography is defined less by its focus and more by its adherence to strictly numeric measures. Finally, critical geography, sometimes known as humanistic or cultural geography, uses qualitative methods to explore how geography impacts various cultural characteristics. These divisions, while instructive of the methods and diversity of geographic thought, do not prevent geographers from using the insights and methods of multiple schools.

Central Concepts in Population Geography

The following section will identify some of the core concepts in the study of populations.

Crude birth rate: the annual number of childbirths for every 1,000 people.

Crude death rate: the annual number of mortalities, or deaths, for every 1,000 people.

Demographic transitions: A population goes through a demographic transition when there is a distinct and drastic change in death and birth rates. Population geographers divide transitions into three major demographic transition models, or DTMs. In the first DTM, a population begins with relatively high birth and death rates. Then the death rate drops. Next, the birth rate drops. Eventually the birth and death rates stabilize again, but at much lower rates than the population experienced before the drop. This pattern describes the typical transitions experienced by Western nations that went through industrialization in the 1800s. In the second DTM, which describes some regions in Central Europe, populations have declines in both birth and death rates, but the death rate continues to drop lower than the birth rate. When the rates do stabilize, the birth rate remains considerably higher than the death rate. Finally, in the third DTM, which describes much of Asia, Africa, and South America, the population will experience declining death rates, but there is no significant decline in birth rates. Population geographers debate what factors might cause the difference in these major transition models.

Development geography: Geographers concerned with development geography study how population dynamics and spatial relationships can affect the standard of living for individuals within a population. This approach often combines geographic techniques with economic and sociological theories.

Economic geography: This term describes the distribution of economic activities. Economic geographers study how different economic activities form links between different regions and populations. One of the critical issues in economic geography is the study of how the natural distribution of resources is exploited and transported.

Infant mortality rate: This figure measures the number of infant deaths for every 1,000 infants within a year. An infant is defined as any child less than one year old. Traditionally, infant mortality rates are used to assess the general state of healthcare in a population. A population with a high infant mortality rate can be assumed to have poor or no access to healthcare.

Language demography: the study of the spread of a language. Language demographers attempt to estimate the number of speakers a language has. They also try to distinguish between regional dialects and identify ways in which population changes may impact a language.

Life expectancy: the average age to which the members within a community can be expected to live. For reasons biological and cultural, women tend to live longer than men. To account for this, life expectancies are often given separately for males and females. In the United States, the life expectancy of a male is about 75 years and the life expectancy for a female is about 80 years.

Morbidity rate: the incidence of people contracting a selected illness within a population. Given the differences between diseases, there is no standard unit for morbidity rates and researchers must decide meaningful measures for the problem they wish to study. This should not be confused with **mortality rate**, a measure of the number of deaths in the population.

Population density: a measure of how many individuals of a population exist in a given unit of space. There is no standard measure for population density, so researchers must determine a meaningful unit of space before they can accurately describe population density.

Religious demography: the study of the number and distribution of adherents to various religions or belief systems. There are numerous problems facing religious demographers, notably the sometimes bewildering diversity of belief among religious adherents who identify themselves as members of the same faith.

Urban geography: Geographers have applied tools originally devised to study widespread distributions of populations to densely populated urban environments. The result is the field known as urban geography. Urban geographers study the efficiency of urban development schemes, the way in which social and ethnic groups are distributed through an urban area, and how urban space influences human activities, from employment to crime.

▶ Practice Questions

1. A region in the tropical zone is most likely to experience which of the following weather conditions?
   a. tornados
   b. monsoons
   c. blizzards
   d. droughts
   e. cold snaps

2. If a cartographer were making a map of London, what feature could he or she use to best indicate that the city was situated in the northern hemisphere?
   a. title
   b. key
   c. scale bar
   d. locator globe
   e. compass rose

3. In terms of the hydrologic cycle, all of the following are considered reservoirs EXCEPT
   a. rainfall.
   b. glaciers.
   c. a lake.
   d. the atmosphere.
   e. groundwater.

Use the following map to answer question 4.

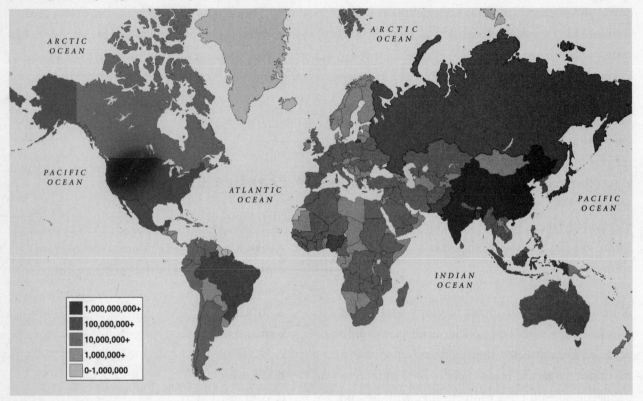

4. Which of the following countries has the greatest number of residents?

a. Canada

b. Egypt

c. Greenland

d. Brazil

e. Australia

5. The scale bar of a map converts inches into miles. The scale is 1 to 20. If two points are represented as four inches apart, how far apart are the points in real life?

a. 4 miles

b. 5 miles

c. 20 miles

d. 40 miles

e. 80 miles

6. Which of the following often correlates with high infant mortality rates?

a. high levels of immigration

b. violent civil unrest

c. uneven ratio of male to female births

d. tropical zone location

e. densely populated urban communities

7. The advance and retreat of a glacier is likely to produce all of the following geographic features EXCEPT

a. a gravel plane.

b. a lake.

c. a cirque.

d. a valley.

e. a mountain ridge.

8. Which of the following reasons for human migration would be considered a "push factor"?
   a. family relations
   b. increased security
   c. limited job market
   d. improved medical care
   e. religious freedom

9. As a nation's economy grows more developed, few citizens tend to work in which of the following fields?
   a. agriculture
   b. law
   c. military
   d. medicine
   e. education

10. Which of the following would be best described as a thematic map?
   a. a sketch on a party invitation showing invitees how they can get to the party by automobile
   b. a map showing the political boundaries of the nations in South America
   c. a map of the United States with each state shaded red or blue to indicate how its presidential electors voted
   d. a poster that shows several different bus routes through a city
   e. a map showing the mountains, forests, cities, roads, and waterways of Arizona

▶ **Answers**

1. b
2. d
3. a
4. d
5. e
6. b
7. e
8. c
9. a
10. c

12▶ Economics

The CLEP divides the field of economics into microeconomics and macroeconomics. **Microeconomics** focuses on the theories that describe the behavior of individual consumers and businesses. **Macro-economics** concerns itself with the behaviors of entire economic systems, often on the national or international scale. This chapter will follow this distinction. The first section will cover crucial concepts in micro-economics. The second section will focus on essential macroeconomic concepts. Finally, the first five review questions will cover microeconomic concepts while the last five questions will focus on macroeconomic subjects.

▶ Microeconomics

Microeconomics studies how individuals and businesses use their limited resources in a market economy. Included in this field are the behaviors of competitive markets, the descriptions of common business structures, and how rational agents determine the value of goods based on numerous factors. What follows are core micro-economic concepts that may appear as topics on the CLEP exam.

Corporation

The modern business corporation is a business structure that, for legal purposes, is a separate entity apart from the identity of its various members. It is, in the eyes of the law, a person. This status as a legal being gives the corporation some special capacities:

1. Corporations can participate in legal proceedings. They may initiate and be the target of lawsuits.

2. Like a human, corporations may own assets. The property of a corporation is understood as belonging to the legal entity of the corporation and not the members of the company.

3. A corporation has the right to create its own bylines to regulate its internal activities. These rules are understood to originate from the company and not the members of the corporation.

4. The employer/employee relationship is between the individual employee and the legal entity of the corporation. The corporation can hire, fire, promote, or demote employees and other agents.

5. Like any other human agent, corporations can enter into contracts. Then it is legally the corporation's responsibility to meet its contractual obligations.

For identification purposes, corporations are either **S corporations** or **C corporations**. The former is, for whatever reason, not subject to federal income tax, while the latter is. Further, a corporation may also be identified as a limited liability company, or **LLC**. In an LLC, the individual owners enjoy the benefit of an agreement that caps their financial obligations to the company. In short, their financial liability stemming from their involvement with the company can only be accounted to a certain level (usually equal to the value of their investment), regardless of the performance or actions of the company. There are other managerial implications to organizing as an LLC, but it is chiefly the risk-minimizing element of the agreement that makes the LLC such an attractive proposition.

Most modern corporations also include transferable shares of ownership, most likely but not necessarily in the form of stock. The importance of this feature is tied to the corporation's identity as a legal entity. The corporation's identity is not altered by changes in ownership.

Finally, corporations are generally characterized by their capacity to outlast the leadership of any given managers. This is to say that personnel changes, even those at the very highest levels of management, do not change the legal identity of the corporation.

Diminishing Returns

The law of diminishing returns says that, in a production system, each increase in variables intended to increase production yields less actual production in proportion to the amount added. The ultimate result is that producers eventually start investing more and more for smaller and smaller increases in efficiency. Economies of scale describe just the opposite situation (see the following section).

Economies of Scale

In some situations, increases in the scope of production lead to a drop in the costs of production. There are several reasons this might happen. Increases in the labor pool might allow for greater specialization, which in turn could lead to greater efficiency. The cost of raw materials might decrease when bought in bulk. Economies of scale refute the law of diminishing returns (see the previous section).

Imperfect Competition

A considerable portion of microeconomics assumes perfect competition (see Perfect Competition). However, there are a number of real-world conditions that may create imperfect competition. A restricted number of producers or purchasers will create imperfect competition. A **monopoly**, the sole producer for a specific good, and **oligopoly**, a single purchaser for a good, can exert influence over the pricing of goods that can overwhelm the regular logic of competitive markets.

Pricing strategies might create imperfect competition. Price discrimination, when a single provider offers the same good at different prices to different customers, is one such practice. A company might adopt a policy of predatory pricing or supra-competitive pricing. The former involves slashing prices to a level lower than the market will bear in order to force competitors to make the same damaging move. The latter involves just the opposite: It is a policy of inflating prices past what the market will support. Companies benefiting from unique competitive or legal advances might engage in either strategy and either strategy would result in imperfect competition.

Perhaps the most common cause of imperfect competition is government regulation. Paradoxically, government regulators often work to create both perfect and imperfect competition. When regulators enforce antimonopoly laws, they are acting to promote perfect competition. However, the government also enforces various consumer protection laws, hiring laws, safety laws, and environmental regulations. Any of these might require a company to make noncompetitive policies, the impact of which would be reflected in the cost of the goods it brought to market.

Partnership

A partnership is a business structure in which multiple owners or investors all share in the profits and losses of the company they collectively own. There are three major forms of partnership: general, limited, and limited liability partnership (LLP).

A general partnership is formed between two or more owners, and each and every one of the owners is personally liable for the company's debts and legal troubles. Legally, all the partners are considered equal managers.

In a limited partnership, there are two kinds of partners: general partners and limited partners. General partners have all the rights, authority, and liabilities of partners in a general partnership. Limited partners, on the other hand, benefit from limited liability. The tradeoff is that they also lack any managing authority.

An LLP combines the characteristics of a general partnership and an LLC. All the partners in an LLP benefit from limited liability, but there is no division between general and limited partners. All the partners share management authority.

Some states allow limited liability partnerships, but this is still relatively rare. Such companies limit the liability of all partners, but have two different classes of partners, just like a limited partnership.

Perfect Competition

The phrase *perfect competition* describes a theoretical market in which only the logic of supply and demand can influence prices. Most economists assume that perfect competition maximizes the efficient use of resources and maximizes profits.

Perfect competition requires a series of important assumptions. First, perfect competition requires that no single producer or consumer has enough power to influence the market in its own favor. This imaginary market of small and autonomous producers and consumers is called the atomic market. Perfect competition also requires the idea that all similar goods are perfectly interchangeable. In this hypothetical market, all companies produce essentially the same product. This aspect of perfect competition is called homogeneity. In this hypothetical market, every agent knows the price every provider is charging. It assumes that a consumer is never fooled by advertising or false claims about products. The firms involved in perfect competition all have equal access to customers and resources. There are also no bars to a producer entering the market. Finally, perfect competition assumes all the agents in the market act in full freedom and independence.

Price Elasticity of Demand

Price elasticity of demand (PED) describes the relationship between the price of a good and changes in demand. Goods can be placed on a spectrum of perfectly inelastic to perfectly elastic. If a product is perfectly inelastic, then changes in price do not affect the demand for the good. With goods that are perfectly elastic, even the tiniest rise in price will completely eliminate demand. Few goods are perfectly elastic or perfectly inelastic; however, all products fall somewhere on the spectrum.

One good indication of the elasticity of a good is the possibility of substitution by a consumer. When faced with a rise in price, consumers will try to substitute the now expensive good for something less costly. Inelastic goods are necessary and cannot be replaced. If a sick man needs a specific kind of medicine, he must buy that kind of medicine or go without. There is no possibility of substitution. However, when buying a brand of candy at a movie snack counter, unless the consumer is unusually picky, the consumer can freely trade one treat for another and pick the least costly treat.

Profit

Profit, in economic terms, is wealth an investor gains on his or her initial investment after all the costs of the business he or she has invested in are taken into account. In perfect competition, a business would eventually make what is known as normal profit. The definition of normal profit is a bit tricky. A business is making normal profit when total revenues are equal to the total costs of business. Initially this sounds as if the investors would not be making money. The reason for the confusion is that paying the investors enough return on their investment to ensure their continued support is considered part of the total cost.

It is important to note that accountants use the term *profit* differently than economists. Accountants distinguish among several forms of profit. Gross profit is the amount of wealth gained minus the cost of goods sold (the costs directly related to producing whatever the firm sells). Net profit is the wealth earned after all costs have been paid, including employee wages, administrative costs, and such things. Finally, optimum profit describes the amount of profit that the owners of the firm have determined is what the firm should be earning. This may or may not match the economists' conception of normal profit.

Revenue

The money a business gets from the normal sale of goods is called revenue. When discussing a particular firm's revenue, it is standard practice to focus only on those activities that are considered a normal part of the firm's business. The reason for this is that revenue is an important consideration in financial planning. If a firm wants to project future economic activity, it would want its projections to be based on the typical revenues of the company. Taking into account atypical or one-time infusions of money would give the firm an unrealistic picture of what normal revenues were.

Single Ownership

This is a business structure with a single owner. This business has no identity separate from the identity of the owner. Although the owner does not enjoy the protections of limited liability, there are advantages that make the administration of the business easier.

Taxes

Questions on the CLEP may require identifying different types of taxation. Following are some of the common types of taxes found in the United States.

Ad valorem **tax:** taxes attached to certain services and goods. The tax is calculated on the basis of the value of the good to which it is attached. Sales tax on a new pair of shoes would be an example of an *ad valorem* tax.

Capital gains tax: a tax levied on capital gains. Capital gains are wealth earned from the sale of capital assets. Capital assets are a special subset of assets and can be considered an asset that creates property. For example, a shoe factory is an asset, as a firm owns it, and it has value. However, it is a capital asset because it creates shoes, which are property and potential saleable. Capital gains are usually taxed at a rate below the rate applied to standard income.

Income tax: a tax levied on the income of an individual or a legal entity like a corporation.

Property tax: a tax on the presumed market value of any property. This usually includes real estate, but it may include mobile property as well. Vehicle registration fees are considered a form of property tax. Technically, this is often also a form of *ad valorem* tax, with the property value being the value on which the tax is based.

▶ Macroeconomics

Microeconomics studies the behavior of individual buyers, sellers, and business firms. In contrast, **macroeconomics** is the term given to the study of large-scale economic activities. Macroeconomics studies the behavior of nations, entire industries, and global systems. The following sections will briefly review concepts and terms that are likely to appear on the CLEP macroeconomics exam.

Business Cycle

The business cycle describes changes in an economic system's overall performance. The cycle includes several stages:

1. **Recovery.** This period of expansion is characterized by an increase in the gross domestic product's (GDP) rate of growth. Typically the unemployment rate decreases as well. This period follows a period of economic contraction.
2. **Prosperity.** This is an extended period of economic expansion. It is characterized by sustained growth in the GDP and an unusually low unemployment rate. In times of prosperity, capacity utilization (the ratio of actual production output to potential production output) approaches 1.
3. **Recession.** This is a period of economic contraction. Typically, it is characterized by negative GDP growth, a slightly raised unemployment rate, and a decrease in capacity utilization.
4. **Depression.** This is an extended period of economic contraction. It is characterized by sustained negative GDP growth and a decrease in capacity utilization. As a general rule, the distinction between a recession and a depression is that the unemployment rate is even worse in a depression, and a depression persists for a long period.

Circular Flow of Income

The circular flow of income is a greatly simplified model of the relation between production and consumption. The consumer gets wages, goods, and services from producers. Producers get revenue and the capacity to purchase needed supplies, called the *factors of production* in this model. In a perfect world, the flow in both directions would reach equilibrium. In fact, government interventions, foreign trade, and leakages (unexpected, one-time adjustments) ensure that equilibrium is never maintained.

Federal Reserve Banking System

In 1913, the United States established the **Federal Reserve** as its central bank system. The intention was to create an organization that could regulate the money supply in an elastic way to meet periodic changes in money demand and act as a last resort lender to commercial banks that were in desperate need of a loan. At the time, its chief function was to defend the nation's banks against bank runs, sudden mass withdrawals from a bank by its depositors.

The Federal Reserve, or Fed for short, is a quasi-public bank system. That means it is a mix of government and privately run institutions. It includes a board of governors appointed by the president of the United States, a financial policy group known as the Federal Open Market Committee, 12 regional federal banks, many privately owned banks, and numerous special advisory committees.

The modern Federal Reserve has four goals. First, it moderates long-term interest rates. Second, it helps create economic growth. Third, it tries to decrease unemployment. And fourth, it helps stabilize prices.

To achieve these goals, the Fed has three significant tools at its disposal. The first of these is **open market operations**. Open market operations are methods for expanding or constricting the money supply through the sale or loan of government bonds or similar items. The Fed mainly uses an economic tool called an overnight repurchase agreement, which acts like a loan. With these repurchase agreements, the Fed can take money in and out of circulation. The amount of money in circulation has an important impact on inflation (see Inflation, page 169).

The Fed can also encourage or discourage spending by adjusting **interest rates** on the loans commercial banks make to one another. Because banks frequently lend money to one another, this rate change is eventually felt at the level of the individual borrower.

Finally, the Fed can set the level of **monetary reserves** all of the member banks must maintain. Because this money cannot be loaned out or otherwise invested, it is effectively taken out of circulation. If the Fed wishes to shrink the money supply, it raises the level of reserves required. If it wishes to increase the monetary supply, it decreases the mandatory reserve level.

Because it uses interest-generating loans as one of its major tools, the Fed does generate a profit off the loans it makes to its member banks. After paying its operational costs, the Fed's remaining profits are returned to the United States government and included in the federal budget.

There have been numerous criticisms of the Federal Reserve. Some economists have accused the Fed of being too susceptible to short-term economic pressures, arguing that its policies reflect the desires of changing political administrations rather than sound economic thinking. Others allege that any artificial manipulation of the money supply interferes with the logic of the market. Some economists even go so far as to argue that the Fed's manipulation of the money supply is what creates the boom and bust cycles in the economy. Other common criticisms are that the decisions of the Fed are not open to enough public scrutiny, and that the tools the Fed uses to control inflation are too imprecise, and their effects too irregular, to provide any accurate level of control.

Fiscal Policy

Generally speaking, the term *fiscal policy* refers to the use of government powers to affect the performance of the national economical system. Fiscal policy is often contrasted with **monetary policy**, which is the effort to affect the economy through the regulation of interest rates and the expansion or contraction of the monetary supply.

If the Fed is the chief agent of monetary policy, the federal government is the United States' chief agent of fiscal policy. The most important tools of fiscal policy are taxation and government spending. These tools impact the economy by altering demand for certain goods and by redistributing wealth among the agents within an economic system.

Unfortunately, a fiscal policy that uses a combination of low taxes and extensive government spending has an important down side: the creation of a **deficit**. When government expenditures overtake the tax revenue, the result is a public debt called the deficit. Eventually, the deficit will have to be paid and this means that, sooner or later, the citizens will have to be taxed enough to raise the money. A good fiscal policy will encourage economic growth while minimizing the debt burden on the government and its citizens. Traditionally, the United States government has simply carried a deficit, spending more than it gains through tax revenues. For a brief period in the twentieth century, the government was actually operating at a surplus. However, entering the twenty-first century, the U.S. government was operating with a deficit of more than $300 billion.

Three- and Four-Sector Economy

Some economists like to divide the economy up into three or four sectors, depending on the profit motive of the economic agents involved in each sector. The first sector is known as the private sector and includes for-profit businesses and their customers. The second sector, or public sector, includes government-owned or state operated institutions. The third sector encompasses nonprofit and charitable operations. This sector is known as the social sector.

Finally, some economists like to add a fourth sector to the model. This sector is called the informal sector and includes exchanges that society does not regulate, such as exchanges between family members or friends. The black market, which includes all illegal transactions, might be considered part of the informal economy.

Transfer Payment

A transfer payment is any payment a government makes to a person without an expectation of a direct exchange of goods or services. In the United States, the money paid out through Social Security and welfare would be considered transfer payments.

Gross National Product (GNP) and Gross Domestic Product (GDP)

The GNP is the market value of all the final goods and services produced by the citizens of a country within a year, no matter where those citizens might be geographically. In contrast, the GDP represents the market value of all the final goods and services produced within a country in a single year. The GDP is often considered the single most important measure in macroeconomics. It represents the ultimate financial restriction on any given national economic system and is the closest thing economists have produced to providing an accurate measure of a nation's real wealth.

Inflation

Inflation is an increase in the average prices in a given economic system. Typically, the term is used to describe consumer price inflation, which specifically refers to an increase in the price of consumer goods. It is often measured in percent change of the cost of a selected set of goods.

The most common cause of inflation is an increase in the money supply, literally the amount of money available within an economic system. Changes in the supply of goods may also contribute to inflation. Inflation has many clear negative effects. It reduces the spending power of most agents in an economy. It also pushes up wages (which is helpful for employees, but hurts employers) and distorts the prices of trade goods. Still, some slight inflation is not necessarily a bad thing. It may encourage investment and purchases as money saved becomes less valuable as inflation goes on.

Inflation can be countered in economic systems that have a central bank, like the Federal Reserve Bank. Central banks can slow inflation by raising interest rates and slowing the growth of the money supply. The money supply can also be restricted by altering the exchange rate between money and some other commodity, like gold, or by increasing taxation while cutting government spending. In the United States, the Federal Reserve Bank generally tries to keep inflation under 2%. The opposite of inflation is **deflation**.

International Trade

The modern economy is now a global phenomenon. In 1944, the International Monetary Fund was established to create a global currency system through the monitoring of exchange rates and balance of payments (payments from any one country to all other countries). In 1995, the World Trade Organization was formed with the purpose of removing barriers to international trade. Globalization is the term for the integration that trade, migration, and the spread of technology have brought. The study of international trade is a rich and complex field and this single chapter could not cover every concept and idea international economists have developed, but the concepts that follow are crucial to understanding some of the modern issues surrounding international trade.

Balance on goods and services: Also known as the trade balance, the balance of services and goods equals the value of exports minus the value of imports.

Comparative advantage: Some countries have material or legal advantages in the production of specific goods. This lowers their opportunity cost—not only the cost of producing the good, but also the money lost by not focusing on the production of other goods. It benefits countries to produce items with low opportunity costs and trade for items with high opportunity costs.

Currency appreciation/depreciation: When a currency rises in value in relation to other currencies, it is an example of currency appreciation. A currency depreciates when it loses value relative to other currencies. The value of a currency is related to a number of factors, including the GDP of a country, the volume and direction of the country's international trade, and interest rates within the country. A strong currency would be stable (resistant to inflation) and come from a country with high interest rates (which would make investing attractive to a foreign investor).

Import/export quotas: A government may restrict access to foreign markets or restrict competition by foreign producers by placing a quantity limit on imported and exported goods.

Non-tariff barriers: A non-tariff barrier is any restriction on international trade that is not a tariff. Environmental regulations that barred the important of certain vehicles would be an example of a non-tariff barrier.

Tariffs: Tariffs are taxes on imported goods. Tariffs increase the price of foreign goods and make domestically produced goods more attractive to consumers. They are used by nations to protect domestic producers from foreign competition.

Voluntary export restraints: When two governments agree to limit the volume of a particular exported good, they establish a voluntary export restraint.

▶ Practice Questions

1. Which of the following describes the point where a consumer has maximized total utility within income and price restraints?
   a. shut-down point
   b. point elasticity of demand
   c. saturation point
   d. consumer equilibrium
   e. breakeven point

2. All of the following are assumptions necessary for perfect competition EXCEPT
   a. the market does not distinguish between goods on the market.
   b. all consumers within the market operate under identical income constraints.
   c. no consumers have special knowledge of price variations.
   d. all the firms providing a service or good have complete access to the market.
   e. no producers are so large as to unilaterally affect the market.

3. Which of the following best explains why a firm would adopt a policy of cost plus pricing?
   a. The firm wishes to take advantage of a peak period when demand and marginal costs are higher.
   b. The firm is operating in a market with minimal or no entry or exit barriers.
   c. The firm plans to use predatory pricing to put pressure on competing firms.
   d. The firm is a producer in a oligopolistic market place and following the polices of the price leader.
   e. The firm lacks information necessary to set prices according to the $MR = SMC$ rule.

4. Which of the following best describes a situation in which low-quality products drive high-quality products out of a market because of differences in the information held by buyers and sellers?
   a. adverse selection
   b. market signaling
   c. monopsony
   d. short run equilibrium
   e. decreasing cost industry

5. Which best describes why a long-run average cost curve might fall as output expands?
   a. diminishing returns
   b. output elasticity
   c. economies of scale
   d. income effect
   e. market saturation

6. If a country experiences currency appreciation, which of the following is most likely to happen?
   a. an increase in tourists visiting the county
   b. an increase in imports
   c. an increase in citizens traveling abroad
   d. an increase in foreign investment
   e. an increase in exports

7. All of the following are typical reasons for outsourcing EXCEPT
   a. access to larger talent pools.
   b. reduction in time to market.
   c. access to intellectual property.
   d. savings in labor costs.
   e. reduction in staff turnover.

8. All of the following practices are associated with protectionist trade policies EXCEPT
   a. import quotas.
   b. custom duty reduction.
   c. subsidies.
   d. import licensing.
   e. tariffs.

9. Which of the following is most likely to cause an increase in the transaction demand for money?
   a. a rise in GDP
   b. a rise in inflation
   c. a fall in GDP
   d. a trade surplus
   e. an increase in unemployment

10. Which of the following open market operations is characteristic of monetary policy?
   a. legislative regulation of industry
   b. reductions in government spending
   c. the creation of trade barriers
   d. the adjustment of interest rates
   e. the regulation of tax rates

▶ **Answers**

1. d
2. b
3. e
4. a
5. c
6. c
7. e
8. b
9. a
10. d

13▶ Sociology

Sociology is the organized study of social phenomena. These phenomena include the ways in which an individual may interact with his or her culture as well as large-scale features that emerge only when people come together to form groups. This chapter will cover some of the major sociological paradigms and then cover some individual subjects that have traditionally been important topics for sociological research.

▶ The Major Paradigms of Sociology

The four major sources of sociological theory all appear, nearly simultaneously, in the latter half of the nineteenth century. Since that time, the field has adopted political ideologies, rejected and rediscovered basic principles, and transformed its methods and ideas to keep pace with the changes of society. It would be impossible to cover every shift within the social science even in a book twice this size. However, it is possible to follow the general development of sociology's most important schools of thought. This section will trace the development of sociology, highlight some of its more important practitioners, and outline some of the essential sociological theories.

Positivism

The existence of sociology as a unique branch of study can be traced to **Auguste Comte**, a nineteenth-century French philosopher. Comte not only coined the term *sociology*, but also stressed the importance of empirical research in the study of social phenomena. Unlike the study of philosophy, which advanced through observation and speculation, Comte felt that sociologists had to apply the scientific method to the study of society. In fact, Comte felt only information gained through the scientific method was worthwhile. Everything else was just speculation.

Comte's positivism was attacked almost immediately by others who wanted to push the newly founded science in a different direction. Despite this, Comte's positivism continues to exert a profound influence on the theories and methods of sociology. Most would say that, even today, it is an adherence to a scientific framework that defines and distinguishes sociology.

Marxism

In contrast to Comte's positivism, the nineteenth-century German philosopher **Karl Marx** and his followers felt that dialectical materialism should be the basis of all study of society. Dialectical materialism was a complex set of philosophical positions that, among other things, claimed that societies develop through the conflict of opposites. For Marx, the conflict between social classes was the greatest of these conflicts. Marx saw most of history as the conflict between the haves and the have-nots. Marx further believed that the laboring class was destined to rise up and dominate the upper class.

Marx's ideas were only partially accepted by sociologists. Few modern sociologists are dialectical materialists, but many of the concepts studied by Marx are now an important part of the field. Understanding social conflict, the existence of separate and distinct social classes within societies, and the study of forces that promote or restrict social change are all typical preoccupations of sociologists.

Humanistic Sociology

Another nineteenth-century challenge to positivism came from a loose group of like-minded German sociologists, the most famous being **Max Weber**. Weber believed that certain aspects of human society were unique to humans. The creation of meaning, the development of rules and norms, and the sharing of values were all without parallel in the natural world. Therefore, a positivist approach that treated everything humans did as just another physical phenomenon would be bound to miss some of the most crucial aspects of social life.

Weber's own book *The Protestant Ethic and the Spirit of Capitalism* is a landmark example of humanistic sociology. In it, Weber explains how the values of Protestantism were one of the major reasons Western society developed capitalistic economic systems. Weber claimed positivist and materialistic approaches would be unable to explain this phenomenon. The material conditions in other societies were no different from conditions in Europe. It was European values and systems of meaning that made the difference.

Structural Functionalism

The work of **Émile Durkheim**, a French sociologist, was the inspiration for the fourth great source of sociology: **structural functionalism**. Durkheim felt that societies were collections of social facts. These are phenomena that are external to the efforts of individual members. In essence, social facts are larger than the decisions of the individual members of a society. For example, the definition of a social role, such as *father,* has a reality beyond the behavior of a single man acting or failing to act as a father. Taken collectively, these social facts reveal how a society is organized. That's the *structural* part of structural functionalism.

The *functional* part proposes that societies are organized for the collective fulfillment of biological and social needs. The structural elements that make up a society work interdependently to ensure the continued existence of the society. Anything that exists is assumed to play some ongoing role in the survival of a society.

▶ Modern Movements

In the early twentieth century, sociologists modified or expanded the four seminal paradigms of the nineteenth century. Out of humanistic sociology's interest in shared meanings and values came **symbolic interactionism**. Sociologists working from symbolic interactionist assumptions hold that the social individual is a performance that humans adopt to interact. These sociologists closely study the strategies and techniques people adopt to present themselves to others in their society.

Social constructionism is another important product of the humanistic school of sociology. Social constructionists study how knowledge is derived through social interaction, be it from informal interactions with peer groups or more formal interactions with institutions like schools. Social constructionists pay special attention to the ways in which social norms, biases, and stereotypes are constructed and then mistaken for objective reality.

Marxist sociology produced **conflict theory**, a sociological approach that studies the role of power and conflict in social organizations. Much of conflict theory continues to emphasize the struggle between labor and owners that Marx identified as the key driving force in social development, but some sociologists have expanded their focus to include gender, religion, and race as sites of conflict.

Positivist sociology, with its commitment to quantitative analysis, remains a vital (perhaps even dominant) force in the field. Its most recent and influential offshoot is social networking theory, which views all social organizations as webs of nodes and ties. The nodes are individual agents in a network. The scale of the nodes can vary depending on the network being discussed. In a classroom, the teacher and the students might be the nodes. If the network is the oil industry, then the nodes might be oil companies, national governments, and international regulatory agencies. Connecting the nodes are ties. There can be many different types of ties. Every possible connection among the nodes needs to be indicated, and each different type of relationship must be indicated by a different type of tie. Properly mapped out, a social network can be used to run complex simulations of social behavior.

Finally, the rise and fall of postmodern sociological theories had an impact on the field as a whole. **Postmodernism** was a term coined to identify a broad group of philosophies and approaches. Though the individual theories of postmodern sociologists differed greatly, certain traits could be generally ascribed to the movement. First, postmodern thinkers rejected notions of absolute reality. All knowledge was a social construct maintained by the application of coercive force. Second, postmodernists rejected the importance of the actor in social interactions. If all social roles were the product of social forces and not free will, then it was assumed free will was irrelevant. Despite the intellectual extremism of these positions, postmodern sociology proved remarkably adept at crossing disciplinary boundaries in academia. Its most lasting contribution to sociology was to introduce to the field observational methods from anthropology and cultural studies. Postmodernism also brought renewed attention to finding creative models for some classical sociological concepts, such as deviance. Ultimately, postmodern sociology's radical stance was impossible to maintain. The extreme rejection of objectivity hampered its ability to progress (or even admit the possibility of progress). Still, the variety of methods now available to sociologists is richer due to the influence of postmodernism.

▶ Important Sociological Concepts

Sociologists have studied a bewildering array of social organizations, from the mundane to the most exotic. There is no way to range across the entire body of concepts and theories generated by the discipline. There are, however, some concerns that appear again and again. By reviewing these key concepts, one can grasp the issues sociologists seem to perennially revisit.

Social Organization and Change

A **social organization** is any group that organizes its members into roles and provides connections among the various members. Sociologists identify five major social organizations that have been present in civilization: governments, educational institutions, religious institutions, economic systems, and family units. As one might expect, it is common for any individual to have a role in several of these institutions at any given time.

The forms these major institutions might take can vary widely across societies or even within a society. Sociologists have competing theories to explain just why different societies and groups produce different social organizations. One popular nineteenth-century theory of organization and change involved a circular pattern of social growth and decay. This early sociological theory had its roots in classical historical studies that held that civilizations follow a predictable pattern of rise and fall. Modern sociologists now feel that this is too simplistic a model to explain how societies organize themselves and why they change over time. However, some recent studies of population growth rates suggest that some social phenomena, such as birth rates, may follow a general cycle, rising and falling predictably in reaction to a host of external factors.

A nineteenth-century theory that has proven more durable is the **Darwinian model** of social evolution. Herbert Spenser, an early proponent of evolutionary thought, proposed that societies act like a species of animal under the influence of natural selection. The forms a society's social organizations take are the product of natural selection. Organizational forms that were not successful in perpetuating a society's existence failed, and forms that promoted the successful persistence of the society were continued. Early evolutionary sociologists believed that this process of selection naturally improved and perfected societies. This bias has been long overturned. Adaptation, it is now believed, is an immediate reaction to the environment and has no long-term goal or end result. This modernized view of social evolution is somewhat similar to the ideas of structural functionalists, who hold that the persistence of any social organization is evidence that it helps maintain the society. This persistence is a morally indifferent fact, and not proof that a society is getting better or improving over time.

Traditional Marxists placed the growth and development of all societies on the same track. According to traditional Marxists, societies grow increasingly complex in order to take advantage of natural resources. The division of labor is an example of this increase in complexity. By specializing in a job, the person doing the job can do it better. However, this increasing complexity creates social inequalities, especially once the concept of private property is developed within a society. Marx felt that these inequalities would destroy a society and, from that destruction, a new order of communal property and collective control of resources would arise. Few modern sociologists believe Marx's predictions are a given. However, many continue to emphasize the ways in which systemic inequalities and conflicts between social groups explain how unique social organizations are created.

Finally, Max Weber, a key figure from the humanistic school, proposed that rationalization was the constant driving force behind the development of society. According to Weber, as societies develop over time, an increasing number of social interactions are shaped by the need for greater efficiency. Influences like traditional values and emotional needs are replaced by the value of increased efficiency. This drive for efficiency eventually remakes the institutional organizations of a society. For example, smaller shops are often pushed out of the market by larger and less personal, but more efficient, so-called "big box" stores. In turn, these stores feel increasing pressure from even more efficient online stores. Proponents of Weber's theory point to the late twentieth- and early twenty-first-century trend of globalization as evidence of Weber's thesis. However, critics feel Weber overstates his case. Many countries, especially those with theocratic governments, have proved exceptionally resistant to some forms of rationalization. In such cases, the influence of traditional values would seem considerably more powerful than Weber predicted.

Demography

At its most general, demography is the statistical study of populations. Traditionally, demography focuses on measuring just a handful of factors, usually those that alter the number or composition of a population: birth rates, death rates, and rates of migration. Demographers collect this data though direct and indirect means. Direct means include getting data from official sources of information. In the United States, the census is the most comprehensive source of demographic information. In situations where reliable sources of direct data are unavailable, demographers must rely on indirect methods. One common indirect method is to ask people to report data on others in the community. Demographers might ask subjects to provide data on not only themselves, but also other members of their extended family. Another indirect method involves applying mathematic population models to the data. For example, demographers noticed that certain factors tend to produce what is known as population momentum. Countries where a large percentage of the population is under the age of 18 usually experience population growth. Even if a demographer could not determine an actual birth rate, evidence that a large percentage of the population is young would suggest growth. Add this assumption to other pieces of data and a demographer could provide a useful estimation of the birth rate.

Sociologists often rely on demographic data to determine quantitative facts about the groups they study. Indirect methods are especially valuable for sociologists who study populations that, for one reason or another, might not be revealed in direct sources. For example, illegal immigrants would be hesitant to report their immigration status to official data collectors. Sociologists wishing to study the population of illegal immigrants must apply indirect demographic methods to the issue of identifying population size.

Family

For a term people recognize immediately, creating a widely accepted sociological definition of what constitutes a **family** proves remarkably tricky. The traditional notion of biological kin relations does not apply universally. Nor do traditional notions of cohabitation necessarily apply. Given this tangle, sociologists have tended to adopt a somewhat self-justifying definition of family: A family is whatever the societal norms define as a family. Sociologists have identified three main ideal family structures, all of which are the dominant model of family life somewhere in the world. Matrifocal families consist of a mother and her children. Consanguineal families consist of a mother, her children, and relatives of the mother. Finally, conjugal families consist of a mother, a father, and children. Remember, these are ideal families, meaning they are considered the norm. All societies include families that, for one reason or another, do not conform to the ideal. Whether these non-ideal families are subject to social controls or not depends on the society.

Although the definition of a family unit varies, there is very little disagreement about the social function of the family. Nearly all sociologists agree that the family unit performs two crucial functions. First, through assisting biological reproduction and providing for the care of young, the family unit maintains the population of a society. Second, the family is the first institution that provides new members of the society with social training.

In the United States, research has focused on the nuclear family, defined as a conjugal family consisting of a mother, a father, and their offspring. This family model is often thought to be the social norm of American society. Some sociologists have studied the origins of this particular form, citing either economic pressures of industrialization (which broke the nuclear family off from the more traditional extended family) or the values and traditions of Judaism and Christianity. Another important area of study has been the increasing diversity of family organizations and their impact on American society as a whole. For example, the increasing incidence of divorce is a popular topic of study. Divorce rates, the causes for divorce, the demographic distribution of divorce, and the impact on the socialization of any children are hotly debated topics. The sociological implications of same-sex couples raising children is another recent, and controversial, topic of study.

Deviance

In sociology, **deviance** is defined as any variation from the social norm that is met with some degree of formal or informal social control. Not all variation is considered deviance. For example, having red hair would put a subject in a statistical minority, but it is not a violation of a social norm (the codified and informal rules of a social group), and is not subject to control. It is also important to remember that deviance need not necessarily be a crime. Crime is the formal, codified, and institutional expression of social norms, but forms of deviance might be subject to non-legal control. For example, wearing the wrong type of clothes to a social event would probably not result in somebody being arrested, but it may be considered deviance, and controls in the form of public censure or exclusion from further events might result.

One of the important and perpetually studied topics is the source of deviance. Structural functionalists, following a theory Durkheim first proposed to explain suicide, suggest that deviance is a product of a subject's faulty connection to the structures of society. Durkheim claimed that all individuals in a society could be ranked on two characteristics: their level of integration into the social norms and the amount of regulation controlling their actions. Persons who are poorly integrated and poorly controlled are most likely to engage in deviant behavior.

Another important theory of deviance suggests that deviant behavior stems from conflicts between a subject's acceptance of the dominant social goals and the subject's acceptance of the accepted institutional means a society gives the subject to obtain those goals. The tension between the goals of a society and the means of achieving them can lead to positive innovations. However, it can also lead to deviant behavior. For example, accumulating wealth is considered an accepted goal in capitalist society. However, stealing is not considered an accepted means toward achieving that goal. A person who believes in the goals of society but does not use the accepted means to achieve those goals might engage in deviant behavior. This theory is known as **stress theory**.

Schools of thought that emphasize the conflict between elements within a society, such as Marxism and conflict theory, view deviance and the application of social control in terms of the use of power and the maintenance of the institutions that benefit the most powerful people in a society. In traditional Marxist theories, the inequalities inherent in a society produce deviance. This deviant behavior is an implicit and ineffectual revolt against the status quo and an excuse for the segments of society to apply oppressive social controls on the lower classes. In this way, what is actually class conflict is redefined as question of law and order. Less class-based conflict theories suggest that social control is applied to all classes with the purpose of maintaining order throughout the society. In these theories, the act of constantly looking for deviance produces an ever longer and longer list of potentially deviant behaviors, ensuring that all the members in a society are constantly under some pressure of social control.

Finally, humanistic schools of sociology tend to emphasize how the use of shared definitions of *right, wrong,* and other common indicators of deviance can create deviants and deviant behavior. One popular humanistic theory of deviance is called labeling theory. This theory holds that giving actions the label of deviance tends to become a self-fulfilling prophecy. A person identified as a criminal, for example, might find it harder to find legitimate work. This might possibly lead to further criminal activity. Furthermore, it might make him or her reluctant to discuss the past. When people learn that this person has been labeled a criminal, this reluctance may be taken as proof that he or she is untrustworthy and is hiding the past to avoid further detection. Humanistic sociologists emphasize that the

process of working through definitions of deviance essentially trains the subject to behave in deviant ways. Another popular humanistic explanation of deviance, called the subcultural theory, holds that within any society, smaller subgroups necessarily form around shared affinities. These subgroups, or subcultures, generate their own norms. When the norms of a subculture differ noticeably from the norms of the dominant culture, the result is deviant behavior. This is especially likely in situations where the organization of society makes it difficult for the members of a subculture to achieve success in the dominant culture.

A special subset of the study of deviance is the study of criminal activity. Many criminologists studying criminal activities use general theories of deviance to explain why subjects might engage in criminal acts. However, there is one important theory specific to criminology that attempts to explain why subjects commit crimes. This theory is called **rational choice theory**. Rational choice theory proposes that subjects who commit crimes do so of their own free will after weighing the benefits and risks. Before committing a crime, subjects will consider their need for whatever benefits they might receive from the successful commission of a crime and balance this against what they assume to be the effort involved and the likelihood that they will be caught and punished. Some rational choice theorists go so far as to say that crime is so normal that wherever the opportunity exists and the effort is minimal and the chances of being caught are slim, almost any given subject will commit a crime. This assumption, called the **routine activity theory**, has proven helpful in describing certain widespread crimes such as music piracy. Rational choice theory does not assume that subjects always make the right choice. In fact, subjects often incorrectly assess both the benefits and risks of criminal activity. Self-serving biases and the selective use of available information can lead subjects to make decisions on the basis of faulty assumptions. For example, a recent study by economist Steven Levitt concluded that most people involved in the illegal sale of narcotics make no more than the minimum wage. There is, according to Levitt, no financial incentive for the added legal risks a drug dealer takes. Rational choice theorists might point to pervasive media imagery that suggests dealing drugs is a fast way to earn large sums of money. The prevalence of this mostly unrepresentative imagery leads decision-makers to greatly overestimate the potential benefits of drug dealing.

Once deviance is identified by society, **social controls** are applied. Social control is any action meant to limit and correct deviant behavior.

Some researchers have suggested that social controls can be divided into four distinct types: direct, indirect, internal, and control by satisfaction. Direct control describes the application of punishments for deviant behavior. Indirect control refers to the psychological control applied by the subject's conscience. Internal controls are controls applied because the subject does not want to damage important social links. For example, the desire to avoid alienating close friends would be an example of an internal control. Finally, control by satisfaction describes the use of rewards to ensure behavior that conforms to the norm.

Social Stratification

For most societies, some sort of hierarchy of social classes is the norm. Describing and explaining this stratification is a common goal of sociologists.

Each major school of sociology has approached the question of social stratification through its own set of assumptions. Structural functionalist sociologists assume that stratification must contribute to the continued persistence of society or stratification would not be such a common and enduring element of social organizations. The structural functionalist Talcott Parsons theorized that diversification was essential to the survival of societies. Without diversification, societies would not be efficient enough to supply the basic needs of their members. Parsons felt that this diversification led inevitably to the creation of imbalances of power, chains of command, and other elements of social stratification.

Where structural functionalists see stratification as a social fact beyond human control, Marxists and conflict theorists stress the role that humans play in actively creating and maintaining social stratification. For these theorists, the labor of the lower classes creates advantages, most typically wealth, for the upper classes. The upper classes then use their advantages to maintain the inequality of power that ensures their privileged status.

Humanistic sociologists tend to agree with Marxists and conflict theorists that stratification is an active process and the product of deliberate action on the part of different members of society. Where they would differ is in the emphasis Marxists and conflict theorists have placed on economic factors. Humanistic sociologists believe that tradition and value systems play an important role in creating and maintaining social hierarchies. For example, the uneven balance of power between a priest and a layperson in a church has little to do with economic factors. Instead, religious conviction, the shared values of the church that bind the priest and layperson, are the source of the power the priest has in the relationship.

▶ Practice Questions

1. Which of the following best describes lavish expenditures made solely for the purpose of displaying wealth and social status?
   a. differential accumulation
   b. economic materialism
   c. utility maximization
   d. conspicuous consumption
   e. social solidarity

2. Which of these is an example of the "condemnation of the condemner" neutralization strategy?

    a. If I had been given more opportunities, I would not have done wrong.

    b. People pretend to be upset by my behavior because they secretly do what I do.

    c. It is not a real crime unless somebody is clearly hurt by it.

    d. Standing by your friends is more important than following the letter of the law.

    e. The so-called victims got what they deserved.

3. All of these positions are typical of conflict theory EXCEPT

    a. all social development tends toward greater rationalization.

    b. social inequalities exist between the classes in every society.

    c. changes in social structures are the result of human actions.

    d. powerful groups typically use their power to stay in power.

    e. religion, gender, and race may all be sources of social conflict.

4. According to positivist, what best distinguishes sociology's approach to the study of human society?

    a. an interest in furthering social development for the greater good

    b. a rejection of materialistic explanations of social behavior

    c. a commitment to empirical and scientific methods

    d. a focus on typically Western social organizations

    e. an emphasis on the study of the importance of the family unit

5. Which of the following is best described as a norm that is the product tradition and routine, the violation of which is not usually considered a serious threat to social order?

    a. a correlation

    b. a more

    c. a negative sanction

    d. a law

    e. a folkway

6. Which of the following best describes a research method intended to study a subject or group over an extended period?

    a. participant observation

    b. longitudinal study

    c. survey research

    d. content analysis

    e. experimental research

7. Which of the following sociologists argued that the collective interest of a small group of power elites in society rendered the actions and motivations of ordinary citizens irrelevant?

    a. Max Weber

    b. Auguste Comte

    c. C. Wright Mills

    d. George Herbert Mead

    e. Talcott Parsons

8. All of the following characterized the Frankfurt School of Sociology EXCEPT

    a. an interest in the impact of mass and popular culture.

    b. a rejection of strictly positivist approaches.

    c. the use of psychological concepts to explain social phenomena.

    d. strong criticism of the inequalities of capitalism.

    e. a commitment to evolutionary theories of social change.

9. The potential to move up and down the hierarchy of social class is called
   a. mobility.
   b. assimilation.
   c. affinity.
   d. anomie.
   e. association.

10. All of the following are characteristics of a total institution EXCEPT
   a. restricted geographic limits.
   b. no distinctions between members are recognized.
   c. all activities are carried out collectively.
   d. all rules are implicit rather than explicit.
   e. strict scheduling of activities.

▶ **Answers**

1. d
2. b
3. a
4. c
5. e
6. b
7. c
8. e
9. a
10. d

CHAPTER

14 ▶ Anthropology

The CLEP does not have a separate anthropology exam. However, the CLEP does include anthropology topics in the Social Sciences and History exam. According to the College Board, anthropology material constitutes about 6% of the exam. This chapter will cover issues and concepts that are likely to appear on the exam.

▶ Cultural Anthropology and Ethnology

Broadly speaking, **anthropology** is the study of humanity. It is a holistic field, meaning it draws methods and concepts from a broad range of sources. There are four general approaches to the field. The cultural approach studies the cultural organization of a specific group of people. This is what most people think of when they think of anthropology. **Cultural anthropology** relies heavily on qualitative methods and extended observations. The biological approach focuses on the development of the human race's physical form. The specific study of humanity's biological evolution is known as **paleoanthropology**. The **linguistic** approach to anthropology studies the development and spread of language. Finally, **archaeology** approaches the study of human history through the examination of material artifacts. An archaeologist looks at the tools, decorations, art, buildings, and other material remnants of a culture to see what these artifacts reveal about the people who used them. The CLEP emphasizes cultural anthropology, its chief method ethnography, and paleoanthropology.

Cultural anthropology has its origins in the rise of the military and economic European powers of the Victorian era. At that time, European anthropologists gathered data from explorers, missionaries, and others involved in the colonial enterprise. They then organized this data, most often looking for similarities in cultural practices and beliefs. The great goal of these early anthropologists was to determine whether there was a single evolutionary path for all cultures and, if there was, to rank existing societies according to their progress on this path.

By the twentieth century, two components of Victorian-era anthropology had fallen out of favor. First, modern anthropologists reject the notion of a universal path of evolution. The American anthropologist Julian Steward proposed a more nuanced model of cultural evolution called cultural ecology. Stewart proposed that a culture is shaped by it immediate environment. Where there are parallels between cultures, the two cultures must share some environmental element. However, these adaptations are local and can only be found in cultures facing the same environmental challenge. The French anthropologist Claude Lévi-Strauss proposed a non-evolutionary explanation for similarities across societies. Lévi-Strauss was a proponent of a philosophy called structuralism, which holds that humans build meaning out of conceptual differences and oppositions. Some of these oppositions, like life/death or day/night, are so basic as to be universal. Because humans build their culture on top of these oppositions, it is not surprising that some cultural elements, especially those dealing with basic concepts, show some similarities.

The second major development was methodological. The early anthropologists were, for the most part, gatherers of secondhand information. They would sort and sift through reports from sources spread throughout various colonies. By the twentieth century, anthropologists shifted toward what would be the dominant approach of modern cultural anthropology: **ethnography**. This approach combines insights from multiple disciplines with extensive fieldwork. Ethnography requires firsthand observation or participation in a cultural system. These observations must be made over an extended period. It stresses interaction with the individuals being studied, through either informal conversation or formal interviews. It may or may not combine these observations with indirect research, such as interactions with other specialists, case studies, and genealogical records. Ethnology's ultimate goal is to discover the intellectual beliefs of the subjects studied and explain how these beliefs shape their interactions within their culture and with their environment. Though originally conceived as a method used for non-Western, non-industrialized societies, ethnology has proved remarkably adaptable. It has been fruitfully applied to subcultures within industrialized Western cultures, such as the residents of ethnic urban enclaves or the members of specific professions.

Because it treats living humans as the objects to be studied, ethnographic methods demand a constant awareness of research ethics. Critics of ethnology have described several potential ethical conflicts within the ethnological approach. First, because ethnologists do not want to prejudice subject behavior or unintentionally influence the data, they must often deceive their subjects. These deceptions might not be serious in and of themselves, but this practice goes contrary to the idea that people should be the subjects of study only on the condition of their fully informed and freely given consent. Second, ethnography's reliance on qualitative methods means that an ethnologist's results are vulnerable to subjective interpretations. Despite this unavoidable subjectivity, ethnologists often present their findings as if they were objective results. To help minimize the impact of these ethical problems, most anthropologists create research protocols meant to increase methodological clarity and decrease the possibility of observer bias.

▶ Major Anthropological Theorists

This section will discuss major contributors to the field of anthropology.

Franz Boas

Boas was a German-American anthropologist who studied the native population of the Pacific Northwest. Although Boas recognized the importance of evolution to explain biological phenomena, he fought against theories that proposed a single universal evolutionary path for all human cultures. Boas proposed alternatives that would, in time, inform the idea of cultural ecology.

Boas's other essential contribution was the idea of **cultural relativism**. The values and perceptions of a culture become instilled in the members of each culture through educational processes. The values are based on the culture's experience of its environment. New experiences are interpreted through the values of the culture, either by reconciling the new experiences with perceived truths or by shifting the perceived truths to account for the new experience. To the degree that all humans exist within a culture, all humans interpret experience through the filter of their cultural values. There are two important consequences of this assumption. First, value judgments do not automatically communicate across cultural boundaries. What is reasonable in one culture is not always reasonable in another. This means that anthropologists should avoid making value judgments about the cultures they are studying. Second, ethnologists must be careful not to impose their values on the observations. Because ethnologists also come from a culture, their tendency will be to interpret the actions of their subject according to the values of the ethnologist's cultural standards and not the subject's. One of the main reasons ethnological studies must be conducted over a long period is to give researchers a chance to shed some of their cultural perceptions and learn to see their subjects in terms of their own culture.

Donald Brown

Brown is an American anthropologist best known for his efforts to identify what he calls **human universals**. Human universals would be cultural features that appear at all times and in all cultures. Brown has identified more than 100 of these supposed universal features. Some universals are abstract concepts. For example, all cultures appear to have logical notions for distinguishing parts from the whole. Other notions are more complicated and involve extensive cultural practices to maintain. For example, all cultures create the means for avoiding incest and all cultures have some method for trying to heal sick and injured members.

Clifford Geertz

Geertz was one of the chief proponents of what would be called **symbolic anthropology**. This approach to anthropology defines culture as the network of concepts and representations a population uses to make meaning in the world around it. For Geertz, the ultimate purpose of anthropology was to attempt to identify the critical and essential symbols of a culture. To do this, anthropologists must add another method to their ethnological toolbox: thick description. The goal of thick description is to describe a social activity in objective terms, while also providing the larger context that makes the activity meaningful to the actors. For example, an objectively accurate description of a professional baseball game would include details like the length of a game, the rules governing play, and the behavior of the fans. A thick description would have to include a discussion of what baseball means. It might include historical details, discuss gender roles and racial issues, and explore the different ways in which regional identification translates into loyalty for certain sports franchises.

Marvin Harris

An American anthropologist who conducted fieldwork in Mozambique, Harris founded an approach to anthropology called **cultural materialism**. An outgrowth of Marxism, cultural materialism focuses on how material conditions shape the institutions of a culture. Harris did not, however, believe in the Marxist notion of the dialectic, and he rejected the idea that Marxism's insights into cultural structures revealed that capitalism was evil and communism was the moral future of mankind. For Harris, there were four levels of social activity. The first three were what he called *etic*, or understood by the subject culture. The first of these levels was the **infrastructure**, the society's relationship to the environment including the means of production and population dynamics. The next level is the **structure**, which includes social codes and behavioral norms. The final etic level is the **superstructure**, which includes the symbolic exchanges in a culture including the arts and various religious rituals. Above all these Harris placed what he called the **emic superstructure**, which consists of the intellectual structures that made all the other levels make sense. In contrast to the etic levels, the subjects of a study would be unable to communicate at the emic level. The anthropologist's goal is to extrapolate the structures of the emic superstructure from their observations of the other three levels.

Melville J. Herskovits

Herskovits, an American anthropologist, expanded the notions of what constituted the legitimate field of study for anthropology by applying the techniques of the field to the study of African Americans and their unique culture. He identified average physical characteristics, social structures, and even traced the roots of some cultural practices to Africa. He pre-figured critical anthropologists, who use anthropological methods to advance social and political reforms. Herskovits used his research to overturn then-prevalent stereotypes and argue against European colonialism in Africa.

Clyde and Florence Kluckhohn

This husband and wife team of American anthropologists developed, with the help of others, the **values orientation theory**. This proposed that societies could be understood and classified by their orientation toward five important concepts. The first concept was the inherent moral character of humans: Were humans naturally good, bad, or a mix of the two? The second feature was the relationship between humankind and nature: Was humankind dominant? Was nature dominant? Were nature and humankind supposed to be in harmony? Time was the third crucial concept: All societies placed a dominant value on the past, the present, or the future. Next, all societies could be divided by their emphasis on active or passive action. Finally, all societies could be described by their social organization: hierarchical, collective, or individualistic.

Marcel Mauss

Although this French anthropologist never did any fieldwork, he made significant contributions to the discipline. Mauss combined the functionalism of social anthropology with insights from psychology. Mauss focused on how individual actors in a cultural exchange each understood their unique roles in the act, emphasizing that individuals understood cultural contexts at the same time they maintained a distinctly individual viewpoint. Mauss also helped establish a method of research in which the focus is not on an entire culture, but a single act. This act is then explored exhaustively, connecting to other aspects of the culture and revealing the large social factors surrounding it. His study on gift giving in various cultures is a famous example of this approach.

Margaret Mead

Perhaps the best known of all anthropologists, Mead is notable less for her contributions to the field than for her public persona. Mead was an American anthropologist who studied oceanic communities. Mead specialized in sexual behaviors as well as formal and informal education systems. Influenced by Franz Boas, Mead used cultural relativism as a tool of social critique, going so far as to state what she believed to be the superiority of the some of the systems and ideals of so-called "primitive" cultures. In this, she can be thought to have set the stage for what came to be called critical anthropology, a politically oriented anthropology that makes goals like anti-colonialism and native sovereignty an explicit part of its project. Mead is also considered a predecessor of what is now called feminist anthropology. Feminist anthropologists would not only focus attention on gender roles in numerous societies, but would also question some of the biased assumptions they believed underpinned various anthropological theories and studies.

George Peter Murdock

Associated with positivist methods, Murdock originated the Cross-Cultural Survey. This massive project gathered quantitative data on thousands of different cultures and sorted them into an easy-to-access database. Through his project, he promoted the use of quantitative methods, despite the bias toward qualitative observation inherent in the ethnological approach.

Marshall Davis Sahlins

Sahlins, an American anthropologist who studied cultures in the south Pacific, produced a model of cultural evolution that proposes there are two distinct levels of evolution. The first level is called **general evolution** and it is universal to all cultures. General evolution describes the tendency of cultures to expand and grow more complex over time. The second level of evolution is called **specific evolution**. This describes all the different ways in which cultures react specifically to their environmental conditions, producing unique arrangements according to the culture's needs. Specific evolution can be driven by something unique in a culture's environment, or it can be driven by exchanges of ideas and technologies between cultures, a process called diffusion. Because every culture's specific evolution has been different, it will react in a unique way to the introduction of a new cultural quality. Therefore, diffusion not only alters the cultures involved, but it transforms the qualities being diffused.

A. R. Radcliffe-Brown

Radcliffe-Brown, an English anthropologist who studied communities in the Andaman Islands, Australia and Africa, was one of the founders of social anthropology. Influenced by theories of functionalism in sociology, Radcliffe-Brown shifted the emphasis of anthropology from the search for the primitive roots of Western culture to describing how the beliefs, practices, and social organizations of all cultures persisted because they ensured the survival of the culture and met the needs of the culture's members. For example, Radcliffe-Brown studied the practice of ancestor worship, where members of a society would ritualistically pay homage to the supposedly still living spirits of their ancestors. Radcliffe-Brown explained this not in terms of superstition, but in terms of social function. He claimed ancestor worship sustained the authority of the male head of the family and served to provide moral force to family responsibilities.

Edward Sapir

A German-American linguist and anthropologist, Sapir studied several of the languages of the Native American people. Sapir proposed the theory that language is the dominant means through which people experience the world. He believed a thorough description of a language would reveal the fundamental building blocks of a culture's perceptions of the world.

Leslie White

An American anthropologist who studied the native populations of the American southwest, White proposed a model of cultural evolution that held that the primary function of cultural processes was to control energy in order to perform work. Technology, meaning not just tools, but also the techniques for their use, was the driving force behind cultural evolution. White believed that differences in technology helped explain the socioeconomic advantages some cultures had over others. If technology was the material and cultural effort to solve problems and the successful use of technology demanded the efficient capture and use of energy, then societies that could best capture and use energy would be at an advantage in any conflict with less technologically efficient societies. White's ideas remain controversial; critics feel that they are ethnocentric and unjustly imply that some cultures are primitive or backward.

▶ Paleoanthropology

Paleoanthropology is a branch of anthropology that focuses on the origins and development of early human life and its nearest relatives. Because the chief objects of study passed away several million years ago, paleoanthropologists cannot rely on ethnological methods. Instead, paleoanthropologists study fossilized remains, using their knowledge of anatomy and the theory of evolution to piece together the story of mankind's physical development. Paleoanthropologists also study artifacts, material remnants of prehistoric life, to identify milestones in the development of humanity's intellectual powers.

Human Evolution

The field of paleoanthropology began in the nineteenth century. At that time, three different fossil specimens of Neanderthal were discovered at separate sites in Europe. These finds were given special importance by the publication of Charles Darwin's *On the Origin of Species.* That book, which set forth one of the first full arguments for the theory of evolution, avoided any discussion of human evolution. However, both advocates and critics found the implication obvious: If the theory of evolution was correct, modern humans must be the result of evolutionary processes and there must exist evidence of pre-human stages of existence. Neanderthal seemed to fit that description. Modern researchers debate the fate of Neanderthal. Some researchers believe that Neanderthal interbred with human ancestors, eventually being assimilated into the evolutionary line of humanity. Others, pointing to DNA evidence, suggest that Neanderthal never contributed to the human gene pool and simply died out.

In China, from 1903 to 1929, paleoanthropologists discovered fossil evidence of another possible human ancestor. The first clues to the existence of what would come to be called "Peking Man" came in the form of ancient, but recognizably human teeth that were being sold as ingredients for home remedies in a Chinese apothecary in Beijing. Over the next few decades, enough fossil remains were collected to firmly establish that a non-Neanderthal predecessor to modern humans existed in Asia.

For many years, the discovery of Peking Man caused most paleoanthropologists to believe that the human species originated in Asia. But, from the 1920s to now, a long series of important discoveries in Africa has forced paleoanthropologists to recognize Africa as the birthplace of the human race.

In 1924, the skull discovery of *Australopithecus africanus* was made in Taung, Botswana. This discovery, know as the Taung Child, was nicknamed "the southern ape of Africa" by anthropologist Raymond Dart. For a time, it was believed this species was the last common ancestor leading to the genus *Homo*, which contains all the various species of proto-humans and modern humanity. Recently, more weight is given to the idea that *Australopithecus* developed in another genus. If this is true, then it represents a branch of the family tree that contains modern humans, but is not a direct ancestor.

The bones of *Homo habilis* ("skilled man"), currently believed to be the first species in the genus *Homo*, the same genus as modern humans, were discovered between 1962 and 1964. *Homo ergaster* ("working man") and its descendant, the very humanlike *Homo erectus* ("upright man"), were identified as separate species in the 1970s and 1980s. Whether *Homo erectus* is the direct ancestor of modern man, or of *Homo sapiens* ("knowing man"), is still debated. Still, lacking definitive proof to the contrary, most paleoanthropologists seem to have agreed to treat *Homo erectus* as humanity's immediate predecessor.

For modern paleoanthropologists, modern humans are the products of several evolutionary trends that slowly affect the entire family of human and proto-human species. First, there is the development of bipedal motion. Unlike apes, which generally rely on all four limbs for motion, humans have come to rely solely on their feet. Second, the size of the brain cavity increased as the species approached the modern human form. This, anthropologists believe, allowed for the development of uniquely human mental capacities. Third, humans developed a weaker, but more precise grip through changes in hand muscle and bone structure. Fourth, humans developed a different set of teeth, with smaller canine teeth, optimized for omnivorous diets. Finally, the throat structure of humans changed to allow for a greater range of vocalizations. This allowed for the use of spoken languages.

There are two major theories of how exactly moderns became the globally dominant species of primate. The first is called the multiregional hypothesis. It proposes that modern humans evolved in a separate, but parallel, fashion from different ancestors in Africa, Europe, Asia, and Australia. Anthropologists who hold to the multiregional hypothesis also suggest that these different groups intermingled with other species of humans, producing the unique regional differences in modern humans. The more popular theory is known by several names, including the recent single-origin hypothesis, the out-of-Africa model, the replacement hypothesis, and the recent African origin hypothesis. Proponents of this theory claim that modern humans first appeared in southern Africa. They spread through Africa, and then Asia and Australia. Finally, nearly 10,000 years ago, humans crossed over into North and South America. Along the way, they replaced the other species in the *Homo* genus, through either direct or indirect conflict over space and resources.

Prior to 10,000, most humans lived in hunter-gatherer groups. These groups were small and nomadic. Between 10,000 and 12,000 years ago, humanity underwent what is now called the Neolithic Revolution. During this time, humans began to transition from a nomadic to a settled way of life. Agricultural techniques and the domestication of animals decreased reliance on hunting as a source of food. The abundance created by farming encouraged an economy based on trade with other human groups. This abundance also allowed human communities to support larger populations, leading to a boom in the human population.

► Practice Questions

1. Which of the following terms describes anthropological analysis that approaches a subject at a single and specific point in time, instead of taking a more historical view?

   a. ahistoric

   b. diachronic

   c. contextualized

   d. chronological

   e. synchronic

2. The theory that culture develop through the cross-cultural transmission of material and conceptual items is known as

   a. historical materialism.

   b. diffusionism.

   c. progressivism.

   d. social Darwinism.

   e. unilinealism.

3. Which of the following anthropologists is most associated with neoevolutionary theories of cultural development?

   a. Paul Radin

   b. Ruth Benedict

   c. Edward Sapir

   d. Julian Steward

   e. Margaret Mead

4. All of the following are consequences of the Neolithic Revolution EXCEPT

   a. invention of written language.

   b. manufacture of secondary products.

   c. elevated birth rates and larger social groups.

   d. development of the trade economy.

   e. increased immunity to some diseases.

5. Which of the following species of the genus *Homo* is usually credited with being the first to use tools?

   a. *Homo georgicus*

   b. *Homo ergaster*

   c. *Homo habilis*

   d. *Homo erectus*

   e. *Homo sapiens*

6. Which of the following describes the theory that the environment may set limits on certain forms of cultural development, but does not completely determine the final shape a culture may take?

   a. ethnocentrism

   b. possibilism

   c. Darwinism

   d. determinism

   e. cultural materialism

7. "Courtesy, modesty, good manners, conformity to definite ethical standards are universal, but what constitutes courtesy, modesty, very good manners, and definite ethical standards is not universal. It is instructive to know that standards differ in the most unexpected ways." Which of the following concepts does this quotation exemplify?

   a. ethnographic realism

   b. postcolonialism

   c. positivism

   d. cultural relativism

   e. ethnocentrism

8. Which of the following anthropologists argued that cultural development depended entirely on the ability to store and efficiently use energy?

a. Franz Boas
b. Ruth Benedict
c. Leslie White
d. Margaret Mead
e. George Dalton

9. Which of the following terms describes an informal economic system of unrestricted sharing or giving done without expectation of receiving any good or service in return?

a. general reciprocity
b. moral reciprocity
c. symmetrical reciprocity
d. negative reciprocity
e. balanced reciprocity

10. "The aim is to draw large conclusions from small, but very densely textured facts; to support broad interpretations about the role of culture in the construction of collective life by engaging them exactly with complex specifics." Which of the following ethnographic techniques does this quotation describe?

a. extended subject interviews
b. observer participation
c. quantitative survey
d. thick description
e. longitudinal study

▶ **Answers**

1. e
2. b
3. d
4. a
5. c
6. b
7. d
8. c
9. a
10. d

15▶ Psychology

Psychology is the study of the mental processes of human beings. It can refer both to the general study of psychological principles in an experimental setting and to the practice of treating patients suffering from psychological disorders.

In general, psychologists can be loosely divided into four large schools. Each school contains researchers (who advance new concepts and test them in an experimental setting) and practitioners (who treat patients). From here, the disciplines are further divided into a large number of separate specializations. Despite a pattern of ever-increasing specialization, it is possible to get a broad overview of the field. This chapter will cover the four main schools of psychology, including some of the notable psychologists and important concepts associated with each school. Then the chapter will cover some of the crucial concepts in the field. Finally, the methods used by psychological researchers will be covered.

▶ The Four Schools of Psychology

There are four chief schools of modern psychology, which can be arranged in the following rough chronological order: **scientific psychology**, **behaviorism**, **humanistic psychology**, and **cognitive psychology**. This order is helpful, but it should be kept in mind that the schools overlap one another and that the insights of one school are often adopted and adapted by psychologists in other schools.

Scientific Psychology

The dominant period of scientific psychology starts in 1879 and lasts roughly until the 1920s. Prior to this period, the study of the mental life of humans was a philosophical or religious endeavor. The scientific psychologists broke with this tradition and tried to replace philosophical speculation with systems of experiments and recorded observations.

In 1879, the first psychology department was founded at Leipzig University in Germany. By 1890, enough progress had been made that American psychologist William James could produce the field's first major textbook, *The Principles of Psychology*.

In Russia, an experimental psychologist named Ivan Pavlov conducted a series of important animal experiments to study how learning happens. The model he developed to explain the learning process is known as **classical conditioning**.

The last important development of the classical period was the explosive rise of Freudian psychoanalysis. Sigmund Freud was an Austrian psychologist who developed a theoretical system of human development, explanations for numerous mental conditions, and a method of treatment called **psychoanalysis**. Freud's ideas were incredibly popular in his time, gaining him and psychoanalysis global recognition. Though research psychologists would criticize Freud for what they perceived as the unscientific basis of his theories, his ideas and methods would dominate the clinical practice of psychology from the turn of the century until the 1960s.

Key Figures

Sigmund Freud: The creator of psychoanalysis, Freud made a strong argument for the existence of an unconscious mind. Operating without conscious control and submerged beneath the threshold of self-examination, the unconscious mind is a repository for ideas too dangerous or painful to be left open to scrutiny in the conscious mind. The process of burying feelings, ideas, and memories in the unconscious is called repression. Repressed ideas and feelings continue to affect the conscious mind, though in obscure and indirect ways. When the conscious mind becomes overwhelmed by these influences, the result is a mental condition. Later, Freud suggested a more complex system of mental elements. Instead of the conscious and unconscious mind, Freud claimed humans possessed an ego, superego, and id. The ego is a sense of self. The superego is an internal censor that represses ideas to protect the ego. The id is the opposite of the superego, an unconscious drive for unregulated pleasure. Freud's numerous theories were all extensions of this basic architecture.

William James: A noted author and philosopher, William James attempted to establish a uniform methodology for the study of psychology. James tried to establish four key methods of research. The first method, **analysis**, involved critically studying past and current work in the field. The next method James called **introspection**. James felt psychologists should study their own minds for insights into mental phenomenon. **Scientific experimentation** was James's third method. Finally, he proposed statistical studies, a process he called **comparison** that could help psychologists. Only the method of introspection is no longer used by modern psychologists.

Ivan Pavlov: Through extensive experimentation with dogs, Pavlov created an intricate theoretical system explaining how ideas are learned on a conscious and unconscious level. By training dogs to associate certain stimuli, such as the tone of a bell with being fed, Pavlov could then identify what associations and reactions dogs would make under different conditions. Through repetition, Pavlov learned that some associations could be made strong enough to evoke counterintuitive reactions. For example, ring a bell every time a dog is fed and eventually the dog will salivate at the sound of the bell, even if no food is provided. Pavlov also investigated the effects of positive and negative reinforcement, or rewards and punishments, on the process of association. His system is known as **classical conditioning**.

Wilhelm Wundt: Wundt established the identity of scientific psychology by creating the first laboratory for psychological research. He stressed the impact of the physical aspects of the human brain on thought and sensation. He theorized that consciousness was made up of separate distinct elements. This view of human consciousness was later dubbed structuralism. Wundt also pioneered the field of social and cultural psychology, using psychological methods to attempt to understand broad social and cultural phenomenon.

Behaviorism

Many psychologists reacted negatively to what they felt were unscientific assumptions underlying psychoanalysis. Their attempt to get psychology on a more firmly scientific footing created the second major school, **behaviorism**.

Behaviorism was so named because the psychologists who belonged to the movement decided that only observable changes and actions could properly be studied. This restricted what could be researched to external behaviors. Concepts like Freud's id were dismissed as philosophical abstractions. The dismissal of

any sort of inner life created an assumption that behavior was also the product of external forces. In the famed debate of nature versus nurture, behaviorists were almost entirely on the side of nurture.

Behaviorism was dogged by controversies. The popular application of behaviorist ideas made behaviorists public figures and their provocative statements occasionally overshadowed their work. Pioneer behaviorist B.F. Skinner, for example, dismissed concepts like freedom and dignity as unscientific. Aside from provocative public statements, behaviorists' experiments were sometimes controversial. Noted behaviorist John Watson conducted an experiment to create a phobia of rats in an orphan infant known only as "Albert B." By today's standards, his experiment would be considered unethical.

Despite such controversies, behaviorism became the dominant approach to the field in the early twentieth century. This was especially true in America, where its empirical rigor and schematic approach to behavior modification was appreciated by progressive educators, marketing and public relations professionals, and academics in other fields.

Behaviorism ultimately became a victim of its own success. In the search for greater scientific precision, psychologists applied advanced technology to the study of human behavior. This greatly expanded what was now considered observable. Psychologists also used increasingly sophisticated statistical methods to their research. The wealth of new data these advances produced overturned the assumption that external forces were the chief influence on the psychology of an individual. The concerns of behaviorism, if not all the basic assumptions, became the concerns of the cognitive psychologists.

Key Figures

Clark L. Hull: One of Hull's major contributions to behaviorism was to integrate it with evolutionary theory. For Hull, behaviors developed in response to the environment. Behaviors that helped subjects adapt to their environments would persist. Hull theorized that subjects actively experiment on their environments and their psychology "evolves" as their experiments succeed and fail. Hull also extensively studied hypnosis.

B. F. Skinner: An influential researcher, Skinner innovated research technologies and observational methods that helped behaviorists quantify human responses to experimental stimulus. Skinner expanded the conditioning model advanced by Pavlov, adding a more nuanced understanding of the use of rewards to the model. Skinner also produced a body of research on the importance of conditioning in the acquisition of spoken language. Skinner was, for many years, the public face of behaviorism.

Edward Tolman: Using test animals to explore conditioning, Tolman invented the concept of the cognitive map: a purely mental model or belief system subjects use to interpret complex situations.

John Watson: Watson was another behaviorist who began with Pavlov's work and added detail to the model of conditioning. Watson rejected the importance of reinforcement and instead explored the role association played in developing behavior. Watson focused specifically on child development and the link between thought and speech. In 1920, Watson conducted a controversial experiment in creating fear response in an infant. This experiment is known as the Little Albert experiment.

Humanistic Psychology

Just as behaviorism was a reaction to the more philosophical aspects of psychoanalysis, a movement of psychologists reacted to what they felt was the reductive thinking of behaviorism. Less a coherent movement than several contemporary movements with some general similarities, the **existential humanists** reemphasized the role of nonobservable, purely mental processes. They also rebelled against some of the basic premises of behaviorism. They rejected the notion that all mental processes could be broken down in smaller independent actions and behaviors. They stressed that all human activity takes place in a complex living context of desires, responsibilities, and negotiations with others. Furthermore, they stressed that humans innately possess self-awareness, creativity, and a drive to find meaning in the world around them.

Another major distinction between humanistic psychologists and their behaviorist predecessors was the emphasis humanistic psychologists placed on the medical practice of psychology. Like some of the earliest scientific psychologists, many humanistic psychologists developed their theories from the observation and treatment of patients. When doing experimental research, a humanistic psychologist was likely to focus on qualitative aspects of the phenomenon being studied rather than quantitative aspects.

Given its emphasis on psychotherapy, it is perhaps unsurprising that the greatest achievements in humanistic psychology came in the form of innovative approaches to treatment. Often these approaches were called holistic treatments, as they were intended to take into account all the needs of a patient and the patient's context in the world. Gestalt therapy was prominent holistic treatment. The creation of two German psychologists and one American philosopher, Gestalt theory pulled together elements of psychology, philosophy, Eastern religions, and artistic practices in an effort to create a flexible and all-inclusive approach to therapy. Rather than advancing a particular theory of mental life, Gestalt therapy was a set of practices meant to encourage self-awareness in the patient. Once the patient was aware of unhelpful psychological symptoms, the patient could better avoid negative behaviors and spur positive mental growth.

From its start in the 1950s, humanistic psychology became the dominant school through the 1960s and 1970s. Eventually, **cognitive psychology**, which reemphasized empirical research and the scientific method, replaced it as the dominant model.

Key Figures

Gordon Allport: Allport is considered the first psychologist to focus his studies on personality. Allport theorized that all personalities are made up of a collection of traits. These traits are organized into three categories. Secondary traits are traits that appear only in certain contexts or situations. Central traits are the constant elements of personality and they are found in all humans. Cardinal traits are rare traits that act as powerful organizers of an entire personality.

R. D. Laing: A controversial figure, Laing believed that much of what was labeled mental illness was simply an attempt to communicate needs and concerns that, because of context, were misunderstood or incorrectly treated as pathology. Laing worked to develop approaches to therapy that he thought would be less invasive and confrontational.

Abraham Maslow: The **hierarchy of needs**, Maslow's most lasting contribution to psychology, states the humans have several needs. These needs can be organized into five categories. At the bottom of the hierarchy are basic needs. In the most basic category, one finds physical needs, such as the need for food. The next step up the hierarchy includes those things that keep the physical needs met. These so-called safety needs include employment, good health, and physical security. Next are the interpersonal needs. Friendship, family affection, and sexual intimacy are found there. The fourth rank includes self-esteem and respect in the community. Finally, at the top, one finds the higher abstractions, such as the exercise of morality and creativity.

Maslow's ranking served as a therapeutic blueprint and as counter-model to the more mechanistic models of the human psyche advanced by the behaviorists.

Carl Rogers: Rogers developed the client-centered approach to therapy. In client-centered therapy, the therapist attempts to develop a personal relationship with the client in the hopes that, through this relationship, the therapist can convince the client to solve his or her own problems. This approach is still being used today.

Cognitive Psychology

The biggest single innovation in cognitive psychology was the computer. Computers made it easier for psychologists to use more complicated statistical methods. Computer programmers, finding parallels between the creation of software and the creation of mental faculties, introduced new ideas to the field. Computer-driven imaging technologies allowed psychologists to observe the functioning of the brain at the cellular level. Finally, powerful computers allowed scientists to sequence and study human DNA, unlocking new information about what is and is not innate to our biological being.

Advances in medicine and chemistry also played huge roles in revolutionizing the field. Cognitive psychologists, working with chemists and biologists, revealed the biological and chemical processes that allow the human brain to work. This has created vast new fields of study and powerful, if controversial, applications in therapy.

Like the humanistic psychologists, it is best to think of cognitive psychology less as a movement and more as a collection of research methods and some general common assumptions. As a general rule, cognitive psychologists find that psychology must advance through the scientific method and the use of quantitative data. In this, they differ radically from the humanistic psychologists. However, cognitive psychologists differ from behaviorists in that they believe many, maybe even most, of our mental faculties are innate properties and not the product of external influences. This latter assumption has led to the greatest triumph and most controversial aspect of the primacy of cognitive psychology: the dominance of pharmaceutical treatment.

The discovery of the role various biological and chemical processes played in the role of human psychology led to the development of pharmaceutical treatments for many mental disorders. Though such treatments have been around for as long as psychology has, the late twentieth century witnessed a boom in the number of ailments treated with drugs and an increase in the number of patients currently taking such treatments. Though the positive impact on patients is well documented, detractors say that the scope of these treatments is disturbing and they suggest that such treatments merely suppress symptoms rather than cure patients.

Key Figures

John Robert Anderson: Anderson is best known for his Adaptive Control of Thought—Rational (ACT-R) theory. ACT-R is a cognitive architecture, a computer program that simulates human thought processes. The architecture describes the most basic elements of the thought process. Notably, ACT-R divides all human knowledge into two categories: declarative and procedural. Declarative thoughts are data stored as memories. Procedural thoughts are unconscious skills. ACT-R is one of many such models created by cognitive psychologists.

Elizabeth Loftus: Loftus has studied how memories change over time. Loftus's work has shown that new ideas, changes in environment, and suggestions by others can alter the content of remembered information, sometimes without the subject being aware of any change. She is a controversial figure for her work on suppressed memories and the creation of false memories.

Steven Pinker: Pinker is one of the chief proponents of evolutionary psychology: the research into how evolutionary processes shaped the psychology of humans. Pinker has specialized in the study of the innate capacity to learn and use language and in the biological processes of visual perception.

▶ Important Psychological Concepts

Abnormal psychology: the study of behaviors that are rare in the general population, harmful to the subject, unacceptable in the subject's social context, and irrational. Such behaviors are known as **psychopathologies**.

Attachment: the emotional link between an infant and its main caregiver.

Attribution: the action of assigning a cause to a behavior.

Big Five theory: a currently popular theory of the personality that posits five major factors to a subjects' personality: openness, conscientiousness, extraversion, agreeableness, and neuroticism. These factors can be identified by the acronym OCEAN.

Cognitive dissonance: a contradiction between thoughts and behaviors.

Defense mechanisms: psychological processes used to protect the ego from the conflict between the id and superego.

Difference (or absolute) threshold: the minimum amount of change in a condition that can be registered by a subject.

Dual-code theory: a theory that holds visual and auditory data are processed in two distinctly different ways.

Encoding: the process of turning data into a memory.

Figure-ground: the distinction made between an object being viewed and the surrounding visual data.

Heuristics: mental "rules of thumb" that subjects develop to help make sense of the world around them.

Language acquisition device: a theoretical mental architecture that is the source of humans' inherent ability to learn a language.

Locus of control: a description of where a subject believes the dominant force of control of his or her life resides. Subjects with an internal locus believe they control their lives. A subject with an external locus believes outside forces are dominant.

Motivational bias: a tendency to ascribe specific attributions to actions.

Neurotransmitters: a chemical action that allows nerve signals to travel over a synapse.

Perceptual set: a plan of assumptions that helps subjects interpret stimuli.

Plasticity: the capacity of the human brain to adapt its shape over time as a healing process.

Reinforcement schedule: in conditioning, the set of rules that determine when positive and negative reinforcement is applied.

Reflex: actions that require no cognitive process.

Social psychology: the study of the influence of other humans on the development and working of mental processes. The study of interpersonal attraction, the effects of persuasion, and the creation of stereotypes are common areas of study for social psychologists.

Social-cognitive theory: a theory that claims the personality is influenced by internal (ideas and beliefs) and external (the observation of others) behavior.

Socialization: the term for the process of learning about a social group and finding one's role within it. Psychologists emphasize the role of external agents in the process of socialization, especially the family, schools, and peer groups. Other institutions (such as churches) and the mass media may also play a role in socialization.

Synapse: the gap within neurons where nerve signals travel.

Talk therapy: any psychological treatment that relies mainly on regular communication between patient and therapist.

Working memory: a process in which the subject simultaneously processes short- and long-term memories.

▶ Psychological Methods

What distinguishes psychology from more philosophical and religious efforts to study human nature is its reliance on agreed upon scientific methods. To help them between understand the human mind, psychologists have developed many different research techniques. This section will cover some of the most common.

Animal studies: Animal subjects have been essential in studying the learning process, memory, and behavior development. Animals, because they can be better controlled, are useful for experiments where limiting the variables on a human subject would be difficult or impossible.

Computer modeling: Many cognitive psychologists find it helpful to simulate mental behaviors through the use of complex computer programs. Computer modeling allows the psychologist total control over the variables involved in an experiment. However, even with modern computers, the number of variables must remain relatively small.

Controlled human experiments: In laboratory conditions, psychologists can apply scientific methods to human research subjects. By using human subjects, the research can avoid having to generalize human behaviors from observed behaviors in other animals. However, the use of human subjects introduces a host of ethical concerns. Most modern researchers comply with an ethical code known as the Declaration of Helsinki. Among other things, this declaration requires subjects be able to give informed consent, allows for subjects to quit an experiment at any time in the process, and requires researchers to always put the welfare of the subject before the consequences of the experiment.

Naturalistic observation: Psychologists may make qualitative and quantitative observations of a subject in an uncontrolled real-world environment.

Neurological observation: Modern technologies, such as MRI scanners, make it possible for scientists to study brain activity on a scale that was impossible before. Using these new technologies, scientists may study the otherwise invisible brain activity of human subjects. A common strategy is to study subjects with known mental impairments to see if their brain activity reveals some distinctly unusual pattern.

Statistical surveys: Using a scientifically determined sample set (a group that represents the broader demographic being studied), psychologists may use interviews, questionnaires, online surveys, or other information gathering devices. This is the easiest way to get a broad sample, but the researcher loses some control over the quality of the data the subjects choose to report.

▶ Practice Questions

1. In classical conditioning, which of the following describes a consequence of action that increases the frequency of the action?
   a. generalizer
   b. negative reinforcement
   c. promoter
   d. positive reinforcement
   e. punishment

2. Which of the following is an example of an implicit or procedural memory?
   a. remembering the name of your fifth-grade teacher
   b. answering a question in a trivia contest
   c. following a set of directions to a friend's house
   d. leaving your signature on a piece of paper
   e. recalling the names of characters from a movie

3. According to Howard Gardner, all of these are types of intelligence EXCEPT
   a. musical intelligence.
   b. linguistic intelligence.
   c. spatial intelligence.
   d. kinesthetic intelligence.
   e. chronologic intelligence.

4. In Piaget's preoperational stage of child development, which of the following describes a developing child's inability to understand the perspectives of other people?
   a. centration
   b. transductive reasoning
   c. egocentrism
   d. seriation difficulties
   e. irreversibility

5. Cognitive scientists have linked the varying experience of and reaction to stress to the operation of which organ?
   a. the midbrain
   b. the amygdala
   c. the hippocampus
   d. the fungilform papillae
   e. the hypothalamus

6. Which of the following persuasion techniques is an example of the *foot-in-the-door technique*?
   a. A child promises to behave in exchange for a toy. The child further promises to do more chores.
   b. A repairman asks for an unreasonable amount of money to fix a car. When this is rejected, he lowers the price.
   c. A company uses the names and likeness of well-known sports stars to promote a new energy drink.
   d. A friend asks for a ride. When the ride is given, the friend then asks if his four friends can have a ride as well.
   e. A saleswoman, while convincing a customer to buy a video game, states that the copy the customer wants is last one in the shop.

7. All of the following are Freudian defense mechanisms EXCEPT
   a. confirmation.
   b. rationalization.
   c. displacement.
   d. sublimation.
   e. undoing.

8. Which of the following is an example of a biomedical treatment for a mental disorder?
   a. Gestalt therapy
   b. pharmacotherapy
   c. psychoanalysis
   d. person-centered therapy
   e. rational-emotive therapy

9. Which of the following is characteristic of humanistic psychological approaches?

a. the reduction of all human activity to external behaviors

b. a reliance on pharmaceutical treatments for most minor mental disturbances

c. holistic models of personality that include internal and external influences

d. a preference for quantitative research methods over qualitative observations

e. extensive use of animal studies as a research method

10. Which of the following is most likely to be prescribed to an epileptic patient?

a. an antipsychotic

b. a mood stabilizer

c. a stimulant

d. an antidepressant

e. an anticonvulsant

▶ **Answers**

1. a
2. d
3. e
4. c
5. b
6. d
7. a
8. b
9. c
10. e

SECTION

3 ▶ About the CLEP College Mathematics Exam

The College Mathematics exam assesses your understanding of the basic principles and concepts of mathematics. The examination does not cover material requiring advanced mathematical knowledge. The examination does include material taught in a college course for non-math majors. At least 50% of the examination focuses on straightforward problems, while the remainder of the test requires an understanding of mathematical concepts and an ability to apply those concepts.

The test questions include material on logic, sets, equations, functions and their graphs, probability, statistics, and data analysis. Complex numbers, logarithms and exponents, and applications from algebra and geometry are covered, but to a lesser degree. Candidates should be familiar with key terms, symbols, notation, and vocabulary.

The examination is 90 minutes long and includes 60 questions. Pretest questions are inserted into the examination, but they are not scored. Time spent on tutorials or in inserting personal/registration information is not counted against the 90 minutes allotted for the exam.

The College Mathematics examination requires very little arithmetic calculation. You are not required to use a calculator to answer the questions, although an online calculator is available through the examination software.

The following is an overview of the material on this exam. While this overview is extensive, it is wise to review the concepts and problems you know and then set aside time to practice working with those areas that you need to strengthen.

The College Mathematics examination includes questions on the following topics:

- **Sets** (10%): This includes union and intersection, subsets, Venn diagrams, and Cartesian product.
- **Logic** (10%): This section includes truth tables, conjunctions, disjunctions, implication, and negations. Also included in this section are necessary and sufficient conditions; converse, inverse, and contrapositive; and hypotheses, conclusions, and counterexamples.
- **Real Number Systems** (20%): This portion of the examination includes prime and composite numbers, odd and even numbers, factors and divisibility, rational and irrational numbers, absolute value and order, and open and closed intervals.
- **Functions and Their Graphs** (20%): This section includes concepts such as properties and graphs of functions, domain and range, and composition of functions and inverse functions.

- **Probability and Statistics** (25%): The following concepts may appear in this section: counting problems, including permutations and combinations; computation of probabilities of simple and compound events; simple conditional probability; mean, median, mode, and range; and standard deviation.
- **Additional Topics from Algebra and Geometry** (15%): This section may include questions on complex numbers; logarithms and exponents; applications from algebra and geometry; perimeter and area of plane figures; properties of triangles, circles, and rectangles; the Pythagorean theorem; parallel and perpendicular lines; and algebraic equations and inequalities.

CLEP College Mathematics Pretest

Before reviewing topics that will be covered on the CLEP College Mathematics exam, test your existing skills by taking the pretest that follows. You will encounter 60 questions that are similar to the type you will find on the CLEP College Mathematics exam. The questions cover six content areas:

- the real number system
- sets
- logic
- functions and their graphs
- probability and statistics
- algebra and geometry

For now, ignore the time restraints of the official CLEP; take as much time as you need to complete each question.

Answer every question; however, if you are not sure of an answer, put a question mark by the question number to note that you are making a guess. On the official CLEP, you are not penalized for unanswered or incorrect answers, so making a good guess is an important skill to practice.

When you are finished, check the answer key on page 218 carefully to assess your results. Your pretest score will help you determine how much preparation you need and in which areas you need the most careful review and practice.

▶ CLEP College Mathematics Pretest

1.	ⓐ ⓑ ⓒ ⓓ				21.	ⓐ ⓑ ⓒ ⓓ				41.	ⓐ ⓑ ⓒ ⓓ		
2.	ⓐ ⓑ ⓒ ⓓ				22.	ⓐ ⓑ ⓒ ⓓ				42.	ⓐ ⓑ ⓒ ⓓ		
3.	ⓐ ⓑ ⓒ ⓓ				23.	ⓐ ⓑ ⓒ ⓓ				43.	ⓐ ⓑ ⓒ ⓓ		
4.	ⓐ ⓑ ⓒ ⓓ				24.	ⓐ ⓑ ⓒ ⓓ				44.	ⓐ ⓑ ⓒ ⓓ		
5.	ⓐ ⓑ ⓒ ⓓ				25.	ⓐ ⓑ ⓒ ⓓ				45.	ⓐ ⓑ ⓒ ⓓ		
6.	ⓐ ⓑ ⓒ ⓓ				26.	ⓐ ⓑ ⓒ ⓓ				46.	ⓐ ⓑ ⓒ ⓓ		
7.	ⓐ ⓑ ⓒ ⓓ				27.	ⓐ ⓑ ⓒ ⓓ				47.	ⓐ ⓑ ⓒ ⓓ		
8.	ⓐ ⓑ ⓒ ⓓ				28.	ⓐ ⓑ ⓒ ⓓ				48.	ⓐ ⓑ ⓒ ⓓ		
9.	ⓐ ⓑ ⓒ ⓓ				29.	ⓐ ⓑ ⓒ ⓓ				49.	ⓐ ⓑ ⓒ ⓓ		
10.	ⓐ ⓑ ⓒ ⓓ				30.	ⓐ ⓑ ⓒ ⓓ				50.	ⓐ ⓑ ⓒ ⓓ		
11.	ⓐ ⓑ ⓒ ⓓ				31.	ⓐ ⓑ ⓒ ⓓ				51.	ⓐ ⓑ ⓒ ⓓ		
12.	ⓐ ⓑ ⓒ ⓓ				32.	ⓐ ⓑ ⓒ ⓓ				52.	ⓐ ⓑ ⓒ ⓓ		
13.	ⓐ ⓑ ⓒ ⓓ				33.	ⓐ ⓑ ⓒ ⓓ				53.	ⓐ ⓑ ⓒ ⓓ		
14.	ⓐ ⓑ ⓒ ⓓ				34.	ⓐ ⓑ ⓒ ⓓ				54.	ⓐ ⓑ ⓒ ⓓ		
15.	ⓐ ⓑ ⓒ ⓓ				35.	ⓐ ⓑ ⓒ ⓓ				55.	ⓐ ⓑ ⓒ ⓓ		
16.	ⓐ ⓑ ⓒ ⓓ				36.	ⓐ ⓑ ⓒ ⓓ				56.	ⓐ ⓑ ⓒ ⓓ		
17.	ⓐ ⓑ ⓒ ⓓ				37.	ⓐ ⓑ ⓒ ⓓ				57.	ⓐ ⓑ ⓒ ⓓ		
18.	ⓐ ⓑ ⓒ ⓓ				38.	ⓐ ⓑ ⓒ ⓓ				58.	ⓐ ⓑ ⓒ ⓓ		
19.	ⓐ ⓑ ⓒ ⓓ				39.	ⓐ ⓑ ⓒ ⓓ				59.	ⓐ ⓑ ⓒ ⓓ		
20.	ⓐ ⓑ ⓒ ⓓ				40.	ⓐ ⓑ ⓒ ⓓ				60.	ⓐ ⓑ ⓒ ⓓ		

▶ Pretest Questions

1. Given $g(x) = \frac{x}{4} - 2$, find $g^{-1}(x)$.
 a. $g^{-1}(x) = 4x + 8$
 b. $g^{-1}(x) = 2 - \frac{x^2}{4}$
 c. $g^{-1}(x) = 8x - 8$
 d. $g^{-1}(x) = \frac{x}{4} + \frac{1}{2}$

2. Both p and q are prime numbers. Which of the following is the largest number by which both p^5q^7 and p^3q^8 will be divisible?
 a. pq
 b. p^3q^8
 c. p^3q^7
 d. p^5q^7

3. "I am not warm" is the negation for
 a. I am warm.
 b. I am cold.
 c. you are warm.
 d. you are cold.

4. $\log_7(\frac{b}{49})$ is equivalent to
 a. $\log_7(b) + 2$.
 b. $\log_7(b) - 2$.
 c. $49\log_7(b)$.
 d. $\log_7(b) - \log_7(2)$.

5. How many different ways can the letters T, R, E, and K be arranged?
 a. 8
 b. 12
 c. 20
 d. 24

6. Three consecutive even numbers add to 66. What is the value of the smallest number of the three?
 a. 20
 b. 21
 c. 23
 d. 25

7. Given $g(x) = x^3$ and $f(x) = x^2 + 5$, find $(f \circ g)$.
 a. $x^5 + 5$
 b. $x^6 + 5$
 c. $(x^2 + 5)^5$
 d. $x^3 + x^2 + 5$

8. During a soccer game, only three players on the Phantoms scored. Knowing which variable would enable the completion of the entire chart?

	# GOALS 1ST HALF	# GOALS 2ND HALF	TOTAL # GOALS
Sam	a	b	3
Lisa	c	0	d
Jem	e	f	5
Total # Goals	g	4	h

 a. c
 b. d
 c. e
 d. h

9. Use the remainder theorem to evaluate $f(x) = 2x^4 + x^2 + 2x + 3$ at $x = -3$.
 a. 0
 b. 54
 c. 168
 d. 180

10. Given that the mean of i, j, k, and l is 8 and the mean of i and j is 4, what is the mean of k and l?

   a. 4

   b. 8

   c. 10

   d. 12

11. The graph of $y = f(x)$ is shown here. Which of the following could be the graph of $y = 2f(x)$?

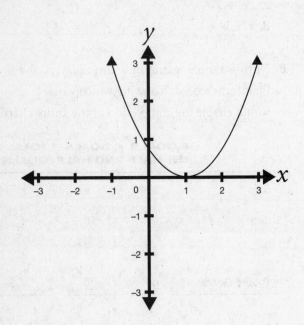

a.

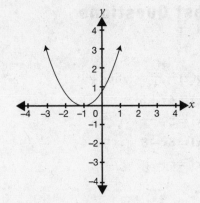

b.

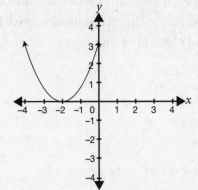

c.

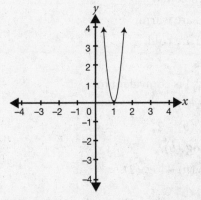

d.

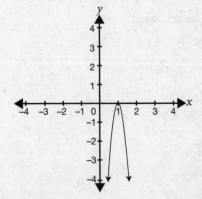

12. Given $\frac{c}{d} = e$ and e is a composite number, which of the following must be true?

   a. c must be a prime number.

   b. c must be a composite number.

   c. d must be a prime number.

   d. d must be a composite number.

13. Which of the follow statements best describes the normal distribution of data?

   a. There are at least two outliers.

   b. Individual values are, overall, close to the average.

   c. The standard deviation would be equal to zero.

   d. The standard deviation would be negative.

14. Given A = {l, m, n, o, p}, B = {m, o, q}, C = {q, r, s, t}, and D = {n, q, t}, which of the two sets are disjoint?

   a. A and B

   b. B and D

   c. C and D

   d. A and C

15. The function $f(x)$ is a linear function. $f(1) = 5$ and $f(3) = 13$, so $f(10) =$

   a. 14

   b. 20

   c. 41

   d. 53

16. What was the range of temperatures for the week? Refer to the chart:

DAY	MON	TUE	WED	THURS	FRI	SAT	SUN
Temperature (in degrees F)	61	64	62	64	67	66	68

   a. 3 degrees

   b. 4 degrees

   c. 7 degrees

   d. 9 degrees

17. The graph shown here may be the graph for which of the following inequalities?

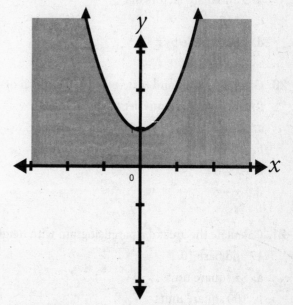

   a. $y \le \left(\frac{1}{2}x\right)^2$

   b. $y \le \left(\frac{1}{2}x\right)^2 + 2$

   c. $y < \left(\frac{1}{2}x\right)^2$

   d. $y < \left(\frac{1}{2}x\right)^2 + 2$

18. If the truth value of $p \wedge q$ is true, which of the following statements are true?

I. $p \wedge \sim q$

II. $q \wedge p$

III. $\sim p \wedge \sim q$

a. I only

b. II only

c. II and III only

d. I, II, and III

19. If q is divisible by 15 and $q \times 2 = r$, which of the following statements must be true?

a. 2 and 3 are factors of q

b. 3 and 5 are factors of r

c. $\frac{r}{2} = 15$

d. r is divisible by $\frac{q}{2}$

20. Given $f(x) = -x$ and $(g \circ f)x = -6 - x$, which of the following is equivalent to $g(x)$?

a. $x - 6$

b. $x + 6$

c. $-x - 6$

d. $-x + 6$

21. Calculate the area of a parallelogram with height 17 and base 10.

a. 85 square units

b. 100 square units

c. 170 square units

d. 289 square units

22. Which of the following is the complex conjugate of $5 - 3i$?

a. $-5 - 3i$

b. $-5 + 3i$

c. $5 - 3i$

d. $5 + 3i$

23. Considering "If I am a mother, then I am a female," which of the following is also true?

a. Being a mother is necessary for my being female.

b. My being a female is sufficient to state that I am a mother.

c. Being a mother is sufficient for stating that I am a female.

d. Being a female is necessary for my not being a mother.

24. What is the prime factorization of 84?

a. 21×4

b. $1 \times 2 \times 2 \times 3 \times 7$

c. $2 \times 2 \times 3 \times 7$

d. $4 \times 3 \times 7$

25. Given $g(x) = 2x^2 - 6$ and $h(x) = x^2 + 6$, find $(g - h)x$.

a. x^2

b. $x^2 - 12$

c. $4x^4 - 24x^2 + 42$

d. $x^4 + 12x^2 + 30$

26. How many different combinations can be made if three signs are to be chosen out of six possible signs?

a. 18

b. 20

c. 120

d. 720

27. Which of the following is an example of a rational number?

a. $\frac{\sqrt{2}}{1}$

b. $\sqrt{3}$

c. $\sqrt{5}$

d. $\frac{3}{1}$

28. In the Music Club, 45 students are in band, and 30 students are in chorus. Fifteen of these students are in both band and chorus. One student will be chosen at random to win a prize. What is the probability that the student chosen will be a student who participates only in chorus?

a. $\frac{1}{4}$

b. $\frac{1}{6}$

c. $\frac{3}{4}$

d. none of the above

29. If $\cup = \{2, 4, 6, 8, 10, 12\}$, $A' = \{6, 8, 10\}$, and $B = \{2, 4, 12\}$, which of the following statements is true?

I. B is a subset of A

II. A and B are equivalent sets

III. A is a proper subset of B

a. I and II only

b. I only

c. III only

d. I and III only

30. The graph of function $f(x)$ is shown here. What is the range of $f(x)$?

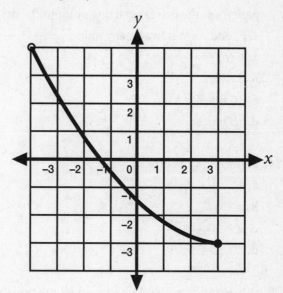

a. $-3 \le y \le 4$

b. $-3 \le y < 4$

c. $-3 < y \le 4$

d. $-3 \le y < 3$

31. On a test for a class with 30 students, the mean score was 65.3 points. The teacher rescored the test by adding 7 points to each test. What is the new mean?

a. 72.3

b. 73.2

c. 75.5

d. 74.2

32. Given $p \rightarrow q$, which of the following is the contrapositive?

a. $p \leftrightarrow q$

b. $\sim p \rightarrow \sim q$

c. $q \rightarrow p$

d. $\sim q \rightarrow \sim p$

33. A driver goes west for 2 miles, then north for 6 miles, then east for 10 miles. The straight-line path from the driver's starting point to the driver's endpoint is how many miles?

    a. 6 miles

    b. 8 miles

    c. 10 miles

    d. 18 miles

34. Reduce $\frac{(z^4)^7}{z^4 \times z^7}$.

    a. 1

    b. z^{39}

    c. z^{-31}

    d. z^{17}

35. $\frac{P}{Q} = R$ and $\frac{S}{P} = T$. If P, Q, R, S, and T are positive integers, which of the following statements must be true?

    a. S is divisible by R

    b. Q is divisible by S

    c. P is a factor of R

    d. Q is a factor of R

36. There are two zeros for which of the following functions?

    a. $f(x) = -|x| - 4.5$

    b. $f(x) = -|x| + 4.5$

    c. $f(x) = |x - 4.5|$

    d. $f(x) = -|x - 4.5|$

37. There is a 40% chance that it will rain on Monday. There is also a 70% chance that Kayla will get her braces off on Monday. What is the probably that Monday will be rainy and Kayla will NOT get her braces off?

    a. 12%

    b. 15%

    c. 28%

    d. 70%

38. Using the pie chart, if 15 people prefer apple pie, how many prefer cherry?

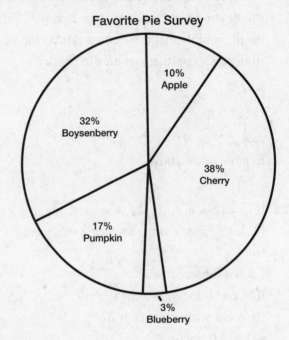

Favorite Pie Survey

10% Apple

32% Boysenberry

38% Cherry

17% Pumpkin

3% Blueberry

    a. 38

    b. 60

    c. 57

    d. 50

39. A right triangle has short side lengths of 5 units and 12 units. What is its perimeter?

    a. 17 units

    b. 30 units

    c. 60 units

    d. 169 units

40. Given $U = \{a, b, c, d, e\}$, $B = \{c, d, e\}$, and $A' = \{a, b\}$, find $A \cap B$.

    a. B

    b. B'

    c. U

    d. Ø

41. If n and p are prime numbers, n^3p^6 and n^5p^5 will both be divisible by which of the following?

   a. n^3p^6

   b. n^5p^6

   c. n^5p^5

   d. n^3p^5

42. The function $f(x)$ is defined as $f(x) = \frac{1}{x-2}$. All of the following may be in the domain of $f(x)$ EXCEPT

   a. -2

   b. 0

   c. 1

   d. 2

43. Let m be the slope of line L. Let m' be the slope of line L'. L' is perpendicular to L. Which of the following is equivalent to $mm' - (mm')^2$?

   a. -2

   b. -1

   c. 1

   d. 2

44. Given that the range of a set of numbers is x, variance is y, and the median is z, which of the following must be equal to the standard deviation?

   a. $\sqrt{x}$

   b. y

   c. $\sqrt{z}$

   d. $\sqrt{y}$

45. If $U = \{1, 2, 3, 4, 5\}$, $A = \{1, 2, 3, 4\}$, and $B = \{2, 3, 4, 5\}$, find $A' \times B'$.

   a. $\varnothing$

   b. $\{(5, 1)\}$

   c. $\{(1, 2), (1, 3), (1, 4), (1, 5)\}$

   d. $A \cap B$

46. Given s is odd, $t = s + 2$, and $u = t - 1$, which of the following is correct?

   a. u is even.

   b. u is odd.

   c. t is divisible by 2.

   d. u is not divisible by 2.

47. Given $f(x) = 2x - 4$ and $g(x) = x - 2$, find $(\frac{f}{g})x$.

   a. $2x - 8$

   b. $2x - 6$

   c. 2

   d. $2x$

48. Four hiking trails pass through both Lookout 1 and Lookout 2. Five hiking trails connect Lookout 2 to Lookout 3. There is no direct trail between Lookout 1 and Lookout 3; all hikers must pass through Lookout 2. If no trail is to be used twice, how many different routes exist for a hike from Lookout 1 to Lookout 3 and back?

   a. 400

   b. 320

   c. 240

   d. 144

49. Which of the following is equivalent to **v**?

r	s	v
T	T	T
T	F	F
F	T	T
F	F	F

   a. $\sim\sim s$

   b. $\sim s$

   c. $\sim r$

   d. $\sim\sim r$

50.

a. $|r| < |q| < |p|$
b. $q < p < |r|$
c. $|q| > |p| > r$
d. $|r| > |q| > |p|$

51. As indicated on the following histogram, only three students scored between which interval?

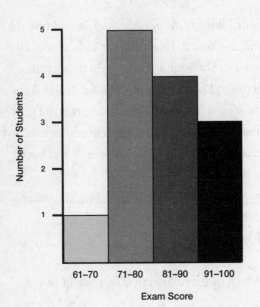

a. 61–70
b. 71–80
c. 81–90
d. 91–100

52. When considering an upcoming team uniform order, the jersey is available in five different colors. One of four different inks must be chosen for the jersey. How many choices are available?

a. 5
b. 9
c. 20
d. 120

53. Which of the following Venn diagrams represents $(A \cap C) \cap (B \cap C)$?

a.

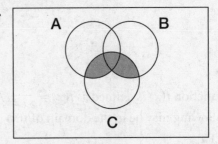

b.

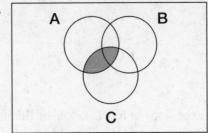

c.

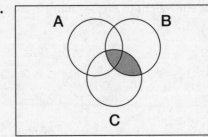

d.

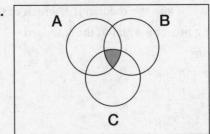

54. If b is an odd, negative integer, which of the following must be an even, positive number?

I. $b + 7$

II. $\sqrt{b^2} + 1$

III. $2|b|$

a. II and III

b. I and II

c. I only

d. III only

55. The function $f(x)$ is defined as $f(x) = x^2 - 9$. When compared with $f(x)$, what happens to the graph of $f(x + 9)$?

a. $f(x)$ slid downward by nine units.

b. $f(x)$ slid left by nine units.

c. $f(x)$ slid upward by nine units.

d. $f(x)$ reflected about the y-axis.

56. v $\vee$ l may represent which of the following?

a. I bought corn and I bought peppers.

b. I bought corn or I bought peppers.

c. If I bought corn, then I bought peppers.

d. I bought corn if, and only if, I bought peppers.

57. If $U = \{10, 20, 30, 40, 50\}$, $A = \{10, 30, 50\}$, and $B = \{20\}$, find $A \cup B$.

a. $\varnothing$

b. $\{20\}$

c. $\{10, 20, 30, 40, 50\}$

d. $\{10, 20, 30, 50\}$

58. Which of the following is an example of an irrational number?

a. $\sqrt[3]{8}$

b. $\sqrt{(\sqrt{16})}$

c. $\sqrt{121}$

d. $\sqrt{11}$

59. Vijay knows that b is a three-digit number with a hundreds digit of 2 and a units digit of 1. If he has one guess as to the value of b, what is the probability that he will get the number right?

a. $\frac{1}{4}$

b. $\frac{1}{5}$

c. $\frac{1}{9}$

d. $\frac{1}{10}$

60. Given $f(x) = -x$ and $g(x) = x + 5$, the composition $(g \circ f)x$ is the same as

a. applying a reflection that moves the graph down by five units.

b. applying a reflection that moves the graph up by five units.

c. applying a translation that moves the graph down by five units.

d. applying a translation that moves the graph up by five units.

▶ Answers

1. a. To solve, first rewrite the function in terms of x and y. To do this, replace $g(x)$ with y:

$y = \frac{x}{4} - 2$

Next, switch the x and y and solve for y:

$x = \frac{y}{4} - 2$

$x + 2 = \frac{y}{4}$

$4(x + 2) = y$

$4x + 8 = y$

Finally, replace the y with $g^{-1}(x)$.

$g^{-1}(x) = 4x + 8$

Thus, **a** is correct. Choice **b** is incorrect because $2 - \frac{x}{4}$ is the additive inverse of $\frac{x}{4-2}$, which is not the inverse of the function. If you chose **c**, you accidentally subtracted 2 instead of adding 2 when rearranging the equation. If you chose **d**, you accidentally divided by 4 instead of multiplying by 4.

2. c. If you compare p^5q^7 and p^3q^8, looking at the exponents for p, you see a 5 and a 3. The answer will have p^3 in it, as p^3q^8 will not be divisible by p with an exponent larger than 3. Looking at the exponents for q, you see a 7 and an 8. The answer will have q^7 in it, as p^5q^7 will not be divisible by q with an exponent larger than 7. You are looking for the largest number, so although both numbers are divisible by pq, choice **a** is incorrect. Therefore, choice **c**, p^3q^7, is the correct answer.

3. a. A negation is the equivalent to "not p," or $\sim p$. If the statement, p, is "I am warm," then $\sim p$ would be "I am not warm." Choice **b** is incorrect because it has nothing to do with the statement. Choices **c** and **d** are incorrect because the word *cold* is used or because the word *you* is used.

4. b. Use $\log_b(\frac{m}{n}) = \log_b(m) - \log_b(n)$, so you get $\log_7(\frac{b}{49}) = \log_7(b) - \log_7(49)$. $\log_7(49) = 2$ because $7^2 = 49$. Therefore, $\log_7(b) - \log_7(49)$ can be simplified to $\log_7(b) - 2$, and **b** is correct. If you chose **a**, you probably solved $\log_b(mn)$ by mistake. If you chose **c**, you may have used $\log_b(m_n)$ by mistake. Choice **d** is incorrect because $\log_7(\frac{b}{49}) = \log_7(b) - \log_7(49)$.

5. d. Use $_nP_r$ where n is the total number of elements that can be selected and r is the number of elements that will actually be selected.

$_nP_r = \frac{n!}{(n-r)!}$

In this case n and r are the same: there are four letters to be selected from and we are selecting four letters. The formula becomes

$_4P_4 = \frac{4!}{(0)!}$

Recall 0!, by definition = 1. So the answer is 4! $= 4 \times 3 \times 2 \times 1 = 24$. There are 24 different possible arrangements, so choice **d** is correct.

6. a. Consecutive even numbers will increase by 2. If the smallest even number is x, the next even number will be $x + 2$, and the next even number will be $x + 4$. We know these will add to 66, so write the equation $x + (x + 2) + (x + 4) = 66$. This simplifies to $3x + 6 = 66$, so $3x = 60$, and x is 20. Because x is the smallest of the three numbers, the answer is 20. If you set this equation up to be three consecutive numbers, x, $x + 1$, and $x + 2$, you may have chosen the incorrect choice **b**. Choices **c** and **d** are both odd numbers, so they are incorrect.

7. b. $(f \circ g)x$ is equivalent to $f(g(x))$, so substituting in the given functions, you get $(x^3)^2 + 5 = x^6 + 5$, so **b** is correct. If you chose **a**, you added the exponents instead of multiplying them. If you chose **c**, you probably calculated $(g \circ f)x$ by mistake. If you chose **d**, you probably calculated $(f + g)x$ by mistake.

8. c. If you knew the value of e, you could solve both goals for the first half and all of Jem's goals, which you could then solve across the rows. Knowing any of the other variables won't help because you can only figure out a full column or a full row. To see how this works, try filling this chart in four times with $e = 2$, $c = 1$, $d = 1$, and $h = 9$. Knowing e, you will be able to fill all columns and rows; with the others, you will figure out some variables, but not all.

9. c. Put the -3 outside of the L. This is the number you are dividing into the coefficients that you see in the equation. The top row inside the L lists all of the coefficients in the equation. Have all the powers of x descend and add in any necessary 0 coefficients for any powers not present: $2x^4 + 0x^3 + 1x^2 + 2x + 3x^0$. Always bring down the leftmost coefficient in the L; in this case, we bring down a 2.

The -3 outside of the L multiplies with this 2, and we fill in -6 in the next right column inside the L. Add down to get $0 - 6 = -6$ at the bottom. The -3 outside of the L multiplies with this -6, and we fill in 18 in the next right column inside the L. Add down to get $1 + 18 = 19$ at the bottom. The -3 outside of the L multiplies with this 19, and we fill in -57 in the next right column inside the L. Add down to get $2 - 57 = -55$. The -3 outside of the L multiplies with this -55, so we fill in 165 in the next right column inside the L. Add down to get $3 + 165 = 168$.

-3	2	0	1	2	3
		-6	18	-57	165
	2	-6	19	-55	168

When evaluating $x = -3$, synthetic division gives us the remainder of 168, so the value of $f(x)$ at $x = -3$ is 168, and **c** is correct. If you chose **a**, then you may have guessed that $x = -3$ would be a zero of $f(x)$, which is not true. If you chose **b**, you forgot to make a column for 0 for the $0x^3$ in your synthetic division L. If you chose **d**, you made a multiplication error, one that did not account for the negative sign in the -3.

10. d. Recall that to calculate the mean, you add all the numbers and divide by the total number of numbers. For $i, j, k,$ and l, $\frac{(\text{sum of all})}{4} = 8$. Cross multiply to find that the sum of all 4 variables must be 32. For i and j, $\frac{(\text{sum of all})}{2} = 4$, so the sum of these two variables is 8. The sum of all four variables, minus the sum of just i and j, would be $32 - 8 = 24$. This value, 24, is the sum of the two remaining variables, k and l. To find the mean of k and l, divide by 2 to get 12.

11. c. Multiplying $f(x)$ by 2 will double the y value. This will squeeze the graph as shown in **c**. Choice **a** represents a translation, or a slide, to the left by one unit. This would happen if $y = f(x - 1)$. Choice **b** also represents a slide, to the left, this time by two units. This would happen if $y = f(x - 2)$. Choice **d** squeezes the graph, but also inverts it. This could be the graph of $y = -2f(x)$. Because there is no negative sign being applied, the graph will not be inverted, and **d** is incorrect.

12. b. A prime number is a positive integer that has only two distinct positive divisors, 1 and the number itself. A composite number is a positive integer that has a positive divisor other than 1 or itself. Rearranging $\frac{c}{d} = e$ yields $d \times e = c$. Because we know e is composite, d times the composite number e must yield a composite number. Thus, c must also be composite.

13. b. Outliers are the values that are not in accordance with the mean or the other values. For a data set with a normal distribution, individual values are close to the average (overall). Choice **b** is correct, and **a** is incorrect. The standard deviation would only equal zero if all the values in the data sets were the same—every value would equal the mean. This is not normally the case, so **c** is incorrect. Standard deviations are never negative, so **d** is incorrect.

14. d. Sets are disjoint when they have no elements in common. Because $A \cap C = \varnothing$, they are disjoint; these two sets have no elements in common. None of the other answer choices yield the empty set when the two sets intersect.

15. c. The problem states that $f(x)$ is linear, so you know it must follow the formula $y = mx + b$. First use $\frac{(y_2 - y_1)}{(x_2 - x_1)}$ to find the slope.

$\frac{(y_2 - y_1)}{(x_2 - x_1)} = \frac{(13 - 5)}{(3 - 1)} = \frac{8}{2} = 4$.

The slope is 4. With a slope of 4, $y = mx + b$ becomes $y = 4x + b$, and when you substitute in, you get $5 = 4(1) + b$, so $b = 1$. The equation is $y = 4x + 1$. $f(10) = 4(10) + 1 = 41$. Choice **c** is correct. If you chose **a**, you may have mistakenly thought the rule was $f(x) = x + 4$ because this works for $f(1)$. However, this rule does not work on $f(3)$ and is incorrect. If you mistakenly selected choice **b**, you may have thought that because $f(3) = 13$, the rule was $x + 10$. This does not work with $f(1)$, so this is an incorrect rule.

16. c. Recall that the range is the difference between the highest number and lowest number of a set. Choice **c** is the correct answer because the highest temperature was 68 degrees and the lowest temperature was 61 degrees, and the difference is 7 degrees. Choice **a** is incorrect because it's the difference between the lowest temperature and the median. Choice **b** is incorrect because it's the difference between the highest temperature and the median. Choice **d** is incorrect because it is not the difference between the highest and lowest numbers.

17. b. First notice that the parabola is made with a solid curve (as opposed to a dashed curve), so the ≤ symbol should be used in the inequality. This makes **c** and **d** incorrect without further scrutiny. Next, notice that the turning point of the parabola is not at $(0, 0)$, so this makes **a** incorrect, because the turning point of $(\frac{1}{2}x)^2$ would be at $(0, 0)$. Choice **b**, $y \le (\frac{1}{2}x)^2 + 2$ is the only choice that can possibly be represented by the given graph, as the parabola is drawn as a solid parabola and is moved upward from the origin.

18. b. The conjunction $p \wedge q$ will be true only if both p and q are true. This conjunction is logically equivalent to $q \wedge p$. The technical name for this equivalence is commutation, but it is easy to think about it in terms of English: p and q will be logically equivalent to q and p.

19. b. Because q is divisible by 15, and 3 and 5 are factors of 15, choice **b** is correct, as r would then also be divisible by these numbers. We know that q is divisible by 3 and 5 because it is divisible by 15, so it must have the factors of 3 and 5. We cannot, however, say that it must have the factors of 2 and 3, so **a** is incorrect. $\frac{r}{2}$ would equal 2, but q being divisible by 15 doesn't make q equal to 15. For example, q may be 30, so **c** is incorrect. We know r is divisible by 15 and 2, but we cannot say that r must be divisible by q, so **d** is incorrect.

20. a. The composition $(g \circ f)x$ is $-6 - x$, which is the same as $-x - 6$. Because $f(x) = -x$, you know that the composition is equal to $f(x) - 6$, so $g(x) = x - 6$. Choices **b**, **c**, and **d** represent computation errors in which one or both of the signs is incorrect.

21. c. The formula for the area of a parallelogram is $A = \text{base} \times \text{height}$. Here the height is 17 and the base is 10, so $A = 17 \times 10 = 170$. Choice **a** is incorrect; it is $\frac{1}{2}$ base $\times$ height. Choice **b** represents 10×10, so it is incorrect. Choice **d** is incorrect because it represents 17×17.

22. d. To solve, leave the real part the same and change the sign for the imaginary part. Leave the 5, and change $-3i$ to $+3i$. Thus, the answer is $5 + 3i$. Choice **a** is incorrect because it changed the sign of the real part. Choice **b** is incorrect because it changed the sign on both parts. Choice **c** is incorrect because it did not change the sign on the imaginary part.

23. **c.** In this case, let p be "I am a mother" and q be "I am a female." For sufficient conditions, given that $p \rightarrow q$ is true, then knowing that p is true would be sufficient for statement q to be true. In this case, knowing that I am a mother would be sufficient for stating that "I am a female" is true. This is represented correctly in choice **c**. This is represented backward (and incorrectly) in choice **b**. For necessary conditions, given that $p \rightarrow q$ is true, in order for p to be true, q has to be true. This would be represented correctly by stating "My being a female is necessary for my being a mother." Choice **a** has this backward and is incorrect. Choice **d** is incorrectly stating that p would be sufficient for $\sim q$.

24. **c.** A prime number is a positive integer that has only two distinct positive divisors, 1 and the number itself. Prime factorization of a number is accomplished by writing the number as the product of only prime numbers. Choice **c** is the only choice that multiplies to 84 and contains only prime numbers. (Another way to represent the prime factorization of 84 is $2^2 \times 3 \times 7$.) Note that choice **b** is incorrect because 1 is not prime.

25. **b.** $(g - h)x$ is the same as $g(x) - h(x)$, so subtract the given functions to get $2x^2 - 6 - (x^2 + 6) = 2x^2 - 6 - x^2 - 6$, which simplifies to $x^2 - 12$, so **b** is correct. If you selected choice **a**, you probably forgot to distribute the minus sign into the parentheses while subtracting the two functions. If you chose **c**, you calculated $g \circ h$ by mistake. If you chose **d**, you calculated $h \circ g$ by mistake.

26. **b.** Use $_nC_r$ where n is the total number of elements that can be selected and r is the number of elements that will actually be selected.

$$_nC_r = \frac{n}{r!(n-r)!}$$

In this case, $n = 6$ and $r = 3$: There are 6 signs to be selected from and we are selecting 3 signs. The formula becomes:

$$_6C_3 = \frac{6!}{3!(6-3)!} = \frac{6!}{3!3!} = \frac{6 \times 5 \times 4 \times 3 \times 2 \times 1}{3 \times 2 \times 1 \times 3 \times 2 \times 1} =$$

$\frac{6 \times 5 \times 4}{3 \times 2 \times 1} = \frac{120}{6} = 20$ different combinations. Choice **b** is correct. Choice **a** is a distracter, 3×6 (a tempting guess). If you selected choice **c**, you may have computed $_6P_3$ by mistake. If you selected choice **d**, you probably solved 6! by mistake.

27. **d.** Rational numbers can be expressed as the ratio of two integers in the form $\frac{a}{b}$. Choice **d** is in this form and is the correct answer. Taking the square root of a perfect square such as $\sqrt{16}$ will always yield a rational number. If you cannot think of a whole number that when squared will give you the number under the radical sign, then the number you are dealing with is an irrational number—one that cannot be expressed in the form $\frac{a}{b}$. Thus, $\sqrt{2}, \sqrt{3}, \sqrt{5}$ are all irrational numbers. The square root of these numbers will result in numbers with nonterminating, nonrepeating decimal extensions.

28. a. To make sure all students are accounted for only once, make up a formula, such as
Total = Band + Chorus − Both
Solve to get $45 + 30 − 15 = 60$ students in all. 30 total chorus students − 15 students in "both" = 15 students in only chorus. The probability that the student chosen will be a student who participates only in chorus would then be $\frac{15}{60} = \frac{1}{4}$. You may have selected choice **b** in error if you got the total by incorrectly adding all three numbers given in the problem. If you selected choice **c**, you may have incorrectly gotten a probability of $\frac{45}{60}$.

29. a. Given $\cup = \{2, 4, 6, 8, 10, 12\}$ and $A' = \{6, 8, 10\}$, we take the complement of A' to get A, so A is $\{2, 4, 12\}$. Recall that the complement of A is all of the elements in the universe that are not in A. Thus, you can just take the complement of the complement to get A. Every element in A is also in B, so B is a subset of A, so I is true. For A to be a proper subset of B, A would be a subset of B, but B would not be a subset of A. However, B is a subset of A, so III is false. Because I and II are true, **a** is the correct answer.

30. b. The range consists of the *y* values that are possible. Notice that the largest point of the interval for *y* is 4, but *y* cannot equal 4. The smallest *y* value is −3. Thus, the range is $−3 \leq y < 4$, so choice **b** is correct. Choice **a** is incorrect as the $\leq$ symbol is used instead of $<$. Choice **c** uses $\leq$ and $<$ in the wrong places. Choice **d** is incorrect as it uses the highs and lows for the *x* values instead of the *y* values.

31. a. Choice **a** is the correct answer because if you add 7 points to each score, it would be the same thing as adding 7 points to the overall mean. For example, if all 30 students received a 65.3, the mean would be 65.3. When the teacher adds 7 points to each test, each student would have 72.3, and the new mean would be 72.3. If you selected choice **b**, **c**, or **d**, you probably made a computational error.

32. d. To generate the contrapositive of a conditional statement, switch the antecedent and the consequent and negate them both. The contrapositive of $p \rightarrow q$ would be $\sim q \rightarrow \sim p$, so **d** is correct. Choice **a** is a biconditional statement, and is incorrect. Choice **b** is the inverse and is incorrect. Choice **c** switched the antecedent and the consequent, which is the converse, so this choice is incorrect.

33. c. Draw a diagram to see what is going on:

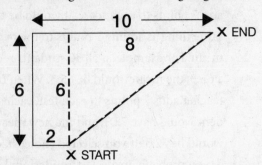

Notice the right triangle that is created by the dashed lines. The driver went west for 2 miles, so you know the top side of the triangle is 8 miles. The driver drove north for 6 miles, so you know the left side of the triangle is 6 miles. This is a 6-8-10 right triangle. If you did not know that, you could use the Pythagorean theorem, $a^2 + b^2 = c^2$ to get $6^2 + 8^2 = c^2$; $c^2 = 100$; $c = 10$ miles. Choice **c** is correct. Choice **a** represents the distance traveled north and is incorrect. Choice **b** represents one leg of the right triangle that is created and is incorrect. Choice **d** represents the total distance that the driver drove and not the straight-line path between the two points.

34. d. First, multiply the exponents in the numerator using the rule $(x^m)^n = x^{mn}$.

$$\frac{(z^4)^7}{z^4 \cdot z^7} = \frac{z^{28}}{z^4 \cdot z^7}$$

Next, you can add the exponents in the denominator according to the rule $x^m \times x^n = x^{m+n}$.

$$\frac{z^{28}}{z^4 \cdot z^7} = \frac{z^{28}}{z^{11}}$$

Now use the rule $x^m \div x^n = x^{m-n}$.

$$\frac{z^{28}}{z^{11}} = z^{28-11} = z^{17}$$

35. a. A number is divisible by its factors. Rearranging $\frac{P}{Q} = R$ yields $Q \times R = P$. Both Q and R are factors of P; P is divisible by Q and R. Similarly, rearranging $\frac{S}{P} = \frac{TP}{Q} = R$ yields $P \times T = S$. Both P and T are factors of S; S is divisible by P and T. Because $Q \times R = P$, S is divisible by both Q and R. Choice **a** must be true.

36. b. Choice **b** will have two zeros, when $x = 4.5$ and when $x = -4.5$. Choice **a** is incorrect. Because $|x|$ is always positive, $-|x|$ will be negative and you have a negative number (or zero in the case of $x = 0$) minus 4.5, so $f(x)$ will always be negative. Choice **c** will have one zero, when x is 4.5. Choice **d** will have one zero, when x is 4.5.

37. a. This question deals with independent events. The probability is then $P(\text{Event 1}) \times P(\text{Event 2})$. In this case, Event 1 is that it will rain on Monday. The odds are 40%. Event 2 is the probability that Kayla will NOT get her braces off. There is a 70% chance that Kayla will get her braces off on Monday, so the probability that she won't is 30%. $P(\text{Event 1}) \times P(\text{Event 2}) = 40\% \times 30\% = 0.4 \times 0.3 = 0.12 = 12\%$. If you selected choice **c**, you probably found the probability for $P(\text{rain}) \times P(\text{braces off})$ by mistake. If you selected choice **d**, you probably added 40% + 30%, which is incorrect.

38. c. Fifteen people prefer apple pie, and this is 10% of the total. 10% is the same as $\frac{1}{10}$. 15 is $\frac{1}{10}$ of 150. Now that we know the total, we can take 38% of the 150 to find out how many people prefer cherry pie. 38% = .38 and .38 × 150 is 57, so **c** is correct. Choice **a** is incorrect because the total amount of people is not 100. Choice **b** is incorrect; you may have selected this answer if you approximated 38% as 40%. Choice **d** is incorrect; you may have picked this if you tried to make a quick estimation.

39. b. This is a 5-12-13 right triangle. If you did not know that, you could use the Pythagorean theorem, $a^2 + b^2 = c^2$ to get $5^2 + 12^2 = c^2$; $c^2 = 169$; $c = 13$. To find the perimeter, add up all of the sides: $5 + 12 + 13 = 30$ units. Thus, **b** is correct. Choice **a** is the sum of the two given sides, and is incorrect. Choice **c** is the product of the two given sides and is incorrect. Choice **d** is the sum of the squares of the two given sides and is incorrect.

40. a. Knowing that $U = \{a, b, c, d, e\}$, $A' = \{a, b\}$, and that the complement of A is all of elements in the universe that are not in A, you can just take the complement of the complement to get $A = \{c, d, e\}$. Next $A \cap B = \{c, d, e\}$, so A and B are equivalent sets, and choice **a**, B, is the correct answer.

41. d. Because both n and p are prime numbers, n^3p^6 and n^5p^5 represent prime factorizations. In order for one number, x, to be divisible by another number, y, y must divide evenly into x. The only numbers that will divide evenly into both n^3p^6 and n^5p^5 will contain n^3, n^2, n^1, n^0 separate or combined with p^5, p^4, p^3, p^2, p^1, p^0. This is because a number with any power higher than 3 for n will not divide evenly into n^3p^6 and any number with any power higher than 5 for p will not divide evenly into n^5p^5. Thus, the only answer choice that fits the criteria is **d**, n^3p^5.

42. d. The denominator of the fraction cannot equal zero, so x cannot equal 2. The domain cannot include 2, so **d** is correct.

43. a. The slope of a line is represented as m. The slope of a perpendicular line will have a slope equal to $\frac{-1}{m}$. L has a slope of m and L' has a slope of m'. This means that $m' = \frac{1}{-m}$. Given the equation $mm' - (mm')^2$, substitute $(\frac{-1}{m})$ for m'.
$$mm' - (mm')^2$$
$$= m(\frac{-1}{m}) - (m(\frac{-1}{m}))^2$$
$$= -1 - (-1)^2$$
$$= -1 - 1$$
$$= -2$$
Choice **a** is correct. Choices **b**, **c**, and **d** represent incorrect answers due to errors in adding and multiplying signed numbers.

44. d. Recall that the range for a given set of values is found by subtracting the lowest value from the highest value. The median for a given set of values is found by ordering all of the values and citing the middle number as the median for an odd number of values and averaging the two middle numbers if there is an even number of values. The variance, S^2, is the average squared deviation of values from mean. The standard deviation is represented by S and it is the square root of the variance. In this question, knowing the range and the median is not relevant. The variance is equal to y. To solve for the standard deviation, take the square root of the variance: $\sqrt{y}$, so choice **d** is correct. Choice **a** is incorrect; it is the square root of the range and this is not the standard deviation. Choice **b** is incorrect because it is the variance, and this is not equal to the standard deviation. Choice **c** is incorrect: It is the square root of the median, and this is not the standard deviation.

45. b. To solve, first we need to find A' and B'. A' means the complement of A. Recall that the complement of A will be all of elements in the universe that are not in A. The same rule holds for finding B'. Thus, A' = {5} and B' = {1}. Next, to find the Cartesian product, A' × B', list all possible ordered pairs that would result by taking the first coordinate from set A' and the second coordinate from set B'. Solving, we get {(5, 1)}. Choice **b** is correct. Choice **c** has too many ordered pairs. Choice **a** is incorrect because there are elements in the solution set. A ∩ B would equal {2, 3, 4}, and this is not the same as the Cartesian product of A' and B'.

46. a. Given s is odd and $t = s + 2$, we know t is odd, and thus not divisible by 2. Choice **c** is incorrect. Because an odd number minus 1 will yield an even number, u must be even. Thus, choice **a** is correct, and choice **b** is incorrect. Choice **d** is incorrect because even numbers, like u, are divisible by 2.

47. c. $\left(\frac{f}{g}\right)x$ is equivalent to $\frac{f(x)}{g(x)}$, so substituting the numbers into the function, you get $\frac{2x-4}{x-2} = \frac{2(x-2)}{x-2} = 2$, so **c** is correct. This is an example of a constant function. If you chose **a**, you calculated $f \circ g$ by mistake. If you chose **b**, you calculated $g \circ f$ by mistake. If you chose **d**, you accidentally included the variable x in the new function.

48. c. Four hiking trails pass through both Lookout 1 and Lookout 2, and five hiking trails connect Lookout 2 to Lookout 3. Applying the counting principle, this gives $4 \times 5 = 20$ possibilities on the way there. On the way back, between Lookouts 3 and 2, there are now only 4 choices. Similarly, between Lookouts 2 and 1, there are now only 3 choices. Apply the counting principle again to get $4 \times 3 = 12$ possible ways back. In all, there are $20 \times 12 = 240$ possible routes. Choice **a** is incorrect; you may have multiplied 20×20 by mistake. Choice **b** is incorrect; it is a distracter that uses "familiar" digits—the numbers that are used in the question. Choice **d** is incorrect; you may have mistakenly multiplied 12×12 if you selected this choice.

49. a Looking at the truth values for **v**, you should notice that they are identical to the truth values for **s**. Because **s** is not a choice, ~~**s**, which is equivalent to **s**, is the answer.

s	~s	~~s
T	F	T
F	T	F
T	F	T
F	T	F

50. a. Looking at the number line, $p = -2.5$, $q = -1$, and $r = .5$. The absolute values of these numbers would then be $|p| = 2.5$, $|q| = 1$, and $|r| = .5$. Substituting the numerical values, choice **a** would be $.5 < 1 < 2.5$, which is correct. Choice **b** would be $1 < -2.5 < .5$, which is correct. Choice **c** would be $1 > 2.5 > .5$, which is incorrect. Choice **d** would be $.5 > 1 > 2.5$, which is incorrect.

51. d. Choice **d** is the correct answer because according to the histogram, the number of students who scored within the class interval labeled 91–100 is equal to 3. The *y*-axis tells us how many students fall within each class interval. Choice **a** is incorrect because the number of students scoring in the range 61–70 is equal to 1. Choices **b** and **c** are incorrect because the number of students that fall within these intervals are 5 and 4, respectively.

52. c. The counting principle states that given event A can occur in *a* ways and event B can occur in *b* ways, the two events can occur together in $a \times b$ ways. In this case, there are five "ways" for color and four "ways" for ink. Solving, we get $5 \times 4 = 20$ different choices. Choice **c** is correct. Choice **a** may have been chosen in error if $_5C_4$ was calculated by mistake. If you selected choice **b**, you may have added the two numbers instead of multiplying. If you selected choice **d**, you may have computed $_5P_4$ by mistake.

53. d. Recall that ∩ means intersection (find what the sets have in common) and ∪ means union (combine the two sets). Do whatever is in the parentheses (or innermost set of parentheses) first. (A ∩ C) looks like this:

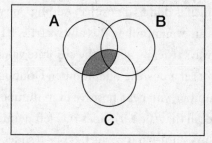

and (B ∩ C) looks like this:

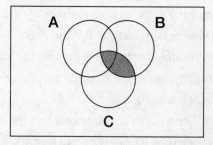

If you selected **b** or **c**, you incorrectly picked a partial answer. Next, take the intersection of these two to get:

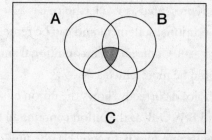

Choice **a** is (A ∩ C) ∪ (B ∩ C), where the union was taken at the last step instead of the intersection.

54. a. First, look at all three statements. I is not always true; it only holds true in some situations. For example, it is true for –5, but not true for 0 and –9. This tells you that choices **b** and **c** are incorrect. Next, look at II. $\sqrt{b^2} = b$, which is odd and positive. Adding one gives us an even number. II is always true. III is also always true. By taking the absolute value of b, you get a positive odd number. Doubling this number, you get a positive even number.

55. b. Recall that $f(x + a)$ slides $f(x)$ left a units. Thus, choice **b** is correct. $f(x) - a$ slides $f(x)$ down a units, so **a** is incorrect. $f(x) + a$ slides $f(x)$ up a units, so **c** is incorrect. $f(-x)$ flips $f(x)$ over the y-axis, so **d** is incorrect. Note that in this case you are applying the rule of the function to $x + 9$, which means the graph slides left by 9.

56. b. v $\vee$ l represents a disjunction and the symbol $\vee$ means *or*. The only choice that v $\vee$ l may represent would be **b**, *I bought corn or I bought peppers.* Choice **a** is a conjunction (conjunctions use the word *and*) and could be represented as v $\wedge$ l. Choice **c** is a conditional statement and can be represented as v $\rightarrow$ l. Choice **d** is a biconditional and could be represented as v $\leftrightarrow$ l.

57. d. Choice **d** correctly shows the union of sets A and B, A $\cup$ B, as the union contains all elements in A and B. In choice **a**, the null set (empty set) is incorrect because the union of the two sets does contain elements. Choice **b** is the intersection of the two sets, A $\cap$ B, not the union. Choice **c** is incorrect; it is the universe.

58. d. Irrational numbers cannot be expressed in the form $\frac{a}{b}$. Rational numbers can be expressed as the ratio of two integers in the form $\frac{a}{b}$. If you cannot think of a whole number that, when squared, will give you the number under the radical sign, then the number you are dealing with is an irrational number. So $\sqrt{11}$ is the irrational number because there is no number that when squared will equal 11. Choice **d** is correct. $\sqrt[3]{8} = 2$, which is a rational number, so **a** is incorrect. $\sqrt{(\sqrt{16})} = \sqrt{4} = 2$, which is a rational number, so **b** is incorrect. $\sqrt{121} = 11$, which is a rational number, so **c** is incorrect.

59. d. Given b is a three-digit number with a tens digit of 2 and a units digit of 1, b can be written as 2_1, where _ can be any of the digits that we use in our base 10-number system: 0 1 2 3 4 5 6 7 8 9. There are 10 potential values to fill in the blank with and only one will be correct. Thus, the probability that he will get it right is 1 out of 10, or $\frac{1}{10}$.

60. **d.** The graph of $f(x)$ moves up by five units, so **d** is correct.

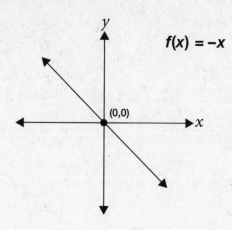

$f(x) = -x$

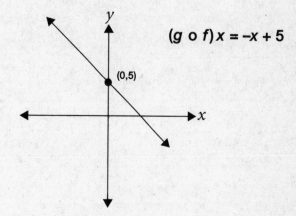

$(g \circ f)x = -x + 5$

The proper term for this transformation is a translation, so **a** and **b** are incorrect. The graph moves upward because you are adding 5, so **d** is correct.

CHAPTER

16 ▶ The Real Number System

Real numbers are not imaginary. Imaginary numbers involve the square root of −1. Real numbers can be divided into several subcategories.

▶ Types of Numbers

The real number system is subcategorized into several number sets.

> The **counting numbers**, also known as the natural numbers, are the numbers you would count on your fingers, and then some. The set of counting numbers is {1, 2, 3, 4, 5, . . .}.
>
> The set of **whole numbers** includes all of the counting numbers, but additionally includes zero. The set of whole numbers is {0, 1, 2, 3, 4, . . . }.
>
> **Integers** contain all of the counting numbers and whole numbers, but also contain the negative counterpart for all the counting numbers. The set of integers is { . . . −4, −3, −2, −1, 0, 1, 2, 3, 4, . . . }.

So far, the number types discussed include numbers that do not include fractional parts or decimal extensions.

Rational numbers are real numbers that can be expressed in the form $\frac{a}{b}$, where both a and b are integers. Note that the denominator of a fraction can never be equal to zero, so when expressing this ration, $b \neq 0$. The form $\frac{a}{b}$ just means we are taking the ratio of two integers.

Irrational numbers are real numbers that cannot be expressed as the ratio of two integers in the form $\frac{a}{b}$. Note that the denominator of a fraction can never be equal to zero, so when expressing this ratio, $b \neq 0$. These numbers have decimal extensions that do not repeat and do not truncate (end). $\sqrt{7}$ and π are both irrational numbers.

Example

For each number in the table, check the box or boxes that correctly classify that number.

	COUNTING #	WHOLE #	INTEGER	RATIONAL #	IRRATIONAL #
0	☐	☐	☐	☐	☐
$0.\overline{3}$	☐	☐	☐	☐	☐
−3	☐	☐	☐	☐	☐
2	☐	☐	☐	☐	☐
$-\frac{1}{2}$	☐	☐	☐	☐	☐
$\sqrt{2}$	☐	☐	☐	☐	☐

By remembering or reviewing the definitions, the chart can be correctly completed as follows:

	COUNTING #	WHOLE #	INTEGER	RATIONAL #	IRRATIONAL #
0		√	√	√	
$0.\overline{3}$				√	
−3			√	√	
2	√	√	√	√	
$-\frac{1}{2}$				√	
$\sqrt{2}$					√

▶ Absolute Value and Order

To find the **absolute value** of a number, you simply find its distance from zero. $|x|$ means "the absolute value of x."

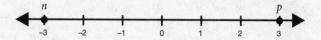

Points n and p are both three units from zero.
$|n| = |p| = 3$

When considering the order of numbers relative to one another, it is helpful to use the following mathematical symbols:

$<$ less than
$>$ greater than
$\leq$ less than or equal to
$\geq$ greater than or equal to
$=$ equal to

Referring back to the number line, we can create inequalities that correctly state the order of the marked numbers.

$n < 0 < p$
$0 < |n|$
$0 < |p|$
$p > n$
$p > 0 > n$

▶ Open and Closed Intervals

When considering inequalities, if there is an "or equal to" component on the symbol, the interval is a **closed interval**. For example, look at $-1 \leq x \leq 1$:

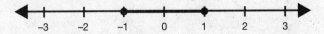

If there is no "or equal to" component on the symbol, the interval is an **open interval**. For example, look at $-1 < x < 1$:

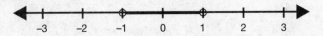

You can also have a mix of the two, and this is called a **half-open interval** or **half-closed interval**. $-1 \leq x < 1$ is such an example:

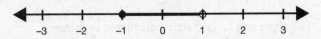

Example

Write an inequality for this number line. Is this an open or closed interval?

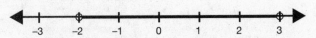

The inequality is $-2 < x < 3$, and this is an open interval. x cannot equal -2 or 3 but can equal any value in between. The circles that enclose the points -2 and 3 are therefore not filled in.

▶ Factors, Products, and Multiples

When multiplying two numbers or quantities, you have:

$$\text{factor} \times \text{factor} = \text{product} \text{ or } f_1 \times f_2 = P$$

When looking at a particular number, a **factor** of that number is an integer that goes into that number evenly. f_1 and f_2 are both factors of P.

Example

Given $a \times 3 = c$, where a and c are nonzero integers, list the factors of c.

The factors of c would be a and 3, because if you divide c by either a or 3, there will be no remainder. Let's consider two nonzero integers as the factors f_1 and f_2 in the equation of $f_1 \times f_2 = P$. The product, P, will be **divisible** by both of these factors. If you were to divide P by either f_1 or f_2, there would be no remainder. Another way of looking at it is that f_1 and f_2 both divide evenly into P.

Example

If a positive whole number x is divisible by 6, what other numbers must x be divisible by?

Because 6 is divisible by 2 and 3, x will also be divisible by 2 and 3.

Multiples of a number are all the numbers that number goes into evenly. Multiples are all the numbers you say when you count by that number. You can find multiples of your number by multiplying by integer values. Zero will be a multiple of your number, as will the number itself, and your number will have many negative multiples as well.

Some multiples of 2 are −2,000; −8; −2; 0; 2; 4; 5,000; 1,000,000.

Example

Consider the following rule.

Given that a and b are multiples of x, $a \times b$, $a + b$, and $a - b$ and are all multiples of x.

See if this rule holds true for 70 and 80, two multiples of 10.

$a \times b = 70 \times 80 = 5{,}600$, which is a multiple of 10.

$a + b = 70 + 80$, which is a multiple of 10.

$a - b = 70 - 80 = -10$, which is a multiple of 10.

▶ Odd and Even Numbers

Integers are **even** if they are divisible by 2. Integers are **odd** if they cannot be divided by 2 evenly.

Example

Given the odd number y, list the three next greater even numbers.

Because y is odd, $y + 1$ will be even. The next greater even number will be +2 more, $y + 3$. The next greater even number will be +2 more, $y + 5$.

▶ Prime and Composite Numbers

A positive integer is regarded as **prime** if it has two distinct factors (and only two): 1 and itself. The smallest prime number is 2.

A **composite number** is a positive integer that is divisible by 1, itself, and another distinct number (or some other distinct numbers).

If you look closely at both of these definitions, you can see that 1 is neither prime nor composite.

Example

For each number, check the box that correctly classifies that number.

	PRIME #	COMPOSITE #
0	☐	☐
1	☐	☐
2	☐	☐
3	☐	☐
4	☐	☐
5	☐	☐
6	☐	☐
7	☐	☐

The chart can be correctly completed as follows:

	PRIME #	COMPOSITE #
0		
1		
2	√	
3	√	
4		√
5	√	
6		√
7	√	

▶ Prime Factorization

Composite numbers can be written as the product of prime numbers, and this is called **prime factorization**. One way to solve for prime factorization is to make a factor tree, as for the number 24:

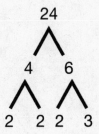

Thus, the prime factorization of 24 is $2 \times 2 \times 2 \times 3$, or $2^3 \times 3$.

Example

Draw factor trees for the prime factorization of 85 and for the prime factorization of 88.

and

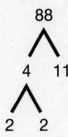

17 ▶ Basic Set Concepts and Terminology

A set is a collection of **objects**. A set is described in a way that makes it easy for someone to tell whether or not an object belongs to that particular set.

For example, it would be easy to tell whether or not a number belongs to the set of all odd integers. "All odd integers" is well defined would be an example of a set. "All ninth graders at Elm Street High School" is well defined and would also be an example of a set. On the other hand "the best meals" is not well defined. Who would get to decide what meals are best? What are the criteria? What does "best" mean? "The best meals" would not be an example of a set.

Sets include **members** or **elements**. These terms can be used interchangeably.

When using the **roster notation** of a set, a capital letter represents a set and brackets enclose the elements of the set. For example, set B contains the elements 2, 4, 5, 8, and 10. Set B is shown here represented in roster notation:

B = {2, 4, 6, 8, 10}

The number of elements within a set is called its **cardinal number**.

Example

B = {12, 14, 16, 18, 20}

What is the cardinal number of set B?

This set contains five elements, so the cardinal number of set B equals 5.

In this example, set B was shown using the roster notation. Another way sets can be shown is with the **set-builder notation**. Using the set-builder notation, set B would be:

{$x \mid x$ is a positive even integer less than 11}

An **infinite set** is one that will go on and on forever. For example, the set of whole numbers is equal to {0, 1, 2, 3, 4, 5, . . . } whereby the ellipses indicates that this set continues on infinitely.

▶ Symbols Used When Working with Sets

Two symbols are used to show whether or not an element belongs to a particular set. $\in$ means "is an element of" and $\notin$ means "is not a member of."

Example

Let's refer to set B again.

B = {2, 4, 6, 8, 10}

Which symbol belongs in the blank?

(Choose $\in$ or $\notin$)

2 ___ B

5 ___ B

You can see that 2 is an element of set B, so $2 \in B$. 5 is not one of the members of set B, so $5 \notin B$.

For sets with no elements, or when solving a set question for which the answer would be "no elements," the **empty set** symbol, $\emptyset$, is used. Another way to show the empty set is to use a set of empty brackets, { }. Another name for the empty set is the **null set**.

▶ Types of Subsets and Set Equality

If set A is a subset of set B, we show this by using the symbol $\subset$.

A $\subset$ B

When this symbol is used, we know that set A is a **subset** of set B. This means that every member of set A is also in set B. By this definition, if set A is a subset of set B, there is also the possibility that set A and set B are identical.

If the symbol $\subseteq$ is used instead, such as A $\subseteq$ B, we know that set A contains *some but not all* of the members of set B. The symbol $\subseteq$ is used to denote a **proper subset**. For proper subsets, A is a subset of B, but B is *not* a subset of A.

If set A and set B are identical, that is, if set A is a subset of B *and* set B is a subset of A, we would have what is called **set equality**.

Example

Given P = {1} and Q = {1, 3, 4}, which symbol should be used in the blank?

P ___ Q

In this case, P is a subset of Q, but Q is *not* a subset of P, so this is a proper subset, and the symbol $\subseteq$ would be used:

P $\subseteq$ Q

► The Universal Set

The set from which we select all of the sets we are listing is called the **universal set**. We use the symbol U to show the universal set in any given situation.

Let's say that $U = \{1, 2, 3, 4, 5, 6, 7, 8\}$

$A = \{2, 3, 4\}$

$B = \{3, 4, 5, 6\}$

$C = \{1, 2, 7, 8\}$

We can now look at ways to relate sets A and B. What elements do they have in common? What happens when we combine them?

We can also relate set A or set B to the **universe**.

► Intersection

We use $\cap$ to take the **intersection** of two sets. The intersection of two sets will be a set containing all elements both sets have in common.

Example

Using sets A and B, what is $A \cap B$?

The sets are:

$A = \{2, 3, 4\}$

$B = \{3, 4, 5, 6\}$

$A \cap B$ consists of only the elements found in both A and B. $A \cap B = \{3, 4\}$.

► Disjoint Sets

Sets are **disjoint** when they have no elements in common. These sets can also be referred to as independent or mutually exclusive.

Example

Using sets B and C, what is $B \cap C$?

$B = \{3, 4, 5, 6\}$

$C = \{1, 2, 7, 8\}$

This is a case of disjoint sets because B and C have no elements in common.

We would write $B \cap C = \{\}$ or $B \cap C = \emptyset$.

► Union

We use $\cup$ to make a new set that contains all of the elements in two sets, and this is called the union.

Example

Using the sets defined in the previous section:

$U = \{1, 2, 3, 4, 5, 6, 7, 8\}$

$A = \{2, 3, 4\}$

$B = \{3, 4, 5, 6\}$

$C = \{1, 2, 7, 8\}$

What is $A \cup B$?

$A \cup B = \{2, 3, 4, 5, 6\}$ because we would use all elements in A and all elements in B.

► Complement

The **complement** of a particular set is a set containing all the elements that are in the universe that are not found in that particular set.

An apostrophe, ', is used to denote the complement.

Example

In this example, we will still be considering the universal set as defined previously.

$U = \{1, 2, 3, 4, 5, 6, 7, 8\}$

$A = \{2, 3, 4\}$

$B = \{3, 4, 5, 6\}$

$C = \{1, 2, 7, 8\}$

What is B'?

Compare the universal set and B. What does the universal set have that B doesn't? $\{1, 2, 7, 8\}$. So B' = $\{1, 2, 7, 8\}$. Note that B' and C are exactly the same. In this case, B' = C would also be a correct answer.

The relationship between B and B' is shown in the diagram:

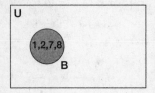 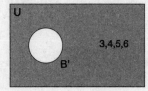

▶ Venn Diagrams

In the previous example, we used a diagram to represent a set (set B) and we used shading to show where elements would be found.

Venn diagrams use circles and overlapping to show common areas. Shading is used to show concepts such as "union." These diagrams let us visualize sets.

In the following examples, circles are used for sets A and B, and they are shaded to show union and intersection, respectively.

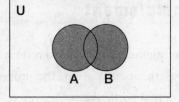

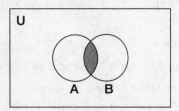

▶ The Cartesian Product

The elements of two sets can be combined into ordered pairs by finding the **Cartesian product** of the two sets. The symbol used is ×. A × B is found by listing all possible ordered pairs that would result by multiplying one first coordinate from set A (the first set) with a coordinate from set B (the second set).

Examples

A = {2, 3, 4}
B = {3, 4, 5, 6}

Using sets A and B, find A × B.

Create all possible ordered pairs using A to generate the first coordinate and B to generate the second coordinate:

A × B = {(2, 3), (2, 4), (2, 5), (2, 6), (3, 3), (3, 4), (3, 5), (3, 6), (4, 3), (4, 4), (4, 5), (4, 6)}

▶ Quick Symbol Summary

U the universal set
∩ intersection
∪ union
Ø the empty set
∈ is an element of
∉ is not an element of
⊆ is a proper subset of
⊂ is a subset of
' complement
× Cartesian product

▶ Practice Questions

Given:

$U = \{2, 3, 4, 5, 8, 9, 11\}$
A = $\{5, 8, 9\}$
B = $\{3, 5\}$
C = $\{8, 9, 11\}$

1. What is the cardinal number of A?

2. What is the cardinal number of B?

3. True or False: $3 \in C$

4. Find A'.

5. Find B ∩ C.

6. True or False: B and C are disjoint.

7. Find A × B.

8. Find B ∪ C.

9. True or False: A ∈ C

▶ **Answers**

1. **3**, because there are 3 elements in set A.

2. **2**, because there are 2 elements in set B.

3. **False.** $3 \in C$ is false because 3 is not an element in set C. $3 \notin C$ would be the proper expression.

4. **A' = {2, 3, 11}** because these are all the elements in the universe that are not in set A.

5. **B ∩ C = {}** because when you intersect these sets, you get the null set. They are disjoint.

6. **True.** "B and C are disjoint" is true—they have no elements in common.

7. **×** is the symbol for Cartesian product. A × B = {(5, 3), (5, 5), (8, 3), (8, 5), (9, 3), (9, 5)}

8. **∪** is the symbol for union. B ∪ C = {3, 5, 8, 9, 11}

9. **False.** A ∈ C is false because 5 is not an element of C. All three elements in A would need to be in C.

18▶ Logic

A statement is a declarative sentence that is either true or false and is thus said to have a **truth value**. A statement must be either true or false.

It is commonplace to use *p* to represent a statement. The **negation** of this statement would be "not *p*" and would be represented as **~*p***. If we represent the statement "I am cold" as *p*, then ~*p* would be the same as saying "I am not cold." If the truth value for *p* is true, then the truth value for ~*p* would be false.

Examples

Evaluate the following as true or false statements, and write the negation for each.

All children have red hair. _____

A lot of people enjoy movies. _____

Three plus six equals nine. _____

The first sentence "All children have red hair," is a false statement, as not all children have red hair. "A lot of people enjoy movies," and "Three plus six equals nine," are both true statements. The negations would be "All children do not have red hair," "A lot of people do not enjoy movies," and "Three plus six does not equal nine."

When two statements are combined by the use of connectives, a **compound statement** results.

The two connectives you should know are *and* and *or*.

Conjunctions use *and* to join two statements into a compound statement. **Disjunctions** use *or* to join two statements.

Connective	Name of Connective	Symbol
and	conjunction	$\wedge$
or	disjunction	$\vee$

Example

If p represents the statement "I will go to the dance," and q represents the statement "I will go to the store," use logic notation to represent "I will go to the dance and I will go to the store."

Because *and* is used, you would write $p \wedge q$.

▶ Truth Tables

For the conjunction $p \wedge q$ to be true, both p and q need to be true. A truth table is a table that represents all of the possible combinations of truth values regarding whatever scenario you are considering. In this case, it lists all possible combinations of both statements and the truth value of the conjunction.

p	q	$p \wedge q$
T	T	T
T	F	F
F	T	F
F	F	F

Notice that the only time the conjunction $p \wedge q$ is true is when both p and q are true—at the top row of the truth table.

Example

Complete the following truth table:

p	q	$p \vee q$
T	T	
T	F	
F	T	
F	F	

For the disjunction $p \vee q$ to be true, either p or q needs to be true. The disjunction is also true when both p and q are true. In completing the truth table, the only time the disjunction will be false is when both p and q are false—this is the case in the bottom row of the truth table:

p	q	$p \vee q$
T	T	T
T	F	T
F	T	T
F	F	F

Example

Complete the following truth table:

q	~q
T	
F	

This truth table lists the value of the negation of q, or "not q." If q is true, it follows that "not q" is false, and vice versa:

q	~q
T	F
F	T

▶ Conditional Statements

A **conditional statement** uses *if* and *then*. A conditional statement is represented as:

$$p \rightarrow q$$

This means if p, then q. The statement before the arrow is called the **antecedent**. The statement after the arrow is called the **consequent**. If p is true, then q must be true. Conditional statements will produce a value of false only if the first antecedent is true and the consequent is false.

Example

Complete the truth table for the following conditional statement.

p	q	$p \rightarrow q$
T	T	
T	F	
F	T	
F	F	

The conditional statement will be false only if the consequent occurs when the antecedent does not. In other words, if q occurs without p, then $p \rightarrow q$ would be false. This happens in row 2 in the following table

p	q	$p \rightarrow q$
T	T	T
T	F	F
F	T	T
F	F	T

▶ Implications

Implications involve the use of implied relationships and are represented as:

$$p \Rightarrow q$$

This means that p implies q, or that q is a logical consequence of p.

Consider the statement, "Studying implies passing." Note that there is a causal relationship present: The relationship implies that studying causes passing.

Example

Let p represent: I studied.

Let q represent: I passed.

Let: $p \Rightarrow q$ represent "Passing is a logical consequence of studying."

Complete the truth table for the following implication

p	q	$p \Rightarrow q$
T	T	
T	F	
F	T	
F	F	

Note the wording: "Passing is a logical consequence of studying." The consequence (passing), q, is what results when p (studying) is true.

The implication will be false only if the consequence occurs when the antecedent does not. In other words, if q occurs without p, then $p \Rightarrow q$ would be false. This happens in row 2

p	q	$p \Rightarrow q$
T	T	T
T	F	F
F	T	T
F	F	T

▶ Double-Lined Arrows or Single-Lined Arrows?

Strictly speaking, implications use arrows with two lines, $p \Rightarrow q$, and conditionals use arrows with one line, $p \rightarrow q$. Strictly speaking, implications will always use the word *implies*, and conditionals will always use *if-then* statements. Many logical books and courses, however, don't adhere strictly to these definitions.

It is wise to understand the difference between the two, but it is acceptable to use the arrow with one line for both, and you might see the single used in both cases on the CLEP test as well.

▶ Converse

The converse of a conditional statement switches the antecedent and the consequent.

The converse of $p \rightarrow q$ would be $q \rightarrow p$.

Example

Let p represent: I am working out.

Let q represent: I am hot.

Write the conditional statement "If I am working out, then I am hot" using logic notation. Write the converse both in a sentence and also using logic notation.

The conditional statement would be represented as $p \rightarrow q$. The converse would be written as "If I am hot, then I am working out," and is represented as $q \rightarrow p$.

Note that the converse is not logically equivalent to the conditional statement. I could be hot because I am standing by a bonfire.

▶ Inverse

The inverse of a conditional statement negates both the antecedent and the consequent.

The inverse of $p \rightarrow q$ would be $\sim p \rightarrow \sim q$.

Example

Let p represent: I have headphones.
Let q represent: I have music.

Write the conditional statement "If I have headphones, then I have music" using logic notation. Write the inverse both in a sentence and also using logic notation.

The conditional statement would be represented as $p \rightarrow q$. The inverse would be written as "If I do not have headphones, then I do not have music," and is represented as $\sim p \rightarrow \sim q$.

Note that the inverse is not logically equivalent to the conditional statement. I could have music because a car pulled up next to me with its radio blasting.

▶ Contrapositive

To generate the contrapositive of a conditional statement, switch the antecedent and the consequent and negate them both.

The contrapositive of $p \rightarrow q$ would be $\sim q \rightarrow \sim p$.

Example

Let p represent: I am drinking coffee.
Let q represent: My heart is beating fast.

Write the conditional statement "If I am drinking coffee, then my heart is beating fast" using logic notation. Write the contrapositive both in a sentence and also using logic notation.

The conditional statement would be represented as $p \rightarrow q$. The contrapositive would be written as "If my heart is not beating fast, then I am not drinking coffee," and is represented as $\sim q \rightarrow \sim p$.

Note that the contrapositive is indeed logically equivalent to the conditional statement. Because of the casual relationship, I would not be able to drink coffee and not have my heart beat fast. Therefore, if my heart is not beating fast, I must not be drinking coffee.

▶ Counter Examples

When making an argument, a **counter example** is an exception to the proposed general rule.

Considering "All girls have blonde hair," a counter example would be proof of the existence of a girl with non-blonde hair.

▶ Valid Argument Patterns

In the last example, we saw that the contrapositive is indeed logically equivalent to the original conditional statement. This section contains a list of valid argument patterns.

Affirming the Antecedent
Given $p \rightarrow q$ and p is true, it is valid to say that q is true.

Denying the Consequent
Given $p \rightarrow q$ and $\sim q$ is true, it is valid to say that $\sim p$ is also true.

Chain Argument
Given $p \rightarrow q$ and $q \rightarrow r$, it is valid to say that $p \rightarrow r$.

Disjunctive Argument
Given $p \vee q$ and $\sim p$ is true, it is valid to say that q is true.
Given $p \vee q$ and $\sim q$ is true, it is valid to say that p is true.

Example

Given:

I will go to the dance or I will go to the store.

I will not go to the store.

What valid argument can be made?

"I will go to the dance or I will go to the store" is represented as $p \lor q$.

"I will not go to the store" is represented as $\sim q$.

Because $\sim q$ is true, for $p \lor q$ to be true, p has to be true. By using the disjunctive argument, you can argue that I will go to the dance.

▶ Truth Functional Equivalencies

The following is a list of truth functional equivalencies. These show more than one way to say the same thing.

- **Double Negation**

  $p \leftrightarrow \sim\sim p$

- **Commutation**

  $(p \land q) \leftrightarrow (q \land p)$

  $(p \lor q) \leftrightarrow (q \lor p)$

  $(p \to q) \leftrightarrow (\sim p \lor q)$

- **Contraposition**

  $(p \to q) \leftrightarrow (\sim q \to \sim p)$

  $\sim(p \land q) \leftrightarrow (\sim p \lor \sim q)$

  $\sim(p \lor q) \leftrightarrow (\sim p \land \sim q)$

▶ Hypothesis and Conclusions

When considering hypothetical if-then statements, the antecedent (the clause presented after the *if*) is considered the **hypothesis**, and the consequent (the clause presented after the *then*) is considered the **conclusion**.

One clue that you are looking at a hypothetical situation is the word *suppose*. The if-then statement is creating a logical fantasy, and your reasoning is considered **hypothetical reasoning**.

▶ Necessary Conditions and Sufficient Conditions

Let's say you are trying to come up with a conditional statement regarding divisibility, and you proclaim:

"If a number is divisible by 15, then it is divisible by 5."

Given the antecedent "a number is divisible by 15," we are trying to prove the consequent "it is divisible by 5."

Notice that if a number is divisible by 15 (p has a truth value of true), then it is necessary that the number is also divisible by 5 (q has a truth value of true).

A condition that must be satisfied for a statement to be true is called a **necessary condition**.

For necessary conditions, if statement p implies statement q, q is a necessary condition of statement p.

This is just another way of looking at the truth table we saw earlier in the section

p	q	p $\Rightarrow$ q
T	T	T
T	F	F
F	T	T
F	F	T

Given that $p \Rightarrow q$ is true, in order for p to be true, q has to be true. This is shown in the first row of the truth table.

A condition that, if satisfied, ensures a statement's truth is called a **sufficient condition**.

In this case, when a number divisible by 15 is satisfied (p has a truth value of true), this assures that it is divisible by 5 (q has a truth value of true). Therefore, "a number is divisible by 15" is a sufficient condition for saying that number is divisible by 5.

If p implies q, then statement p is a sufficient condition of statement q.

Looking at the same truth table for implications:

p	q	$p \Rightarrow q$
T	T	T
T	F	F
F	T	T
F	F	T

Given that $p \Rightarrow q$ is true, then knowing that p is true would be sufficient for statement q to be true.

Example

Circle the correct type of condition:

A number being divisible by 10 is necessary/sufficient for it being even.

The two statements can be written in the form of the implication:

"Being divisible by 10 implies being even."

Thus, we have $p \Rightarrow q$, where p is "being divisible by 10" and q is "being even."

The example focuses on p, a number being divisible by 10, and we need to decide if p is necessary or sufficient.

We have this information:

$p \Rightarrow q$ is true

p is true

In the definition of necessary conditions, we saw:

Given that $p \Rightarrow q$ is true, in order for p to be true, q has to be true.

In the definition of sufficient conditions, we saw that:

Given that $p \Rightarrow q$ is true, knowing that p is true would be sufficient for statement q to be true.

The information we have is a match for the second definition, so we know that a number being divisible by 10 is **sufficient** for it being even.

If you think about it, you'll realize that this makes sense: A number being divisible by 10 is sufficient for knowing the number is even. It is not necessary for a number to be divisible by 10 for it to be even—there are many even numbers that are not divisible by 10.

▶ Biconditional Statements and Necessary and Sufficient Statements

Statements that use **if and only if** are called **biconditional statements**. In other words, if $p \rightarrow q$ and $q \rightarrow p$ are both true, we can also say "p if and only if q."

Note that p would be both **necessary and sufficient** for q and vice versa.

Let p represent: I am punished.

Let q represent: I am caught.

The biconditional statement: "I am punished if and only if I am caught" is represented by $p \leftrightarrow q$.

Example

Let *p* represent: I am punished.

Let *q* represent: I am caught.

Let $p \leftrightarrow q$ represent: "If I am punished if and only if I am caught"

Complete the truth table for the following biconditional statement.

p	*q*	$p \leftrightarrow q$
T	T	
T	F	
F	T	
F	F	

We added two columns to show $p \rightarrow q$ and $q \rightarrow p$. The biconditional statement will be true only when $p \rightarrow q$ and $q \rightarrow p$ are both true. Note that this occurs only when *p* and *q* have the same truth value. This happens in row 1 and row 4 here:

p	*q*	$p \rightarrow q$	$q \rightarrow p$	$p \leftrightarrow q$
T	T	T	T	T
T	F	F	T	F
F	T	T	F	F
F	F	T	T	T

CHAPTER

19 ▶ Functions and Their Graphs

A **function** of *x*, written as $f(x)$, applies a rule for calculating a *y* value. In order to be a function, the process of $x \rightarrow y$ must yield only one *y* value for every *x* value.

Consider the function $f(x) = x + 1$. For every *x* to which you apply the rule, you will get one and only one *y* value.

$f(x) = x + 1$ looks like this:

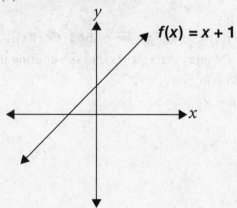

$f(x) = x + 1$

You can apply the **vertical line test** to determine whether $x + 1$ is a function. Mentally draw a vertical line anywhere on the graph and make sure that your line crosses only one point.

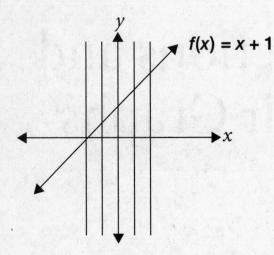

Example

Given $f(x) = 3x - 1$, find $f(5)$.

To solve, substitute 5 for x:

$f(5) = 3(5) - 1 = 15 - 1 = 14$

▶ Domain and Range

The **domain** of a function consists of all the x values that you can plug into the function. This may be the set of real numbers, for example.

Example

Given $f(x) = \frac{15}{x^2}$, what is the domain of this function?

Looking at $f(x) = \frac{15}{x^2}$, and remembering that the denominator of a fraction cannot be zero, we know that x cannot be zero. The domain is all real numbers with x not equaling 0.

The **range** of a function consists of all the y values that the rule produces.

Example

Given $f(x) = \frac{15}{x^2}$, what is the range of this function?

Recall that the domain is all real numbers not equal to 0. Once these nonzero real numbers are plugged into the function, the output will be a positive number. The range is all real numbers greater than 0.

▶ Combining Functions

Functions can be combined with operations you are very familiar with, such as $+, -, \times,$ and $\div$, as well as with composition functions, which are just functions of functions.

The sum $(f + g)(x) = f(x) + g(x)$

Example

Given $f(x) = 2x$ and $g(x) = 3x$, find $(f + g)(x)$.

$(f + g)(x) = f(x) + g(x)$, so substituting the two functions in, you get:

$f(x) + g(x) = 2x + 3x = 5x$

The difference $(f - g)(x) = f(x) - g(x)$

Example

Given $f(x) = \frac{1}{3}x$ and $g(x) = 2x$, find $(f - g)(x)$.

$(f - g)(x) = f(x) - g(x)$, so substituting the two functions, you get:

$f(x) + g(x) = \frac{1}{3}x - 2x = -1\frac{2}{3}x$

The product $(f \times g)(x) = f(x) \times g(x)$

Example

Given $f(x) = \frac{5}{2}x$ and $g(x) = \frac{2}{3}x$, find $(f \times g)(x)$.

$(f \times g)(x) = f(x) \times g(x)$, so substituting the two functions in, you get:

$f(x) \times g(x) = \frac{5}{2}x \times \frac{2}{3}x = \frac{5}{3}x$

The quotient $(f \div g)(x) = f(x) \div g(x)$

Example

Given $f(x) = 5x$ and $g(x) = x + 1$, find $(f \div g)(x)$.

$(f \div g)(x) = f(x) \div g(x)$, so substituting the two functions, you get:

$$f(x) \div g(x) = 5x \div (x+1) = \frac{5x}{(x+1)} \text{ where } x \neq -1$$

▶ Compositions of Functions

Compositions of functions are just functions of functions. The symbol used is o.

For example, the composition g o f of x is:

$(g \circ f)(x) = g(f(x))$

The composition f of g of x is:

$(f \circ g)(x) = f(g(x))$

Example

Given $f(x) = 2x$ and $g(x) = x + 1$, find $(g \circ f)(x)$ and $(f \circ g)x$.

$(g \circ f)(x) = g(2x) = 2x + 1$

$(f \circ g)(x) = f(x + 1) = 2(x+1) = 2x + 2$

▶ Inverse Functions

The **inverse function** of a function is a rule that inverts or undoes the original function and is represented as $f^{-1}(x)$.

If $f(x)$ is a rule such that $f(20) = 10$, then $f^{-1}(x)$ would be a rule that, when applied to 10, would yield 20.

Sometimes it will be obvious what the inverse function is.

If $f(x) = \frac{1}{2}x$, this rule halves x. $f^{-1}(x)$ should be doubling the x so we can get our original number back. $f^{-1}(x)$ would then equal $2x$.

Sometimes it is not so obvious what the inverse function is. In these cases, follow these steps:

First, rewrite the function in terms of x and y. To do this, replace $f(x)$ with y.

Next, switch the x and y and solve for y.

Finally, replace the y with $f^{-1}(x)$.

Example

Use these steps to find the inverse function for $f(x) = \frac{1}{2}x$.

To solve, first rewrite the function in terms of x and y. To do this, replace $f(x)$ with y:

$f(x) = \frac{1}{2}x$ becomes $y = \frac{1}{2}x$

Next, switch the x and y and solve for y:

$y = \frac{1}{2}x$ becomes $x = \frac{1}{2}y$

$2(x = \frac{1}{2}y)$

$y = 2x$

Finally, replace the y with $f^{-1}(x)$:

$y = 2x$ becomes $f^{-1}(x)$

▶ Simple Transformations of Functions

Translations are "slides." If you have the function $f(x) = x + 1$, you can slide this graph down to the origin using a translation. In this case, the translation would be $g(x) = x - 1$.

Notice that $(g \circ f)(x) = g(x + 1) = (x + 1) - 1 = x$, so the new line will be $y = x$.

Reflections flip the function about a line of symmetry, such as the x-axis or the y-axis.

Considering $f(x) + x = 1$, the function $g(x) = -x$ will flip the line across the y-axis.

Note that $(g \circ f)(x) = -(x + 1)$

All y values that were positive in $f(x)$ are now negative and vice versa.

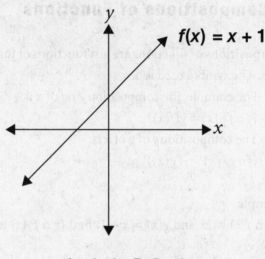

$f(x) = x + 1$

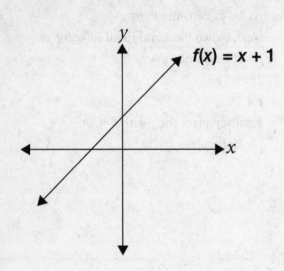

$f(x) = x + 1$

Apply the Reflection

$g(x) = -x$

Apply the Translation

$g(x) = x - 1$

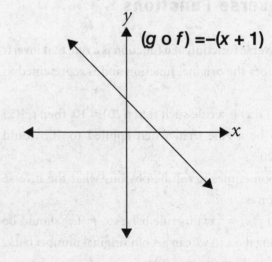

$(g \circ f) = -(x + 1)$

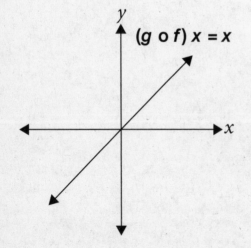

$(g \circ f) x = x$

Rules for Simple Transformations

Familiarity with these rules will help you spot simple transformations—namely translations and reflections.

$f(x + a)$	slides $f(x)$ left a units
$f(x - a)$	slides $f(x)$ right a units
$f(x) + a$	slides $f(x)$ up a units
$f(x) - a$	slides $f(x)$ down a units
$-f(x)$	flips $f(x)$ over the x-axis
$f(-x)$	flips $f(x)$ over the y-axis
$a(f(x))$ where $a \neq 0$	squishes or stretches the graph, depending on the value of a; if a is negative, the graph will also be inverted.

Example

The function $f(x)$ is defined as $f(x) = 2x^2 - 1$. When compared with $f(x)$, the graph of $f(x + 5)$ is

_____

_____

Note that $f(x) + a$ slides $f(x)$ up a units. This makes sense because you are applying the rule of the function (this gives you y) and then you are adding a. This increases y by a, which means the graph slides up. Because you are finding $f(x + 5)$, when compared with $f(x)$, the graph will "slide" five units upward.

20▶ Probability and Statistics

The **addition principle for counting** is good for situations where you are dealing with groups that may or may not have some elements in common. If you know that Group A has *a* elements and Group B has *b* elements, and they don't have any elements in common, you would just add $a + b$ to get the total. This relates to set theory: For any two disjoint sets A and B, the number of elements in A $\cup$ B will be equal to the number of elements in set A plus the number of elements in set B.

If Group A has *a* elements and Group B has *b* elements, and these groups have *c* elements in common, then you cannot count these elements twice. The total would be $a + b - c$. This relates to set theory too: A $\cup$ B will be equal to the number of elements in set A plus the number of elements in set B minus the number of elements in A $\cap$ B.

Sometimes you will encounter a situation where two groups are described: They have some elements in common, but it is also clear that there exist elements that belong to neither of these groups. In this case, you can consider an N group (a "neither" group) with *n* elements. The total would be $a + b - c + n$. In set theory, you would see this exact situation if set A and set B were not disjoint (that is to say that some elements are in both A and B), but there were also other elements that were in a different set, such as set C.

Example

In the Environment Club, 40 students are in the Marine Science subcommittee, while 30 students are in the Land Cleanup subcommittee. Fifteen of these students are in both subcommittees. There are also 5 board members who are in neither of these subcommittees. How many students are in the club all together?

To make sure all students are accounted for only once, make up a formula, such as:

Total = Marine + Land − Both + Neither
Substitute the given values:
Total = 40 + 30 − 15 + 5 = 60
Thus, there are 60 students in the Environment Club.

The **multiplication principle for counting** states that if event A can occur in *a* ways and event B can occur in *b* ways, the two events can occur together in $a \times b$ ways. This also works with more than two events; for example, if event A can occur in *a* ways, event B can occur in *b* ways, and event C can occur in *c* ways, then the three events can occur together in $a \times b \times c$ ways.

You can also use the multiplication principle for counting when you have a multi-step process, such as filling five seats in a row with five people. If you have five seats and five people, when you fill the first seat, you have five choices; when you fill the next seat, you have four choices; then three, then two, then one. Another way to express $5 \times 4 \times 3 \times 2 \times 1$ is 5!, which is 5 factorial. It gets tricky, though, when you have three seats and five people. For this situation, you would need to use the permutation formula if the order of the individuals matters.

Example

Joan has three shirts to choose from and six pairs of pants to choose from. How many different outfits can she create?

Event A (picking a shirt) can occur in *a* ways and event B (picking a pair of pants) can occur in *b* ways, so the two events can occur together in $a \times b$ ways. Because there are three shirts and six pairs of pants, this formula becomes $3 \times 6 = 18$.

Joan can create 18 different outfits using these shirts and pants.

Example

Five children will perform on stage. How many different ways can they be ordered in line?

When placing the first child, you have five choices; when placing the second, you have four choices; when placing the third, you have three choices; when placing the fourth, you have two choices; when placing the fifth, you have one choice. Multiply all these "ways" together to get $5 \times 4 \times 3 \times 2 \times 1 = 120$.

▶ Factorials

The **factorial** of *n*, denoted, **n!**, is the product of all the positive integers less than or equal to *n*. By definition, $0! = 1$. Note that *n* cannot be negative.

Example

Find 6!

$$6! = 6 \times 5 \times 4 \times 3 \times 2 \times 1 = 720$$

Permutations are used for finding all possible ordered sequences of objects or events. Permutations are used to see how many ways you can arrange the order of objects without repetition. Here, A B C is regarded as different from C B A because the order is different.

Use $_nP_r$ where *n*, is the total number of elements that can be selected, and *r* is the number of elements that will actually be selected.

$$_nP_r = \frac{n!}{(n-r)!}$$

Example

Three of five children will be chosen to perform on stage in a line. How many different orders are possible?

Recall that n is the total number of elements that can be selected, so $n = 5$. r is the number of elements that will actually be selected, so $r = 3$. Because order matters, use:

$$_nP_r = \frac{n!}{(n-r)!}$$

$$_5P_3 = \frac{5!}{(5-3)!} = 5 \times 4 \times 3 \times 2 \times 1 = 5 \times 4 \times 3 = 60$$

different possible orders.

Combinations are used when finding groups of objects or events where order does not matter. Combinations are concerned with the groups, not the order within a group. Here, A B C is regarded as the same as C B A because the group is the same.

Use $_nC_r$, where n is the total number of elements that can be selected, and r is the number of elements that will actually be selected.

$$_nC_r = \frac{n!}{r!(n-r)!}$$

Example

Three of five children will be chosen to perform on stage in a line. How many different combinations of children are possible?

Recall n is the total number of elements that can be selected, so $n = 5$. r is the number of elements that will actually be selected, so $r = 3$. If your children are represented as A B C D E, the same group can occur in any order: A B C = C B A = B A C. This question is asking only about the *combinations* of children, and not how they are ordered. Because order does not matter, use:

$$_nC_r = \frac{n!}{r!(n-r)!}$$

$$_5C_3 = \frac{5!}{3!(5-3)!} = \frac{5 \times 4 \times 3 \times 2 \times 1}{3 \times 2 \times 1 \times 2 \times 1} = \frac{5 \times 4 \times 3}{2 \times 1} = \frac{60}{2} = 30$$

▶ Probabilities

Simple events are events that have exactly one outcome. The probability of an event, P(E), is expressed as:

$$P(E) = \frac{\text{number of favorable outcomes}}{\text{total number of possible outcomes}}$$

The probability of an event is always between 0 and 1 (inclusive). This means that the probability of an event can be 0, 1, or any value in between these two numbers. A probability of zero means there is no possibility of an event's occurrence. A probability of 1 represents the event is certain to occur.

When considering all of the possible outcomes for a simple event, the sum of all these probabilities must equal 1. For example, if you flip a coin, the probability for heads is $\frac{1}{2}$ and the probability for tails is $\frac{1}{2}$. These are the only two possibilities, and the sum of both these probabilities is $\frac{1}{2} + \frac{1}{2} = 1$.

Similarly, the probability of an event occurring plus the probability of that event not occurring will also always add to 1. If you flip a coin, the probability for heads is $\frac{1}{2}$ and the probability for "not heads" is $\frac{1}{2}$. The sum of both these probabilities is $\frac{1}{2} + \frac{1}{2} = 1$.

Example

Today, 15 freshmen, 25 sophomores, 30 juniors, and 35 seniors entered a school contest to win a trip to a conference. If one winner is to be chosen at random, what is the probability that a senior will win the trip?

The probability of a simple event can be expressed as:

$$P(E) = \frac{\text{number of favorable outcomes}}{\text{total number of possible outcomes}}$$

In this case, the number of favorable outcomes equals the number of seniors: 35. The total number of possible outcomes will be the total number of possible winners, which is $15 + 25 + 30 + 35 = 105$. Thus:

$$P(E) = \frac{35}{105} = \frac{1}{3}.$$

▶ Compound Events

A **compound event** is a combination of simple events. Sometimes these simple events are mutually exclusive. For example, if you and I enter a raffle, it would be possible to calculate the probability of either of us winning. I have my tickets, and you have your tickets. Either of us winning is considered a mutually exclusive event because my winning excludes your winning and vice versa. To solve the probability of this mutually exclusive event, we would write:

$P(\text{me or you}) = P(\text{me}) + P(\text{you})$
For two simple, mutually exclusive events E and F:
$P(E \text{ or } F) = P(E) + P(F)$

Example
Today 15 freshmen, 25 sophomores, 30 juniors, and 35 seniors entered a school contest to win a trip to a conference. If one winner is to be chosen at random, what is the probability that a senior or a freshman will win the trip?

This question is a variation of the last question. To solve, use:
$P(S \text{ or } F) = P(S) + P(F)$

You know that P(S), the probability that a senior will win, is $\frac{35}{105}$. The probability that a freshman will win is $\frac{15}{105}$.

$$P(S \text{ or } F) = \frac{35}{105} + \frac{15}{105} = \frac{50}{105} = \frac{10}{21}$$

Conditional probability considers the probability of one event given that another event has occurred. The probability of A given B is written as: $P(A|B)$ You can calculate the odds of rolling a 6 and then a 5 on a die, for example. You would write $P(5|6)$, which means: the probability of rolling a 5, given that a 6 was just rolled.

Example
If the cards are not replaced, what is the probability of choosing two jacks in a row from a standard deck of cards?

Note that after the first jack is drawn, there are only 51 cards to choose from, and only 3 are jacks.

$$P(A|B) =$$
$$P(J|J) = \frac{3}{51}$$

▶ Data Analysis—Terms and Calculations

For a given set of values, the **range** is the value that is obtained when you subtract the smallest value from the largest value.

When looking at a collection of data, it is helpful to look at the location of the "middle." When measuring the location of the center of a distribution, you are finding the **central tendency**. The common measures of central tendency are mean, median, and mode.

To calculate the **mean** (otherwise known as the average), add all the numbers and divide by the total number of numbers.

Example
Given the set of numbers: 5, 3, –2, –2, find the mean.

The mean is $\frac{5 + 3 + (-2) + (-2)}{4} = \frac{4}{4} = 1$

To calculate the **median**, list the values in order and note the middle value—this is the median. If there are an even number of values, you will have two middle numbers. When this is the case, the median is the mean of these two middle numbers.

Example

Find the median of 5, 3, –2, –2.

First, arrange the numbers in order: –2, –2, 3, 5

The middle numbers are –2 and 3. Take the mean of these to get the median:

$$\frac{-2+3}{2} = \frac{1}{2} = 0.5$$

The **mode** is the number that occurs the most often.

Example

Find the mode of 5, 3, –2, –2.

–2 is the "most occurring," so the mode is –2.

▶ Standard Deviation Concepts

You have seen a few different calculations that we can make for a set of data. Think about what the mean tells you about your data. It is the sum of all the numbers divided by the number of numbers. Let's say you were taking the temperature every Groundhog Day for ten years. You then looked at the average. Are most of the numbers in your set of data close to your average, or do you see extremes?

A **normal distribution** of data will have values that are (overall) close to the average, rather than having values off in the extremes.

This is where the idea of the **bell curve** comes in. The peak represents your mean, and the "fatness" or "skinniness" of your bell gives you an idea of how different from the mean your values are.

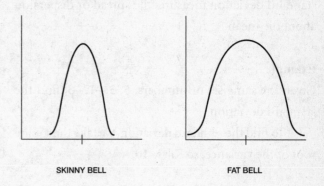

SKINNY BELL   FAT BELL

If the bell is skinny, then your values are pretty close to the mean. If your bell is fat, then your values **deviate** more from the mean—in other words, they are more different.

Visually, this makes sense, but in order to put numbers on this, you need to understand two terms: **variance** and **standard deviation**.

The **variance**, S^2, is the **average squared deviation** of values from the mean. To find the average squared deviation, you find every deviation, square each, and then take the average of all these values.

Example

Given the set of numbers: 5, 3, –1, –3, find the variance.

To solve, you must first know the mean:

The mean is $\frac{5+3+(-1)+(-3)}{4} = \frac{4}{4} = 1$

To find the variance, S^2, we need to find the average squared deviation of values from the mean.

$S^2 = [(1-5)^2 + (1-3)^2 + (1-(-1))^2 + (1-(-3))^2] \div 4$

$= [(-4)^2 + (-2)^2 + (2)^2 + (4)^2] \div 4$

$= [16 + 4 + 4 + 16] \div 4$

$= [40] \div 4$

$= 10$

The **standard deviation** is represented by S, and it is the square root of the variance. For a set of data, the standard deviation measures the spread or dispersion about the mean.

Example

Given the same set of numbers: 5, 3, –1, –3, find the standard deviation.

To find the standard deviation, we take the square root of the variance, so $S = \sqrt{10}$.

▶ Data Interpretation and Representation

When you collect data in the field and write it down or otherwise store it, you are gathering **raw data**. This data can be analyzed and represented visually in many ways. An **independent variable** is the variable that is changed, and the **dependent variable** is the response or outcome that is measured. The independent variable can be varied without manipulation; for example, the passage of time occurs naturally. Alternatively, the independent variable may be manipulated by the experimenter; for example, a scientist may change the temperature with a thermostat. The dependent variable *depends* on the independent variable. This sets up a cause-effect situation where the independent variable is the cause that elicits an effect (change in dependent variable). Depending on the research and data at hand, different visual representations will lend themselves to be more or less appropriate.

When comparing values across different groups or categories, **bar graphs** are a great way to represent your data. The x-axis will be labeled as to what it represents (for example, "Days of the Week"), but will also contain a label for each group or category at the base of each bar (for example, "Monday," "Tuesday," and so on). The bar rises to the point where the dependent variable falls on the y-axis. The units should be clearly notated and the y-axis should be labeled. Sometimes the y-axis will represent the mean. Other times it can represent a total. The graph should also have a title.

In the following example, the groups are Freshmen, Sophomores, Juniors, and Seniors. The y-axis represents the average number of days absent per student for the first quarter.

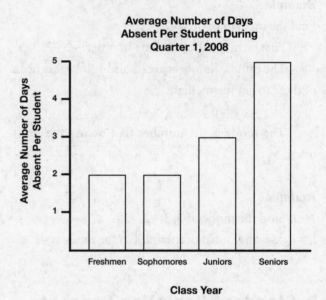

When you would like to continuously display how a dependent variable changes over time, **line graphs** are a good way to display your data visually. The x-axis shows the independent variable, and the y-axis shows the independent variable. Again, be sure to label both axes and title the graph.

In the following example, the number of dandelions is charted over time.

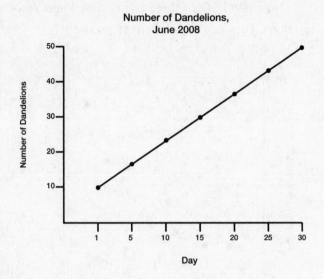

Number of Dandelions, June 2008

Sometimes you will have data that fits into different **class intervals**. A class interval is just a non-overlapping interval, such as "ages 20–29" and "ages 30–39." In these cases, it is helpful to construct a **histogram**. Histograms use bars that touch each other.

In the following example, the histogram shows the average yearly income (*y*-axis) based on four class intervals (the age intervals shown on the *x*-axis).

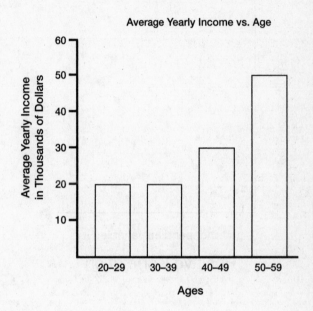

Average Yearly Income vs. Age

Pie charts, also known as **circle graphs**, are used to represent part-to-whole relationships. The whole pie represents 100%. Each piece represents a proportional part of the whole. Pie charts should always have titles, and there will either be a color key for the slices or each slice will be directly labeled.

In the following example, the whole circle represents all of the money (100% of the money) spent during August. Each slice represents where different percentages of that money was spent.

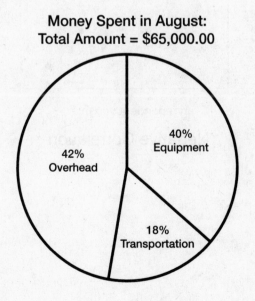

Money Spent in August: Total Amount = $65,000.00

If you are trying to see whether one variable is related to another, you can construct a **scatterplot**. The independent variable would go along the *x*-axis and the dependent variable would go along the *y*-axis. You would plot your data points and see if a **line of best fit** can be drawn. You may note the following relationships:

Note that both of these graphs have linear relationships. These are shown here, respectively:

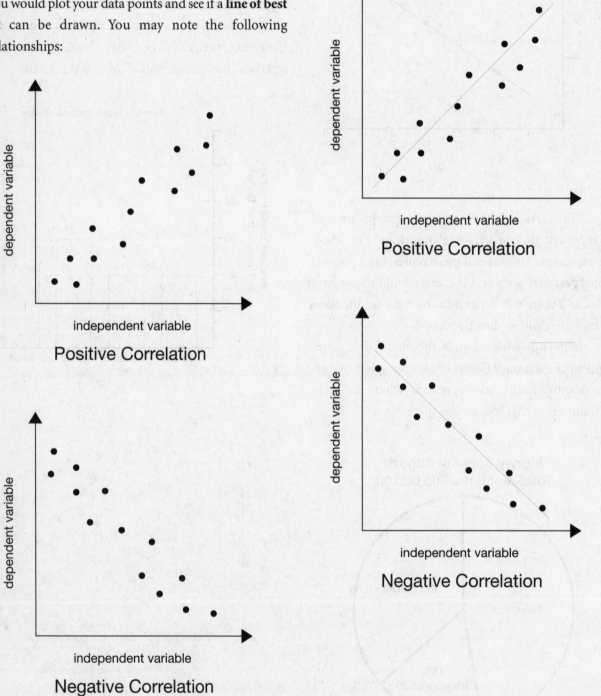

Positive Correlation

Positive Correlation

Negative Correlation

Negative Correlation

21 ▶ Additional Topics from Algebra and Geometry

When you raise a number to a whole number **exponent** that is greater than 1, this number indicates how many times you should multiply your number by itself. For example, $x^5 = x \times x \times x \times x \times x$. When you have an exponent of zero, $x^0 = 1$ (where $x \neq 0$). When you have an exponent of 1, $x^1 = x$. When you raise a number to an integer value exponent that is less than zero, $x^{-m} = \frac{1}{x^m}$ (where $x \neq 0$). The rules of exponents are listed here.

Products of powers: $x^m \times x^n = x^{m+n}$
Quotients of powers: $x^m \div x^n = x^{m-n}$
Power of a power: $(x^m)^n = x^{mn}$
Power of a product: $(x \times y)^m = x^m \times y^m$
Power of a quotient: $\left(\frac{x}{y}\right)^m = \frac{x^m}{y^m}$

Example
Reduce $\frac{(x^3)^2}{x^5}$.

To solve, use the rule $(x^m)^n = x^{mn}$ to change the numerator to x^6. Next, using the rule $(x^m)^n = x^{mn}$, the whole expression, $\frac{x^6}{x^5}$, simplifies to x.

Logarithms are related to exponents; in fact, the log function inverses the exponential functions. The logarithm of your number will be the exponent to which you need to raise the base in order to get your number.

$$\log_{\text{base}}(\text{your number}) = \text{answer}$$
$$\text{base}^{\text{answer}} = \text{your number}$$

Just like there are rules you need to know for exponents, there are rules you need to know for logs:

$$\log_b(mn) = \log_b(m) + \log_b(n)$$
$$\log_b(\tfrac{m}{n}) = \log_b(m) - \log_b(n)$$
$$\log_b(m^n) = n \times \log_b(m)$$

Example

Expand $\log_5(\frac{25}{b})$.

Use $\log_b(\frac{m}{n}) = \log_b(m) - \log_b(n)$, so you get $\log_5(\frac{25}{b}) = \log_5(25) - \log_5(b)$. Notice that $\log_5(25) = 2$ because $5^2 = 25$. Thus, $\log_5(25) - \log_5(b)$ can be simplified to $2 - \log_5 b$.

Example

Expand $\log_2(128^h)$.

Use $\log_b(m^n) = n \times \log_b(m)$ to change $\log_2(128^h)$ into $h \times \log_2 128$. Notice that $\log_2 128 = 7$ because $= 2^7 = 128$. So $h \times \log_2 128$ simplifies to $7h$.

Complex numbers involve the imaginary number i. i is the square root of -1.

$$i = \sqrt{-1}$$

This also means that $i^2 = -1$.

Example

Express in terms of i: $\sqrt{-25}$.

To solve, first separate the square root of -1:
$$\sqrt{-25} = \sqrt{-1} \times \sqrt{25}$$
The square root of -1 is i:
$$\sqrt{-1} \times \sqrt{25} = i\sqrt{25} = 5i$$

Example

Express in terms of i: $\sqrt{-5} \times \sqrt{-5}$.

To solve, first pull out i from under each radical:
$$\sqrt{-5} \times \sqrt{-5} = i\sqrt{5} \times i\sqrt{5} = i^2\sqrt{5 \times 5} = i^2\sqrt{25}$$
$$= (-1)\sqrt{25} = (-1)(5) = -5$$

Example

What is the numerical value of $(3 + 2i)(3 - 2i)$?

To solve, first use **FOIL**. Recall that FOIL means you multiply the first terms, then you multiply the outer terms, then you multiply the inner terms, and then you multiply the last terms, and you add all of these products together.

$$\text{F} \quad \text{O} \quad \text{I} \quad \text{L}$$
$$(3 + 2i)(3 - 2i) = 9 - 6i + 6i - 4i^2$$

$9 - 6i + 6i - 4i^2$ simplifies to $9 - 4i^2$. Next, knowing that $i^2 = -1$, this can be simplified further to $9 - 4(-1) = 13$.

It is best to avoid having i in the denominator. To convert to proper form, multiply by an equivalent of one, such as $\frac{i}{i}$.

Example

$\frac{5 + i}{i} =$

To get the i out of the denominator and yet still retain the same value, you can multiply by $\frac{i}{i}$, because any number divided by itself is 1, and any number times 1 is itself.

So

$\frac{5 + i}{i} \times 1$ will retain its value

and

$\frac{5+i}{i} \times \frac{i}{i}$ will not change the value of this expression.

First, isolate the numerator in parentheses so that you will multiply correctly later.

$\frac{(5+i)}{i} \times \frac{i}{i}$

$= \frac{i(5+i)}{i^2}$

$= \frac{i(5+i)}{-1}$

$= \frac{(5i+i^2)}{-1}$

$= \frac{(5i-1)}{-1}$

$= \frac{5i}{-1} - \frac{1}{-1}$

$= -5i + 1$

To find the complex conjugate for an expression involving a complex number, simply take whatever the imaginary part is and change the sign while keeping the real part as is. For example, the complex conjugate of $a - bi$ would be $a + bi$.

Example

Find the complex conjugate of $9 - 4i$.

To solve, leave the real part the same and change the sign for the imaginary part. Leave the 9, and change $-4i$ to $+4i$. Thus, the answer is $9 + 4i$.

▶ Applications from Algebra and Geometry

Plane figures have two dimensions—length and width. If you calculate the distance around a plane figure, you are finding the **perimeter**, and in the case of a circle, this is called the **circumference**. Perimeter and circumference are always measured in units of length. For example, to find the perimeter of a square with a side equal to 3 cm, you would add up all four sides: 3 cm + 3 cm + 3 cm + 3 cm = 12 cm. Notice that the units used, cm,

are units of length. Areas, on the other hand, are measured in units squared. The square with side = 3 cm would have an area of 9 cm². You should be familiar with the following formulas:

Formulas for Perimeter and Area of Plane Figures

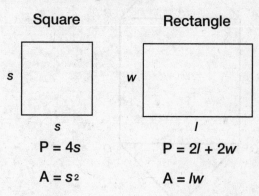

Square

$P = 4s$

$A = s^2$

Rectangle

$P = 2l + 2w$

$A = lw$

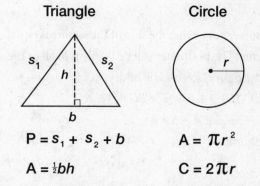

Triangle

$P = s_1 + s_2 + b$

$A = \frac{1}{2}bh$

Circle

$A = \pi r^2$

$C = 2\pi r$

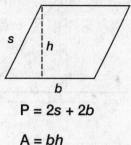

Parallelogram

$P = 2s + 2b$

$A = bh$

These basic formulas can be used in combination. Try the following example.

Example

Ryan draws square ABCD and then adds two triangles to the diagram as shown here. What is the perimeter of the figure?

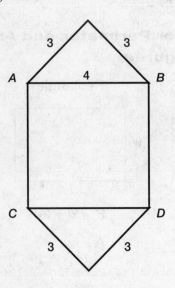

To solve, notice that the side of the square is equal to four units. The perimeter will be the sum of all of the sides of the figure, so you will add:

Side AD + 3 + 3 + Side BC + 3 + 3

= 4 + 3 + 3 + 4 + 3 + 3

= 20 units

Example

Find the area of the trapezoid:

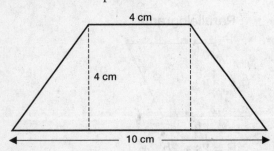

If you know the formula for the area of a trapezoid, $\frac{1}{2}(b_1 + b_2)h$, you can use it. If not, you can find the area by noticing that there is a square on the inside combined with two triangles. The area of the square is

$s^2 = 4^2 = 16$ cm^2. Because the base of the trapezoid at the bottom is 10 and the top base is 4, the difference of 6 will be split between the two triangles. This means that the base of each triangle is 3 cm. The area of each triangle is then $\frac{1}{2}bh = \frac{1}{2}(3)(4) = 6$ cm^2. The total area would be the sum of the area of the square plus the area of the 2 triangles: 16 cm^2 + 6 cm^2 + 6 cm^2 = 28 cm^2.

Let's test this against the trapezoid formula:

$A = \frac{1}{2}(b_1 + b_2)h$

$= \frac{1}{2}(4 + 10)(4)$

$= \frac{1}{2}(14)(4)$

$= 28$ cm^2

Example

What is the area of the annulus shown here?

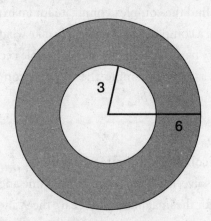

An annulus is just a large circle with a small circle cut out. To find the area of the annulus, you would find the area of the large circle and subtract the area of the smaller circle. Let's call the radius of the large circle R and the radius of the small circle r. The area of the annulus would then be:

$A = \pi R_2 - \pi r_2$

$= \pi(6)_2 - \pi(3)_2$

$= 36\pi - 9\pi$

$= 37\pi$ units squared

▶ Properties of Triangles, Circles, and Rectangles

One plane figure can be **similar** to another plane figure. This means that both figures are in proportion to one another. Every square is similar to every other square, so there is no fun in exploring similar squares. A rectangle that has a width of 3 cm and a length of 4 cm would be similar to any rectangle that multiples this length and width by a constant. For example, a rectangle that is 3 cm × 4 cm may be a scale model for a plot of land that is 3 km by 4 km, or 30 km by 40 km.

For the most part, the CLEP exam focuses on similar triangles. Triangle ABC will be similar to triangle $A'B'C'$ if a constant, k, can be found such that $A' = kA$, $B' = kB$, and $C' = kC$.

Example

Triangle $A'B'C'$ is similar to triangle ABC shown here. If $A'B' = 12$, what is the perimeter of triangle $A'B'C'$?

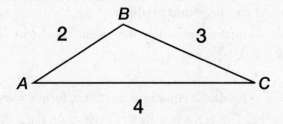

The relationship between AB and $A'B'$ is such that $A'B'$ is 6 times the value of AB. Use this relationship to find the other two sides. Because $BC = 3$, $B'C'$ would equal $3 \times 6 = 18$. Because $AC = 4$, $A'C'$ will equal $4 \times 6 = 24$. The sum of all sides for $A'B'C'$ is then $12 + 18 + 24 = 54$ cm.

Right triangles are special cases because you can use the **Pythagorean theorem** to relate two legs of the triangle to the **hypotenuse** of the triangle. The hypotenuse is the side of the triangle that is opposite the right angle; it is the longest side, and it is represented as

c. The two other sides are called legs and are represented as a and b. These sides are related by the Pythagorean theorem:

$a^2 + b^2 = c^2$

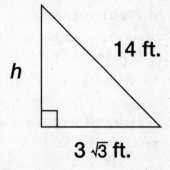

$$a^2 + b^2 = c^2$$

Example

A 14-foot-long ladder leans against a building. The base of the ladder is $3\sqrt{3}$ feet away from the base of the building. At what height does the top of the ladder touch the building?

First, sketch a diagram:

14 ft.

h

3 √3 ft.

Next, use $a^2 + b^2 = c^2$ to solve:

$(3\sqrt{3})^2 + h^2 = 14^2$

$(9 \times 3) + h^2 = 196$

$27 + h^2 = 196$

$h^2 = 169$

$h = 13$ feet

A brief review of the properties of circles, triangles, and rectangles follows.

Properties of Circles

- In the interior, circles have 360°.
- The radius is the distance from the center of the circle to the surface (edge) of the circle.
- The diameter passes through the center of the circle and touches two points on its surface.
- A semicircle is created when the circle is sliced exactly in half.

Properties of Triangles

- The interior angles of a triangle add up to 180°.
- A right triangle contains a 90° angle, and the Pythagorean theorem can be used to find the lengths of the sides
- Similar triangles are in proportion to one another.
- The sum of any two sides of a triangle will be greater than the third side.
- The largest side is opposite the largest angle, and the smallest side is opposite the smallest angle.

Properties of Rectangles

- The interior angles of a rectangle add to 360°.
- Rectangles have four right angles.
- The diagonals of a rectangle are equal and bisect each other.
- If all four sides of a rectangle are the same length, then the rectangle is also a square.

▶ Algebraic Equations

You should be able to spot linear and quadratic equations. Many questions on linear equations will involve parallel and perpendicular lines. Many questions on quadratic equations deal with stretching and flipping parabolas—you saw this in Chapter 19, but we will look more closely at it here.

Linear equations are in the form $y = mx + b$, where m is the slope (the change in y divided by the change in x), and b is the y-intercept. If m is positive, then the slope is positive. If m is negative, then the slope is negative.

It is important to remember that the slopes of parallel lines have the same value.

Example

Given the line $y = 5x + 8$, is the line $y = 5x - 92$ parallel?

First, make sure both equations are in the form $y = mx + b$, and they are. Next, compare the values for m. Both of these equations have a value of 5, so they are indeed parallel.

It is also important to remember that the slopes of perpendicular lines are negative reciprocals of each other. For a line with a slope of m, a perpendicular line will have a slope of $\frac{-1}{m}$.

Example

Line L has a slope of $\frac{1}{3}$. Line R is perpendicular to line L. What is the slope of line L?

Because line L has a slope of $\frac{1}{3}$, the negative reciprocal can be found by flipping the numerator and denominator and adding the $-$ sign. The slope of line R will be -3.

Quadratic equations are in the form $y = ax^2 + bx + c$. This is the equation of a parabola. If $a > 0$, the parabola opens upward. If $a < 0$, the parabola opens downward. The line of symmetry is at $x = \frac{-b}{2a}$, where x is the x-coordinate of the turning point. Most CLEP questions on this topic require you to tell what will happen to the graph of a parabola when you make a change to the equation. In the functions chapter, you saw that by multiplying $y = x^2$ by -1, you will flip your parabola over the x-axis. In the following example, you will look closer at the equation for the parabola, and try to recognize the difference between two transformations.

Example

Given $f(x) = x^2$, describe the difference between the graphs of $y = 2x^2$ and $y = (2x)^2$.

In the first case, you are squaring x and then doubling this value:

x	y
−2	8
−1	2
0	0
1	2
2	8

In the second case, you are doubling x and then squaring this value:

x	y
−2	16
−1	8
0	0
1	8
2	16

Thus, the parabola for $y = (2x)^2$ will be more "squished" than the parabola $y = 2x^2$.

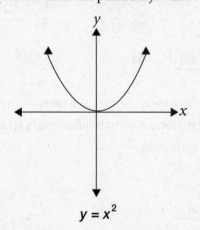

$y = x^2$

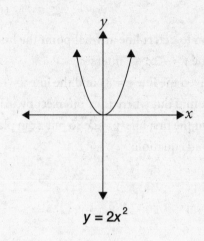

$y = 2x^2$

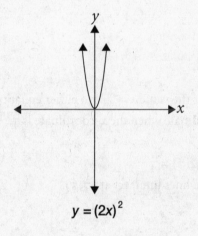

$y = (2x)^2$

▶ Systems of Linear Equations

Systems of linear equations involve more than one line. There are two ways to see how these lines are related to each other. One way is to substitute a variable from one equation into the other equation. The second way is to solve a **simultaneous equation**, which just means you are adding or subtracting the two given equations so that you can find the value where they will be equal.

Example

Use substitution to determine at what point the line $y = 2x$ and the line $y = -2x + 1$ intersect.

You are given the line $y = 2x$ and the line $y = -2x + 1$, so you can find out where they intersect by using substitution. For the first line, $y = 2x$, so put $2x$ in place of y in the second equation:

$$y = -2x + 1$$
$$2x = -2x + 1$$

Isolating the variable and simplifying, you get:

$$4x = 1$$
$$x = \frac{1}{4}$$

Next, put the value $x = \frac{1}{4}$ into either equation to get the y-coordinate when the x-coordinate is $\frac{1}{4}$.

$$y = 2x = 2\left(\frac{1}{4}\right) = \frac{1}{4} = \frac{1}{2}$$
Thus, the lines intersect at $(\frac{1}{4}, \frac{1}{2})$.

Example

Use a simultaneous equation to determine at what point the line $y = 2x$ and the line $y = -2x + 1$ intersect.

The goal of simultaneous equations is to be able to cross out one of the variables when you add or subtract the equations. The first line has a $2x$ and the second line has a $-2x$. Thus, if we add the two equations, these variables will cancel out.

$$y = 2x$$
$$+ y = -2x + 1$$
$$\overline{2y = 1}$$
$$y = \frac{1}{2}$$

Now, put the value $y = \frac{1}{2}$ into either equation to get the x-coordinate when the y-coordinate is $\frac{1}{2}$.

$$y = 2x$$
$$\frac{1}{2} = 2x$$
$$\frac{1}{2} \div 2 = x$$
$$x = \frac{1}{4}$$
Thus, the lines intersect at $(\frac{1}{4}, \frac{1}{2})$.

Example

Use a simultaneous equation to determine at what point the line $3y = 4x - 8$ and the line $y = 2x + 1$ intersect.

The goal of simultaneous equations is to be able to cross out one of the variables when you add or subtract the equations. The first line has a $4x$ and the second line has a $2x$. If we double the entire second equation and subtract it from the first, we will be able to cross out a $4x$.

$$3y = 4x - 8$$
$$-(y = 2x + 1)$$

is the same as:

$$3y = 4x - 8$$
$$-2(y = 2x + 1)$$

Note that doubling an entire equation does not change the equation.

Distributing the 2, we get:

$$3y = 4x - 8$$
$$-(2y = 4x + 2)$$

Note that the parentheses are still there—this is a reminder that the subtraction must affect every term of the equation. Subtracting, we get:

$$3y = 4x - 8$$
$$-(2y = 4x + 2)$$
$$\overline{y = -10}$$

When y is -10, we can solve for x with:

$y = 2x + 1$
$-10 = 2x + 1$
$-11 = 2x$
$\frac{-11}{2} = x$
$x = -5.5$

Thus, the lines intersect at $(5.5, -10)$.

▶ Graphing Inequalities

If, instead of being given the line $y = x$, you are given $y > x$, you would notice that y cannot equal x and that all values above the line $y = x$ would be in the solution set. To graph this, you would use a dashed line for $y = x$, and you would shade the part of the graph that is above the line.

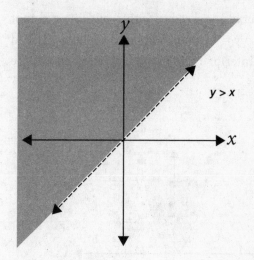

Example

Sketch the graph of $x \leq y \leq 4$.

This example also involves the graph of $y = x$, except this time y is allowed to equal x, so you would draw a solid line for $y = x$. Next, notice that y must be less than or equal to 4. Graph $y = 4$ as a solid line, because y can equal 4.

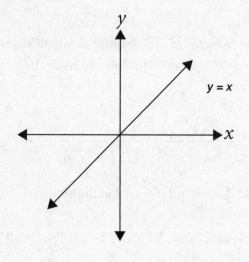

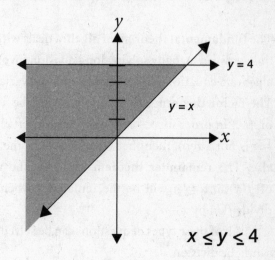

Example

Sketch the graph of $x^2 \leq y < 16$.

This example involves the graph of $y = x^2$ and $y = 16$. Note that $y = 16$. Because y can equal x^2, the parabola should be sketched with a solid line. y cannot equal 16, so $y = 16$ should be sketched with a dashed line. The interior region that is created should be shaded.

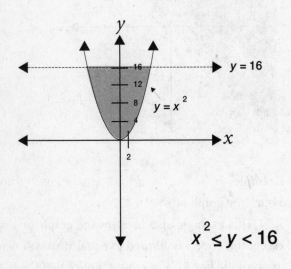

$$x^2 \leq y < 16$$

▶ Algebraic Theorems

The **fundamental theorem of algebra** deals with the link between actually solving long division involving algebraic equations and manipulating the variables. The **factor theorem** says that $x = a$ must be a zero of $f(x)$ in order for $x - a$ to be a factor of $f(x)$. If $x = a$ is not a zero, then that value can tell something else. The **remainder theorem** says that the value of $f(x)$ at $x = a$ will be the remainder when you divide $f(x)$ by $x - a$.

All of these types of questions can be solved with synthetic division.

Example

Given $f(x) = 2x^5 + 2x^2 + 5x$, what will the remainder be when $f(x)$ is divided by $x - 2$?

The remainder theorem says that the value of $f(x)$ at $x = 2$ will be the remainder when you divide $f(x)$

by $x - 2$. First, set $x - 2$ equal to zero to get $x = 2$. The value of $f(x)$ at $x = 2$ will be the remainder when you divide $f(x)$ by $x - 2$. If this value equals zero, then $x = 2$ is a root of the equation, also called a zero of the equation.

Using synthetic division is a quick way to find out the remainder.

The 2 outside of the L is the number you are dividing into the coefficients that you see in the equation. The top row inside the L lists all of the coefficients in the equation. Have all the powers of x descend and add in any necessary 0 coefficients for any powers not present: $2x^5 + 0x^4 + 0x^3 + 2x^2 + 5x + 0x^0$. Always bring down the leftmost coefficient in the L; in this case, we bring down a 2.

```
2 |  2    0    0    2    5    0
     ↓
     2
```

The 2 outside of the L multiplies with this 2, and we fill in a 4 in the next right column inside the L.

```
2 |  2    0    0    2    5    0
          4
     2
```

Add down to get $0 + 4 = 4$ at the bottom.

```
2 |  2    0    0    2    5    0
          4
     2    4
```

The 2 outside of the L multiplies with this 4, and we fill in 8 in the next right column inside the L.

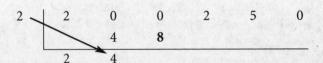

Add down to get $0 + 8 = 8$ at the bottom.

2	2	0	0	2	5	0
		4	8			
	2	4	**8**			

The 2 outside of the L multiplies with this 8, and we fill in 16 in the next right column inside the L.

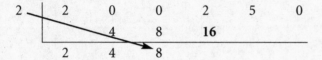

2	2	0	0	2	5	0
		4	8	**16**		
	2	4	8			

Add down to get $2 + 16 = 18$.

2	2	0	0	2	5	0
		4	8	16		
	2	4	8	**18**		

The 2 outside of the L multiplies with this 18, and we fill in 36 in the next right column inside the L.

2	2	0	0	2	5	0
		4	8	16	**36**	
	2	4	8	18		

Add down to get $5 + 36 = 41$.

2	2	0	0	2	5	0
		4	8	16	36	
	2	4	8	18	**41**	

The 2 outside of the L multiplies with this 41, and we fill in 82 in the next right column inside the L.

2	2	0	0	2	5	0
		4	8	16	36	**82**
	2	4	8	18	41	

Add down to get $0 + 82 = 82$.

2	2	0	0	2	5	0
		4	8	16	36	82
	2	4	8	18	41	**82**

When $2x^5 + 2x^2 + 5x$ is divided by $x - 2$, the remainder is 82, and thus, 82 is the answer to this question.

This question could have also been asked another way: You could have be asked to evaluate $f(2)$ for $f(x) = 2x^5 + 2x^2 + 5x$. The remainder theorem says that the value of $f(x)$ at $x = 2$ will be the remainder when you divide $f(x)$ by $x - 2$, so this is just another way of asking the same question.

The third way this question could have been asked would have been to ask whether $x = 2$ is a root of $f(x) = 2x^5 + 2x^2 + 5x$. Had $x = 2$ been a root, synthetic division would have given us a remainder of 0.

The fourth way this question could have been asked would have been to ask whether $x = 2$ is a zero of $f(x) = 2x^5 + 2x^2 + 5x$. Had $x = 2$ been a zero of $f(x) = 2x^5 + 2x^2 + 5x$, synthetic division would have given us a remainder of 0.

4 ▶ About the CLEP Natural Sciences Exam

he Natural Sciences section of the CLEP examination includes various topics covered in college-level freshman and sophomore biology and physical science courses. This content usually satisfies the university requirements for biology and physical science credits for non-majors. That is, the Natural Sciences examination is not appropriate for science majors.

While the Natural Sciences examination does not assume knowledge of specific and factual details, this test does examine your knowledge and understanding of principles and concepts in science. The Natural Sciences exam will also require you to understand key science issues in current or present-day culture.

Successful completion of this examination will enable you to demonstrate your skill, level of knowledge, and comprehension with material covered in courses that meet the general education requirement in the sciences. Colleges or related institutions will grant up to six hours to individuals making a satisfactory score on the exam. In some cases, colleges will grant you course credit for your total score covering a two-semester survey course for biology and physical science.

You will be given 90 minutes to complete 120 questions on the examination. Please note that some of the questions are only pretest questions. These will not be scored. Your time spent on tutorials or in providing personal data is not part of the actual test time.

The following is a description of content in the exam and the percentage of the exam devoted to a specific content area:

- basic principles, facts, and concepts (40% of the examination)
- interpreting and comprehending information given to you in graphs, diagrams, tables, equations, and/or verbal passages (20% of the examination)
- applying knowledge of qualitative and quantitative functions within the principles of science. The material in this section will be presented in the form of graphs, diagrams, tables, verbal passages, and equations. Note that more attention will be given to qualitative than quantitative reasoning (40% of the examination).

The Natural Sciences examination includes material from the following topics. The percentage listed next to each topic represents the approximate number of questions on that topic.

- Biological Sciences (50%)
  - 10% origin of life, evolution, classification of organisms
  - 10% the organization of the cell, cell division, the chemical nature of the gene, bioenergetics and biosynthesis
  - 20% the structure, function, and development of organisms, the patterns of heredity
  - 10% the concepts of population biology with an emphasis on ecology
- Physical Sciences (50%)
  - 7% atomic and nuclear structure and properties, elementary particles, nuclear reactions
  - 10% chemical elements, compounds and reactions, molecular structure and bonding
  - 12% heat, thermodynamics, and states of matter, classical mechanics, relativity
  - 4% electricity and magnetism, waves, light and sound
  - 7% the universe: galaxies, stars, the solar system

- 10% the Earth: atmosphere, hydrosphere, structure, properties, surface features, geological processes, history

Some of the examination questions are interdisciplinary in nature and thus they cannot be easily classified in one of categories listed here. Some questions cover content drawn from areas such as the history and philosophy of science, scientific methods, science applications and technology, and the relationship of science to contemporary problems of society, such as environmental science, global warming, and the depletion of energy. Some of the questions on this examination are laboratory oriented.

▶ Choosing Resources to Prepare for the Exam

As you prepare for the Natural Sciences examination, note that most textbooks used in freshman and sophomore Natural Sciences courses include content in the previous outline. The way the content is arranged may differ across textbooks. Thus, it is wise to review more than one textbook in the biological and physical sciences. Most of these textbooks can be found in college bookstores or libraries. In choosing a textbook, review the table of contents against the material highlighted in the above outline.

Candidates might also maintain an interest in scientific issues, read science articles in newspapers and magazines, watch public television programs such as "Nova," use the Internet to explore ideas and principles in biology and physical science, or work in a health field or do laboratory work. These activities will help you score well on the Natural Sciences examination.

CLEP Natural Sciences Pretest

Before reviewing topics that will be covered on the CLEP Natural Sciences exam, test your existing skills by taking the pretest that follows. You will encounter 120 questions that are similar to the type you will find on the CLEP Natural Sciences exam. The questions are organized by the two content areas:

- biological sciences
- physical sciences

For now, ignore the time restraints of the official CLEP; take as much time as you need to complete each question.

Answer every question; however, if you are not sure of an answer, put a question mark by the question number to note that you are making a guess. On the official CLEP, you are not penalized for unanswered or incorrect answers, so making a good guess is an important skill to practice.

When you are finished, check the answer key on page 310 carefully to assess your results. Your pretest score will help you determine how much preparation you need and in which areas you need the most careful review and practice.

▶ CLEP Natural Sciences Pretest

1. ⓐ ⓑ ⓒ ⓓ ⓔ	41. ⓐ ⓑ ⓒ ⓓ ⓔ	81. ⓐ ⓑ ⓒ ⓓ ⓔ
2. ⓐ ⓑ ⓒ ⓓ ⓔ	42. ⓐ ⓑ ⓒ ⓓ ⓔ	82. ⓐ ⓑ ⓒ ⓓ ⓔ
3. ⓐ ⓑ ⓒ ⓓ ⓔ	43. ⓐ ⓑ ⓒ ⓓ ⓔ	83. ⓐ ⓑ ⓒ ⓓ ⓔ
4. ⓐ ⓑ ⓒ ⓓ ⓔ	44. ⓐ ⓑ ⓒ ⓓ ⓔ	84. ⓐ ⓑ ⓒ ⓓ ⓔ
5. ⓐ ⓑ ⓒ ⓓ ⓔ	45. ⓐ ⓑ ⓒ ⓓ ⓔ	85. ⓐ ⓑ ⓒ ⓓ ⓔ
6. ⓐ ⓑ ⓒ ⓓ ⓔ	46. ⓐ ⓑ ⓒ ⓓ ⓔ	86. ⓐ ⓑ ⓒ ⓓ ⓔ
7. ⓐ ⓑ ⓒ ⓓ ⓔ	47. ⓐ ⓑ ⓒ ⓓ ⓔ	87. ⓐ ⓑ ⓒ ⓓ ⓔ
8. ⓐ ⓑ ⓒ ⓓ ⓔ	48. ⓐ ⓑ ⓒ ⓓ ⓔ	88. ⓐ ⓑ ⓒ ⓓ ⓔ
9. ⓐ ⓑ ⓒ ⓓ ⓔ	49. ⓐ ⓑ ⓒ ⓓ ⓔ	89. ⓐ ⓑ ⓒ ⓓ ⓔ
10. ⓐ ⓑ ⓒ ⓓ ⓔ	50. ⓐ ⓑ ⓒ ⓓ ⓔ	90. ⓐ ⓑ ⓒ ⓓ ⓔ
11. ⓐ ⓑ ⓒ ⓓ ⓔ	51. ⓐ ⓑ ⓒ ⓓ ⓔ	91. ⓐ ⓑ ⓒ ⓓ ⓔ
12. ⓐ ⓑ ⓒ ⓓ ⓔ	52. ⓐ ⓑ ⓒ ⓓ ⓔ	92. ⓐ ⓑ ⓒ ⓓ ⓔ
13. ⓐ ⓑ ⓒ ⓓ ⓔ	53. ⓐ ⓑ ⓒ ⓓ ⓔ	93. ⓐ ⓑ ⓒ ⓓ ⓔ
14. ⓐ ⓑ ⓒ ⓓ ⓔ	54. ⓐ ⓑ ⓒ ⓓ ⓔ	94. ⓐ ⓑ ⓒ ⓓ ⓔ
15. ⓐ ⓑ ⓒ ⓓ ⓔ	55. ⓐ ⓑ ⓒ ⓓ ⓔ	95. ⓐ ⓑ ⓒ ⓓ ⓔ
16. ⓐ ⓑ ⓒ ⓓ ⓔ	56. ⓐ ⓑ ⓒ ⓓ ⓔ	96. ⓐ ⓑ ⓒ ⓓ ⓔ
17. ⓐ ⓑ ⓒ ⓓ ⓔ	57. ⓐ ⓑ ⓒ ⓓ ⓔ	97. ⓐ ⓑ ⓒ ⓓ ⓔ
18. ⓐ ⓑ ⓒ ⓓ ⓔ	58. ⓐ ⓑ ⓒ ⓓ ⓔ	98. ⓐ ⓑ ⓒ ⓓ ⓔ
19. ⓐ ⓑ ⓒ ⓓ ⓔ	59. ⓐ ⓑ ⓒ ⓓ ⓔ	99. ⓐ ⓑ ⓒ ⓓ ⓔ
20. ⓐ ⓑ ⓒ ⓓ ⓔ	60. ⓐ ⓑ ⓒ ⓓ ⓔ	100. ⓐ ⓑ ⓒ ⓓ ⓔ
21. ⓐ ⓑ ⓒ ⓓ ⓔ	61. ⓐ ⓑ ⓒ ⓓ ⓔ	101. ⓐ ⓑ ⓒ ⓓ ⓔ
22. ⓐ ⓑ ⓒ ⓓ ⓔ	62. ⓐ ⓑ ⓒ ⓓ ⓔ	102. ⓐ ⓑ ⓒ ⓓ ⓔ
23. ⓐ ⓑ ⓒ ⓓ ⓔ	63. ⓐ ⓑ ⓒ ⓓ ⓔ	103. ⓐ ⓑ ⓒ ⓓ ⓔ
24. ⓐ ⓑ ⓒ ⓓ ⓔ	64. ⓐ ⓑ ⓒ ⓓ ⓔ	104 ⓐ ⓑ ⓒ ⓓ ⓔ
25. ⓐ ⓑ ⓒ ⓓ ⓔ	65. ⓐ ⓑ ⓒ ⓓ ⓔ	105. ⓐ ⓑ ⓒ ⓓ ⓔ
26. ⓐ ⓑ ⓒ ⓓ ⓔ	66. ⓐ ⓑ ⓒ ⓓ ⓔ	106. ⓐ ⓑ ⓒ ⓓ ⓔ
27. ⓐ ⓑ ⓒ ⓓ ⓔ	67. ⓐ ⓑ ⓒ ⓓ ⓔ	107. ⓐ ⓑ ⓒ ⓓ ⓔ
28. ⓐ ⓑ ⓒ ⓓ ⓔ	68. ⓐ ⓑ ⓒ ⓓ ⓔ	108. ⓐ ⓑ ⓒ ⓓ ⓔ
29. ⓐ ⓑ ⓒ ⓓ ⓔ	69. ⓐ ⓑ ⓒ ⓓ ⓔ	109 ⓐ ⓑ ⓒ ⓓ ⓔ
30. ⓐ ⓑ ⓒ ⓓ ⓔ	70. ⓐ ⓑ ⓒ ⓓ ⓔ	110. ⓐ ⓑ ⓒ ⓓ ⓔ
31. ⓐ ⓑ ⓒ ⓓ ⓔ	71. ⓐ ⓑ ⓒ ⓓ ⓔ	111. ⓐ ⓑ ⓒ ⓓ ⓔ
32. ⓐ ⓑ ⓒ ⓓ ⓔ	72. ⓐ ⓑ ⓒ ⓓ ⓔ	112. ⓐ ⓑ ⓒ ⓓ ⓔ
33. ⓐ ⓑ ⓒ ⓓ ⓔ	73. ⓐ ⓑ ⓒ ⓓ ⓔ	113 ⓐ ⓑ ⓒ ⓓ ⓔ
34. ⓐ ⓑ ⓒ ⓓ ⓔ	74. ⓐ ⓑ ⓒ ⓓ ⓔ	114. ⓐ ⓑ ⓒ ⓓ ⓔ
35. ⓐ ⓑ ⓒ ⓓ ⓔ	75. ⓐ ⓑ ⓒ ⓓ ⓔ	115. ⓐ ⓑ ⓒ ⓓ ⓔ
36. ⓐ ⓑ ⓒ ⓓ ⓔ	76. ⓐ ⓑ ⓒ ⓓ ⓔ	116. ⓐ ⓑ ⓒ ⓓ ⓔ
37. ⓐ ⓑ ⓒ ⓓ ⓔ	77. ⓐ ⓑ ⓒ ⓓ ⓔ	117. ⓐ ⓑ ⓒ ⓓ ⓔ
38. ⓐ ⓑ ⓒ ⓓ ⓔ	78. ⓐ ⓑ ⓒ ⓓ ⓔ	118. ⓐ ⓑ ⓒ ⓓ ⓔ
39. ⓐ ⓑ ⓒ ⓓ ⓔ	79. ⓐ ⓑ ⓒ ⓓ ⓔ	119 ⓐ ⓑ ⓒ ⓓ ⓔ
40. ⓐ ⓑ ⓒ ⓓ ⓔ	80. ⓐ ⓑ ⓒ ⓓ ⓔ	120. ⓐ ⓑ ⓒ ⓓ ⓔ

▶ Pretest Questions

Biological Sciences

1. What type of information can the fossil record provide about conditions on Earth millions of years ago?
   a. whether two ancient species existed at the same point in time
   b. whether ancient hominids mapped constellations
   c. the distance between Earth and Venus
   d. whether there was life on Mars
   e. the percentage of herbivorous dinosaurs that laid infertile eggs

2. What set of data best supports the theory of evolution?
   a. the existence of hydrogen bonds between water molecules
   b. the range of temperature variations across the Earth
   c. the number of reptile species that regenerate tails
   d. the shapes of a particular species of finches' beaks over generations
   e. the range of variation in growth spurts of human adolescents

3. A vestigial structure is a physical trait in an organism that has lost its function over time. For example, whales have small leg bones buried within the back of their body. These small leg bones are remnants of the long legs of their land-dwelling ancestors. Another example of a vestigial structure is
   a. opposable thumbs in humans.
   b. long necks in giraffes.
   c. brightly colored plumes of peacocks.
   d. mitochondria in a bacterium.
   e. wings on an ostrich.

4. Homologous structures are a sign of
   a. biological coincidence.
   b. evolution from a common ancestor.
   c. increasing diversity in a population.
   d. interbreeding.
   e. endangered species.

5. The science of classifying organisms is known as
   a. genetics.
   b. homology.
   c. natural selection.
   d. parsimony.
   e. taxonomy.

6. Which of these organisms shares the most recent common ancestor with humans?

a.

b.

c.

d.

e.

Use the following diagram to answer questions 7–9.

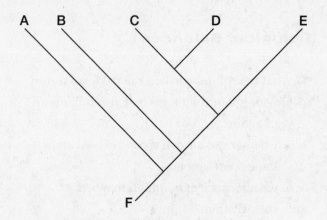

7. Which two species are least closely related?
   a. A and E
   b. A and C
   c. A and B
   d. C and D
   e. B and E

8. Which species is a common ancestor to all the others shown?
   a. species A
   b. species B
   c. species D
   d. species E
   e. species F

9. What is the name of this type of depiction of ancestral relationships?
   a. a pedigree
   b. an allopatry
   c. a phylogenetic tree
   d. a Punnett square
   e. a linkage map

Use the following text and diagram to answer questions 10–12.

In the 1950s, Stanley Miller developed an experiment to determine what conditions were like on the early Earth and how these conditions brought forth the complex organic compounds of the modern planet. Miller included water in one flask and several gases in another flask, and attached the flasks with glass tubing on either side (see figure). Miller's experiment included the gases and a large electrical discharge in the upper chamber, cooling just below the upper chamber, and heating of the lower chamber, which contained water.

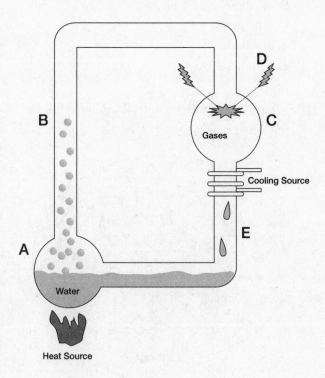

10. Which component of the experimental setup represents the atmosphere of the early Earth?
  a. A
  b. B
  c. C
  d. D
  e. E

11. Miller's experiment suggests that thermal vents found in the oceans may have contributed to chemical evolution by
  a. transmitting electrical impulses into the oceans to spark reactions.
  b. providing a home for deep sea creatures.
  c. producing oxygen for reactions.
  d. facilitating natural selection.
  e. providing thermal energy for the reactions that produced complex compounds.

12. What does this suggest about the possibility of life on other planets?
  a. There is no possibility for life on other planets, even if the conditions are similar to those of the early Earth, because other planets are not as technologically advanced.
  b. There is no possibility for life on other planets because other planets are not warm enough to support life.
  c. There is a possibility for life on another planet if the conditions that existed on the early Earth are all present.
  d. There is a possibility for life on another planet if the life can survive frequent lightning storms.
  e. There is a possibility for life on another planet because many other planets are larger than Earth.

13. Which of the following is NOT found in a prokaryotic cell?
  a. mitochondria
  b. nucleus
  c. cytoplasm
  d. DNA
  e. ribosomes

14. Which of the following statements about mitochondria is false?

   a. They are the powerhouses of a cell.

   b. They contain DNA.

   c. They synthesize some of their own proteins.

   d. They are enclosed by a cell wall.

   e. They contain ribosomes.

15. _____ lower the activation energy of a
reaction.

   a. Mitochondria

   b. Enzymes

   c. Substrates

   d. Molecules of ATP

   e. Thermodynamics

16. In cellular respiration, what is the final electron
acceptor of the electron transport chain?

   a. glucose

   b. carbon dioxide

   c. oxygen

   d. nitrogen

   e. chlorophyll

17. Retroviruses copy RNA information into DNA
through

   a. transcription.

   b. reverse transcription.

   c. translation.

   d. reverse translation.

   e. none of the above

18. What stage of mitosis is depicted in the following
illustration?

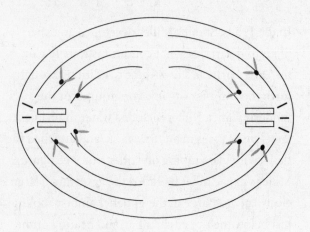

   a. interphase

   b. prophase

   c. metaphase

   d. anaphase

   e. telophase

19. What stage of meiosis is depicted in the following illustration?

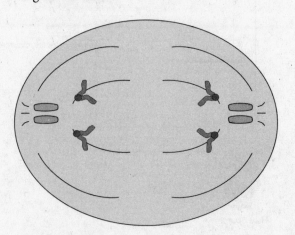

   a. metaphase I

   b. metaphase II

   c. anaphase I

   d. anaphase II

   e. interphase

Use the following diagram to answer questions 20 and 21.   *Use the following diagram to answer questions 22 and 23.*

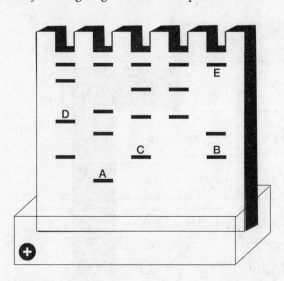

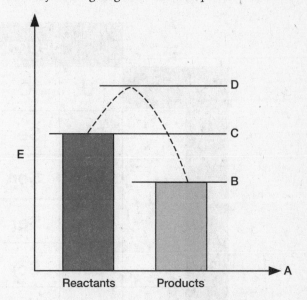

20. In the gel electrophoresis experiment, digested fragments of DNA migrate toward a positively charged electrode at varying rates according to size. Which fragment shown above is the shortest?

a. fragment A

b. fragment B

c. fragment C

d. fragment D

e. fragment E

21. What feature of DNA makes the fragments migrate toward the positively charged electrode?

a. oxygen molecules

b. hydrogen bonds

c. double helix

d. phosphate molecules

e. carbon molecules

22. What type of reaction is shown in the graph?

a. endergonic

b. exergonic

c. metabolic

d. hydrolytic

e. redox

23. Which of the following indicates the activation energy of the reaction?

a. A-B

b. A-C

c. B-D

d. B-C

e. C-D

Use the following diagram to answer question 24.

Second Letter

First Letter		U	C	A	G	Third Letter
		U	**C**	**A**	**G**	
U		Phe	Ser	Tyr	Cys	U
		Phe	Ser	Tyr	Cys	C
		Leu	Ser	STOP	STOP	A
		Leu	Ser	STOP	Trp	G
C		Leu	Pro	His	Arg	U
		Leu	Pro	His	Arg	C
		Leu	Pro	Gln	Arg	A
		Leu	Pro	Gln	Arg	G
A		Ile	Thr	Asn	Ser	U
		Ile	Thr	Asn	Ser	C
		Ile	Thr	Lys	Arg	A
		Met	Thr	Lys	Arg	G
G		Val	Ala	Asp	Gly	U
		Val	Ala	Asp	Gly	C
		Val	Ala	Glu	Gly	A
		Val	Ala	Glu	Gly	G

24. A coding strand of DNA has the sequence 3'-CCCAAAGGG-5.' Which peptide is produced from this strand?

    a. Pro-Lys-Gly

    b. Gly-Lys-Pro

    c. Gly-Phe-Pro

    d. Pro-Phe-Gly

    e. none of the above

25. Which of the following best exemplifies an exception to the law of independent assortment?

    a. linked genes

    b. recessive traits

    c. mutations

    d. test crosses

    e. all of the above

26. In humans, "sex-linked traits" most commonly refer to genes

    a. on the Y chromosome.

    b. on the X chromosome.

    c. that determine sexual traits.

    d. that combine during sexual reproduction.

    e. that mutated during an early stage of fertilization.

27. The farther apart two genes on a single chromosome are, the higher the probability

    a. that they are not developmentally important.

    b. that they code for the same protein.

    c. that one is recessive and one is dominant.

    d. that crossing over will unlink them.

    e. that a point mutation will occur.

28. _____ is a diagnostic technique that analyzes amniotic fluid, extracted from the uterus, for certain genetic disorders in the fetus.

    a. Parthenogenesis

    b. Endometriosis

    c. In vitro fertilization

    d. Blastulation

    e. Amniocentesis

29. The _____ is responsible for maintaining homeostasis in vertebrates by integrating the endocrine and nervous systems.

    a. adrenal gland

    b. thyroid gland

    c. pancreas

    d. pituitary gland

    e. hypothalamus

30. A biological cycle that occurs with a frequency of about 24 hours regardless of any environmental variable is referred to as a

    a. circadian rhythm.

    b. thigmotropism.

    c. photoperiodism.

    d. Krebs cycle.

    e. any of the above

31. The _____ forms the skin and nervous system in human development.

    a. endoderm

    b. mesoderm

    c. ectoderm

    d. none of the above

    e. all of the above

32. A "red tide" may be caused by
   a. slime molds.
   b. diatoms.
   c. dinoflagellates.
   d. ciliates.
   e. fungi.

33. All fungi reproduce _____ by producing _____.
   a. sexually . . . spores
   b. asexually . . . yeasts
   c. asexually or sexually . . . spores
   d. asexually or sexually . . . yeasts
   e. none of the above

34. In alternation of generations in angiosperms, the diploid plant, which is the _____, produces _____ spores by meiosis.
   a. sporophyte . . . haploid
   b. sporophyte . . . diploid
   c. gametophyte . . . haploid
   d. gametophyte . . . diploid
   e. none of the above

35. _____ are the male structures of angiosperms.
   a. Pistils
   b. Flowers
   c. Carpels
   d. Anthers
   e. Sepals

36. The reflex arc in humans does NOT include which of the following?
   a. sensory neuron
   b. spinal cord
   c. central nervous system
   d. brain
   e. motor neuron

Use the following diagram to answer questions 37–39.

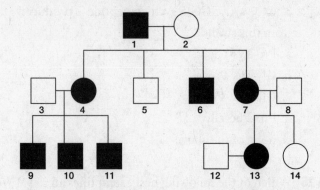

In this figure, shaded shapes represent individuals expressing the phenotype for a certain genetic trait.

37. This type of diagram that traces phenotypes of an organism and its ancestors is referred to as a
   a. Punnett square.
   b. phylogeny.
   c. pedigree.
   d. homology.
   e. cladogram.

38. Which of the following best describes the pattern of heredity of the trait being traced in the figure?
   a. autosomal dominant
   b. sex-linked recessive
   c. deleterious
   d. heterozygous
   e. homozygous

39. Which of the following fully describes the non-affected offspring that individuals 7 and 8 have produced?
   a. one male and one female
   b. one male
   c. one female
   d. one male and two females
   e. two females

Use the following diagram to answer questions 40 and 41.

	F	f
f	Ff	ff
f	Ff	ff

40. This type of cross involving (at least) one homozygous recessive genotype is known as
   a. Mendelian cross.
   b. F1 cross.
   c. F2 cross.
   d. test cross.
   e. genome cross.

41. The ratio of dominant to recessive phenotypes produced in this cross is
   a. 3:1.
   b. 2:1.
   c. 9:3:3:1.
   d. 1:2:1.
   e. 1:1.

Use the following diagram to answer question 42.

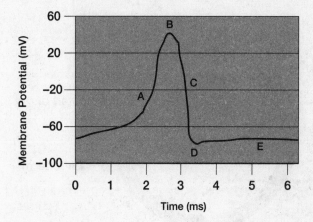

42. Which of the points on the graph represents the depolarization of the neuron?
   a. A
   b. B
   c. C
   d. D
   e. E

Use the following equation to answer questions 43 and 44.

$$6CO_2 + 12H_2O + energy \rightarrow C_6H_{12}O_6 + 6O_2 + 6H_2O$$

43. What reaction is summarized in this equation?
   a. respiration
   b. oxidation
   c. fermentation
   d. photosynthesis
   e. glycolysis

44. Where does the energy in the first part of the reaction come from?
   a. heat
   b. water
   c. light
   d. oxygen
   e. carbon

Use the following diagram to answer questions 45 and 46.

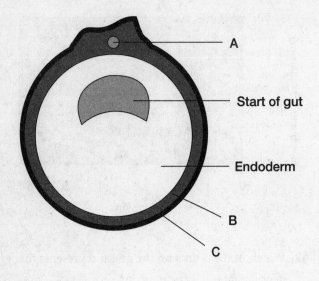

45. The figure represents a human embryo just after gastrulation. What does the structure marked A represent?
   a. zygote
   b. gamete
   c. ectoderm
   d. notochord
   e. placenta

46. The layer marked C in the figure will eventually form
   a. skin and nervous system.
   b. skeletal and muscular systems.
   c. liver and pancreas.
   d. head and neck.
   e. all of the above

Use the following diagram to answer questions 47 and 48.

ABO blood type in humans is a classic example of a genetic trait with multiple alleles. These situations do not follow the standard outcomes of Mendel's original pea plant crosses. One of three possible alleles may be passed on by each parent. Both A and B are codominant over O. The possible genotypes are shown in the following table:

	A	B	O
A	AA	AB	AO
B	AB	BB	BO
O	AO	BO	OO

47. A male with blood type A and a female with blood type O can produce a child with which of the following blood types?
   a. A
   b. AB
   c. B
   d. ABO
   e. none of the above

48. A person with blood type A has the genotype
   a. AA.
   b. AO.
   c. Neither **a** nor **b** is possible.
   d. Either **a** or **b** is possible.
   e. cannot be determined

49. Permafrost is typically found in which of the following biomes?
   a. rain forest
   b. desert
   c. temperate grassland
   d. broadleaf forest
   e. tundra

50. Organisms that undergo photosynthesis are called
   a. autotrophs.
   b. heterotrophs.
   c. carnivores.
   d. herbivores.
   e. omnivores.

Use the following diagram to answer questions 51–53.

The following graph represents the effect of immigration and extinction rates on the number of species on a specific island.

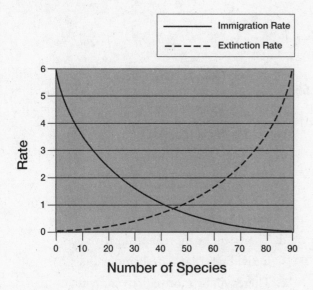

51. Approximately how many species will be present on the island when the immigration rate is equal to the extinction rate?
   a. 0
   b. 25
   c. 45
   d. 75
   e. 90

52. A sudden rise in the extinction rate was noticed, but the number of species remained stable. Which of the following has probably occurred?
   a. The immigration rate has risen.
   b. The immigration rate has fallen.
   c. The immigration rate did not change.
   d. The island is no longer a source of nutrients.
   e. The island has developed a new climate.

53. Which of the following conclusions can be made from this graph?
   a. If the number of species on the island is high, the extinction rate will be high, and the immigration rate will be low.
   b. If the number of species on the island is high, the extinction rate will be low, and the immigration rate will be high.
   c. If the number of species on the island is high, the extinction rate will be low, and the immigration rate will be low.
   d. If the number of species on the island is high, the extinction rate will be high, and the immigration rate will be high.
   e. none of the above

Use the following diagram to answer questions 54–56.

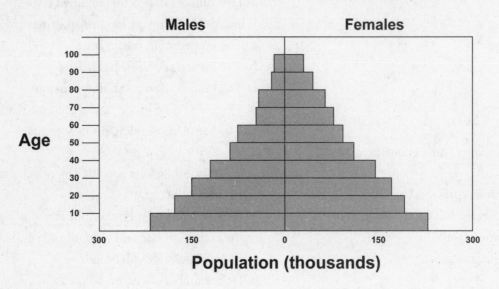

(Reproductive age: 20–40)

54. According to the age pyramid, this population is
   a. expanding.
   b. declining.
   c. stable.
   d. resource-deficient.
   e. economically stable.

55. The age range with the highest number of individuals is
   a. 90–100.
   b. 70–80.
   c. 50–60.
   d. 20–30.
   e. 0–10.

56. Which of the following statements best describes this population 20 years from now, assuming the current trend continues?
   a. The population will decrease.
   b. The population will face a job shortage.
   c. There will be more reproductive-age individuals than children.
   d. There will be more reproductive-age individuals than elderly individuals.
   e. There will be more elderly individuals than children.

Use the following diagram to answer questions 57–59.

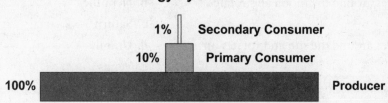

Energy Pyramid

57. Based on the figure, which of the following foods provides the most energy?
   a. beef
   b. chicken
   c. fish
   d. shrimp
   e. carrot

58. A cow would be classified in which level of this pyramid?
   a. producer
   b. primary consumer
   c. secondary consumer
   d. producer or primary consumer
   e. producer or secondary consumer

59. A tertiary consumer would probably have what percentage of energy?
   a. 0%
   b. 0.1%
   c. 0.5%
   d. 20%
   e. 50%

60. A colony of bees has only one permanent member that is reproductively active: the queen. All the bees in a hive are the offspring of the queen. A worker bee will sting an intruder, sacrificing its own life, to protect the queen and hive. This is an example of which of the following?
   a. courtship
   b. foraging
   c. altruism
   d. competition
   e. commensalism

Physical Sciences

61. Which of the following is correct?
    a. Earth revolves around the moon and rotates on its axis.
    b. Earth revolves around the sun and rotates on its axis.
    c. Earth rotates around the moon and revolves on its axis.
    d. Earth rotates around the sun and revolves on its axis.
    e. Earth rotates around the sun and rotates on its axis.

62. The correct order of the parts of the sun is
    a. chromosphere, core, corona, photosphere, and solar wind.
    b. core, corona, chromosphere, photosphere, and solar wind.
    c. photosphere, chromosphere, corona, solar wind, and core.
    d. solar wind, corona, chromosphere, photosphere, and core.
    e. solar wind, photosphere, chromosphere, corona, and core.

63. The average distance from Earth to the sun is a(n)
    a. astronomical unit.
    b. kilometer.
    c. light year.
    d. parsec.
    e. solar.

64. Which of the following is NOT one of the "gas giants"?
    a. Jupiter
    b. Neptune
    c. Saturn
    d. Uranus
    e. Venus

65. The chart shows the distance of four galaxy clusters from Earth and the speed at which each appears to be moving away from Earth.

GALAXY CLUSTER	DISTANCE (MILLIONS OF LIGHT YEARS)	SPEED (KM/S)
W	1×10^2	1×10^3
X	1×10^3	1.5×10^4
Y	2.5×10^3	4×10^4
Z	4×10^3	6×10^4

From this data, the distance a galaxy cluster is from Earth
    a. is directly related to how fast it is moving.
    b. is inversely related to how fast it is moving.
    c. is one-tenth of the speed at which it is moving.
    d. is ten times the speed at which it is moving.
    e. is unrelated to how fast or slow it is moving.

66. "The daily sunspot number is calculated by multiplying the number of groups of sunspots observed and then adding this product to the total count of individual spots. This is sometimes referred to as a Zurich Sunspot Number. However, results vary, because the measurement depends on observer interpretation and experience and on the stability of Earth's atmosphere above the observing site. The use of Earth as a platform from which to record these numbers contributes to this variability, too, because the sun rotates and the evolving spot groups are distributed unevenly across solar longitudes. To compensate for these limitations, each daily international number is computed as a weighted average of measurements made from a network of cooperating observatories."

The best title for this paragraph is
a. "How Daily Sunspot Numbers are Calculated."
b. "How to Define a Zurich Sunspot Number."
c. "Sunspot Distribution on the Sun's Surface."
d. "The Unreliability of Earth for Making Sunspot Counts."
e. "Why the Daily Sunspot Number is Inaccurate."

67. This table gives some data about the planets in a star system. The periods of revolution and rotation are in Earth days.

PLANET	PERIOD OF REVOLUTION	PERIOD OF ROTATION
W	250	2
X	450	10
Y	800	20
Z	1,200	25

Which of the following gives the order—from fewest to most—of the "days" in a "year" for the four planets?
a. W, X, Y, Z
b. X, Y, Z, W
c. Y, X, Z, W
d. Z, Y, X, W
e. W, Z, X, Y

68. In this diagram, the distance from the sun to a nearby star is measured using the parallax method.

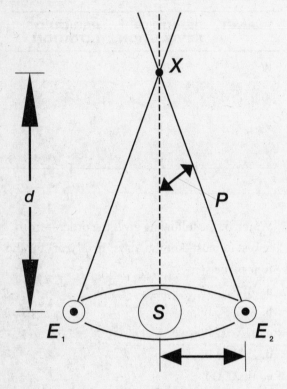

If the parallax angle is 0.5 of an arc second, what is the distance to the star?

a. 0.25 parsec

b. 0.5 parsec

c. 1 parsec

d. 2 parsecs

e. 4 parsecs

69. The table shows some data about comets that travel through the solar system.

COMET	PERIHELION DISTANCE (A.U.)	SEMI-MAJOR AXIS (A.U.)	ORBITAL PERIOD (YR.)
Halley	~0.6	~18	~75
Encke	~0.3	~2.2	~3
Wirtanen	~1.1	~3.1	~6
Borrelly	~1.4	~3.6	~7
Kohoutek	~1.6	~3.4	~6

Which comet has the shortest "year" and passes the closest to the sun?

a. Borrelly

b. Encke

c. Halley

d. Kohoutek

e. Wirtanen

70. The table lists some data about planets in a star system.

PLANET	ORBITAL ECCENTRICITY	APHELION-TO-PERIHELION DISTANCE
Q	0.05	10^9 km
R	0.10	10^8 km
S	0.30	10^9 km
T	0.15	10^8 km
U	0.01	10^7 km

Which planet has the smallest distance from the perihelion to the star?

a. Q
b. R
c. S
d. T
e. U

71. What is the result of binding oxygen and iron?
a. a higher boiling point
b. a lighter color
c. lowered density
d. increased hardness
e. rust

72. Which of the following is NOT a mixture?
a. air
b. baking soda
c. milk
d. sand
e. wood

73. The temperature of 50 milliliters of gas in a container with a fixed volume is doubled. What happens to the pressure of the gas in the container?
a. It doubles.
b. It is halved.
c. It quadruples.
d. It is quartered.
e. It is unchanged.

74. Which of the following is NOT a group of elements on the periodic table?
a. actinides
b. alkaline earths
c. lanthanides
d. nuclides
e. transition metals

75. The table shows the solubility of three compounds in grams per 100 cubic centimeters of water at one atmosphere of pressure and at three different temperatures.

	0° C	10° C	20° C
X	0.6	0.6	0.7
Y	122	128	133
Z	12	16	22

Which compound(s) exhibit(s) the greatest solubility increase(s) as temperature rises when compared to the solubility at 0°?

a. X
b. X and Y
c. Y
d. Y or Z
e. Z

76. The diagram shows the effect a catalyst has on the rate at which a chemical reaction produces oxygen.

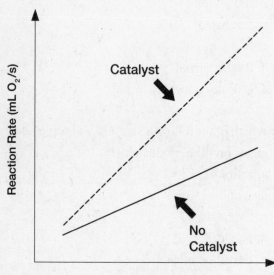

A conclusion that can be drawn from the diagram is that
a. the catalyst doubles the rate of oxygen production as temperature is increased.
b. the catalyst has no effect on the rate of production of oxygen.
c. the catalyst increases the temperature at which the reaction occurs.
d. the catalyst increases the rate of oxygen production as the temperature is increased.
e. the catalyst increases the rate of oxygen production by a constant amount as the temperature is increased.

77. What numbers should replace the question marks in order to balance the following chemical equation?
$$?N_2 + ?H_2 \rightarrow ?NH_3$$
a. 1, 1, and 1
b. 1, 1, and 2
c. 1, 2, and 1
d. 1, 2, and 2
e. 1, 3, and 2

78. Which of the following would balance the chemical reaction $Ca + 2H_2O \rightarrow$?
a. $CaOH + H_2\uparrow$
b. $CaOH_2 + H_2\uparrow$
c. $Ca(OH)_2 + H_2\uparrow$
d. $Ca_2OH_2 + H_2\uparrow$
e. $(CaO)_2H + H_2\uparrow$

79. In the reaction $2KClO_3 \rightarrow 2KCl + 3O_2$, how many moles of potassium chloride are produced if six moles of oxygen are produced?
a. eight
b. four
c. three
d. seven
e. six

80. In the *third-order* reaction-rate equation aA + bB → cC + dD, the concentration of A is 0.05 and the concentration of B is 0.1. Reactant A reacts twice as fast as reactant B, and the reaction rate depends on both reactants. If the reaction rate equation is given by $r = k$ [A]^m × [B]^n, which of the following gives the reaction rate for this system?

a. $k \times 10^{-2}$
b. $5k \times 10^{-3}$
c. $2.5k \times 10^{-3}$
d. $5k \times 10^{-4}$
e. $2.5k \times 10^{-4}$

81. The amount of energy consumed by an electrical device is measured in

a. amperes.
b. kilowatts.
c. kilowatt-hours.
d. ohms.
e. volts.

82. In the diagram, the direction of a magnetic field is shown around a wire in a circuit.

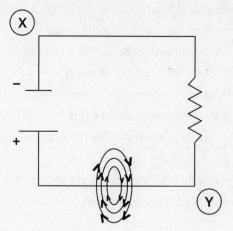

Which of the following statements is untrue?

a. The current flows from Y to X.
b. The electrons flow from X to Y.
c. The magnetic field results from the current flow.
d. The magnetic field results from the electron flow.
e. The magnetic field results from the voltage.

83. A circuit component that can be charged and discharged is a(n)

a. ammeter.
b. capacitor.
c. insulator.
d. resistor.
e. voltmeter.

84. Which of the following is true? "The force between two charges is
  a. directly proportional to the product of the charges and the distance between them."
  b. directly proportional to the square of the distance between the charges."
  c. inversely proportional to the inverse of the distance between the charges."
  d. inversely proportional to the square of the product of the charges."
  e. inversely proportional to the square of the distance between the charges."

Use the following diagram to answer questions 85 and 86.

The following diagram shows alternating voltage changing with time.

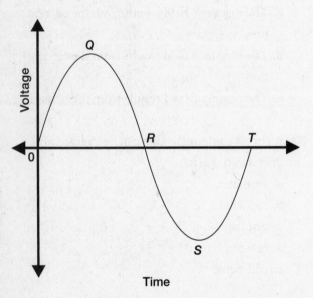

Time

85. The voltage is changing most rapidly
  a. at point Q.
  b. at point R.
  c. at point S.
  d. between points Q and R.
  e. between points R and S.

86. The voltage is positive
  a. at point O.
  b. at point S.
  c. between points O and T.
  d. between points Q and R.
  e. between points R and S.

87. In the circuit shown, $R_1 = 2$ ohms, $R_2 = 3$ ohms, and $R_3 = 4$ ohms.

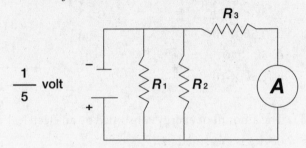

What current appears on the ammeter A in the circuit?
  a. $\frac{1}{45}$ amp
  b. $\frac{1}{26}$ amp
  c. $\frac{29}{30}$ amp
  d. $\frac{30}{29}$ amp
  e. $\frac{26}{25}$ amp

88. The table shows the values of a magnetic field, B, at a specified distance, r, from a wire carrying a current, I.

MAGNETIC FIELD, B (TESLAS)	DISTANCE, r (METERS)	CURRENT, I (AMPERES)
1×10^{-7}	1	2
2×10^{-7}	1	1
4×10^{-7}	2	1

Based on this data, what is the relationship between B, I, and r?
a. $B \propto I \times r$
b. $B \propto I \div r$
c. $B \propto r$
d. $B \propto r \div I$
e. $B \propto 1 \div (r \times I)$

89. A capacitor carries 4×10^{-6} Coulombs in a 200-volt circuit. What is the capacitor's capacitance?
a. 8×10^{-10} μF
b. 8×10^{-4} μF
c. 5×10^{-1} μF
d. 50 μF
e. 200 μF

90. What is the current in milliamps (mA) in a circuit with a source voltage of 2π volts at 50 kilohertz (kH) and an inductance of 25 millihenrys (mH)?
a. 0.125 mA
b. 0.8 mA
c. 80 mA
d. 125 mA
e. 800 mA

91. Which of the following is the correct order of the parts of Earth's interior, starting with Earth's surface?
a. crust, lithosphere, mantle, inner core, outer core
b. crust, lithosphere, mantle, outer core, inner core
c. inner core, outer core, mantle, lithosphere, crust
d. mantle, outer core, inner core, lithosphere, crust
e. outer core, crust, mantle, lithosphere, inner core

92. The order of the epochs in the Tertiary period of the Cenozoic period is
a. Eocene, Miocene, Oligocene, Paleocene, and Pliocene.
b. Miocene, Oligocene, Paleocene, Pliocene, and Eocene.
c. Oligocene, Paleocene, Pliocene, Eocene, and Miocene.
d. Paleocene, Pliocene, Eocene, Miocene, and Oligocene.
e. Pliocene, Miocene, Oligocene, Eocene, and Paleocene.

93. Which of the following is NOT an example of the three basic rock types?
a. clastic
b. granite
c. magma
d. shale
e. slate

94. A single self-contained piece of a mineral found in an aggregate rock is a

a. crystal.

b. fragment.

c. grain.

d. ferroclast.

e. sediment.

95. The table shows the densities and relative hardness of five minerals.

MINERAL	DENSITY (g/cm³)	HARDNESS (Mohs scale)
R	4	10
S	3	7
T	5	6
W	9	3
X	3	1

Which mineral can make a scratch on all of the others?

a. W

b. X

c. R

d. S

e. T

96. The diagram shows the percentage composition of Al_2O_3, FeO, and SiO_2 in three minerals.

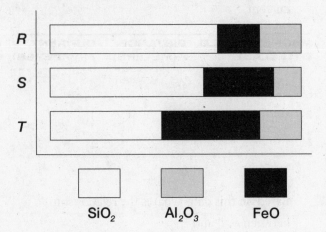

The greatest percentage of SiO_2 and the least percentage of FeO are found in which mineral(s)?

a. R

b. R and S

c. R and T

d. S

e. S and T

97. The table shows the size ranges of different types of rock particles.

PARTICLE TYPE	SIZE RANGE (MM)
clay	$< \frac{1}{300}$
silt	$\frac{1}{300} - \frac{1}{20}$
sand	$\frac{1}{20} - 1$
gravel	$1 - 5$
pebble	$5 - 50$

Which types of particles would pass through a sifting bed with a screen grating that captures rock particles larger than 1.5 mm?
a. all five particle types
b. clay and silt
c. clay, gravel, sand, and silt
d. gravel only
e. sand and silt

98. A seismic wave that registers 6.5 on the Richter scale is how many times larger than a seismic wave that registers 4.5 on the Richter scale?
a. −100
b. −2
c. 2
d. 10
e. 100

99. The slip rate of the rock on one side of a fault line is measured to be about 6 mm/year for the past 2,300 years. How long would it take for the rock to slip a meter?
a. about 3 years
b. about 167 years
c. about 383 years
d. about 6,000 years
e. about 13,800 years

100. The table shows the melting points of rocks.

APPROXIMATE TEMPERATURE (°C)	MINERALS THAT ARE MOLTEN
1,200	All
1,000	Olivine
800	Amphibole
600	Quartz

Which minerals would be molten at 900° C?
a. all
b. amphibole
c. amphibole and quartz
d. amphibole and olivine
e. olivine

101. Water vapor rising from snow is an example of
a. boiling.
b. condensation.
c. evaporation.
d. freezing.
e. sublimation.

102. In the equation for a thermodynamically insulated system, $H = U + pV$, H is
a. emissivity.
b. enthalpy.
c. entropy.
d. external energy.
e. internal energy.

103. All of the following are examples of exothermic processes EXCEPT
a. a burning candle.
b. baking bread.
c. making ice.
d. mixing water and strong acids.
e. rusting iron.

104. Specific heat is calculated according to the formula
   a. $\Delta Q \div \Delta T = m \div c$.
   b. $\Delta Q = m \times c \times \Delta T$.
   c. $\Delta Q \div m = \Delta T \div c$.
   d. $\Delta Q = m \times (c \div \Delta T)$.
   e. $\Delta Q \times \Delta T = m \div c$.

105. The diagram shows what happens to a substance as it is heated and as it changes from a solid to a gaseous state.

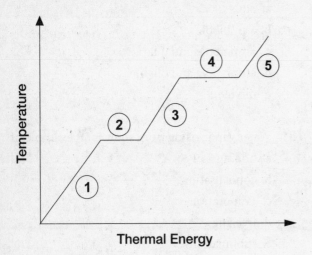

During which parts of the graph is the substance at a constant temperature?
   a. 1 only
   b. 1 and 3
   c. 1, 3, and 5
   d. 2 only
   e. 2 and 4

106. The diagram shows a heat engine cycle for a gasoline automobile engine.

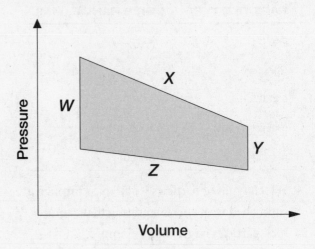

What are the correct names for each of the steps W, X, Y, and Z?
   a. heat added; heat extracted; work done *by* fuel; work done *on* fuel
   b. heat added; heat extracted; work done *on* fuel; work done *by* fuel
   c. heat added; work done *by* fuel; heat extracted; work done *on* fuel
   d. heat added; work done *on* fuel; heat extracted; work done *by* fuel
   e. heat added; work done *on* fuel; work done *by* fuel; heat extracted

107. The outside temperature reading is 50° F. What is the Celsius temperature reading if the Fahrenheit temperature reading is cut in half?
   a. 5° C
   b. 10° C
   c. 25° C
   d. 50° C
   e. 100° C

108. What is the temperature in Kelvin degrees if the temperature is 14 degrees Fahrenheit?
a. $248\frac{5}{9}$ degrees Kelvin
b. 263 degrees Kelvin
c. 277 degrees Kelvin
d. 283 degrees Kelvin
e. $298\frac{5}{9}$ degrees Kelvin

109. The diagram shows the thermodynamic work done across a range of pressures and volumes.

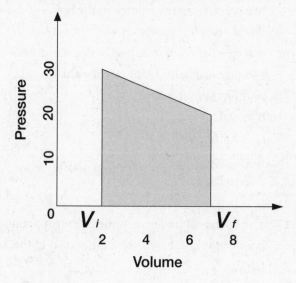

The work done is
a. 40 units.
b. 125 units.
c. 150 units.
d. 175 units.
e. 210 units.

110. The table gives the specific heat of two substances, X and Y, in Joules per gram-Kelvin.

SUBSTANCE	SPECIFIC HEAT
X	0.9
Y	0.4

If the same amount of heat is used to raise both substances by 10 degrees Kelvin, how do the masses, m_X and m_Y, of X and Y compare?

a. $m_X = \frac{4}{9} \times m_Y$
b. $m_X = m_Y$
c. $m_X = \frac{9}{4} \times m_Y$
d. $m_X = 4 \times m_Y$
e. $m_X = 9 \times m_Y$

111. An element is defined by its
a. atomic weight.
b. electrons and neutrons.
c. isotopes.
d. neutrons.
e. protons.

112. All of the following are charged particles EXCEPT
a. alpha particles.
b. beta particles.
c. gamma rays.
d. neutrons.
e. protons.

113. In $^{139}_{56}$ Ba, what does the number 139 represent?
a. the number of electrons
b. the number of electrons and protons
c. the number of neutrons
d. the number of neutrons and protons
e. the number of protons

114. Iron 56 and Iron 58 are best described as

a. inert elements.

b. isotopes.

c. radicals.

d. trace elements.

e. trans-uranium elements.

115. The diagram shows the number of neutrons and protons in an isotope, **I**. Other elements **G**, **H**, **K**, **L**, and **M** and their numbers of neutrons and protons are also shown.

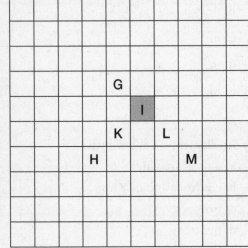

If isotope **I** decays by alpha decay, which of the other elements would result?

a. G

b. H

c. K

d. L

e. M

116. "The radioactive half-life of a given radioisotope is unaffected by the physical or chemical conditions around it. However, a radioisotope may be excreted from a living organism so that it no longer is a source of radiation exposure to the organism. The rate of excretion of such a radioisotope can be defined as an effective biological half-life. The rate of decrease of radiation exposure is then affected by both the physical and biological half-life, giving an effective half-life for the isotope in the body." Based on this explanation, the best way to describe the relationship of biological, effective, and physical half-life is that they are

a. difficult to measure.

b. equal.

c. insignificant.

d. related.

e. unrelated.

117. The relative abundance of the five most abundant isotopes of an element are shown in the table.

ATOMIC WEIGHT	ABUNDANCE (%)
58	68
60	26
61	1
62	4
63	1

What is the chance that a random sample of the element will contain isotopes with an atomic weight of 60, 61, or 62?

a. 1%

b. 4%

c. 5%

d. 27%

e. 31%

118. The graph shows how many grams of a radioactive isotope remain after 800 years, during which time it decays into other isotopes.

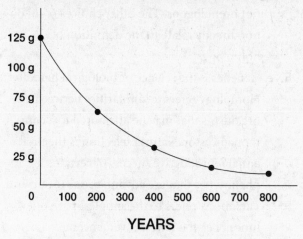

After about how many years has approximately three-fourths of the original mass of radioactive material decayed into other isotopes?

a. 100 years
b. 200 years
c. 400 years
d. 600 years
e. 800 years

119. The table shows the mass, in atomic mass units (u), of a hydrogen atom with one electron and one proton and the masses of a single electron and a single proton.

PARTICLE	MASS (u)
electron	0.0005485
hydrogen atom	1.0078250
proton	1.0072764

What is the mass defect between the hydrogen atom and its constituent particles?

a. 0 u
b. 0.0000001 u
c. 0.0005485 u
d. 2.0145529 u
e. 2.0156499 u

120. The table shows ionization energies of some elements.

ELEMENT	IONIZATION ENERGY (EV)
Fl	17
H	14
He	25
N	15
O	14

Which element(s) would be easiest to excite by adding or subtracting a photon?

a. H
b. H and He
c. H and O
d. H, O, or N
e. He

▶ Answers

1. a. The fossil record contains evidence of life in earlier times. The fossil record also provides evidence that two species were present at the same time. Choices **b**, **c**, and **d** are incorrect because the fossil record does not contain information about whether ancient hominids mapped constellations, the distance between Earth and Venus, or whether there was life on Mars. Choice **e** is incorrect because the fossil record does not contain enough specimens to ascertain the percentage of herbivorous dinosaurs that laid infertile eggs.

2. d. The shapes of a particular species of finches' beaks over generations show how an organism can change over time, and why it may change. The theory of evolution is supported by research that shows the gene pool of a population changes from generation to generation through different processes, such as mutation and natural selection. The existence of hydrogen bonds between water molecules (choice **a**), the range of temperature variations across the Earth (choice **b**), the number of reptile species that regenerate tails (choice **c**), and the range in variation of growth spurts of adolescent humans (choice **e**) do not explain why organisms evolved over time.

3. e. In order to be considered vestigial, a feature must not have any true function in an organism. Opposable thumbs, long necks, and brightly colored plumes are all assets to these creatures, so choices **a**, **b**, and **c** are incorrect. Mitochondria are vital to cellular respiration, so choice **d** is incorrect. Wings on a flightless bird are vestigial, as they are remnants of fully functional wings of flying ancestors.

4. b. Homology specifically refers to similarity attributable to ancestry. Biological coincidence may produce analogous structures, but not homologous. The other choices (**c–e**) do not directly relate to the definition of homology.

5. e. Genetics is the science of biological heredity. Homology refers to similarities between organisms that may be attributed to a common ancestor. Natural selection is the preferential reproductive success of certain phenotypes that are advantageous to survival. Parsimony refers to the simplest path of evolution, i.e., the fewest divergences.

6. a. Orangutans are close relatives to humans evolutionarily, and they share many of the same characteristics. The other organisms shown are members of different taxonomic groups, indicating they converged at a more distant point in evolutionary history.

7. b. A and C are least closely related because there are the most evolutionary steps in between them. All the other choices have fewer nodes in between them, indicating that there are fewer evolutionary steps in between the origin of each species.

8. e. Species F is the root of this phylogenetic tree, from which all other branches arise.

9. c. A phylogenetic tree, like the one shown, is a pictorial representation of evolutionary steps that produced related species. A pedigree shows phenotype information between generations of a lineage to track the inheritance of a specific trait. A Punnett square is used to predict genotypic information about the offspring of two sexually reproducing mates. A linkage map shows the arrangement of genes on chromosomes.

10. c. The upper chamber of the experiment contains the simple gases that were believed to compose the atmosphere of the early Earth. The electrical current represents lightning, and the downward drops in the cooled tube represent rainfall. The water in the lower chamber represents the oceans.

11. e. As represented by the flame under the lower flask, thermal vents in the oceans allowed water vapor to rise and react with the gases of the early atmosphere.

12. c. If life on Earth originated from the set of conditions that were replicated in Miller's experiment, there is no reason that another planet with identical conditions could not also give rise to life.

13. b. The absence of a true nucleus fundamentally distinguishes prokaryotic cells from eukaryotic cells. All the other choices may be found in either type of cell.

14. d. Plant cells, not mitochondria, are typically enclosed by a cell wall. All the other choices are true statements about mitochondria. Mitochondria are commonly referred to as the "powerhouses" of a cell (choice **a**) because they are the main site of ATP synthesis. Mitochondria contain their own DNA (choice **b**); in fact, mitochondrial genetic material is commonly used in tracing evolutionary relationships between organisms. Mitochondria synthesize some of their own proteins (choice **c**) using their own ribosomes (choice **e**).

15. b. Enzymes speed up reactions by lowering the activation energy, or the total energy needed for a reaction to take place. The substrates are the actual reactants on which enzymes work.

16. c. In the final step of the electron transport chain, a pair of electrons is added to oxygen, which combines with two hydrogen ions to form water.

17. b. Transcription is the process in which DNA information is copied into RNA, so reverse transcription describes the opposite process, which is performed by retroviruses. Translation is the process through which RNA information is used to create amino acid chains, or proteins. Reverse translation does not exist.

18. d. In anaphase, the two centromeres of each chromosome come apart, producing two sister chromatids. The chromatids separate and migrate toward opposite poles along the spindle fibers, as shown in the figure. Interphase is the period of the cell cycle when mitosis is not occurring. In prophase, the chromatin fibers become double-stranded chromosomes. In metaphase, the chromosomes line up in the central plane of the nucleus. In telophase, nuclear envelopes form around each set of chromosomes.

19. d. In anaphase II, the two centromeres of each chromosome come apart, producing two single-stranded sister chromatids. The chromatids separate and migrate toward opposite poles along the spindle fibers, as shown in the figure. In anaphase I, tetrads separate into homologous double-stranded chromosomes, which migrate toward opposite poles along the spindle fibers. In metaphase I, homologous chromosomes line up in the central plane of the nucleus. In metaphase II, sister chromatids line up in the central plane of the nucleus. Interphase is the period of the cell cycle when mitosis is not occurring.

20. a. Shorter fragments move through the gel more quickly, so the fragment that is the farthest from the well is the shortest. Fragment A has migrated farther than any other fragment, so it is probably the shortest fragment.

21. d. Phosphate molecules carry a negative charge that is pulled toward the positively charged electrode. Carbon and oxygen molecules in DNA do not contribute polarity, and hydrogen bonds and double helix refer to structural features of DNA.

22. b. In an exergonic reaction, energy is released so that the products have a lower potential energy than the reactants, as per the graph. In an endergonic reaction, energy is absorbed so that the products have a higher potential energy than the reactants. The other choices do not convey information about the energy transfer in the reaction, so these conclusions cannot be made based on the information in the graph provided.

23. e. The activation energy of a reaction is the amount of energy required for the reaction to proceed. The area between regions C and D represents the energy difference between the reactants and the onset of the reaction, so this is the activation energy. A-B indicates the energy of the products. A-C indicates the energy of the reactants. B-D is the difference between the activation energy and the energy of the products. B-C is the energy difference between the reactants and products.

24. c. The complementary RNA strand for this DNA sequence would be GGGUUUCCC, which corresponds to Gly (GGG), Phe (UUU), Pro (CCC).

25. a. The law of independent assortment states that a pair of alleles separates from all other pairs of alleles during gamete formation, so that a trait is passed on separately from all other traits. Genes that are linked on a single chromosome are passed on together, so linked genes are an exception to this rule.

26. b. Most sex-linked traits are carried by genes on the X chromosome, the larger of the two sex chromosomes. Sex-linked genes do not necessarily code for sexual traits, as the X chromosome is present in both males and females.

27. d. Crossing over occurs when the ends of two non-sister chromatids become entangled and switch between chromosomes. Genes that are close to each other along the chromosome are less likely to be separated in the event of a crossover. The position of the gene on the chromosome does not have any relevance regarding what it codes for or the likelihood of a mutation occurring.

28. e. Amniocentesis can be performed to analyze genetic disorders in a fetus before birth. Parthenogenesis is a type of asexual reproduction. Endometriosis is a disorder affecting the endometrium of females. In vitro fertilization is the process of combining male and female reproductive tissue in a lab. Blastulation is a step in early embryonic development.

29. e. The hypothalamus secretes hormones of the posterior pituitary and regulates the anterior pituitary to maintain homeostasis. The adrenal gland secretes hormones in response to stress. The thyroid gland secretes hormones to regulate metabolism and growth. The pituitary gland releases hormones to regulate a variety of physiological functions.

30. a. A circadian rhythm is present in all eukaryotes and persists even in the absence of external cues. Thigmotropism is a response to touch. Photoperiodism is a response to changes in light throughout the course of a day. The Krebs cycle is a process that occurs during aerobic respiration.

31. c. The ectoderm layer contains cells that will become the outside covering of the body, including the skin and outer membranes of the eyes, and the nervous system. Many internal organs arise from the mesoderm layer, and the inner linings of the digestive tract and other organs arise from the endoderm.

32. c. A red tide is a phenomenon wherein phytoplankton such as dinoflagellates accumulate quickly near the ocean's surface. The term *red tide* comes from the reddish color of these organisms.

33. c. Fungi can reproduce asexually or sexually by producing spores. Yeast are a type of single-celled fungi.

34. a. The sporophyte is the diploid plant that produces haploid spores through meiosis. The gametophyte is the haploid plant that produces haploid gametes through mitosis.

35. d. Anthers are the male structures of angiosperms. A flower usually contains both male and female structures. Carpels are the ovule-producing structures of the flower, consisting of a stigma, style, and ovary. Pistils consist of several fused carpels and are the female structures of angiosperms. A sepal is a leaflike covering that protects a flower before it opens.

36. d. The reflex arc in humans involves only the sensory neuron, spinal cord, and motor neuron. When a reflex occurs, it does not involve the brain processing the signal, which is why a person does not need to think about pulling a hand away from a very hot stove. The spinal cord is part of the central nervous system.

37. c. A pedigree tracks a specific genetic trait through generations of offspring to determine its mode of inheritance. A Punnett square predicts the genotypes that will result from mating. Phylogeny refers to the evolutionary history of a species or group of species. Homology is a similarity between two species that can be attributed to common ancestry. A cladogram is a diagram that depicts shared traits among different species.

38. a. This is clear by process of elimination. Sex-linked traits primarily appear in males, but this trait appears commonly in both males and females. It is not clear whether the trait is deleterious from the pedigree. Heterozygous and homozygous refer to genotypes, not to a trait in general. The trait is probably autosomal dominant as it is frequently passed to offspring, regardless of gender.

39. c. Individuals 7 and 8 have two offspring: 13 and 14. A circle represents a female, and shading represents expression of the trait. Only individual 13 expresses the trait, so one female is the correct choice.

40. d. In a test cross, a homozygous recessive genotype is crossed with an unknown genotype to determine whether this parent is heterozygous or homozygous for the dominant trait. If the parent is homozygous for the dominant trait, there should be no offspring displaying the recessive phenotype. Offspring with the recessive phenotype can be produced only if the parent is heterozygous for the dominant trait, as is the case.

41. e. There are only two phenotypes shown in the Punnett square: Ff and ff. Ff will display the dominant trait, and ff will display the recessive trait. Thus, the ratio is 1:1.

42. a. The original and final state of the neuron shown is the resting potential, which is about –70mV. When an action potential occurs, positively charged sodium ions enter the neuron and cause it to depolarize to about 30 + mV, as shown in part A of the graph. After the sodium ions rush in, positively charged potassium ions exit the cell, restoring the membrane potential during repolarization, as shown in part C of the graph. The sodium-potassium pump then returns the distribution of ions to its original state, restoring the resting potential of –70mV, as shown in part E.

43. d. In photosynthesis, plants use light energy to convert carbon dioxide and water to glucose, oxygen, and water. In aerobic respiration, glucose and oxygen are converted into water, carbon dioxide, and energy. In fermentation, glucose is converted into carbon dioxide and alcohol or lactic acid. Glycolysis is one step in respiration.

44. c. Light from the sun is captured by plants to drive the process of photosynthesis. Different pigments in the plant absorb different wavelengths of light in photosynthesis. Water, oxygen, and carbon are involved in photosynthesis in different ways, but light is the primary energy source driving the reaction.

45. d. After gastrulation, the mesoderm layer forms the rodlike notochord. Cells near the notochord signal for the neural crest to form, which will become the brain and spinal cord. A zygote refers to a fertilized egg, the very beginning of embryonic development. A gamete is a haploid sex cell. The ectoderm is labeled C in this figure. The placenta is the structure in a pregnant uterus that nourishes the developing fetus.

46. a. The layer marked C represents the ectoderm of the embryo. This layer differentiates in the cells that will become the outside covering of the body, including the skin and outer membranes of the eyes, and the nervous system. The liver and pancreas arise from the mesoderm layer, which is marked B. The various components of the head and neck are composed of cells from different layers of the embryo.

47. a. A male with blood type A can have a genotype of AA or AO. A female with blood type O must have the genotype OO. Punnett squares for each of the possible crosses are shown here:

	A	O
O	AO	OO
O	AO	OO

	A	A
O	AO	AO
O	AO	AO

Thus, the only possible blood types from these parents are A and O. O does not appear in the choices, so choice **a** is correct.

48. d. Because A is a dominant allele, a person with blood type A can have a homogenic or heterogenic genotype.

49. e. The tundra covers the polar regions of the Earth and is classified by a very cold climate, as well as permafrost—a permanently frozen layer of soil. All other biomes reach temperatures too warm for permafrost.

50. a. Autotrophs are organisms that make their own food; photosynthesis is the process by which an organism uses light energy to do this. Heterotrophs obtain food by eating other organisms. Carnivores are heterotrophs that eat other animals, herbivores are heterotrophs that eat plants, and omnivores are heterotrophs that eat both plants and animals.

51. c. The equilibrium theory of island biogeography, represented in the graph, states that the number of species on an island reaches an equilibrium when the immigration rate and extinction rates are equal. On the graph, this refers to the intersection of the two lines, which occurs at the point corresponding to roughly 45 species.

52. a. If the extinction rate has risen but the number of species has not fallen, there must be another source of new species. This source is immigration, as shown in the graph. If the immigration rate fell or remained stable, the number of species would decline. Choices **d** and **e** cannot be inferred from the information given.

53. a. When the number of species on an island is high, all the available resources are being used, and it is likely that the increased competition will lead to increased extinction. Immigration will be low because the island is already at capacity and cannot provide for any additional species.

54. a. An age graph with a pyramid shape represents an expanding population. A declining population would have a base (young population) that is narrower than the middle (reproductive age population). A stable population would have little difference between the number of individuals in the young age ranges and the reproductive age ranges. There is no information about resource availability or economics in this graph, so choices **d** and **e** are incorrect.

55. e. The width of the bars in the graph corresponds to the number of people in each age group. The widest bar corresponds to the 0–10 range, so this is the group with the most individuals for this population.

56. d. If the trend shown continues, the younger members of society will still outnumber the older members. Thus, there will be more reproductive age individuals than elderly individuals. The population is expanding, so it will not decrease in coming years (choice **a**). There is no information related to job availability, so choice **b** is incorrect.

57. e. A carrot is a vegetable that belongs to the plant kingdom, so it is a producer. Producers have the highest energy level in the energy pyramid because they create their own nutrients using light energy from the sun. The other choices are primary or secondary consumers.

58. b. A cow is a primary consumer because it consumes grass, a producer. A producer makes its own nutrients. A secondary consumer feeds on primary consumers.

59. b. Each level of the energy pyramid passes on 10% of its energy to the next level. A tertiary consumer feeds on secondary consumers, so it would have 10% of the 1% in the secondary consumer group, or 0.1%

60. c. Altruism is a behavior that helps another member of a population at an individual's own expense. Because the worker bee dies while protecting the queen bee, this is an example of altruism. Courtship involves mating rituals in organisms. Foraging refers to food gathering behaviors. Competition is the struggle among organisms for various resources. Commensalism is a relationship between two organisms wherein one organism benefits and the other organism is unaffected.

61. b. The Earth *revolves* around the sun and *rotates* on its axis. Choices **a** and **c** are incorrect because Earth does not revolve around the moon. Choices **d** and **e** are incorrect because the words *revolve* and *rotate* are used incorrectly in each.

62. d. The order given is from space to the center of the sun. Choice **a** is incorrect because the core should be at the beginning or the end of the list. Choice **b** is incorrect because the corona does not follow the core. Choice **c** is incorrect because the photosphere is not the outermost part of the parts listed. Choice **e** is incorrect because the corona is next to the solar wind, not the photosphere.

63. a. An astronomical unit (A.U.) is defined as the average distance from Earth to the sun. Choice **b** is incorrect because a kilometer is a measure of distance, but it is not the standard unit for the average distance from Earth to the sun. Choice **c** is incorrect because a light year is the distance light travels in a year, which is much less than the average distance from Earth to the sun. Choice **d** is incorrect because a parsec is used to measure interstellar distances, not the average distance from Earth to the sun. Choice **e** is incorrect because it is not a recognized unit that refers to the average distance from Earth to the sun.

64. e. Venus is an "inner planet" and not classified as one of the "gas giants" in the solar system. Choices **a–d** are incorrect because all are classified as "gas giants."

65. a. Speed increases as the distance from Earth increases. Choice **b** is incorrect because the speed increases as the distance from Earth increases. Choices **c** and **d** are incorrect because they compare different variables (distance and speed). Choice **e** is incorrect because there appears to be a direct relationship between how far a distance is from Earth and the speed at which it is moving away from Earth.

66. a. This is the best choice, because the paragraph first gives a formula for calculating sunspot numbers, followed by some qualifying information that is used to produce a more accurate count. Choice **b** is incorrect because the Zurich Sunspot Number is the name given to the calculation for the number of the sunspots, and is not the main point of the paragraph. Choice **c** is incorrect because sunspot distribution on the sun's surface is a contributing factor to counting sunspots, but is not the main point of the paragraph. Choice **d** is incorrect because the role of Earth as an observation point is mentioned as a contributing factor to counting sunspots, but is not the main point of the paragraph. Choice **e** is incorrect because the accuracy of the sunspot count is one of the qualifiers to using the Zurich Sunspot Number, but is not the main point of the paragraph.

67. c. The number of "days" in a "year" of each planet is 40 (800 ÷ 20) for Planet *Y*, 45 (450 ÷ 10) for Planet *X*, 48 (1,200 ÷ 25) for Planet *Z*, and 125 (250 ÷ 2) for Planet *W*. Choice **a** is incorrect because the order of the "days" of the "year" is not the order in Earth days of the period of revolution or the order of the period of rotation in Earth days of the four planets. Choices **b**, **d**, and **e** are incorrect because the calculation of the number of "days" or the ordering of the "days" was done incorrectly.

68. d. For very small angles, $d \approx \frac{1}{p}$, so $d \approx 2$ parsecs. Choice **a** is incorrect because $d \neq p^2$. Choice **b** is incorrect because $d \neq p$. Choice **c** is incorrect because $d \neq 2p$. Choice **e** is incorrect because $d \neq \frac{1}{p^2}$.

69. b. Its perihelion (the closest distance to the sun) is less than that of the other comets, and its "year" (orbital period) is less than that of the other comets. Choices **a** and **c–e** are incorrect because their perihelia and orbital periods are less than that of Comet Encke.

70. e. The distance from the perihelion to the star is computed by dividing the aphelion-to-perihelion distance by two, and then multiplying that quotient by the quantity 1–e. For planet *U*, this gives 4.95×10^6 km. Choices **a–d** are incorrect because their distances from perihelion to the star are, respectively,

Q: 4.75×10^8 km; *R:* 4.5×10^7 km; *S:* 3.5×10^8 km; *T:* 4.25×10^7 km.

71. e. Iron reacts with oxygen to form rust.

72. b. Baking soda is sodium bicarbonate, which is a compound, not a mixture. Choices **a**, **c**, **d**, and **e** are incorrect because air, milk, sand, and wood are mixtures of other elements and compounds.

73. a. According to Charles's Law, when the temperature doubles, so does the pressure in a closed container. Choices **b–e** are incorrect because they do not reflect Charles's Law.

74. d. "Nuclides" is not a group of elements on the periodic table. Choices **a–c** and **e** are incorrect because they are all group names on the periodic table.

75. e. The change in compound Z's solubility is greater than the change in the solubility of compounds X or Y as temperature rises. Choice **a** is incorrect because compound X shows no change in solubility when the temperature rises from 0° C to 10° C. Choice **b** is incorrect because the change in solubility of both compounds X and Y as temperature rises is less than the change in solubility for compound Z. Choice **c** is incorrect because the change in compound Y's solubility as temperature rises is not as great as the change in compound Z's solubility as temperature rises. Choice **d** is incorrect because compounds Y and Z exhibit different solubility changes as temperature rises; both cannot be correct.

76. d. The slope of the reaction-rate line is greater when a catalyst is present than when it is not. Choice **a** is incorrect because there is no way to tell by how much the catalyst increases the rate of oxygen production. Choice **b** is incorrect because the presence of a catalyst causes the slope of the reaction rate to increase as temperature increases. Choice **c** is incorrect because temperature is an independent variable just as the absence or presence of the catalyst is. Choice **e** is incorrect because the reaction rate in the presence of a catalyst varies as the temperature increases, and is not constant relative to the reaction rate in the absence of a catalyst.

77. e. The same number of H and N atoms appear on each side of the equation. Choices **a–d** are incorrect because there are different numbers of H and/or N atoms on each side of the equation.

78. c. The same number of Ca, H, and O atoms appear on each side of the equation. Choices **a**, **b**, **d**, and **e** are incorrect because different numbers of Ca, Ho, and/or O atoms appear on each side of the equation.

79. b. Six moles of oxygen represent twice as many moles as are indicated in the basic chemical reaction, so the number of moles of potassium chloride or potassium chlorate produced is two times two, or four moles. Choice **a** is incorrect because eight moles would be four times as many moles of either potassium substance. Choice **c** is incorrect because three moles would correspond to 4.5 moles of oxygen. Choice **d** is incorrect because the number of moles of potassium chloride is not the sum of the coefficients of the moles in the reaction. Choice **e** is incorrect because six moles of potassium chloride would correspond to three times as many moles of oxygen, or nine moles of oxygen.

80. e. $m = 2$ if reactant A reacts twice as fast as reactant B, and $n = 1$, because the reaction rate depends on both reactants A and B; this gives $r = k\,[0.05]^2 \times [0.1]^1$ or $2.5k \times 10^{-4}$. Choices **a–c** are incorrect because they are *second-order* reactions. Choice **d** is incorrect because reactant B is not the faster-reacting reactant.

81. c. Power (kilowatts) is the *rate* of energy consumption, and kilowatt-hours is a measure of the total energy consumption. Choice **b** is incorrect because power (kilowatts) is the *rate* of energy consumption. Choices **a**, **d**, and **e** are units for current, resistance, and voltage, not energy.

82. e. Voltage is not a factor in the magnitude of the magnetic field, but current is. Choices **a** and **b** are incorrect because conventional current flow and electron flow are in opposite directions, i.e., electron flow out of the negative terminal and conventional current flow into the negative terminal. Choices **c** and **d** are incorrect because both are true.

83. b. A capacitor can be charged and discharged in a circuit. Choices **a** and **e** are incorrect because an ammeter and a voltmeter can *register* charging or discharging, but are not the circuit elements that *are* charged or discharged. Choice **c** is incorrect because an insulator is a part of a capacitor but is not the only part of the capacitor that is charged or discharged. Choice **d** is incorrect because a resistor does not charge or discharge in a circuit.

84. e. The force between the charges is given by the formula
$$F = k \times \left(\frac{q^1 \times q^2}{r^2}\right)$$
This means that the force is proportional to the inverse of the square of the distance between the charges. Choice **a** is incorrect because the force is not directly proportional to the distance between the charges. Choice **b** is incorrect because the force is not *directly* proportional to the square of the distance between the charges. Choice **c** is incorrect, because the force is not inversely proportional to the distance between the charges, but to the *square* of the distance. Choice **d** is incorrect because the force is not *inversely* proportional to the product of the charges, but *directly* proportional to their square.

85. b. The slope of the voltage curve is steepest at point R. Choices **a** and **c** are incorrect because the slope of the voltage curve is zero at both points. Choices **d** and **e** are incorrect because the slope of the voltage curve varies between points Q and R and between points R and S.

86. d. The voltage is positive between points Q and R, even though it is decreasing. Choice **a** is incorrect because the voltage is zero at point O. Choice **b** is incorrect because the voltage is negative at point S. Choice **c** is incorrect because the *total* voltage between points O and T is zero. Choice **e** is incorrect because the voltage between points R and S is negative.

87. b. The total resistance of the circuit is $\frac{26}{5}$ ohms. If the voltage is $\frac{1}{5}$ volt and the voltage is the product of the current and the resistance, the current will be $\frac{1}{5} \div \frac{26}{5}$, or $\frac{1}{26}$ amp. Choices **a** and **d** are incorrect because the resistance was calculated incorrectly. Choices **c** and **e** are incorrect because the wrong formula relating current, resistance, and voltage was used.

88. d. When I is doubled, B is doubled, and when r is doubled, B is cut in half. Choices **a–c** and **e** are incorrect because the data does not support the proportionality listed for each choice.

89. e. Capacitance is calculated with the formula $C = \frac{Q}{V}$, which gives $C = (4 \times 10^{-6}) \div 200 = 2 \times 10^{-8}$ or 200 μF. Choices **a** and **b** are incorrect because capacitance is calculated by dividing charge by voltage, not by multiplying. Choices **c** and **d** are incorrect because capacitance is calculated by dividing charge by voltage, not voltage by charge.

90. b. The *inductive reactance* of the circuit is given by $X_L = 2\pi \times f \times L$ or $2\pi \times 50$ kH $\times$ 25 mH or $2,500\pi$ ohms. Current is voltage divided by reactance, or 2π volts divided by $2,500\pi$ ohms or 0.8 milliamps. Choices **a** and **d** are incorrect because the formulas for current and reactance were used incorrectly. Choices **c** and **e** are incorrect because the conversion from amperes to milliamperes was done incorrectly.

91. b. Choice **a** reverses the order of the inner and outer cores. Choice **c** is the correct order of the parts but starts at Earth's center, not at its surface. The parts in choices **d** and **e** are in the wrong order.

92. e. This is the correct order of the epochs from youngest to oldest. Choices **a–d** are incorrect because they only partially reflect the correct order of the epochs from oldest to youngest or vice versa.

93. c. Magma is not an example of one of the three basic rock types; it is molten material that precedes the formation of igneous rock. Choices **a**, **b**, **d**, and **e** are incorrect because all are examples of the three basic rock types.

94. c. A grain is a self-contained piece of a mineral found in an aggregate rock. Choice **a** is incorrect because a crystal could be formed from more than one material and is a larger component of a mineral than a grain. Choice **b** is incorrect because "fragment" does not have a precise geological meaning. Choice **d** is incorrect because it does have a denotation in geology. Choice **e** is incorrect because "sediment" is a much larger geologic structure than a "grain," and could contain grains of a variety of minerals.

95. c. Minerals with greater hardness numbers can make scratches on minerals with lesser hardness numbers. Choice **a** is incorrect because a greater density does not mean a greater hardness. Choice **b** is incorrect because a mineral cannot mark a mineral with a greater hardness number. Choices **d** and **e** are incorrect because their hardness numbers are less than that of mineral *R*.

96. a. Mineral *R* contains the greatest percentage of SiO_2 *and* the least percentage of FeO. Choices **b–e** are incorrect because they do not contain the greatest percentage of SiO_2 *and* the least percentage of FeO.

97. c. The grating would pass clay, silt, sand, and some gravel (≤ 1.5 mm). Choice **a** is incorrect because pebbles would not pass through the grating (5 mm $>$ 1.5 mm). Choices **b** and **e** are incorrect because the grating would pass clay, sand, silt and some gravel. Choice **d** is incorrect because the grating would pass some gravel ($>$ 1 mm and ≤ 1.5 mm) but also all smaller particles.

98. e. A difference of 2 on the Richter scale is equivalent to a multiple of 10^2 or 100 times. Choice **a** is incorrect because the question is how much larger the 6.5 amplitude wave is than the 4.5 amplitude wave, not the other way around. Choices **b** and **c** are incorrect because the amplitude of the waves is not found by subtracting one Richter value from the other. Choice **d** is incorrect because the difference between 6.5 and 4.5 is 2, not one, which would mean that one wave had an amplitude 10 times the other.

99. b. 6 mm/year is 0.006 m/year, and 1 meter divided by 0.006 m/year is about 167 years. Choice **a** is incorrect .6 mm/year is not 6,000 m/year, and dividing 6,000 m/year by 2,300 years does not give a meaningful physical quantity (m per years squared). Choice **c** is incorrect because dividing 2,300 years by 6 mm/year does not give a meaningful physical quantity (year squared per mm). Choice **d** is incorrect because 6,000 years is an unreasonable answer if the slip rate is 6 mm/year. Choice **e** is incorrect, because 2,300 years times 6 mm/year gives 13,800 mm, not 13,800 years.

100. c. Amphibole and quartz have melting points below 900° C. Choice **a** is incorrect because all minerals would be molten at 1,200° C, but not at 900° C. Choice **b** is incorrect because amphibole is not the only mineral of those listed that would be molten at 900° C; so would quartz. Choices **d** and **e** are incorrect because olivine would not be molten at 900° C.

101. e. Some of the water molecules in the snow absorb enough energy in the melting process to be in a gaseous state and escape to create a "fog" of water vapor above the snow mass. Choices **a** and **c** are incorrect because boiling and evaporation are changes from a liquid to a gaseous state. Choice **b** is incorrect because condensation is a change from the gaseous to a liquid state. Choice **d** is incorrect because freezing is a change from the liquid to a solid state.

102. b. The equation relates enthalpy (H) to a system's internal energy (U), pressure (p), and volume (V). Choice **a** is incorrect because emissivity is not a unit of energy. Choice **c** is incorrect because entropy is not a unit of energy. Entropy is a measure of disorder. Choice **d** is incorrect because external energy is not a part of this equation. Choice **e** is incorrect because the internal energy is U, not H.

103. b. Baking bread is not an exothermic process. Choices **a** and **c–e** are all exothermic processes in which energy is released.

104. b. Specific heat (c) is the amount of heat (ΔQ) needed to raise the temperature (ΔT) of one gram (m) of a substance one degree Kelvin. In formulaic form,

$$\frac{\Delta Q}{\Delta T} = m \times c \text{ or } \Delta Q = m \times c \times \Delta T$$

Choice **a** is incorrect because c divided by m does not give Joules per Kelvin degree. Choice **c** is incorrect because the quotients $\Delta Q \div m$ and $\Delta T \div c$ do not give meaningful physical units, e.g., Joules per unit of mass versus degrees Kelvin per gram-degree Kelvin. Choices **d** and **e** are incorrect because $\Delta Q \times \Delta T$ is Joule-degrees, whereas $m \div c$ is Joules *per* degree and $m \times c$ is grams squared per Joule-degrees.

105. e. The temperature is constant as the thermal energy increases. Choices **a**, **b**, and **c** are incorrect because the temperature is increasing as the thermal energy increases. Choice **d** is incorrect because part 4 is also at a constant temperature.

106. c. Heat engines add energy to fuel, which does work, after which heat is removed, and work is done on the fuel by reducing its volume and increasing its pressure in the automobile engine cylinders. Choices **a** and **b** are incorrect because if the heat was extracted after it had been added, no work would be done (adiabatic). Choices **d** and **e** are incorrect because work cannot be done on the fuel until after the heat has been extracted from doing work.

107. a. The Celsius temperature reading is found according to the formula

$$C = \frac{5}{9} \times (F - 32)$$

If $F = 50$, then $C = \frac{5}{9} \times (50 - 32)$, or 10. Half of 10 is 5. The Celsius temperature reading is 5° C.

108. b. 14° is −10° Celsius, which is 263 degrees Kelvin. Choices **a** and **e** are incorrect because the wrong formula was used to calculate Celsius temperature from Fahrenheit. Choice **c** is incorrect because the Fahrenheit temperature was added to 273 to get the Kelvin temperature; the Celsius temperature (−10) should have been added to 273. Choice **d** is incorrect because +10 degrees Celsius was added to 273, not −10 degrees Celsius.

109. b. The work done is the *area* of the shaded region on the pressure-volume plot, i.e., $\frac{1}{2} \times$ (10 × 5) plus (20 × 5), or 125 units. Choice **a** is incorrect because the work done is not the difference of the pressure-volume product at two units of volume and the pressure-volume product at 7 units of volume. Choice **c** is incorrect because the work done is not the product of the highest pressure and the difference of the final and initial volume values. Choice **d** is incorrect because the work done is not the product of the pressure that corresponds to the midpoint of the final and initial volumes and the final volume. Choice **e** is incorrect because the work done is not the product of the highest pressure and volume values.

110. a. This is correct because $Q_X = Q_Y$; $0.9 \times 10 \times m_X = 0.4 \times 10 \times m_Y$; $9 \times m_X = 4 \times m_Y$; $m_X = \frac{4}{9} \times m_Y$. Choices **b**–**e** are incorrect because they are incorrect applications of the basic specific heat formula $Q = m \times c \times \Delta T$.

111. e. An element's proton number is unique to that element. Choice **a** is incorrect because "atomic weight" can apply to compounds or elements, and for elements is the sum of its neutrons *and* protons, which varies by isotope of the element. Choice **b** is incorrect because the sum of an element's electrons and neutrons can vary, by isotope. Choice **c** is incorrect because an element's *isotopes* can vary according to the number of neutrons in the nucleus of the element. Choice **d** is incorrect because the number of neutrons can vary in isotopes of the same element.

112. c. Gamma rays are not particles and have no charge. Choices **a**, **b**, and **e** are particles, but all carry charges. Choice **d** is a particle that has no charge.

113. d. Here, 139 is the atomic weight, which consists of the number of protons (56) and the number of neutrons (83). Choice **a** is the same as the number of protons (56), and choice **b** is the sum of the number of electrons and protons (112). Choice **c** is the number of neutrons (83), and choice **e** is the number of protons (56).

114. b. The best description of those listed is isotopes. Choice **a** is incorrect because none of iron's isotopes are inert. Choice **c** is incorrect, because the iron isotopes are electrically neutral (zero net charge), unlike a radical. Choice **d** is incorrect because it is not the best description of the iron isotopes. Choice **e** is incorrect because iron's atomic weight is not greater than that of uranium.

115. b. The isotope would lose two protons and two neutrons. Choice **a** is incorrect because the isotope does not gain a proton and loses two neutrons, not one. Choice **c** is incorrect because the isotope loses two protons and neutrons, not one. Choice **d** is incorrect because the isotope does not gain a neutron, but loses two neutrons and two protons. Choice **e** is incorrect because the isotope loses two neutrons, and does not gain them.

116. d. It is the only choice that is supported by the passage. Choice **a** is incorrect because there is nothing in the passage about measurement of half-life. Choice **b** is incorrect because there is nothing in the passage to suggest that the three half-life concepts are equivalent. Choice **c** is incorrect because there is nothing in the passage to suggest that any of the three half-life measurements are insignificant. Choice **e** is incorrect because the passage suggests that a radioisotope's effective half-life in a living organism is a function of its biological and physical half-life.

117. e. The chance of a sample containing isotopes with atomic weights of 60, 61, *or* 62 is the sum of the percentage abundances— 26 + 1 + 4—or 31%. Choices **a** and **b** are incorrect because they are the abundance of the isotopes with atomic weight 61 and 62 alone. Choice **c** is incorrect because it is sum of the abundance of the isotopes with atomic weights 61 or 62 only. Choice **d** is incorrect because it is sum of the abundance of the isotopes with atomic weights 60 or 61 only.

118. c. About one-fourth (30 grams) of the original amount remains, which means that about three-fourths of the original amount has decayed into other isotopes. Choice **a** is incorrect since about three-fourths of the original mass of radioactive material remains after 100 years. Choices **b**, **d**, and **e** are the times after which one-half, one-eighth, and one-sixteenth, respectively, of the original mass of radioactive material remains.

119. b. The sum of the electron and proton mass is 1.0078249 u and the mass of the hydrogen atom is 1.0078250; the difference of the two is 0.0000001 u. Choice **a** is incorrect because there is a non-zero mass defect between the hydrogen atom's mass and the mass of its constituent particles. Choice **c** is incorrect because the mass defect of this system is not the mass of the electron. Choices **d** and **e** are incorrect because the mass defect is the difference between the mass of the hydrogen atom system and the *sum* of the masses of its constituent particles, not some other combination of these three masses.

120. c. The lower the ionization energy, the easier it is to change the energy level of an atom by the addition or removal of a photon (energy); H and O have the lowest ionization energies in the table. Choice **a** is incorrect because O also has the same ionization energy as H. Choices **b** and **e** are incorrect because He is the most difficult element on the list to excite by the addition or removal of a photon (energy). Choice **d** is incorrect because N's ionization energy is slightly higher than that of H and O, so it is not the easiest element to ionize on the list.

22 ▶ Biological Science

All living things are made up of one or more of the basic functional units called cells. Some living things have one simple cell and others several specialized types of cells that are responsible for particular functions. All cells arise from preexisting cells and pass on genetic information in the form of DNA (deoxyribonucleic acid) and RNA (ribonucleic acid) through the process of reproduction. All living things get **energy** for their life functions by either producing or consuming food. The food is digested and broken down into smaller nutrients, the essential building blocks for cellular structures and processes. All living things also regulate their internal environment in order to maintain a stable condition, known as homeostasis. Living things respond to stimuli, changes in the internal and external environment, in ways to maintain homeostasis. For example, a person shivers in a cold environment in order to maintain a constant body temperature.

All living things reproduce to create offspring with similar traits and appearances. As generations of living things reproduce, variations in these traits and appearances arise. **Asexual reproduction** involves one parent and is the primary form of reproduction for single-celled organisms, like bacteria and protists. Some multicellular organisms reproduce asexually also, such as many plants and fungi. **Sexual reproduction** involves the union of genetic information from two parents. Flowering plants and animals reproduce sexually. Asexual reproduction occurs much faster than sexual reproduction. Sexual reproduction results in increased genetic diversity among offspring and parents.

▶ Cell Biology

All cells have a cell membrane that regulates the transport of nutrients and wastes in and out of the cell by the processes of diffusion, osmosis, and active transport. Some cells also have cell walls. The membrane surrounds cytoplasm where genetic materials and cellular structures are located. All cells contain ribosomes, which are responsible for producing proteins from amino acids. Prokaryotic cells (bacteria and cyanobacteria) lack a true nucleus and organelles, and have a cell wall. Eukaryotic cells have a membrane-bound nucleus storing DNA on chromosomes inside. These cells also have differentiated membrane-bound structures called organelles, which are responsible for specific cellular functions. Chloroplasts are found only in eukaryotic cells of autotrophs and contain chlorophyll to carry out photosynthesis. Mitochondria are the cell power plants, generating most of the cells' supply of energy in the form of ATP. The nucleolus is found in the nucleus and contains RNA and protein; its principle function is to produce and assemble ribosomes. The Golgi complex processes proteins and other macromolecules for cell secretion. Lyosomes contain enzymes used in digestion. Vacuoles are found in the cytoplasm of most plants and some animal cells and serve as storage areas for food, water, or waste.

Cells replicate into identical cells in order for an organism to grow and reproduce. **Prokaryotes** (single cell microorganisms) reproduce by binary fission, or division of identical cells. **Eukaryotic** cells follow a more complex process of reproduction described by the cell cycle. Most of a cell's life is spent in interphase, when it grows and replicates DNA. In late interphase, DNA replication produces sister chromatids, identical chromosome strands joined at a centromere. This is followed by mitosis, which is divided into prophase, metaphase, anaphase, and telophase. During prophase, DNA condenses into chromosomes, followed by metaphase, when chromosomes are aligned at the central metaphase plate. Next, in anaphase, sister chromatids separate and are pulled apart forming sister chromosomes. Finally, nuclear membranes form around the sister chromosomes in telophase, creating two nuclei. Now the cell is ready to split into two daughter cells, known as cytokinesis.

Mitosis

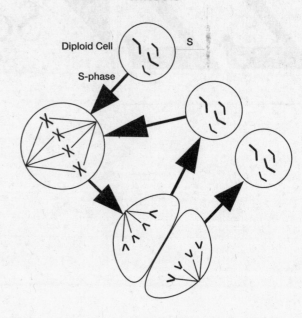

Living things vary in cellular complexity. Prokaryotic cells lack a nucleus, and organelles are found only in bacteria and cyanobacteria (blue-green algae). Eukaryotic cells have a nucleus and small structures within the cell, organelles, that carry out specific functions. The simplest living things are unicellular microorganisms, consisting of only one cell. This includes bacteria and protists. More complex living things are multicellular organisms, and have many cells that take on specific functions. This includes some algae, plants, and animals. A collection of specialized cells that perform a similar function form tissue. These tissues form structures and organs, which compose organ systems that work together to carry out the life functions of an organism.

Plants have **vascular tissue** that transports fluid and nutrients throughout the plant. The primary components of vascular tissue are xylem, which transports water and mineral nutrients from the root up the plant, and phloem, which transports sugars and nutrients to parts throughout the plant. Plants without vascular tissue lack the specialized structures to transport water and are often low-growing and found in moist environments.

Leaves are specialized organs that make food through the process of photosynthesis. Epidermis tissue forms the outer surface of leaves and has pores called stomata that allow carbon dioxide to enter the leaf. The carbon dioxide enters the cell chloroplasts, small structures that contain chlorophyll, which use the sun's energy to produce sugar for food. Plants maintain homeostasis of water content by controlling stomata. Water evaporates from the leaves in a process called transpiration when stomata are open, and water loss is reduced by the plant closing stomata.

Most plants grow **flowers** to reproduce. The stamen is the male part of a flower, which contains the anther that produces pollen. To reproduce, pollen attaches to the female part of a flower, the pistil, which contains the ovary and the egg cells. After pollen makes contact with the eggs of the pistil, seeds are made.

Vertebrate animals, including humans, have four types of tissue that compose their organs and organ systems. Epithelial tissue covers organ surfaces, such as skin and the inner lining of the digestive system. **Epithelial tissue** is responsible for protection, secretion, and absorption. **Connective tissue** holds everything together, and includes bone and cartilage, ligaments and tendons, blood, and adipose (fat). **Muscle tissue** is contractile tissue, which provides force and movement, either as motion or movement within internal organs. Muscle tissue includes visceral or smooth muscle, which is found in the inner lining of organs, skeletal muscle, which is attached to bone and provides mobility, and cardiac muscle, which is only found in the heart. **Nervous tissue** makes up the brain, spinal cord, and peripheral nervous system.

Humans have many **organ systems** working together. The **integumentary system** is the outermost organ system covering the body and is its largest organ. It includes the skin and associated glands, hair, and nails. Skin consists of epidermis (thinner, outermost layer) and dermis (thicker, innermost layer). Below the skin is the subcutaneous tissue. The integumentary system cooperates with the immune system to protect against infection and dehydration, regulates body temperature, provides sensation, and synthesizes vitamin D.

The **skeletal system** includes bones, cartilage, tendons, and ligaments, which give the body structural support and protection. With the muscular system, it allows for body movement. Bones store calcium and contain marrow to produce red and white blood cells and platelets. Bones come together at flexible joints, which are held together by ligaments. Muscles are connected to bones by tendons. Cartilage is a flexible yet strong tissue found in the joints, nose, and ears.

The **nervous system** is the command center of the body, consisting of the central nervous system of the brain and spinal cord, and the peripheral nervous system of all the nerves branching from the spinal cord. The brain's functions are broken up into three parts: the cerebral hemispheres responsible for higher functions, like speech and rational thought; the cerebellum, which maintains subconscious activities and balance functions; and the brain stem, which is in charge of automated functions, such as breathing and circulation. Nerve cells called neurons pass along signals through the nervous system. Signals are transmitted through long axons and are received by the dendrites, which are branched structures from neurons. The space between axons and dendrites is known as a synapse. Reflexes are unconscious reactions to stimuli that bypass the brain. Sensory receptors are part of the peripheral nervous system and send signals to the brain to be processed as vision, sound, taste, smell, and touch.

The **muscular system** provides force and movement. Muscle tissue can only contract and is generally attached to bone to work in opposing motions. Voluntary muscle (skeletal) is controlled by conscious thought; involuntary muscle (visceral, smooth) is controlled by the nervous system; and cardiac muscle (heart muscle, striated, and smooth) is specialized tissue that contracts spontaneously and is controlled by the nervous system.

The **respiratory system** involves the lungs, nose, trachea, bronchi, and diaphragm. Its primary function is to take in oxygen and eliminate carbon dioxide. Air enters through the mouth or nose and passes through the trachea, which branches into bronchi at the lungs. The bronchi branch off into smaller bronchioles and end with capillary rich alveoli, which exchange oxygen and carbon dioxide with the circulatory system. The diaphragm is the muscle responsible for expanding and contracting the volume of the chest cavity, which in turn forces air in and out of the lungs.

The **cardiovascular system** is the heart, blood vessels, and blood working together to transport oxygen, carbon dioxide, nutrients, and wastes throughout the body to other organ systems. Arteries and arterioles are blood vessels that carry blood that is oxygen and nutrient rich away from the heart. Veins and venules carry blood to the heart that has more carbon dioxide and wastes. Capillaries are beds of tiny blood vessels found in tissue and are the site of the exchange of gases and nutrients. Arteries are thick walled because they carry the blood at high pressure, and veins are thin walled because the blood returns at lower pressure. Blood rate is slowest in the capillaries to allow for material exchange. The human heart has four chambers, two upper atria and two lower ventricles. Blood is pumped from the right ventricle to the lungs by the

pulmonary arteries and is returned to the left atrium of the heart through pulmonary veins. This is known as the pulmonary circuit. Blood is then pumped from the left ventricle to all the tissues of the body through the aorta, the largest artery in the body, and is returned to the right atrium of the heart. This is known as the systemic circuit. Red blood cells contain hemoglobin, which carries oxygen and gives blood its red color. White blood cells protect the body from infectious diseases and foreign bodies. Platelets in the blood primarily help blood to clot.

The **endocrine system** is a group of glands and tissues that secrete hormones. Hormones are substances that facilitate communication between the organ systems. Hormones secreted by the pituitary gland regulate growth and stimulate the thyroid. Thyroid hormones help control the rate of metabolism. Hormones produced by the pancreas maintain blood glucose levels; insulin decreases glucose levels, and glucagon increases glucose levels. Adrenaline, otherwise known as the "fight or flight" hormone, is produced by the adrenal glands.

The **immunological system** protects the body from infection. It consists of the lymphatic system, which includes the spleen, tonsils, thymus gland, and bone marrow (producing white blood cells). The lymphatic system is responsible for recycling body fluids and fighting disease. Immunity occurs when the immune system recognizes antigens, harmful pathogens, and produces antibodies to get rid of the antigen. The immune system has the ability to distinguish its own body's molecules from antigens and other foreign bodies. Unfortunately, this means the immune system will attack transplanted tissue from another person. The immune system is able to remember formerly encountered antigens and reacts quickly when exposed again, which is called acquired immunity.

The **digestive** (or **gastrointestinal**) **system** consists of the gastrointestinal tract, which includes the mouth, esophagus, stomach, small intestine, large intestine, and anus. Accessory organs, such as the teeth, tongue, liver, pancreas, and gall bladder, aid in the digestion of food. The function of the digestive system is to break down food, absorb nutrients and energy, and eliminate wastes. Digestion starts in the mouth where the food is broken down into smaller pieces by the teeth, and enzymes in saliva begin digestion of carbohydrates. In the stomach, hydrochloric acid and pepsin further digest food. Then food goes into the small intestine, where pancreatic enzymes and bile continue digestion and nutrients are absorbed. Pancreatic enzymes include trypsin to digest proteins, lipase to digest fats, and amylase to digest carbohydrates. The large intestine absorbs water and minerals and eliminates waste as feces through the anus. The liver processes nutrients absorbed by the small intestine and produces bile that emulsifies fats and is stored in the gall bladder. The liver is also responsible for detoxification.

The **renal** (or **excretory**) **system** uses the kidneys to filter blood to remove nitrogenous waste and toxic byproducts and retain necessary nutrients, like glucose and amino acids. The kidneys contain excretory units called nephrons, where blood is filtered. This process also allows the renal system to regulate water and salt balance and control blood pH. Waste is passed through the ureters as urine and is stored in the bladder until it is excreted out of the body through the urethra.

The **reproductive system** consists of external genitalia and internal reproductive organs. In males, the scrotum and penis are external genitalia, and the testes, prostrate gland, and ducts to transport sperm are internal reproductive organs. In females, the clitoris and two sets of labia are external organs, and the ovaries, fallopian tubes, uterus, vagina, and cervix are the internal system.

The male sperm and female egg (ovum) are gametes, which contain half the correct number of chromosomes. The ovaries contain thousands of eggs, and about once a month, an egg is released from one ovary into the fallopian tube. Sperm is produced in the seminiferous tubules in the testes and travels through the vas deferens and the penis to fertilize an egg in the female uterus. If the egg is not fertilized, menstruation occurs and the cycle continues. If the egg is fertilized, it becomes a zygote with the correct number of chromosomes and attaches to the uterus wall and grows into an embryo. The embryo grows into a baby during a nine-month gestation period and exits the uterus through the cervix and vagina.

▶ Chemistry of Life

All living things need energy to survive. Organisms use a molecule called **ATP** (adenosine triphosphate) to obtain the energy they need. ATP can be produced from carbohydrates (sugars) or lipids (fats) within an organism's cells. Some organisms, such as plants, are autotrophs because they produce their own energy in the form of glucose (sugar) using the energy of the sun. This process of **photosynthesis** is represented by the following reaction:

$$6\,CO_2 + 6\,H_2O \rightarrow 6\,O_2 + C_6H_{12}O_6$$

carbon dioxide + water → oxygen + glucose

Plants later use the glucose produced to release energy and form ATP. Organisms that acquire energy by eating food, instead of producing their own food, are heterotrophs. Heterotrophs also use glucose digested from food to release energy and make ATP in the process of cellular respiration:

$$C_6H_{12}O_6 + 6\,O_2 \rightarrow 6\,CO_2 + 6\,H_2O + ATP$$

glucose + oxygen → carbon dioxide + water + ATP

This is an aerobic reaction because oxygen is present to be used in the reaction. If oxygen is not present, organisms release energy from glucose by the anaerobic process of fermentation:

$$C_6H_{12}O_6 \rightarrow \ 2\,C_2H_5OH \ + 2\,CO_2$$
$$\text{glucose} \rightarrow \text{ethyl alcohol} + \text{carbon dioxide}$$

▶ Genetics and Reproduction

Organisms pass on genetic information to their offspring through **chromosomes**, DNA strands that provide the blueprint for cells to build complex proteins that carry out cellular functions. DNA is found in the nucleus of eukaryotic organisms and is composed of two complementary strands of nucleotides that coil around each other forming a double helix. The nucleotide strands provide structure through a sugar-phosphate backbone and are held to each other through the hydrogen bonds of complementary bases. For example, adenine (A) pairs with thymine (T), and guanine (G) pairs with cytosine (C).

The sequence of bases on DNA forms genes that represent codes for specific proteins. The code is organized by groups of three bases called codons. In protein synthesis, DNA is read during transcription to produce a complementary copy, messenger RNA (mRNA), which is able to travel from the nucleus to the cytoplasm of the cell. Instead of using thymine (T) in mRNA, uracil (U) is used, which bonds to adenine (A). Once in the cytoplasm, mRNA attaches to the ribosome, which is the site of protein synthesis. Ribosomal RNA (rRNA) in the ribosome is the main component coordinating the decoding of mRNA to make specific proteins through the process of translation. Transfer RNA (tRNA) contains anticodons that are complementary to the codons of mRNA. tRNA brings amino acids into the ribosome and sequences them into proteins according to the sequences of codons on mRNA.

Organisms that reproduce sexually use haploid **gametes** that have half the required chromosomes as in the diploid eukaryotic cells. During meiosis, the diploid cell undergoes one round of DNA replication and two rounds of division (mitosis), forming four haploid gametes. Gametes from male parents are called sperm and from female parents are called eggs, which combined form a diploid zygote. Genetic variation is introducing during the round of DNA replication due to genetic recombination, which occurs when there is chromosomal crossover between chromosomal pairs. This results in gametes with different combinations of genes than their parent cells, leading to genetic diversity and new traits in offspring.

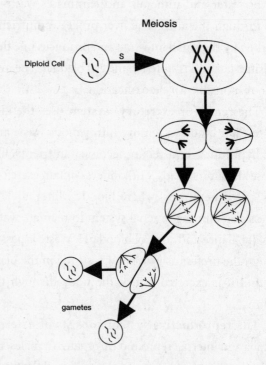

Meiosis

Diploid Cell

gametes

Humans have 23 pairs of chromosomes in their diploid cells, 22 pairs of somatic chromosomes and one pair of sex (gender) chromosomes. Males have one X chromosome and one Y chromosome and females have two X chromosomes. Different species have other chromosomes that determine gender.

Unfortunately, there are genetically inherited diseases created by mutations, changes in the DNA sequence of chromosomes. Examples include Huntington's disease, Tay-Sachs disease, sickle-cell anemia, hemophilia, Parkinson's disease, and cystic fibrosis. Some genetic mutations are sex-linked, and will be seen more in one gender, as in hemophilia, which is linked to the X chromosome and seen mostly in men. Sometimes during sexual reproduction, there is an abnormal gain or loss of chromosomes that can lead to genetic disorders. For instance, Down syndrome is usually caused by an extra chromosome 21.

Many of these conditions are rare, because they are recessive traits. If a person has one dominant chromosome and one recessive chromosome, the dominant trait will be expressed, but the recessive chromosome will be carried in the cells and may be passed on to its offspring. If two parents pass recessive disorders to their offspring, the genetic condition can become present.

▶ Molecular Biology

Cells are made up of four types of **macromolecules**: carbohydrates, lipids, proteins, and nucleic acids. Carbohydrates and fats are used as energy sources. Proteins provide the cell's structure, control a cell membrane's specific functions, and, in the form of an enzyme, act as a catalyst for cellular reactions and functions.

Macromolecules are often polymers of simple components referred to as monomers. Carbohydrates are made up of monomers of monosaccharides. Glucose is an important monosaccharide, and lactose found in milk is a disaccharide (two saccharides bonded together). Many saccharides bonded together form polysaccharides (complex carbohydrates), such as starch and cellulose. Proteins consist of monomers of amino acids, which link together to form long polypeptide chains. These chains fold into complex shapes due to molecular forces and interactions along the polypeptide. The shape of the protein determines its function. DNA and RNA consist of strands of nucleotide

monomers. The polynucleotide strand forms a sugar-phosphate backbone and the sequence of the nitrogenous bases of each nucleotide forms the genetic code.

Monomers used by the cells to form macromolecules are transported across the cell membrane along with other needed nutrients. Transport is made possible by diffusion, movement of molecules from an area of high concentration to one of lower concentration, and active transport, which uses proteins and energy to pump material through the cell membrane against a concentration gradient.

▶ Molecular Genetics

Gregor Mendel is considered the father of classical genetics for the experiments he conducted on the varying traits of garden peas. His work helped formulate the idea that traits are inherited from parents. Earlier ideas of genetics suggested a blending theory of characteristics from parents, much like blending paint colors. However, Mendel's experiments disproved this theory, and heredity is now understood to be controlled by **dominant** and **recessive** traits.

Offspring receive one gene or allele from each parent for a specific trait. If the allele is dominant, then the trait will be expressed. The recessive allele can be present and not expressed when it is with a dominant allele. However, if two recessive alleles are present, the recessive trait will be expressed. For example, a mother can express the dominant trait of brown eyes and carry the recessive allele for blue eyes. If this mother gives the recessive trait to her offspring along with the recessive allele from the father, then the offspring will express the recessive trait of blue eyes. The combination of alleles is referred to as genotype, and phenotype describes the observed trait expressed by the two alleles. If the alleles are the same (both dominant or both recessive), an organism is described as being homozygous for that gene. If the alleles are different, it is heterozygous.

A **Punnett square** is used to make predictions of the genotypes of offspring from two parents. In the Punnett square, dominant alleles are represented with uppercase letters, and recessive alleles are represented with lowercase letters. For example, Mendel's experiments looked at the colors expressed by pea flowers; purple flowers are the dominant trait (P), and white flowers are the recessive trait (p). In the initial generation (P generation), homozygous dominant plants (PP) were crossed with homozygous recessive plants (pp). The resulting generation (F1 generation) yielded all heterozygous plants (Pp) that expressed the dominant purple flower trait. Plants from the F1 generation were crossed and created mostly dominant plants and some recessive plants in the F2 generation. This is because there is a possibility for offspring to receive one recessive allele from both parents. According to the Punnett square for the F2 generation, 25% will be homozygous dominant (PP), 50% will be heterozygous (Pp), and 25% will be homozygous recessive (pp). In some organisms, it is possible to express incomplete dominance with a heterozygous genotype. For instance, RR for red flowers and rr for white flowers could yield Rr offspring presenting pink flowers.

	P	p
P	PP	Pp
p	Pp	pp

▶ Evolution

There is evidence supporting the theory that the diversity of life is the result of evolution, mutations, and natural selection. There is early fossil evidence that prokaryotic bacteria appeared around 3.5 billion years ago. **Fossils** are the remains of creatures found in rock layers and sedimentary layers. Fossil records reveal several variations in organs and structures of vertebrate animals. These variations were most likely the result of genetic mutations, changes in genetic code that are passed on to offspring. More favorable mutations help an organism survive, while less favorable mutations are reduced. Charles Darwin developed the theory of **natural selection** and proposed that organisms best fit for their environment will survive (survival of the fittest). Favorable mutations become adaptations that are passed on to offspring and help them survive in their environment.

Organisms are classified by similarity to other organisms and placed in a system of **taxonomy**, or hierarchical groups of related organisms. For instance, birds are classified with other organisms that fly, which are classified with other warm-blooded animals, which are classified with other animals. The classification has been revised several times, and currently includes eight levels of classification: Domain, Kingdom, Phylum (Division for plants), Class, Order, Family, Genus, and Species.

The three **domains** of organisms are archaea, bacteria, and eukaryotes. Archaea are a small group of prokaryotic single-celled organisms. Prokaryotes lack a nucleus and other cellular organelles. Many of these organisms have adapted to live in extreme conditions, like high temperatures and salty environments, but have also been found in all habitats. Bacteria are unicellular prokaryotic microorganisms. Bacteria vary in shape and include spheres, rods, and spirals. Bacteria are found in every habitat on Earth, and, when compared with Archaea, have differences in the compositions of their cell membrane, DNA replication, and other structures. All other living things comprise the domain Eukaryota. Eukaryotes are organisms whose cells have a nucleus and specialized organelles, and most eukaryotes are multicellular.

There are six **kingdoms** of living things: Archaebacteria, Eubacteria, Protista, Fungi, Plantae, and Animalae. Archaebacteria and Eubacteria are unicellular prokaryotes. Protists are either unicellular, like amoebas and protozoa, or multicellular without specialized tissue, like algae. There are autotrophs (make their own food) and heterotrophs (find food from other sources) classified as protists, which are found in aquatic environments or in other organisms as parasites. Fungi are multicellular heterotrophs that exist only on land. Fungi reproduce asexually and sexually using pores. Some fungi play an essential role in ecosystems by decomposing dead matter and replacing nutrients in the soil. Plants are multicellular autotrophs that live on land and have cell walls containing cellulose. Plant growth only happens at sites of actively dividing cells, meristems, which are located at the tips and edges of the plant. Bryophytes are nonvascular plants that lack vascular tissue to circulate fluids. Vascular plants have tissue systems that circulate water and nutrients through the plant. These plants are either seedless or have seeds to reproduce. There are two types of vascular seed plants: gymnosperms with seeds from cones, and angiosperms, flowering plants. Animals are multicellular heterotrophs that live on land and in water, and their cells lack cell walls. Animals are either invertebrates (without backbones) or vertebrates (with backbones). Invertebrate animals include the phyla of sponges, jellyfish, worms, mollusks, arthropods, and starfish. Mollusks include gastropods (snails and slugs), bivalves (clams and mussels), and cephalopods (octopi and squid). Arthropods are animals with hard exoskeletons and have segmented bodies with appendages on at least one segment; insects have six legs, and arachnids (spiders and scorpions) have eight legs. Vertebrate animals make up the phylum chordata (along with some closely related invertebrates) and include fish, amphibians, reptiles, birds, and mammals. Birds and mammals are considered warm-blooded because they can maintain their body temperature, while other cold-blooded animals cannot. **Mammals** (of which humans are a part) are characterized by having milk-producing glands to feed offspring, growing hair, and giving birth to live young instead of laying eggs (with the exception of the duck-billed platypus).

Viruses are microscopic parasites that are unable to reproduce without a host cell. In order to reproduce, viruses need to infect an organism and inject genetic material into a cell for replication. Viral infections usually lead to disease in animals and humans, and require an immune response to overcome. Antibiotics have no effect on viruses (they treat bacterial infections); vaccines are used to produce lifelong immunity. Antiviral drugs have also been developed to treat infections. Viruses contain DNA or RNA surrounded by a protein coat but lack metabolic activity, a nucleus, and other cellular organelles. With this in mind, many scientists consider viruses to be nonliving.

▶ Ecology

Ecology is the study of interactions between organisms and their environment. Organisms depend on other organisms for energy. Plants are primary producers that use the sun's energy to create chemical energy in the form of glucose through photosynthesis. Plants form the base in an ecosystem's food chain or food web, and are eaten by primary consumers for their energy. Secondary consumers will eat primary consumers for energy, thus moving the energy from the base to the top of the food chain. This type of relationship is known as a predator-prey relationship.

There are many other types of relationships in a food chain. Symbiotic relationships are when two organisms closely interact for the benefit of one or both organisms. Mutualism is when both organisms benefit from the relationship, like a bird eating nectar from a flower and pollinating the flower at the same time. A parasitic relationship is when one organism (the parasite) benefits and the other (the host) is harmed, such as a flea feeding from the blood of a dog. Commensalism is when an organism benefits from the relationship with another organism, but the other is not harmed nor helped, as with orchids growing on trees. Competition between organisms happens when they must use a limited resource, like animals competing for water or plants competing for sunlight.

Organisms are organized into **trophic levels** according to their role in the food chain. Plants and other autotrophs occupy the first level, because they produce energy from sunlight. Herbivores occupy the second level, because they feed off the plants. The third level is for carnivores that eat second level animals. At the fourth level are carnivores that eat other carnivores. As energy moves up the levels, some of it is used by organisms within the trophic, making it less available for higher-level organisms. As a result, primary producers have the most biomass and top-level carnivores have the least.

An **ecosystem** is a group of all living organisms (biotic factors) interacting with all of the nonliving (abiotic) factors of the environment. For example, all the aquatic animals and plants in a lake, and the water, food, and wastes make up an ecosystem. Energy and matter move through biotic and abiotic factors according to biogeochemical cycles. For instance, the carbon cycle describes the movement of carbon through the uptake of carbon dioxide by plants and ocean surface reactions, and its release to the atmosphere by respiration of organisms, decomposition of carbon compounds by bacteria and fungi, and combustion of fossil fuels. The water cycle is the movement of water in the ecosystem through the processes of evaporation, precipitation, runoff, and use by organisms. Living organisms rely on the nitrogen cycle for nitrogen to produce proteins, because they cannot use nitrogen abundantly found in the atmosphere. Only specific bacteria can fix nitrogen into a usable form, and are responsible for returning it back into the atmosphere. Other molecules follow cycles in ecosystems and also rely on the food chains between living organisms.

A group of species interacting with each other is called a **population**. The maximum population growth under ideal environmental conditions is considered the population's **biotic potential**. Systems of different species interacting with each other create a community. Factors within the community will act to limit a population's actual growth, like food sources, competition, predators, and climate. The number of individuals an ecosystem can support is called its carrying capacity. Succession is the process of communities changing over time. When organisms form a new community in previously uninhabited areas, like a lava flow area, it is called primary succession. When an existing community is destroyed by a disturbance, as with a forest fire, it is considered a secondary succession.

Biomes are large geographical areas that share similar types of plants, animals, and climate conditions. Biomes are larger than ecosystems and are similar across the world at the same latitude or similar altitudes. Tundra consists of polar regions and alpine locations with a permanently frozen subsoil layer called permafrost and tiny plants that grow only during the short summer seasons. The land tends to be boggy in the summer and animals are migratory. Tundra is a very windy area. Taiga is characterized by coniferous forest, like spruce and fir, and covers much of the northern hemisphere. Winters are long and cold, and summers are short and dry. Temperate deciduous forest consists of trees that lose their leaves each winter, like maple, birch, and oak. There are cold winters and hot summers with plenty of rainfall for trees and plants. There is a great diversity of animal and plant life. Tropical seasonal forests and rain forests are areas in the tropics that are warm and wet most of the year. Some areas have distinct wet and dry seasons. Biodiversity is at a maximum in these regions, which contain at least half of the Earth's land plants and animal species. Grasslands and prairies have warmer summers than deciduous forests, but with less rainfall. Grasslands have rich soil, which supports farmlands and large populations of grazing animals. Due to hot, dry summers, grasslands experience fires, which is a natural part of this biome. Deserts are very dry with little precipitation. Plants and animals have special adaptations to conserve water. Aquatic biomes are freshwater and marine. Freshwater includes streams, rivers, ponds, lakes, and wetlands. Marine regions include oceans, estuaries, and coral, and have saltwater. Marine life is diverse and these ecosystems are divided into zones: pelagic (open water), benthic (deep water), abyssal (deepest ocean), and intertidal (exposed at low tide).

23 ▶ Physical Science

Everything is made up of **matter**. Matter has mass and takes up space. Matter exists in one of three states: **solid**, **liquid**, or **gas**. Solids have distinct shape and occupy definite volume. The particles making up a solid are packed closely together and maintain fixed positions. Liquids take on the shape of their container and have a definite volume. A liquid's particles are free to move within the boundaries of the liquid within its container. Gases do not have a distinct shape or a definite volume. The particles of gas are in constant motion and are farther apart than liquids and solids. Gas will expand to fill the entire space that contains it, like the air in a room.

When matter goes from one state to another, it is referred to as a change of state. State changes are controlled by temperature and pressure. As temperature increases, matter will change state from solid to liquid to gas. This is because increasing temperature increases the movement of particles, which is highest in a gaseous state. As pressure is increased, matter moves from gas to liquid to solid. This is because increasing pressure forces particles to get closer; particles are closest in a solid state. The process of moving from a solid state into a liquid state is called **melting**; the temperature at this change is referred to as its **melting point**. Moving from liquid to gas is called **boiling**, and the corresponding temperature is the **boiling point**. When gas changes to a liquid state, it is called **condensation**. When liquid changes to a solid state, it is called **freezing** or **crystallization**, and this corresponding temperature is the **freezing point**. The freezing point is the same as the melting point for any substance. The temperature and pressure at which a substance can exist in equilibrium in its three states of matter is called the **triple point**. When a substance changes state from a solid to gas without first turning into a liquid, it is referred to as **sublimation**.

▶ Atoms and Atomic Theory

Matter is made up of **atoms**, and each element, like carbon, oxygen, or hydrogen, is characterized by a distinct atom. Atoms are made up of subatomic particles: protons, neutrons, and electrons. **Protons** and **neutrons** make up the nucleus of an atom and give an atom its mass; each has an amu (atomic mass unit) of 1. **Electrons** are in motion around the nucleus and have a negligible mass. Electrons are distributed in specific orbitals around the nucleus and each orbital consists of increasing energy levels referred to as shells (*s, p, d, f*). Protons are positively charged and neutrons are not charged, leaving the nucleus positively charged. The electrons distributed around the nucleus have a negative charge. If the number of protons is equal to the number of electrons, then the atom will be neutral. Sometimes, an atom will give up an electron or take an electron to become electronically stable, and will have a net positive (cation) or negative charge (anion), respectively.

Neil Bohr devised a model to describe the structure of atoms. It depicts electrons as orbiting around the central nucleus. An electron can be excited by a quantum of energy, moving it to an outer orbit (excited level). The electron can then emit radiation (energy) to fall back to its original orbit (ground state). The electrons in the outer orbit are referred to as valence electrons and are in the last energy level. These electrons are loosely held and are responsible for the bonding with other elements and electrons. According to the octet rule, an element is most stable when it has eight valence electrons.

Orbitals are represented as specific shapes; *s* orbitals are spherical, and *p* orbitals are dumbbell-shaped. Pauli's Exclusion Principle states that an orbital can hold two electrons if they are of opposite spins. However, according to Hund's Rule, the most stable arrangement of electrons in the same energy levels is one in which electrons have parallel spins. Therefore, when filling the *p, d,* or *f* levels, each orbital must first have one electron before a second electron occupy an orbital. The distribution of electrons in orbitals can be written as an electron configuration. Starting with the innermost orbital, energy levels are written with their corresponding orbitals. A superscript denotes the number of electrons in each orbital. For example, Chlorine (Cl) would be written: $1s^2 2s^2 2p^6 3s^2 3p^5$.

The **atomic number** of an element represents the number of protons in its nucleus, Z. This can be written as $_Z X$. The mass number or atomic mass, A, is the sum of protons and neutrons in the nucleus. This can be written as $^A X$. The atomic number determines the identity of an element. However, an element can have a different atomic mass depending on the number of neutrons in the nucleus. This is called an isotope of an element and most often is an unstable form of the element.

Radioactivity is the spontaneous emission of particles from an unstable nucleus. This radioactive decay can form isotopes or new elements, and can release energy. An alpha particle is a positively charged particle emitted from a heavy nucleus. A beta particle is an electron emitted from an element. During a beta emission, a neutron is converted into a proton, thus increasing the atomic number and changing the identity of the element. Gamma radiation typically occurs with alpha and beta emissions. Gamma rays are high-energy photons that do not change the atomic number or mass of an element.

The **half-life** is the amount of time for half of the atoms of a radioactive sample to decay. This is an important characteristic of isotopes used to determine when radioactive material is safe to handle or to calculate the age of ancient things, as in carbon dating.

Fission is the nuclear reaction of a large isotope breaking apart into two or more smaller elements. This can be accomplished by bombarding the isotope with a smaller unit, usually a neutron. This reaction releases a lot of energy, which has been harnessed in atomic bombs and nuclear power plants.

A **fusion reaction** is essentially the reverse of a fission reaction; two smaller nuclei are fused into one heavier nucleus. This is the same reaction that powers the sun. Fusion reactions release an extraordinary amount of energy. This was first demonstrated by detonating the hydrogen bomb, which is approximately 1,000 times as powerful as an atomic bomb. Scientists have tried for several decades to safely harness the energy from a fusion reaction. If this reaction is controlled, it has the potential to provide a limitless electricity supply with no pollution.

Elements are categorized by the periodic table in order of increasing number of protons. Elements arranged in columns, referred to as families or groups, have the same number of valence electrons and share similar characteristics. Some important families are alkali metals (IA), alkaline earth metals (IIA), halogens (VIIA), and noble gases (VIIIA). The rows of the periodic table are called periods, and the elements of each period do not have any similarities. Moving from left to right along a period, the atomic radius increases and the ability to gain electrons increases, referred to as electronegativity. Moving from top to bottom in a family, the atomic radius increases and the electronegativity decreases.

hydrogen 1 H																	helium 2 He
lithium 3 Li	beryllium 4 Bd											boron 5 B	carbon 6 C	nitrogen 7 N	oxygen 8 O	fluorine 9 F	neon 10 N
sodium 11 Na	magnesium 12 Mg											aluminium 13 Al	silicon 14 Si	phosphorus 15 P	sulfur 16 S	chlorine 17 Cl	argon 18 Ar
potassium 19 K	calcium 20 Ca	scandium 21 Sc	titanium 22 Ti	vanadium 23 V	chromium 24 Cr	manganese 25 Mn	iron 26 Fr	cobalt 27 Co	nickel 28 Ni	copper 29 Cu	zinc 30 Zn	gallium 31 Ga	germanium 32 Ge	arsenic 33 As	selenium 34 Se	bromine 35 Br	krypton 36 Kr
rubidium 37 RB	strontium 38 Sr	yttrium 39 Y	zirconium 40 Zr	niobium 41 Nb	molybdenum 42 Mo	technetium 43 Tc	ruthenium 44 Ru	rhodium 45 Rh	palladium 46 Pd	silver 47 Ag	cadmium 48 Cd	indium 49 In	tin 50 Sn	antimony 51 Sb	tellurium 52 Te	iodine 53 I	xenon 54 Xe
caesium 55 Cs	barium 56 Ba	57-70 *	lutetium 71 Lu	hafnium 72 Hf	tantalum 73 Ta	tungsten 74 W	rhenium 75 Re	osmium 76 Os	iridium 77 Ir	paltinum 78 Pt	gold 79 Au	mercury 80 Hg	thallium 81 Tl	lead 82 Pb	bismuth 83 Bi	polonium 84 Po	astatine 85 At	radon 86 Rn
francium 87 Fr	radium 88 Ra	89-102 **	lawrencium 103 Lr	rutherfordium 104 Rf	dubnium 105 Db	seaborgium 106 Sg	bohrium 107 Bh	hassium 108 Hs	meitnerium 109 Mt	unummilium 110 U	unununium 111 Uuu	ununbium 112 Uub		ununquadium 114 Uuq			

* Lanthanide series	lanthanum 57 La	cerium 58 Ce	prasedymium 59 Pr	neodymium 60 Nd	promethium 61 Pm	samarium 62 Sm	europium 63 Eu	gadolinium 64 Gd	terbium 65 Tb	dysprosium 66 Dy	holmium 67 Ho	erbium 68 Er	thulium 69 Tm	ytterbium 70 Yb
** Actinide series	actinium 89 Ac	thorium 90 Th	protactinium 91 Pa	uranium 92 U	neptunium 93 Np	plutonium 94 Pu	americium 95 Am	curium 96 Cm	berkelium 97 Bk	californium 98 Cf	ensteinium 99 Es	fermium 100 Fm	mendelevium 101 Md	nobelium 102 No

Metals are elements that have high densities, are good conductors of electricity and heat, shiny, malleable, and are solid at room temperature. Metals have a greater tendency to lose their valence electrons and are grouped in the left side of the periodic table (families I–III). **Nonmetals** are elements that react easily with other substances, are poor conductors, readily accept electrons, and are gaseous at room temperature. Nonmetals are found in the upper right side of the periodic table. **Metalloids** are nonmetallic elements with properties in between those of metals and nonmetals, like semiconductivity. They are found between metals and nonmetals on the periodic table. **Halogens** in family VIIA are nonmetal gases at room temperature that usually exist diatomically, such as Fluorine (F_2). **Noble gases** are in the far right column of the periodic table and have a full number of valence electrons, making them stable and unreactive to others substances.

► Compounds

Molecules are two or more atoms bonded together, as with oxygen O_2. A **compound** is a combination of two or more elements and is named according to the bonds that hold them together. Covalent compounds share one or more electron pairs between atoms, and are typically two nonmetal elements. Polar covalent compounds have stronger bonds due to one atom pulling the electron pair more than the other. The resulting molecule has a dipole between the atoms; one end has a negative charge and the other a positive charge. Polar molecules are attracted to other polar molecules and form strong hydrogen bonds between them. Ionic compounds are formed from the combination of cations (positively charged) and anions (negatively charged). Ionic bonds are the result of unequal sharing of electrons.

Binary covalent compounds (two elements present) are named according to the number of atoms. Prefixes are used with the name to indicate the number of atoms present, such as carbon dioxide (CO_2) and dinitrogen tetroxide (N_2O_4). Ionic compounds tend to be a combination of metal and nonmetal elements. They are named with the metal first, followed by the nonmetal whose ending is changed to -*ide*, such as lithium sulfide (Li_2S). Other times it is a compound of positive or negative polyatomic ions, like ammonium carbonate ($NH_4)_2CO_3$.

A **mixture** is a combination of two or more compounds to form a solution. The two substances are not chemically bonded to each other and can be separated out. The liquid of a mixture is called the solvent, and the solute is the compound dissolved into the solvent.

Acids are proton donors (according to Bronsted-Lowery Theory) or electron acceptors (according to Lewis Theory). Acids release hydrogen ions (H^+) in water and decrease pH. Bases are proton acceptors (Bronsted-Lowery) or electron donors (Lewis). Bases release hydroxide ions in (OH^-) water and increase pH. The acidity of a solution is reported within the pH scale 0 to 14. Acidic solutions have a pH below 7 and strong acids have a low pH. A neutral solution has a pH of 7, such as water. Basic solutions have a pH above 7 and strong bases have a high pH. Each unit on the pH scale represents a change in acidity of 10 times. Therefore, a solution with a pH of 4 is 10 times as acidic as one with a pH of 5, and 100 times as acidic as a solution with a pH of 6. Buffer solutions resist a change in pH when acids or bases are added.

► Stoichiometry

Compounds interact with other chemical compounds to change their composition. Reactions can be the decomposition of reactants into simpler molecules or the synthesis of complex products from simpler molecules. Combustion is the burning of molecules with oxygen as a reactant and always results in the products of carbon dioxide and water.

Oxidation-reduction (redox) reactions involve the transfer of electrons from one molecule to another. Oxidation represents the loss of electrons and reduction represents the gain of electrons. In a redox reaction, the number of electrons lost is always equal to the number of electrons gained.

The law of conservation of mass states that mass cannot be created or destroyed. Therefore, in chemical reactions, the mass of the initial molecules (reactants) must equal the mass of the final molecules (products), even if the molecules have formed new compounds. Therefore, the atoms in chemical equations need to be balanced between reactant and products. This can be accomplished by balancing both sides of the equation by trial and error. When determining the mass of reactants or products, the number of moles of an atom must be used. A mole is the mass of a substance equal to 6.022×10^{23} molecules (Avogadro's number). One mole of an element is equal to its atomic mass. For instance, one mole of carbon is equal to 12 grams. The molecular mass is the sum of the atomic masses of its elements, which is also the same as its molar mass (g/mol). For example, one mole of CO_2 has a molar mass of 44 grams/mole (12g/mol + 2 × 16g/mol).

Reaction Rates and Equilibrium

A reaction has a **reaction rate** related to its activation energy. **Activation energy** is the minimum amount of energy required for reactants to be changed into products. The higher the activation energy needed, the slower the reaction rate will be. Some reactions are reversible; products can transform into reactants. Equilibrium occurs when the rates for the forward reaction and reverse reaction are the same.

Reactions that release energy, usually in the form of heat, are called **exothermic reactions**. Exothermic reactions have low activation energies for the forward reaction, because the reactants are unstable and easily changed. Combustion reactions are examples of exothermic reactions. **Endothermic reactions** have high activation energies and require energy or heat in order for the reaction to get started. Highly endothermic reactions have stable reactants, and it is difficult to move them toward the forward reaction. The amount of energy given off or taken in would be equal to the energy needed or given off in the reverse reaction.

Reactions require molecules to come in contact with each other and rates are affected by various factors. As temperature increases, rates increase, because particles move faster and have more collisions at higher temperatures. Smaller particles react faster, because they collide often at any temperature and concentration. A higher concentration of reactants increases the number of particles available for reaction and increases the rate. Catalysts increase the reaction rate by lowering the activation energy. A catalyst does not get used up during a reaction.

Units of Measure

The metric system is commonly used for measurement in science. Length is measured in meters (m), mass in grams (g), volume in liters (L), time in seconds (s), and temperature in degrees Celsius (ºC). The magnitude of these units can be increased or decreased by powers of ten and represented by a corresponding prefix. For instance, one-hundredth of a meter is a centimeter (cm), and 1,000 grams is a kilogram (kg).

Mechanics

Energy is the ability to do work. The law of conservation of energy (**first law of thermodynamics**) states that energy cannot be created or destroyed, but can be transformed into other forms. Kinetic energy is energy of motion. Potential energy is stored energy that has potential to be converted into another form of energy. Chemical energy is the energy stored in the bonds between elements. Thermal energy is related to temperature, and electrical energy is related to the movement of electrons. Mass energy refers to Einstein's Theory of Relativity and is defined as $E = mc^2$, where m is equal to mass and c is equal to the speed of light.

The **second law of thermodynamics** states that when work is done, some energy is lost as heat. This process increases a system's entropy, which is a measure of energy unavailable to do work. Heat is the transfer of energy from areas of high energy (or temperature) to low energy. Conduction moves heat through matter from areas of high temperature to low temperature. Convection transfers heat through the movement of currents within fluids (liquids and gases). The units of heat include the joule (J), British Thermal Unit (BTU), and calorie (cal).

Measuring potential energy can be difficult. Kinetic energy is easily measured by temperature. A temperature measurement is the average kinetic energy of particles. There are three temperature scales. The Celsius scale is set at 0º C and 100º C for the freezing point and boiling point of water, respectively. The Fahrenheit scale is set at different conditions and is related to the Celsius scale as follows: ºF = 1.8º C + 32. The Kelvin scale measures absolute temperature, with 0º K referred to as absolute zero, where particles have minimal motion and can be no colder.

Velocity (v) is the rate of change of the position of an object expressed as distance divided by time ($v = \frac{d}{t}$). Acceleration (a) is the rate of change of velocity (an increase or decrease in velocity). Acceleration is determined as the change in velocity ($v_2 - v_1$) divided by the period of time. Gravity is expressed as acceleration with a constant rate of 9.8 m/s^2.

Classical physics is based largely on the work of Sir Isaac Newton. Newton's first law of motion describes inertia, an object's resistance to change its state of motion. An object at rest will stay at rest and an object in motion will stay in motion unless there is an unbalanced force acting on it. Force causes an object to accelerate (change speed and/or direction).

Newton's second law of motion involves the momentum of an object. It defines the net force on an object as the product of its mass and acceleration ($F = ma$) and is measured in Newtons (N). The greater the mass of an object or the greater the acceleration, the greater its net force will be.

Newton's third law of motion states that every action has an equal and opposite reaction. In other words, when object A exerts a force on object B, object B exerts an equal and opposite force on object A.

Quantum mechanics describes energy and matter on a microscopic scale that classical mechanics was unable to explain. In particular, quantum mechanics theories address electron orbits of atoms, black body radiation, and motion in space. Einstein's theory of special relativity states that speed of light is the same regardless of the motion of observer. This is important to prove that the laws of physics remain constant regardless of the point of reference, and show that space and time are relative concepts. Einstein developed the theory of general relativity to apply to broader concepts, such as gravitational theory.

▶ Wave Motion

Waves carry and transfer energy from one point to another without carrying matter. Some examples include sound waves, light waves, radio waves, ocean waves, and seismic waves of earthquakes. Waves have crests (highpoints) and troughs (low points), and oscillate with a definite period (T), the time for one wave to complete its cycle. The frequency (f) of a wave is the number of crests that pass a fixed point per second; frequency is the reciprocal of the period, $f = \frac{1}{T}$. The wavelength (λ) is the distance between crests, and the amplitude (*A*) is the distance between the crest and trough. The velocity of the wave is the product of wavelength and frequency, λ*f*. Frequency and wavelength are inversely related, so that a wave with a long wavelength has a short frequency and vice versa.

Light and Sound

Sound waves are created by the vibration of matter. Sound waves travel as longitudinal waves (compression waves), which create changes in pressure of the medium they travel through. The speed of sound varies depending on the medium it travels through. Sound cannot travel through a vacuum.

Electromagnetic radiation is the transmission of energy as waves. These waves include radio waves, microwaves, infrared radiation, visible light, ultraviolet radiation, X-rays, and gamma rays. Waves in the beginning of this range are associated with longer wavelengths and low energy. Waves at the end of the range, such as ultraviolet radiation and X-rays, have short wavelengths and high energy.

Light is part of the visible spectrum of electromagnetic radiation. Light has properties of both particles and waves. Light travels in straight lines and can be reflected, bounced off a surface in a straight line of travel at an angle equal to its incoming angle. Light can also be refracted, which is the bending of light as it travels through different media, like the transition from water to air. The visible spectrum is broken down into different wavelengths or frequencies that represent colors observable by the human eye.

▶ Electricity and Magnetism

The interaction of the subatomic particles of matter involves **electromagnetic forces**. Electrical forces are either positive or negative. Similar charges repel each other and opposite charges attract each other. The unit for electrical charge is the coulomb (C). Coulomb's

law states that the electric force between two electric charges is directly proportional to the product of the magnitudes of each charge and inversely proportional to the square of the distance between them. Normally, objects contain a net charge of zero (equal amounts of positive and negative charges). By applying an external electric field or force on the object, its net charge can be altered to pick up more positive or negative charges. This situation is referred to as **static electricity**.

Conductors easily allow the flow of electron movement or electrical current. Insulators resist the flow of electrical current. Semiconductors have properties in between that of a conductor and an insulator. Electrical current is measured by the unit ampere (A) and is equal to the amount of electrical charge per second. The volt (V) is the potential difference across a conductor and can be represented as joules per coulomb (J/C). The electrical resistance between two points of a conductor is measured in ohms (Ω) and is the measure of a substance's ability to oppose electrical current. Ohm's law describes the relationship of electrical current as directly proportional to the voltage and inversely proportional to the resistance ($I = \frac{V}{R}$). A watt (W) measures power, or the ability to do work using electricity, and can be calculated by the product of volts and amperes, $V \times A$.

Magnetism is an attractive or repulsive force between objects. Magnetic forces are affected by the charge of the object and its relative motion. Magnetic fields surround electric currents and exert a magnetic force on moving electric charges and magnetic dipoles.

▶ The Solar System

The **solar system** consists of the eight planets and their moons and three dwarf planets (Ceres, Pluto, and Eris) orbiting the sun. The planets from closest to farthest from the sun are Mercury, Venus, Earth, Mars, Jupiter, Saturn, Uranus, and Neptune. Moons orbit six of the eight planets. The origin of Earth's moon is not known, but the accepted theory is that Earth was struck by a giant object and material from the impact was put into orbit, eventually forming the moon. The moon has no atmosphere or water, and has been struck by meteorites that have formed various lunar craters. Lunar eclipses occur when the moon passes through some portion of the entire shadow cast by the Earth from the sun. Solar eclipses occur when the moon passes between the Earth and sun, partially or totally blocking the view of the sun.

There are many other small bodies orbiting the solar system. **Comets** are loose collections of ice, dust, and small rock particles that regularly orbit the solar system. On Earth, they are observed as patches of light with long tails. **Asteroids** are small, planetlike bodies in orbit around the sun and in between the orbits of Mars and Jupiter; some may be the remains of comets that have burned out. Smaller particles are considered meteoroids, and when they become visible entering the Earth's atmosphere, they are called meteors. A meteorite is a part of the meteoroid of that is not destroyed by entering the atmosphere and reaches the ground.

The solar system is located in the Milky Way galaxy, a barred spiral galaxy that contains about 200 billion stars. The Milky Way is one of billions of galaxies in the universe. The Big Bang theory proposes that the universe was created about 14 billion years ago from an initial state of extremely high density and temperature that expanded rapidly into its current state. From this expansion stars, like the sun, were formed. The first stage of a star is in the form of a nebula, a cloud of dust, hydrogen, and plasma. A star initially consists of hydrogen and helium, which are fused together to make heavier elements inside the core of the star. The fusion reactions at a star's core release vast amounts of energy that radiates into outer space. Once the hydrogen fuel at the core is used up, a star can become a red giant and continue fusion of heavier elements. When fusion is no longer possible, the star will either burn out or explode in a supernova. Depending on the size of the star, the supernova can leave a neutron star, or, in the case of the largest stars, a black hole.

▶ Geology

The age of the Earth is about 4.6 billion years. Earth's geological time scale is divided into eons, eras, periods, epochs, and stages corresponding to specific life forms and climate. There is geological evidence that the land masses initially existed as a single land mass referred to as Pangaea. Pangaea existed during the Paleozoic and Mesozoic eras, about 250 million years ago. The Precambrian era is Earth's early history and consists of three eons from 4.5 billion to 542 million years ago. Fossil records are poor, but early life included bacteria and marine algae. Toward the end of the Precambrian era, marine invertebrates were present.

The current eon is Phanerozoic and is divided into three eras. The Paleozoic era started with the Cambrian period 542 million years ago and ended with the Permian period 251 million years ago. During this era, the sea level retreated and advanced over the continents. Marine vertebrates and land plants evolved, and tall forests emerged. There were several ice ages during this time that resulted in mass extinctions. Giant amphibians, early reptiles, and insects appeared by the end of the Paleozoic era.

The Mesozoic era lasted from 251 million years ago until 65 million years ago. The continents gradually split from Pangaea during this time. The climate was exceptionally warm and many new animal species evolved. During the Triassic period, there was a mass extinction known as the "Great Dying"; most sea and land species became extinct. Dinosaurs dominated the Jurassic period until the Cretaceous period, when there was another mass extinction, most likely caused by a meteor impact—all terrestrial dinosaurs became extinct. Late in the Mesozoic era, flowering plants appeared.

The Cenozoic era covers the last 65 million years to present time. This was a time of long-term cooling, significant volcanic activity, and is considered the age of new life. Flowering plants, insects, and birds substantially evolved. Large mammals and the first primates appeared. During the Quaternary period, the last ice age occurred. Hominids appeared about 250 million years ago and modern humans evolved about 160,000 years ago.

The Earth has different layers, or spheres, each with its particular characteristics. Earth's metallic core is composed mostly of iron and some nickel, and has a solid inner core and liquid outer core. The circulation of liquid iron in the core generates Earth's magnetic field. Outside of the core is **mantle**. The mantle is mostly solid and comprises about 70% of the Earth's volume. The upper layer of the mantle reaches 10–50 km below the Earth's surface and has produced the Earth's crust, the rocky outer shell of the planet.

The **lithosphere** consists of a thin upper part of mantle and the outermost crust. Below the lithosphere, the asthenosphere contains malleable rock that can move over time. The rock of the lithosphere consists of cooler, brittle rock. The crust under the ocean is about 10 km deep and under the continents is about 50 km thick. The lithosphere is broken up into several **tectonic plates** that shift along the surface of the asthenosphere. As these plates move in relation to each other, the collision or separation of the plates exerts forces that cause continental drift, earthquakes, volcanoes, and the formation of mountains and ocean trenches. Fault lines or zones are the areas of tectonic plate movement, and are the location of most earthquakes.

Tectonic plates consist of continental and oceanic crust. Continents are much thicker than oceanic crust and contain mountain ranges of very old rock. The continental shelf extends from the continent and gradually submerges below the ocean's water to a depth of roughly 140 meters. The depth dramatically becomes steeper at the continental slope and extends out to the deep ocean floor, the abyssal plain. Along the ocean floor, there are areas of deep ocean trenches due to the subduction, the sliding of one tectonic plate underneath another as they move toward each other. In other areas, plate tectonics form underwater mountain ranges called mid-ocean ridges.

The crust contains a variety of rocks. **Igneous rock** is molten magma that has cooled under the surface of the Earth, and is usually associated with volcanic activity. **Sedimentary rock** is created by underwater sediments in the ocean compacted by pressure as the sediment layer builds up. **Metamorphic rock** is formed when either igneous or sedimentary rock is subject to extreme heat and pressure.

Soil is a naturally occurring mixture of broken rock fragments, clay, and decomposing organic matter (humus). Erosion is the process that changes the surface of the Earth by wearing away rock and carrying away soil through agents of current, like wind and water, natural disasters, or chemical erosion, such as acid rain and overuse of fertilizer. Weathering is the decomposition for rocks, soil, and minerals through exposure to the Earth's atmosphere. This differs from erosion, which requires forces of movement.

▶ The Atmosphere

The atmosphere has a mixture of gases: nitrogen (78%), oxygen (21%), argon (0.9%), and carbon dioxide (0.038%). Water vapor depends on the climate and ranges from 0.3% to 4%.

The atmosphere is divided into four layers. The **troposphere** is near the surface of the Earth and rises about 15 km. Weather takes place in the troposphere and is the location of almost all clouds. Pressure and temperature decrease with height in the troposphere. The next layer is the **stratosphere**, up to about 50 km. The atmosphere is less dense and temperature increases with height, because ozone in this layer absorbs much of the ultraviolet energy from the sun. The following layer is the **mesosphere**, which extends to 80 km. Temperature again decreases with altitude, and this is where most meteors burn up when entering the atmosphere. Beyond the mesosphere, the atmosphere varies greatly. The air in the **thermosphere** is extremely thin, and there is an abundance of ions. Temperature increases with height and reaches 2,000° C.

▶ Hydrology

The **hydrosphere** is all the water on the Earth's surface, groundwater, and water in the atmosphere. Water is vital to living things and an important factor in climate, weather, and erosion. The ocean covers about 71% of the Earth's surface and contains about 97% of the total water on Earth. The ocean acts as a temperature buffer, and ocean currents affect climates by transferring cold and warm air and precipitation to land.

Clouds consist of condensed water droplets that are sources of precipitation and reflect some sunlight back into space. Rain occurs when the air becomes saturated with water vapor. Weather is the daily conditions of temperature, precipitation, and wind. Weather is largely affected by temperature differences created by incoming solar energy, referred to as insolation. Temperature differences result in pressure differences. Winds transport air from high pressure to low pressure, moving weather systems throughout the atmosphere.

SECTION

5 ▶ About the CLEP Humanities Exam

The CLEP Humanities exam assesses your background and knowledge in the area of literature and the fine arts. The Humanities exam extends from the classical through the contemporary period and includes a range of topics and questions in the fields of art, architecture, music, dance, film, theater, poetry, and prose. You will be expected to recall specific information, comprehend concepts, and apply your knowledge of these concepts. The exam also requires that you demonstrate an ability to interpret and analyze different examples of art and literature.

The 90-minute CLEP Humanities exam includes 140 questions. Time allotted for tutorials or for filling in your personal information does not count as actual test time. Test takers who achieve a successful, satisfactory score many receive up to six semester hours of college credit.

On the CLEP Humanities exam, test takers will encounter questions that test the following:

- specific factual information about authors and their works (50% of the questions)
- knowledge of techniques such as rhyme scheme, medium, and matters of style, and the ability to associate them with certain writers, artists, schools, or periods (30% of the questions)
- the ability to interpret and comprehend literary passages and art reproductions (20% of the questions)

The material in the CLEP Humanities exam is very similar to the material covered in a college-level humanities course. The CLEP Humanities exam is divided into the following content areas:

- 50% Literature
  - 10% Drama
  - 10–20% Poetry
  - 15–20% Fiction
  - 10% Nonfiction (including philosophy)
- 50% Fine Arts
  - 20% Visual Arts (including painting, sculpture, and photography)
  - 15% Performing Arts (including music)
  - 10% Performing Arts (including film and dance)
  - 5% Visual Arts (including architecture)

Questions on the CLEP Humanities exam are taken from the entire history of art and culture, evenly divided across the following periods: Classical, Medieval, Renaissance, seventeenth century, eighteenth century, nineteenth century, and twentieth century.

Up to 10% of the questions address humanities topics from cultures in Asia, Africa, or Latin America. In some instances, a question will explore several disciplines or periods.

You will not be required to know a foreign language in order to respond to literacy works, as all of the works chosen for the exam have English translations.

The subject of humanities is very broad—there is no simple way to cover all the material that may be covered on the CLEP Humanities exam. Chapters 24 and 25 of *CLEP Test Prep* will each give you a solid list of humanities topics and, in turn, the right foundation to address many of the questions you are likely to encounter. Although it is certainly not complete, the goal is to present a snapshot of humanities through different time periods.

This section will provide the names of important works, people, and movements in the humanities. If any of these names are unfamiliar to you, we suggest researching them online or at a local library.

The Humanities exam is one of the more challenging parts of the CLEP. This subject is extremely diverse, and there is no easy way to cover all the material that may appear on the official test. Don't be overwhelmed as you begin to tackle the lists in Chapters 24 and 25. You can, however, prepare yourself for the official test by exposing yourself to as many cultural topics as possible. There are several ways to accomplish this:

- Read cultural news in local and international publications.
- Visit libraries.
- Take trips to museums.
- Attend readings at local bookstores or universities.

CLEP Humanities Pretest

Before reviewing topics that will be covered on the CLEP Humanities exam, determine your existing skills by taking the pretest that follows. You will encounter 140 questions that are similar to the type you will find on the CLEP Humanities exam. The questions cover two main content areas:

- literature
- fine arts

Ignore the time restraints of the official CLEP for now, and take as much time as you need to complete each question.

Answer every question; however, if you are not sure of an answer, put a question mark by the question number to note that you are making a guess. On the official CLEP, you are not penalized for unanswered or incorrect answers, so making a good guess is an important skill to practice.

When you are finished, check the answer key on page 385 carefully to assess your results. Your pretest score will help you determine how much preparation you need and in which areas you need the most careful review and practice.

▶ CLEP Humanities Pretest

1. ⓐ ⓑ ⓒ ⓓ ⓔ	51. ⓐ ⓑ ⓒ ⓓ ⓔ	101. ⓐ ⓑ ⓒ ⓓ ⓔ
2. ⓐ ⓑ ⓒ ⓓ ⓔ	52. ⓐ ⓑ ⓒ ⓓ ⓔ	102. ⓐ ⓑ ⓒ ⓓ ⓔ
3. ⓐ ⓑ ⓒ ⓓ ⓔ	53. ⓐ ⓑ ⓒ ⓓ ⓔ	103. ⓐ ⓑ ⓒ ⓓ ⓔ
4. ⓐ ⓑ ⓒ ⓓ ⓔ	54. ⓐ ⓑ ⓒ ⓓ ⓔ	104 ⓐ ⓑ ⓒ ⓓ ⓔ
5. ⓐ ⓑ ⓒ ⓓ ⓔ	55. ⓐ ⓑ ⓒ ⓓ ⓔ	105. ⓐ ⓑ ⓒ ⓓ ⓔ
6. ⓐ ⓑ ⓒ ⓓ ⓔ	56. ⓐ ⓑ ⓒ ⓓ ⓔ	106. ⓐ ⓑ ⓒ ⓓ ⓔ
7. ⓐ ⓑ ⓒ ⓓ ⓔ	57. ⓐ ⓑ ⓒ ⓓ ⓔ	107. ⓐ ⓑ ⓒ ⓓ ⓔ
8. ⓐ ⓑ ⓒ ⓓ ⓔ	58. ⓐ ⓑ ⓒ ⓓ ⓔ	108. ⓐ ⓑ ⓒ ⓓ ⓔ
9. ⓐ ⓑ ⓒ ⓓ ⓔ	59. ⓐ ⓑ ⓒ ⓓ ⓔ	109 ⓐ ⓑ ⓒ ⓓ ⓔ
10. ⓐ ⓑ ⓒ ⓓ ⓔ	60. ⓐ ⓑ ⓒ ⓓ ⓔ	110. ⓐ ⓑ ⓒ ⓓ ⓔ
11. ⓐ ⓑ ⓒ ⓓ ⓔ	61. ⓐ ⓑ ⓒ ⓓ ⓔ	111. ⓐ ⓑ ⓒ ⓓ ⓔ
12. ⓐ ⓑ ⓒ ⓓ ⓔ	62. ⓐ ⓑ ⓒ ⓓ ⓔ	112. ⓐ ⓑ ⓒ ⓓ ⓔ
13. ⓐ ⓑ ⓒ ⓓ ⓔ	63. ⓐ ⓑ ⓒ ⓓ ⓔ	113 ⓐ ⓑ ⓒ ⓓ ⓔ
14. ⓐ ⓑ ⓒ ⓓ ⓔ	64. ⓐ ⓑ ⓒ ⓓ ⓔ	114. ⓐ ⓑ ⓒ ⓓ ⓔ
15. ⓐ ⓑ ⓒ ⓓ ⓔ	65. ⓐ ⓑ ⓒ ⓓ ⓔ	115. ⓐ ⓑ ⓒ ⓓ ⓔ
16. ⓐ ⓑ ⓒ ⓓ ⓔ	66. ⓐ ⓑ ⓒ ⓓ ⓔ	116. ⓐ ⓑ ⓒ ⓓ ⓔ
17. ⓐ ⓑ ⓒ ⓓ ⓔ	67. ⓐ ⓑ ⓒ ⓓ ⓔ	117. ⓐ ⓑ ⓒ ⓓ ⓔ
18. ⓐ ⓑ ⓒ ⓓ ⓔ	68. ⓐ ⓑ ⓒ ⓓ ⓔ	118. ⓐ ⓑ ⓒ ⓓ ⓔ
19. ⓐ ⓑ ⓒ ⓓ ⓔ	69. ⓐ ⓑ ⓒ ⓓ ⓔ	119 ⓐ ⓑ ⓒ ⓓ ⓔ
20. ⓐ ⓑ ⓒ ⓓ ⓔ	70. ⓐ ⓑ ⓒ ⓓ ⓔ	120. ⓐ ⓑ ⓒ ⓓ ⓔ
21. ⓐ ⓑ ⓒ ⓓ ⓔ	71. ⓐ ⓑ ⓒ ⓓ ⓔ	121. ⓐ ⓑ ⓒ ⓓ ⓔ
22. ⓐ ⓑ ⓒ ⓓ ⓔ	72. ⓐ ⓑ ⓒ ⓓ ⓔ	122. ⓐ ⓑ ⓒ ⓓ ⓔ
23. ⓐ ⓑ ⓒ ⓓ ⓔ	73. ⓐ ⓑ ⓒ ⓓ ⓔ	123. ⓐ ⓑ ⓒ ⓓ ⓔ
24. ⓐ ⓑ ⓒ ⓓ ⓔ	74. ⓐ ⓑ ⓒ ⓓ ⓔ	124. ⓐ ⓑ ⓒ ⓓ ⓔ
25. ⓐ ⓑ ⓒ ⓓ ⓔ	75. ⓐ ⓑ ⓒ ⓓ ⓔ	125. ⓐ ⓑ ⓒ ⓓ ⓔ
26. ⓐ ⓑ ⓒ ⓓ ⓔ	76. ⓐ ⓑ ⓒ ⓓ ⓔ	126. ⓐ ⓑ ⓒ ⓓ ⓔ
27. ⓐ ⓑ ⓒ ⓓ ⓔ	77. ⓐ ⓑ ⓒ ⓓ ⓔ	127. ⓐ ⓑ ⓒ ⓓ ⓔ
28. ⓐ ⓑ ⓒ ⓓ ⓔ	78. ⓐ ⓑ ⓒ ⓓ ⓔ	128. ⓐ ⓑ ⓒ ⓓ ⓔ
29. ⓐ ⓑ ⓒ ⓓ ⓔ	79. ⓐ ⓑ ⓒ ⓓ ⓔ	129. ⓐ ⓑ ⓒ ⓓ ⓔ
30. ⓐ ⓑ ⓒ ⓓ ⓔ	80. ⓐ ⓑ ⓒ ⓓ ⓔ	130. ⓐ ⓑ ⓒ ⓓ ⓔ
31. ⓐ ⓑ ⓒ ⓓ ⓔ	81. ⓐ ⓑ ⓒ ⓓ ⓔ	131. ⓐ ⓑ ⓒ ⓓ ⓔ
32. ⓐ ⓑ ⓒ ⓓ ⓔ	82. ⓐ ⓑ ⓒ ⓓ ⓔ	132. ⓐ ⓑ ⓒ ⓓ ⓔ
33. ⓐ ⓑ ⓒ ⓓ ⓔ	83. ⓐ ⓑ ⓒ ⓓ ⓔ	133. ⓐ ⓑ ⓒ ⓓ ⓔ
34. ⓐ ⓑ ⓒ ⓓ ⓔ	84. ⓐ ⓑ ⓒ ⓓ ⓔ	134. ⓐ ⓑ ⓒ ⓓ ⓔ
35. ⓐ ⓑ ⓒ ⓓ ⓔ	85. ⓐ ⓑ ⓒ ⓓ ⓔ	135. ⓐ ⓑ ⓒ ⓓ ⓔ
36. ⓐ ⓑ ⓒ ⓓ ⓔ	86. ⓐ ⓑ ⓒ ⓓ ⓔ	136. ⓐ ⓑ ⓒ ⓓ ⓔ
37. ⓐ ⓑ ⓒ ⓓ ⓔ	87. ⓐ ⓑ ⓒ ⓓ ⓔ	137. ⓐ ⓑ ⓒ ⓓ ⓔ
38. ⓐ ⓑ ⓒ ⓓ ⓔ	88. ⓐ ⓑ ⓒ ⓓ ⓔ	138. ⓐ ⓑ ⓒ ⓓ ⓔ
39. ⓐ ⓑ ⓒ ⓓ ⓔ	89. ⓐ ⓑ ⓒ ⓓ ⓔ	139 ⓐ ⓑ ⓒ ⓓ ⓔ
40. ⓐ ⓑ ⓒ ⓓ ⓔ	90. ⓐ ⓑ ⓒ ⓓ ⓔ	140. ⓐ ⓑ ⓒ ⓓ ⓔ
41. ⓐ ⓑ ⓒ ⓓ ⓔ	91. ⓐ ⓑ ⓒ ⓓ ⓔ	
42. ⓐ ⓑ ⓒ ⓓ ⓔ	92. ⓐ ⓑ ⓒ ⓓ ⓔ	
43. ⓐ ⓑ ⓒ ⓓ ⓔ	93. ⓐ ⓑ ⓒ ⓓ ⓔ	
44. ⓐ ⓑ ⓒ ⓓ ⓔ	94. ⓐ ⓑ ⓒ ⓓ ⓔ	
45. ⓐ ⓑ ⓒ ⓓ ⓔ	95. ⓐ ⓑ ⓒ ⓓ ⓔ	
46. ⓐ ⓑ ⓒ ⓓ ⓔ	96. ⓐ ⓑ ⓒ ⓓ ⓔ	
47. ⓐ ⓑ ⓒ ⓓ ⓔ	97. ⓐ ⓑ ⓒ ⓓ ⓔ	
48. ⓐ ⓑ ⓒ ⓓ ⓔ	98. ⓐ ⓑ ⓒ ⓓ ⓔ	
49. ⓐ ⓑ ⓒ ⓓ ⓔ	99. ⓐ ⓑ ⓒ ⓓ ⓔ	
50. ⓐ ⓑ ⓒ ⓓ ⓔ	100. ⓐ ⓑ ⓒ ⓓ ⓔ	

▶ Pretest Questions

Directions: Each of the following questions has five suggested answer choices. Select the one that is best.

1. In a poem by Samuel Taylor Coleridge, the speaker wakes from a dream or vision and announces that if people knew what he had seen, they would shun him and cry out a warning:

   Beware, Beware!
   His flashing eyes, his floating hair
   Weave a circle round him thrice
   And close your eyes in holy dread,
   For he on honey-dew hath fed,
   And drunk the milk of Paradise.

   What poem are these lines from?
   a. *The Rime of the Ancient Mariner*
   b. *Christabel*
   c. *Frost at Midnight*
   d. *Kubla Khan*
   e. *The Pains of Sleep*

2. Who stated that "the poets and philosophers before me discovered the unconscious"?
   a. Albert Camus
   b. Socrates
   c. Sigmund Freud
   d. William Shakespeare
   e. Emily Dickinson

3. The title of Joseph Campbell's book *The Hero With a Thousand Faces* is meant to convey the
   a. many villagers whose lives are changed by the story the hero has to tell.
   b. fact that the hero journeys into many different imaginary countries.
   c. universality of the myth of the hero who journeys into the wilderness.
   d. many languages into which the myth of the hero has been translated.
   e. deformed hero who discovers beauty within.

4. In that book, Joseph Campbell writes that the "human kingdom, beneath the floor of the comparatively neat little dwelling that we call our consciousness, goes down into unsuspected Aladdin caves. There not only jewels but dangerous jinn abide. . . ." These *Aladdin caves* are most likely to be found in
   a. the mountains.
   b. fairy tales.
   c. the fantasies of the hero.
   d. the unconscious mind.
   e. a treasure trove of jewels.

5. Wolfgang Amadeus Mozart became interested in music because
   a. his father thought it would be profitable.
   b. he was forced to take lessons.
   c. he saw his sister learning to play.
   d. he came from a musical city.
   e. his wife saw it as a way to support the family.

6. Mozart's father had a plan to take Mozart and his sister on tour to play before the European courts. He had set his sights on the capital of the Hapsburg Empire, Vienna. On their way to Vienna, the family stopped in Linz, where Mozart gave his first public concert. What was the consequence of Mozart's first public appearance?

a. He charmed the emperor and empress of Hapsburg.

b. Leopold set his sights on Vienna.

c. Word of Mozart's genius spread to the capital.

d. He mastered the violin.

e. He succumbed to stage fright.

7. As a child, Mozart passed the long uncomfortable hours in the imaginary Kingdom of Back, of which he was king. He became so engrossed in the intricacies of his make-believe court that he persuaded a family servant to make a map showing all the cities, villages, and towns over which he reigned. This anecdote about Mozart's Kingdom of Back illustrates

a. Mozart's admiration for the composer Johann Sebastian Bach.

b. that Mozart was often ignored by his family.

c. that Mozart was mentally unstable.

d. that Mozart's friends were imaginary people and family servants.

e. Mozart's lack of geographical skills.

8. The swing style of jazz can be most accurately characterized as

a. complex and inaccessible.

b. appealing to an elite audience.

c. lively and melodic.

d. lacking in improvisation.

e. slow tempo and somber.

9. In the 1940s, you would most likely find bebop being played where?

a. church

b. a large concert hall

c. in music schools

d. small clubs

e. in small cities in the South

10. One of the most significant innovations of the bebop musicians was

a. to shun older musicians.

b. to emphasize rhythm.

c. to use melodic improvisations.

d. to play in small clubs.

e. to alienate African-American musicians.

11. The late 1980s found the landscape of popular music in America dominated by a distinctive style of rock and roll featuring over-styled hair, makeup, and wardrobe worn by the genre's ostentatious rockers. This type of rock music was known as

a. glam metal.

b. ska.

c. rhythm and blues.

d. indie rock.

e. new wave.

12. This style of music got its start in the Pacific Northwest during the mid-1980s, the offspring of the metal-guitar driven rock of the 1970s, and the hardcore, punk music of the early 1980s. Nirvana had simply brought into the mainstream a sound and culture that got its start years before with bands like Mudhoney, Soundgarden, and Green River. This style of music is known as

a. Britpop.

b. grunge.

c. folk rock.

d. psychedelic rock.

e. surf rock.

13. This novel is the tale of a male infant discovered by a rich gentleman. After many troubled years, the child ends up a wanderer with ill fortune. The novel's author is interested in human behavior and motives, though not in psychologies, as he is more explanatory than exploratory.
  a. *The Red Badge of Courage*
  b. *Native Son*
  c. *Tom Jones, the Foundling*
  d. *Ulysses*
  e. *Ordinary People*

14. The piano was invented in which country?
  a. Russia
  b. England
  c. Germany
  d. Austria
  e. Italy

15. The dance characterized by a frenzied tempo and performed in 6/8 time is called
  a. waltz.
  b. tarantella.
  c. polka.
  d. salsa.
  e. swing.

16. What is the term for a combination of three or more tones in music?
  a. chord
  b. scale
  c. melody
  d. syncopation
  e. crescendo

17. *West Side Story* was choreographed by
  a. Gene Kelly.
  b. Jerome Robbins.
  c. Bob Fosse.
  d. Twyla Tharp.
  e. Stephen Sondheim.

18. What is the name of the first primarily African-American dance company?
  a. Dance Theatre of Harlem
  b. Apollo
  c. Harlem Dance Troupe
  d. Nigerian Ballet Company
  e. American Ballet Theatre

19. In the 1960s, Chubby Checker increased the popularity of what dance craze?
  a. alligator
  b. twist
  c. mashed potato
  d. bugaloo
  e. pony

20. This novel, told from the first-person point of view, is Charles Dickens's most autobiographic novel. It is preceded by seven novels and followed by seven more.
  a. *David Copperfield*
  b. *Oliver Twist*
  c. *A Tale of Two Cities*
  d. *A Christmas Carol*
  e. *Great Expectations*

21. The protagonist of this book begins with the narration, "If you really want to hear about it, the first thing you'll probably want to know is where I was born, and what my lousy childhood was like, and how my parents were occupied and all before they had me, and all that David Copperfield kind of crap, but I don't feel like going into it."
   a. *The Great Gatsby*
   b. *The Catcher in the Rye*
   c. *Bonfire of the Vanities*
   d. *Grapes of Wrath*
   e. *Oliver Twist*

22. The poet e.e. cummings makes numerous references to this Christian allegory in his "The Enormous Room." This allegory has been translated into more than 200 languages and never been out of print.
   a. *The Lord of the Rings*
   b. *The Faerie Queene*
   c. *Republic*
   d. *The Pilgrim's Promise*
   e. *The Romance of the Rose*

23. In *Gulliver's Travels,* the Lilliputians are used as a symbol of
   a. pursuers of knowledge that has no real-life use.
   b. existence governed by sense and moderation.
   c. misplaced human pride.
   d. insufficiency.
   e. travel to foreign lands.

24. "Before I had left America, that is to say in the year 1781, I had received a letter from M. de Marbois, of the French legation in Philadelphia, informing me he had been instructed by his government to obtain such statistical accounts of the different states of our Union, as might be useful for their information; and addressing to me a number of queries relative to the state of Virginia. I had always made it a practice whenever an opportunity occurred of obtaining any information of our country, which might be of use to me in any station public or private, to commit it to writing. These memoranda were on loose papers, bundled up without order, and difficult of recurrence when I had occasion for a particular one."

—Thomas Jefferson, *Paris*

This passage may be identified as part of an autobiography by
   a. its use of the third person.
   b. its use of specific details known only by the author.
   c. its use of the first person.
   d. its references to actual persons and places.
   e. its author being a U.S. president.

Use the following passage to answer questions 25 and 26.

We sailed from Peru (where we had continued by the space of one whole year), for China and Japan, by the South Sea; taking with us victuals for twelve months; and had good winds from the east, though soft and weak, for five months space, and more. But then the wind came about, and settled in the west for many days, so as we could make little or no way, and were sometimes in purpose to turn back. But then again there arose strong and great winds from the south, with a point east, which carried us up (for all that we could do), towards the north; by which time our victuals failed us, though we had made good spare of them. So that finding ourselves, in the midst of the greatest wilderness of waters in the world, without victuals, we gave ourselves for lost men and prepared for death. Yet we did lift up our hearts and voices to God above, who showeth his wonders in the deep, beseeching him of his mercy, that as in the beginning he discovered the face of the deep, and brought forth dry land, so he would now discover land to us, that we might not perish.

—Francis Bacon, *The New Atlantis,* 1627

25. *The New Atlantis* shows evidence of Bacon's inspiration from
a. Western European society.
b. the *King James Bible.*
c. contemporary explorers of the New World.
d. ancient survivor myths.
e. the Far East.

26. Bacon's vision of Atlantis, an ideal world, may have been based on all of the following EXCEPT
a. Eden.
b. Thomas Moore's *Utopia* (1516).
c. the Elysian Fields of Greek mythology.
d. Hades, Roman mythology's underworld.
e. Christianity.

27. Bruce Springsteen's song, "The Promised Land" refers to a major tenet of what religion?
a. Christianity
b. Buddhism
c. Mormonism
d. Judaism
e. Hinduism

28. Read the following poem.

Crossing the Bar

Sunset and evening star,
And one clear call for me!
And may there be no moaning of the bar,
When I put out to sea.
But such a tide as moving seems asleep,
Too full for sound and foam,
When that which drew from out the boundless
   deep
Turns again home!
Twilight and evening bell,
And after that the dark!
And may there be no sadness of farewell,
When I embark;
For though from out our bourn of Time and
   Place
The flood may bear me far,
I hope to see my Pilot face to face
When I have crost the bar.

                        —Alfred, Lord Tennyson

Who is the "Pilot" Tennyson refers to in the next-to-last line of the poem?
a. his lover
b. his muse
c. God
d. the commander of his ship
e. his mother

29. Prior to the 1830s, dancing between men and women was done with little or no physical contact. That changed with the introduction of what dance?
a. salsa
b. the jive
c. flamenco
d. Paso Doble
e. Viennese waltz

30. What do the polka and the tango have in common?
a. They both originated in Europe.
b. They both use flamenco music.
c. They both gained popularity in brothels.
d. They both involve an embrace by the dancers.
e. They both stress changing partners.

31. Which idea about the tango is true?
a. The tango remains a dance of the less privileged classes.
b. The dances of Europe were superior to the tango of South America.
c. The exact origins of the tango are unknown.
d. The tango was outlawed in dance halls and brothels in Argentina.
e. The name *tango* describes the dance form, but not the music that accompanies it.

32. What conclusion can be drawn about a similarity between ancient Egypt and ancient Greece, based on the images?

PASHT, THE CAT-HEADED GOD.

a. The mythologies of both cultures included figures that were part human and part animal.

b. Both cultures worshipped women.

c. Both cultures used imposing figures at the entrance of tombs.

d. The artists of both cultures worked exclusively in limestone.

e. The artists of both cultures were from the lower classes.

Use the following passage to answer questions 33 and 34.

(1) Many years ago there lived an Emperor, who was so excessively fond of grand new clothes that he spent all his money upon them, that he might be very fine. He did not care about his soldiers, nor about the theatre, and only liked to drive out and show his new clothes. He had a coat for every hour of the day; and just as they say of a king, "He is in council," so they always said of him, "The Emperor is in the wardrobe."

(2) In the great city in which he lived it was always very merry; every day came many strangers; one day two rogues came: they gave themselves out as weavers, and declared they could weave the finest stuff anyone could imagine. Not only were their colors and patterns, they said, uncommonly beautiful, but the clothes made of the stuff possessed the wonderful quality that they became invisible to any one who was unfit for the office he held, or was incorrigibly stupid.

(3) "Those would be capital clothes!" thought the Emperor. "If I wore those, I should be able to find out what men in my empire are not fit for the places they have; I could tell the clever from the dunces. Yes, the stuff must be woven for me directly!"

(4) And he gave the two rogues a great deal of cash in hand, that they might begin their work at once.

(5) As for them, they put up two looms, and pretended to be working; but they had nothing at all on their looms. They at once demanded the finest silk and the costliest gold; this they put into their own pockets, and worked at the empty looms till late into the night.

—Excerpt from Hans Christian Andersen's
The Emperor's New Clothes

33. Paragraph 3 uses which literary device?

   a. foreshadowing

   b. irony

   c. metaphor

   d. alliteration

   e. assonance

34. Which sentence best describes the dominant theme of the passage?

   a. Vanity blinds a man to truth.

   b. Cleverness can make one rich.

   c. The clothes make the man.

   d. Rulers can be easily manipulated.

   e. A kind ruler makes a wise ruler.

Use the following image to answer questions 35 and 36.

35. This Aztec work represents an art form used throughout civilization by many cultures called

   a. decorative columns.

   b. relief sculpture.

   c. utilitarian pottery.

   d. religious painting.

   e. kinetic sculpture.

36. Which answer choice provides the best description of the sculpture's composition?

   a. The headdresses on the two figures anchor the middle of the sculpture.

   b. The decorative friezes on the top left and side left provide symmetry.

   c. The dissimilarity in size of the two gods symbolizes the uneven power between them.

   d. The open book at the bottom of the work provides balance.

   e. Although the two gods are dissimilar in size, they are balanced through use of the large sticklike object that bisects the image diagonally.

37. Stephen Sondheim is one of the preeminent American composers and lyricists of the twentieth century. He uses the genre of musical theater to communicate

   a. psychological truths.

   b. stereotypical characters.

   c. startling art forms.

   d. the legacy of Oscar Hammerstein.

   e. common stereotypes.

38. What is one way in which Stephen Sondheim's musicals differ from the works of other artists?

   a. He used Japanese poetry as a subject.

   b. He relied on the guidance he received from the legendary Oscar Hammerstein and Leonard Bernstein.

   c. His characters had more depth than the typical two-dimensional musical figures.

   d. He created the most popular musical of all time, *West Side Story*.

   e. He used the nineteenth-century English class system as a subject.

Use the following poem to answer questions 39 and 40.

A Parting Guest

What delightful hosts are they—
Life and Love!
Lingeringly I turn away,
This late hour, yet glad enough
They have not withheld from me
Their high hospitality.
So, with face lit with delight
And all gratitude, I stay
Yet to press their hands and say,
"Thanks.—So fine a time! Good night."

—James Whitcomb Riley

39. Riley uses which literary device in his poem?
  a. hyperbole
  b. personification
  c. imagery
  d. oxymoron
  e. irony

40. Who is the Parting Guest?
  a. life
  b. the poet
  c. love
  d. a friend of the hosts
  e. death

Use the following passage to answer questions 41 and 42.

It is a melancholy object to those who walk through this great town or travel in the country, when they see the streets, the roads, and cabin doors, crowded with beggars of the female sex, followed by three, four, or six children, all in rags and importuning every passenger for an alms. These mothers, instead of being able to work for their honest livelihood, are forced to employ all their time in strolling to beg sustenance for their helpless infants. . . .

I think it is agreed by all parties that this prodigious number of children in the arms, or on the backs, or at the heels of their mothers, and frequently of their fathers, is in the present deplorable state of the kingdom a very great additional grievance; and, therefore, whoever could find out a fair, cheap, and easy method of making these children sound, useful members of the commonwealth, would deserve so well of the public as to have his statue set up for a preserver of the nation . . .

I shall now therefore humbly propose my own thoughts, which I hope will not be liable to the least objection.

I have been assured by a very knowing American of my acquaintance in London, that a young healthy child well nursed is at a year old a most delicious, nourishing, and wholesome food, whether stewed, roasted, baked, or boiled; and I make no doubt that it will equally serve in a fricassee or a ragout.

I do therefore humbly offer it to public consideration that . . . children . . . may, at a year old, be offered in the sale to the persons of quality and fortune through the kingdom; always advising the mother to let them suck plentifully in the last month, so as to render them plump and fat for a good table. A child will make two dishes at an entertainment for friends; and when the family dines alone, the fore or hind quarter will make a reasonable dish, and seasoned with a little pepper or salt will be very good boiled on the fourth day, especially in winter.

—from Jonathan Swift,
A Modest Proposal

41. In this excerpt, Swift is both
   a. acknowledging a societal problem and using satire to address it.
   b. using humor and being satirical.
   c. acknowledging a societal problem and proposing a feasible solution.
   d. using humor and venting frustration with the monarchy.
   e. using humor and ignoring social realities.

42. The Ireland that Swift is writing about
   a. needs more affordable housing.
   b. needs the mothers and children who are begging in the streets to join the labor force and become "useful members of the commonwealth."
   c. could be improved through the implementation of his proposal.
   d. is in a cycle of poverty caused by the laziness of the less fortunate.
   e. is being governed by "persons of quality and fortune" who are doing nothing to help the less fortunate.

Use the following poem to answer questions 43 and 44.

The Sun just touched the morning;
The morning, happy thing,
Supposed that he had come to dwell,
And life would be all spring.
She felt herself supremer,—
A raised, ethereal thing;
Henceforth for her what holiday!
Meanwhile, her wheeling king
Trailed slow along the orchards
His haughty, spangled hems,
Leaving a new necessity,—
The want of diadems!
The morning fluttered, staggered,
Felt feebly for her crown,—
Her unanointed forehead
Henceforth her only one.

—Emily Dickinson

43. This poem predominantly uses which literary device?
   a. personification
   b. alliteration
   c. euphemism
   d. parody
   e. assonance

44. The word *diadems* in line 12 means
   a. hammers.
   b. pens.
   c. fences.
   d. crowns.
   e. horses.

45.

In this painting depicting Marc Antony crowning Julius Caesar as dictator of Rome, the artist suggests that Caesar was

a. a power-hungry man, eager for control.

b. despised by the citizens of Rome.

c. uncomfortable with the idea being appointed dictator.

d. distrustful of Mark Antony.

e. a confidant of Mark Antony.

46. Which of the following songs begins with the three bars shown here?

a. "She'll Be Coming around the Mountain"

b. "The Star Spangled Banner"

c. "Yankee Doodle"

d. "How Much is that Doggie in the Window?"

e. "Little Johnny Jones"

47. "In most of us . . . was the great desire to [be] able to read and write. We took advantage of every opportunity to educate ourselves. [Punishments] were very harsh if we were caught trying to learn or write."

—John W. Fields

This quotation is an excerpt from Mr. Fields's narrative describing his life as

a. a prison inmate.

b. a slave.

c. a private in the Northern army during the Civil War.

d. a sharecropper.

e. a prisoner of war.

Use the following passage to answer questions 48 and 49.

Sinclair Lewis's novel *Main Street*, published in 1920, examines the stifling effects of small town life. Its protagonist, Carol Kennicott, is a sophisticated outsider in the setting of Gopher Prairie, Minnesota. She brings with her a love of art and literature as well as a desire to enact social reform. Kennicott is rejected by the town's homogeneous population, who view any form of intellectualism as a threat.

48. Lewis's Kennicott would most likely have embraced which historic or cultural event of the 1920s?

a. prohibition

b. dance marathons

c. women's suffrage

d. industrial mass production

e. the Palmer Raids

49. What sentence best describes a major theme of *Main Street,* according to the passage?

   a. In *Main Street,* Sinclair Lewis presents a critique of Americans who are content with their provincial lives.

   b. Lewis's character Carol Kennicott represents the outsider and helps to rationalize Americans' fear of immigrants exemplified in the Red Scare.

   c. *Main Street* is a call to citizens of every small town, who are urged to conform rather than face rejection.

   d. Lewis captures the joys and sorrows of small-town American life in his uplifting novel *Main Street.*

   e. Lewis's character Carol Kennicott represents the outsider who learns that it is best to be satisfied with small-town life.

50. Read the following poem.

The Eagle
He clasps the crag with crooked hands;
Close to the sun in lonely lands,
Ringed with the azure world he stands.
The wrinkled sea beneath him crawls;
He watches from his mountain walls,
And like a thunderbolt he falls.

Given the tone of the poem, and noting especially the last line, what is the eagle most likely doing in the poem?

   a. dying of old age

   b. hunting prey

   c. learning joyfully to fly

   d. keeping watch over a nest of young eagles

   e. fleeing from a predator

51. What is the tone of this quote?

"I'm always making a comeback, but nobody ever tells me where I've been."

—Billie Holiday

   a. sincere

   b. ironic

   c. humorous

   d. nostalgic

   e. melancholy

52. Look at the following picture.

This picture can be described by saying that

   a. it is detail-oriented.

   b. it is the work of an Impressionist painter.

   c. it favors symmetry and embraces the concepts of neoclassicism.

   d. its perspective, that of the boy on the curb, is unique.

   e. its perspective, that of the boy on the curb, is common the time period of this piece.

53. Which of the following is the first Disney Broadway musical based on its film version?

a. *Beauty and the Beast*
b. *The Lion King*
c. *Mary Poppins*
d. *The Little Mermaid*
e. *Aida*

Use the following passage to answer questions 54 through 56.

What's Wrong with Commercial Television?

(1) Kids who watch much commercial television ought to develop into whizzes at the dialect; you have to keep so much in your mind at once because a series of artificially short attention

(5) spans has been created. But this in itself means that the experience of watching the commercial channels is a more informal one, curiously more "homely" than watching BBC [British Broadcasting Corporation].

(10)   This is because the commercial breaks are constant reminders that the medium itself is artificial, isn't, in fact, "real," even if the gesticulating heads, unlike the giants of the movie screen, are life-size. There is a kind of built-in alienation

(15) effect. Everything you see is false, as Tristan Tzara gnomically opined. And the young lady in the St. Bruno tobacco ads who currently concludes her spiel by stating categorically: "And if you believe that, you'll believe anything," is saying no more

(20) than the truth. The long-term effect of habitually watching commercial television is probably an erosion of trust in the television medium itself.

   Since joy is the message of all commercials, it is as well they breed skepticism. Every story has a

(25) happy ending, gratification is guaranteed by the conventions of the commercial form, which contributes no end to the pervasive unreality of it all.

Indeed, it is the chronic bliss of everybody in the

(30) commercials that creates their final divorce from effective life as we know it. Grumpy mum, frowning dad, are soon all smiles again after the ingestion of some pill or potion; minimal concessions are made to mild frustration (as they

(35) are, occasionally, to lust), but none at all to despair or consummation. In fact, if the form is reminiscent of the limerick and the presentation of the music-hall, the overall mood—in its absolute and unruffled decorum—is that of the

(40) uplift fables in the Sunday school picture books of my childhood.

   —Angela Carter, from *Shaking a Leg* (1997)

54. According to the author, what is the main difference between commercial channels and public television stations like the BBC?

a. Commercial television is very artificial.
b. Public television is more informal and uplifting.
c. Commercial television teaches viewers not to believe what they see on TV.
d. Commercial television is more like the movies than public television.
e. Commercial television is more informative and educational.

55. Which of the following would the author most likely recommend?

a. Don't watch any television at all; read instead.
b. Watch only the BBC.
c. Watch only commercial television.
d. Watch what you like, but don't believe what commercials claim.
e. Protest commercial television until the government enforces regulations on the medium.

56. According to the author, what is the main thing that makes commercials unrealistic?
   a. Everyone in commercials always ends up happy.
   b. The background music is distracting.
   c. Commercials are so short.
   d. The people in commercials are always sick.
   e. There is always a suitable pill for every ailment.

57. In the late 1940s, big film studios like Warners were forced to divest themselves from owning lucrative theater chains. Many Hollywood stars were making their last films (or were about to make their final film) under long-term contracts with these studios. These stars include all but which of the following?
   a. Olivia de Havilland
   b. Bette Davis
   c. Humphrey Bogart
   d. Marilyn Monroe
   e. Errol Flynn

58. Igor Stravinsky's ballet features Petrouchka, who is a
   a. swan.
   b. young girl.
   c. puppet.
   d. magician.
   e. old woman.

Use the following poem to answer questions 59 and 60.

War Is Kind

Do not weep, maiden, for war is kind.
Because your lover threw wild hands toward the sky
And the affrighted steed ran on alone,
Do not weep.
War is kind.
Hoarse, booming drums of the regiment
Little souls who thirst for fight,
These men were born to drill and die
The unexplained glory flies above them
Great is the battle-god, great, and his kingdom—
A field where a thousand corpses lie.
Do not weep, babe, for war is kind.
Because your father tumbled in the yellow
   trenches,
Raged at his breast, gulped and died,
Do not weep.
War is kind.
Swift, blazing flag of the regiment
Eagle with crest of red and gold,
These men were born to drill and die
Point for them the virtue of slaughter
Make plain to them the excellence of killing
And a field where a thousand corpses lie.
Mother whose heart hung humble as a button
On the bright splendid shroud of your son,
Do not weep. War is kind.
                                    —Stephen Crane, 1899

59. The speaker repeats the line *War is kind* five times in the poem. Why?
   a. He wants to emphasize the truth of this line.
   b. It is the theme of the poem.
   c. He is talking about several wars.
   d. He believes that readers will not understand the importance of this line.
   e. It will take a lot to convince listeners that this line is true.

60. Which of the following best conveys the theme of the poem?
  a. War is unkind, but necessary.
  b. There is no virtue in war.
  c. We should not weep for soldiers, because they died in glory.
  d. Everyone must sacrifice in a war.
  e. War without causalities is not really war.

Use the following passage to answer questions 61 and 62.

Beginning in 1958 . . . local NAACP [National Association for the Advancement of Colored People] chapters organized sit-ins, where African Americans, many of whom were college students, took seats and demanded service at segregated all-white lunch counters. It was, however, the sit-in demonstrations at Woolworth's store in Greensboro, North Carolina, beginning on February 1, 1960, that caught national attention and sparked other sit-ins and demonstrations in the South. One of the four students in the first Greensboro sit-in, Joe McNeil, later recounted his experience: " . . . we sat at a lunch counter where blacks never sat before. And people started to look at us. The help, many of whom were black, looked at us in disbelief too. They were concerned about our safety. We asked for service, and we were denied, and we expected to be denied. We asked why we couldn't be served, and obviously, we weren't given a reasonable answer, and it was our intent to sit there until they decided to serve us."

Sources: www.congresslink.org and Henry Hampton and Steve Fayer (eds.) *Voices of Freedom: An Oral History of the Civil Rights Movement from the 1950s through the 1980s.* Vintage Paperback, 1995.

61. Joe McNeil has not directly stated, but would support, which of the following statements?
  a. Without the sit-in in Greensboro, NC, the Civil Rights movement would never have started.
  b. Woolworth's served affordable lunches.
  c. Local NAACP chapters were causing trouble and upsetting citizens.
  d. The college students showed courage when they participated in the Greensboro sit-in.
  e. Woolworth was one of the few places instituting a policy of segregation.

62. What is the author's purpose in including Joe McNeil's quotation?
  a. to show that young people are the most likely to push for societal change
  b. to demonstrate that everyone has a different point of view
  c. to give a firsthand account of what has become a historic event
  d. to discount the importance of the Civil Rights movement
  e. to bring fame and credit to Joe McNeil

63.

Source: India Picture Gallery,
www.historylink102.com/india/index.htm.

The statue pictured here shows
a. the Hindu God Siva in warrior mode.
b. the Hindu God Siva representing the three-fold qualities of nature: creation, preservation, and destruction.
c. the Hindu God Siva in benevolent mode.
d. the Hindu God Siva in androgynous form.
e. the Hindu God Siva in a state of agitation.

64. Who or what was most responsible for the fostering and development of ballet?
a. Renaissance Italians
b. French and Italian ruling classes of the fifteenth and sixteenth centuries
c. the ballet school founded by King Louis XIV
d. Catherine de Medici
e. Louis XIV

65. What was a likely consequence of the demise of ballet as a court fad?
a. Ballet reached a wider audience.
b. The king embraced a new dance form.
c. Peasant dances returned to favor.
d. Professional ballet dancers were unemployed.
e. Ballet was not performed for many years.

66. How did early Italian *balleti* differ from the peasant dances on which they were based?
a. The peasants danced in courts rather than in their rural communities.
b. They were embellished with costumes and scenery.
c. They were performed by professional French dancers.
d. They were performed by Italian noblemen.
e. They were based on different patterns, steps, and rhythms.

67.

Source: India Picture Gallery,
http://historylink102.com/india/index.htm.

The Taj Mahal, pictured here, is an example of
a. perfect symmetry.
b. classic western architecture.
c. a historic monument within an urban setting.
d. how perspective can be distorted when viewing an object from a distance.
e. Greek architecture.

68.

Which of the following is NOT a prominent architectural characteristic of medieval castles featured in the engraving?

a. turrets

b. moats

c. stone walls

d. dungeons

e. defensive walls

69. Which of the following statements is NOT true?

a. German printer Johannes Gutenberg is often credited with the invention of the first printing press to use movable type.

b. Johannes Gutenberg used handset type to print the Gutenberg Bible in 1455.

c. Chinese printers used movable block prints and type made of clay as early as 1040.

d. Korean printers invented movable copper type about 1392.

e. Chinese and Korean printers learned their methods from the work of Gutenberg.

Use the painting to answer question 70.

Lucas Cranach the Elder, Portrait of Johannes Cuspinian, 1502–03. (Dr. Oskar Reinhart Collection, Winterthur, Switzerland.)

70. Typical of portraits painted in the sixteenth century, Cranach's subject is

a. a fellow painter.

b. a member of the court.

c. a writer.

d. a commoner.

e. a writer.

71. What time period did Edgar Allan Poe refer to as "the glory that was Greece, the grandeur that was Rome!"?

a. Classical Antiquity

b. the Renaissance

c. the medieval era

d. the Age of Enlightenment

e. the Dark Ages

72. Whose life in the eighth or seventh century is often taken as marking the beginning of Classical Antiquity?
a. Alexander the Great
b. Homer
c. Aristotle
d. Hesiod
e. Plato

73. Who formally recorded the creation of an inverted image formed by light rays passing through a pinhole into a darkened room?
a. Alhazen
b. Aristotle
c. Leonardo da Vinci
d. Giovanni Battista Della Porta
e. Mo-Ti

74. The term *camera obscura* was first used by what astronomer?
a. Galileo
b. Giovanni Cassini
c. John Babtist Riccioli
d. Johannes Kepler
e. Nicolaus Copernicus

75. In what book, written by Giovanni Battista Della Porta in 1558, was the use of camera obscura recommended as an aid for drawing for artists?
a. *Academia Secretorum Naturae*
b. *A Concise History of Photography*
c. *Magiae Naturalis*
d. *The New Method of Making Common-Place Book*
e. *Essay Concerning Human Understanding*

76. In 1727, Professor J. Schulze mixed chalk, nitric acid, and what other ingredient in a flask, noticing darkening on the side of the flask exposed to sunlight?
a. gold
b. water
c. vinegar
d. pewter
e. silver

77. In what year did Thomas Wedgwood make "sun pictures" by placing opaque objects on leather treated with silver nitrate?
a. 1592
b. 1650
c. 1776
d. 1800
e. 1845

Use the following poem to answer questions 78 through 81.

(1) My mistress' eyes are nothing like the sun;
Coral is far more red than her lips' red;
If snow be white, why then her breasts are dun;
If hairs be wires black wires grow on her head.

(5) I have seen roses, damasked, red and white,
But no such roses see I in her cheeks;
And in some perfumes is there more delight
Than in the breath that from my mistress reeks.
I love to hear her speak, yet well I know

(10) That music hath a far more pleasing sound;
I grant I never saw a goddess go;
My mistress, when she walks, treads on the
    ground.
And yet, by heaven, I think my love as rare

(15) As any she belied with false compare.
                              —William Shakespeare

78. This poem is an example of a(n)
  a. elegy.
  b. epic.
  c. lyric.
  d. sonnet.
  e. limerick.

79. Line 1 is an example of
  a. hyperbole.
  b. metaphor.
  c. personification.
  d. simile.
  e. satire.

80. In the poem, Shakespeare mocks the conventional love poem format. This is called a(n)
  a. soliloquy.
  b. epiphany.
  c. parody.
  d. elegy.
  e. speech.

81. The final rhyming couplet expresses
  a. sincere love.
  b. sarcastic love.
  c. symbolic love.
  d. satirical love.
  e. unrequited love.

82. At its winter meeting in January, the American Library Association announces its children's book award winners. Which of the following is NOT one of the association's awards?
  a. Randolph Caldecott
  b. John Newbery
  c. Theodor Seuss Geisel
  d. William Allen White
  e. Batchelder

83. *The lonely tree wept.* This is an example of
  a. hyperbole.
  b. metaphor.
  c. personification.
  d. simile.
  e. alliteration.

Use the following passage to answer questions 84 and 85.

All the streets and lanes was just mud, they warn't nothing else *but* mud—mud as black as tar, and nigh about a foot deep in some places; and two or three inches deep in *all* the places. The hogs loafed and grunted around, everywheres. You'd see a muddy sow and a litter of pigs come lazying along the street and whollop herself right down in the way, where folks had to walk around her, and she'd stretch out and shut her eyes, and wave her ears, whilst the pigs were milking her, and look as happy as if she was on salary.

—*The Adventures of Huckleberry Finn,*
Mark Twain

84. The writing style used in the passage is
   a. colloquialism.
   b. dialect.
   c. jargon.
   d. slang.
   e. sarcasm.

85. This paragraph excerpt is an example of
   a. descriptive writing.
   b. expository writing.
   c. persuasive writing.
   d. technical writing.
   e. informative writing.

86. In Robert Frost's poem *The Road Not Taken,* the forked road represents choices in life. The road in the poem's title is an example of a
   a. personification.
   b. metaphor.
   c. simile.
   d. symbol.
   e. rhyme.

87. George Orwell wrote *Animal Farm* in the style of a
   a. comedy.
   b. fable.
   c. legend.
   d. tall tale.
   e. almanac.

88. Which author has NOT written significant material in the genre of fantasy?
   a. Lloyd Alexander
   b. Susan Cooper
   c. Stephen King
   d. J. R. R. Tolkien
   e. C. S. Lewis

89. Which genre of literature has no known authors but is passed down over time through word of mouth, reflecting the beliefs, customs, and dreams of peoples?
   a. horror
   b. folklore
   c. historical fiction
   d. science fiction
   e. conspiracy fiction

90. Victorian writers are known for
   a. criticism of their society.
   b. drama.
   c. poetry.
   d. psychological exploration of characters.
   e. two-dimensional characters.

91. During what period was the printing press invented?
   a. the Middle Ages
   b. the Gothic period
   c. the Byzantine era
   d. the Enlightenment
   e. the Renaissance

92. The Woodstock Music and Art Fair—better known to its participants and to history simply as "Woodstock"—took place in which year?
   a. 1960
   b. 1965
   c. 1969
   d. 1970
   e. 1972

93. Approximately how many people attended the three-day Woodstock festival?
   a. 30,000
   b. 90,000
   c. 125,000
   d. 500,000
   e. 750,000

94. Which of the following statements about O'Connell Street in Dublin, Ireland, is NOT true?
   a. The street is named for Daniel O'Connell, an Irish patriot.
   b. It is home to a monument on a sturdy column, surrounded by four serene angels seated at each corner of the monument's base.
   c. Although it is not a particularly long street, Dubliners will tell the visitor proudly that it is the widest street in all of Europe.
   d. On the street is the famous General Post Office that, during the 1916 rebellion, was taken over and occupied by the Irish rebels to British rule, sparking weeks of armed combat in the city's center.
   e. This street was modeled after the Champs-Elysees in Paris.

95. What novel by Nobel Prize winner Toni Morrison takes place in the African-American section of Medallion, Ohio, a community called "the Bottom," where people, and even natural things, are apt to go awry, to break from their prescribed boundaries, a place where bizarre and unnatural happenings and strange reversals of the ordinary are commonplace?
   a. *The Bluest Eye*
   b. *Song of Solomon*
   c. *Sula*
   d. *Beloved*
   e. *Jazz*

Use the following poem to answer questions 96–99.

A Narrow Fellow in the Grass

A narrow fellow in the grass
Occasionally rides;
You may have met him—did you not?
His notice sudden is.
The grass divides as with a comb,
A spotted shaft is seen,
And then it closes at your feet
And opens further on.
He likes a boggy acre,
A floor too cool for corn,
Yet when a boy, and barefoot,
I more than once at noon
Have passed, I thought, a whip-lash
Unbraiding in the sun,
When, stooping to secure it,
It wrinkled, and was gone.
Several of nature's people
I know and they know me;
I feel for them a transport
Of cordiality;
But never met this fellow,
Attended or alone,
Without a tighter breathing
And zero at the bone.

96. Who or what is the *fellow* in this poem?
   a. a whip-lash
   b. a snake
   c. a gust of wind
   d. a boy
   e. a bird

97. The phrase *Without a tighter breathing/And zero at the bone* most nearly indicates
   a. fright.
   b. cold.
   c. grief.
   d. awe.
   e. joy.

98. The phrase *nature's people* means
   a. nature lovers.
   b. children.
   c. animals.
   d. neighbors.
   e. parents.

99. The speaker of this poem is most likely
   a. an adult woman.
   b. an adult man.
   c. Emily Dickinson, the poet.
   d. a young boy.
   e. a young girl.

100. What is the name of the hand-woven rugs made in India? Today, they are usually made of wool, but they are descendants of cotton floor and bed coverings.
   a. Persian
   b. Dhurrie
   c. loom-woven
   d. Navajo
   e. Gond

101. Which of the following statements about the play *Waiting for Godot* is accurate?

   a. The 1955 production of *Waiting for Godot* was the play's first performance.

   b. *Waiting for Godot* was written by Peter Hall.

   c. The sets and characters in *Waiting for Godot* were typical of London stage productions in the 1950s.

   d. *Waiting for Godot* was not first performed in English.

   e. The play consists of three acts.

102. Which of the following statements is NOT accurate?

   a. *Waiting for Godot* has only five characters and a minimal setting.

   b. The character of Mr. Godot appears halfway through Act II.

   c. In a statement that was to become famous, the critic Vivian Mercer has described Godot as "a play in which nothing happens twice."

   d. On opening night, the line, "Nothing happens, nobody comes, nobody goes. It's awful," was met by a loud rejoinder of "Hear! Hear!" from an audience member.

   e. Harold Hobson's review in *The Sunday Times* managed to recognize the play for what history has proven it to be, a revolutionary moment in theater.

103. Moscow has a history of chaotic periods of war that ended with the destruction of a once largely wooden city and the building of a "new" city on top of the rubble of the old. What is the result of this history?

   a. Moscow is a layered city, with each tier holding information about a part of Russia's past.

   b. The people of Moscow are more interested in modernization than in preservation.

   c. The Soviet government destroyed many of the historic buildings in Russia.

   d. Much of the city's history has been erased.

   e. Moscow has prohibited any new development.

104. Dramatist Lorraine Hansberry's political beliefs had their origins in her experience as

   a. the daughter of politically active parents.

   b. a successful playwright in New York.

   c. a resident of Southside Chicago.

   d. an intellectual in Greenwich Village.

   e. an African immigrant living in New York City.

105. Each of the following Hansberry accomplishments occurred posthumously, EXCEPT

   a. a dramatic adaptation of her autobiography, *To Be Young, Gifted, and Black,* was released based on Hansberry's plays, poems, and other writings.

   b. her play *Les Blancs,* a drama set in Africa, was produced.

   c. *A Raisin in the Sun* was adapted as a musical.

   d. *A Raisin in the Sun* won a Tony award.

   e. her play *The Sign in Sidney Brustein's Window* was produced.

106. Hansberry's father earned his living as
   a. a civil rights worker.
   b. a banker.
   c. a real estate broker
   d. an artist and activist.
   e. a writer.

107. Hansberry's main purpose in writing *A Raisin in the Sun* was to
   a. win her father's approval.
   b. break down stereotypes.
   c. show people how interesting her own family was.
   d. earn the right to produce her own plays.
   e. win New York Drama Critic's Circle Award for Best Play of the Year.

108. The term *panopticon* was coined by Jeremy Bentham in the late eighteenth century. A panopticon is a
   a. prison cell.
   b. place in which everything can be seen by others.
   c. tower that provides a panoramic view.
   d. house that is transparent.
   e. place in which surveillance cameras and other monitoring equipment are in use.

109. There is little information available about the legendary blues guitarist Robert Johnson, and the information that is available is as much rumor as fact. What is undisputable, however, is Johnson's impact on the world of rock and roll. Some consider Johnson to be the father of modern rock. Which of the following artists was NOT influenced by Johnson?
   a. Muddy Waters
   b. Led Zeppelin
   c. the Rolling Stones
   d. Allman Brothers Band
   e. Metallica

110. What rock guitarist has said that "Robert Johnson to me is the most important blues musician who ever lived. . . . I have never found anything more deeply soulful than Robert Johnson"?
   a. Eric Clapton
   b. Jimmy Hendrix
   c. Jimmy Page
   d. Joe Walsh
   e. Slash

111. There are more than 50 types of blues music, including all but which of the following?
   a. Chicago blues
   b. Memphis blues
   c. juke joint blues
   d. acoustic country blues
   e. five-step blues

112. Because they have the ability to evoke an emotional response in readers, political cartoons can serve as a vehicle for swaying public opinion and can contribute to reform. Thomas Nast (1840–1902) demonstrated the power of his medium when he used his art to expose the corruption of
a. Fernando Wood.
b. Fiorello LaGuardia.
c. Boss Tweed.
d. William Mooney.
e. Andrew Jackson.

113. Rich cultural diversity evolved in China during the Yuan (*first* or *beginning*) Dynasty (1279–1368), under the governance of the Mongol leader Khubilai Khan, as it had in other periods of foreign dynastic rule. Major achievements included all the following EXCEPT the
a. development of drama and the novel.
b. increased use of the written vernacular.
c. introduction of foreign musical instruments.
d. introduction of the production of thin glass to Europeans.
e. advances in the fields of travel literature.

114. When it was first developed, chiaroscuro printmaking was valued because it
a. effectively mimicked the appearance of fine drawings.
b. was employed by the most renowned artists in Europe.
c. enabled printmakers to use several colors on one print.
d. cost less than other types of printmaking.
e. reliably reproduced designs originally created for etchings.

115. Among the most sought-after prints today are those of Rembrandt van Rijn (1606–69). Rembrandt himself pulled the first prints from his etched plates, but so great were the demands by collectors that further printings had to be made by other craftsmen. The history of one print offers clues to the dates at which Rembrandt's plates were reworked. A 1789 reworking added the inscription "No. 122" to Rembrandt's original; on the version in a volume published in 1809, however, the inscription has been erased and shading added across the top. This print is
a. *Flight into Egypt.*
b. *Tobias and the Angel.*
c. *The Pancake Woman.*
d. *Christ Healing the Sick.*
e. *The Abduction of Europa.*

Use the following passage to answer questions 116–120.

(1) It is sometimes said that a "good subject" for a short story should always be capable of being expanded into a novel. The principle may be defendable in special cases; but it is certainly a

(5) misleading one on which to build any general theory. Every "subject" (in the novelist's sense of the term) must necessarily contain within itself its own dimensions; and one of the fiction-writer's essential gifts is that of discern-

(10) ing whether the subject which presents itself to him, asking for incarnation, is suited to the proportions of a short story or of a novel. If it appears to be adapted to both the chances are that it is inadequate to either.

(15) It would be as great a mistake, however, to try to base a hard-and-fast theory on the denial of the rule as on its assertion. Instances of short stories made out of subjects that could have been expanded into a novel, and that are yet

(20) typical short stories and not mere stunted novels, will occur to everyone. General rules in art are useful chiefly as a lamp in a mine, or a handrail down a black stairway; they are necessary for the sake of the guidance they give, but (25) it is a mistake, once they are formulated, to be too much in awe of them.

There are at least two reasons why a subject should find expression in novel-form rather than as a tale; but neither is based on the num- (30) ber of what may be conveniently called incidents, or external happenings, which the narrative contains. There are novels of action which might be condensed into short stories without the loss of their distinguishing quali- (35) ties. The marks of the subject requiring a longer development are, first, the gradual unfolding of the inner life of its characters, and secondly the need for producing in the reader's mind the sense of the lapse of time.

(40) Outward events of the most varied and exciting nature may without loss of probability be crowded into a few hours, but moral dramas usually have their roots deep in the soul, their rise far back in time; and the suddenest- (45) seeming clash in which they culminate should be led up to step by step if it is to explain and justify itself.

There are cases, indeed, when the short story may make use of the moral drama at its culmi- (50) nation. If the incident dealt with be one which a single retrospective flash sufficiently lights up, it is qualified for use as a short story; but if the subject be so complex, and its successive phases so interesting, as to justify elaboration, the (55) lapse of time must necessarily be suggested, and the novel-form becomes appropriate.

The effect of compactness and instantaneity sought in the short story is attained mainly by the observance of two "unities"—the old tradi- (60) tional one of time, and that other, more modern and complex, which requires that any rapidly enacted episode shall be seen through only one pair of eyes . . . .

One thing more is needful for the ultimate (65) effect of probability; and that is, never let the character who serves as reflector record anything not naturally within his register. It should be the storyteller's first care to choose this reflecting mind deliberately, as one would (70) choose a building-site, or decide upon the orientation of one's house, and when this is done, to live inside the mind chosen, trying to feel, see and react exactly as the latter would, no more, no less, and, above all, no otherwise. (75) Only thus can the writer avoid attributing incongruities of thought and metaphor to his chosen interpreter.

116. According to the author, Edith Wharton, which factor(s) determine whether a subject is suitable for a novel instead of a short story?
I. the number of incidents in the story
II. the need to show the development of the character(s)
III. the need to reflect the passage of time
a. I only
b. I and II only
c. II and III only
d. I and III only
e. all of the above

117. In line 42, the phrase *moral drama* can best be defined as
   a. an uplifting story.
   b. a story of religious values.
   c. a story of ethical challenge(s).
   d. a religious play.
   e. a story without action elements.

118. In lines 48–56, the author
   a. contradicts the rule established in the previous paragraph.
   b. clarifies the rule established in the previous paragraph.
   c. shows an example of the rule established in the previous paragraph.
   d. justifies the rule established in the previous paragraph.
   e. provides a new rule.

119. According to the author, two defining characteristics of a short story are
   a. complexity and probability.
   b. moral dilemmas and sudden clashes.
   c. retrospection and justification.
   d. metaphor and congruity.
   e. limited time and point of view.

120. In line 69, *this reflecting mind* refers to
   a. the author.
   b. the narrator.
   c. the reader.
   d. a story's translator.
   e. a story's editor.

121. What violinist made his or her American concert debut on New Year's Eve, 1982 with the New York Philharmonic?
   a. Bach
   b. Akiko Ono
   c. Midori
   d. David Rubinoff
   e. Bin Huang

122. What instrument is the ancestor of the modern violin?
   a. rabab
   b. pan-pipe
   c. hydraulic organ
   d. tambourine
   e. rattler

123. What ancient instrument had exactly three strings stretched across its bowl-shaped body, with each string tuned to a particular pitch? A musician played this instrument by plucking its strings.
   a. parthenioi
   b. paidikoi
   c. kitharistoerioi
   d. lyre
   e. drill-flute

124. Which of these events happened first in music history?
   a. The rabab was invented by the Arabs.
   b. Stradivari began making his violins.
   c. Niccolo Paganini wrote his caprices.
   d. The rebec appeared in Europe.
   e. The sarod was developed.

125. Archaeologists working in Manege Square in Russia uncovered the commercial life of eight centuries. By excavating five meters deep, archaeologists provided a picture of the evolution of commercial Moscow. Among the finds were all but which of the following?
  a. wooden street pavement from the time of Ivan the Terrible (sixteenth century)
  b. a wide cobblestone road from the era of Peter the Great (early eighteenth century)
  c. street paving from the reign of Catherine the Great (mid- to late eighteenth century)
  d. a wealthy merchant's estate (nineteenth century)
  e. a cobbler's shop (nineteenth century)

126. The 1937 painting *The Eternal City* by American painter Peter Blume portrays
  a. fascist Italy under Mussolini.
  b. Italian fascism that appears to improve everyday conditions.
  c. Mussolini as a benevolent dictator.
  d. the fall of Italian fascism.
  e. ancient Rome.

127. *Guernica* by Pablo Picasso was his interpretation of
  a. the Versailles Peace Conference.
  b. Hitler's invasion of France.
  c. Nazi bombings of Guernica, Spain, during the Spanish Civil War.
  d. the effect of prohibition on American culture.
  e. the fall of Rome.

128. The majority of Salvador Dali's work demonstrates the twentieth-century style of painting known as
  a. Dadaism.
  b. the Fauvres.
  c. cubism.
  d. surrealism.
  e. Impressionism.

129. The architectural mandate that "form follows function" was from what school of architecture?
  a. the Oxford Movement
  b. the Bauhaus school
  c. the Bloomsbury circle
  d. Gothic
  e. Romanesque

130. Georgia O'Keeffe and Edward Hopper were
  a. twentieth-century American painters.
  b. jazz pianists.
  c. literary historians of the ninetieth century.
  d. inventors of skyscrapers.
  e. British literary figures of the twentieth century.

Use the following image to answer question 131.

131. The illustration is of a six-panel folding screen illustrated with ink on paper. It is part of a pair of screens depicting the four seasons; this one shows fall (right) and winter (left). It was drawn by Soami (1472–1525), a famous Japanese painter, art critic, poet, landscape gardener, and master of the tea ceremony and flower arrangement. A historian could use this screen to support which of the following positions?

a. Empty space is important in Japanese art.

b. Japan is a densely populated country.

c. Samurai used brightly colored screen-paintings with gold-leaf backgrounds to display their wealth.

d. all of the above

e. none of the above

Use the following two songs to answer question 132.

"I Didn't Raise My Boy to Be a Soldier" (1915)

Lyrics by Al Bryan, music by Al Piantadosi
I didn't raise my boy to be a soldier,
I brought him up to be my pride and joy.
Who dares to place a musket on his shoulder
To shoot some other mother's darling boy?
Let nations arbitrate their future troubles,
It's time to lay the sword and gun away;
There'd be no war today if mothers would all say,
"I didn't raise my boy to be a soldier."

"Over There" (1917)

Music and lyrics by George Cohan
Johnnie get your gun, get your gun, get your gun.
Take it on the run, on the run, on the run.
Hear them calling you and me, every son of
   liberty;
Hurry right away, no delay, go today.
Make your daddy glad to have had such a lad
Tell your sweetheart not to pine; to be proud
   her boy's in line.

132. These two popular American songs deal with the position of the United States at the time of World War I. What is the best conclusion based on these two sources?
   a. American parents were proud to have their children join the army.
   b. Singers and songwriters should stay out of politics.
   c. American soldiers in World War I fought for liberty.
   d. World War I was unnecessary.
   e. World War I was controversial and elicited different points of view.

133. The kingdom of Benin, in the area around present-day Nigeria, produced remarkable brass (often called bronze by Europeans) artwork from the twelfth century to the seventeenth century. Which conclusion can be drawn based on Benin bronze?
   a. This practice spread to other areas of Africa.
   b. West Africans understood principles of metallurgy.
   c. Benin's artists did not comprehend the difference between bronze and brass.
   d. West Africans were uncivilized.
   e. All social classes created brass artwork in Benin.

134. Why did Gordon Parks choose the name *American Gothic* for his photograph?
   a. because the photograph was dark and mysterious
   b. because the photograph exactly duplicated the images of Grant Wood's painting with the same name
   c. because the photograph had a composition similar to Grant Wood's painting
   d. because Parks admired Grant Wood's life and work
   e. because Ella Watson bore an uncanny resemblance to the farmer's wife in Grant Wood's painting

Use the following photograph and text to answer question 135.

Source: National Archives and Records Administration.

After 72 years of campaigning and protest, women were granted the right to vote in 1920. Passed by Congress and ratified by 36 of the then 48 states, the Nineteenth Amendment of the U.S. Constitution states, "The right of citizens of the United States to vote shall not be denied or abridged by the United States or by any State on account of sex."

135. With which of the following statements would women in the photograph most likely agree?
   a. Women should behave in a dignified and orderly manner even if they are protesting.
   b. Women stand outside the gates of governmental power.
   c. The suffragettes would be more effective if they had more powerful slogans.
   d. Demonstrations are the most effective ways to influence lawmaking.
   e. Demonstrations are always ineffective.

Use the following passage to answer questions 136 and 137.

The Scream is a powerful work of art that has true aesthetic value. In its raw depiction of the unavoidable human emotions of alienation, anxiety, and fear, *The Scream* invites meaningful introspection as the viewer internalizes its message of the vulnerability of the human psyche.

   The Scream is a very dynamic and yet frightening painting. The blood-red sky and eerie water/air seem to be moving and twirling, even enveloping the screaming man's mind as he stands on a bridge completely disregarded by passers-by who do not share in his horror. Viewers of the painting cannot help but ask: Why is the man screaming? And why is he alone in his scream? What is he afraid of? Or, what has he realized or seen that is making him scream? Why aren't the others as affected as he? The threat must be internal, yet the brushstrokes, colors, and perspective seem to indicate that the horror is also bound to something in nature, something outside of the man. In any case, the agony and alienation are inescapable. Something horrible has happened or been realized by the man who cannot contain his horror, but it has not affected the others on the bridge.

   That the people in the background are calm and do not share this horror conveys a truth regarding the ownership of our own feelings. We are often alone in our feelings, as can be especially noticed when we are in pain. The horror is the man's own; he must carry it himself.

   In this expressionist piece, the black, red, and orange colors are both bold and dark, illuminating and haunting at the same time. Remarkably, the light from the blood-reds and vibrant oranges in the distant sky seem to be somewhat detached from the figure in the forefront, failing to reach his persona, suggesting that there is little to illuminate his (and the viewer's) fears. The man's face is nondescript; in fact, it almost looks more like a skull than a living man's face, hollow with two simple dots to indicate the nostrils, no hair, and no wrinkles of the skin. This could be any man or woman, left to deal with his or her own horrors.

136. Which of the following best describes what is depicted in Edvard Munch's 1893 painting *The Scream*?

  a. a man screaming as he falls through the sky

  b. a man standing alone on a bridge and screaming

  c. several people on a bridge, with the man in the forefront screaming

  d. several people on a bridge, all of them screaming

  e. something horrible happening to people on a bridge

137. You can infer that Munch left the face of the screamer "nondescript" because he

  a. wanted to show that we are all the screamer.

  b. did not like to paint detailed portraits of people, especially their faces.

  c. couldn't decide how to make the person look.

  d. wanted the person to look childlike and innocent.

  e. wanted the hollow face to contrast with the swirling sky.

138. When did almanacs begin predicting the weather?

  a. in medieval times

  b. in the sixteenth century

  c. in the seventeenth century

  d. They have always predicted the weather.

  e. They do not predict the weather.

139. What was unique about "Davy Crockett" almanacs?

  a. They included tall tales.

  b. They were sold only in the United States.

  c. They included stories about Davy Crockett.

  d. They were printed during the Civil War.

  e. They included facts about the Civil War.

140. What was the purpose of the first almanacs?

  a. to predict the weather

  b. to list church holidays

  c. to publish poetry

  d. to print humorous stories

  e. to chart the movement of the stars

▶ Answers

1. d. These lines are from *Kubla Khan, or, A Vision in a Dream: A Fragment.* This poem has strange, dreamy imagery and can be read on many levels. *Kubla Khan* was never finished.

2. c. This quote is from Sigmund Freud, a Czech Austrian psychiatrist who founded the psychoanalytic school of psychology. He is best known for his theories of the unconscious mind.

3. c. Campbell's hero is archetypal. An archetype is a personage or pattern that occurs in literature and human thought often enough to be considered universal. He has ventured outside the boundaries of the village and, after many trials and adventures, has returned with the boon that will save or enlighten his fellows. The faces in the title belong to the hero, not to villagers, countries, languages, or adventures (choices **a**, **b**, **d**, and **e**).

4. d. The quote states that the kingdom of the unconscious mind goes down into unsuspected Aladdin caves. The story of Aladdin is a fairy tale (choice **b**), but neither this nor the other choices are in the passage.

5. c. Mozart's older sister Maria Anna, who the family called Nannerl, was learning the clavier, an early keyboard instrument, when her three-year-old brother took an interest in playing. As Nannerl later recalled, Mozart "often spent much time at the clavier, picking out thirds, which he was always striking, and his pleasure showed that it sounded good."

6. c. After Mozart's first public appearance at Linz, word of his genius traveled to Vienna.

7. d. The anecdote emphasizes Mozart's imagination. The phrase *engrossed in the intricacies of his make-believe court* suggests a child with a lively imagination.

8. c. Swing can be described as *lively*. Jazz soloists in big bands improvised from the melody, indicating that the music was *melodic*.

9. d. In the 1940s, you would most likely hear bebop being played in clubs, such as Minton's Playhouse in Harlem.

10. b. Rhythm is the distinguishing feature of bebop, and in small groups, the drums became more prominent. Setting a driving beat, the drummer interacted with the bass, piano, and the soloists, and together the musicians created fast, complex melodies.

11. a. This music was known as glam metal or hair metal. Bands like Poison, White Snake, and Mötley Crüe popularized glam rock with their power ballads and flashy style, but the product had worn thin by the early 1990s.

12. b. Grunge rockers derived their fashion sense from the youth culture of the Pacific Northwest: a melding of punk rock style and outdoors clothing like flannel shirts, heavy boots, worn-out jeans, and corduroy pants. At the height of the movement's popularity, when other Seattle bands like Pearl Jam and Alice in Chains were all the rage, the trappings of grunge were working their way to the height of American fashion.

13. c. This summary describes *Tom Jones, the Foundling,* written by Henry Fielding in 1749. Some consider this one of the first prose works describable as a novel.

14. e. The piano was originally invented in Florence, Italy, in 1709. The man responsible was Bartolomeo Cristofori.

15. b. The tarantella, which takes its name from the dance performed to cure a person who has been bitten by the tarantella spider, is an Italian dance in 6/8 time.

16. a. In music, a combination of three or more tones is referred to as a chord.

17. b. The original 1957 Broadway production of *West Side Story* was choreographed by Jerome Robbins.

18. a. The Dance Theatre of Harlem was a dance company for African-American ballet dancers, cofounded by Arthur Mitchell and Karel Shook.

19. b. The twist is an African-American folk dance step. However, it appeared as a new dance craze when Chubby Checker released his single "The Twist."

20. a. Charles Dickens's *David Copperfield* was referred to as his "favourite child." This book, also known as *The Personal History, Adventures, Experience and Observation of David Copperfield the Younger of Blunderstone Rookery* (which he never meant to publish on any account), was first published in 1850. Many elements within *David Copperfield* follow events in the author's own life.

21. b. These are the first words of Holden Caulfield, the narrator of *The Catcher in the Rye* by J. D. Salinger.

22. d. This work is *The Pilgrim's Progress* by John Bunyan, published in February of 1678. It is regarded as one of the most significant works of English literature.

23. c. Jonathan Swift uses the Lilliputians as symbols of humankind's excessive pride. They are the tiniest race visited by Gulliver, but also the smuggest, both collectively and individually.

24. c. An autobiography is an author's account of his or her own life. The use of first-person pronouns (*I* and *me*) is a common device in the genre.

25. c. Bacon was writing during the "Age of Discoveries," in which European explorers sailed around the globe, encountering previously unknown cultures and continents. There is no evidence to support the other answer choices.

26. d. Hades is the underworld, or Hell, of Roman mythology, and as such is the opposite of Atlantis.

27. d. In Genesis, God promises Abraham a land that will be an eternal possession, where he and his descendants can create a nation that is a model for the rest of the world.

28. c. The entire poem uses figurative language to compare death to being "put out to sea." The "Pilot" the poet hopes to see face to face when he dies is God.

29. e. In the Viennese waltz, couples faced one another and embraced. The dance became a craze in Europe.

30. d. The polka was a popular dance employing the embrace. The tango took the embrace of the waltz and the polka a step further, as dancers pressed their cheeks and chests together, and entwined their legs during the complicated footwork.

31. c. In Argentina, the tango was developed not in literary society, which might be counted on to record the development, but rather in the dance halls and brothels. These venues were frequented by the less privileged and uneducated classes who left little evidence of their existence, let alone their dance habits.

32. a. Both images are of figures that are part human and part animal. The images provide no solid evidence of worship practices (choice **b**), and do not appear to be at the entrance of tombs (choice **c**). There is also no indication of the materials used by ancient Greek and Egyptian artists (choice **d**). There is no information about the artists (choice **e**).

33. b. The emperor states that with his new clothes, he could "tell the clever from the dunces." But it is clear to the reader that *he* is the dunce, for believing the rogues about their ability to make invisible clothing. This discrepancy between what the character says and what the reader knows to be true is known as *irony.*

34. a. The passage, an excerpt from Hans Christian Andersen's *The Emperor's New Clothes,* centers on a ruler whose obsession with his wardrobe prevents him from seeing the truth (that the rogues are lying).

35. b. The work is clearly a sculpture, and is referred to as *relief* because its features or form stand out from a background.

36. e. The sticklike object, with its thin shaft and large decorative top, bisects the work diagonally and provides balance for the unequally sized figures. It does not provide commentary on their power (choice **c**). Choice **a** is incorrect because the headdresses are found at the top and middle of the work and do not stand out as anchoring features. Because the friezes are found only at the left top and left side of the work surrounding the larger figure, they cannot be said to provide symmetry (choice **b**). The open book at the bottom of the sculpture (choice **d**) is barely noticeable, and does not provide balance.

37. a. Sondheim had a desire to explore and reveal psychological truths.

38. c. Other artists used Japanese poetry or the nineteenth-century English class system as subjects (choices **a** and **e**). Other artists did receive guidance from Hammerstein and/or Bernstein (choice **b**). Sondheim did not create *West Side Story* (choice **d**), but rather wrote its lyrics.

39. b. The poet endows the abstract concepts of Love and Life with human characteristics. They are hosts who provide hospitality and have hands that are held by the poet.

40. b. The poet uses the first-person pronouns *I* and *me* to indicate that he is the guest who has enjoyed the hospitality of his hosts, Life and Love, and turns away to bid them good night.

41. a. Swift is addressing a societal problem with satire.

42. e. Swift's satire highlights the grave situation facing Ireland's growing impoverished population. The kingdom is in a "deplorable state," and no one has stepped forward to offer a solution (one who did, Swift writes, would "have his statue set up for a preserver of the nation").

43. a. By referring to the dawn as *she,* and the sun as *he* and *wheeling king,* Dickinson is using personification. Alliteration (choice **b**) is the repetition of consonant sounds; euphemism (choice **c**) is the substitution of an agreeable word or idea for one less pleasant; parody (choice **d**) is ridicule by imitation; and assonance (choice **e**) is the repetition of vowel sounds. These literary devices are not used in the poem.

44. d. Diadems are described as a necessity of the *wheeling king* with *haughty, spangled hems,* making *crown* the most logical choice.

45. c. By portraying Julius Caesar turning his back and putting up his hand in an almost defiant gesture toward Antony's offer of the crown, the artist succeeds in conveying the idea that Caesar was uncomfortable with the idea of being appointed dictator.

46. a. The notes show the beginning of the popular American folk song "She'll Be Coming around the Mountain."

47. b. Prisoners, army privates, sharecroppers, and prisoners of war were not forbidden to learn how to read and write. Slave owners imposed this restriction on their slaves in order to maintain their authority.

48. c. Kennicott is described as an outsider who has *a love of art and literature and a desire to enact social reform.* Dance marathons and industrial mass production have nothing to do with this description. Prohibition and the Palmer Raids were the product of a segment of society who wanted people's rights restricted. Kennicott would have more likely embraced women's suffrage, a movement that allowed women to vote in national elections beginning in 1920.

49. a. Choices **b, c,** and **e** describe the opposites of *Main Street* themes. Kennicott is an outsider, but her character is used not to rationalize fear of the outsider but to critique that fear. Similarly, the desire to conform rather than face rejection is also critiqued. Choice **d** misses the tone of the novel as captured in the passage. Words such as *stifling, rejected,* and *threat* do not describe an *uplifting* novel.

50. b. Saying that the eagle watches and then falls *like a thunderbolt* implies alertness and striking, so the most logical choice is that the eagle is hunting.

51. c. Holiday jokingly uses the word *comeback* in the second part of the sentence to refer to a physical return, rather than a return to her career. The joke cannot accurately be described as sincere, nor is it nostalgic, because it does not indicate a desire to return to a sentimentalized time in the past. If she was ironic, she would use the word to mean the opposite of its literal meaning.

52. a. Using the process of elimination, choice **a** is the only correct answer. The style and subject indicate it is not the work of an Impressionist, and although the image could possibly be described as neo-classic, symmetry is not a feature. Finally, the perspective is not that of the boy, because he is a part of the wider scene, one that includes much more than simply his perspective.

53. a. Disney's first Broadway musical was *Beauty and the Beast,* based on its film version of *Beauty and the Beast* (released in 1991).

54. c. The author states in lines 10–12 that *commercial breaks are constant reminders that the medium itself is artificial* and that *the long term effect of habitually watching commercial television is probably an erosion of trust in the television medium itself* (lines 20–22). Thus, commercial television teaches viewers not to believe what they see or hear on TV.

55. d. The author doesn't seem to think watching television—whether it is commercial or public—is inherently a bad thing; rather, she is emphasizing that we should not (indeed, can't) believe everything we see on commercial TV (choice **d**).

56. a. The author writes that *Every story has a happy ending . . . which contributes no end to the pervasive unreality of it all* (lines 24–27) and *it is the chronic bliss of everybody in the commercials that creates their final divorce from effective life as we know it* (lines 28–30).

57. d. All the other stars listed were making their last films under long-term contracts with film studios—Olivia de Havilland in 1946, Bette Davis in 1949 (with *Beyond the Forest*), Humphrey Bogart in 1951 (with *The Enforcer*), and Errol Flynn in 1953.

58. c. *Petrouchka* is the story of a Russian puppet who comes to life and discovers how to love.

59. e. Throughout the poem, the speaker shows how war is not kind: It kills a lover, a father, and a son; it leaves fields littered with thousands of corpses.

60. b. The tone of the poem makes it clear that war is not kind and that there is no virtue in slaughter or excellence in killing.

61. d. Although McNeil does not state that the college students were brave, the firsthand account notes that the African-American Woolworth's employees "were concerned" about the students' safety. This implies that the students could not be sure of what consequences they would face.

62. c. This quotation from a participant in this sit-in gives the passage a firsthand perspective on the historical event.

63. c. This Indian statue clearly shows the Hindu god in a benevolent pose. There is nothing to suggest a warrior (choice **a**), the three qualities of nature (choice **b**), androgyny (choice **d**), or agitation (choice **e**).

64. b. Although answer choices **a, c, d,** and **e** are important to the development of ballet, it was the ruling classes of both countries (including Catherine de Medici and Louis XIV) that fostered and helped develop ballet.

65. a. When court dances fell out of favor, dancers found work in theaters. Ballet dancers performed in theaters instead of courts, and they reached wider audiences.

66. b. Elaborate scenery and costumes transformed the peasant dances.

67. a. The Taj Mahal is perfectly symmetrical, with each half constructed as the mirror image of the other.

68. d. While it may be assumed that the pictured castle includes a dungeon, it is not featured in the engraving.

69. e. Although Gutenberg is given credit for the invention of movable type, others in different parts of the world at different time periods had used a similar technique. This does not lessen the great effect that Gutenberg's invention had on European culture.

70. b. Portraits during this time period were typically of royal or noble subjects.

71. a. The term *Classical Antiquity* typically refers to Greek and Roman civilization, from Homer to Constantine. This encompasses both the Greek and Latin languages and their literature, including poetry, drama, history, philosophy, rhetoric, and religion.

72. b. Classical Antiquity is the study of Greek and Roman civilization marked at the beginning by the life of Homer.

73. e. Mo-Ti called this darkened room a "collecting place" or the "locked treasure room."

74. d. The German astronomer Johannes Kepler first used this term in the early seventeenth century. He used it for astronomical applications and had a portable tent camera for surveying in Upper Austria.

75. c. Giovanni Battista Della Porta's most famous work, entitled *Magiae Naturalis (Natural Magic),* covered a variety of the subjects, including the study of occult philosophy, astrology, alchemy, mathematics, meteorology, and natural philosophy.

76. e. Chalk, nitric acid, and silver resulted in this reaction.

77. d. This event occurred in 1800. The resulting images deteriorated rapidly, however, if displayed under light stronger than that from candles.

78. d. It is a poem of 14 lines of iambic pentameter. This Shakespearean sonnet consists of three quatrains followed by a rhyming couplet.

79. d. A simile is the comparison of two objects using the words *like* or *as.*

80. c. A parody is a literary form that does mock other work. Shakespeare does not give his lover a glowing description, but tells it as he sees it.

81. a. In spite of expressing a less than pleasing picture of his lover, the writer loves her for who she is.

82. d. The William Allen White Award is the children's state award in Kansas.

83. c. Personification allows the writer to give animals, plants, and ideas the qualities of a human.

84. b. Dialect is the local language of the people. This includes the accent, vocabulary, grammar, and idioms.

85. a. Descriptive writing seeks to paint a vivid picture so that the reader is pulled into the writer's experience.

86. d. A symbol is a concrete object that represents an idea or concept.

87. b. A fable is a story with a moral principle using animals or birds as the protagonists.

88. c. Stephen King writes in the science fiction and horror genres.

89. b. Folklore includes fables, folk tales, tall tales, myths, legends, Mother Goose rhymes, nursery tales, and folk songs.

90. a. Following the Industrial Revolution, novel writers like Charles Dickens, the Bronte sisters, and, later, Thomas Hardy and George Eliot wrote about the problems of contemporary life.

91. e. The invention of the printing press occurred during the Renaissance.

92. c. Woodstock opened on August 15, 1969. Woodstock is considered the defining moment for an entire generation.

93. d. Fences that were supposed to facilitate ticket collection never materialized, and all attempts at gathering tickets were abandoned. Crowd estimates of 30,000 kept rising; by the end of the three days, people estimated the crowd at 500,000.

94. e. O'Connell Street was not modeled after the Champs-Elysees. In fact, when Dubliners call O'Connell Street the widest street in Europe, this claim usually meets with protests, especially from French tourists, claiming the Champs-Elysees of Paris as Europe's widest street. But the witty Dubliner will not relinquish bragging rights easily and will trump the French visitor with a fine distinction: The Champs-Elysees is a *boulevard,* while O'Connell is a *street.*

95. c. The very naming of the setting of *Sula* is a turning-upside-down of the expected; the Bottom is located high up in the hills. The novel is furthermore filled with images of mutilation, both psychological and physical. A great part of the lives of the characters, therefore, is taken up with making sense of the world, setting boundaries, and devising methods to control what is essentially uncontrollable.

96. b. The *fellow* is a snake, which frightens the speaker.

97. a. *Tighter breathing* indicates fear, as does *zero at the bone* (one is sometimes said to be cold with fear). Also, the subject is a snake, which is generally a feared animal.

98. c. In context, the speaker is discussing animals, because he follows with his contrasting attitude toward this fellow, meaning the snake. The other choices are all human beings.

99. b. Stanza 2 contains the phrase *when a boy,* implying that the speaker was a boy in the past and is now, therefore, an adult man. (This is the reason it cannot be the poet speaking, her name being *Emily.*)

100. b. In fact, the name *Dhurrie* comes from the Indian word *dari,* which means threads of cotton. The rugs are noted for their soft colors and their varieties of design and make a stunning focal point for any living room or dining room.

101. d. The first line of the passage describes the English language premiere of the play, indicating it had been previously performed in a different language.

102. b. The character of Mr. Godot never shows up.

103. a. In some areas of the city, archaeologists have reached the layer from 1147, the year of Moscow's founding. Among the findings from the various periods of Moscow's history are carved bones, metal tools, pottery, glass, jewelry, and crosses.

104. a. Born in Chicago in 1930, Hansberry was a member of a prominent family devoted to civil rights.

105. e. This play is about an intellectual in Greenwich Village, New York City, a man who is open-minded and generous of spirit and who, as Hansberry wrote, "cares about it all. It takes too much energy not to care." Lorraine Hansberry died on the final day of the play's run on Broadway. Her early death, at the age of 34, was unfortunate, as it cut short a brilliant and promising career, one that, even in its short span, changed the face of American theater.

106. c. Her father definitely worked in the cause of civil rights (choice **a**), but he did not earn his living that way.

107. b. One of Hansberry's central artistic efforts was to free many people from the smothering effects of stereotyping by depicting the wide array of personality types and aspirations that exist within one Southside Chicago family.

108. b. A *panopticon* is defined as a place in which everything is in full view of others. Bentham was describing an idea for how prisons should be designed. The prisoners' cells would be placed in a circle with a guard tower in the middle. All walls facing the center of the circle would be glass. In that way, every prisoner's cell would be in full view of the guards. The prisoners could do nothing unobserved, but would be unable to see the guard tower. They would know they were being watched—or rather, they would know that they could be watched—but because they would not see the observer, they would never know when the guard was actually monitoring their actions.

109. e. All the other answer choices contain musicians who claim to have been influenced by Robert Johnson.

110. a. Eric Clapton even recorded *Me and Mr. Johnson,* an album of the legendary Johnson's works. Clapton remembers first hearing Johnson's music as a teenager, and he has been playing Johnson's songs for nearly 40 years.

111. e. This is not one of the more than 50 types of blues music. All the other answer choices contribute to this rich blues variety, which comes as no surprise to those who recognize the blues as a fundamental American art form. Indeed, in its resolution to name 2003 the Year of the Blues, Congress declared that the blues is "the most influential form of American roots music." In fact, the two most popular American musical forms—rock and roll and jazz—owe their genesis in large part (some would argue entirely) to the blues.

112. c. Nast exposed the Boss Tweed Ring in New York City. Created under tight deadlines for ephemeral, commercial formats like newspapers and magazines, cartoons still manage to have lasting influence. Although they tackle the principal issues and leaders of their day, they often provide a vivid historical picture for generations to come.

113. d. During this time, certain key Chinese innovations—such as printing techniques, porcelain playing cards, and medical literature—were introduced in Europe, while European skills, including the production of thin glass and cloisonné, became popular in China.

114. a. The early popularity of chiaroscuro related to its reproductions of fine drawings.

115. c. The Rembrandt van Rijn print in question is *The Pancake Woman.*

116. c. In paragraph 3, Wharton states the two chief reasons a subject should find expression in novel-form: first, the gradual unfolding of the inner life of its characters, and second, the need to produce in the reader's mind the sense of the lapse of time (lines 35–39). Lines 27–32 contradict the factor mentioned in statement I, the number of incidents the narrative contains.

117. c. The author is referring to a story in which a character or characters must make decisions about moral, or ethical, dilemmas. This can be inferred from a close reading of this paragraph and the next. She does not mention religion (choices **b** and **d**), nor does she intimate that moral dramas are always uplifting (choice **a**). A moral drama certainly may have action elements (choice **e**), though they may not predominate.

118. b. Wharton uses this paragraph to clarify the "rules" she established in the previous paragraph by describing more specifically that if a subject can be dealt with in a single retrospective flash, it is suitable for a short story while those that justify elaboration or need to suggest the lapse of time require the novel form. This clarification is not a contradiction (choice **a**), an example (choice **c**), a justification (choice **d**), or a new rule (choice **e**).

119. e. In lines 57–63, Wharton writes that short stories observe two unities: that of time (which is limited to achieve the effect of compactness and instantaneity), and that of point of view, telling the story through only one pair of eyes. The other characteristics are not mentioned in this passage.

120. b. This paragraph expands on the final idea of the previous paragraph, that of the limited point of view. In line 66, Wharton refers to the character who serves as reflector—thus, in line 69, *this reflecting mind* is that same person, the one who tells the story, the narrator.

121. c. After Midori's surprise appearance on New Year's Eve, word of her great artistry started spreading slowly. Midori's success has brought her other rewards. In 1992, she established a foundation called Midori and Friends. Midori is committed to giving other children the same kinds of opportunities that she had as a child. This nonprofit organization provides lessons to youngsters whose families can't afford to pay for music instruction. It also lends and inexpensively leases musical instruments to underprivileged kids.

122. a. Music historians believe that the Arab rabab is an ancestor of the modern violin. The rabab was a pear-shaped piece of wood on which one, two, or three strings were stretched. A musician played this instrument by drawing a bow across the strings.

123. d. This describes the ancient lyre, an ancestor of the violin.

124. a. The correct chronology of these events begins with the invention of the rabab. Later, by about 1200, it was combined with the lyre to make a rebec. The sarod also was developed as a result of the rabab being invented. Stradivari began making violins in the late 1600s. Paganini wrote his caprices in the late 1700s and early 1800s.

125. e. This was not one of the discoveries. However, smaller finds—a belt and buckle, a gold chain, shoes, locks, and a horse harness—provide rich details about the lives of Muscovites of the past. The citizens of the present are determined that history will not repeat itself and that the past will be uncovered and celebrated, rather than shrouded and forgotten. As a result of this respectful approach to modernization, Moscow, a city with more and more modern structures appearing all the time, remains largely distinguished by Byzantine cathedrals, fifteenth- and sixteenth-century stone buildings, and the ostentatious estates of the eighteenth and nineteenth centuries.

126. a. Peter Blume (1906–1992) was an American painter who emigrated from Russia to New York City in 1906. He painted *The Eternal City,* which depicts the process of rebuilding civilization out of its own destruction and portrays fascism under Mussolini's Italy.

127. c. In this 1937 painting, Picasso portrayed the bombing of Guernica by 28 bombers on April 26, 1937.

128. d. Most of Dali's work typified surrealism, which was popular during the 1920s and 1930s in Europe and often produced bizarre, dreamlike images.

129. b. In the 1910s, *form follows function* was effectively adopted by the Bauhaus school and applied to the production of everyday objects.

130. a. Georgia O'Keeffe, Thomas Hart Benton, and Edward Hopper were all American painters of the 1920s.

131. a. The folding screen, known in Japanese as *byobu,* is one of the most distinctive and beautiful forms of Japanese art. Screens could serve as room partitions or settings for special events. They offered large surfaces to paint, and many of Japan's finest artists worked in this format. This screen does not have bright colors or a gold leaf, so choices **c** and **d** are incorrect. However, large patches of unpainted space indicate that choice **a** is correct (thereby invalidating choice **e**—none of the above). Japan (in general) is a densely populated country, but this screen gives no indication of that, so choice **b** is incorrect.

132. e. The two songs take opposed views as to the value of enlisting and fighting in World War I. Choices **a** and **c** are supported by "Over There" but not by "I Didn't Raise My Boy to Be a Soldier." Choice **d** is incorrect for the opposite reason; it is proposed by Al Bryan but rejected by George Cohan. Some people believe choice **b**, but there is no evidence to support this position in these songs; everyone is allowed to express an opinion in a democratic society.

133. b. Metallurgy relates to the science and technology of working with metals and alloys.

134. c. Parks's photograph echoes the composition of Grant Wood's famous painting.

135. b. By portraying the women picketing outside the tall gates of the White House, the photographer is making a visual statement that concurs with choice **b**. The photograph provides no information to support any of the other answer choices.

136. c. The man stands on a bridge and is completely disregarded by passers-by.

137. a. This could be any man or woman, left to deal with his or her own horrors, suggesting that the reason the face is nondescript is to enable us all to identify with the screamer. There is no evidence that Munsch did not like to paint faces (choice **b**) or that he couldn't decide how to make the person look (choice **c**). He may have wanted the person to look innocent (choice **d**) or to create contrast between the face and the sky (choice **e**), but there is no suggestion of this in the review.

138. b. In the sixteenth century, almanacs included predictions on the weather based on previous weather patterns. Early almanacs were charts of the stars and did not include other information.

139. a. Almanacs printed in the United States from 1835 to 1856, called "Davy Crockett" almanacs, included many tall tales of the frontier.

140. e. In the beginning, almanacs showed the movement of the stars over a period of several years.

24 ▶ Literature

The literature questions on the CLEP Humanities exam assess your ability to comprehend, interpret, and contextualize literature throughout different historical periods. The literature section will test knowledge of drama, poetry, fiction, and nonfiction. You should be able to respond to themes and motifs, as well as analyze religious and philosophical ideas and their significance in shaping various cultures.

The following list consists of time periods accompanied by important literary events and people. With this list, you will become familiar with many important names, places, and cultural movements, which will help you tackle questions on the CLEP Humanities exam. While it is not complete, the objective of this list is to introduce you to a "snapshot" of literature throughout history.

▶ 800–400 B.C.E.

Events
- This period was dominated by Homer and other Greek tragedians.
- the epic tradition
- Drama begins.
- the lyric tradition

People
- Aeschylus
- Archilochus
- Aristophanes
- Demosthenes
- Euripedes (*Medea*)
- Homer (*The Iliad*, *The Odyssey*)
- Pindar
- Sappho
- Solon
- Sophocles (*Oedipus the King*)
- Tyrtaeus

▶ 250 B.C.E.–150 C.E.

Events
- Writers of the Roman Empire are most noted in this time period.

People
- Catullus
- Cicero
- Horace
- Julius Caesar
- Juvenal (Satires)
- Lucretius
- Marcus Aurelius (*The Meditations*)
- Ovid
- Petronius
- Seneca
- Suetonius (*Lives of the Twelve Caesars*)
- Tacitus (*Germania*)
- Virgil (*The Aeneid*)

▶ 450–1066 B.C.E.

Events
- the rise of haiku poetry
- *Beowulf*

People
- Murasaki Shibiku (*Tale of Genji*)

▶ 1066–1500

Events
- Provençal tradition of lyric poetry grows in Southern France.
- Romance genre is developed by Chrétien.
- invention of the printing press (1450)

People
- Boccacio (1313–1375)
- Geoffrey Chaucer (1343–1400)
- Dante (1307–1321)
- Gower
- Langland
- Petrarch (1304–1374)
- Rumi (1207–1273)

▶ 1500–1660

Events
- the Renaissance
- Elizabethan age (1558–1603)

- the Globe Theatre built (1599)
- Jacobean age (1603–1625)
- Caroline age (1625–1649)
- Commonwealth period (1649–1669)

People
- Miguel de Cervantes (1605–1615)
- John Donne (1572–1631)
- Ben Johnson (1572–1637)
- Ben Jonson
- Christopher Marlowe (1564–1593)
- Andrew Marvel (1621–1678)
- John Milton (1608–1674)
- Francois Rabelais (1490–1553)
- William Shakespeare (1564–1616)
- Sir Philip Sidney
- Edmund Spenser
- Henry Vaughan (1621–1695)

▶ 1660–1785

Events
- the neoclassical period
- the Restoration (1660–1700)
- the Augustan Age, "Age of Pope" (1700–1745)
- Puritan/Colonial literature in America (1650–1750)
- the first gothic novel, *The Castle of Otranto* (1764)

People
- Corneille
- Daniel Defoe (1660–1731)
- John Dryden
- Jonathan Edwards
- Thomas Gray
- Samuel Johnson (1709–1784)
- Moliére (1622–1673)
- Alexander Pope (1688–1744)

- Racine
- Jean-Jacques Rousseau (1712–1778)
- Jonathan Swift (1667–1745)
- Voltaire (1694–1778)
- Horace Walpole
- Johann Wolfgang von Goethe (1749–1832)

▶ 1750–1800

Events
- the Age of Reason (America)

People
- Patrick Henry
- Thomas Jefferson
- Thomas Paine
- Phyllis Wheatley (1753–1784)

▶ 1785–1830

Events
- the Romantic period
- the Gothic period (estimated 1785–1820, though it lasted longer in America)

People
- Jane Austen (1775–1817)
- Charles Baudelaire
- William Blake (1757–1827)
- Lord Byron (1788–1824)
- Samuel Taylor Coleridge (1772–1834)
- James Fenimore Cooper (1789–1851)
- Henry Fielding
- Johann Goethe
- John Keats (1795–1821)
- Klinger
- Samuel Richardson

- Dante Gabriel Rossetti
- Sir Walter Scott
- Mary Shelley (1797–1851)
- Percy Bysshe Shelley (1792–1822)
- Alfred, Lord Tennyson (1809–1892)
- William Wordsworth (1770–1850)

▶ 1832–1901

Events

- the Victorian period
- the Pre-Raphaelites (1848–1860)
- transcendentalism in America (1840–1860)
- age of realism in America (1865–1900)

People

- Bronson Alcott
- Louisa May Alcott
- Charlotte Bronte (1816–1855)
- Emily Brontë (1818–1848)
- Elizabeth Barrett Browning (1806–1861)
- Robert Browning (1812–1889)
- Kate Chopin
- James Fenimore Cooper
- Stephen Crane (1871–1900)
- Charles Dickens (1812–1870)
- Emily Dickinson (1830–1886)
- Fyodor Dostoevsky
- Frederick Douglass (1818–1895)
- Paul Lawrence Dunbar (1872–1906)
- George Eliot, a.k.a. Marian Evans
- Ralph Waldo Emerson
- Gustave Flaubert
- Margaret Fuller
- Nikolai Gogol
- Nathaniel Hawthorne
- Anthony Hopkins
- Victor Hugo

- Henrik Ibsen (1828–1906)
- Harriet Jacobs (1813–1897)
- Henry James (1843–1916)
- Herman Melville
- Charlotte Perkins Gilman
- Edgar Allan Poe (1809–1849)
- William Makepeace Thackeray
- Henry David Thoreau
- Leo Tolstoy
- Mark Twain, a.k.a. Samuel Clemens (1835–1910)
- Walt Whitman
- Emile Zola

▶ 1901–1914

Events

- the Edwardian period (Europe)
- naturalism (America)

People

- Joseph Conrad (1857–1924)
- W. E. B. DuBois
- Jack London (1876–1916)
- Edith Wharton (1862–1937)

▶ 1914–1945

Events

- the Modern period

People

- Sherwood Anderson
- Albert Camus (1913–1960)
- Willa Cather (1873–1947)
- T.S. Eliot
- William Faulkner (1897–1962)
- F. Scott Fitzgerald (1896–1940)

- Robert Frost (1874–1963)
- Ernest Hemingway (1899–1961)
- Langston Hughes (1906–1967)
- Zora Neale Hurston (1891–1960)
- Edna St. Vincent Millay (1892–1950)
- George Orwell (1903–1950)
- John Steinbeck (1902–1968)
- Tennessee Williams (1911–1983)

▶ 1950–Present

Events

- postmodernism
- the Beat movement
- slam poetry

People

- Rudolfo Anaya (1927–)
- Maya Angelou (1928–)

- Ray Bradbury (1920–)
- Sandra Cisneros (1954–)
- Ralph Ellison (1914–1994)
- Louise Erdrich (1954–)
- William Golding (1911–1993)
- Joseph Heller (1923–)
- Jack Kerouac (1922–1969)
- Ken Kesey (1935–2001)
- Maxine Hong Kingston (1940–)
- John Knowles (1926–)
- Arthur Miller (1915–2005)
- Toni Morrison (1931–)
- Eugene O'Neill (1888–1953)
- Sylvia Plath (1932–1963)
- Chaim Potok (1929–2002)
- J. D. Salinger (1919–)
- Amy Tan (1952–)
- Alice Walker (1944–)
- Elie Wiesel (1928–)

25 ▶ Fine Arts

The fine arts questions on the CLEP Humanities exam assess your ability to comprehend, interpret, and contextualize the visual and performing arts. These arts have served to express humanity's basic spiritual beliefs and the need to organize its environment from prehistoric times to the present.

The fine arts section of the CLEP Humanities exam will test knowledge of painting, sculpture, photography, music, film, dance, and architecture. You should be able to understand basic elements of form and content in the visual arts.

The following are brief descriptions of the different fine arts. Along with these descriptions are lists of important works, events, or people. These lists are not complete; however, the objective is to introduce you to a "snapshot" of fine arts throughout history.

▶ Sculpture

Sculpture encompasses the art of molding shapes into three-dimensional forms. Sculptures may be cast, which is when molten metals poured into molds to create bronze figures. They can also be cast from wood, stone, or marble, or shaped from clay. Today, sculptures are even welded together from pieces of metal.

Works
- *Ara Pacis* (Altar of Peace)
- bust of Emperor Constantine
- *Caesar Augustus*
- Charioteer from Delphi
- death mask of Pacal the Great
- *The Discus Thrower*
- Equestrian statue of Marcus Aurelius
- Hellenistic sculpture
- *Hermes*
- *The Kiss*
- Lady Justice statue
- Palette of King Narmer
- Pharaoh Akhenaton and his Queen, Nefertiti
- The Pieta
- Realism in Greek sculpting
- Savannah Bird Girl Statue
- sculptures at Tell Asmar
- the Sphinxes
- The Statue of David
- Statue of Liberty
- *The Thinker*
- *Trajan's Column*
- The *Venus de Milo*
- *Venus of Willendorf*
- *Winged Victory of Samothrace*

Sculptors
- Frederic Bartholdi
- Gian Lorenzo Bernini
- Constantin Brancusi
- Alexander Calder
- Anthony Caro
- Jay Hall Carpenter
- Christo
- Anthony Cragg

- Jacopo Della Quercia
- Donatello
- Marcel Duchamp
- David Evison
- Lorenzo Ghiberti
- Julio González
- Frederick Hart
- Youssef Howayek
- Philip King
- Karsten Konrad
- Norbert Kricke
- Jacques Lipshitz
- Tullio Lombardo
- Michelangelo
- Henry Moore
- Robert Morris
- Isamu Noguchi
- Andrea Pisano
- Praxiteles
- Man Ray
- Tilman Riemenschneider
- Auguste Rodin
- George Segal
- Sylvia Shaw Johnson
- David Smith
- William G. Tucker
- Verrocchio

▶ Painting

The art of painting is a two-dimensional way of re-creating reality or arranging abstract forms in color on a flat surface. Paintings have traditionally been created on surfaces like walls, wooden panels, canvas, paper, parchment, or decorative objects like vases.

Color is usually applied with a brush, using different pigments. Some of the more predominate forms of painting include watercolor, oil, tempera, and acrylic.

When creating a fresco, a painter applies pigment directly over wet plaster. This seals the piece on the surface (usually a wall or ceiling).

Other Types of Two-Dimensional Art

Two other types of two-dimensional art are drawing and printmaking. Drawing, which can be in color or black and white, is done with graphite, ink applied by pen or brush, chalk, or crayons. Printmaking is the process of making art by printing, normally on paper.

There are many variations on these methods, including etching, woodcuts, and lithographs. In these methods, multiple copies of a drawing or print are made by creating either a raised or recessed surface that takes ink and pressing paper against the surface.

Works
- *Adoration*
- *Both Members of This Club*
- *Campbell Soup Cans*
- *Cliff Dwellers*
- *Dream of Love*
- *Drowning Girl*
- *Flag*
- Frescoes of St. Francis's life at Assisi
- *Just What Is It That Makes Today's Homes So Different, So Appealing?*
- *The Kiss*
- *Le Guitariste*
- *Magenta, Black, Green on Orange*
- *Mona Lisa*
- *One: Number 31, 1950*
- *People of Chilmark*
- *Portrait of Master Bill*
- *Portrait of Picasso*
- *Ralph's Diner*
- *The Scream*
- Sistine Chapel ceiling
- *Snow in New York*
- *St. Anne and the Virgin*
- *Still Life*
- Trinity fresco
- *View of Toledo*
- *Woman with a Guitar*

Artists
- Linda Bacon
- George Bellows
- Bernini
- Botticelli
- François Boucher
- Carpaccio
- Mary Cassatt
- Paul Cezanne
- Chuck Close
- Jacques Louis David
- Leonardo da Vinci
- Eugene Delacroix
- Audrey Flack
- Fragonard
- Jane Frank
- Theodore Gericault
- El Greco
- Laura Marie Greenwood
- Robert Henri
- Edward Hopper
- Jasper Johns
- Gustav Klimt
- Lee Krasner
- Roy Lichtenstein
- Reginald Marsh
- Henri Matisse
- Claude Monet
- Pablo Picasso

- Jackson Pollock
- Poussin
- Raphael
- Rembrandt
- Pierre Auguste Renoir
- Rubens
- Vincent van Gogh
- Vasari
- Jan Vermeer
- Andy Warhol

Events

- early Renaissance (1350–1500)
- high Renaissance (1500–1520)
- Venetian Renaissance (1500–1600)
- baroque (1600–1700)
- realistic painting (1720–1800)
- French classicism and romanticism (1800s)
- Impressionism (1800s–early 1900s)
- Cubism (early 1900s)
- expressionism (mid-1900s)
- American realism and regionalism (1930s)
- abstract expressionism (1950s)
- pop art (1950s–1960s)
- photorealism (1960s–present)

▶ Photography

Photography is an artistic process that records pictures by capturing light on a light-sensitive medium, such as a film or electronic sensor. Different forms of photography include color, black and white, and digital. Photography has many uses for both business and pleasure. As such, it can be viewed as a commercial and artistic endeavor.

Events

- accidental creation of the first photosensitive compound (1727)
- The stereoscopic era begins (1855).
- Direct positive images on glass (ambrotypes) and metal (tintypes or ferrotypes) become popular in the United States (1855–1857).
- The camera obscura is combined with photosensitive paper (1816).
- A permanent (negative) image is created using paper soaked in silver chloride and fixed with a salt solution (1834).
- Louis Daguerre is awarded a pension by the French government in exchange for publication of methods and the rights by others to use the Daguerreotype process (1837).
- Calotype process is patented (1841).
- Carte-de-visite photography is developed in Paris, leading to worldwide boom in portrait studios for the next decade (1854).
- The color separation method is first demonstrated (1861).
- Mathew Brady and his staff photograph images of the American Civil War (1861–1865).
- U.S. Congress sends photographers out to the West (1870s).
- The "dry plate" process is proposed (1871).
- The first Kodak camera is created (1888).
- Jacob Riis publishes *How the Other Half Lives*, images of tenement life in New York City (1890).
- J. P. Morgan finances Edward Curtis to document the traditional culture of the North American Indian (1906).
- Lewis Hine is hired by the U.S. National Child Labor Committee to photograph children working in mills (1909).
- inception of Technicolor for movies, where three black and white negatives were made in the same camera under different filters (1932)

- Fuji photo film founded (1934)
- The camera phone introduced in Japan by Sharp/J-Phone (2000).

People

- Ansel Adams
- Alhazen, aka Abu Ali al-Hasan Ibn al-Haitham
- Diane Arbus
- Frederick Scott Archer
- Aristotle
- Giovanni Battista Della Porta
- Margaret Bourke-White
- Mathew Brady
- Robert Capa
- James Clerk-Maxwell
- Imogen Cunningham
- Louis Daguerre
- Adolphe Disderi
- Elsa Dorfman
- George Eastman
- Walker Evans
- Reinerus Gemma-Frisius
- Ducas de Hauron
- William Jackson
- Johannes Kepler
- Dorothea Lange
- Mo-Ti
- Eadweard Muybridge
- Carl Mydans
- Nicéphore Niépce
- Tim O'Sullivan
- Arthur Rothstein
- Professor J. Schulze
- W. Eugene Smith
- Alfred Stieglitz
- Hiroshi Sugimoto
- Henry Fox Talbot
- Felix Toumachon
- Willard Van Dyke
- Roman Vishniac
- Thomas Wedgwood
- Edward Weston

▶ Architecture

Architecture is the organization of space and form to provide structure, whether for living, working, worshipping, or civil needs. Architectural styles have always been connected to technology, building materials, and community needs.

Works

- Angkor, Cambodia
- Athenian Treasury
- Badshahi Mosque, Pakistan
- Brunelleschi
- Burj Dubai
- the Cache at Deir el Bahri
- construction of pyramids in Egypt
- the Empire State Building
- Erectheion
- Europe's Gate, Madrid
- Fourth Temple of Hera
- the Freedom Tower
- Gare do Oriente Railway Station
- Gothic cathedrals
- Great Pyramid at Giza
- Great Wall of China
- the Karnak temple complex
- King Tut's Tomb
- Knossos
- La Rotonda
- Lenin's Mausoleum
- Lion Gate
- Machu Picchu
- Ollantaytambo
- the Parthenon

- Perspolis Palace of Persia
- the Petronas Twin Towers
- Saint Basil's Cathedral
- The Sears Tower
- Simonas Petras Monastery
- Sphinx of Giza
- Step Pyramid Complex
- Stoa of Attalus
- Sydney Opera House
- Taipei 101
- Temple of Apollo
- Temple of Artemis
- Temple of Athena Nike
- Temples of Paestum
- Theater at Epidauros
- Tombs of the Nobles
- The Turning Torso
- The Wainwright Building
- Wells Cathedral, England
- The White House

Events

- In ancient Egypt, Greece, and Rome, civilizations built enormous temples and shrines (3000–337 B.C.E.).
- European architecture moved from the rectangular basilica forms to the classically inspired Byzantine style (373–500 C.E.).
- As Rome spread across Europe, heavier, stocky Romanesque architecture with rounded arches emerged (500–1200).
- Innovative builders created the great cathedrals of Europe (1200–1400).
- A return to classical ideas ushered an "age of 'awakening'" in Italy, France, and England (1400–1600).
- In Italy, the Baroque style is reflected in opulent and dramatic churches with irregular shapes and extravagant ornamentation (1600–1800).

- During the last phase of the Baroque period, builders constructed elegant white buildings with sweeping curves (1650–1790).
- European settlers in the New World borrowed ideas from their homelands to create their own brand of architecture (1600–1780).
- Georgian was a stately, symmetrical style that dominated in Great Britain and Ireland and influenced building styles in the American colonies (1720–1800).
- A renewed interest in ideas of the Renaissance inspired a return of classical shapes in Europe, Great Britain, and the United States (1750–1880).
- Antebellum homes in the American South were often built in the Greek Revival style (1790–1850).
- Victorian styles include Gothic Revival, Italianate, Stick, Eastlake, Queen Anne, Romanesque, and Second Empire (1840–1900).
- The Arts and Crafts movement revived an interest in handicrafts and sought a spiritual connection with the surrounding environment, both natural and manmade (1860–1900).
- Art Nouveau was first expressed in fabrics and graphic design, and the style spread to architecture and furniture in the 1890s. Art Nouveau buildings often have asymmetrical shapes, arches, and decorative surfaces with curved, plantlike designs (1890–1914).
- Zigzag patterns and vertical lines create a dramatic effect on jazz-age Art Deco buildings (1925–1935).
- Twentieth-century trends include art moderne and the Bauhaus school coined by Walter Gropius, deconstructivism, formalism, modernism, structuralism, and postmodernism (1900–present).

People

- Abbot Suger
- Anthemius of Tralles
- Apollodorus of Damascus
- Callicrates
- Leonardo da Vinci
- Renaud de Cormont
- Thomas de Cormont
- Demetrios
- Frank Gehry
- Villard de Honnecourt
- Iktinos
- Imhotep
- Isidore of Miletus
- Kallikrates
- Jean de Loup
- Lu Ban
- Robert de Luzarches
- Marcus Agrippa
- Mnesicles
- Jean d'Orbais
- Paeonius
- Andrea Palladio
- Gaucher de Reims
- Rhoikos
- Senemut
- Bernard de Soisons
- Louis Sullivan
- Mies van der Rohe
- Vernacular
- Vitruvius
- John Webb
- Elizabeth Mytton Wilbraham
- Christopher Wren
- Frank Lloyd Wright
- Yu Hao

▶ Music

The art of music is the arrangement of sounds for voice and musical instruments. Throughout history, music has been a byproduct of a community or ethnic group's need for expression or celebration. Music has often been linked to storytelling and poetry.

People

- Louis Armstrong
- Johann Sebastian Bach
- Joan Baez
- the Beach Boys
- The Beatles
- Ludwig van Beethoven
- Leonard Bernstein
- David Bowie
- James Brown
- Francesca Caccini
- Jose Carreras
- The Clash
- Patsy Cline
- Phil Collins
- John Coltrane
- Elvis Costello
- Bing Crosby
- Crosby, Stills, Nash, and Young
- Celia Cruz
- The Cure
- Dee-Lite
- Depeche Mode
- Joaquin Desprez
- Destiny's Child
- Placido Domingo
- The Doors
- Guillaume Dufay
- Bob Dylan
- Duke Ellington
- George Gershwin

- Gilbert and Sullivan
- Pope Gregory the Great
- The Grateful Dead
- Guido of Arezzo
- George Frederick Handel
- Jimi Hendrix
- Faith Hill
- Billie Holiday
- Janet Jackson
- Janis Joplin
- Jefferson Airplane
- Carole King
- Hector Lavoe
- Annie Lenox
- Loretta Lynn
- Lully
- Madonna
- Bob Marley
- Felix Mendelssohn
- Glenn Miller
- Claudio Monteverdi
- Jelly Roll Morton
- Wolfgang Amadeus Mozart
- Muddy Waters
- Roy Orbison
- Outkast
- Dolly Parton
- Luciano Pavarotti
- The Police
- Elvis Presley
- Prince
- Public Enemy
- Tito Puente
- Purcell
- Queen
- Rameau
- The Ramones
- Lou Reed
- The Rolling Stones

- Gioacchino Rossini
- Franz Peter Schubert
- Robert Schumann
- Selena
- Tupac Shakur
- Carly Simon
- Simon and Garfunkel
- Nina Simone
- Frank Sinatra
- Sly and the Family Stone
- Bessie Smith
- Patti Smith
- The Supremes
- Troubadours
- U2
- Andrew Lloyd Webber
- The Who
- Stevie Wonder

Works

- "Amazing Grace"
- "The Barber of Seville"
- "Blood on the Fields"
- "Down Hearted Blues"
- "Euridice"
- Gregorian chants
- "The Mikado"
- "Moon River"
- "Oh, Susannah"
- "Porgy and Bess"
- "Rapper's Delight"
- "Rhapsody in Blue"
- "Stars and Stripes Forever"
- "Swan Lake"
- "Thriller"
- "Wedding March"
- "When Johnny Comes Marching Home"
- "White Christmas"

Events

- The spread of Christianity in the western world spurred the development of European music (325 B.C.E.).
- The English Madrigal School is firmly established (1588).
- Beethoven completes his "Symphony No. 5," which many consider the most popular classical work ever written (1807).
- The slave trade introduces West African rhythms, work songs, chants, and spirituals to America (1860).
- Thomas Edison invents sound recording (1877).
- Carnegie Hall opens in New York (1891).
- Ragtime, a combination of West Indian rhythm and European music, is born (1896).
- *Billboard* magazine publishes a list of the most popular vaudeville songs (1913).
- the swing era of the 1930s and 1940s
- Electric guitars debut (1936).
- The National Academy of Recording Arts and Sciences sponsors the first Grammy Award ceremony for music recorded (1959).
- Woodstock music festival occurs (1969).
- The Jamaican film *The Harder They Come,* starring Jimmy Cliff, launches the popularity of reggae music in the United States (1973).
- Punk roars out of Britain during the late 1970s, with bands such as the Sex Pistols and the Clash expressing nihilistic and anarchistic views in response to a lack of opportunity in Britain, boredom, and antipathy for the bland music of the day.
- *Saturday Night Fever* sparks the disco inferno (1977).
- The Sugar Hill Gang releases the first commercial rap hit, "Rapper's Delight," bringing rap off the New York streets and into the popular music scene (1979).
- John Lennon of the Beatles is shot dead in New York City (1980).
- MTV goes on the air running around the clock music videos, debuting with "Video Killed the Radio Star" (1981).
- Michael Jackson releases *Thriller,* which sells more than 25 million copies, becoming the biggest-selling album in history (1982).
- The Rock and Roll Hall of Fame Museum opens in Cleveland, Ohio (1995).
- Winton Marsalis wins first the Pulitzer Prize for jazz (1997).

▶ Dance

The art form of dance is based on movement and expression. Dance is performed by individuals, couples, or groups. In history, folk and tribal dancing were connected to communal celebration or religious ritual. The dance forms of ballet and musical theater are choreographed to implement strict steps and gestures.

Types

- Bachata
- ballet
- ballroom
- bellydance
- bhangra
- breakdance
- Capoiera
- ceremonial dance
- cha-cha
- country/western dance
- cumbia
- folk dance
- foxtrot
- Irish step dance
- jazz

- jitterbug
- jive
- krumping
- Lindy hop
- line dance
- Mambo
- meringue
- Paso Doble
- polka
- pom
- quickstep
- ritual dance
- rumba
- salsa
- samba
- step dance
- square dance
- swing
- tango
- tap
- waltz
- Western promenade dances

Dancers

- Fred Astaire
- Mikhail Baryshnikov
- Sammy Davis, Jr.
- Isadora Duncan
- Margot Fonteyn
- Savion Glover
- Martha Graham
- Gregory Hines
- Michael Jackson
- Gene Kelly
- Arthur Murray
- Rudolf Nureyev
- Anna Pavlova
- Twyla Tharpe
- John Travolta

Events

- Dance Biennial in France, largest gathering of U.S. dance companies (1990)
- Documentary film *Rize* is released, highlighting two distinct styles of dance—clowning and krumping (2005).
- *Mad Hot Ballroom,* a documentary film by director Marilyn Agrelo about a ballroom dance program for fifth graders in the New York City public school system, premiered (2005).

▶ Film

Film is an art form that is produced by recording images from the world with cameras, or by creating images using animation techniques or special effects. This art form is credited as

- a source of popular entertainment
- a powerful method for educating audiences
- a universal communication device

Films have become popular worldwide by using dubbing or subtitles that translate the dialogue into various languages. There are dozens of film genres, including documentary, film noir, western, action, comedy, horror, and musical.

Works

- *Ben-Hur*
- *The Birth of a Nation*
- *The Blair Witch Project*
- *Breakfast at Tiffany's*
- *Casablanca*
- *Citizen Kane*
- *Forrest Gump*
- *Gone with the Wind*
- *The Great Train Robbery*

- *Harry Potter and the Sorcerer's Stone*
- *Lost in Yonkers*
- *Midnight Cowboy*
- *My Big Fat Greek Wedding*
- *Philadelphia*
- *Potemkin*
- *Psycho*
- *One Flew Over the Cuckoo's Nest*
- *On the Waterfront*
- *Saturday Night Fever*
- *Schindler's List*
- *Shrek*
- *The Sound of Music*
- *Star Wars*
- *West Side Story*

People

- Marlon Brando
- Charlie Chaplin
- James Dean
- Thomas Edison
- Sergei Eisenstein
- Greta Garbo
- Jean-Luc Godard
- Tom Hanks
- Audrey Hepburn
- Alfred Hitchcock
- Elia Kazan
- Auguste and Louis Lumière
- Marilyn Monroe
- Edwin S. Porter
- Roberto Rossellini
- George C. Scott
- Steven Spielberg
- Spencer Tracy
- Orson Welles

Events

- The Edison Corporation establishes the first motion-picture studio, a Kinetograph production center nicknamed the Black Maria, which is slang for a police van (1894).
- The first movie theater opens in Pittsburgh, Pennsylvania (1905).
- Walt Disney creates his first cartoon, *Alice's Wonderland* (1924).
- The Academy Awards are distributed for the first time (1928).
- As head of the Motion Picture Producers and Distributors of America, William Hays establishes a code of decency that outlines what is acceptable in films (1930).
- The Cannes Film Festival debuts in France (1946).
- The Hollywood Ten—a group of writers, producers and directors—are called as witnesses in the House Committee's investigation of un-American activities. They are jailed for contempt of Congress when they refuse to disclose whether they are Communists (1948).
- At the 1972 Academy Awards, Sacheen Littlefeather stands in for Marlon Brando and refuses his Best Actor Oscar for his role in *The Godfather* as protest of the U.S. government's treatment of Native Americans (1973).
- The Steadicam is used for the first time in *Rocky* (1976).
- *Titanic* is released; it is the most expensive film of all time, costing between $250 and $300 million (1997).

SECTION

6 ▶ Practice Tests

CLEP English Composition Practice Test 1

You are now familiar with the kinds of questions and answer formats you will see on the official CLEP English Composition exam. Now, take Practice Test 1 to identify any areas that you may need to review in more depth before the test day.

On this practice test, you will encounter 50 questions and one essay that are similar to the type you will find on the official CLEP English Composition with Essay exam. The questions are organized into three content areas:

- Identifying Sentence Errors
- Improving Sentences
- Revising Works in Progress

To simulate the test conditions, use the time constraints of the official CLEP English Composition exam. Allow yourself 90 minutes to complete this practice test.

Remember, on the official CLEP, there is no penalty for incorrect answers, so always make a guess if you are unsure of an answer.

When you are finished, check the answer key on page 429 carefully to assess your results.

► CLEP English Composition Practice Test 1

1.	ⓐ ⓑ ⓒ ⓓ ⓔ		21.	ⓐ ⓑ ⓒ ⓓ ⓔ		41.	ⓐ ⓑ ⓒ ⓓ ⓔ
2.	ⓐ ⓑ ⓒ ⓓ ⓔ		22.	ⓐ ⓑ ⓒ ⓓ ⓔ		42.	ⓐ ⓑ ⓒ ⓓ ⓔ
3.	ⓐ ⓑ ⓒ ⓓ ⓔ		23.	ⓐ ⓑ ⓒ ⓓ ⓔ		43.	ⓐ ⓑ ⓒ ⓓ ⓔ
4.	ⓐ ⓑ ⓒ ⓓ ⓔ		24.	ⓐ ⓑ ⓒ ⓓ ⓔ		44.	ⓐ ⓑ ⓒ ⓓ ⓔ
5.	ⓐ ⓑ ⓒ ⓓ ⓔ		25.	ⓐ ⓑ ⓒ ⓓ ⓔ		45.	ⓐ ⓑ ⓒ ⓓ ⓔ
6.	ⓐ ⓑ ⓒ ⓓ ⓔ		26.	ⓐ ⓑ ⓒ ⓓ ⓔ		46.	ⓐ ⓑ ⓒ ⓓ ⓔ
7.	ⓐ ⓑ ⓒ ⓓ ⓔ		27.	ⓐ ⓑ ⓒ ⓓ ⓔ		47.	ⓐ ⓑ ⓒ ⓓ ⓔ
8.	ⓐ ⓑ ⓒ ⓓ ⓔ		28.	ⓐ ⓑ ⓒ ⓓ ⓔ		48.	ⓐ ⓑ ⓒ ⓓ ⓔ
9.	ⓐ ⓑ ⓒ ⓓ ⓔ		29.	ⓐ ⓑ ⓒ ⓓ ⓔ		49.	ⓐ ⓑ ⓒ ⓓ ⓔ
10.	ⓐ ⓑ ⓒ ⓓ ⓔ		30.	ⓐ ⓑ ⓒ ⓓ ⓔ		50.	ⓐ ⓑ ⓒ ⓓ ⓔ
11.	ⓐ ⓑ ⓒ ⓓ ⓔ		31.	ⓐ ⓑ ⓒ ⓓ ⓔ			
12.	ⓐ ⓑ ⓒ ⓓ ⓔ		32.	ⓐ ⓑ ⓒ ⓓ ⓔ			
13.	ⓐ ⓑ ⓒ ⓓ ⓔ		33.	ⓐ ⓑ ⓒ ⓓ ⓔ			
14.	ⓐ ⓑ ⓒ ⓓ ⓔ		34.	ⓐ ⓑ ⓒ ⓓ ⓔ			
15.	ⓐ ⓑ ⓒ ⓓ ⓔ		35.	ⓐ ⓑ ⓒ ⓓ ⓔ			
16.	ⓐ ⓑ ⓒ ⓓ ⓔ		36.	ⓐ ⓑ ⓒ ⓓ ⓔ			
17.	ⓐ ⓑ ⓒ ⓓ ⓔ		37.	ⓐ ⓑ ⓒ ⓓ ⓔ			
18.	ⓐ ⓑ ⓒ ⓓ ⓔ		38.	ⓐ ⓑ ⓒ ⓓ ⓔ			
19.	ⓐ ⓑ ⓒ ⓓ ⓔ		39.	ⓐ ⓑ ⓒ ⓓ ⓔ			
20.	ⓐ ⓑ ⓒ ⓓ ⓔ		40.	ⓐ ⓑ ⓒ ⓓ ⓔ			

▶ Part I: Multiple Choice

Identifying Sentence Errors

Directions: The following sentences test your knowledge of grammar, usage, diction (choice of words), and idiom. Some sentences are correct as written. No sentence contains more than one error.

You will find that the error, if there is one, is underlined and lettered. Assume that elements of the sentence that are not underlined are correct and cannot be changed. In choosing answers, follow the requirements of standard written English.

If there is an error, selected the one underlined part that must be changed to make the sentence correct. If there is no error, select choice **e**.

1. "There is a famous quote by Ernest Hemingway that <u>says,</u> 'Do not ask <u>for whom</u> the bell <u>tolls; it tolls for thee</u>,'"
$\quad\quad\quad\quad\quad\quad\quad\quad\quad\quad\quad\quad\quad\quad\quad\quad$ **a** $\quad\quad\quad\quad\quad\quad$ **b** $\quad\quad\quad\quad\quad\quad\quad\quad\quad$ **c**

explained Mrs. Hutchinson to her <u>English class</u>. <u>No error.</u>
$\quad\quad\quad\quad\quad\quad\quad\quad\quad\quad\quad\quad$ **d** $\quad\quad\quad\quad$ **e**

2. The <u>worlds</u> greatest <u>speeches</u> have <u>enduring messages</u> that speak to <u>people's hearts</u> as well as their minds.
$\quad\quad$ **a** $\quad\quad\quad\quad\quad\quad$ **b** $\quad\quad\quad\quad\quad$ **c** $\quad\quad\quad\quad\quad\quad\quad\quad$ **d**

<u>No error.</u>
e

3. <u>Although both of us</u> bicker on a daily basis, <u>Katherine and myself</u> agree on some important things
$\quad$ **a** $\quad\quad\quad\quad\quad\quad\quad\quad\quad\quad\quad\quad\quad\quad\quad\quad$ **b**

<u>such as pineapple</u> should never go on pizza, Pink Floyd is still the best band ever, and <u>there is no nicer city</u>
$\quad$ **c** $\quad\quad\quad\quad\quad\quad\quad\quad\quad\quad\quad\quad\quad\quad\quad\quad\quad\quad\quad\quad\quad\quad\quad\quad\quad$ **d**

on the planet than Portland, Oregon. <u>No error.</u>
$\quad\quad\quad\quad\quad\quad\quad\quad\quad\quad\quad\quad\quad\quad$ **e**

4. The <u>most popular teachers</u> at the school <u>was the ones</u> that <u>graded fairly</u>, taught passionately, cared deeply,
$\quad\quad$ **a** $\quad\quad\quad\quad\quad\quad\quad\quad\quad\quad\quad$ **b** $\quad\quad\quad\quad$ **c**

and communicated <u>effectively</u> with all of the students. <u>No error.</u>
$\quad\quad\quad\quad\quad\quad\quad$ **d** $\quad\quad\quad\quad\quad\quad\quad\quad\quad\quad\quad$ **e**

5. <u>Each of the vitamin supplements</u> the nutritionist suggested <u>were supposed</u> to be taken with food,
$\quad$ **a** $\quad\quad\quad\quad\quad\quad\quad\quad\quad\quad\quad\quad\quad\quad\quad\quad$ **b**

<u>so she planned</u> to take all of them <u>when she ate dinner</u> that evening. <u>No error.</u>
$\quad$ **c** $\quad\quad\quad\quad\quad\quad\quad\quad\quad$ **d** $\quad\quad\quad\quad\quad\quad\quad\quad$ **e**

6. <u>Although</u> the news media often portrays a different picture, according to the Bureau of Justice <u>statistics,</u>
$\quad$ **a** $\quad\quad\quad\quad\quad\quad\quad\quad\quad\quad\quad\quad\quad\quad\quad\quad\quad\quad\quad\quad\quad\quad\quad\quad\quad\quad\quad\quad$ **b**

<u>the number of school shootings are</u> actually on a steady decline and <u>has been</u> for the last several years. <u>No error.</u>
$\quad$ **c** $\quad\quad\quad\quad\quad\quad\quad\quad\quad\quad\quad\quad\quad\quad\quad\quad\quad\quad\quad$ **d** $\quad\quad\quad\quad\quad\quad\quad\quad\quad\quad\quad$ **e**

7. Whenever <u>anyone calls</u> Dr. Hutton's cell phone, <u>he answers</u> because he knows that while the caller
                 a   **b**

might be a telemarketer, <u>he or she</u> may also be calling with what <u>they consider</u> a life or death situation.
                        c   **d**

<u>No error.</u>
  e

8. Once <u>a person</u> has decided what kind of career to pursue, it is essential that <u>he or she explore</u> the different
      a   **b**

educational possibilities <u>open to you</u> in order to make the wisest and most compatible choice with
                    c

<u>one's interests</u>, talents, and abilities. <u>No error.</u>
  d   **e**

9. The saying that there are <u>no certainties</u> in life other than <u>death and taxes</u> is an <u>uncannily</u> correct one, as
                       a   **b**   **c**

<u>everything else</u> contains some element of choice. <u>No error.</u>
  d   **e**

10. Lilah slipped on <u>each pair</u> of snow boots; she <u>could not decide</u> <u>which</u> was the <u>most comfortable</u> to wear
                   a   **b**   **c**   **d**

when she was out in the snow. <u>No error.</u>
                          e

11. <u>Although the thunderstorm</u> <u>had passed</u> almost an hour ago, there <u>wasn't no</u> chance of the sun <u>returning</u>
      a   **b**   **c**   **d**

any time that afternoon. <u>No error.</u>
                    e

12. It <u>quickly became clear</u> that the strange image Belinda <u>had seen earlier</u> that afternoon had <u>actually been</u>
        a   **b**   **c**

some kind of <u>allusion</u>. <u>No error.</u>
          d   **e**

13. The <u>new hospital intern</u> spent his entire night <u>filling out</u> charts, <u>calming frightened patients</u>, emptying
      a   **b**   **c**

multiple bedpans, <u>mopped up</u> a number of spills, and listening to nurses complain about the doctors.
                    d

<u>No error.</u>
  e

14. Bruce Willis, a famous actor <u>and who has starred</u> in a series of *Die Hard* movies, <u>has been entertaining audiences</u>
  a   b

ever since his first years on <u>television's</u> *Moonlighting,* where <u>he played the role</u> of detective David Addison.
                               c   d

<u>No error.</u>
  e

15. The architect had just rolled up <u>his blueprints</u> when someone knocked on the door, <u>putting a rubber band</u>
                                         a   b

around them and <u>putting them</u> into a portfolio to keep them in the <u>right order</u>. <u>No error.</u>
                  c   d   e

16. The Wallace Street Bookstore <u>is a fascinating place</u> that specializes in <u>highly collectible</u> books <u>sold</u> by
                                       a   b   c

helpful volunteers <u>with surprisingly high prices</u>. <u>No error.</u>
                    d   e

17. Thanks to the <u>incredible rise</u> in department store-type competition, many small, <u>independent bookstores</u>
                       a   b

have either <u>going out of business</u> or been <u>forced to file bankruptcy</u>. <u>No error.</u>
             c   d   e

18. The <u>nonstop presidential coverage</u> is being shown on <u>every single television channel</u>, <u>so</u> we have no choice
             a   b   c

but to <u>watch it or find something else</u> to do. <u>No error.</u>
         d   e

19. It did not take me long to realize that <u>instead</u> of spending <u>our entire afternoon</u> shooting hoops, we
                                                a   b

<u>should of been</u> studying for <u>our history midterms</u>. <u>No error.</u>
  c   d   e

20. This afternoon, I <u>finally</u> took the time to pull out some <u>stationary</u> and write a <u>long letter</u> to my
                           a   b   c

grandparents <u>who live</u> in Florida. <u>No error.</u>
              d   e

Improving Sentences

Directions: In each of the following sentences, part of the sentence or the entire sentence is underlined. After each sentence, you will find five versions of the underlined part. Choice **a** repeats the original; the other four are different.

Choose the answer that best expresses the meaning of the original sentence. If you think the original is better than any of the other alternatives, choose **a**; otherwise, choose one of the others. Your choice should produce the most effective sentence—one that is clear and precise, without awkwardness or ambiguity.

21. <u>My homework assignment is late and that is because</u> I had to work an extra shift last night and did not get home until long after midnight.
    a. My homework assignment is late and that is because
    b. My homework assignment is late was because
    c. My homework assignment is late because
    d. My homework assignment is late and that was because
    e. My homework assignment late because

22. <u>Beeping constantly to signal multiple voice messages, I reached for my cell phone to see who was calling so often.</u>
    a. Beeping constantly to signal multiple voice messages, I reached for my cell phone to see who was calling so often.
    b. Beeping constantly to signal multiple voice messages, to see who was calling so often, I reached for my cell phone.
    c. To see who was calling so often, I reached for my cell phone, beeping constantly to signal multiple voice messages.
    d. Who was calling so often, I reached for my cell phone to see as it was beeping constantly to signal multiple voice messages.
    e. I reached for my cell phone to see who was calling so often because it was beeping constantly to signal multiple voice messages.

23. The weekend <u>had finally arrived I could not wait</u> to get started on washing and detailing my car because I had only had it for two weeks.
    a. had finally arrived I could not wait
    b. had finally arrived; I could not wait
    c. had finally arrived, I could not wait
    d. had finally arrived: I could not wait
    e. had finally arrived although I could not wait

24. <u>If one is patient enough,</u> it is possible to get a squirrel to come all the way to your back door and wait for you to sit down and hand feed it.
    a. If one is patient enough
    b. If you is patient enough
    c. If one were patient enough
    d. If you are patient enough
    e. If one are patient enough

25. The toddler was having a wonderful time playing with the blocks, creating a fort, building a wall, and <u>he arranged the blocks in order of height</u> during the afternoon.

   a. he arranged the blocks in order of height
   b. he arranges the blocks in order of height
   c. arranging the blocks in order of height
   d. arranges the blocks in order of height
   e. he has arranged the blocks in order of height

26. Having the confidence to do both radio and television interviews <u>with poise is a skill that most people never get the chance to actually develop.</u>

   a. with poise is a skill that most people never get the chance to actually develop.
   b. with poise are a skill that most people never get the chance to actually develop.
   c. with poise, is a skill that most people never get the chance to actually develop.
   d. with poise are skills that most people never get the chance to actually develop.
   e. with poise were skills that most people never get the chance to actually develop.

27. <u>Running the 5k race faster than anyone else in the high school</u> had ever attempted and set a new state record.

   a. Running the 5k race faster than anyone else in the high school
   b. He ran the 5k race faster than anyone else in the high school
   c. Running the 5k race he was faster than anyone else in the high school
   d. He runs the 5k race faster than anyone else in the high school
   e. He did run the 5k race faster than anyone else in the high school

28. I had to admit that the baby was <u>cute as a button and a dead ringer for her father.</u>

   a. cute as a button and a dead ringer for her father.
   b. cute and a lot like her father.
   c. adorable and looked just like her father.
   d. cute as a button and looked like her dad.
   e. adorable and a dead ringer for her father.

29. The new student, <u>which was from a remote area in China,</u> joined Lisa's writing group and introduced herself to everyone.

   a. which was from a remote area in China
   b. that was from a remote area in China
   c. which is from a remote area in China
   d. who was from a remote area in China
   e. who were from a remote area in China

30. Although snail mail continues to serve certain business functions, person-to-person communication <u>has been taken over by e-mails,</u> and letter writing is becoming an ancient art.

   a. has been taken over by e-mails
   b. have been taken over by e-mails
   c. had been taken over by e-mails
   d. are taken over by e-mails
   e. is been taken over by e-mails

Revising Works in Progress

Directions: Each of the following passages consists of numbered sentences. Because the passages are part of longer writing samples, they do not necessarily constitute a complete discussion of the issues presented.

   Read each passage carefully and answer the questions that follow. The questions test your awareness of a writer's purpose and of characteristics of prose that are important to good writing.

Use the following passage to answer questions 31–35.

(1) Do you know people who shriek and run if faced with a snake or spider? (2) Perhaps you are one of those people yourself. (3) In a recent study from the University of Queensland, researchers have looked closely at why certain people have specific phobias. (4) Although the original hypothesis of why people are so afraid of these creatures put it down to evolutionary instinct, this study has a different theory.

(5) This new idea properly places the blame not on human instinct but on the media. (6) Dr. Helena Purkis, one of the researchers, stated that "people tend to be exposed to a lot of negative information regarding snakes and spiders, and we argue this makes them more likely to be associated with phobia." (7) Clearly, the blame is on newspapers and magazines.

(8) What is the purpose of this study? (9) The researchers hope to find keys to what factors make a person phobic. (10) Even though they hope this information will help them treat and counsel these people. (11) "[This] could give us some information about the way people need to deal with snakes and spiders in order to minimize negative emotional responses," she added.

31. Which of the following is a valid criticism of the passage as a whole?
   a. It is inconsistent in its use of tenses.
   b. It is organized in an illogical order.
   c. It switches from first person to third.
   d. It is biased in its approach to the theory.
   e. It does not include any quotes from authorities.

32. The quotation in sentence 6
   a. supports the idea in the previous sentence.
   b. is completely irrelevant and should be deleted.
   c. proves that the study was really performed.
   d. shifts the focus of the passage to past research studies.
   e. demonstrates why Dr. Purkis participated in this study.

33. What should be done with sentence 7?
   a. It should be left as it is.
   b. It should be removed entirely.
   c. It should be moved to the next paragraph.
   d. It should be rewritten from third person to first person.
   e. It should be enclosed within a set of parentheses.

34. Which of the following is the best way to combine sentences 8 and 9 (reproduced here)?
   What is the purpose of this study? The researchers hope to find keys to what factors make a person phobic.
   a. What is the purpose of this study, it is to help researchers find keys to what factors make a person phobic.
   b. The researchers hope to find keys to what factors make a person phobic and that is the purpose of the study.
   c. The purpose of this study is to help researchers find keys to what factors make a person phobic.
   d. The researchers, which is the purpose of the study, hope to find keys to what factors make a person phobic.
   e. What factors make a person phobic is what researchers hope to find the keys to through this study.

35. What would be the best choice to replace *Even though* in sentence 10?
   a. Meanwhile
   b. However
   c. Fortunately
   d. On the other hand
   e. In turn

Use the following passage to answer questions 36–40.

(1) I bet you have all seen them either in person or on television. (2) They are the people who enter competitive eating contests and are somehow able to eat quantities of food that most people would never even consider. (3) How they manage to do it has become an intriguing mystery for gastroenterologists who want to understand the mechanics of power eating.

(4) "These competitive eaters are an interesting group of people who seem to have abilities that many people in the normal population don't have," said one physician. (5) These eaters apparently use a combination of skills and tricks to gulp down as much food as they do in one sitting. (6) One trick that helps is that they drink a great deal of water for several days before the contest. (7) This helps the stomach to stretch. (8) It can hold more food that way.

(9) On the other hand, another trick these people may use is to fill the stomach beforehand with high-fiber, low-calorie foods such as cabbage. (10) These foods remain in the stomach a while before breaking down. (11) This suppresses the release of the hormones that tell a person's brain he or she is full. (12) If competitive eaters can stop that signal from reaching their brains, they can keep eating long after he is actually full.

36. The main problem with the introductory sentence is that
   a. it does not have anything to do with the rest of the passage.
   b. it does not have any connection to the sentence that follows.
   c. it uses a cliché that most readers would not understand.
   d. it is written in first person and the rest of the passage is not.
   e. it contains an unidentified quote that confuses the reader.

37. In context, the best phrase to replace *they* in sentence 6 would be
   a. gastroenterologists.
   b. the population.
   c. physicians.
   d. tricks.
   e. competitive eaters.

38. Which of the following is the best way to combine sentences 7 and 8 (reproduced here)?
   This helps the stomach to stretch. It can hold more food that way.
   a. This helps the stomach to stretch and it can hold more food that way.
   b. This helps the stomach to stretch and hold more food.
   c. This helps the stomach to stretch and the stomach can hold more food.
   d. This helps the stomach stretch and hold more food that way too.
   e. This helps the stomach to stretch with more food that way.

39. What would be the best choice to replace *On the other hand* in sentence 9?

  a. Whereas

  b. Unfortunately

  c. In addition

  d. Meanwhile

  e. For example

40. Which of the following is a valid criticism of sentence 12?

  a. It uses the wrong pronoun and verb form in the last part of the sentence.

  b. It does not have any connection the sentence before it.

  c. It contains an error in punctuation.

  d. It repeats the same information as in the second paragraph.

  e. It uses technical terms that have not been adequately explained.

Use the following passage to answer questions 41–45.

(1) There is no question in the medical world that burns are one of the most painful injuries for most people to endure. (2) However, Loyola University in Illinois has a new treatment that seems to be making a real difference in pain levels for patients. (3) It isn't a new medication or therapy. (4) Instead it will be an interactive, virtual reality video game known as Snow World.

(5) To play Snow World, the player has to immerse him- or herself mentally in an environment that features piles of snow, penguins, polar bears, igloos, and icy rivers. (6) All of these images help distract the patient from the painful treatment and therapy they are undergoing.

(7) While being treated for burns, the patient wears a helmet that shows him or her a three-dimensional world of winter. (8) Headphones allow the burn victim to hear what is going on in this icy world, as well as his favorite music and a mouse allows him to throw snowballs. (9) The player can block other's snowballs with his or send a torrent of snowballs out to explode snowmen and knock over penguins. (10) So far, all studies have shown that this game has been able to significantly reduce the amount of perceived pain in patients, especially younger ones.

41. What should be done to sentence 4?

  a. Change the verb tense from future to present.

  b. Move it to later on in the essay.

  c. Put it in quotation marks.

  d. Eliminate it from the essay completely.

  e. Add more details to it about the cost of the game.

42. Which of the following is a valid criticism of sentence 6?

  a. It does not fit in with the information in the rest of the paragraph.

  b. It introduces an entirely different perspective to the essay.

  c. It changes verb tense and uses the wrong pronoun.

  d. It does not support the main idea of the entire essay.

  e. It changes the main subject and belongs elsewhere in the essay.

43. The function of sentence 10 is to
  a. list the statistics gathered regarding pain reduction in patients.
  b. introduce simple information about the effect of this therapy.
  c. refer the reader to a resource for further details about the game.
  d. describe the basic ways that the interactive game works.
  e. explain why pain relief is a necessary part of burn treatment.

44. From this passage, you can conclude that its author
  a. is sympathetic to the experiences of burn victims.
  b. is a huge fan of interactive games.
  c. is a doctor who works with burn victims.
  d. has sympathy for those dealing with burns.
  e. works for Loyola University in Illinois.

45. The passage concentrates on
  a. what burn treatment is available.
  b. how interactive games basically work.
  c. new research being done at Loyola University.
  d. creative ways of treating chronic illnesses.
  e. an innovative way to help burn victims cope with pain.

Use the following passage to answer questions 46–50.

(1) Hearing about burglary in today's culture is not remotely unusual. (2) Hearing about it in the world of nature, however, is relatively uncommon. (3) Despite this, there are some sneaky robbers roaming about many forests. (4) Almost 200 species are keeping busy stealing the food of other birds.

(5) Some of the birds swoop through and in midair, they grab food out of the beaks of other birds. (6) Others just chase and chase a bird until, exhausted, it gives up and drops the food. (7) This typically involves a complex, zigzagging flight through the skies overhead, full of cackling and official bird harassment.

(8) Researchers have figured out several things about these thieves with wings. (9) The species tend to live in open areas where there is a lot of room for chasing. (10) They tend to be birds that chow down on meatier meals like fish and mice, rather than those who dine only on insects. (11) Finally, these birds appear to have large brains in comparison to its body. (12) This proves that it doesn't take brute force to be a bird bully. (13) It just takes a big brain!

46. From this passage, you can conclude that the author
  a. is an avid birdwatcher.
  b. works in an aviary.
  c. really doesn't like birds.
  d. thinks birds are a nuisance.
  e. has done research on bird behavior.

47. Which of the following is the best way to combine sentences 1 and 2 (reproduced here)?

Hearing about burglary in today's culture is not remotely unusual. Hearing about it in the world of nature, however, is relatively uncommon.

a. Hearing about burglary in today's culture is not remotely unusual, but hearing about it in the world of nature is relatively uncommon.

b. Hearing about burglary in today's culture is not remotely unusual unless hearing about it in the world of nature is relatively uncommon.

c. Hearing about burglary in today's culture is not remotely unusual meanwhile hearing about it in the world of nature is relatively uncommon.

d. Hearing about burglary in today's culture is not remotely unusual because hearing about it in the world of nature is relatively uncommon.

e. Hearing about burglary in today's culture is not remotely unusual even though hearing about it in the world of nature is relatively uncommon.

48. The function of sentence 8 is to introduce

a. an opposing opinion.

b. a new thesis statement.

c. a quote from an expert.

d. a concluding statement.

e. a description of the birds.

49. Which of the following is a valid criticism of sentence 10?

a. It does not feature any relevant details.

b. It switches from first to third person.

c. It uses slang terms that should be replaced.

d. It contradicts earlier information.

e. It uses the wrong verb forms and tenses.

50. Which of the following is the best way to combine sentences 12 and 13 (reproduced here)?

This proves that it doesn't take brute force to be a bird bully. It just takes a big brain!

a. This proves that it doesn't take brute force to be a bird bully but it just takes a big brain.

b. This proves that it doesn't take brute force to be a bird bully, it just takes a big brain.

c. This proves that it doesn't take brute force to be a bird bully meanwhile it just takes a big brain.

d. This proves that it doesn't take brute force to be a bird bully; it just takes a big brain.

e. This proves that it doesn't take brute force to be a bird bully, for example, it just takes a big brain.

▶ Part II: Essay

Directions: You will have 45 minutes to plan and write an essay on the topic specified. Read the topic carefully. You are expected to spend a few minutes considering the topic and organizing your thoughts before you begin writing. *Do not write on a topic other than the one specified. An essay on a topic of your own choice is not acceptable.*

The essay is intended to give you an opportunity to demonstrate your ability to write effectively. You should therefore take care to express your thoughts on the topic clearly and exactly and to make them interesting to the reader. Be specific, using supporting examples whenever appropriate. Remember that how well you write is more important than how much you write.

James Twitchell once wrote that materialism is "the thing that everybody loves to hate." Should modern society be criticized for being materialistic? Plan and write an essay in which you develop your point of view on this issue. Support your position with reasoning and examples taken from your reading, studies, experience, or observations.

▶ Answers

Part I: Multiple Choice

1. e. This sentence has no error.

2. a. The word *worlds* is possessive and not plural, so it requires an apostrophe.

3. b. *Myself* should be *I*; it is the subject of agree; *myself* is a reflexive pronoun.

4. b. *Was* should be *were* because *teachers* is plural, and the subject and verb need to agree in number.

5. b. *Were* should be *was* because *each* is singular, and the subject and verb need to agree in number.

6. c. *Are* should be *is* because *number* is singular, and the subject and verb need to agree in number.

7. d. *They* should be *he or she* because the antecedent *caller* is singular.

8. c. *You* should be *one* or *him or her* because the antecedent is *person*.

9. e. This sentence has no error.

10. d. *Most* should be *more*.

11. c. This is a double negative; it should be *was not any* or *there was no*.

12. d. This is a commonly confused word; *allusion* should be *illusion*.

13. d. This is an example of faulty parallelism; it should read *mopping up*.

14. a. The sentence parallels a noun with a dependent clause; the correct wording is *who has,* omitting the word *and*.

15. b. The participial phrase has no word in the sentence to modify. Who is putting the rubber band on? It isn't the door.

16. d. The phrase *with surprisingly high prices* is misplaced. The phrase should appear after *collectible books*.

17. c. *Going out of business* is the wrong verb tense; it should be *gone out of business*.

18. e. This sentence has no error.

19. c. *Should of been* should be *should have been*.

20. b. This is an example of a commonly confused word; the correct spelling is *stationery* and not *stationary*.

21. c. This choice keeps the original meaning but eliminates the wordiness. Choice **b** changes the verb tense. Choice **d** is still too wordy, and choice **e** is missing a verb.

22. e. This revision takes the misplaced modifier and puts it next to *the phone* instead of *I*. The other choices mix up the words so that they do not make sense.

23. b. It connects the two complete sentences with a semicolon, which is the correct punctuation. Choice **c** uses a comma, which creates a comma splice. Choice **d** uses a colon, which is incorrect, and **e** inserts a conjunction that does not fit the meaning of the sentence.

24. d. This choice replaces *one* with the correct pronoun *you*, but keeps the correct verb tense and keeps it singular to match the subject.

25. c. Choice **b** does not use the right verb to maintain the parallelism. Choice **d** eliminates the pronoun but still uses the wrong verb, and choice **e** also uses the wrong form of the verb to match the rest of the sentence.

26. a. There are no errors in this sentence. The verb should be present tense and singular, and only choice **a** does this.

27. b. The sentence is missing a subject, so one needs to be inserted. The verb tense has to be maintained correctly, however.

28. c. This sentence contains two idioms or clichés that need to be replaced with strong phrases that convey the meaning clearly.

29. d. The correct word is *who* because it refers to a person. *Which* and *that* are not correct. The correct verb tense and singularity must also be kept in place.

30. a. There are no errors in this sentence. Only choice **a** maintains the correct verb form.

31. d. The use of *clearly* and *properly* in the second paragraph reveals the author's bias.

32. a. The quote expands on the idea stated in sentence 5.

33. b. This sentence does not add anything to the essay and shows personal bias.

34. c. This is the only sentence that retains the meaning of both and is not overly wordy.

35. e. This is the only choice that shows the correct relationship between the previous sentence and this one.

36. d. The first sentence uses *I*, but the first person is not used anywhere else in the passage.

37. e. The pronoun is vague, but it refers to the competitive eaters.

38. b. This is the only combination that maintains the meaning and eliminates excess wordiness.

39. c. This is the only transition that makes sense with the sentences before and after it.

40. a. In the last part of the sentence, the pronoun switches to *he* instead of *they*, and *are* changes to *is*.

41. a. This is correct. Moving it would put it out of order. It's not a quote, and it should not be eliminated; details about the cost are irrelevant.

42. c. This is correct. For *patient*, the pronoun should be *she or he*, and the verb should be *is*.

43. b. The point of this sentence is to mention that the game has been an effective distraction method for burn victims.

44. d. There is nothing to indicate any of these are true, except choice **d**, because the author seems aware of how painful burn treatment can be and why distraction is so helpful.

45. e. All of the other choices are either too generic or irrelevant to the main idea of the passage.

46. e. This is the only choice that is supported by the details in the passage.

47. a. This requires a transition word that indicates contrast, and only this choice does that.

48. b. This statement introduces what the rest of the paragraph will be talking about.

49. c. *Chow down* is a slang phrase that should be replaced.

50. d. Combining the two sentences with a semicolon makes this a correct choice. Other punctuation does not work, and the transition words or conjunctions in other choices do not make sense.

Part II: Essay

Example: 6 points

When I hear the word <u>materialistic</u>, I think of other vague terms that are tossed around in today's society. It is a word that means different things to different people and because of that, determining if it is something to criticize or something to admire is too subjective to truly answer. In my opinion, being materialistic means spending unreasonable amounts of money on things that do not actually mean much to the owner. It means collecting things for the sake of collecting rather than for passion or appreciation. When people begin purchasing items for no other reason than to have something to do, then materialism has gone too far.

I have an uncle who collects snow globes, for example. He started the tradition when he was only ten years old and he moved for the first time. He received a snow globe as a going away gift from his neighbor and he was fascinated by it. Since then, he has collected a globe from every place he has traveled in his lifetime.

This is not a case of materialism, but a case of passion.

My cousin, on the other hand, spends money constantly. He never uses it for anything important. He just buys more and more expensive items, most of which he just throws in a pile in his room and never thinks about again. I often think of all the things he could do with that money that could benefit others. To me, spending money for the sake of spending instead of doing beneficial things for others is what materialism really means.

Money is nothing more than a tool within our society. We can use it to buy things that we do not really need, or deep underneath, even want. Or we can help people and pursue our passions with this tool. If we choose the former instead of the later, then society has every right to criticize us.

Example: 4 points

Materialism is an insult. It is a blatant waste of money. In a world that needs money for so many different things, to see if wasted on nonessential items is tragic. I hate it. Yet, I see it happening all the time throughout the nation and even in the city where I live.

One look at the nightly news is enough to see how people waste their money. Celebrities buy ridiculous things. The government runs the national deficit up higher and higher. It is little wonder that children and young adults who have been raised with the media have little respect for the ways money could be spent. After all, with Madonna singing "I'm living in a material world and I am a material girl" to the masses, why should they think to object?

I am not materialistic. I spend my money wisely. I try to only buy locally and even though I am often tempted to do otherwise, I try to only spend my money on things I truly need rather than just on what I want. That is my way of fighting back against materialism. Because really, it's a terrible thing and a waste of money.

Example: 2 points

To be materialistic, you got to have money. I don't. I know some who do but me and my family aren't. It sucks too because I sure would like to have some.

Our soceity loves money. The more you make, the better person you are. It seems like it anyway. I don't think that's fair. I think you can be a good person and be poor at the same time.

Maybe one day, I will be materialistic. That'd be cool. I'd blow my money on stupid stuff. Like all the game systems. And games. I want to do that. Then I wouldn't care if people insulted me.

CLEP English Composition Practice Test 2

Now take CLEP English Composition Test 2 for additional practice. On this practice test, you will encounter 90 multiple-choice questions that are similar to the type you will find on the official CLEP English Composition Exam without Essay. The questions are organized by the five content areas:

- Identifying Sentence Errors
- Improving Sentences
- Restructuring Sentences
- Revising Works in Progress
- Analyzing Writing

To simulate the test conditions, use the time constraints of the official CLEP English Composition Exam. Allow yourself 90 minutes to complete this practice test.

Remember, on the official CLEP, there is no penalty for incorrect answers, so always make a guess if you are unsure of an answer.

When you are finished, check the answer key on page 459 carefully to assess your results.

▶ CLEP English Composition Practice Test 2

1.	ⓐ	ⓑ	ⓒ	ⓓ	ⓔ	31.	ⓐ	ⓑ	ⓒ	ⓓ	ⓔ	61.	ⓐ	ⓑ	ⓒ	ⓓ	ⓔ
2.	ⓐ	ⓑ	ⓒ	ⓓ	ⓔ	32.	ⓐ	ⓑ	ⓒ	ⓓ	ⓔ	62.	ⓐ	ⓑ	ⓒ	ⓓ	ⓔ
3.	ⓐ	ⓑ	ⓒ	ⓓ	ⓔ	33.	ⓐ	ⓑ	ⓒ	ⓓ	ⓔ	63.	ⓐ	ⓑ	ⓒ	ⓓ	ⓔ
4.	ⓐ	ⓑ	ⓒ	ⓓ	ⓔ	34.	ⓐ	ⓑ	ⓒ	ⓓ	ⓔ	64.	ⓐ	ⓑ	ⓒ	ⓓ	ⓔ
5.	ⓐ	ⓑ	ⓒ	ⓓ	ⓔ	35.	ⓐ	ⓑ	ⓒ	ⓓ	ⓔ	65.	ⓐ	ⓑ	ⓒ	ⓓ	ⓔ
6.	ⓐ	ⓑ	ⓒ	ⓓ	ⓔ	36.	ⓐ	ⓑ	ⓒ	ⓓ	ⓔ	66.	ⓐ	ⓑ	ⓒ	ⓓ	ⓔ
7.	ⓐ	ⓑ	ⓒ	ⓓ	ⓔ	37.	ⓐ	ⓑ	ⓒ	ⓓ	ⓔ	67.	ⓐ	ⓑ	ⓒ	ⓓ	ⓔ
8.	ⓐ	ⓑ	ⓒ	ⓓ	ⓔ	38.	ⓐ	ⓑ	ⓒ	ⓓ	ⓔ	68.	ⓐ	ⓑ	ⓒ	ⓓ	ⓔ
9.	ⓐ	ⓑ	ⓒ	ⓓ	ⓔ	39.	ⓐ	ⓑ	ⓒ	ⓓ	ⓔ	69.	ⓐ	ⓑ	ⓒ	ⓓ	ⓔ
10.	ⓐ	ⓑ	ⓒ	ⓓ	ⓔ	40.	ⓐ	ⓑ	ⓒ	ⓓ	ⓔ	70.	ⓐ	ⓑ	ⓒ	ⓓ	ⓔ
11.	ⓐ	ⓑ	ⓒ	ⓓ	ⓔ	41.	ⓐ	ⓑ	ⓒ	ⓓ	ⓔ	71.	ⓐ	ⓑ	ⓒ	ⓓ	ⓔ
12.	ⓐ	ⓑ	ⓒ	ⓓ	ⓔ	42.	ⓐ	ⓑ	ⓒ	ⓓ	ⓔ	72.	ⓐ	ⓑ	ⓒ	ⓓ	ⓔ
13.	ⓐ	ⓑ	ⓒ	ⓓ	ⓔ	43.	ⓐ	ⓑ	ⓒ	ⓓ	ⓔ	73.	ⓐ	ⓑ	ⓒ	ⓓ	ⓔ
14.	ⓐ	ⓑ	ⓒ	ⓓ	ⓔ	44.	ⓐ	ⓑ	ⓒ	ⓓ	ⓔ	74.	ⓐ	ⓑ	ⓒ	ⓓ	ⓔ
15.	ⓐ	ⓑ	ⓒ	ⓓ	ⓔ	45.	ⓐ	ⓑ	ⓒ	ⓓ	ⓔ	75.	ⓐ	ⓑ	ⓒ	ⓓ	ⓔ
16.	ⓐ	ⓑ	ⓒ	ⓓ	ⓔ	46.	ⓐ	ⓑ	ⓒ	ⓓ	ⓔ	76.	ⓐ	ⓑ	ⓒ	ⓓ	ⓔ
17.	ⓐ	ⓑ	ⓒ	ⓓ	ⓔ	47.	ⓐ	ⓑ	ⓒ	ⓓ	ⓔ	77.	ⓐ	ⓑ	ⓒ	ⓓ	ⓔ
18.	ⓐ	ⓑ	ⓒ	ⓓ	ⓔ	48.	ⓐ	ⓑ	ⓒ	ⓓ	ⓔ	78.	ⓐ	ⓑ	ⓒ	ⓓ	ⓔ
19.	ⓐ	ⓑ	ⓒ	ⓓ	ⓔ	49.	ⓐ	ⓑ	ⓒ	ⓓ	ⓔ	79.	ⓐ	ⓑ	ⓒ	ⓓ	ⓔ
20.	ⓐ	ⓑ	ⓒ	ⓓ	ⓔ	50.	ⓐ	ⓑ	ⓒ	ⓓ	ⓔ	80.	ⓐ	ⓑ	ⓒ	ⓓ	ⓔ
21.	ⓐ	ⓑ	ⓒ	ⓓ	ⓔ	51.	ⓐ	ⓑ	ⓒ	ⓓ	ⓔ	81.	ⓐ	ⓑ	ⓒ	ⓓ	ⓔ
22.	ⓐ	ⓑ	ⓒ	ⓓ	ⓔ	52.	ⓐ	ⓑ	ⓒ	ⓓ	ⓔ	82.	ⓐ	ⓑ	ⓒ	ⓓ	ⓔ
23.	ⓐ	ⓑ	ⓒ	ⓓ	ⓔ	53.	ⓐ	ⓑ	ⓒ	ⓓ	ⓔ	83.	ⓐ	ⓑ	ⓒ	ⓓ	ⓔ
24.	ⓐ	ⓑ	ⓒ	ⓓ	ⓔ	54.	ⓐ	ⓑ	ⓒ	ⓓ	ⓔ	84.	ⓐ	ⓑ	ⓒ	ⓓ	ⓔ
25.	ⓐ	ⓑ	ⓒ	ⓓ	ⓔ	55.	ⓐ	ⓑ	ⓒ	ⓓ	ⓔ	85.	ⓐ	ⓑ	ⓒ	ⓓ	ⓔ
26.	ⓐ	ⓑ	ⓒ	ⓓ	ⓔ	56.	ⓐ	ⓑ	ⓒ	ⓓ	ⓔ	86.	ⓐ	ⓑ	ⓒ	ⓓ	ⓔ
27.	ⓐ	ⓑ	ⓒ	ⓓ	ⓔ	57.	ⓐ	ⓑ	ⓒ	ⓓ	ⓔ	87.	ⓐ	ⓑ	ⓒ	ⓓ	ⓔ
28.	ⓐ	ⓑ	ⓒ	ⓓ	ⓔ	58.	ⓐ	ⓑ	ⓒ	ⓓ	ⓔ	88.	ⓐ	ⓑ	ⓒ	ⓓ	ⓔ
29.	ⓐ	ⓑ	ⓒ	ⓓ	ⓔ	59.	ⓐ	ⓑ	ⓒ	ⓓ	ⓔ	89.	ⓐ	ⓑ	ⓒ	ⓓ	ⓔ
30.	ⓐ	ⓑ	ⓒ	ⓓ	ⓔ	60.	ⓐ	ⓑ	ⓒ	ⓓ	ⓔ	90.	ⓐ	ⓑ	ⓒ	ⓓ	ⓔ

▶ Part I: Multiple Choice

Identifying Sentence Errors

Directions: The following sentences test your knowledge of grammar, usage, diction (choice of words), and idiom. Some sentences are correct as written. No sentence contains more than one error.

You will find that the error, if there is one, is underlined and lettered. Assume that elements of the sentence that are not underlined are correct and cannot be changed. In choosing answers, follow the requirements of standard written English.

If there is an error, selected the one underlined part that must be changed to make the sentence correct. If there is no error, select choice **e**.

1. In Pacific Northwest <u>cities</u> like Seattle and Portland, there <u>isn't</u> hardly a <u>single day</u> when <u>no rain</u> falls.
                         a   **b**   **c**   **d**

    <u>No error.</u>
      e

2. Of the two digital cameras he <u>showed</u> me, I liked the silver one <u>the best</u>, <u>not only</u> because of its high pixels,
                                     a   **b**   **c**

    but also because of <u>its</u> price. <u>No error.</u>
                d   **e**

3. If you plan on missing more than two basketball practices, you <u>should contact</u> your coach <u>directly</u> or, if
                                                 a   **b**

    you cannot reach her, <u>one must call</u> the school administration office as soon as <u>possible</u>. <u>No error.</u>
                        c   **d**   **e**

4. The <u>gathering</u> of dark storm clouds, <u>clearly indicated</u> on the meteorologist's map, <u>were</u> <u>definitely</u> indicative
         a   **b**   **c**   **d**

    of an upcoming major weather event. <u>No error.</u>
                                   e

5. Much to the <u>dismay and disappointment</u> of thousands of fans, <u>neither</u> the *Buffy, the Vampire Slayer* <u>nor</u>
                 a   **b**   **c**

    the *Angel* series is going <u>to be renewed</u> for television. <u>No error.</u>
                           d   **e**

6. The telephone rang <u>so</u> <u>unexpected</u>, and there was such chaos already going on in the dorm room, that it
                        a   **b**

    was <u>virtually</u> impossible to hear who was <u>speaking</u> on the other end. <u>No error.</u>
         c   **d**   **e**

7. <u>To write</u> a research paper <u>good</u>, you must <u>not only understand</u> the basics of grammar, spelling, and
      a   **b**   **c**

punctuation, you must also be able to tell the difference between reliable facts and <u>someone's</u> personal
                                                                       d

opinion. <u>No error.</u>
         e

8. <u>All year round</u>, tourists <u>come</u> to Oregon <u>to hike</u> the tree-covered hills, explore the pine forests, ski on the
    a   **b**   **c**

snowy mountains, visit the sandy coast, and <u>swimming in the chilly ocean.</u> <u>No error.</u>
                                      d   **e**

9. If one truly appreciates movies with <u>unbelievable and unexpected</u> twists, <u>you</u> certainly have to see
                                  a   **b**

<u>every single movie</u> M. Night Shyamalan has ever <u>produced</u>. <u>No error.</u>
    c   **d**   **e**

10. Horror <u>writers</u>, such as Stephen King, Dean Koontz, Clive Barker, and John Saul, <u>commonly appears</u> at
           a   **b**

national conventions where <u>they</u> meet with fans, <u>sign their books</u>, and speak to crowds. <u>No error.</u>
                       c   **d**   **e**

11. The <u>cost</u> of first-class postage stamps continues <u>to rise</u> every <u>few years, however</u>, the price is still
        a   **b**   **c**

<u>relatively miniscule</u> considering how far one stamp can take an envelope. <u>No error.</u>
    d   **e**

12. When Caroline <u>opened</u> the front door of her apartment, the guests and the family members <u>who had come</u>
               a   **b**

from near and far jumped up from <u>his or her</u> hiding places and <u>shouted</u>, "Surprise!" <u>No error.</u>
                             c   **d**   **e**

13. Although <u>volunteering looks good</u> on a resume and can increase a <u>high school student's</u> chance of
                 a   **b**

obtaining a scholarship, <u>they</u> take other elements into <u>consideration</u>, including grades, test scores, and
                       c   **d**

financial background. <u>No error.</u>
                   e

14. Neither of the contestants <u>are</u> planning <u>to pursue</u> a career in entertainment after their <u>dismal failure</u> in
                            a   **b**   **c**

front of the judges of "American Idol," even though <u>they</u> still wanted to be performers. <u>No error.</u>
                                           d   **e**

15. The second haunted house was definitely the <u>scariest</u> of the two, <u>although</u> it was not quite as dark inside
                                     a   **b**

and had <u>a lot less</u> small, <u>screaming children</u> running through it. <u>No error.</u>
        c   **d**   **e**

16. Flightless birds, such as ostriches and emus, retain <u>their wings</u>, which they <u>primarily use</u> for balance when
                                      a   **b**

<u>they run, they</u> even have been known to flap their wings up and down in order <u>to maintain</u> a comfortable
  c   **d**

temperature. <u>No error.</u>
        e

17. <u>Although</u> castles were <u>commonly cold</u> and uncomfortable places, <u>they</u> were <u>cunningly designed</u> to
    a   **b**   **c**   **d**

withstand the siege of enemy forces, thanks to small windows, stone walls, and protective towers. <u>No error.</u>
                                                                  e

18. The naïve first-year <u>college student</u> <u>frequently</u> sleeps too late and parties too much, which, not <u>surprisingly</u>,
                    a   **b**   **c**

can lead to <u>their failing</u> a class or even losing a scholarship. <u>No error.</u>
        d   **e**

Improving Sentences

Directions: In each of the following sentences, part of the sentence or the entire sentence is underlined. After each sentence, you will find five versions of the underlined part. Choice **a** repeats the original; the other four are different.

Choose the answer that best expresses the meaning of the original sentence. If you think the original is better than any of the other alternatives, choose **a**; otherwise, choose one of the others. Your choice should produce the most effective sentence—one that is clear and precise, without awkwardness or ambiguity.

19. Although meteorologists continue to get more and more advanced technology and equipment, <u>their weather forecasts wrong</u> about 50% of the time.
   a. their weather forecasts wrong
   b. their weather forecasts which is wrong
   c. their weather forecasts are wrong
   d. is their weather forecasts wrong
   e. their weather forecasts that is wrong

20. Some couples have their first children before they have learned any real parenting skills, <u>while a few reading books and attending seminars as soon as they find out they are expecting a child.</u>
   a. while a few reading books and attending seminars as soon as they find out they are expecting a child.
   b. while a few, reading books and attending seminars as soon as they find out they are expecting a child.
   c. but a few reading books and attending seminars as soon as they find out they are expecting a child.
   d. however, a few reading books and attending seminars as soon as they find out they are expecting a child.
   e. while a few begin reading books and attending seminars as soon as they find out they are expecting a child.

21. The number of grocery store shoppers that carry a wallet full of coupons with them <u>is growing, approximately 50%</u> of those in line have at least one applicable coupon to apply to their purchases.
   a. is growing, approximately 50%
   b. is growing; approximately 50%
   c. is growing, although approximately 50%
   d. is grown, approximately 50%
   e. is to grown, approximately 50%

22. <u>Raymond's new vacuum worked beautifully</u> on the interior of his new car, he still was not able to get the pine needles from last year's Christmas tree out of the side pockets.

a. Raymond's new vacuum worked beautifully

b. Because Raymond's new vacuum worked beautifully

c. Although Raymond's new vacuum worked beautifully

d. Raymond's new vacuum worked beautifully,

e. Whenever Raymond's new vacuum worked beautifully

23. <u>After watching television for more than seven hours straight, the couch no longer felt very comfortable to the boys.</u>

a. After watching television for more than seven hours straight, the couch no longer felt very comfortable to the boys.

b. After watching television for more than seven hours straight, the boys were no longer very comfortable on the couch.

c. Watching television for more than seven hours straight, the couch no longer felt very comfortable to the boys.

d. The boys were no longer very comfortable on the couch, after they had watched television for more than seven hours straight.

e. For more than seven hours straight the boys had watched television, the couch no longer felt very comfortable to them.

24. To keep her house completely clean, she spends at least three hours a day dusting the furniture, vacuuming the floors, and <u>she puts away a minimum of two loads of laundry.</u>

a. she puts away a minimum of two loads of laundry.

b. next, she puts away a minimum of two loads of laundry.

c. finally, she putting away a minimum of two loads of laundry.

d. putting away a minimum of two loads of laundry she does.

e. putting away a minimum of two loads of laundry.

25. The character of Clark Kent has been around for decades, <u>because no one has made him quite as popular as Tom Welling has in *Smallville.*</u>

a. because no one has made him quite as popular as Tom Welling has in *Smallville.*

b. although no one has made him quite as popular as Tom Welling has in *Smallville.*

c. since no on has made him quite as popular as Tom Welling has in *Smallville.*

d. for no one has made him quite as popular as Tom Welling has in *Smallville.*

e. whenever no one had made him quite as popular as Tom Welling has in *Smallville.*

26. Because the *Serenity* movie was quite popular in the movie theatres and on home video, there are still no plans to bring back the *Firefly* series, according to former producer Joss Whedon.

    a. Because the *Serenity* movie was quite popular in the movie theatres and on home video

    b. Although the *Serenity* movie was quite popular in the movie theatres and on home video

    c. Since the *Serenity* movie was quite popular in the movie theatres and on home video

    d. However, the *Serenity* movie was quite popular in the movie theatres and on home video

    e. For the *Serenity* movies was quite popular in the movie theatres and on home video

27. The Parkinsons have decided to cancel their Saturday afternoon barbeque by the pool while the weather forecast is calling for massive thunderstorms throughout the entire weekend.

    a. while the weather forecast is calling

    b. so the weather forecast is calling

    c. although the weather forecast is calling

    d. however the weather forecast is calling

    e. because the weather forecast is calling

28. Situation comedies have been popular with audiences of all ages for the last several decades, some of them have become entrenched into our culture in a number of ways.

    a. for the last several decades, some of them have become entrenched

    b. for the last several decades, become entrenching some of them have

    c. some of them, for the last several decades, have become entrenched

    d. for the last several decades; some of them have become entrenched

    e. becoming entrenched, for the last several decades, they have

29. In the United States, a growing number of families that do not have much spare time on their hands and end up in the drive-through lanes at convenient fast-food restaurants.

    a. and end up in the drive-through lanes

    b. so end up in the drive-through lanes

    c. end up in the drive-through lanes

    d. ends up in the drive-through lanes

    e. ending up in the drive-through lanes

30. Countless music groups and individual singers have recorded a version of "Unchained Melody," no one can perform it better than the original Righteous Brothers though.

    a. no one can perform it better than the original Righteous Brothers though

    b. since no one can perform it better than the original Righteous Brothers though

    c. in performing, no one can do it better than the original Righteous Brothers

    d. the Righteous Brothers perform it better because they are the original

    e. but no one can perform it better than the original Righteous Brothers

31. Whenever the telephone rings, everyone in the house knows that it is going to be for Nicole, since she has a social life that is busy enough for at least three people.

    a. Whenever the telephone rings,

    b. The telephone, whenever it rings,

    c. Ringing, whenever the telephone does

    d. Because the telephone rings

    e. The telephone rings

32. Originally designed to help people control their diabetes, the physician informed the fascinated audience that this medication would also assist thousands in losing significant amounts of weight.

a. Originally designed to help people control their diabetes, the physician informed the fascinated audience that this medication would also assist thousands in losing significant amounts of weight.

b. Designed to help people control their diabetes originally, the physician informed the fascinated audience that it would also assist thousands in losing significant amounts of weight.

c. Originally designed to help people control their diabetes, this medication would also assist thousands in losing significant amounts of weight, the physician told the fascinated audience.

d. The physician told the fascinated audience that although originally designed to help people control their diabetes, significant amounts of weight could be lost as well with this medication.

e. Losing significant amounts of weight could be done with the medication originally designed to help people control their diabetes, said the physician to his fascinated audience.

33. While numerous horror novels try to persuade readers that psychopaths are hiding around every corner, other authors much more optimistic.

a. other authors much more optimistic.

b. other authors are much more optimistic.

c. other authors is much more optimistic.

d. other authors which are much more optimistic.

e. other authors although much more optimistic.

34. Television detectives miraculously have the ability to solve the most complicated crimes in less than an hour, few can do it with as much style and obsessiveness as the main character on *Monk*.

a. an hour, few can do it

b. an hour since few can do it

c. an hour, for few can do it

d. an hour; few can do it

e. an hour, while few can do it

35. The curious student asked the museum curator endless questions from the local high school history class.

a. The curious student asked the museum curator endless questions from the local high school history class.

b. From the local high school history class, the museum curator was asked endless questions by the curious student.

c. The curious student from the local high school history class asked the museum curator endless questions.

d. Endless questions were asked by the curious student from the local high school to the museum curator.

e. The museum curator asked the curious student from the local high school endless questions.

36. The high wind warning <u>had been issued in the evening; people were already tying down</u> their possessions and preparing for the worst.

   a. had been issued in the evening; people were already tying down

   b. had been issued in the evening, people were already tying down

   c. had been issued in the evening, since people were already tying down

   d. had been issued in the evening; already tying down

   e. had been issued in the evening for people were already tying down

Restructuring Sentences

Directions: Revise each of the following sentences according to the directions that follow it. Some directions require you to change only part of the original sentence, while others require you to change the entire sentence. You may need to omit or add words in constructing an acceptable revision, but you should keep the meaning of the revised sentence as close to the meaning of the original sentence as the directions permit. Your new sentence should follow the conventions of standard written English and should be clear and precise.

For each question, look at answer choices **a** through **e** for the exact word or phrase that is included in your revised sentence, and select that answer choice. If you have thought of a revision that does not include any of the words or phrases listed, try to revise the sentence again so that it does include the wording in one of the answer choices.

37. *Owing to his knowledge of government policy, Mayor Fitzpatrick had many supporters.*

   Begin with <u>Many people supported</u>.

   Your new sentence will contain

   a. so

   b. while

   c. although

   d. because

   e. and

38. *Coming to America as a young woman, she found a job as a nanny.*

   Change <u>Coming</u> to <u>She came</u>.

   Your new sentence will contain

   a. and so she found

   b. and had found

   c. and there she found

   d. and then finding

   e. and found

39. *When we consider how reality television dominates much of today's programming, we can understand why many of the newest "celebrities" are not trained actors.*

   Change <u>we can understand</u> to <u>explains.</u>

   Your new sentence will begin with

   a. Programming dominating

   b. On account of reality television's dominating

   c. The fact of reality television's domination

   d. Due to the domination of reality television

   e. The domination of reality television

40. *Much is known of the acai berry's origin and its life-enhancing benefits.*

    Start with <u>Many know</u>.

    Your new sentence will contain

a. and it

b. and if

c. and how

d. and life-enhancement

e. and life-enhancing

41. *John had done some very clever songwriting; the audience was amused, and the critic was baffled.*

    Start with <u>John amused</u>.

    Your new sentence will contain

a. critic by

b. critic of

c. critic being

d. critic doing

e. critic with

42. *The embarrassment Sam endured during his first presentation was less stressful than his fear that he might get an incomplete grade for not showing up.*

    Start with <u>The fear</u>.

    Your new sentence will contain

a. was as

b. was the

c. was more

d. was less

e. being that

43. *The council has recently become concerned about the mayor's corruption or innocence.*

    Start with <u>Whether</u>.

    Your new sentence will contain

a. corrupt has

b. corrupt was

c. corrupt became

d. corrupt being

e. corrupt man

44. *Most people who like to play soccer have little appreciation for the sacrifices required to become an all-star like David Beckham.*

    Start with <u>Few people</u>.

    Your new sentence will contain

a. appreciate

b. appreciating

c. hardly appreciating

d. lack of appreciation

e. have to appreciate

45. *Unfortunately for the Democratic candidate, rebuttals were not allowed by the debate moderator because of time restraints.*

    Change <u>allowed</u> to <u>allow</u>.

    Your new sentence will contain

a. moderator due to

b. moderator were

c. moderator that

d. moderator did

e. moderator having

46. *Many states adhere to the No Child Left Behind Act for assessment requirements, but a few leave the decision to school districts.*

    Start with <u>Although</u>.

    Your new sentence will contain

a. states leave

b. states left

c. states can be left

d. states will have left

e. states to be leaving

47. *Readers are treated to adult themes and a more sophisticated approach to fiction by Judy Blume's later works.*

> Start with The later works of Judy Blume.
> Your new sentence will contain

a. cause the treating of the readers
b. enable to readers to be treated
c. treat readers
d. treats the readers
e. is treating

48. *Moving to New York City as a young child, Raven-Symoné became a principal character on* The Cosby Show.

> Change Moving to Raven-Symoné moved.
> Your new sentence will contain

a. and therefore she became
b. and became
c. and once there becoming
d. and then becoming
e. and had became

49. *A gene that appears to lead to obesity has been discovered by scientists.*

> Start with Scientists.
> Your new sentence will contain

a. were discovered
b. who discovered
c. to have discovered
d. discovering
e. have discovered

50. *AIDS, a disease caused by the human immunodeficiency virus, has been an increasing health crisis in African nations over the last decade.*

> Start with The human immunodeficiency virus.
> Your new sentence will contain

a. that has been
b. which has been
c. which are
d. having been
e. to be

Revising Works in Progress

Directions: Each of the following passages consists of numbered sentences. Because the passages are part of longer writing samples, they do not necessarily constitute a complete discussion of the issues presented.

Read each passage carefully and answer the questions that follow. The questions test your awareness of a writer's purpose and of characteristics of prose that are important to good writing.

Use the following passage to answer questions 51–59.

(1) Year after year, one of the most popular Halloween costumes for children and adults alike is Batman. (2) And this superhero was created in 1939 and known worldwide continues to be one of the most popular comic strip characters ever created.

(3) Batman was the brainchild of comic book artist Bob Kane. (4) Who was just 22 years old when he was asked to create a new superhero for DC Comics. (5) Superman was a phenomenal success, and DC Comics wanted another hero, just as powerful, to appeal to its readers. (6) Kane's idea for Batman reportedly came from Leonardo da Vinci's famous sketch of a man flying with batlike wings and the heroes in the *Shadow* and *Zorro* series who wore masks.

(7) Kane's Batman was a success that was big right from the start. (8) The masked hero soon moved from comic books to his own newspaper strip, and in 1943, Batman episodes were aired on the radio. (9) In 1966, live-action Batman shows hit the TV screen. (10) The series was wildly popular, and the syndicated show still airs today on channels like the Cartoon Network.

(11) Batman is really Bruce Wayne, a millionaire who witnessed the murder of his parents as a child. (12) Why was Batman so popular? (13) The answer may lie in the background Kane gave his character. (14) He vowed to avenge their deaths and the bringing of criminals to justice. (15) He didn't have any supernatural powers. (16) Instead, he devotes his life to training his body and mind to fight crime and used his wealth to develop high-tech crime-fighting tools and weapons, like his famous Batmobile. (17) Thus Kane created a superhero who is just as human as the rest of us. (18) In Batman, Kane gave us an image of our own superhero potential.

51. Which of the following is the best way to revise the underlined portion of sentence 2 (reproduced here)?

And *this superhero was created in 1939 and known worldwide continues* *to be one of the most popular comic strip characters ever created.*

a. this superhero, was created in 1939 and known worldwide, continues

b. this superhero, having been created in 1939 and known worldwide, continues

c. this superhero, created in 1939 and known worldwide, continues

d. this superhero, was created in 1939 and known worldwide, and continuing

e. this superhero, who was created in 1939 and being known worldwide, continues

52. Which of the following is the best way to revise and combine sentences 3 and 4 (reproduced here)?

Batman was the brainchild of comic book artist Bob Kane. Who was just 22 years old when he was asked to create a new superhero for DC Comics.

a. Batman was the brainchild of comic book artist Bob Kane, that was just 22 years old when he was asked to create a new superhero for DC Comics.

b. Batman was the brainchild of comic book artist Bob Kane; who was just 22 years old when he was asked to create a new superhero for DC Comics.

c. Just 22 years old when he was asked to create a new superhero for DC Comics, comic book artist Bob Kane was the brainchild of Batman.

d. Batman was the brainchild of comic book artist Bob Kane, who was just 22 years old when he was asked to create a new superhero for DC Comics.

e. Batman was the brainchild of comic book artist Bob Kane, while he was just 22 years old when he was asked to create a new superhero for DC Comics.

53. Which of the following is the best way to revise sentence 6 (reproduced here)?

Kane's idea for Batman reportedly came from Leonardo da Vinci's famous sketch of a man flying with batlike wings and the heroes in the Shadow *and* Zorro *series who wore masks.*

a. Kane's idea for Batman reportedly came from the famous sketch of a man flying with batlike wings from Leonardo da Vinci and the heroes in the *Shadow* and *Zorro* series who wore masks.

b. Kane's idea for Batman reportedly came from Leonardo da Vinci's famous sketch of a man flying with having wings like a bat and the heroes in the *Shadow* and *Zorro* series who wore masks.

c. Kane's idea for Batman reportedly came from Leonardo da Vinci's famous sketch of a man flying with batlike wings. And the heroes in the *Shadow* and *Zorro* series who wore masks.

d. Kane's idea for Batman was reported coming from Leonardo da Vinci's famous sketch of a man flying with batlike wings and the heroes in the *Shadow* and *Zorro* series who wore masks.

e. Kane's idea for Batman reportedly came both from Leonardo da Vinci's famous sketch of a man flying with batlike wings and from the heroes who wore masks in the *Shadow* and *Zorro* series.

54. Which of the following is the best version of the underlined portion of sentence 7 (reproduced here)?

Kane's Batman <u>was a success that was big</u> *right from the start.*

a. no change

b. was a big success

c. was successful in a big way

d. was successfully big

e. is a successful thing

55. Which of the following would best replace *And* at the beginning of sentence 2?

a. In fact,

b. Instead,

c. Despite this,

d. Nevertheless,

e. Excepting this,

56. Which of the following is the best version of the underlined portion of sentence 14 (reproduced here)?

He vowed to avenge their deaths <u>and the bringing of criminals to justice</u>.

a. no change

b. and brought criminals to justice

c. and will bring criminals to justice

d. and bring criminals to justice

e. and that he would bring criminals to justice

57. Which of the following is the best way to revise sentence 16 (reproduced here)?

Instead, he devotes his life to training his body and mind to fight crime and used his wealth to develop high-tech crime-fighting tools and weapons, like his famous Batmobile.

a. Instead, he devoted his life to training his body and mind to fight crime and used his wealth to develop high-tech crime-fighting tools and weapons, like his famous Batmobile.

b. Instead, he devotes his life to training his body and mind fighting crime and used his wealth to develop high-tech crime-fighting tools and weapons, like his famous Batmobile.

c. Instead, he devotes his life to training his body and mind fighting crime and used his wealth to develop high, tech crime-fighting tools and weapons, like his famous Batmobile.

d. Instead, he devotes his life to training his body, and mind to fight crime and used his wealth to develop high-tech crime-fighting tools and weapons, like his famous Batmobile.

e. Instead, he devotes his life to training his body and mind to fight crime and used his wealth developing high-tech crime-fighting tools and weapons, like his famous Batmobile.

58. The writer of the passage could best improve sentence 18 by revising the sentence and adding which of the following?

a. However, Batman was someone in whom Kane

b. Therefore, in Batman, we are given

c. More importantly, in Batman, Kane gives us

d. On the other hand, in Batman, we see

e. Thankfully, it is in Batman that we have

59. Which of the following is the best way to revise sentence 8 (reproduced here)?

The masked hero soon moved from comic books to his own newspaper strip, and in 1943, Batman episodes were aired on the radio.

a. The masked hero soon moved from comic books to his own newspaper strip, and in 1943, Batman episodes were aired on the radio.

b. The masked hero soon moved from comic books to his own newspaper strip to the radio.

c. In 1943, the masked hero soon moved from comic books to his own newspaper strip, and Batman episodes were aired on the radio.

d. In 1943, the masked hero soon moved from comic books to his own newspaper strip to the radio.

e. The masked hero soon moved from comic books to his own newspaper strip, and Batman episodes were aired on the radio.

Use the following passage to answer questions 60–70.

(1) One of today's hottest fads is also one of the world's oldest practices the ancient art of yoga. (2) Yoga is different from other fitness activities because it is not only physical. (3) In the correct form, yoga is a practice of unification: an emotional, spiritual, and physical exercise.

(4) A simple sitting pose such as staff pose, for example, requires you to tighten and lengthen stomach, back, and arm muscles as you stretch your legs out in front of you and place your hands by your side. (5) More difficult poses, such as brave warrior, require you to balance on one leg and hold a pose that strengthens leg, back, and stomach muscles. (6) Though it may seem easy to those who have never practiced, yoga poses require great concentration, and they are surprisingly effective in stretching and strengthening muscles.

(7) For example yoga tones and strengthens the body, it also tones and strengthens the mind. (8) Many poses can be only held if you are completely focused on the task, and full benefit of the poses are coming only through proper breathing. (9) Concentrated, deep breathing during yoga helps you extend more fully into the poses. (10) Thereby gaining greater benefit from the stretch. (11) And the steady circulation of breath through you're body both calms and energizes.

(12) I am still relatively new to the practice of yoga. (13) I have been practicing yoga for only one year. (14) I am addicted to yoga unlike any other physical activity because it is also a spiritual practice. (15) Through yoga, I am able to release tensions that lodge in various parts of my body: the tight shoulders, the cramped legs, the belly that is in knots. (16) The physical release is also a spiritual release. (17) I feel calm after doing yoga, reconnected to my body, and reconnected to my inner self.

60. Which of the following is the best version of the underlined portion of sentence 1 (reproduced here)?

> One of <u>today's hottest fads is also one of the world's oldest practices the ancient art</u> of yoga.

  a. no change

  b. today's hottest fads is also one of the world's most old practices the ancient art

  c. today's hottest fads, is also one of the world's oldest practices the ancient art

  d. today's hottest fads is also one of the world's oldest practices: the ancient art

  e. todays hottest fads is also one of the world's oldest practices the ancient art

61. Which of the following is the best version of the underlined portion of sentence 3 (reproduced here)?

> <u>*In the correct form*</u>, *yoga is a practice of unification: an emotional, spiritual, and physical exercise.*

  a. no change

  b. Formed in the correct manner

  c. Done correctly

  d. Being done correctly

  e. Doing it in the correct way

62. Which of the following is the best version of the underlined portion of sentence 4 (reproduced here)?

> *A simple sitting pose such as staff pose, for example, <u>requires you to tighten</u> and lengthen stomach, back, and arm muscles as you stretch your legs out in front of you and place your hands by your side.*

  a. no change

  b. requiring that you tighten

  c. it requires you to tighten

  d. requires tightening

  e. in which you are required to tighten

63. The writer could best improve the passage by doing what to sentence 6?

  a. removing sentence 6

  b. moving sentence 6 to follow sentence 3

  c. moving sentence 6 to begin paragraph 2

  d. moving sentence 6 to follow sentence 4

  e. moving sentence 6 to follow sentence 7

64. Which of the following is the best way to revise sentence 8 (reproduced here)?

Many poses can be held only if you are completely focused on the task, and full benefit of the poses are coming only through proper breathing.

a. Many poses can be held only if you are completely focused on the task, and full benefit of the poses are coming only through proper breath.

b. Many poses can be held only if you are completely focused on the task and full benefit of the poses are coming only through proper breathing.

c. Many poses can be held only if you are completely focused on the task, and benefiting fully of the poses are coming only through proper breathing.

d. Many poses can be held only if you are completely focused on the task, and full benefit of the poses comes only through proper breathing.

e. Many poses can only be held if you are completely focused on the task, but full benefit of the poses are coming only through proper breathing.

65. Which of the following is the best version of the underlined portions of sentences 9 and 10 (reproduced here)?

Concentrated, deep breathing during yoga helps you extend more fully into the <u>poses. Thereby</u> gaining greater benefit from the stretch.

a. poses, thereby

b. poses; thereby

c. poses, so thereby

d. poses, but

e. poses. But

66. Which of the following is the best version of the underlined portion of sentence 11 (reproduced here)?

And the steady circulation <u>of breath through you're body</u> both calms and energizes.

a. no change

b. of breath through your body both

c. of breath, through your body, both

d. through your body of breath both

e. of breath through you're body

67. Which of the following is the best way to revise and combine sentences 12 and 13 (reproduced here)?

I am still relatively new to the practice of yoga. I have been practicing yoga for only one year.

a. I am still relatively new to yoga, the practice of which I have been doing for only one year.

b. I am still relatively new to the practice of yoga, of which I have only been practicing for one year.

c. I am still relatively new to yoga, which I have been practicing for only one year.

d. I have only been practicing yoga for one year, which means I am still relatively new to the practice.

e. Because I am still relatively new to yoga, I have only been practicing for one year.

68. Which word or phrase would best fit at the beginning of sentence 14?

a. Since

b. Surprisingly,

c. In the end,

d. Similarly,

e. However,

69. Which of the following is the best version of the underlined portion of sentence 15 (reproduced here)?

Through yoga, I am able to release tensions that lodge in various parts of my body: the tight shoulders, the cramped legs, the belly that is in knots.

a. no change
b. the belly with knots
c. the knots in the belly
d. the knotted belly
e. the belly having knots

70. Which of the following would best replace *For example* at the beginning of sentence 7?

a. While
b. Otherwise
c. For instance
d. To put it differently
e. Here

Analyzing Writing

Directions: The following passages are excerpts from longer pieces, and they do not necessarily completely address a topic. Read each passage, and answer the questions that follow. The questions test your ability to recognize key writing elements, including the writer's purpose and the organizational structure of a passage.

Use the following passage to answer questions 71–74.

(1) In any good fiction, there is always something at stake for the main character. (2) There has to be, or why would we readers care? (3) What is at stake is occasionally obvious, but more often than not, the author withholds critical information in the story. (4) The author may hint at something, and this hint may jumpstart a journey of circumstances and consequences. (5) The author's decision to withhold information whets the reader's appetite. (6) The dramatic tension builds as the writer continues to withhold important information in a story. (7) Every opportunity to delay the key information further develops the tension.

(8) In *An Early Winter* by Marion Dane Bauer, a young boy must accept that his grandfather has changed. (9) Early on, the boy and the reader learn that the grandfather is not well. (10) Other family members believe that the grandfather is not capable of taking care of himself anymore. (11) The boy does not believe this, and he sets out to prove the family wrong. (12) The boy and his grandfather go fishing and soon the boy realizes that his grandfather's limitations—his grandfather has begun to show signs of dementia—are more serious than he thought. (13) The boy must decide how he will handle and accept his grandfather's illness and limitations.

71. Which of the following is the best function of sentence 2?

a. Sentence 2 is a connector between sentence 1 and sentence 3.
b. By asking the reader a question, sentence 2 engages the reader and begins a dialogue with the reader.
c. Sentence 2 should be omitted, as it serves no purpose at all.
d. Sentence 2 is the thesis statement.
e. Sentence 2 provides details.

72. Which of the following best describes the relationship between the two paragraphs in the story?

   a. The second paragraph restates what is said in the first paragraph.

   b. Paragraph 2 gives a concrete illustration of what is said in paragraph 1.

   c. Paragraph 2 generalizes about paragraph 1.

   d. The second paragraph offers an opposite point of view to paragraph 1.

   e. The first and second paragraphs both give specific illustrations.

73. What should be done with sentence 7?

   a. It should begin with the word *so,* joined with sentence 6.

   b. It should appear after sentence 8.

   c. It should be removed from the passage.

   d. It should appear after sentence 1.

   e. It should be the first sentence in paragraph 1.

74. The main implication of this passage is that

   a. dramatic tension emerges when the reader doesn't have all of the answers.

   b. dramatic tension is not a critical element in good fiction.

   c. when an author withholds information, it is usually because he or she does not have the answers.

   d. most stories are about families.

   e. only mystery writers know how to create dramatic tension.

Use the following passage to answer questions 75–78.

(1) The coast of the state of Maine is one of the most irregular in the world. (2) A straight line running from the southernmost coastal city to the northernmost coastal city would measure about 225 miles. (3) If you followed the coastline between these points, you would travel more than ten times as far. (4) This irregularity is the result of what is called a drowned coastline. (5) The term comes from the glacial activity of the ice age. (6) At that time, the whole area that is now Maine was part of a mountain range that towered above the sea. (7) As the glacier descended, however, it expended enormous force on those mountains, and they sank into the sea.

(8) As the mountains sank, ocean water charged over the lowest parts of the remaining land, forming a series of twisting inlets and lagoons of contorted grottos and nooks. (9) The highest parts of the former mountain range, nearest the shore, remained as islands. (10) Mt. Desert Island was one of the most famous of all the islands left behind by the glacier. (11) Marine fossils found here were 225 feet above sea level, indicating the level of the shoreline prior to the glacier.

(12) The 2,500-mile-long rocky and jagged coastline of Maine keeps watch over nearly 2,000 islands. (13) Many of these islands are tiny and uninhabited, but many are home to thriving communities. (14) Mt. Desert Island is one of the largest, most beautiful of the Maine coast islands. (15) Measuring 16 miles by 12 miles, Mt. Desert was very nearly formed as two distinct islands. (16) It is split almost in half by Somes Sound, a very deep and very narrow stretch of water seven miles long.

(17) For years, Mt. Desert Island, particularly its major settlement, Bar Harbor, afforded summer homes for the wealthy. (18) Recently though, Bar Harbor has become a burgeoning arts community as well. (19) But, the best part of the island is the unspoiled forest land known as Acadia National Park. (20) Since the island sits on the boundary line between the temperate and sub-Arctic zones, the island supports the flora and fauna of both zones as well as beach, inland, and alpine plants. (21) It also lies in a major bird migration lane and is a resting spot for many birds. (22) The establishment of

Acadia National Park in 1916 means that this natural monument will be preserved and that it will be available to all people, not just the wealthy. (23) Visitors to Acadia may receive nature instruction from the park naturalists as well as enjoy camping, hiking, cycling, and boating. (24) Or they may choose to spend time at the archeological museum learning about the Stone Age inhabitants of the island.

(25) The best view on Mt. Desert Island is from the top of Cadillac Mountain. (26) This mountain rises 1,532 feet, making it the highest mountain on the Atlantic seaboard. (27) From the summit, you can gaze back toward the mainland or out over the Atlantic Ocean and contemplate the beauty created by a retreating glacier.

75. Which of the following lists of topics best outlines the information in the selection?

a. ■ ice-age glacial activity
   ■ the islands of Casco Bay
   ■ formation of Cadillac Mountain
   ■ summer residents of Mt. Desert Island

b. ■ formation of a drowned coastline
   ■ the topography of Mt. Desert Island
   ■ the environment of Mt. Desert Island
   ■ tourist attractions on Mt. Desert Island

c. ■ mapping the Maine coastline
   ■ the arts community at Bar Harbor
   ■ history of the National Park system
   ■ climbing Cadillac Mountain

d. ■ the effect of glaciers on small islands
   ■ stone-age dwellers on Mt. Desert Island
   ■ the importance of biodiversity
   ■ hiking in Acadia National Park

e. ■ descending glaciers
   ■ fossils of Maine
   ■ Maine tourism
   ■ Atlantic Ocean

76. Which of the following statements best expresses the main idea of paragraph 4 (sentences 17–24) of the selection?

a. The wealthy residents of Mt. Desert Island selfishly kept it to themselves.

b. Acadia National Park is one of the smallest of the national parks.

c. On Mt. Desert Island, there is great tension between the year-round residents and the summer tourists.

d. Due to its location and environment, Mt. Desert Island supports an incredibly diverse animal and plant life.

e. Maine's Cadillac Mountain offers hikers a spectacular vantage point.

77. According to the selection, the large number of small islands along the coast of Maine is the result of

a. glaciers forcing a mountain range into the sea.

b. Maine's location between the temperate and sub-Arctic zones.

c. the irregularity of the Maine coast.

d. the need for summer communities for wealthy tourists and artists.

e. the unique Maine floral and fauna.

78. The content of paragraph 4 (sentences 17–24) indicates that the writer believes that

   a. the continued existence of national parks is threatened by budget cuts.

   b. the best way to preserve the environment on Mt. Desert Island is to limit the number of visitors.

   c. national parks allow large numbers of people to visit and learn about interesting wilderness areas.

   d. Mt. Desert Island is the most interesting tourist attraction in Maine.

   e. an abundance of tourism has hurt the native floral and fauna in Arcadia National Park.

Use the following passage to answer questions 79–84.

(1) Today, bicycles are elegantly simple machines that are common around the world. (2) Many people ride bicycles for recreation, while others use them as a means of transportation. (3) The first bicycle, called a *draisienne,* was invented in Germany in 1818 by Baron Karl de Drais de Sauerbrun. (4) Because it was made of wood, the *draisienne* wasn't very durable nor did it have pedals. (5) Riders moved it by pushing their feet against the ground.

(6) In 1839, Kirkpatrick Macmillan, a Scottish blacksmith, invented a much better bicycle. (7) Macmillan's machine had tires with iron rims to keep them from getting worn down. (8) He also used foot-operated cranks similar to pedals so his bicycle could be ridden at a quick pace. (9) It didn't look much like the modern bicycle, though, because its back wheel was substantially larger than its front wheel. (10) Although Macmillan's bicycles could be ridden easily, they were never produced in large numbers.

(11) In 1861, Frenchman Pierre Michaux and his brother Ernest invented a bicycle with an improved crank mechanism. (12) They called their bicycle a *vélocipède,* but most people called it a "bone shaker" because of the jarring effect of the wood and iron frame. (13) Despite the unflattering nickname, the *vélocipède* was a hit. (14) After a few years, the Michaux family was making hundreds of the machines annually, mostly for fun-seeking young people.

(15) Ten years later, James Starley, an English inventor, made several innovations that revolutionized bicycle design. (16) He made the front wheel many times larger than the back wheel, put a gear on the pedals to make the bicycle more efficient, and lightened the wheels by using wire spokes. (17) Although this bicycle was much lighter and less tiring to ride, it was still clumsy, extremely top-heavy, and ridden mostly for entertainment.

(18) It wasn't until 1874 that the first truly modern bicycle appeared on the scene. (19) Invented by another Englishman, H.J. Lawson, the safety bicycle would look familiar to today's cyclists. (20) The "safety bicycle" had equal-sized wheels, which made it much less prone to toppling over. (21) Lawson also attached a chain to the pedals to drive the rear wheel. (22) By 1893, the safety bicycle had been further improved with air-filled rubber tires, a diamond-shaped frame, and easy braking. (23) With the improvements provided by Lawson, bicycles became extremely popular and useful for transportation. (24) Today they are built, used, and enjoyed all over the world.

79. There is enough information in this passage to show that

  a. several people contributed to the development of the modern bicycle.

  b. only a few *vélocipèdes* built by the Michaux family are still in existence.

  c. for most of the nineteenth century, few people rode bicycles just for fun.

  d. bicycles with wheels of different sizes cannot be ridden easily.

  e. John Starley was resentful that he did not receive more credit for inventing the bicycle.

80. The writer mentions that the first person to use a gear system on bicycles was

  a. H. J. Lawson.

  b. Kirkpatrick Macmillan.

  c. Pierre Michaux.

  d. James Starley.

  e. Baron Karl de Drais de Sauerbrun.

81. This passage was most likely written in order to

  a. persuade readers to use bicycles for transportation.

  b. describe the problems that bicycle manufacturers encounter.

  c. compare bicycles used for fun with bicycles used for transportation.

  d. tell readers a little about the history of the bicycle.

  e. display the effects of bicycles on the environment.

82. The writer explains that Macmillan added iron rims to the tires of his bicycle to

  a. add weight to the bicycle.

  b. make the tires last longer.

  c. make the ride less bumpy.

  d. make the ride less tiring.

  e. add an aesthetic detail to the bicycle.

83. Read the following sentence from paragraph 4 (sentences 15–17):

  Ten years later, James Starley, an English inventor, made several innovations that <u>revolutionized</u> bicycle design.

  As it is used in the sentence, the word *revolutionized* most nearly means

  a. cancelled.

  b. changed drastically.

  c. became outdated.

  d. exercised control over.

  e. abandoned conventions.

84. Which of the following statements from the passage represents the writer's opinion?

  a. The safety bicycle would look familiar to today's cyclists.

  b. Two hundred years ago, bicycles didn't even exist.

  c. The Michaux brothers called their bicycle a *vélocipède*.

  d. Macmillan's machine had tires with iron rims.

  e. The earliest version of the bicycle was made of wood.

Use the following passage to answer questions 85–90.

(1) Tradition has it that Newton was sitting under an apple tree when an apple fell on his head, and this made him understand that earthly and celestial gravitation are the same. (2) A contemporary writer, William Stukeley, recorded in his *Memoirs*

of Sir Isaac Newton's Life a conversation with Newton in Kensington on April 15, 1726, in which Newton recalled "when formerly, the notion of gravitation came into his mind. (3) It was occasioned by the fall of an apple, as he sat in contemplative mood. (4) Why should that apple always descend perpendicularly to the ground, thought he to himself. (5) Why should it not go sideways or upwards, but constantly to the earth's centre."

(6) Sir Isaac Newton, English mathematician, philosopher, and physicist, was born in 1642 in Woolsthorpe-by-Colsterworth, a hamlet in the county of Lincolnshire. (7) His father had died three months before Newton's birth, and two years later his mother went to live with her new husband, leaving her son in the care of his grandmother. (8) Newton was educated at Grantham Grammar School. In 1661 he joined Trinity College, Cambridge, and continued there as Lucasian professor of mathematics from 1669 to 1701. (9) At that time the college's teachings were based on those of Aristotle, but Newton preferred to read the more advanced ideas of modern philosophers such as Descartes, Galileo, Copernicus, and Kepler. (10) In 1665, he discovered the binomial theorem and began to develop a mathematical theory that would later become calculus.

(11) However, his most important discoveries were made during the two-year period from 1664 to 1666, when the university was closed due to the Great Plague. (12) Newton retreated to his hometown and set to work on developing calculus, as well as advanced studies on optics and gravitation. (13) It was at this time that he discovered the Law of Universal Gravitation and discovered that white light is composed of all the colors of the spectrum. (14) These findings enabled him to make fundamental contributions to mathematics, astronomy, and theoretical and experimental physics.

(15) Arguably, it is for Newton's Laws of Motion that he is most revered. (16) These are the three basic laws that govern the motion of material objects. (17) Together, they gave rise to a general view of nature known as the clockwork universe. (18) The laws are (1) every object moves in a straight line unless acted upon by a force. (2) The acceleration of an object is directly proportional to the net force exerted and inversely proportional to the object's mass. (3) For every action, there is an equal and opposite reaction.

(19) In 1687, Newton summarized his discoveries in terrestrial and celestial mechanics in his *Philosophiae naturalis principia mathematica* (*Mathematical Principles of Natural Philosophy*), one of the greatest milestones in the history of science. (20) In this work he showed how his principle of universal gravitation provided an explanation both of falling bodies on the earth and of the motions of planets, comets, and other bodies in the heavens. (21) The first part of the *Principia*, devoted to dynamics, includes Newton's three laws of motion; the second part to fluid motion and other topics; and the third part to the system of the world, in which, among other things, he provides an explanation of Kepler's laws of planetary motion.

(22) This is not all of Newton's groundbreaking work. (23) In 1704, his discoveries in optics were presented in *Opticks,* in which he elaborated his theory that light is composed of corpuscles, or particles. (24) Among his other accomplishments were his construction (1668) of a reflecting telescope and his anticipation of the calculus of variations, founded by Gottfried Leibniz and the Bernoullis. (25) In later years, Newton considered mathematics and physics a recreation and turned much of his energy toward alchemy, theology, and history, particularly problems of chronology.

(26) Newton achieved many honors over his years of service to the advancement of science and

mathematics, as well as for his role as warden, then master, of the mint. (27) He represented Cambridge University in Parliament, and was president of the Royal Society from 1703 until his death in 1727. (28) Sir Isaac Newton was knighted in 1705 by Queen Anne. (29) Newton never married, nor had any recorded children. (30) He died in London and was buried in Westminster Abbey.

85. Based on Newton's quote in sentences 2–5 of the passage, what can best be surmised about the famous apple falling from the tree?
   a. There was no apple falling from a tree—it was entirely made up.
   b. Newton never sat beneath apple trees.
   c. Newton got distracted from his theory on gravity by a fallen apple.
   d. Newton used the apple anecdote as an easily understood illustration of the Earth's gravitational pull.
   e. Newton invented a theory of geometry for the trajectory of apples falling perpendicularly, sideways, and up and down.

86. In sentence 17, what does the term *clockwork universe* most nearly mean?
   a. eighteenth-century government
   b. the international dateline
   c. Newton's system of latitude
   d. Newton's system of longitude
   e. Newton's Laws of Motion

87. According to the passage, how did Newton affect Kepler's work?
   a. He discredited Kepler's theory at Cambridge, choosing to read Descartes instead.
   b. He provided an explanation of Kepler's laws of planetary motion.
   c. He convinced the dean to teach Kepler, Descartes, Galileo, and Copernicus instead of Aristotle.
   d. He showed how Copernicus was a superior astronomer to Kepler.
   e. He did not understand Kepler's laws, so he rewrote them in English.

88. Which of the following is NOT an accolade received by Newton?
   a. Member of the Royal Society
   b. Order of Knighthood
   c. Master of the Royal Mint
   d. Prime Minister, Parliament
   e. Lucasian Professor of Mathematics

89. Of the following, which is last in chronology?
   a. *Philosophiae naturalis principia mathematica*
   b. *Memoirs of Sir Isaac Newton's Life*
   c. Newton's Laws of Motion
   d. *Optiks*
   e. invention of a reflecting telescope

90. Which description best summarizes the life of Sir Isaac Newton?

    a. distinguished inventor, mathematician, physicist, and great thinker of the seventeenth century

    b. eminent mathematician, physicist, and scholar of the Renaissance

    c. noteworthy physicist, astronomer, mathematician, and British Lord

    d. from master of the mint to master mathematician: Lord Isaac Newton

    e. Isaac Newton: founder of calculus and father of gravity

▶ Answers

1. b. This statement uses a double negative. Both *isn't* and *hardly* are negatives. The *isn't* should be changed to *is*.

2. b. When two things are compared, an adjective in the comparative degree is needed. The *best* should be *better*.

3. c. This question contains an error in pronoun shift. The sentence begins with *you* but changes at the end to *one*. The use of pronouns should be consistent all the way through from beginning to end.

4. c. The subject of the sentence is *gathering*, which is singular. The verb should also be singular, so *were* should be *was*.

5. e. There is no error in this example.

6. b. There is an error in diction in this sentence. An adverb is needed to modify the verb *rang*. *Unexpected* should be *unexpectedly*.

7. b. This question tests an error in diction. Adverbs modify active verbs; *well*, rather than *good*, should modify the verb *to write*.

8. d. This sentence contains faulty parallelism. Coordinating elements in a series should have parallel grammatical form. *Swimming in the chilly ocean* should be *swim in the chilly ocean*.

9. b. The problem here is the pronoun shift. The sentence starts in the third person, using *one*. To be consistent, the next pronoun used should be *one*, not *you*.

10. b. This sentence demonstrates a problem with subject-verb agreement. The subject is *writers*, which is plural. This requires a plural verb, so *appears* should be *appear*.

11. c. You should not use *however* as a conjunction between independent clauses. Either a semicolon or a period should be used to join the clauses.

12. c. This is an example of a problem with pronoun-antecedent agreement. The antecedents are *guests* and *members*, which are plural, so the pronoun should be plural also. *His or her* should be *their*.

13. c. Here is a problem with pronoun reference. The pronoun *they* does not refer to any specific noun or pronoun.

14. a. The subject is *neither*, which is singular. The verb needs to be singular, too, so the *are* should be *is*.

15. a. This is a question about faulty comparison. A comparison of two things uses the comparative degree by adding -*er*. The word *scariest* should be *scarier*.

16. c. This is a run-on sentence. You cannot join two independent clauses with a comma. It needs to be replaced with either a period or semicolon.

17. e. There is no error in this question.

18. d. It is incorrect to use a pronoun in the wrong number. The subject is singular (*student*) and the pronoun should also be singular. The word *their* should be *his or her*.

19. c. This is a sentence fragment because it is missing a verb. Only choice **c** adds the verb in the right tense.

20. e. The second part of this sentence is a fragment and is missing the complete verb. Choice **e** adds the verb *begin* to make it correct.

21. b. This is a run-on sentence with two independent clauses joined by a comma. The way to correct the error is to join the clauses with a semicolon, as in choice **b**.

22. c. To correct this run-on sentence, you can turn the first independent clause into a dependent one. To do this successfully, however, you have to choose a subordinate conjunction (*although*) to show how the two sentences relate to each other. *Because* and *whenever* do not do this.

23. b. This is an example of a misplaced modifier. The introductory clause should modify *the boys,* not *the couch*.

24. e. This sentence contains faulty parallelism. All three verbs must be the same. The first two end in *-ing,* so the third one needs to be changed so that it does, too.

25. b. These two independent clauses are joined by a subordinate conjunction. Only *although* will show the correct relationship between the two thoughts, however.

26. b. The dependent clause in the first half of this sentence does not have the right relationship to the second half. Only the addition of the word *although* connects the two halves.

27. e. You need to look at the relationship between the two independent clauses. The subordinate conjunction has to connect the clauses so that they make sense. Only the word *because* does this.

28. d. This is a run-on sentence that is best repaired by adding a semicolon. The conjunctions in the other examples do not show the relationship between the sentences correctly.

29. c. In the original form, the word *that* creates a dependent clause in the first part of the sentence. Putting the word *and* between the subject and verb makes the sentence confusing and incorrect. The best solution is to take any word in that position out, as in choice **c**.

30. e. Here is a run-on sentence. You can fix this problem by using the appropriate coordinating conjunction. In this case, the best one is the word *but*.

31. a. The original form is the best.

32. c. This is an example of a misplaced modifier. The introductory clause should modify *the medication,* not *the physician*.

33. b. The second part of this sentence is an independent clause, but it is missing a verb. Choice **b** adds the verb and maintains the subject-verb agreement.

34. d. This is an example of a run-on sentence, and adding a semicolon repairs the error. Inserting the conjunctions would change the meaning of the sentence.

35. c. In this sentence, the phrase *from the local high school history class* is modifying *student,* so it needs to be shifted without changing the meaning of the sentence.

36. a. The original form is the best.

37. d. Your rephrased sentence will probably read, "Many people supported Mayor Fitzpatrick *because* he had knowledge of government policy."

38. e. Your rephrased sentence will probably read, "She came to the city as a young woman *and found* a job as a nanny."

39. e. Your rephrased sentence will probably read, "*The domination of reality television* explains why many of the newest television celebrities are not trained actors."

40. c. Your rephrased sentence will probably read, "Many know where the acai berry comes from *and how* it enhances lives."

41. e. Your rephrased sentence will probably read, "John amused the audience and baffled the *critic with* his very clever songwriting."

42. c. Your rephrased sentence will probably read, "The fear that he might get an incomplete grade for not showing up *was more* stressful than the embarrassment Sam endured during his first presentation."

43. a. Your rephrased sentence will probably read, "Whether the mayor is innocent or *corrupt has* become a concern of the council."

44. a. Your rephrased sentence will probably read, "Few people who like to play soccer *appreciate* the sacrifices required to become an all-star like David Beckham."

45. d. Your rephrased sentence will probably read, "Unfortunately for the Democratic candidate, the debate *moderator did* not allow rebuttals because of time restraints."

46. a. Your rephrased sentence will probably read, "Although some states adhere to the No Child Left Behind Act for assessment requirements, other *states leave* the decision to school districts."

47. c. Your rephrased sentence will probably read, "The later works of Judy Blume *treat readers* to adult themes and a more sophisticated approach to fiction."

48. b. Your rephrased sentence will probably read, "Raven-Symoné moved to New York City as a young child *and became* a principal character on *The Cosby Show.*"

49. e. Your rephrased sentence will probably read, "Scientists *have discovered* a gene that appears to lead to obesity."

50. b. Your rephrased sentence will probably read, "The human immunodeficiency virus casuses AIDS, *which has been* an increasing health crisis in African nations over the last decade."

51. c. The nonessential information in this sentence is best set off by commas, and choice **c** is the only version that is grammatically correct. Choice **a** is incorrect because the information set off by commas is incomplete (*was* should be deleted, or *who* should be inserted before *was*). Choice **b** is incorrect because the verb phrase *having been created* is incorrect; the correct helping verb would be *had,* not *having,* and the clause would require *which* before *had.* Choice **d** is incorrect for the same reason as **a,** and because the verb *continuing* should be in the past tense. Choice **e** is incorrect because the verb *being* should be either the present or past tense, not a present participle.

52. d. Sentence 4 is best attached to sentence 3 as a nonessential *who* clause, thus providing extra information regarding the creation of Batman. Choice **a** is incorrect because *that* is used to refer to a group or thing. Kane is a person, so *who* should be used instead of *that.* Choice **b** is incorrect because a semicolon can only be used between two complete sentences (independent clauses), and sentence 4 is an incomplete sentence. Choice **c** is correct, but it changes the meaning of the original sentence. Batman was the brainchild of Kane, not the other way. Choice **e** is incorrect because it is wordy and awkward.

53. e. The modifier *who wore masks* should be moved after *heroes* to be as close as possible to the noun it modifies. Choice **a** is incorrect because *Leonardo da Vinci's* should be as close as possible to the noun it modifies, *sketch.* Choice **b** is incorrect because *batlike wings* is a more concise modifier than *having wings like a bat;* also, the verb *having* cannot follow *flying with.* Choice **c** is incorrect because the new sentence beginning with *and* would be a fragment (incomplete sentence). In choice **d,** the verb phrase *was reported coming* is incorrect.

54. b. This is the most concise and correct way to convey this idea. Choice **a** is unnecessarily wordy. Choice **c** is too informal (*in a big way* is slang). Choice **d** is awkward and states that the size was a success, not that the comic strip was a success. Choice **e** is incorrect because *thing* is too general; a more precise noun should be used.

55. a. The message of sentence 2 gives additional support to the idea in sentence 1. The only answer choice that contains a transitional word or phrase that shows addition is choice **a.**

56. d. This choice uses parallel structure and is correct and concise. Choice **a** is incorrect because *to* requires the verbs *avenge* and *bring* to be in their infinitive forms. Choice **b** is incorrect for the same reason; *brought* is in the past tense, not the infinitive form. Likewise, choice **c** uses the future tense (*will bring*), so it is incorrect. Choice **e** is grammatically correct, but it is wordy and less effective than the parallel structure in choice **d.**

57. a. The tenses are inconsistent (present tense *devotes* and past tense *used*). The other sentences about Batman's background are in the past tense, so *devotes* should be changed to the past tense *devoted.* Choice **b** is incorrect because *to* is necessary to show the relationship between *mind* and *fight;* a gerund (*fighting*) would not make sense here. Choice **c** is incorrect because *high* and *tech* work together to create one modifier, so the hyphen between them is necessary. Choice **d** is incorrect because there are only two items in the list (*body* and *mind*), so there should not be a comma between them. Choice **e** is incorrect because the gerund *developing* would not make sense here.

58. c. The most effective transitional phrase to begin this sentence is *More importantly.* The idea expressed in this sentence—that Batman gives us *an image of our own superhero potential*—is the most powerful explanation for why so many people were drawn to the Batman character. Choice **a** is incorrect because the idea in sentence 18 does not contrast with the idea in sentence 17. While choice **b** is logical (the idea in sentence 18 is an "effect" of the idea in sentence 17), choice **c** is more appropriate in the context. Choice **d** is incorrect because sentence 18 does not contrast the idea in sentence 17. Choice **e** is incorrect because it is wordy, and the transitional word *thankfully* seems out of place in both style and context.

59. a. This sentence is best as written. The revised sentences change either the meaning or timeline of the original sentence. From the original sentence, we can only surmise that Batman episodes being aired on the radio happened in 1943. Also, deleting the year unnecessarily removes important information.

60. d. Colons are used to introduce lists, quotations, and explanations. In this sentence, *the ancient art of yoga* "explains" what one of the world's oldest practices is. Choice **e** is incorrect because the apostrophe is necessary to show possession (a *fad* belonging to *today*). Choice **b** is incorrect because the superlative of one-syllable words is formed by adding *-est*. Choice **c** is incorrect because commas should not be placed between subjects and verbs.

61. c. This is the most concise and correct choice. The phrase should have a verb, because the action is what must be performed correctly, so choice **a** is incorrect. Choice **b** is incorrect because it is wordy and awkward. Choice **d** is incorrect because *being* is unnecessary and ungrammatical. Choice **e** is awkward and wordy, adding the pronoun *it* to confuse the sentence.

62. a. *Pose* is the subject, so the verb must be *requires* to agree. Choice **b** is incorrect because it uses the present participle form of the verb. Choice **c** is incorrect because it adds a second subject, it. Choice **d** has the correct form of the verb, but it disrupts the parallel structure of the sentence; *lengthen* would also have to be changed to *lengthening*. Choice **e** is incorrect because it creates a sentence fragment.

63. c. Sentence 6 introduces the idea of how yoga poses stretch and strengthen muscles. It is therefore best placed at the beginning of paragraph 2 before sentence 4, which provides a specific example of a pose that stretches and strengthens muscles. Removing the sentence (choice **a**) would remove the transition needed between paragraphs 1 and 2 and would make sentence 4, which has the phrase for example, awkward. Choice **b** is incorrect because sentence 6 introduces the ideas discussed in paragraph 2, not paragraph 1. Choice **d** is incorrect because the sentence states the general idea that sentence 4 provides a specific example of; therefore, it must precede sentence 4. Choice **e** is incorrect because sentence 7 is in paragraph 3, which discusses a different idea (the mental aspect of yoga).

64. d. The sentence requires the simple present tense comes, not the present participle *are coming*. Choice **a** is incorrect because it is breathing that is required, not simply breath. Choice **b** is incorrect because the sentence is a complex sentence with two independent clauses connected with the coordinating conjunction *and*; because the sentences are long, they should have a comma between them. Choice **c** is incorrect because *benefit* needs to be a noun with its adjective *full*, not a verb (*benefiting*) with an adverb (*fully*). Choice **e** is incorrect because the word *but* in place of *and* changes the meaning of the original sentence.

65. a. Sentence 10 is an incomplete thought (sentence fragment) and must be connected to sentence 9. A semicolon can only be placed between two independent clauses (complete thoughts), *so* choice **b** is incorrect. Choice **c** is incorrect because *so* and *thereby* together creates an awkward transition between sentences, and *so* does not convey the correct relationship between sentences. Choice **d** is incorrect because the word *but* as a transition changes the intended meaning of the original sentences. Choice **e** is wrong because sentence 10 is unnecessary information and should be set off by commas. The sentence fragment must be corrected.

66. b. *You're* is a contraction of *you are*; the sentence requires the possessive *your*. Choice **a** is incorrect because *you're* must be corrected. Choice **c** is incorrect because *through your body* is a prepositional phrase necessary for the meaning of the sentence, so it should not be set off by commas. Choice **d** creates an awkward word order by moving *breath* farther away from *circulation*, so it is incorrect. *Both* could be deleted, but the sentence still requires the possessive *your*, so choice **e** is incorrect.

67. c. This is the most concise and correct choice. Choice **a** contains an awkward and wordy phrase, *the practice of which I have been doing.* Choice **b** is also awkward and wordy, repeating *practice* and using an unnecessary *of* before *which*. Choice **d** is grammatically correct, but turns the idea order around, and is also wordy with the repetition of *practice*. Choice **e** is incorrect because it is a run-on sentence; *because* makes the first clause dependent.

68. e. Sentence 14 offers a contrast to the information in sentence 13, so *however* is the best transition between the sentences. Choice **a** is incorrect because *since* is a subordinating conjunction and makes sentence 14 a fragment. Choice **b** is incorrect because it does not fit the context of the paragraph or passage. Choice **c** is incorrect for the same reason. Choice **d** is incorrect because sentence 14 does not offer an idea similar to the one in sentence 13.

69. d. Choice **d** gives the sentence parallel structure; the other items in the list follow the adjective, noun pattern of *the knotted belly.* Choices **a**, **b**, **c**, and **e** are all incorrect because they do not correct the lack of parallel structure.

70. a. The sentence is showing sequence; yoga tones and strengthens the body at the same time it tones and strengthens the mind. The only answer choice that contains a transitional word or phrase that shows sequence is choice **a.**

71. b. The use of a question pulls the audience into this passage and tries to make them really consider the author's message.

72. b. Paragraph 2 supports paragraph 1 by giving examples from a novel.

73. c. This sentence repeats sentence 5.

74. a. In sentence 6, the author specifically states, *The dramatic tension builds as the writer continues to withhold important information in a story.*

75. b. Choice **b** includes the main points of the selection and is not too broad. Choices **a** and **e** feature minor points from the selection. Choice **c** also features minor points, with the addition of *history of the National Park system*, which is not included in the selection. Choice **d** lists points that are not discussed in the selection.

76. d. Choice **d** expresses the main idea of paragraph 4 of the selection. The information in choices **a**, **b**, and **c** is expressed in paragraph 3, while the information in choice **e** is stated in paragraph 4.

77. a. Choice **a** is correct, according to paragraph 2, sentence 9. Choices **b**, **c**, and **e** are mentioned in the selection, but not as causing the islands; choice **d** is not mentioned in the selection.

78. c. Paragraph 5 discusses the visitors to Acadia National Park in a positive light; therefore, choice **c** is correct. Choices **a**, **b**, **d**, and **e** are not mentioned in the selection.

79. a. This is the best choice because each paragraph of the passage describes an inventor whose machine was a step toward the modern bicycle. There is no evidence to support choices **b** or **e**. Choices **c** and **d** are incorrect because they both make statements that, according to the passage, are untrue.

80. d. The fourth paragraph states that James Starley added a gear to the pedals.

81. d. The passage gives the history of the bicycle. Choice **a** is incorrect because few opinions are included in the passage. There is no support for choices **b**, **c**, or **e**.

82. b. This information is clearly stated in the second paragraph. The iron rims kept the tires from being worn down, and therefore, the tires lasted longer. Choice **a** is incorrect because although the iron rims probably did make the machine heavier, that was not Macmillan's goal. Choice **c** is incorrect because no information is given about whether iron-rimmed or wooden tires moved more smoothly. There is no support for choice **d** or **e**.

83. b. Based on the paragraph, this is the only possible choice. Starley *revolutionized* the bicycle; that is, he made many innovative changes. In this context, the other choices make no sense.

84. a. This is the only choice that states an opinion. The writer cannot be certain that the safety bicycle would look familiar to today's cyclists; it is his or her opinion that this is so. The other choices are presented as facts.

85. d. The anecdote contrasts with the ensuing quote in paragraph 1 and depicts a plausible reason for the apple story—Newton wanted to make his theory understood to the general public. Speaking in physics terminology is abstract, but using an illustration that regular people have witnessed again and again would aid in understanding. The quote gives credence to the anecdote, ruling out choice **a**. Choices **b** and **e** are never mentioned, and choice **c** is not backed up by the passage.

86. e. In paragraph 4, Newton's Laws of Motion are said to govern the motion of objects and are the basis for the concept of the clockwork universe. Nowhere in the passage is it stated that Newton or his laws are responsible for the international date line (choice **b**), latitude (choice **c**), or longitude (choice **d**). Choice **a** plays on the word *govern* and is misleading.

87. b. The passage specifically states that Newton provided an explanation of Kepler's laws.

88. d. All of the other titles were bestowed on Newton during his lifetime.

89. b. William Stukeley published *Memoirs of Sir Isaac Newton's Life* in 1726, after Newton's death. The other choices are all accomplishments of Newton in his lifetime.

90. a. Choice **a** is correct because it lists the proper
accolades and the proper timeframe in which
he lived. Choice **b** is incorrect because he did
not live in the Renaissance; choices **c** and **d**
are incorrect because he was not a lord, but
a knight; and choice **e** is incorrect because
it is not the best summary of his vast
accomplishments.

CLEP Social Sciences and History Practice Test 1

You are now familiar with the kinds of questions and answer formats you will see on the official CLEP Social Sciences and History exam. Now take Practice Test 1 to identify any areas that you may need to review in more depth before the test day.

On this practice test, you will encounter 120 questions that are similar to the type you will find on the official CLEP Social Sciences and History exam.

To simulate the test conditions, use the time constraints of the official CLEP Social Sciences and History exam. Allow yourself 90 minutes to complete this practice test.

Remember, on the official CLEP, there is no penalty for incorrect answers, so always make a guess if you are unsure of an answer.

When you are finished, check the answer key on page 487 carefully to assess your results.

► CLEP Social Sciences and History Practice Test 1

#					
1.	a	b	c	d	e
2.	a	b	c	d	e
3.	a	b	c	d	e
4.	a	b	c	d	e
5.	a	b	c	d	e
6.	a	b	c	d	e
7.	a	b	c	d	e
8.	a	b	c	d	e
9.	a	b	c	d	e
10.	a	b	c	d	e
11.	a	b	c	d	e
12.	a	b	c	d	e
13.	a	b	c	d	e
14.	a	b	c	d	e
15.	a	b	c	d	e
16.	a	b	c	d	e
17.	a	b	c	d	e
18.	a	b	c	d	e
19.	a	b	c	d	e
20.	a	b	c	d	e
21.	a	b	c	d	e
22.	a	b	c	d	e
23.	a	b	c	d	e
24.	a	b	c	d	e
25.	a	b	c	d	e
26.	a	b	c	d	e
27.	a	b	c	d	e
28.	a	b	c	d	e
29.	a	b	c	d	e
30.	a	b	c	d	e
31.	a	b	c	d	e
32.	a	b	c	d	e
33.	a	b	c	d	e
34.	a	b	c	d	e
35.	a	b	c	d	e
36.	a	b	c	d	e
37.	a	b	c	d	e
38.	a	b	c	d	e
39.	a	b	c	d	e
40.	a	b	c	d	e
41.	a	b	c	d	e
42.	a	b	c	d	e
43.	a	b	c	d	e
44.	a	b	c	d	e
45.	a	b	c	d	e
46.	a	b	c	d	e
47.	a	b	c	d	e
48.	a	b	c	d	e
49.	a	b	c	d	e
50.	a	b	c	d	e
51.	a	b	c	d	e
52.	a	b	c	d	e
53.	a	b	c	d	e
54.	a	b	c	d	e
55.	a	b	c	d	e
56.	a	b	c	d	e
57.	a	b	c	d	e
58.	a	b	c	d	e
59.	a	b	c	d	e
60.	a	b	c	d	e
61.	a	b	c	d	e
62.	a	b	c	d	e
63.	a	b	c	d	e
64.	a	b	c	d	e
65.	a	b	c	d	e
66.	a	b	c	d	e
67.	a	b	c	d	e
68.	a	b	c	d	e
69.	a	b	c	d	e
70.	a	b	c	d	e
71.	a	b	c	d	e
72.	a	b	c	d	e
73.	a	b	c	d	e
74.	a	b	c	d	e
75.	a	b	c	d	e
76.	a	b	c	d	e
77.	a	b	c	d	e
78.	a	b	c	d	e
79.	a	b	c	d	e
80.	a	b	c	d	e
81.	a	b	c	d	e
82.	a	b	c	d	e
83.	a	b	c	d	e
84.	a	b	c	d	e
85.	a	b	c	d	e
86.	a	b	c	d	e
87.	a	b	c	d	e
88.	a	b	c	d	e
89.	a	b	c	d	e
90.	a	b	c	d	e
91.	a	b	c	d	e
92.	a	b	c	d	e
93.	a	b	c	d	e
94.	a	b	c	d	e
95.	a	b	c	d	e
96.	a	b	c	d	e
97.	a	b	c	d	e
98.	a	b	c	d	e
99.	a	b	c	d	e
100.	a	b	c	d	e
101.	a	b	c	d	e
102.	a	b	c	d	e
103.	a	b	c	d	e
104.	a	b	c	d	e
105.	a	b	c	d	e
106.	a	b	c	d	e
107.	a	b	c	d	e
108.	a	b	c	d	e
109.	a	b	c	d	e
110.	a	b	c	d	e
111.	a	b	c	d	e
112.	a	b	c	d	e
113.	a	b	c	d	e
114.	a	b	c	d	e
115.	a	b	c	d	e
116.	a	b	c	d	e
117.	a	b	c	d	e
118.	a	b	c	d	e
119.	a	b	c	d	e
120.	a	b	c	d	e

▶ Practice Test Questions

Directions: Each of the questions or incomplete statements in this exam is followed by five suggested answers or completions. Select the one that is best in each case.

Western Civilization

1. Note the following ideas:
- early civil rights stance
- one novel by this author
- losing childhood innocence

These ideas are associated with which book?

a. *Gone with the Wind*—Margaret Mitchell

b. *For Whom the Bell Tolls*—Ernest Hemingway

c. *To Kill a Mockingbird*—Harper Lee

d. *Huckleberry Finn*—Mark Twain

e. *The Sound and the Fury*—William Faulkner

2. Which of the following pairs is correct?

a. I Have a Dream—Malcolm X

b. Fear but Fear Itself—Martin Luther King

c. Ich bin ein Berliner—John F. Kennedy

d. Tear Down This Wall—George W. Bush

e. Gettysburg Address—Thomas Jefferson

3. Which of the following pairs is correct?

a. Samuel Clemens—*Leatherstocking Tales*

b. Homer—*Faust*

c. Adam Smith—*Wealth of Nations*

d. Walter Rostow—*The Theory of the Leisure Class*

e. Johann Wolfgang Goethe—*Moll Flanders*

4. Read the following.

"We little thought when we first put on our overalls and caps and enlisted in the Munitions Army how much more inspiring our life was to be then we had dared to hope. Though we munitions workers sacrifice our ease we gain a life worth living. Our long days are filled with interest and with the zest of doing work for our country in the grand cause of Freedom."

This passage depicts an experience from

a. the women's suffrage movement.

b. the cause of the abolitionists during the Civil War.

c. the families of the Underground Railroad.

d. the female nurses involved in World War II.

e. the World War I women's movement to working in factories.

5. The three European nations that established trading centers on the coasts of India during the sixteenth century were

a. France, Germany, and Ireland.

b. Spain, Monaco, and Hungary.

c. Greece, Italy, and Turkey.

d. England, the Netherlands, and Portugal.

e. England, France, and Italy.

6. Read the following quote from the autobiography of Stefan Zweig.

"A rapid excursion into the romantic, a wild, manly adventure—that is how the war of 1914 was painted in the imagination of the simple man, and the younger people were honestly afraid that they might miss the most wonderful and exciting experience of their lives; that is why they hurried and thronged to the colors, and that is why they shouted and sang in the trains that carried them to the slaughter; wildly and feverishly the red wave of blood course through the veins of the entire nation."

This passage describes the beginning of
a. the Revolutionary War.
b. the Civil War.
c. World War I.
d. World War II.
e. the Vietnam War.

7. Which of the following astronomers was originally responsible for the concept that the planets all revolved around the sun?
a. Galileo
b. Kepler
c. Ptolemy
d. Copernicus
e. Halley

8. Which of the following philosophers is correctly paired with his or her philosophy?
a. Wollstonecraft—Vindications of the Rights of Women
b. Voltaire—The Support of Muhammad
c. Smith—The Decline and Fall of the Roman Empire
d. Hume—Philosophic Letters on the English
e. Beccaria—The Progress of the Human Mind

9. In the eighteenth century, which of the following types of medical practitioners was considered the most elite?
a. surgeons
b. apothecaries
c. faith healers
d. midwives
e. physicians

10. I was born in Corsica and went to military school in France. I rose quickly through the ranks and by age 25, I was a brigadier general. I soon became a national hero and eventually emperor. My wife Josephine and I were later exiled to Elba and then to Saint Helena, a tiny island in the south Atlantic.
Who is speaking?
a. Lafayette
b. Louis XVI
c. de Gouges
d. Robespierre
e. Napoleon

11. Which of the following set of years most accurately defines the cold war era?
a. 1911–1915
b. 1929–1931
c. 1932–1945
d. 1947–1989
e. 1991–2007

12. Read the following quote.

"We sent the Americans a note saying that we agreed to remove our missiles and bombers on the condition that the president give us his assurance that there would be no invasion of Cuba by the forces of the United States or anybody else."

Who is speaking and about which president?

a. Gorbachev and Reagan

b. Stalin and Truman

c. Hitler and Roosevelt

d. bin Laden and Bush

e. Khrushchev and Kennedy

13. In the 1960s, Charles de Gaulle worked hard to

a. maintain France's independence from the Soviet Union and the United States.

b. fight against both armored warfare and military aviation.

c. stop the production of atomic weapons.

d. show his opposition to control inflation and industrial growth in France.

e. keep the original constitution of the Fourth Republic.

14. Who wrote the book *Perestroika*?

a. Gorbachev

b. de Gaulle

c. Lenin

d. Khrushchev

e. Stalin

15. Which president challenged the Soviet Union to "tear down this wall"?

a. Carter

b. Ford

c. Reagan

d. Nixon

e. Bush

16. Who was the female politician who earned the nickname "the Iron Lady"?

a. Eleanor Roosevelt

b. Nancy Reagan

c. Raisa Gorbachev

d. Margaret Thatcher

e. Shirley Chisholm

17. The "women's lib" movement in postwar times was primarily spearheaded by teacher and author

a. Margaret Sanger.

b. Susan B. Anthony.

c. Gloria Steinem.

d. Germaine Greer.

e. Simone de Beauvoir.

18. Jackson Pollock was known for what style of painting?

a. impressionism

b. abstract expressionism

c. primitivism

d. surrealism

e. post-impressionism

World History

19. During the Russian Revolution, which of the following events occurred first?

a. murder of Rasputin

b. Civil War

c. tsar abdicates

d. Lenin arrives in Russia

e. Brest-Litovsk Treaty

20. During the regime of Nazi Germany, which of the following events happened last?

a. Hitler is made chancellor.

b. Nuremburg laws

c. *Kristallnacht*

d. Enabling Act

e. Reichstag fire

21. When Pope Innocent VII was looking for something on which to blame the Black Death, he stated that he thought the cause was

a. rats.

b. tainted water.

c. witches.

d. lack of sanitation.

e. evil spirits.

22. I became queen at the age of 18. I listened closely to the advice of my husband Prince Albert, as well as that of my Prime Minister, Lord Melbourne. I gave birth to nine children but then tragically lost my husband at a young age. I wore black every day from that day forward. I became a symbol of the British Empire and was in power for 64 years, the longest in British history. Which queen is described here?

a. Elizabeth II

b. Anne

c. Mary

d. Victoria

e. Elizabeth I

23. The Boxer Uprising in 1899–1900 was due to what circumstances?

I. economic hardship

II. anti-foreign feelings due to Christian missionaries' actions

III. a strong belief in superstition held by the uneducated lower classes

a. I only

b. II only

c. III only

d. I and III

e. I, II, and III

24. A newspaper reporter stated, "Just an old man in a loincloth in distant India; yet, when he died, humanity wept." What 1948 historical event was he referring to?

a. the assassination of Count Folke Bernadotte

b. the assassination of Gandhi

c. the death of Jan Masaryk

d. the assassination of Jorge Eliecer Gaitan

e. the death of Babe Ruth

25. Which of the following events in world history occurred first?

a. assassination of Egyptian President Anwar Sadat

b. Chernobyl nuclear accident

c. Emperor Hirohito of Japan dies at age 87

d. the Chunnel links England and France

e. Construction of the Berlin Wall

26. In what country were same-sex marriages first legally permitted?

a. Sweden

b. Canada

c. Denmark

d. Japan

e. United States

27. In what year did Saddam Hussein's trial begin?

a. 2003

b. 2004

c. 2005

d. 2006

e. 2007

28. In 2006, the world's population reached

a. five billion.

b. five and a half billion.

c. six billion.

d. six and a half billion.

e. seven billion.

United States History

29. Which of the following was Lincoln's primary reason for creating the Emancipation Proclamation?

a. to encourage the abolitionists

b. to punish the Southerners

c. to support the suffrage movement

d. to preserve the Union

e. to free the slaves

30. The purpose of the Marshall Plan was to

a. support the concept of Manifest Destiny.

b. expand on the concepts in the Emancipation Proclamation.

c. accompany the original draft of the Bill of Rights.

d. provide the money for the search for weapons of mass destruction.

e. rebuild Europe through U.S. funding following World War II.

31. The presidential candidate associated with the Florida voting confusion in 2000 was

a. Ronald Reagan.

b. Dan Quayle.

c. Bill Clinton.

d. John Edwards.

e. Al Gore.

32. Note the following:

- Seward's Folly
- $7.2 million
- polar bear garden
- Russia

These ideas are associated with the

a. Articles of Confederation.

b. purchase of Alaska.

c. Homestead Act.

d. impeachment of Andrew Jackson.

e. Louisiana Purchase.

33. Read the following excerpt from a famous speech.

"No matter how long it may take us to overcome this premeditated invasion, the American people in their righteous might will win through to absolute victory."

What speech is this from?

a. Darrow's "Mercy for Leopold and Loeb"

b. Carter's "A Crisis of Confidence"

c. King's "I've Been to the Mountaintop"

d. Debs's "The Issue"

e. Roosevelt's "Pearl Harbor Address to the Nation"

34. When Hitler made his officers take a "blood oath of allegiance," it stated that what two things were to be held sacred?

a. family and government

b. standards and flags

c. war and prisoners

d. the Nazi Party and the swastika

e. officers and soldiers

35. Which president coined the term *war on terrorism*?

a. Ronald Reagan

b. George Bush

c. Bill Clinton

d. Jimmy Carter

e. George W. Bush

36. Authors who called themselves part of the "Lost Generation" used their novels to criticize

a. materialism.

b. politics.

c. war.

d. prejudice.

e. marriage.

37. What national crisis did Herbert Hoover have to handle right after he was elected president?

a. World War II

b. acts of terrorism

c. the Depression

d. the Dust Bowl

e. the Cuban Missile Crisis

38. Which of the following factors contributed to the steady economic growth of the 1950s and 1960s?

I. continued military spending

II. dramatic increase in birthrate

III. decrease in college enrollment

a. I only

b. III only

c. I and II

d. II and III

e. I, II, and III

39. The Internet was originally created in the 1960s and was intended to be used only by the Department of

a. Commerce.

b. Defense.

c. Agriculture.

d. Education.

e. Treasury.

40. When the Japanese attacked Pearl Harbor, Hawaii was an

a. state.

b. nation.

c. territory.

d. archipelago.

e. lagoon.

41. Which of the following presidents was elected to four terms?

a. Ronald Reagan

b. George W. Bush

c. Bill Clinton

d. Harry Truman

e. Franklin D. Roosevelt

42. What is one of the most influential reasons that Hitler did NOT exploit the possibility of nuclear fission?
 a. Hitler's Germany did not know about the scientific technology yet.
 b. Science was not a high priority to Hitler's Nazi regime.
 c. Albert Einstein warned Hitler against getting involved with fission.
 d. Hitler's attitude toward Jews drove away some of Germany's best scientists.
 e. President Roosevelt refused to share the technical information with Hitler.

43. Article 5 of the North Atlantic Treaty stated, "The parties agree that an armed attack against one or more of them in Europe or North America shall be considered an attack against them all."

What organization did this statement result in creating?
 a. NAFTA
 b. NATO
 c. NASA
 d. NSA
 e. NTSB

44. The main action that Rosa Parks inspired was
 a. riots.
 b. jail time.
 c. boycotts.
 d. looting.
 e. new laws.

45. Which of the following presidents stated, "The torch has been passed to a new generation" during his inaugural speech?
 a. Hoover
 b. Truman
 c. Kennedy
 d. Ford
 e. Reagan

46. Which of the following is not a name used for the hallucinogenic discovered by Albert Hofmann in 1943?
 a. acid
 b. LSD
 c. LSD-25
 d. crack
 e. d-lysergic acid diethylamide

47. Which of the following presidents was responsible for opening up relations with the Soviets and the Chinese?
 a. Richard Nixon
 b. Dwight Eisenhower
 c. Lyndon Johnson
 d. Calvin Coolidge
 e. Gerald Ford

48. Which constitutional amendment is responsible for setting the national voting age?
 a. the Second Amendment
 b. the Fifth Amendment
 c. the Tenth Amendment
 d. the Fifteenth Amendment
 e. the Twenty-Sixth Amendment

Government/Political Science

49. In which of the following cases did the U.S. Supreme Court make the decision that the death penalty is constitutional?
   a. *Marbury v. Madison*
   b. *Abrams v. United States*
   c. *Gregg v. Georgia*
   d. *Miranda v. Arizona*
   e. *Roe v. Wade*

50. The *Plessy v. Ferguson* trial was one that established
   a. the doctrine of separate but equal.
   b. the Supreme Court's ability to overrule congressional law.
   c. school segregation is unconstitutional.
   d. the states can no longer ban abortions.
   e. schools cannot require students to pray in school.

51. Read the following quote.
   "As long as my record stands on federal court, any American citizen can be held in prison or concentration camps without trial or hearing. I would like to see the government admit they were wrong and do something about it, so this will never happen again to any American citizen of any race, creed, or color."

   From which court case does this quote come?
   a. *Gideon v. Wainwright*
   b. *Tinker v. Des Moines*
   c. *Regents of CA v. Bakke*
   d. *Korematsu v. United States*
   e. *New Jersey v. T.L.O.*

52. The first American government, which consisted of 13 states called a confederation, did NOT have the power to
   a. declare war.
   b. tax its citizens.
   c. sign treaties.
   d. create a postal system.
   e. mint money.

53. In the case of both the president and vice president of the United States dying, becoming incapacitated, or unable to perform their jobs, the next person in line to head the country is the
   a. Speaker of the House.
   b. President Pro Tempore of the Senate.
   c. Attorney General.
   d. Secretary of State.
   e. Secretary of the Interior.

54. George Washington once said that one historical document was "little more than the shadow without the substance." To which document was he referring?
   a. Declaration of Independence
   b. U.S. Constitution
   c. Bill of Rights
   d. Articles of Confederation
   e. Federalist Papers

55. The process of becoming an American citizen has a number of requirements, including which of the following?

I. be able to read, write, speak, and understand basic English

II. have lived in the United States as a legal resident for at least five years

III. be of good moral character and loyal to the United States

a. I only
b. II only
c. I and II
d. II and III
e. I, II, and III

56. All of the following are powers of the national government EXCEPT

a. printing money.
b. issuing licenses.
c. making treaties.
d. establishing post offices.
e. regulating interstate trade.

57. Concurrent powers include all of the following EXCEPT

a. collecting taxes.
b. building roads.
c. borrowing money.
d. conducting elections.
e. chartering banks.

58. A proposal to alter the language or provisions of an act is known as a(n)

a. bill.
b. hearing.
c. amendment.
d. ratification.
e. veto.

59. A long speech that cannot be stopped except by a vote from senators is referred to as a(n)

a. monologue.
b. debate.
c. lecture.
d. amendment.
e. filibuster.

60. The requirements to become a U.S. senator include which of the following?

I. a minimum of 30 years old

II. a citizen for at least nine years at the time of election

III. a resident of the state one is elected to represent

a. I only
b. II only
c. I and II
d. II and III
e. I, II, and III

61. What happens if the Electoral College does NOT give one of the presidential candidates at least 270 votes?

a. The people's votes determine the winner.
b. The House of Representatives decides who won.
c. The political campaign starts all over again.
d. Election Day is repeated across the United States.
e. An additional presidential debate is held.

62. What do Salmon P. Chase and William H. Rehnquist have in common?

I. They were both chief justices.

II. They both served as Speakers of the House.

III. They both sat as judges in presidential impeachments.

a. I only

b. II only

c. I and II

d. II and III

e. I and III

63. Which of the following states votes by mail only?

a. Indiana

b. South Dakota

c. New York

d. Oregon

e. California

64. To be considered a potential presidential candidate for the United States, you must be

a. born in the United States.

b. at least 40 years old.

c. married.

d. a U.S. resident for at least 25 years.

e. Christian.

Geography

65. Another word for a group of islands is

a. atoll.

b. lagoon.

c. archipelago.

d. keys.

e. isles.

66. "Boat people" were refugees coming from

a. Cuba and Haiti.

b. Mexico.

c. China and Taiwan.

d. Canada.

e. Ireland and Scotland.

67. Which of the following steps best defines the greenhouse effect?

I. Carbon dioxide and other gases from Earth's surface escape into space.

II. Greenhouse gases trap whatever does not escape and re-radiates them back to Earth.

III. Human-made artificial sources of gases are interfering with the stratospheric ozone.

a. I only

b. II only

c. III only

d. I and II

e. II and III

68. Which of the following is a cold winter desert?

a. Kalahari

b. Gobi

c. Mojave

d. Sahara

e. Sonoran

69. The Common Market was the first name given to what is now known as the

a. Council for Mutual Economic Assistance.

b. Kyoto Protocol.

c. European Union.

d. North Atlantic Treaty Organization.

e. European Economic Community.

70. A karst is a type of landscape that is characterized by which of the following qualities?

I. limestone or dolomite foundation

II. susceptible to erosion

III. commonly found in southern China

a. I only

b. II only

c. I and II

d. II and III

e. I, II, and III

71. What does the term *per capita* mean?

a. per unit

b. per person

c. per dollar

d. per square mile

e. per city

72. You spend the entire day studying the climate, soil, and various landforms of the Earth's surface, so you are most likely a

a. cartographer.

b. climatologist.

c. physical geographer.

d. geomorphologist.

e. cultural geographer.

73. Zero population growth exists when the birth rates are

a. larger than the death rates.

b. higher than in the past.

c. smaller than the death rates.

d. steadily slowing.

e. equal to the death rates.

74. An absolute mathematical location is expressed in

a. degrees, minutes, and seconds.

b. north, south, east, and west.

c. square miles or kilometers.

d. longitude only.

e. latitude only.

75. What is considered to be the most common harmful component of acid rain?

a. carbon dioxide

b. oxygen

c. sulfuric acid

d. nitrous oxide

e. arsenic

76. A species of plants or animals found exclusively in one area is known as

a. endangered.

b. endemic.

c. imported.

d. extinct.

e. threatened.

77. The term *gentrification* is characterized by

I. urban neighborhoods.

II. retired couples.

III. dispossession of minorities.

a. I only

b. II only

c. III only

d. I and III

e. II and III

Sociology

78. Which theory is associated with the right sociologist?

   a. Piaget—Looking Glass Self

   b. Freud—Development of Personality

   c. Cooley—Ability to Reason

   d. Mead—Rationalization of Society

   e. Asch—Role Taking

79. A family that is made up of members who were formerly part of other families is called

   a. blended.

   b. nuclear.

   c. dominant.

   d. multiple.

   e. single.

80. The concept that birth and residence in a country impart basic rights is known as

   a. alienation.

   b. democracy.

   c. citizenship.

   d. community.

   e. socialization.

81. Feeling bewildered, confused, or anxious when encountering situations where the norms of one's culture no longer apply is

   a. cultural lag.

   b. culture contact.

   c. cultural diffusion.

   d. culture shock.

   e. cultural leveling.

82. The number of children an average woman bears is referred to as

   a. intergenerational mobility.

   b. life span.

   c. grade inflation.

   d. pluralism.

   e. fertility rate.

83. Gated communities are examples of what type of discrimination?

   a. sexual

   b. social class

   c. gender based

   d. racial

   e. age

84. The concept of the ego, id, and superego was created by

   a. Ogburn.

   b. Freud.

   c. Marx.

   d. Malthus.

   e. Jung.

85. What is it called when two people with similar characteristics marry each other?

   a. polygamy

   b. monogamy

   c. homogamy

   d. bigamy

   e. trigamy

86. If you lived in a society that focused on women's authority, it would be a(n)

   a. oligarchy.

   b. anarchy.

   c. monarchy.

   d. matriarchy.

   e. patriarchy.

87. Socialism is characterized by which of the following?

I. It is an economic system.

II. It has distribution of goods without a profit motive.

III. It focuses on private ownership.

a. I only

b. II only

c. III only

d. II and III

e. I and II

88. Wearing a Rolex watch or driving a Porsche are examples of

a. caste system.

b. status symbols.

c. social class.

d. upward social mobility.

e. social network.

89. The acronym *WASP* stands for White Anglo-Saxon

a. Person.

b. People.

c. Protestant.

d. Proletariat.

e. Population.

Psychology

90. Drugs that are commonly prescribed to help treat certain anxiety disorders are known as

a. antidepressants.

b. antipsychotics.

c. dopamine.

d. endorphins.

e. barbiturates.

91. I want what I want and I do not care if I am breaking a law or using others. Their feelings are of no relevance. In fact, I don't feel anything for them, so why should they feel anything about me?

The person who would say this would most likely be diagnosed as

a. bipolar.

b. dissociative amnesia.

c. delusions of grandeur.

d. generalized anxiety disorder.

e. antisocial personality disorder.

92. Thinking, knowing, problem-solving, and remembering are all different kinds of

a. cognitive dissonance.

b. cognitive processes.

c. cognitive therapies.

d. cognitive psychology.

e. cognitive maps.

93. A person who has a constant drive to wash her hands is exhibiting what kind of behavior?

a. amnesia

b. bulimia

c. compulsion

d. delusion

e. fixation

94. A chemical that is released by the brain in order to either reduce pain or elevate mood is known as a(n)

a. hormone.

b. depressant.

c. narcotic.

d. endorphin.

e. neurotransmitter.

95. The part of the brain that controls levels of hunger, thirst, body temperature, and sexual behavior is the
  a. Broca's area.
  b. brainstem.
  c. corpus callosum.
  d. frontal lobe.
  e. hypothalamus.

96. It was a lot like going to sleep, except I could hear everything going on around me. It was amazing how much I could remember, however, and the suggestions that the therapist made to me have truly stuck.

  What kind of procedure has this person just gone through?
  a. arousal
  b. hypnosis
  c. biofeedback
  d. manic episode
  e. electroconvulsive therapy

97. Paranoid schizophrenia is characterized by
  I. persecution.
  II. delusions of grandeur.
  III. loss of memory.
  a. I only
  b. II only
  c. III only
  d. I and II
  e. II and III

98. When an inert substance is given to participants in an experiment's control group, the substance is generally referred to as a
  a. depressant.
  b. lithium.
  c. prototype.
  d. sample.
  e. placebo.

99. The period of sleep known as REM stands for rapid eye
  a. motion.
  b. movement.
  c. modulation.
  d. mechanism.
  e. maneuver.

100. When a person assumes something about another based on widely shared beliefs, what is it called?
  a. homeostasis
  b. social norms
  c. modeling
  d. insightful
  e. stereotyping

101. Schizophrenia is characterized by which of the following?
  I. loss of contact with reality
  II. disturbance in thinking
  III. hallucinations and delusions
  a. I only
  b. II only
  c. I and II
  d. II and III
  e. I, II, and III

Anthropology

102. Which of the following numbers correctly represents how many years ago anthropologists believe the first humans came to North America?
  a. 6,000
  b. 8,000
  c. 10,000
  d. 15,000
  e. 20,000

103. Read the following quote.

"I have spent most of my life studying the lives of other peoples—faraway peoples—so that Americans might better understand themselves."

Which famous anthropologist said this?

a. Dian Fossey

b. Ruth Underhill

c. Mary Nichol Leakey

d. Margaret Mead

e. Zora Neale Hurston

104. Which work or idea is associated with the correct anthropologist?

a. Claude Levi-Strauss—Father of American Anthropology

b. Ruth Benedict—Coming of Age in Samoa

c. Franz Boas—the Florida Everglades

d. Margaret Mead—Gorilla Fund International

e. Jane Goodall—Gombe Stream National Park

105. Which of the following would study how different cultures use plants and animals?

a. ethnobiologist

b. paleontologist

c. linguist

d. archaeologist

e. biologist

106. Which of the following subjects is NOT considered part of cultural anthropology?

a. language

b. religion

c. heredity

d. behavior

e. culture

107. If you have spent your entire day using small tools to dust off and excavate a piece of ancient pottery, you are most likely a(n)

a. linguist.

b. archaeologist.

c. scientist.

d. primatologist.

e. biologist.

108. What was one of the first human characteristics to appear right after the split between the human and chimpanzee lineages?

a. using language

b. walking upright

c. developing fire

d. creating crafts

e. wearing clothes

Economics

109. Another economic action that means virtually the same thing as trade is

a. capital.

b. barter.

c. demand.

d. sell.

e. discount.

110. Collective ownership of resources and planning is a hallmark characteristic of which kind of government?

a. democracy

b. communism

c. capitalism

d. monarchy

e. socialism

111. A decline in overall price levels for at least two years is referred to as
   a. deflation.
   b. depression.
   c. inflation.
   d. recession.
   e. stagflation.

112. The U.S. federal budget fiscal year begins on
   a. January 1.
   b. March 1.
   c. April 15.
   d. October 1.
   e. December 30.

113. Which of the following economists and theories is correct?
   a. John Maynard Keynes—Classical
   b. Roy Forbes Harrod—Monetarist
   c. Irving Fisher—Keynesian
   d. Friedrich August von Hayek—Classical
   e. Milton Friedman—Monetarist

114. What economic theory states that while population tends to grow in a geometric progression, food production tends to grow in an arithmetic progression?
   a. crude quantity theory
   b. quantity theory
   c. Malthusian theory
   d. rational expectations
   e. national monopoly

115. Which of the following countries has the longest average workweek?
   a. North America
   b. Germany
   c. France
   d. Denmark
   e. England

116. To calculate the nation's unemployment rate, the number of unemployed is divided by the
   a. interest rate.
   b. minimum wage.
   c. supply and demand.
   d. total revenue.
   e. labor force.

117. What is the term for when the government imposes a minimum price?
   a. price ceiling
   b. price discrimination
   c. price index
   d. price floor
   e. price system

118. In most businesses, profit is the difference between total revenue and total
   a. cost.
   b. labor force.
   c. interest.
   d. inventory.
   e. budget.

119. A tariff is a type of
   a. fine.
   b. tax.
   c. fee.
   d. reward.
   e. bonus.

120. Adam Smith's book, *The Wealth of Nations*, wrote about economy at the dawn of the
   a. Civil War.
   b. Industrial Revolution.
   c. Information Age.
   d. Renaissance.
   e. Agricultural Revolution.

► Answers

1. c. *Gone with the Wind* was about the Civil War, *For Whom the Bell Tolls* was about World War II, and Hemingway wrote more than one book. *Huck Finn* wasn't about war, and Twain wrote multiple novels; *The Sound and the Fury* is not about war, and Faulkner wrote multiple novels as well. Only *To Kill a Mockingbird* fits all three choices.

2. c. I Have a Dream was King, We Shall Overcome was Johnson, the Evil Empire was Reagan, and the Gettysburg Address was Lincoln.

3. c. *Leatherstocking Tales* was Cooper, *Faust* was Goethe, *The Theory of the Leisure Class* was Thorstein Veblen, and *Moll Flanders* was Defoe.

4. e. The clues are *overalls, Munitions Army,* and the *cause of Freedom.* Although this is about women, there is no reference to working for the vote. Nor is there any clue that the passage is about the fight to free the slaves; there are no references to transporting slaves to safety. Nothing in the passage touches on the field of nursing or World War I.

5. d. During the sixteenth century, England, Portugal, and the Netherlands, all possessing large numbers of capable ships and sailors, established ports and trading centers on the coasts of India.

6. c. The key in the speech is the date of 1914. That is long after the Revolutionary and Civil Wars and before World War II and Vietnam.

7. d. The Copernican model was the one that first suggested that the sun was in the middle and planets revolved around it. Other astronomers built off of this idea, but it was Copernicus who first suggested it.

8. a. Voltaire should be matched with *Philosophical Letters on the English*, Beccaria was associated with *An Essay on Crime and Punishment*, Hume is attached to *Scottish Enlightenment*, and Smith wrote *The Wealth of Nations*.

9. e. Surgeons were right under physicians, but were not as respected because they were still associated with the work of barbers. Apothecaries handed out medicine, but were not held in high regard. Faith healers were losing ground as the culture became more scientific and less religious, and the work of midwives had been slowly taken over by physicians.

10. e. The keys in this speech are the place of birth and becoming emperor, as well as the exile. None of the other people listed meet those criteria.

11. d. The first set of years encompasses all of World War I; the second set is the Great Depression; the third set encompasses much of the prelude and all of World War II; and the fifth set is way past the cold war era, into the war on terrorism.

12. e. The keys are *Cuba* and *missiles*, referring to the Cuban Missile Crisis. None of the other pairs of people had anything to do with this crisis.

13. a. De Gaulle was in favor of armored warfare and military aviation. He invested heavily in the nuclear arms race. He was also pushing for industrial growth and wanted to change/improve the constitution.

14. a. None of the authors wrote anything similar to this in title or theme.

15. c. On June 12, 1987, Reagan made a speech at Brandenburg Gate urging the powers that be to tear down the Berlin Wall.

16. d. This was a common nickname for Thatcher and no one else.

17. e. Sanger championed the idea of birth control, Anthony worked for the right to vote, Steinem worked for women's lib in the 1970s, and Greer wrote about it in *The Female Eunuch* in the 1970s.

18. b. He is the one that created the style, often doing his paintings on canvas on the floor. None of the other artists listed followed that style.

19. a. The murder occurred in late 1916, and all other events listed occurred between 1917 and 1918.

20. c. *Kristallnacht* occurred on November 9–10, 1938, and all of the other events occurred between 1933 and 1935.

21. c. Although rats, tainted water, and lack of sanitation were often causes of epidemics, the Pope was not aware of this. He sent his men to search out the witches causing the problem.

22. d. The only queen who had a reign this long was Victoria.

23. e. All three of these elements played an important role in the Boxer Uprising.

24. b. The clues here are *loincloth* and *India*. None of the other deaths had anything to do with those ideas, nor with the concept of *peacekeeper*.

25. e. All of the events listed occurred years after the original construction of the Berlin Wall in 1961. Sadat died in 1981, Chernobyl was in 1986, Hirohito died in 1989, and the Chunnel was completed in 1994.

26. c. Denmark was the first in 1983.

27. c. The trial officially began in 2005. He was captured in 2003.

28. d. This is the correct number, according to the most recent census.

29. d. Choice **a** is incorrect, because the abolitionists did not need further encouragement. Choice **b** is incorrect, because the president had no desire to punish the people of the South. Choice **c** is incorrect because the Proclamation had nothing directly to do with the women's voting movement, and choice **e** is incorrect because it took more to free the slaves than just the Proclamation.

30. e. Choice **a** is incorrect because the Marshall Plan took place in 1948, long after Manifest Destiny. Choice **b** is incorrect for the same reason; it had nothing to do with the issues of the Civil War. Choice **c** is incorrect because the Bill of Rights was decades before this plan, and choice **d** deals with the war on terrorism, which took place decades after the plan. The Marshall Plan was part of the post–World War II recovery.

31. e. None of the other candidates were part of the 2000 election. They were in elections before or after 2000.

32. b. All of the clues deal with the purchase of Alaska because it was called Seward's Folly, cost $7.2 million, nicknamed "polar bear garden," and was purchased from Russia. None of the other choices had to deal with any of the clues.

33. d. This is an excerpt from Debs's speech "The Issue."

34. b. The oath made Hitler's Nazi soldiers swear to uphold all flags and the standards upheld by his reign. None of the other elements were ever mentioned in the oath.

35. e. The war on terrorism is the current war and was so named by Bush. The other presidents were in power before this war began.

36. **a.** These authors included Hemingway, Fitzgerald, Pound, and others. They were critical of the culture's focus on wealth and materialism and did not comment on the other distracters in their famous novels.

37. **c.** Hoover was elected in March 1929, just a few months before the Depression began. World War II was a decade later; acts of terrorism began in 2001; the Dust Bowl occurred in the 1930s, after the Depression; and the Cuban Missile Crisis was under Kennedy's watch.

38. **c.** While I and II would have a strong effect on improving the economy, III would have little effect, and any that it did would be negative and not positive.

39. **b.** The Internet was originally created as a way for members within the Department of Defense to connect with each other. It was not initially designed for widespread use.

40. **c.** At the time of Pearl Harbor, Hawaii was still considered a U.S. territory. It had not become a state yet, and it has never been a nation. It is not considered an archipelago, although it is an island; while it has lagoons, the lagoons are a feature, not the main definition of the state.

41. **e.** Reagan served two, Bush served two, Clinton served two, and Truman served two terms. Only Roosevelt served four terms.

42. **d.** Hitler was aware of some of this technology, science was of very high significance to the Nazi party, Einstein warned the United States against allowing Hitler to have information about fission, and Roosevelt never was asked to share information with Hitler.

43. **b.** NAFTA is the North American Free Trade Agreement, which came into effect in 1994; NASA is the National Aeronautics and Space Administration and has nothing to do with the speech. The NSA is the National Security Agency and the NTSB is the National Transportation Safety Board.

44. **c.** When Rosa Parks was kicked off the bus, many African Americans, who relied heavily on the mass transit system, boycotted the buses, making an immediate economic impact.

45. **c.** This particular quote was spoken only by Kennedy. None of the others used the phrase in their speeches.

46. **d.** Choices **a**, **b**, **c**, and **e** are all accurate names of the drug. *Crack*, however, refers to an entirely different drug and has nothing to do with LSD.

47. **a.** Nixon was the only president in the list of choices that focused on establishing a strong relationship with China.

48. **e.** The Second Amendment refers to the right to bear arms. The Fifth Amendment deals with due process. The Tenth Amendment focuses on powers reserved to the states or to the people, and the Fifteenth Amendment deals with racial suffrage.

49. **c.** Choice **a** deals with judicial review in the United States. Choice **b** dealt with civil rights under the First Amendment. Choice **d** dealt with reading an accused person his or her rights under the law, and choice **e** dealt with the legality of abortion.

50. **a.** None of the other choices are part of the *Plessy v. Ferguson* case. They are other famous court cases.

51. d. Choice **a** dealt with the fact that attorneys must be provided to the accused even if they cannot afford one. Choice **b** focused on students who wore black armbands to school to protest the Vietnam War. Choice **c** was about affirmative action programs in college admissions, and choice **e** was about unreasonable searches.

52. b. The confederation organized itself partly in opposition to Great Britain's policy of taxation for the 13 colonies. To avoid imitating the common enemy, Great Britain, the confederation did not tax itself.

53. a. According to national law, this is the next person in line for the position.

54. d. He wrote that statement in 1785.

55. e. All three of these are requirements for American citizenship.

56. b. This is a state-level power instead of national. The rest are all national.

57. d. Concurrent powers are those shared by national and state governments. All of the powers listed are examples except **d**, which is state only.

58. c. A bill is an act, a hearing is provided to listen to both sides of the bill, ratification is the voting on the bill, and veto is the stopping of a bill.

59. e. A monologue is just a speech by one person and is not political, a debate is between two or more, a lecture is a speech intended to teach, and an amendment is a change to an existing law.

60. e. All three of these are requirements for becoming a U.S. senator.

61. b. According to national law, this is what is done to determine the winner in this highly unlikely scenario.

62. e. Neither of these men were speakers of the House.

63. d. Oregon is the only state in the country that has mail-in only voting.

64. a. You have to be at least 35 years old, not 40. You do not have to be married. You must be a U.S. resident for at least 14 years. You do not have to be Christian.

65. c. An atoll is a coral island surrounding a central lagoon, a lagoon is a body of water, keys are a set of islands, and isles are simply small islands.

66. a. A term that came into use in the late 1970s, it traditionally refers to people who come to the United States in boats, primarily from Cuba and Haiti. They do not approach by boat from these other countries.

67. c. The first two choices are just normal processes, while the third is the basic cause for concern in greenhouse effect/global warming.

68. b. All of the other distracters are hot deserts.

69. c. The Common Market was formed in 1957 and changed its name in 1993. None of the other names apply.

70. e. All three choices define what makes karst.

71. b. The definition of the words mean *per person*. The other terms do not apply.

72. c. A cartographer is a mapmaker. A climatologist studies the effects of weather. A geomorphologist studies Earth's landforms, and a cultural geographer studies how people have altered and adapted to the Earth.

73. e. *Zero population growth* refers to having only the same amount of babies as the number of people who have died.

74. a. This type of location is precisely defined by these three terms and not direction, measurements, or latitude and longitude.

75. c. Oxygen is not harmful. The other elements are in small quantities.

76. b. Endangered and threatened mean its numbers are limited. Extinct means it is gone, and imported means it has been brought in from another location.

77. d. Gentrification is usually characterized by young couples just starting out and able to devote a lot of time to improvements.

78. b. Looking Glass Self was the theory of Cooley. Ability to Reason was the theory of Piaget's. Rationalization of Society was Max Weber, and Role Taking was George Robert Mead.

79. a. A nuclear family is husband, wife, and children. A dominant family is not a psychological term. A multiple family is more than one family sharing one house. A single family is a single parent with one child.

80. c. This is the definition of the term. Alienation is a sense of not belonging. Democracy means a form of government that is run by elected representatives. Community is a group of people with some shared element, and socialization is the ability to interact with others.

81. d. Cultural lag is when human behavior lags behind technological innovations. Culture contact is when people from different cultures come into contact with one another. Cultural diffusion is the spread of cultural characteristics from one group to another, and cultural leveling is the process by which cultures become similar to one another.

82. e. Intergenerational mobility is the change that family members make in social class from one generation to the next. Life span is how long people live. Grade inflation refers to giving higher grades for the same work. Pluralism is the diffusion of power among interest groups.

83. b. Gated communities are available only to those people in the economic upper class. Both men and women are allowed in (choices **a** and **c**), as are all races and ages—if they can all afford it.

84. b. None of the other people listed as distracters were involved in developing these terms.

85. c. Polygamy is more than one spouse. Monogamy is one spouse only. Bigamy is two spouses. Trigamy is having been married three separate times.

86. d. Oligarchy is a government governed by only a few people. Anarchy is a lack of any system of rules. Monarchy is a government ruled by a king or queen. A patriarchy is one run by men only.

87. e. Statement III is incorrect because socialism believes in production that is primarily owned and controlled collectively.

88. b. A caste system is a form of social stratification in which one's status is determined by birth. Social class is a large number of people with similar amounts of income and education who work at jobs that are roughly comparable in status. Upward social mobility refers to movement up the social class ladder, and social network is the social ties radiating outward from the self that link people together.

89. c. The other words have nothing to do with the acronym.

90. a. Antipsychotic medicines are used to control severe psychotic symptoms like delusions or hallucinations. Dopamine is a neurotransmitter, and endorphins are chemicals produced naturally by the brain. Barbiturates are drugs that act as depressants to the central nervous system.

91. e. A bipolar person has severe mood swings, and dissociative amnesia refers to a loss of memory of limited periods in life. Delusions of grandeur have a person imagining he or she is another person, and generalized anxiety disorder has to do with uncontrolled worry.

92. b. Cognitive dissonance occurs when people become aware of inconsistencies in their behaviors. Cognitive therapies assume that maladaptive behavior results from irrational thoughts, beliefs, and ideas. Cognitive psychology studies mental processes, and a cognitive map is a mental representation of a spatial arrangement.

93. c. Amnesia means memory loss; bulimia is an eating disorder that has to do with binging and purging. Delusions are like hallucinations, and a fixation is the arrested development at a psychosexual stage.

94. d. Hormones do not have this ability, depressants are not released by the brain, narcotics are drugs that are not released by the brain, and neurotransmitters are released by the brain but do not reduce pain or elevate the mood.

95. e. Broca's area controls speech. The brain stem does not control any of these things. The corpus callosum transfers information between the two sides of the brain. The frontal lobe controls voluntary body movements, speech, and impulse control.

96. b. Arousal is a sexual stage and is not described here. Biofeedback is a process of learning to control internal physiological functions. A manic episode is characterized by anxiety and rising stress levels, the opposite of what is being described. Electroconvulsive therapy is done with electric shocks and is not remotely like the description.

97. d. Loss of memory, or amnesia, is not a classic symptom of paranoid schizophrenia.

98. e. This is the definition of a placebo and does not describe any of the other distracters.

99. b. This is the technical term.

100. e. Homeostasis is the tendency of the body to maintain a balanced internal state. Social norms are the standards of behavior expected of members of a particular group. Modeling is another name for observational learning. Insightful is just an irrelevant adjective.

101. e. All three of these behaviors are elements of the condition.

102. d. This is the current standard of thought.

103. d. Dian Fossey did not study people; she studied apes. Ruth Underhill studied the Papago women in the 1930s. Leakey studied fossils, and Hurston studied the Florida Everglades.

104. e. Coming of Age in Samoa should be linked with Mead, Gorilla Fund International is Dian Fossey, the father of American anthropology is Franz Boas, and the Florida Everglades was Zora Neale Hurston.

105. a. A paleontologist studies fossils from prehistoric or geologic times, a linguist studies ancient languages, an archaeologist studies objects from the past, and biologists study living and once living things.

106. c. All of these factors are part of anthropology, but not heredity.

107. b. A linguist deals with language and words, a scientist is a generic term that would not apply, a primatologist studies gorillas and other primates, and a biologist studies the field of biology.

108. b. All other distracters came after the ability to walk upright.

109. b. Capital refers to all means of production created by people. Demand is when goods or services are wanted. Sell means to trade a product for money. Discount means to sell for less but still for money. Trading and bartering are done without money.

110. b. Collective ownership is not part of any of the other types of government listed. It is a key element in communism.

111. a. A depression is a longer and deeper economic downturn, inflation is when there's a general rise in price level, recession is a decline in GDP for two consecutive quarters, and stagflation is a combination of recession and inflation at the same time.

112. d. This is the official day the fiscal year begins for the federal budget. The other dates are irrelevant.

113. e. Keynes is Keynesian, Harrod is the Harrod Domar Model, Fisher is neoclassical, and Hayek is liberalism/capitalism.

114. c. Crude quantity theory is the belief that changes in the money supply are directly proportional to changes in price levels. Quantity theory is basically the same belief. Rational expectations is the theory that people learn through experience to anticipate the consequences of changes in monetary and fiscal policy; they act immediately to protect their interests, and all resource and product markets are purely competitive.

115. a. According to the International Labor Organization, Americans worked 350 hours more per year than any European country.

116. e. All of the other factors would not have any relevance to this formula.

117. d. Price ceiling is the maximum price something can be. Price discrimination refers to a seller who charges two or more prices for the same product/service. Price index is the average price of goods as they change over time; and price system is the mechanism that allocates resources, goods, and services based on supply and demand.

118. a. All of the other factors would not have any relevance to this formula.

119. b. It is a type of tax, not a punishment or a positive monetary option.

120. b. *The Wealth of Nations* was written in 1776, so the Civil War and the Information Age had not occurred yet. The Renaissance was centuries past, and the Agricultural Revolution had barely gotten started.

CLEP Social Sciences and History Practice Test 2

Now take CLEP Social Sciences and History Practice Test 2 for additional CLEP practice. Similar to the official exam, you will answer 120 questions. Again, we suggest that you follow the time constraints of the official CLEP Social Sciences and History exam (90 minutes).

Remember, on the official CLEP, there is no penalty for incorrect answers, so always make a guess if you are unsure of an answer.

When you are finished, check the answer key on page 514 carefully to assess your results.

► CLEP Social Sciences and History Practice Test 2

1. (a) (b) (c) (d) (e)
2. (a) (b) (c) (d) (e)
3. (a) (b) (c) (d) (e)
4. (a) (b) (c) (d) (e)
5. (a) (b) (c) (d) (e)
6. (a) (b) (c) (d) (e)
7. (a) (b) (c) (d) (e)
8. (a) (b) (c) (d) (e)
9. (a) (b) (c) (d) (e)
10. (a) (b) (c) (d) (e)
11. (a) (b) (c) (d) (e)
12. (a) (b) (c) (d) (e)
13. (a) (b) (c) (d) (e)
14. (a) (b) (c) (d) (e)
15. (a) (b) (c) (d) (e)
16. (a) (b) (c) (d) (e)
17. (a) (b) (c) (d) (e)
18. (a) (b) (c) (d) (e)
19. (a) (b) (c) (d) (e)
20. (a) (b) (c) (d) (e)
21. (a) (b) (c) (d) (e)
22. (a) (b) (c) (d) (e)
23. (a) (b) (c) (d) (e)
24. (a) (b) (c) (d) (e)
25. (a) (b) (c) (d) (e)
26. (a) (b) (c) (d) (e)
27. (a) (b) (c) (d) (e)
28. (a) (b) (c) (d) (e)
29. (a) (b) (c) (d) (e)
30. (a) (b) (c) (d) (e)
31. (a) (b) (c) (d) (e)
32. (a) (b) (c) (d) (e)
33. (a) (b) (c) (d) (e)
34. (a) (b) (c) (d) (e)
35. (a) (b) (c) (d) (e)
36. (a) (b) (c) (d) (e)
37. (a) (b) (c) (d) (e)
38. (a) (b) (c) (d) (e)
39. (a) (b) (c) (d) (e)
40. (a) (b) (c) (d) (e)

41. (a) (b) (c) (d) (e)
42. (a) (b) (c) (d) (e)
43. (a) (b) (c) (d) (e)
44. (a) (b) (c) (d) (e)
45. (a) (b) (c) (d) (e)
46. (a) (b) (c) (d) (e)
47. (a) (b) (c) (d) (e)
48. (a) (b) (c) (d) (e)
49. (a) (b) (c) (d) (e)
50. (a) (b) (c) (d) (e)
51. (a) (b) (c) (d) (e)
52. (a) (b) (c) (d) (e)
53. (a) (b) (c) (d) (e)
54. (a) (b) (c) (d) (e)
55. (a) (b) (c) (d) (e)
56. (a) (b) (c) (d) (e)
57. (a) (b) (c) (d) (e)
58. (a) (b) (c) (d) (e)
59. (a) (b) (c) (d) (e)
60. (a) (b) (c) (d) (e)
61. (a) (b) (c) (d) (e)
62. (a) (b) (c) (d) (e)
63. (a) (b) (c) (d) (e)
64. (a) (b) (c) (d) (e)
65. (a) (b) (c) (d) (e)
66. (a) (b) (c) (d) (e)
67. (a) (b) (c) (d) (e)
68. (a) (b) (c) (d) (e)
69. (a) (b) (c) (d) (e)
70. (a) (b) (c) (d) (e)
71. (a) (b) (c) (d) (e)
72. (a) (b) (c) (d) (e)
73. (a) (b) (c) (d) (e)
74. (a) (b) (c) (d) (e)
75. (a) (b) (c) (d) (e)
76. (a) (b) (c) (d) (e)
77. (a) (b) (c) (d) (e)
78. (a) (b) (c) (d) (e)
79. (a) (b) (c) (d) (e)
80. (a) (b) (c) (d) (e)

81. (a) (b) (c) (d) (e)
82. (a) (b) (c) (d) (e)
83. (a) (b) (c) (d) (e)
84. (a) (b) (c) (d) (e)
85. (a) (b) (c) (d) (e)
86. (a) (b) (c) (d) (e)
87. (a) (b) (c) (d) (e)
88. (a) (b) (c) (d) (e)
89. (a) (b) (c) (d) (e)
90. (a) (b) (c) (d) (e)
91. (a) (b) (c) (d) (e)
92. (a) (b) (c) (d) (e)
93. (a) (b) (c) (d) (e)
94. (a) (b) (c) (d) (e)
95. (a) (b) (c) (d) (e)
96. (a) (b) (c) (d) (e)
97. (a) (b) (c) (d) (e)
98. (a) (b) (c) (d) (e)
99. (a) (b) (c) (d) (e)
100. (a) (b) (c) (d) (e)
101. (a) (b) (c) (d) (e)
102. (a) (b) (c) (d) (e)
103. (a) (b) (c) (d) (e)
104. (a) (b) (c) (d) (e)
105. (a) (b) (c) (d) (e)
106. (a) (b) (c) (d) (e)
107. (a) (b) (c) (d) (e)
108. (a) (b) (c) (d) (e)
109. (a) (b) (c) (d) (e)
110. (a) (b) (c) (d) (e)
111. (a) (b) (c) (d) (e)
112. (a) (b) (c) (d) (e)
113. (a) (b) (c) (d) (e)
114. (a) (b) (c) (d) (e)
115. (a) (b) (c) (d) (e)
116. (a) (b) (c) (d) (e)
117. (a) (b) (c) (d) (e)
118. (a) (b) (c) (d) (e)
119. (a) (b) (c) (d) (e)
120. (a) (b) (c) (d) (e)

▶ Practice Test Questions

Directions: Each of the questions or incomplete statements in the exam is followed by five suggested answers or completions. Select the one that is best in each case.

Western Civilization

1. Which of the following dates back to the Paleolithic period?
   a. stone tools
   b. Lascaux cave paintings
   c. invention of the bow and arrow
   d. domestication of dogs and reindeer
   e. Olmec culture in Mesoamerica

2. Which of the following titles and authors are a correct match?
   a. Dante—*The Divine Comedy*
   b. Chaucer—*The Decameron*
   c. Machiavellli—*The Reformation*
   d. Boccaccio—*Canterbury Tales*
   e. Hillerbrand—*The Prince*

3. At the beginning of the fourteenth century, what happened to severely diminish the European population?
   a. excessive flooding
   b. religious hangings
   c. widespread famine
   d. sudden drought
   e. economic depression

4. The Hundred Years' War lasted
   a. 37 years.
   b. 54 years.
   c. 100 years.
   d. 116 years.
   e. 200 years.

5. In Renaissance Italy, marriages were
   a. rare.
   b. casual.
   c. private.
   d. spontaneous.
   e. arranged.

6. Who of the following is generally considered to be the father of Italian Renaissance humanism?
   a. Petrarch
   b. Machiavelli
   c. Bruni
   d. Plato
   e. Mirandolo

7. Which of the following works of art was designed to honor the beauty of the human body?
   a. Michelangelo's *Creation of Adam*
   b. Raphael's *The Alba Madonna*
   c. Michelangelo's *David*
   d. Durer's *Adoration of the Magi*
   e. da Vinci's *Mona Lisa*

8. The book *Malleus Maleficarum* focused on the best ways to deal with
   a. young children.
   b. dictators.
   c. church rules.
   d. witches.
   e. the Inquisition.

9. Which of the following best characterizes the philosophy of mercantilism?
I. dominant school of thought in the seventeenth century
II. the concept that the total volume of trade is unchangeable
III. a nation's prosperity depended on its supply of gold and silver

a. I only
b. I and II
c. II and III
d. I and III
e. I, II, and III

10. I revealed the secrets of the universe in *The Starry Messenger*. I used a telescope to make my observations and saw amazing things, including the moon's craters and Venus's sunspots. I shocked most people by stating that the other planets were made out of basically the same elements as Earth. I was also a strong proponent of the heliocentric system. Who am I?

a. Kepler
b. Copernicus
c. Galileo
d. Brahe
e. Newton

11. This style of art appeared in the early eighteenth century. It emphasized grace, curves, and interlaced designs. It was a secular philosophy that focused on happiness and love. What style was it?

a. baroque
b. impressionism
c. abstract
d. realism
e. rococo

12. During the American Revolution, which of the following events happened last?

a. passing of the Stamp Act
b. adoption of the Bill of Rights
c. battle at Lexington and Concord
d. creation of the Treaty of Paris
e. ratification of the Constitution

13. How did the invention of the steam engine affect the Industrial Revolution?

a. sped it up
b. hindered its progress
c. was quite irrelevant
d. created a lot of jobs
e. secured its victory

14. In the nineteenth century, healthcare went through a revolution that combined clinical observation with knowledge gained from

a. traditional autopsies.
b. extensive medical histories.
c. thorough X-rays.
d. common surgeries.
e. responses to medication.

15. The discovery of electricity helped to spur on additional inventions, including all of the following EXCEPT

a. commercial generators.
b. light bulbs.
c. streetcars and subways.
d. steam engines.
e. conveyor belts.

16. Which of the following incidents spurred the beginning of World War I?

a. Germany gave an ultimatum to Russia.

b. Archduke Francis Ferdinand was assassinated.

c. Germany declared war on France and Russia.

d. Belgium was invaded by German troops.

e. Great Britain declared war on Germany.

17. Which of the following events from World War II occurred in 1937?

a. Soviet Union invaded Poland.

b. Hitler became chancellor.

c. Japan invaded China.

d. Germany annexed Austria.

e. Hitler formed a German air force.

18. What was the first event in the long cold war period?

a. Korean War

b. Truman Doctrine

c. Berlin Crisis

d. Vienna Summit

e. Marshall Plan

World History

19. In the Seven Years' War, which of the following countries sided with Britain?

a. Austria

b. France

c. Sweden

d. Spain

e. Prussia

20. Which of the following elements characterizes a tariff?

I. It is applied to imports.

II. It is applied to exports.

III. It is applied to the government.

a. I only

b. II only

c. III only

d. I and II

e. II and III

21. British scientist Edward Jenner was responsible for

a. the Spinning Jenny.

b. smallpox vaccination.

c. water frame.

d. high-pressure steam engine.

e. the cotton gin.

22. At which 1813 battle did the French Army lose badly?

a. Leipzig

b. Lutzen

c. Bautzen

d. Dresden

e. Austerlitz

23. I was a Swiss philanthropist. I was present for the Battle of Solferino and saw thousands of people die. I saw soldiers fall on the battlefield and no one helped them to safety. I couldn't stand it any longer and swore to do something about it. I founded the Red Cross Organization. Who am I?

a. Florence Nightingale

b. Gottfried Daimler

c. Louis Lumiere

d. J. E. B. Stuart

e. Henry Dunant

24. The first crossing of Australia was done by Robert Burke and William Wills riding
   a. horses.
   b. mules.
   c. camels.
   d. donkeys.
   e. carriages.

25. Who followed up on the theories and ideas on evolution that Darwin started?
   a. Joseph Lister
   b. John McAdam
   c. Louis Daguerre
   d. Samuel Morse
   e. Alfred Russel Wallace

26. Fascism developed after which of the following wars?
   a. Revolutionary War
   b. Civil War
   c. World War I
   d. World War II
   e. the war on terrorism

27. The acronym *SALT* stands for Strategic Arms Limitation
   a. Talks.
   b. Techniques.
   c. Tallies.
   d. Tariffs.
   e. Tension.

28. "Gibraltar of the Pacific" refers to
   a. Florida Keys.
   b. Oregon Coast.
   c. Kuril Islands.
   d. Pearl Harbor.
   e. Staten Island.

United States History

29. Which of the following men were black men who fought against slavery in the early to mid-1800s?
   I. Gabriel Prosser
   II. Denmark Vesey
   III. Nat Turner
   a. I only
   b. II only
   c. I and II
   d. II and III
   e. I, II, and III

30. Which religious group was most responsible for establishing the first public school system?
   a. Mormons
   b. Puritans
   c. Christians
   d. Catholics
   e. Protestants

31. A blockade-runner is
   a. a rum runner.
   b. an exceptionally fast ship.
   c. an international spy.
   d. a Peace Democrat.
   e. a weapon used at sea.

32. I am standing in a bread line each day. I have been out of work for weeks and all of my bank accounts are empty. Who could have seen this coming? The economy was so strong before. What time period am I living in?
   a. the Salem Witch Trials
   b. the Crusades
   c. the Depression
   d. the Civil War
   e. the American Revolution

33. Northerners who came to the South following the Civil War in hopes of finding business opportunities were known as
   a. carpetbaggers.
   b. abolitionists.
   c. scalawags.
   d. Yankees.
   e. Confederates.

34. Which of the following steps did the Compromise of 1850 accomplish?
   I. banned the slave trade in Washington, D.C.
   II. passed a strict fugitive slave law
   III. forced new territories to support the idea of slavery
   a. I only
   b. II only
   c. III only
   d. I and II
   e. II and III

35. Read the following quote.
   "…so unwilling am I…to quit a peaceful abode for an ocean of difficulties, without that competency, of political skill, abilities, and inclination, which are necessary to manage the helm…"
   Which of the U.S. presidents stated this reluctance to take office?
   a. Lincoln
   b. Washington
   c. Jefferson
   d. Truman
   e. Hoover

36. Read the following quote.
   "While the property and sovereignty of the Mississippi and its waters secure an independent outlet for the produce of the western States … the fertility of the country, its climate, and extent, promise in due season important aids to our treasury …"
   What purchase was Thomas Jefferson referring to in this quote?
   a. Alaska
   b. Louisiana
   c. Texas
   d. Mexico
   e. Europe

37. I am a Shawnee chief. In 1808, I formed a confederation of all Native Americans living east of the Mississippi River. I worked with my brother, Tenskwatawa, who was known as The Prophet. I met with William Henry Harrison and tried to avoid a war between my people and his. Who am I?
   a. Geronimo
   b. Squanto
   c. Sacajawea
   d. Tecumseh
   e. Pocahontas

38. What new age began in the United States in the early 1800s?

   a. the American Revolution

   b. the Age of Enlightenment

   c. the Industrial Revolution

   d. the Age of Exploration

   e. the Communication Revolution

39. Which of the following characterizes the life of Elizabeth Ann Seton?

   I. In 1975, she was made a saint by the Roman Catholic Church.

   II. She founded the first Catholic parochial school system in the United States.

   III. She created a religious order called the Sisters of Charity.

   a. I only

   b. I and II

   c. II and III

   d. I and III

   e. I, II, and III

40. The Homestead Act of 1862 was designed to

   a. encourage farmers to move to the West.

   b. provide settlers with protection from Native Americans.

   c. promise area tribes a place for them to live.

   d. give huge areas of land to pioneers for free.

   e. support the move of immigrants to the North and South.

41. William Frederick Cody earned the nickname Buffalo Bill by

   a. riding buffalo.

   b. training buffalo.

   c. herding buffalo.

   d. selling buffalo.

   e. killing buffalo.

42. Jane Addams's settlement houses were primarily designed to help

   a. orphans.

   b. widows.

   c. prisoners.

   d. homeless.

   e. immigrants.

43. Which president was known for creating the political slogan, "Speak softly but carry a big stick"?

   a. Truman

   b. F. D. Roosevelt

   c. Kennedy

   d. T. Roosevelt

   e. McKinley

44. As a result of the Monica Lewinsky scandal, President Clinton

   a. resigned.

   b. quit.

   c. was impeached.

   d. was fired.

   e. was removed.

45. *Intolerable Acts* is the term used for the laws passed to punish those involved with

   a. slavery.

   b. the Boston Tea Party.

   c. the Holocaust.

   d. the internment of the Japanese.

   e. terrorist acts.

46. What is the difference between libel and slander?

I. Libel is the act of publishing harmful statements.

II. Slander is the act of publicly stating harmful and/or false accusations.

III. Libel is punishable by a jail sentence, but slander is not.

a. III only

b. I and II

c. II and III

d. I and III

e. I, II, and III

47. It carries pioneers across the ground. It keeps them sheltered from rain, snow, and sun. It weighs little and is pulled by a variety of animals. What is it?

a. a prairie schooner

b. a horseless carriage

c. a plastic wagon

d. a Mayflower

e. a boom town

48. Who created the saying, "God helps those who help themselves"?

a. Mark Twain

b. William Shakespeare

c. Ben Franklin

d. Thomas Jefferson

e. Nathaniel Hawthorne

Government/Political Science

49. Which of the following Supreme Court cases ruled that reciting a nondenominational prayer in public school was unconstitutional?

a. *Brown v. Board of Education*

b. *Doe v. Bolton*

c. *New York Times Co. v. United States*

d. *Reed v. Reed*

e. *Engel v. Vitale*

50. All of the following are examples of civil liberties EXCEPT

a. same-sex marriage.

b. freedom of speech.

c. due process.

d. property ownership.

e. privacy.

51. The Civil Rights Act of 1964 outlawed racial discrimination in

I. employment.

II. education.

III. voting.

a. I only

b. III only

c. I and II

d. II and III

e. I, II, and III

52. Those accused of crimes are protected under the
   I. Fourth and Fifth Amendments.
   II. Sixth Amendment.
   III. Eighth Amendment.
   a. I only
   b. II only
   c. III only
   d. I and II
   e. I, II, and III

53. The gender gap in politics refers to the difference between men and women's
   a. government jobs.
   b. public involvement.
   c. personal opinions.
   d. voting choices.
   e. caucus attendance.

54. Which of the following newspapers is a modern example of yellow journalism?
   a. *The New York Times*
   b. *The Wall Street Journal*
   c. *The National Enquirer*
   d. *USA Today*
   e. *Village Voice*

55. What constitutional issue did the 1989 *Texas v. Johnson* case deal with?
   a. the right to have an abortion
   b. the right to equal education
   c. the right to burn an American flag
   d. the right to purchase a gun/bear arms
   e. the right to privacy

56. Which of the following presidents was involved in an executive pardon?
   a. Clinton
   b. Bush
   c. Reagan
   d. Kennedy
   e. Nixon

57. A professional whose job it is to take public opinion surveys is referred to as a
   a. pollster.
   b. delegate.
   c. muckraker.
   d. candidate.
   e. mudslinger.

58. The Stamp Act Congress occurred during the
   a. sixteenth century.
   b. seventeenth century.
   c. eighteenth century.
   d. nineteenth century.
   e. twentieth century.

59. What does the Thirteenth Amendment do?
   a. bans alcohol
   b. provides the right to free speech
   c. bans slavery
   d. allows for free assembly
   e. bans perjury

60. The term *turnout* during an election refers to
   a. the age of the average voter.
   b. the percentage of female voters.
   c. the fraction of people who choose to abstain.
   d. the number of people who come to caucuses.
   e. the number of people who come out to vote.

61. When is an exit poll typically conducted?
a. at each campaign rally
b. on the day of inauguration
c. at presidential debates
d. on Election Day
e. at the first day of the year

62. According to the decision in *New York Times Co. v. Sullivan,* what must be proved in order to support finding of libel against a public figure?
a. perjury
b. intent
c. injury
d. malice
e. guilt

63. Who does the Rule of Four pertain to?
a. convicted felons
b. Supreme Court justices
c. defense attorneys
d. White House delegates
e. key witnesses

64. A collection of legal written documents in a case filed with a court before the trial is known as a(n)
a. tort.
b. writ.
c. brief.
d. testimony.
e. exhibit.

Geography

65. The tundra is characterized by which of the following qualities?
I. short, cool summers
II. limited vegetation
III. long, cold winters
a. I only
b. II only
c. III only
d. I and III
e. I, II, and III

66. It is a crop that traveled from Asia to the New World during the Age of Discovery. Today, it is grown all over the Midwest. It is used as food because of its high protein content, as well as a type of fuel and an element in paint, ink, and other products. What is it?
a. soybeans
b. alfalfa
c. cotton
d. peppers
e. wheat

67. What do the southern Andes Mountains, the northeast Asian island chains of Japan, and the west coast of North America all have in common?
a. They all border the Atlantic Ocean.
b. They are all located in the northern hemisphere.
c. They are all part of the Ring of Fire.
d. They are all part of the same mountain chain.
e. They are all found on or near the 45th parallel.

68. Which of the following is an example of a nonre-newable resource?

a. petroleum
b. oxygen
c. water
d. sunlight
e. timber

69. The wind had reversed direction and had been blowing steadily for weeks now. The summer had brought a lot of rainfall and had been followed by a long dry season all winter. What kind of weather do these factors create?

a. tornado
b. hurricane
c. thunderstorm
d. monsoon
e. cyclone

70. I am shopping in a Middle Eastern city. I wander through twisting and turning close set aisles, each one lined with countless merchant stalls. People call out to me to buy their product and I haggle with them until the price is one I like. Where am I?

a. in a barrio
b. at a collective farm
c. inside a common market
d. at a bazaar
e. outside a hacienda

71. In the Charney effect, the hypothesis states that the less plant cover there is on the ground, the higher the solar energy that is deflected back into the atmosphere and thus, the lower the
I. humidity.
II. drought risk.
III. precipitation.

a. I only
b. II only
c. I and II
d. I and III
e. I, II, and III

72. The Gulf Stream is characterized by which of the following?
I. reaches Europe and becomes part of the North Atlantic drift
II. is a strong ocean current beginning in the tropical Atlantic Ocean
III. skirts along the eastern coasts of the United States

a. I only
b. II only
c. I and II
d. II and III
e. I, II, and III

73. When algae is eaten by small marine animals, fish eat those animals, and humans eat the fish. That is an example of

a. food chain.
b. evolution.
c. life cycle.
d. eating pyramid.
e. ecosystem.

74. I am an animal bred to live in homes with humans. However, I have been forced to live out in the wild on my own. It has taken time, but I finally developed the skills I needed for survival. What kind of an animal am I?
a. domesticated
b. exotic
c. feral
d. tamed
e. wild

75. Which of the following farming techniques is also known as *swidden*?
a. rotational crops
b. slash and burn
c. extensive land use
d. drought avoidance
e. double cropping

76. Computer cartography is used to
a. plot a complex route.
b. pinpoint a location.
c. create electronic maps.
d. teach basic directions.
e. draw precise maps.

77. Which of the following types of maps are designed to highlight terrain and elevation?
a. climate
b. economic
c. physical
d. political
e. topographic

Sociology

78. Pamela had never known a time where her family was not poor. Her parents were, her grandparents were, and according to her relatives, even her great-grandparents were. Pamela's generations are an example of the
a. upper class.
b. middle class.
c. lower class.
d. under class.
e. social class.

79. An example of a cultural taboo is
a. prejudice.
b. cruelty.
c. incest.
d. stealing.
e. homicide.

80. Overall membership in a church, temple, or synagogue tends to increase with
a. age.
b. income.
c. education.
d. family size.
e. health conditions.

81. The sacred, according to Durkheim, should evoke all of the following EXCEPT
a. obedience.
b. awe.
c. fear.
d. reverence.
e. deep respect.

82. Mrs. Hoppas has been identified as someone who practices polyandry. What does this mean?
   a. She refuses to get married.
   b. She has a husband and a wife.
   c. She has more than one husband.
   d. She has one husband.
   e. She has never been married.

83. The political government system in England is known as a
   a. democracy.
   b. monarchy.
   c. oligarchy.
   d. theocracy.
   e. anarchy.

84. The "groupthink" mentality is characterized by
   I. narrowing of thought by a group of people.
   II. perspective that there is only one correct answer.
   III. alternative answers are perceived as disloyalty.
   a. I only
   b. I and II
   c. II and III
   d. I and III
   e. I, II, and III

85. In a typical dyad, how many possible relationships are there?
   a. one
   b. two
   c. three
   d. four
   e. limitless

86. What kind of leader would tend to assign tasks and then praise or condemn the work of others without any kind of explanation?
   a. authoritarian
   b. democratic
   c. instrumental
   d. expressive
   e. *laissez-faire*

87. According to sociologists, all religions began as
   a. tribes.
   b. miracles.
   c. cults.
   d. churches.
   e. sects.

88. The least industrialized nations tend to have such large families because
   I. using birth control is against their religions.
   II. children are considered economic assets.
   III. they live in communities that support the concept.
   a. I only
   b. II and III
   c. I and III
   d. III only
   e. I, II, and III

89. The animal rights crusade is an example of social
   a. change.
   b. control.
   c. network.
   d. movement.
   e. institution.

Psychology

90. The adolescent stage officially begins at

   a. age 12.

   b. puberty.

   c. the teenage years.

   d. childhood.

   e. the beginning of menstruation.

91. I am the gland that controls the hormones that prepare you for emergencies and dealing with stress. What kind of gland am I?

   a. adrenal

   b. lymph

   c. sweat

   d. salivary

   e. thyroid

92. A person who exhibits continuous self-sacrifice, generosity, and kindness would rightfully be called a(n)

   a. patron.

   b. sponsor.

   c. altruist.

   d. benefactor.

   e. martyr.

93. The circadian theory revolves around the importance and relevance of humans and

   a. food.

   b. work.

   c. relationships.

   d. sleep.

   e. nature.

94. Which of the following words best characterizes a compulsion?

   I. irrational

   II. temporary

   III. uncontrollable

   a. I only

   b. II only

   c. III only

   d. I and III

   e. II and III

95. Fetal alcohol syndrome manifests itself in which of the following ways?

   I. mental retardation

   II. physical abnormalities

   III. behavior problems

   a. I only

   b. II only

   c. I and II

   d. II and III

   e. I, II, and III

96. The word *gustation* refers to the sensation of

   a. sight.

   b. sound.

   c. taste.

   d. touch.

   e. smell.

97. I am positive that I have almost every single disease or illness I have ever heard of. I am sure that death is just around the corner and spend a great deal of time studying medical books to get the right diagnosis. What kind of person am I?

   a. a schizophrenic

   b. a hypochondriac

   c. a sociopath

   d. a masochist

   e. a psychopath

98. The debate of nurture versus nature looks at the behavioral influences of which of the following pairs?
   a. genetics and DNA
   b. birth order and career
   c. heredity and environment
   d. childbirth and location
   e. parenting and attitudes

99. A neonate is
   a. unborn.
   b. newborn.
   c. fewer than 24 hours old.
   d. less than one month old.
   e. less than one year old.

100. I am sitting quietly and focusing inwardly, concentrating intensely, and enjoying an altered state of consciousness. What am I doing?
   a. dreaming
   b. studying
   c. sleeping
   d. relaxing
   e. meditating

101. If you recall something that had been kept in your long term memory, that is known as
   a. storage.
   b. retrieval.
   c. emotion.
   d. amnesia.
   e. remembrance.

Anthropology

102. An example of an activity that brings together people from diverse ethnic backgrounds, regions, political parties, social status, and genders is
   a. state conferences.
   b. popular sports.
   c. campaign rallies.
   d. country clubs.
   e. marriage retreats.

103. Anthropology is the study of the human species and its
   a. immediate ancestors.
   b. basic origins.
   c. unique behaviors.
   d. ancient beginnings.
   e. mental workings.

104. A core value is one that is based on
   a. fleeting opinions.
   b. strong basic beliefs.
   c. peer pressure.
   d. temporary phase.
   e. formal education.

105. When Mrs. Clemens was not hired for the job and asked why, she was told it was because hiring a woman was too risky for the corporation. This is an example of
   a. sexual harassment.
   b. sexual stereotyping.
   c. sexual discrimination.
   d. sexual preference.
   e. sexual mores.

106. Joshua lives in a large house with his siblings, parents, grandparents, and great-grandparents. This is an example of a(n)

   a. blended family.

   b. expanded family.

   c. collateral family.

   d. nuclear family.

   e. extended family.

107. This land is located between the Tigris and Euphrates rivers in the area known today as southern Iraq and southwestern Iran. It was here that some of the world's first cities and states were formed. What land is this?

   a. Atlantis

   b. Israel

   c. Syria

   d. Mesopotamia

   e. Saudi Arabia

108. If a person identified him or herself as a monotheist, this means he or she believes in

   a. one god.

   b. no god.

   c. multiple gods.

   d. gods and goddesses.

   e. Greek gods.

Economics

109. A merger between two businesses in the same industry is referred to as

   a. horizontal.

   b. vertical.

   c. blended.

   d. corporate.

   e. acquisition.

110. When inflation is in the double digits and appears to be out of control, it is known as

   a. hyperinflation.

   b. cost-push inflation.

   c. excess demand inflation.

   d. pricing power inflation.

   e. sectoral inflation.

111. When paying on a loan, each payment goes to pay interest and

   a. balance.

   b. premium.

   c. principal.

   d. debt.

   e. escrow.

112. The *laissez-faire* philosophy supports the idea that the economy should function only

   a. with full governmental cooperation.

   b. with governmental assistance.

   c. without governmental permission.

   d. without government interference.

   e. with governmental influences.

113. A third party whose job it is to act as a negotiator between labor and management during collective bargaining is referred to as a

   a. partner.

   b. union leader.

   c. employer.

   d. liaison.

   e. mediator.

114. Profit is defined as the difference between total revenue and total
  a. cost.
  b. interest.
  c. payment.
  d. margin.
  e. exchange.

115. *WTO* stands for the World Trade
  a. Objective.
  b. Organization.
  c. Occupation.
  d. Operation.
  e. Opportunity.

116. Supply side economics is characterized by which of the following?
  I. the role of the government in economics is too big
  II. high tax rates and hurt individuals and businesses
  III. *laissez-faire* philosophies destroy most economies
  a. II only
  b. III only
  c. I and II
  d. II and III
  e. I, II, and III

117. During World War II, IBM, Xerox, and Alcoa were all
  a. individuals.
  b. just opening.
  c. bankrupt.
  d. monopolies.
  e. reorganizing.

118. The Fair Labor Standards Act from 1938 established what economic standard?
  a. minimum wage
  b. international exchange rates
  c. federally guaranteed bank accounts
  d. the rate of overall inflation
  e. national bank loan interest rates

119. What kind of currency is currently used in Europe?
  a. francs
  b. pesos
  c. deutschmarks
  d. euros
  e. shillings

120. Macroeconomics deals with all of the following EXCEPT
  a. national output.
  b. money supply.
  c. government spending.
  d. stock market.
  e. bank deposits.

▶ Answers

1. b. Choices **a**, **c**, **d**, and **e** came long after the Paleolithic period.

2. a. Chaucer wrote *Canterbury Tales*, Machiavelli wrote *The Prince*, Boccaccio wrote the *Decameron*, and Hillerbrand wrote *The Reformation*.

3. c. Several famines due to crop failure struck during the early fourteenth century (1315–1322), which ended up killing millions.

4. d. It began in 1337 and ended in 1453.

5. e. The majority of all marriages were arranged by the parents for the best alliances to strengthen businesses and family ties.

6. a. This is the title given to Francesco Petrarch, an Italian scholar, poet, and humanist.

7. c. *Creation of Adam*, the *Madonna*, and the *Magi* were all created to honor God/religion. The *Mona Lisa* was about femininity, but *David* was about the beauty of the human form itself.

8. d. The book was written by men sent by the Pope to explore the connection between witches and the plague.

9. e. All three choices were relevant factors in mercantilism.

10. c. Only Galileo wrote in *The Starry Messenger*. All of the other choices are astronomers but do not fit the details in the narrative.

11. e. Baroque was very dramatic and grand, being used for art as well as music. Abstract focused on painting things that did not actually look like anything specific. Impressionism was not developed until the late nineteenth and early twentieth centuries and was usually landscapes. Realism was primarily in the midnineteenth century and focused on painting things exactly as they looked.

12. b. The Bill of Rights was adopted in 1791. The Stamp Act passed in 1765, and the battle at Lexington and Concord was in 1775. The Treaty of Paris was 1783, and the Constitution was ratified in 1788.

13. e. The steam engine was the power needed to ensure that the Industrial Revolution continued to expand and develop. It did not necessarily speed it up but guaranteed its overall success. It did not hinder progress and was definitely relevant. It may have indirectly created more jobs down the road, but that was not a direct effect on the Revolution itself.

14. a. None of the other choices were widely available during this time period other than autopsies.

15. d. Choices a, b, c, and e were all based on electrical power, to which the discovery was essential. The steam engine, however, was powered by steam, and so electricity was not relevant to it.

16. b. All of the other choices happened after the assassination of the Archduke.

17. c. The Soviet Union invaded Poland in 1939. Hitler became Chancellor in 1933. Germany annexed Austria in 1938, and Hitler formed a German air force in 1935.

18. b. The Truman Doctrine was in 1947. The Korean War lasted from 1950–1953. The Berlin Crisis was in 1958, the Vienna Summit was in 1961, and the Marshall Plan followed the Truman Doctrine in 1947.

19. e. This is the only country that was on their side. The rest were on the Austrian side.

20. d. A tariff can be applied to either an import or an export but does not apply to the government.

21. b. Hargreaves invented the Spinning Jenny, Richard Arkwright developed the water frame, Oliver Evans invented the high pressure steam engine, and Eli Whitney created the cotton gin.

22. a. While all of these battles were part of the Napoleonic wars, choices **b, c, d**, and **e** are battles where the French either won or came out equal. In Leipzig, they lost badly.

23. e. Florence Nightingale helped people, but she was not Swiss. Daimler was a German automobile inventor. Lumiere was a filmmaker, and Stuart was an American solider in the Civil War.

24. c. Camels were the most durable and reliable in this environment.

25. e. Wallace was a British naturalist and explorer who was one of the primary evolutionary thinkers of the nineteenth century.

26. c. Fascism began around the year 1922, just after World War I but decades before World War II and the war on terrorism.

27. a. This is what the acronym stands for based on it was a series of bilateral talks between the Soviet Union and the United States.

28. d. This was a nickname for the area during World War II. The Keys are not in the Pacific and neither is Staten Island. The Kuril Islands are in Russia, and while the Oregon Coast is the Pacific, it has never been referred to by this nickname.

29. e. All three either plotted or led uprisings of blacks between 1800 and 1831.

30. b. The Puritans' strong focus on religious education led them to establishing some of the earliest schools.

31. b. The definition of this term is a certain type of ship that was designed to be fast enough to break through any blockades and escape too quickly to be caught.

32. c. The keys to this are *bread lines, bank accounts,* and a *strong economy.* Those clues rule out the other choices.

33. a. Abolitionists were those who fought against slavery. Scalawags were white Southerners who supported Reconstruction policies after the American Civil War (usually for self-interest), and Yankees were people from the North. Confederates were those who supported the U.S. confederate states.

34. d. The first two statements were part of the Compromise. The third one, however, is the opposite of what was done. The Compromise stated that new territories could vote on whether to have slavery at the time they wrote their constitutions.

35. b. Washington did not really want to be president, as he was quite worried about the state of the country. This is an excerpt from what he wrote to a friend in a letter from early 1789.

36. b. The key to knowing this was the Louisiana Purchase is the mention to the Mississippi and other western states, which would not work with Alaska. Choices **c, d**, and **e** were not purchases.

37. d. Only Tecumseh had a brother by this name and was a Shawnee. Tecumseh was well known for meeting Harrison and working hard to find a compromise so war was unnecessary.

38. c. This was the time period when factories began to develop quickly, including the machinery needed to help them produce mass quantities of goods.

39. e. All three of those facts are relevant to her life.

40. a. The act gave small amounts of land to people for a small fee to help encourage them to move to new territory. It offered no protection of any kind and did not deal with the Native Americans. The move was from East to West and not to the North or South.

41. e. He claimed to have killed more than 4,000 of the animals in fewer than 18 months.

42. e. Her settlement houses focused on helping immigrants transition to life in America. She brought different cultures together and tried to merge the classes.

43. d. This was one of Theodore Roosevelt's most popular slogans and referred to gaining control of the isthmus of Panama.

44. c. He remained in office and did not leave for any reason.

45. b. In March 1774, Parliament passed a series of laws known as the Coercive Acts. The provisions of those acts were so strict that they became known as Intolerable Acts among the people of the colonies.

46. b. Neither is punishable by a jail term.

47. a. This is the definition of a prairie schooner.

48. c. It was one of Poor Richard's many aphorisms.

49. e. *Brown v. Board of Education* was about ending racial segregation in schools, *Doe v. Bolton* was about overturning the abortion law, *New York Times v. United States* was about newspapers being able to publish the Pentagon Papers, and *Reed v. Reed* was about ending discrimination between the sexes regarding administration of estates.

50. a. Same-sex marriages are not considered a basic civil liberty provided by the Constitution.

51. e. All three areas are covered by the Civil Rights Act of 1964.

52. e. All four amendments deal with protecting those accused of crimes.

53. d. The term *gender gap* is one associated with voting choices and elections. It is not referred to in any of the other choices.

54. c. Yellow journalism is anything that exploits, distorts, or exaggerates the news in order to create sensational news. The only example of a publication that does this is the tabloid *The National Enquirer.*

55. c. This was the issue behind this particular case. All of the other issues have to do with completely different court cases.

56. e. Nixon was the only president in the list that was given an executive pardon.

57. a. A delegate is a person designated to act for or represent another or others. A muckraker is a person who searches out and publicly exposes real or apparent misconduct of a prominent individual or business. A candidate is a person running for a political position. A mudslinger is someone who spreads unkind rumors and statements about an opponent or candidate.

58. c. It was passed in 1765.

59. c. The Thirteenth Amendment officially abolished and prohibited slavery. The Eighteenth Amendment banned alcohol. The First Amendment guarantees free speech and assembly. The Fifth Amendment deals with perjury.

60. e. The term *turnout* is defined by choice **e.** The other factors do not play a part in the definition of use of the term.

61. d. The typical exit poll is given only on Election Day. The other days are irrelevant.

62. d. This is the essential element of what makes something libel instead of just passing on gossip or a rumor or just saying something unkind.

63. b. The Rule of Four is a U.S. practice that allows four of the nine justices to grant a writ of certiorari; this prevents a majority of the court from controlling all the cases it agrees to hear.

64. c. A tort is a wrongful act resulting in an injury or damage. A writ is a single legal document, while testimony is a person's statement made under oath. An exhibit is a physical piece of evidence.

65. e. All three statements are relevant details about what characterizes the tundra.

66. a. Only soybeans meet all of these details. Alfalfa is not used in these ways and neither is cotton. Peppers are not a prominent crop in the Midwest, and while wheat is, it is not used in fuel or other products.

67. c. All of these spots are part of the Ring of Fire, a circle of areas that are active volcanically. None of the other choices fit all of these locations.

68. a. Petroleum is the only one that does not, in some way, replace itself as it is being used.

69. d. This unique set of climatic factors create a monsoon and none of the other weather conditions.

70. d. A barrio is typically a Latino neighborhood. A collective farm is a large-scale farm in the former Soviet Union. Common market is a term for some of the countries that now make up the European Economic Community, and a hacienda is a Spanish term for large rural estates. The question describes a Middle Eastern bazaar.

71. d. The Charney effect states that without enough ground cover, both humidity and precipitation are reduced, which raises the drought risk, not lowers it.

72. e. All of these statements reflect key elements of what characterizes the Gulf Stream.

73. a. Evolution is the process of each generation of species adapting to their environment. Life cycle is how a single creature goes from birth/death. An eating pyramid is the order that some foods are eaten, and an ecosystem is a community of living things and the environment in which they live.

74. c. A domesticated animal is one that depends on living with humans to survive. An exotic animal is a rare one, and a tamed animal is one that was wild in the past but since tamed. A wild animal is one that cannot live with humans.

75. b. *Swidden* is a term used only for slash and burn agriculture.

76. c. Cartography is all about creating maps, and the computer element makes it electronic maps.

77. e. A climate map shows weather patterns and temperatures. The economic map shows spending patterns and other money matters. A physical map illustrates the physical features of an area. A political map indicates state and national boundaries.

78. d. The definition of under class is poverty that lasts across three generations.

79. c. While the other distracters are crimes or bad traits, none of them are examples of a cultural taboo or a norm so strong that it brings revulsion if violated.

80. a. Church membership tends to decrease with a rise in income and education. Family size does not have a significant difference, nor does health conditions. It tends to increase as a person gets older.

81. a. Although obedience is expected with the sacred, that is not an emotion or feeling it evokes.

82. c. The definition of the term is a woman with more than one husband.

83. b. Because the country is run by a queen and prince, that makes it a monarchy.

84. e. All three choices are defining characteristics of the term.

85. a. There are two people in a dyad, which means there is one relationship.

86. a. This is the hallmark behavior of an authoritarian, which is defined as one who leads by giving orders.

87. c. This is an accurate statement, as the definition of a cult is a new religion with few followers.

88. b. While birth control may be against the religion of some of the people in these nations, it is not a defining characteristic.

89. d. They are an organized group working for a common goal or purpose.

90. b. In the world of psychology, the adolescent stage is considered to begin at whatever age puberty begins.

91. a. Lymph glands do not control these hormones. Sweat glands control perspiration, and salivary glands are part of the digestive process. The thyroid gland deals with growth and metabolism.

92. c. A patron supports someone, usually financially. A sponsor pays for someone to do something. A benefactor also tends to support someone, and a martyr is someone who sacrifices for another, but not with an attitude of generosity and kindness.

93. d. This theory studies the patterns and importance of a person's sleep cycles. It has nothing to do with food, relationships, or work.

94. d. Statement II, temporary, is not true, as compulsions tend to be very persistent and constant.

95. e. All three of these elements are defining characteristics of the condition.

96. c. The definition of the word is the act or sensation of tasting.

97. b. The defining characteristic of a hypochondriac is thinking that you have a plethora of different medical conditions.

98. c. These are the elements that define the debate.

99. d. The definition of a neonate is a newborn infant up to one month old.

100. e. Dreaming is part of sleep, so it cannot be done sitting consciously. Studying is not done in an altered state of consciousness. Sleeping is not focusing intently, and relaxing does involve inward focus.

101. b. Storage is putting the memory away and not getting it back. Emotion is just a feeling, while amnesia is the lack of memory. Remembrance is just another word for remembering, not going in to get a particular memory.

102. b. None of the other choices match all of the requirements of the example. State conferences would not cover all regions. Campaign rallies would not cover all political parties. Country clubs would not include all social classes, and marriage retreats would not include all social status.

103. a. This is the definition of the word.

104. b. This is a definition of the word. Core beliefs are the very basic values each person holds.

105. c. Harassment is unwanted sexual advances. Stereotyping is attributing certain behaviors and abilities to a person based on nothing other than a person's gender. Preference refers to the gender of a person's preferred partners, and mores means sexual values.

106. e. An extended family is defined as a nuclear family with other relatives. Blended is a family with members from different original families. Collateral is not an actual term. Nuclear is a mother, a father, and at least one child.

107. d. Atlantis does not exist. Israel is not located in this area, nor is Syria. Saudi Arabia was not the place where cities and states began.

108. a. The definition of a monotheist is a person who believes in only one god. No god would be an atheist. Pantheist is multiple gods.

109. a. That is the definition of the term. A vertical merger is the joining of two firms engaged in different parts of an industrial process. There is no such thing as a blended merger or a corporate merger. An acquisition is the act of contracting or assuming/acquiring possession of something.

110. a. This is the definition of the term. A cost-push inflation is the rising costs of doing business by pushing up prices. The three other terms are not actual types of inflation.

111. c. This is correct. The balance is the amount still owed. The premium is the amount paid on insurance policies. Debt is an amount owed to someone, and escrow is a separate fund to keep money in to pay another debt.

112. d. This is the definition of *laissez-faire* philosophy.

113. e. A partner is an equal co-owner in a business. A union leader is the head of a union, and an employer is a boss. A liaison is a go between but does not typically work with labor and management during collective bargaining.

114. a. This is the official economic formula used to determine profit.

115. b. This is the correct word used in this acronym.

116. c. Statement III is not part of supply side economics. The other two elements are defining characteristics.

117. d. During World War II, these companies were so large that they cornered the market and did not allow for any competition.

118. a. It was the act that established a basic hourly wage for all of the nation.

119. d. Although in the past each country within Europe had its own kind of currency, it changed to euros so that there would not be any confusion over exchange rates.

120. d. All of the other choices are part of macroeconomics, but the stock market is not involved.

CLEP College Mathematics Practice Test 1

You are now familiar with the kinds of questions and answer formats you will see on the official CLEP College Mathematics exam. Now take Practice Test 1 to identify any areas that you may need to review in more depth before the test day.

On this practice test, you will encounter 60 questions that are similar to the type you will find on the official CLEP College Mathematics exam.

To simulate the test conditions, use the time constraints of the official CLEP College Mathematics exam. Allow yourself 90 minutes to complete this practice test.

Remember, on the official CLEP, there is no penalty for incorrect answers, so always make a guess if you are unsure of an answer.

When you are finished, check the answer key on page 534 carefully to assess your results.

► CLEP College Mathematics Practice Test 1

1. (a) (b) (c) (d)
2. (a) (b) (c) (d)
3. (a) (b) (c) (d)
4. (a) (b) (c) (d)
5. (a) (b) (c) (d)
6. (a) (b) (c) (d)
7. (a) (b) (c) (d)
8. (a) (b) (c) (d)
9. (a) (b) (c) (d)
10. (a) (b) (c) (d)
11. (a) (b) (c) (d)
12. (a) (b) (c) (d)
13. (a) (b) (c) (d)
14. (a) (b) (c) (d)
15. (a) (b) (c) (d)
16. (a) (b) (c) (d)
17. (a) (b) (c) (d)
18. (a) (b) (c) (d)
19. (a) (b) (c) (d)
20. (a) (b) (c) (d)

21. (a) (b) (c) (d)
22. (a) (b) (c) (d)
23. (a) (b) (c) (d)
24. (a) (b) (c) (d)
25. (a) (b) (c) (d)
26. (a) (b) (c) (d)
27. (a) (b) (c) (d)
28. (a) (b) (c) (d)
29. (a) (b) (c) (d)
30. (a) (b) (c) (d)
31. (a) (b) (c) (d)
32. (a) (b) (c) (d)
33. (a) (b) (c) (d)
34. (a) (b) (c) (d)
35. (a) (b) (c) (d)
36. (a) (b) (c) (d)
37. (a) (b) (c) (d)
38. (a) (b) (c) (d)
39. (a) (b) (c) (d)
40. (a) (b) (c) (d)

41. (a) (b) (c) (d)
42. (a) (b) (c) (d)
43. (a) (b) (c) (d)
44. (a) (b) (c) (d)
45. (a) (b) (c) (d)
46. (a) (b) (c) (d)
47. (a) (b) (c) (d)
48. (a) (b) (c) (d)
49. (a) (b) (c) (d)
50. (a) (b) (c) (d)
51. (a) (b) (c) (d)
52. (a) (b) (c) (d)
53. (a) (b) (c) (d)
54. (a) (b) (c) (d)
55. (a) (b) (c) (d)
56. (a) (b) (c) (d)
57. (a) (b) (c) (d)
58. (a) (b) (c) (d)
59. (a) (b) (c) (d)
60. (a) (b) (c) (d)

▶ Practice Test Questions

1. If the sum of the whole number $m + 2$ is not divisible by 2, and the sum $n + 2$ is divisible by 4, which of the following must be true?
   a. m is even and n is odd.
   b. n is even and m is odd.
   c. The sum $m + n$ is even.
   d. The solution to $\frac{(m+n)}{4}$ is even.

2. How many different combinations can be made if three balls are to be picked from five different colored balls and placed into a bag?
   a. 10
   b. 15
   c. 60
   d. 120

3. Which of the following is the converse of "If it is raining, then I will wear boots"?
   a. If it is not raining, then I will not wear boots.
   b. I will wear boots if it is raining.
   c. If I will not wear boots, then it is not raining.
   d. It is raining if and only if I will wear boots.

4. Given $f(x) = \frac{1}{3}x$, find $f^{-1}(x)$.
   a. $f^{-1}(x) = -(\frac{1}{3}x)$
   b. $f^{-1}(x) = 3 - x$
   c. $f^{-1}(x) = x - \frac{1}{3}$
   d. $f^{-1}(x) = 3x$

5. A child draws an ice cream cone by constructing a semicircle atop an equilateral triangle. If the triangle has a side length of 10 units, what is the perimeter of the ice cream cone?
   a. $20 + 5\pi$ units
   b. 25π units
   c. 30 units
   d. $30 + 5\pi$ units

6. Tyrone will pack four pairs of shorts for his upcoming trip. How many different combinations of shorts can be packed if there are five pairs to choose from?
   a. 5
   b. 20
   c. 24
   d. 120

7. If $A = \{5, 10, 15, 20, 25, 30\}$ and $B = \{10, 20, 30\}$, which of the following statements is true?
   a. $A \cup B = B$
   b. $B \cap A = A$
   c. $A \subset B$
   d. $B \subset A$

8. Which of the following is an example of a rational number?
   a. $\sqrt{11}$
   b. $\sqrt{13}$
   c. $\sqrt{16}$
   d. $\sqrt{17}$

9. Given $r \lor s$ is true and $\sim s$ is true, which of the following must be true?
   a. $r \land s$ is true.
   b. $\sim r \land \sim s$ is true.
   c. $\sim r$ is true.
   d. r is true.

10. Based on the number line below, which of the following inequalities is correct?

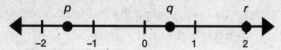

    a. $p > q > r$
    b. $q < |p| < |r|$
    c. $q < p < |r|$
    d. $|q| < r < p$

11. One leg of a right triangle has length 5. The hypotenuse has length 11. What is the length of the triangle's other leg?

    a. $4\sqrt{6}$
    b. $8\sqrt{6}$
    c. $16\sqrt{6}$
    d. 96

12. $(a + bi)(a - bi) =$

    a. $a^2 + b^2$
    b. $a^2 - b^2$
    c. $a^2 + bi$
    d. $a^2 - bi$

13. The numbers 1 through 6 are written on small index cards. How many different ways can these be ordered if the pattern must follow odd-even-odd-even-odd-even?

    a. 72
    b. 36
    c. 360
    d. 720

14. Given p represents "n is an even number," q represents "n is divisible by 2," and considering the definition of the term *even number,* which of the following is true?

    a. $p \leftrightarrow q$
    b. $p \vee q$
    c. $\sim p \wedge q$
    d. $\sim p \rightarrow q$

15. Given $U = \{1, 3, 5, 7, 9, 11, 13, 15\}$, $A = \{1, 3, 5, 7\}$, $B = \{5, 7, 9, 11\}$, and $C = \{9, 11, 13, 15\}$, which sets are disjoint?

    a. A and C
    b. B and C
    c. B' and A
    d. A and B

16. If a and b are both nonzero integers, the solution to which of the following must also be an integer?

    a. $\dfrac{ab + a^3}{a}$
    b. $\dfrac{ab + b^2}{a}$
    c. $\dfrac{b + 2a^2}{a}$
    d. $\dfrac{ab + a^3}{b}$

17. Given $g(x) = 2x + 4$ and $(f \circ g)x = \dfrac{1}{(x + 2)}$, which of the following is equivalent to $f(x)$?

    a. $2x + \dfrac{4}{2}$
    b. $\dfrac{2}{x}$
    c. $\dfrac{1}{x}$
    d. $x + \dfrac{2}{2}$

18. Use the remainder theorem to evaluate $g(2)$ for
$g(x) = 2x^5 + 3x^3 + 2x^2 + 1$.

   a. 33

   b. 49

   c. 65

   d. 97

19. When the following truth table is correctly completed, which of the following statements regarding columns 3 and 4 is true?

p	q	$\sim p \vee \sim q$	$\sim(p \vee q)$
T	T		
T	F		
F	T		
F	F		

   a. They are identical.

   b. They both have two values of true.

   c. They both have two values of false.

   d. None of the above statements are true.

20. If $a = |-17|$, $b = |5^2|$, $c = |-\frac{1}{2}|$, and $d = |-20 - 6|$, which of the following inequalities is correct?

   a. $a < b < c < d$

   b. $a < c < b < d$

   c. $c < a < d < b$

   d. $c < a < b < d$

21. Given $f(x) = \frac{3}{x^3}$, what is the range of this function?

   a. all real numbers

   b. all real numbers greater than or equal to zero

   c. all real numbers except $x = 0$

   d. all real numbers greater than zero

22. Which Venn diagram represents $(A \cap C) \cup B$?

   a.

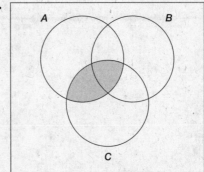

   b.

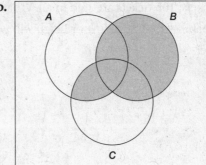

   c.

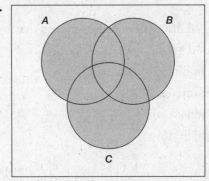

   d.

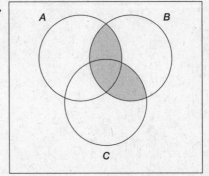

23. Which of the following inequalities represents the number line shown?

    a. $-1.5 \le x < 2$
    b. $-1.5 < x \le 2$
    c. $-1.5 > x \le 2$
    d. $-1.5 \ge x < 2$

24. Adrienne buys 15 raffle tickets and Leigh buys 20 raffle tickets; 105 tickets are sold in all. What is the probability that Adrienne or Leigh will win the raffle?

    a. $\frac{1}{3}$
    b. $\frac{1}{5}$
    c. $\frac{15}{105}$
    d. $\frac{20}{105}$

25. "Doing all of my homework implies that I will get a good grade" is an example of
    a. a biconditional statement.
    b. a conjunction.
    c. a disjunction.
    d. an implication.

26. Given $g(x) = 3x - 12$ and $h(x) = (\frac{1}{3})x$, find $(g \times h)x$.
    a. $x^2 - 4$
    b. $x^2 - 4x$
    c. $x - 4$
    d. $x - 12$

27. Which of the following has the least value?
    a. $|16| - |-15|$
    b. $|15 - 16|$
    c. $1 - |-16|$
    d. $|-15| - 16$

28. Which of the following functions does NOT have a zero?
    a. $f(x) = -|x| + 7$
    b. $f(x) = -|x| - 7$
    c. $f(x) = |x - 7|$
    d. $f(x) = -|x - 7|$

29. Given $A = \{x, y\}$ and $B = \{r, s\}$, find the Cartesian product of sets A and B.
    a. $\{(x, r), (x, s), (y, r), (y, s)\}$
    b. $\varnothing$
    c. $\{r, s, x, y\}$
    d. $\{(x, r), (y, s)\}$

30. Given that p represents the statement "I am thirsty," $\sim p$ would represent
    a. the antecedent.
    b. the consequent.
    c. the negation.
    d. the inverse.

31. A pay-per-use phone costs $5 to activate and 50¢ a minute to use. Which graph may represent the cost (*y*-axis) of using this phone over a given number of minutes (*x*-axis)?

a.

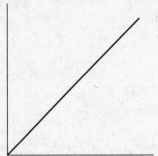

b.

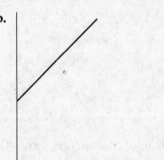

c.

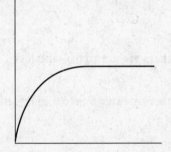

d.

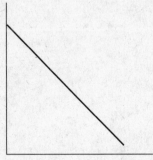

32. Given the set of numbers: 4 , 1, –1, 4, find the variance.

a. 2

b. 4

c. 4.5

d. 5

33. What is the range of the function $y = f(x)$ shown here?

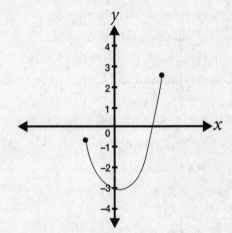

a. $-4 < y < 3$

b. $-4 \leq y \leq 3$

c. $-2 < y < 3$

d. $-2 \leq y \leq 3$

34. A band recently sold out a local show by selling all its 1,000 tickets. There are two types of tickets, regular and children's tickets. If regular tickets are $10 and children's tickets are $5, and the band made $8,000 in ticket sales, how many more regular tickets were sold than children's tickets?

a. 200

b. 400

c. 500

d. 600

35. If k is even and $3l$ is even, which of the following must be true?

a. $k + l$ is even.

b. $k + l$ is odd.

c. $\frac{(k + l)}{3}$ is even.

d. $3(k + l)$ is odd.

36. The function $h(x)$ is defined as $h(x) = \sqrt{\frac{x}{5}}$. When compared with $h(x)$, the graph of $h(x) - 2$ is

a. $h(x)$ slid downward by two units.

b. $h(x)$ slid upward by two units.

c. $h(x)$ reflected about the line $y = 2x$.

d. $h(x)$ reflected about the line $y = -2x$.

37. If $U = \{1, 2, 3, 4, 5, 6, 7, 8, 9, 10, 11\}$, $A = \{2, 3, 5, 7, 11\}$, and $B = \{3, 6, 9\}$, find $A \cap B$.

a. $\{\}$

b. $\{3\}$

c. $\{2, 3, 5, 6, 7, 9, 11\}$

d. $\{1, 2, 3, 4, 5, 6, 7, 8, 9, 10, 11\}$

38. If $a = |-13|$, $b = -2$, $c = a - b$, and $d = |b - a|$, which of the following inequalities is correct?

a. $a < b < c < d$

b. $a < b < d < c$

c. $b < a < c < d$

d. $b < a < c \leq d$

39. Which of the following is true regarding $h(x)$ and $-h(x)$?

a. $-h(x)$ is $h(x)$ reflected about the y-axis.

b. $-h(x)$ is $h(x)$ reflected about the x-axis.

c. $-h(x)$ is $h(x)$ reflected about the line $y = x$.

d. $-h(x)$ is $h(x)$ reflected about the line $y = -x$.

40. Rahul draws a 7 from a standard deck of cards. The card is not placed back into the deck. What is the probability that the next card he draws will also be a 7?

a. $\frac{4}{52}$

b. $\frac{3}{52}$

c. $\frac{4}{51}$

d. $\frac{3}{51}$

41. If k is a prime number less than 10, what is the least possible value of $k \times 2 \times 5$?

a. 10

b. 15

c. 20

d. 30

42. What is the domain of the function shown here?

$$f(x) = \left\{ \begin{array}{l} \frac{1}{2}x \text{ if } 5 < x \leq 15 \\ \frac{2}{3} \text{ if } 15 < x \leq 18 \end{array} \right\}$$

a. all real numbers greater than 5 and less than 18

b. all real numbers greater than 5 and less than or equal to 18

c. all real numbers $\neq 0$

d. all real numbers $\neq 15$

43. Five seniors and seven sophomores enter a raffle. If one winner is to be chosen at random, what is the probability that a sophomore will win the raffle?

   a. $\frac{5}{7}$

   b. $\frac{5}{12}$

   c. $\frac{7}{12}$

   d. $\frac{7}{35}$

44. This graph would best be classified as

SCATTER PLOT

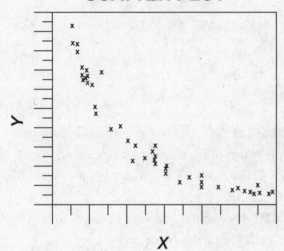

   a. having no correlation.

   b. having an exponential relationship.

   c. having an inverse linear relationship.

   d. having a direct linear relationship.

45. Given $f(x) = \frac{x}{5}$ and $g(x) = 10x + 1$, find $(f \circ g)x$.

   a. $2x + \frac{1}{5}$

   b. $2x + 1$

   c. $x + \frac{1}{5}$

   d. $\frac{1}{5}x$

46. A farmer has $500 to spend on a new fence to enclose a small rectangular plot of land. One side of the plot borders the barn, so the farmer only needs to build fencing on three sides. Fencing material costs $10 per foot of fence. If the side of the plot bordering the barn is 10 feet long, what will be the total area of the enclosed space, assuming the farmer spends all $500 on the fence?

   a. 100 ft.²

   b. 150 ft.²

   c. 200 ft.²

   d. 400 ft.²

47. There is a 20% chance that Justin will decide to go to the school play. There is a 50% chance that Sierra will decide to go to the same play. If Justin's and Sierra's decision about attending are not related, what is the probability that both Justin and Sierra will attend the play?

   a. 10%

   b. 20%

   c. 30%

   d. 70%

48. The number that results when simplifying $\sqrt{(\sqrt{121})}$ is an example of

   a. an imaginary number.

   b. a prime number.

   c. a rational number.

   d. an irrational number.

49. If five consecutive odd integers have a median value of x, what is their average?

   a. $x + 1$

   b. $x - 2$

   c. $5x$

   d. x

50. Use the table below to determine the amount of pixels per inch for the Star 100 Scanner in terms of x.

SCANNER MODEL	PIXELS PER INCH
Star 1,000	x
Star 500	$\frac{1}{4}$ of the pixels of the Star 1,000
Star 200	$\frac{1}{4}$ of the pixels of the Star 500
Star 100	$\frac{1}{4}$ of the pixels of the Star 200

a. $\frac{x}{4}$

b. $\frac{x}{16}$

c. $\frac{x}{64}$

d. $\frac{x}{128}$

51. Given the following values of the functions f and g, $f(g(8))$ is equivalent to what value?

X	5	6	7
f(x)	2	3	4

X	7	8	9
g(x)	4	6	8

a. 2

b. 3

c. 4

d. 6

52. The graph shown here may be the graph for which of the following inequalities?

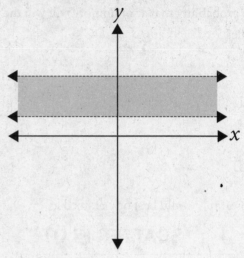

a. $3 \leq y < 9$

b. $-3 < y < 9$

c. $3 < y \leq 9$

d. $3 < y < 9$

53. All of the values in a given data set are equal. Which of the following statements are true?

I. The mean is equal to any given value within the set.

II. The standard deviation is equal to zero.

III. The range is equal to zero.

a. I

b. II and III only

c. I and III only

d. I, II, and III

54. The graph of function $h(x)$ is shown below. What is the range of $h(x)$?

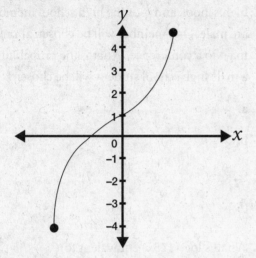

a. $-5 \leq y \leq 6$
b. $-4 \leq y \leq 3$
c. $-5 \leq y < 6$
d. $-5 < y \leq 6$

55. Two school districts reported their scores on the state tests. Both schools plotted their data on graphs using the same increments and units. The mean was the same for both schools, but School P had a greater spread than School Q. Referring to the two graphs below, which of the following statements is true?

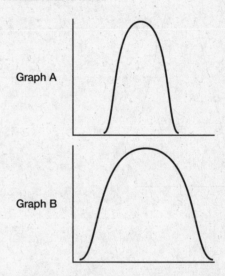

a. Graph A is the bell curve for School P.
b. Graph B is the bell curve for School P.
c. Graph A is the bell curve for School P and School Q.
d. Graph B is the bell curve for School P and School Q.

56. Triangle $A'B'C'$ is similar to triangle ABC shown in the diagram. If $A'B' = 6$, what is the perimeter of triangle $A'B'C'$?

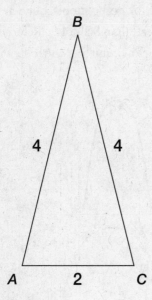

a. 10
b. 12
c. 15
d. 18

57. Which answer choice correctly describes the validity of the following statements?

I. One is a prime number.
II. Two is a prime number.
III. One is a composite number.

a. I and II are true statements.
b. II and III are true statements.
c. Only II is a true statement.
d. Only III is a true statement.

58. If $C = \{y \mid y$ is a positive multiple of $11\}$ and $D = \{z \mid z$ is a positive multiple of $22\}$, find $C \cup D$.

a. D
b. C
c. $\varnothing$
d. C'

59. The East End Environmental Club has 60 members: 40 females and 20 males. 30 members are in high school, and $\frac{1}{3}$ of the high school members are male. One member will be chosen at random to go to a conference. What is the probability that a male high school student will be chosen?

a. $\frac{1}{3}$

b. $\frac{1}{6}$

c. $\frac{2}{3}$

d. $\frac{2}{5}$

60. What is $\log_5(125x)$ equivalent to?

a. 3
b. $3 + \log_5(x)$
c. $\log_5 3 + \log_5(x)$
d. $\log(5x)$

▶ **Answers**

1. b. Because $m + 2$ is not divisible by 2, we know that m must be odd. Because $n + 2$ is divisible by 4, we know $n + 2$ will also be divisible by 2, and n is even. This makes choice **a** incorrect and choice **b** correct. The sum of an odd and even number is odd, so choice **c** is incorrect. $\frac{(m + n)}{4}$ will have an odd number in the numerator because the sum of an odd and even number is odd. Dividing and odd number by 4 will not yield an even number, so choice **d** is incorrect.

2. a. Use $_nC_r$, where n is the total number of elements that can be selected and r is the number of elements that will actually be selected.

$$_nC_r = \frac{n!}{r!(n-r)!}$$

In this case, $n = 5$ and $r = 3$. There are five balls to be selected from, and we are selecting three balls—notice that order does not matter. The formula becomes:

$$_5C_3 = \frac{5!}{3!(5-3)!} = \frac{5!}{3!2!} = \frac{5 \times 4 \times 3 \times 2 \times 1}{3 \times 2 \times 2 \times 1} =$$

$$\frac{5 \times 4}{2} = \frac{20}{2} = 10 \text{ different combinations}$$

Choice **b** is a distracter, equaling 3×5 (a tempting guess). If you selected choice **c**, you may have computed $_5P_3$ by mistake. If you selected choice **d**, you probably solved 5! by mistake.

3. b. "If it is raining, then I will wear boots" is the conditional statement $p \rightarrow q$, where p is "It is raining" and q is "I will wear boots." The converse of a conditional statement switches the antecedent and the consequent, so the converse of $p \rightarrow q$ would be $q \rightarrow p$. This is represented correctly in choice **b**. Choice **a** is the inverse, $\sim p \rightarrow \sim q$, and is incorrect. Choice **c** is the contrapositive, $\sim q \rightarrow \sim p$, and is incorrect. Choice **d** is the biconditional, $p \leftrightarrow q$, and is incorrect.

4. d. To solve, first rewrite the function in terms of x and y. To do this, replace $f(x)$ with y:
$y = \frac{1}{3}x$
Next, switch the x and y and solve for y:
$x = \frac{1}{3}y$
$y = 3x$
Finally, replace the y with $f^{-1}(x)$.
$f^{-1}(x) = 3x$
Thus, choice **d** is correct. Note that $-(\frac{1}{3}x)$ is the additive inverse of $\frac{1}{3}x$, which is not the inverse of the function, so **a** is incorrect. Choices **b** and **c** are distracters—though incorrect, they are tempting guesses because they use numbers from the problem.

5. a. Equilateral triangles have three equal sides; in this case, each side is 10 units in length. The perimeter will be the sum of two sides of the triangle plus $\frac{1}{2}$ the circumference of a circle with diameter of 10. Circumference $= \pi d$, so the circumference of the semicircle is $\frac{1}{2}\pi d = \frac{1}{2}\pi(10) = 5\pi$. Two sides of the equilateral triangle will add to 20 units. In all, the perimeter will be $20 + 5\pi$ units. Choice **a** is correct. Choice **b** is incorrect because you cannot combine the 20 and the 5π to get 25π. Choice **c** represents the perimeter of an equilateral triangle with a side of 10 units. Choice **d** is incorrect; it adds in an extra 10 units, and an extra side of the triangle is added in.

6. **a.** Use $_nC_r$, where n is the total number of elements that can be selected and r is the number of elements that will actually be selected.

$$_nC_r = \frac{n!}{r!(n-r)!}$$

In this case, $n = 5$ and $r = 4$. There are five pairs of shorts to be selected from, and Tyrone is selecting four of them. The formula becomes:

$$_5C_4 = \frac{5!}{4!(5-4)!} = \frac{5!}{4!1!} = \frac{5 \times 4 \times 3 \times 2 \times 1}{4 \times 3 \times 2 \times 1} =$$

5 different combinations. Choice **a** is correct. Choice **b** is a distracter, equaling 4×5 (a tempting guess). If you selected choice **c**, you probably solved 4! by mistake. If you selected choice **d**, you may have computed $_5P_4$ by mistake.

7. **d.** $B \subset A$ is a true statement. $\subset$ means "is a proper subset of." B is a proper subset of A because B is a subset of A, but A is *not* a subset of B. Choice **a** is incorrect because $A \cup B = A$, not B. Choice **b** is incorrect because $B \cap A = B$, not A. A is not a proper subset of B, so choice **c** is incorrect.

8. **c.** Rational numbers can be expressed as the ratio of two integers in the form $\frac{a}{b}$. Taking the square root of a perfect square, such as $\sqrt{16}$, will always yield a rational number. If you cannot think of a whole number that, when squared, will give you the number under the radical sign, then the number you are dealing with is an irrational number—one that cannot be expressed in the form $\frac{a}{b}$. Thus, $\sqrt{11}$, $\sqrt{13}$, and $\sqrt{17}$ are all irrational numbers. The square root of these numbers will result in numbers with nonterminating, nonrepeating decimal extensions. $\sqrt{16} = 4$, which can be represented as $\frac{4}{1}$ and is thus rational. Choice **c** is correct.

9. **d.** Because $\sim s$ is true, s must be false. $r \vee s$, which means "r or s" is true, so r must be true. Choice **d** is correct.

10. **b.** Looking at the number line $p = -1.5$, $q = 0.5$, and $r = 2$. The absolute values of these numbers would then be $|p| = 1.5$, $|q| = 0.5$, and $|r| = 2$. Substituting numerical values, choice **a** would be $-1.5 > 0.5 > 2$, which is incorrect. Choice **b** would be $0.5 < 1.5 < 2$, which is correct. Choice **c** would be $0.5 < -1.5 < 2$, which is incorrect. Choice **d** would be $0.5 < 2 < -1.5$, which is incorrect.

11. **a.** Use the Pythagorean theorem, $a^2 + b^2 = c^2$ to get $5^2 + b^2 = 11^2$, which becomes $25 + b^2 = 121$, and $b^2 = 96$. To find the leg b, take the square root of both sides to get $b = \sqrt{96} = \sqrt{16 \times 6} = 4\sqrt{6}$. Choice **a** is correct. Choices **b** and **c** both pull the 16 out from under the square root incorrectly. Choice **d** is incorrect because it is b^2 and not b.

12. **a.** To solve, use FOIL to multiply the first, outer, inner, and last terms:

$$\overset{\text{F}\quad\text{O}\quad\text{I}\quad\text{L}}{(a + bi)(a - bi) = a^2 - abi + abi - b^2i^2}$$

$a^2 - abi + abi - b^2i^2$ simplifies to $a^2 - b^2i^2$. Next, knowing that $i^2 = -1$, this can be simplified further to $a^2 - b^2(-1) = a^2 + b^2$. Choice **b** is incorrect. You may have made an error with the sign when simplifying $a^2 - b^2(-1)$. The i is only part of the last term, and because it is squared, it is replaced with -1. There will therefore be no i term, so choices **c** and **d** are incorrect.

13. b. There are three spots to fill for odd numbers, and there are three odd cards. The multiplication principle for counting says there will be $3 \times 2 \times 1 = 6$ ways these "odd spots" can be filled up. Similarly, there are three spots to fill for even numbers and there are three even cards, so there are 6 ways to fill these spots. Together the odd-even-odd-even-odd-even can occur in $6 \times 6 = 36$ different ways. If you selected choice **d**, you may have accidentally calculated 6!

14. a. By definition, even numbers are divisible by two. Knowing this, it is clear that both conditionals, "If n is an even number, then n is divisible by 2" and "If n is divisible by 2, then n is an even number," are true, and the biconditional $p \leftrightarrow q$ holds true. Another way of looking at it would be to realize that p and q are logically equivalent. Choice **a** is correct. Choice **b** represents "n is an even number or n is divisible by 2," and is incorrect. Choice **c** represents "n is not an even number and n is divisible by 2," and is incorrect. Choice **d** represents " If n is not an even number, then n is divisible by 2," and is incorrect.

15. a. Disjoint sets have no elements in common. To see what elements two sets have in common, use $\cap$, the intersection. $A \cap C = \emptyset$, which means A and C have no elements in common, so choice **a** is correct. $B \cap C = \{9, 11\}$, so choice **b** is incorrect. $B' = \{1, 3, 13, 15\}$ and $B' \cap A = \{1, 3\}$, so choice **c** is incorrect. $A \cap B = \{5, 7\}$, so choice **d** is incorrect.

16. a. To be an integer, the solution to the expression cannot be a fraction. The infinite set of integers is $\{ \ldots, -3, -2, -1, 0, 1, 2, 3, \ldots \}$. Look for the answer choice that allows you to cancel out the denominator (the bottom of the fraction). In this case, choice **a**, $\frac{ab + a^3}{a}$, can be simplified to $b + a^2$ by dividing both terms in the numerator (top part of the fraction) by a. $b + a^2$ must be an integer. The other answer choices may or may not be integers, so only choice **a** is correct.

17. b. Try to see how $g(x) = 2x + 4$ and $(f \circ g)x = \frac{1}{(x+2)}$ are related. Notice that the denominator of $(f \circ g)x$ is $g(x)$ divided by 2. This is the tipoff that a 2 was factored out. Also, the fact that $(f \circ g)x$ is a fraction and $g(x)$ is not is a tipoff that $f(x)$ involves a variable in the denominator. Looking at the answer choices, setting $f(x) = \frac{2}{x}$ accounts for both of these observations, so choice **b** is correct.

18. d. Put the 2 outside of the L. This is the number you are dividing into the coefficients that you see in the equation. The top row inside the L lists all of the coefficients in the equation. Have all the powers of x descend and add in any necessary 0 coefficients for any powers not present: $2x^5 + 0x^4 + 3x^3 + 2x^2 + 0x + 1x^0$. Always bring down the leftmost coefficient in the L, in this case, we bring down a 2.

The 2 outside of the L multiplies with this 2, and we fill in 4 in the next right column inside the L. Add down to get $0 + 4 = 4$ at the bottom. The 2 outside of the L multiplies with this 4, and we fill in 8 in the next right column inside the L. Add down to get $3 + 8 = 11$ at the bottom. The 2 outside of the L multiplies with this 11, and we fill in 22 in the next right column inside the L. Add down to get $2 + 22 = 24$. The 2 outside of the L multiplies with this 24, and we fill in 48 in the next right column inside the L. Add down to get $0 + 48 = 48$. The 2 outside of the L multiplies with this 48, and we fill in 96 in the next right column inside the L. Add down to get $1 + 96 = 97$.

2		2	0	3	2	0	1
			4	8	22	48	96
		2	4	11	24	48	97

When evaluating $g(2)$, we set $x = 2$, and synthetic division gives us the remainder of 97. $g(2) = 97$, so choice **d** is correct. If you chose **a**, you used 2 3 2 1 as the top row inside your L; you forgot the 0 for the $0x^4$ and the 0 for the $0x$ in your synthetic division L. If you selected choice **b**, you forgot to make a column for 0 for the $0x^4$ in your synthetic division L. If you selected choice **c**, you forgot to make a column for 0 for the $0x$ in your synthetic division L.

19. d. To correctly complete the truth table, $p \lor q$ must be known so that we can negate it in column 4, and $\sim p$ and $\sim q$ must be known, so that we can use those values in column 3:

p	q	$p \lor q$	$\sim p$	$\sim q$	$\sim p \lor \sim q$	$\sim(p \lor q)$
T	T	T	F	F	F	F
T	F	T	F	T	T	F
F	T	T	T	F	T	F
F	F	F	T	T	T	T

The disjunction $\sim p \lor \sim q$ is not the same as $\sim(p \lor q)$, so **a** is incorrect. Choices **b** and **c** are also incorrect because these columns both don't have two values of true, and they both don't have two values of false. Thus, choice **d** is correct.

20. d. First, solve all the absolute values: $a = |-17| = 17$, $b = |5^2| = 25$, $c = |-\frac{1}{2}| = \frac{1}{2}$, and $d = |-20 - 6| = |-26| = 26$. Next, put these in order: $\frac{1}{2}$, 17, 25, 26, which is the same as $c < a < b < d$, so choice **d** is correct.

21. c. The denominator of the fraction cannot equal zero, so x cannot equal 0. Every other real number value is fine. Note that when x is negative, $f(x)$ will also be negative. When x is positive, $f(x)$ will also be positive. This makes choice **c** correct.

22. b. Recall that ∩ means intersection (find what the two sets have in common), and ∪ means union (combine the two sets). Do whatever is in the parentheses (or innermost set of parentheses) first. First take the intersection of A and C to get

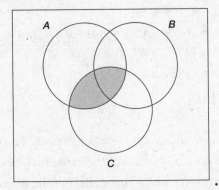

Next, combine that (union) with B to get

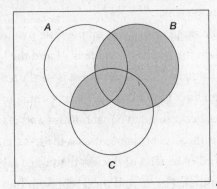

This is the diagram in choice **b**, and is correct. Choice **a** is a partial answer; it is $A \cap C$. Choice **c** is $(A \cup C) \cup B$. Choice **d** is $(A \cup C) \cap B$.

23. b. x cannot equal -1.5 (because the circle is open), and is greater than 1.5, so you are looking for $-1.5 < x$ on one end. x can equal 2 and it is less than 2, so you are looking for $x \leq 2$ on the other end. We know x can equal 2 because the circle is solid. The correct answer is choice **b**, $-1.5 < x \leq 2$.

24. a. The odds of one or the other winning will just be the sum of the probability of each one winning:

$$P(A \text{ or } L) = P(A) + P(L) = \frac{15}{105} + \frac{20}{105} = \frac{35}{105} = \frac{1}{3}$$

Choice **c** represents Leigh's probability of winning. Choice **d** represents Adrienne's probability of winning.

25. d. Implications are in the form "p implies q," which is the form we see in the question, so **d** is correct. A biconditional statement would use the words *if and only if*, so **a** is incorrect. Conjunctions use *and*, so choice **b** is incorrect. Disjunctions use *or*, so choice **c** is incorrect.

26. b. $(g \times h)x$ is the same as $g(x) \times h(x)$, which becomes $(3x - 12) \times (\frac{1}{3})x$ when you substitute the two given functions into the equation. $(3x - 12) \times (\frac{1}{3})x$ simplifies to $x^2 - 4x$, so choice **b** is correct. If you selected choice **a**, you probably made a computational error when simplifying the new function. If you selected choice **c**, you calculated $h \circ g$ by mistake. If you chose **d**, you calculated $g \circ h$ by mistake.

27. c. Solve all of the absolute values in the answer choices: Choice **a** is $|16| - |-15| = 16 - 15 = 1$, choice **b** is $|15 - 16| = |-1| = 1$, choice **c** is $1 - |-16| = 1 - 16 = -15$, and choice **d** is $|-15| - 16 = 15 - 16 = -1$. Thus, choice **c** has the least value.

28. b. Choice **b** is correct; because $|x|$ is always positive, $-|x|$ will be negative; you have a negative number (or zero in the case of $x = 0$) minus 7, so $f(x)$ will always be negative. Choice **a** will have two zeros, when $x = 7$ and when $x = -7$. Choice **c** will have one zero, when x is 4.5. Choice **d** will have one zero, when x is 7.

29. a. To find the Cartesian product, $A \times B$, list all possible ordered pairs that would result by taking the first coordinate from set A and the second coordinate from set B. Solving, we get $\{(x,r),(x,s),(y,r),(y,s)\}$, so **a** is correct. Choice **b** (the empty set) is incorrect because there are elements in the solution set. Choice **c** is not in the form of ordered pairs. Choice **d** does not contain enough ordered pairs.

30. c. Antecedent, consequent, and inverse are all terms used when considering conditional (*if/then*) statements. We are only given one statement, not two joined by *if* and *then*, so choices **a**, **b**, and **d** are all incorrect. Choice **c** is correct. $\sim p$ represents the negation, or "not p," and in this case, "I am not thirsty."

31. b. The cost will obviously increase the more the phone is used, so choices **c** and **d** are incorrect. Note that choice **c** would have the cost level off, even though more and more minutes are being used. Choice **a** does show an increase in cost over time, but is incorrect because the first point is at $(0,0)$ and the initial cost would be $5. Choice **b** is correct because it accounts for the $5 expense when 0 minutes are used.

32. c. To solve, you must first know the mean: The mean is $\frac{(4 + 1 + (-1) + 4)}{4} = \frac{8}{4} = 2$.

To find the variance, S^2, we need to find the average squared deviation of values from mean.

$S^2 = [(2-4)^2 + (2-1)^2 + (2-(-1))^2 + (2-4)^2] \div 4$

$= [(-2)^2 + (1)^2 + (3)^2 + (-2)^2] \div 4$

$= [4 + 1 + 9 + 4] \div 4$

$= [18] \div 4$

$= \frac{18}{4}$

$= 4.5$

Thus, choice **c** is correct. Choice **a** is incorrect as it is the mean, not the variance. Choice **b** is incorrect as it is the mode, not the variance. Choice **d** is incorrect, as it is the range, not the variance.

33. b. The range consists of all possible y values. Here the smallest y value is -4 and the largest y value is 3. Thus, the range is $-4 \le y \le 3$. Note you have to use the less than or equal to symbol because y can equal both -4 and 3. Choice **a** is incorrect because it uses the less than symbol instead of the less than or equal to symbol. The -2 and the 3 represent the boundaries of the domain, and not the range, so choices **c** and **d** are incorrect.

34. a. 1,000 tickets were sold in all. Let r represent the number of regular tickets sold and let $1,000 - r$ represent the number of children's tickets sold. Because regular tickets cost $10, the amount made from the sale of regular tickets would be $10r$. Because children's tickets cost $5, the amount made from the sale of regular tickets would be $5(1,000 - r)$. When these amounts are combined, the total is $8,000.

$$10r + 5(1,000 - r) = 8,000$$
$$10r + 5,000 - 5r = 8,000$$
$$5r + 5,000 = 8,000$$
$$5r = 3,000$$
$$r = 600$$

The number of children's tickets sold is $1,000 - r = 1,000 - 600 = 400$. Because 600 regular tickets were sold and 400 children's tickets were sold, 200 more regular tickets were sold than children's tickets. Choice **a** is correct. Choice **b** represents the number of children's tickets sold and is incorrect. Choice **c** represents $\frac{1}{2}$ the number of all tickets sold and is incorrect. Choice **d** represents the number of regular tickets sold and is incorrect.

35. a. An odd number times an even number will yield an even number, so if $3l$ is even, l must be even. When two even numbers are added together, the sum is an even number, so **a** is correct, and choice **b** is incorrect. $\frac{(k + l)}{3}$ is an even number divided by 3, so the quotient will not be even (choice **c** is incorrect). The sum $k + l$ is even, so $3(k + l)$ is even, and choice **d** is incorrect.

36. a. Recall that $f(x) - a$ slides $f(x)$ down a units, so **a** is correct. $f(x) + a$ slides $f(x)$ up a units, so choice **b** is incorrect. In this case, you are applying the rule of the function (this gives you y), and then you are subtracting 2. This decreases y by 2, which means the graph slides down two units.

37. b. {3} is the intersection of the two sets, $A \cap B$, as it shows what the two sets have in common. Choice **a**, empty set, is incorrect because the intersection of the two sets does contain elements. Choice **c** is incorrect because it is the union, $A \cup B$. Choice **d** is the universe; in this question, $A \cap B$ is {3}, not the universe.

38. d. Simplify all the values for the given variables: $a = |-13| = 13$, $b = -2$, $c = a - b = 13 - (-2) = 13 + 2 = 15$, and $d = |b - a| = |-2 - 13| = |-15| = 15$. Next, put these in order: $-2, 13, 15, 15$, which is the same as $b < a < c \le d$, so choice **d** is correct. The less than or equal to sign, $\le$, is needed between c and d because they are, in fact, equal.

39. b. $-h(x)$ is $h(x)$ reflected about the x-axis. $-h(x)$ is found by finding $h(x)$ and then changing its sign. Thus, if $h(x) = 1$, $-h(x)$ would be -1. The net effect is to reflect the entire line about the x-axis.

40. d. This is a conditional probability question. The probability of A, given B is written as: $P(\frac{A}{B})$. You are finding the probability of a 7 given that a 7 was drawn already. There were 52 cards to begin with, but after the first 7 was drawn, there are 51 cards, of which three cards are 7s. $p(7 \mid 7) = \frac{3}{51}$. Choice **a** is incorrect because it is the probability of drawing the first 7. If you selected choice **b**, you may have forgotten to decrease the number of the cards in the deck by 1. Choice **c** is incorrect because it accounts for four possible cards instead of three after the first draw.

41. c. A prime number is a positive integer that has only two distinct positive divisors, 1 and the number itself. To find the least possible value for $k \times 2 \times 5$, you want to set k equal to the smallest prime number that is less than 10. Two is the smallest prime number. $2 \times 2 \times 5 = 20$, so choice **c** is correct. Setting k equal to 1 (which is not a prime number) would yield the incorrect choice **a**. Setting k equal to 3 (which is not the least prime number) would yield the incorrect choice **d**.

42. b. The domain consists of all the x values that you can put into a function. Here, x has to be greater than 5 and it has to be less than or equal to 18, so choice **b** is correct. Choice **a** is incorrect because if x could not equal 18, the $<$ symbol would have been used instead of the $\leq$ symbol. It is true that x cannot equal zero, but there are additional real number values that are also not in the domain, so choice **c** is incorrect. When $x = 15$, $f(x) = \frac{1}{2}x$, so 15 is in the domain, and choice **d** is incorrect.

43. c. Recall that the probability of a simple event can be expressed as:

$$P(E) = \frac{\text{number of favorable outcomes}}{\text{total number of possible outcomes}}$$

$$P(E) = \frac{\text{number of sophomores}}{\text{total number of students}}$$

There are 7 sophomores entering and 12 students entering in all, thus, the probability that a sophomore will win the raffle $= \frac{7}{12}$. Choice **b** represents the probability that a senior will win, and is incorrect.

44. b. The graph is not linear, but there definitely appears to be a relationship, one that is exponential, so choice **b** is correct. Plots with no correlation indicate no relationship, but that is not the case here, so **a** is incorrect. Choices **c** and **d** are incorrect, as this is not a linear (straight line) relationship.

45. a. $(f \circ g)x$ is the same as $f(g(x))$, so substituting in the given functions, you get $\frac{(10x + 1)}{5} = 2x + \frac{1}{5}$, so **a** is correct. If you selected choice **b**, you probably calculated $(g \circ f)x$ by mistake. If you selected choice **c** or **d**, you probably made a computational error when simplifying.

46. c. The farmer is spending $500 in all, and the fence costs $10/foot. Divide $500 by $10/foot to find that 50 feet of fencing material is purchased; 10 feet of material is needed for the side of the rectangle that is opposite the barn. $50 - 10 = 40$, so there is 40 feet left of fencing material for the other two sides. The other side of the rectangle must then be 20 ft. The farmer has a rectangular plot of 20 ft. by 10 ft., so the enclosed space will be 200 ft.² If you chose **a**, you incorrectly found the enclosed area for a square with a side length of 10 ft. If you selected choice **b**, you found out that 50 feet of fencing material is purchased, but forgot about the side that doesn't need any fencing. If you chose **d**, you incorrectly found the enclosed area for a square with a side length of 20 ft.

47. a. This question deals with independent events. The probability is then $P(\text{Event 1}) \times P(\text{Event 2})$. In this case, Event 1 is that Justin will go to the play and Event 2 is that Sierra will go to the play. $P(\text{Event 1}) \times P(\text{Event 2}) = 20\% \times 50\% = 0.2 \times 0.5 = 0.10 = 10\%$, and choice **a** is correct. Choice **b** is the probability of Justin going. Choice **c** is the difference of the two probabilities. Choice **d** is the sum of the probabilities. The correct calculation requires multiplying the two probabilities, so these are all incorrect.

48. d. Irrational numbers cannot be expressed as the ratio of two integers, $\frac{a}{b}$. If you cannot find a whole number that, when squared, will give you the number under the radical sign, then the number you are dealing with is an irrational number. So $\sqrt{(\sqrt{121})} = \sqrt{11}$ is an irrational number, because there is no number that when squared will equal 11. Choice **d** is correct. Choice **a** is incorrect because imaginary numbers involve i, which is the square root of -1. A prime number is a positive integer that has only two distinct divisors, 1 and the number itself. $\sqrt{11}$ is neither an integer nor a prime number, so choice **b** is incorrect. Choice **c** is incorrect because rational numbers can be expressed as the ratio of two integers in the form $\frac{a}{b}$, which is not the case for $\sqrt{11}$; taking the square root of this number will result in a number with a nonterminating, nonrepeating decimal extension.

49. d. If you set this up algebraically with x as the median, the other values would then be $x - 4$, $x - 2$, $x + 2$, and $x + 4$. In order, these are:

$$x - 4 \qquad x - 2 \qquad x \qquad x + 2 \qquad x + 4$$
$$\text{(median)}$$

The mean is the sum of the numbers divided by the number of numbers and would be:

$$\frac{x-4+x-2+x+x+2+x+4}{5} = \frac{5x}{5} = x$$

50. c. The answer will be $\frac{1}{4}$ of $\frac{1}{4}$ of $\frac{1}{4}$ of x. In math, *of* means "multiply": $(\frac{1}{4})(\frac{1}{4})(\frac{1}{4})x = (\frac{1}{64})x = \frac{x}{64}$.

51. b. You do not have to figure out the rule of each function in order to solve the problem. You can simply read the values off of the tables. To find $f(g(14))$, first find $g(8)$. Reading the second chart, you get $g(8) = 6$. Next find $f(6)$. Reading the first chart you get $f(6) = 3$. Thus, choice **b** is correct. Choice **a** is $f(5)$ and is incorrect. Choice **c** is $f(7)$ and is incorrect. If you selected choice **d**, 6, you probably calculated $g(8)$ by mistake.

52. d. First, notice that the lines are dashed, so the $<$ symbol should be used two times in the inequality. This makes choices **a** and **c** incorrect, as they each include a $\leq$ symbol. Next, both lines are above the x-axis, so both lines would be $y = n$, where n is positive. This makes choice **b** incorrect. Choice **d**, $3 < y < 9$, is the only choice that can possibly be represented by the given graph.

53. d. Because every number in the data set is the same, the mean will be the very same number. Recall that the mean is the sum of all the numbers divided by the number of numbers. The range is found by subtracting the lowest value from the highest value. In this case, when both values are the same, the range will be zero. To find the standard deviation, you need to know the variance. To find the variance, S^2, you find the average squared deviation of values from the mean. Because every value is equal to the mean, the variance will be zero. The standard deviation is equal to the square root of the variance, so when all the values in the data set are the same, the standard deviation is equal to zero. Thus, all three statements are correct, and choice **d** is the correct answer.

54. a. The range consists of the y values that are possible. Notice that the smallest y value is -5 and the largest y value is 6. Thus, the range is $-5 \leq y \leq 6$, so choice **a** is correct. Choice **b** is incorrect; it uses the highs and lows for the x values instead of the y values. Choices **c** and **d** are incorrect because the $\leq$ symbol is missing on one end of the inequality.

55. b. Both schools plotted their data on graphs using the same increments and units. School P had a greater spread than School Q, so the graph that represents School P will be the wider, fatter graph, Graph B. Choice **b** is correct, and choice **a** is incorrect. Both choices **c** and **d** are incorrect because the graphs are visually different for the two schools. The question states that "School P had a greater spread."

56. c. The relationship between AB and $A'B'$ is such that $A'B'$ is $6 \div 4 = 1.5$ times the value of AB. Use this relationship to find the other two sides. Because this is an isosceles triangle, $B'C' = A'B' = 6$. Because $AC = 2$, $A'C'$ will equal $2 \times 1.5 = 3$. The sum of all sides for $A'B'C'$ is then $6 + 6 + 3 = 15$ units. Choice **a** represents the perimeter of triangle ABC and is incorrect. Choice **b** represents the sum of the two equal sides of $A'B'C'$ and does not include the third, so this is incorrect. Choice **d** represents the sum of $6 + 6 + 6$ instead of $6 + 6 + 3$, so this is incorrect.

57. c. A prime number is a positive integer that has only two distinct positive divisors, 1 and the number itself. A composite number is a positive integer that has a positive divisor other than 1 or itself. One is neither prime nor composite, so statements I and III are incorrect and you know that choices **a**, **b**, and **d** are incorrect. Two is a prime number, so only statement II, and thus, choice **c**, is correct.

58. b. Because every member in set D is also in set C, when the union is taken, it is simply set C. Remember, the union will contain all elements in C and D. Choice **a** would represent the intersection $C \cap D$ and is incorrect. Choice **c**, the null set (empty set) is incorrect because the union of the two sets does contain elements. C' is the complement of C (all the elements in the universe that are not in C), but the correct answer would include the element in C.

59. b. $\frac{1}{3}$ of the 30 high school students are male, so $\frac{1}{3} \times 30 = 10$ male high school students. There are 10 male high school students out of 60 members in all, so the probability that a male high school student will be picked is $\frac{10}{60} = \frac{1}{6}$.

60. b. Using the relationship $\log_b(mn) = \log_b(m) + \log_b(n)$, convert $\log_5(125x)$ to $\log_5(125) + \log_5(x)$. Because $5^3 = 125$, $\log_5(125) = 3$. $\log_5(125) + \log_5(x)$ simplifies to $3 + \log_5(x)$, and choice **b** is correct. If you selected choice **a**, you probably forgot to expand the log to include $\log_5(x)$. If you selected choice **c**, you probably solved $\log_5(125) = 3$, but accidentally wrote $\log_5 3$. Choice **d** is incorrect; whenever there is a log with no base listed, it is $\log_{10}$. $\log_{10}(5x)$ is not equal to $\log_5(125x)$.

CLEP College Mathematics Practice Test 2

Now take CLEP College Mathematics Practice Test 2 for additional CLEP practice. Similar to the official exam, you will answer 60 questions. Again, we suggest that you follow the time constraints of the official CLEP College Mathematics exam (90 minutes).

Remember, on the official CLEP, there is no penalty for incorrect answers, so always make a guess if you are unsure of an answer.

When you are finished, check the answer key on page 560 carefully to assess your results.

▶ **CLEP College Mathematics Practice Test 2**

1. (a) (b) (c) (d)
2. (a) (b) (c) (d)
3. (a) (b) (c) (d)
4. (a) (b) (c) (d)
5. (a) (b) (c) (d)
6. (a) (b) (c) (d)
7. (a) (b) (c) (d)
8. (a) (b) (c) (d)
9. (a) (b) (c) (d)
10. (a) (b) (c) (d)
11. (a) (b) (c) (d)
12. (a) (b) (c) (d)
13. (a) (b) (c) (d)
14. (a) (b) (c) (d)
15. (a) (b) (c) (d)
16. (a) (b) (c) (d)
17. (a) (b) (c) (d)
18. (a) (b) (c) (d)
19. (a) (b) (c) (d)
20. (a) (b) (c) (d)

21. (a) (b) (c) (d)
22. (a) (b) (c) (d)
23. (a) (b) (c) (d)
24. (a) (b) (c) (d)
25. (a) (b) (c) (d)
26. (a) (b) (c) (d)
27. (a) (b) (c) (d)
28. (a) (b) (c) (d)
29. (a) (b) (c) (d)
30. (a) (b) (c) (d)
31. (a) (b) (c) (d)
32. (a) (b) (c) (d)
33. (a) (b) (c) (d)
34. (a) (b) (c) (d)
35. (a) (b) (c) (d)
36. (a) (b) (c) (d)
37. (a) (b) (c) (d)
38. (a) (b) (c) (d)
39. (a) (b) (c) (d)
40. (a) (b) (c) (d)

41. (a) (b) (c) (d)
42. (a) (b) (c) (d)
43. (a) (b) (c) (d)
44. (a) (b) (c) (d)
45. (a) (b) (c) (d)
46. (a) (b) (c) (d)
47. (a) (b) (c) (d)
48. (a) (b) (c) (d)
49. (a) (b) (c) (d)
50. (a) (b) (c) (d)
51. (a) (b) (c) (d)
52. (a) (b) (c) (d)
53. (a) (b) (c) (d)
54. (a) (b) (c) (d)
55. (a) (b) (c) (d)
56. (a) (b) (c) (d)
57. (a) (b) (c) (d)
58. (a) (b) (c) (d)
59. (a) (b) (c) (d)
60. (a) (b) (c) (d)

▶ Practice Test Questions

1. If f is an odd number and g and h are both even numbers, which of the following equations would never hold true?
   a. $f + f = g$
   b. $2f = h$
   c. $g + h = f$
   d. $g - f = f$

2. Which of the following is true regarding $g(-x)$ and $g(x)$?
   a. $g(-x)$ is $g(x)$ reflected about the y-axis.
   b. $g(-x)$ is $g(x)$ reflected about the x-axis.
   c. $g(-x)$ is $g(x)$ reflected about the line $y = x$.
   d. $g(-x)$ is $g(x)$ reflected about the line $y = -x$.

3. Given the following scores, what is the sum of the median and the mean?

   7   4   3   7   7   6   8

   a. 12
   b. 13
   c. 14
   d. 15

4. Seven students won a math contest. The principal wants to display pictures of the winners, but only has room to hang four pictures. She decides to arrange pictures of four winners this week and to post the remaining three during the next week. How many different arrangements are possible for this week?
   a. 28
   b. 35
   c. 840
   d. 7!

5. What is the range of the following function?
$$f(x) = \left\{ \begin{array}{l} \frac{1}{2}x \text{ if } 4 \le x \le 12 \\ x + 1 \text{ if } 12 < x \le 20 \end{array} \right\}$$
   a. all real numbers y such that $2 \le y \le 21$
   b. all real numbers y such that $2 < y < 21$
   c. all real numbers y such that $4 < y < 20$
   d. all real numbers y such that $4 < y \le 20$

6. Triangle $A'B'C'$ is similar to triangle ABC shown in the diagram. If $A'B' = 12.5$, what is the perimeter of triangle $A'B'C'$?

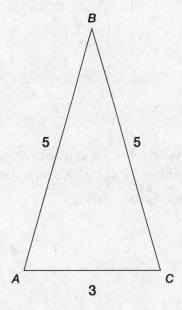

   a. 13
   b. 25
   c. 32.5
   d. 37.5

7. $U = \{101, 102, 103, 104, 105\}$, $A' = \{104, 105\}$, $B' = \{103, 104, 105\}$, and $C = B \cap A$. Which sets are equivalent?
   a. A and B
   b. B and C
   c. A and C
   d. A and B'

8. Given p represents "I am not hungry," and q represents "I have not eaten," which of the following represents "If I am not hungry, then I have not eaten"?

a. $p \rightarrow q$

b. $p \rightarrow \sim q$

c. $p \leftrightarrow q$

d. $\sim p \leftrightarrow \sim q$

9. Nick is using a standard deck of cards. If no cards are replaced, find $P(\frac{K}{Q})$, the probability that he will draw a king followed by a queen.

a. $\frac{4}{52}$

b. $\frac{3}{52}$

c. $\frac{4}{51}$

d. $\frac{3}{51}$

10. If the nonzero integers v and z are both divisible by the whole number y, and $y \neq 0$, which of the following must also be an integer?

a. $\frac{v}{y}$

b. $\frac{y}{z}$

c. $\frac{y}{v}$

d. $\frac{v}{z}$

11. Given $g(x) = 5x + 10$ and $h(x) = (\frac{1}{5})x$, find $(g \times h)x$.

a. $x + 2$

b. $x + 10$

c. $\frac{1}{5}x + 10$

d. $x^2 + 2x$

12. Abigail, Beth, Clara, Darlene, and Evelyn will all be standing in a line on stage. How many different ways can these five girls be arranged in line?

a. 24

b. 25

c. 100

d. 120

13. Given $\frac{(b+1)}{n} = 2$ and $\frac{n}{2}$ is the whole number p, which of the following is true?

a. n is odd.

b. The sum $b + 1$ is odd.

c. b is odd.

d. $n = \frac{2}{(b+1)}$

14. Which Venn diagram represents $(A \cap C) \cup (B \cap C)$?

a.

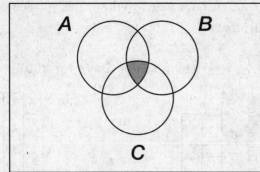

b.

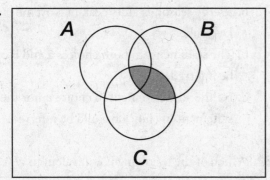

c.

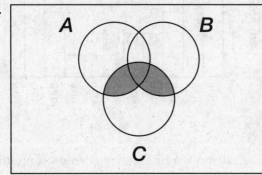

d.

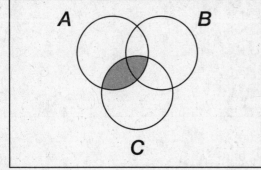

15. Which of the following is a counter example to "all planets have at least one moon"?

a. the existence of a moon without a planet

b. the existence of a planet with three moons

c. the existence of a planet with no moons

d. the existence of a planet surrounded by asteroids

16. Given $g(x) = \frac{x+5}{2}$ and $h(x) = x + 5$, find $(h \circ g)x$.

a. $\frac{x}{2} + 5$

b. $\frac{x}{2} + 7\frac{1}{2}$

c. $x + 7\frac{1}{2}$

d. $\frac{x+10}{2}$

17. $\frac{\sqrt{7}}{1}$ is an example of

a. an imaginary number.

b. an irrational number.

c. a rational number.

d. a prime number.

18. $\frac{(1+i)}{i}$ is equivalent to which of the following?

a. $i + 1$

b. $i - 1$

c. $-i + 1$

d. $-i - 1$

19. The graph of function $g(x)$ is shown here. What is the range of $g(x)$?

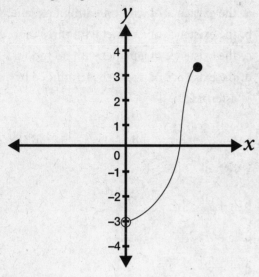

a. $0 < y \leq 4$
b. $-4 < y \leq 4$
c. $-4 \leq y \leq 4$
d. $-4 \leq y < 4$

20. Given $14 < m < 20$, and m is a composite number, which of the following is the least value of m?
a. 15
b. 16
c. 17
d. 18

21. If all of Kevin's sick days were due to environmental allergies, based on this graph, you could infer that

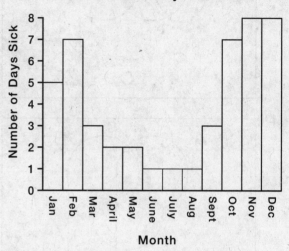

a. allergy season is at a relative low from June through August.
b. allergy season is at its peak in November and December.
c. The statements in both choices **a** and **b** could be inferred.
d. Neither the statement in choice **a** nor the statement in choice **b** could be inferred.

22. Which of the following is equivalent to v?

r	s	v
T	T	T
T	F	F
F	T	T
F	F	T

a. $s \rightarrow r$
b. $r \rightarrow s$
c. $\sim s \rightarrow \sim r$
d. $\sim r \rightarrow \sim s$

23. On Bus 22, 36 of the students take science and 42 of the students take art history. If 12 students take both science and art history, and no students take neither science and art history, how many students are on this bus?
   a. 30
   b. 66
   c. 78
   d. 100

24. Given $f(x) = 4x - 1$, find $f^{-1}(x)$.

   a. $f^{-1}(x) = -(\frac{1}{4}x)$

   b. $f^{-1}(x) = \frac{1}{4}x$

   c. $f^{-1}(x) = \frac{(x+1)}{4}$

   d. $f^{-1}(x) = 1 - 4x$

25. On a test given to five students, Jessica scored 95.2, Vinny got 91.3, Connor and Derek both scored 94.8, and Jade scored 98.0. What was the range of these scores?
   a. 94.82
   b. 94.8
   c. 3.2
   d. 6.7

26. The function $f(x)$ is a linear function. If $f(0) = 2$ and $f(4) = 10, f(20) =$
   a. 22
   b. 26
   c. 36
   d. 42

27. Which of the following statements is false?
   a. All even numbers are divisible by 2.
   b. An even number plus an odd number will add to an odd number.
   c. An odd number plus an odd number will add to an even number.
   d. An even number times an odd number will multiply to an odd number.

28. Given $t \rightarrow s$, which of the following is the inverse?
   a. $s \rightarrow t$
   b. $\sim t \rightarrow \sim s$
   c. $t \leftrightarrow s$
   d. $\sim s \rightarrow \sim t$

29. $U = \{j, k, l, m, n, o, p\}, A' = \{k, m, o\}$, $B = \{n, o, p\}, C' = \{j, k, l, m, o\}$, and $D = A \cap B$. Which sets are equivalent?
   a. C and D
   b. A and B
   c. D and A
   d. B and D

30. If c and d are nonzero integers, when solved, which of the following must also be an integer?
   a. $c + \frac{d}{c}$

   b. $c + \frac{d}{d}$

   c. $\frac{(c \times d)^2}{d^2}$

   d. $\frac{d^2}{c^2}$

31. The function $f(x)$ is defined as $f(x) = \frac{3x^2}{2}$. When compared with $f(x)$, the graph of $f(x) + \sqrt{2}$ is
   a. $f(x)$ slid downward by $\sqrt{2}$ units.
   b. $f(x)$ slid upward by $\sqrt{2}$ units.
   c. $f(x)$ reflected about the line $y = \sqrt{2}x$.
   d. $f(x)$ reflected about the line $y = -\sqrt{2}x$.

32. Which of the following is the negation of $p \lor q$?

  a. $\sim(p \lor q)$

  b. $\sim p \lor \sim q$

  c. $\sim\sim(p \lor q)$

  d. $\sim p \lor q$

33. While redecorating her room, Samantha is in the process of choosing new curtains. The curtains are available in eight different colors, three different opacities, and three different lengths. How many choices are available?

  a. 9

  b. 14

  c. 24

  d. 72

34. Given $f(x) = 5x$ and $(g \circ f)x = 10 - 25x^2$, which of the following is equivalent to $g(x)$?

  a. $10 + x^2$

  b. $10 - x^2$

  c. $-x^2$

  d. x^2

35. Which of the following inequalities represents this number line?

  a. $0 \le x < b$

  b. $0 < x \le b$

  c. $0 \le x < b$

  d. $0 \ge x \le b$

36. Given $A = \{4, 8, 12, 16, 20\}$, which of the following sets is a subset of A?

  a. $B = \{12, 14, 16\}$

  b. $C = \{8, 12, 16\}$

  c. $D = \{2, 4, 6, 8, 16\}$

  d. $E = \{8, 9, 12, 16\}$

37. A farmer grows apples and oranges on his farm. Each apple takes 10 seconds to harvest, while each orange takes 15 seconds. The farmer harvested a total of 800 pieces of fruit, and it took a total of 2.5 hours to harvest all the fruit. How many oranges were harvested?

  a. 150

  b. 200

  c. 250

  d. 600

38. If $a = |-17 + 5|$, $b = |-3^2|$, $c = |\frac{1}{2} - 1|$, and $d = -3$, which of the following inequalities is correct?

  a. $a < b < c < d$

  b. $a < c < b < d$

  c. $d < c < b < a$

  d. $d < a < b < c$

39. If $A = \{1, 2\}$ and $B = \{2, 4\}$, find the Cartesian product of sets A and B.

  a. $\{2\}$

  b. $\{(1, 2), (2, 4), (1, 4)\}$

  c. $\{1, 2, 4\}$

  d. $\{(1, 2), (1, 4), (2, 2), (2, 4)\}$

40. Given $f(x) = \frac{\sqrt{2}}{x^2}$, what is the range of this function?

  a. all real numbers

  b. all real numbers greater than or equal to zero

  c. all real numbers except $x = 0$

  d. all real numbers greater than zero

41. Adam builds a stained glass window in the shape of a square with a semicircle on top of it. The diameter of the semicircle is equal to the side length of the square, which is 10". Brenda builds another stained glass window in the shape of a triangle with base length 6" and height 14". Which window will require more glass to construct, and how much more glass will be required to build it? (Approximate π as 3.)
 a. Adam's is bigger by 58 in.^{2}.
 b. Adam's is bigger by 95.5 in.^{2}.
 c. Adam's is bigger by 133 in.^{2}.
 d. Brenda's is bigger by 95.5 in.^{2}.

42. Given the following values of the functions f and g, $g(f(12))$ is equivalent to what value?

X	11	12	13
$f(x)$	11	11	11

X	10	11	12
$g(x)$	41	45	49

 a. 11
 b. 41
 c. 45
 d. 49

43. Reduce $\frac{x^2 y^2 z^{-4}}{x^{-2} y^7 z^{-4}}$.
 a. $x^{-4} y^9 z^{-8}$
 b. $x^4 y^5 z^8$
 c. $y^{-5} z^{-8}$
 d. $x^4 y^{-5}$

44. The graph shows the temperature fluctuations throughout the course of a day. What is the range shown on the graph in degrees F?

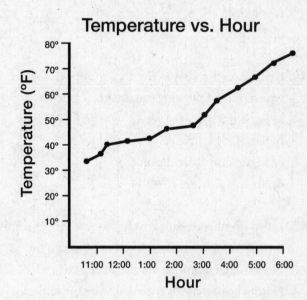

 a. 30°
 b. 40°
 c. 60°
 d. 70°

45. What is $\log_5(x^{25})$ equivalent to?
 a. $\log_5 25 - \log_5(x)$
 b. $\log_5 25 + \log_5(x)$
 c. $5\log x$
 d. $25\log_5 x$

46. Which of the following lines is perpendicular to $y = x - 6$?
 a. $x = y - 6$
 b. $x = y + 4$
 c. $y = 5 - x$
 d. $y = 1 - 6x$

47. If *a*, *b*, *c* is a Pythagorean triple, which of the following is also a Pythagorean triple?
a. $a + 2, b + 2, c + 2$
b. $a, 2b, 3c$
c. a^2, b^2, c
d. $5a, 5b, 5c$

48. Given $A \cup B = C$, $A \cap B = \emptyset$, and $A \cap C = A$, which of the following statements is true?
a. Set *B* is a subset of set *A*.
b. Sets *A* and *B* are disjoint.
c. Sets *A* and *C* are disjoint.
d. Set *C* is a subset of set *B*.

49. If two numbered balls are chosen from the box in the diagram, how many different pairs can be chosen such that their sum is greater than 9? Note: The pair 3, 4 is regarded to be the same as the pair 4, 3.

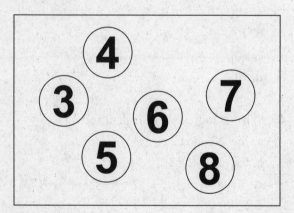

a. 11
b. 13
c. 22
d. 26

50. If the monthly budget total was $3,000, what would be the best estimate for money spent on clothes?

Monthly Budget

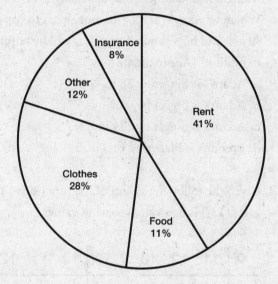

a. $30
b. $600
c. $1,000
d. $2,800

51. If $a = -7$ and $b = 9$, which of the following has the greatest value?
a. $|a + b|$
b. $|a - b|$
c. $|b| + a$
d. $|b + a|$

52. Eight dancers will perform on stage in a line. There are four male and four female dancers. If they will be ordered male-female-male-female-male-female-male-female, how many different orders are possible?

   a. 4^2

   b. 8^2

   c. 24^2

   d. 32^2

53. Given $f(x) = 3x^5 + 2x^2 + 5x + 1$, what will the remainder be when $f(x)$ is divided by $x - 3$?

   a. 0

   b. 115

   c. 451

   d. 763

54. Seven volunteers are on call at the ambulance headquarters when a call comes through. Three volunteers must be sent out such that one (and only one) of the three is an EMT. If three of the volunteers present are EMTs, how many different groups of people can be sent out?

   a. 6

   b. 9

   c. 18

   d. 27

55. What is the mean of a, b, c, and d?

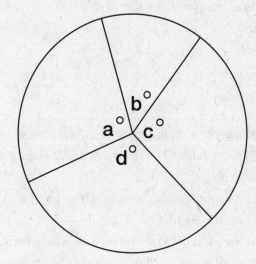

   a. 45

   b. 60

   c. 90

   d. 180

56. What is the range of the function $y = g(x)$ shown here?

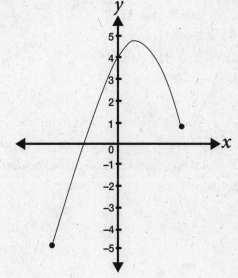

   a. $-4 < y < 4$

   b. $-6 \le y \le 1$

   c. $-6 < y < 6$

   d. $-6 \le y \le 6$

57. Given p is a composite number less than 10, what is the least possible value of $\frac{2p}{2}$?

  a. 3

  b. 2

  c. 1

  d. $\frac{1}{2}$

58. Which of the following is the contrapositive of "If a word describes an action, then a word is an adverb"?

  a. A word describes an action if and only if a word is an adverb.

  b. If a word does not describe an action, then a word is not an adverb.

  c. If a word is an adverb, then a word describes an action.

  d. If a word is not an adverb, then a word does not describe a verb.

59. If n is odd and m is even, which of the following statements is true?

  a. $n + m$ will be even.

  b. $n + n$ will be even.

  c. $n \times m$ will be odd.

  d. $n - m$ will be even.

60. Given that the median of a set of numbers is 1^2, the mean is m^3, and the variance is n^4, which of the following must be equal to the standard deviation?

  a. l

  b. $\sqrt[2]{m^3}$

  c. n^2

  d. n

▶ **Answers**

1. c. You know that f is an odd number and g and h are both even numbers, so look at each answer in terms of how operations work involving odd and even numbers. Choice **a** would be odd + odd = even, so this could be true. Choice **b** would be 2 × odd = even, so this could be true. Choice **c** would be even + even = odd, which will never be true, so choice **c** is the correct answer. Choice **d** would be even − odd = odd, so this could also be true (for example, 6 − 3 = 3).

2. a. $g(-x)$ is $g(x)$ reflected about the y-axis. $g(-x)$ is found by first changing the sign of x and then applying the rule for the function. The net effect is to reflect the entire line about the y-axis.

3. b. For the median, list the scores in order and note the middle number: 3, 4, 6, 7, 7, 7, 8.

The median is 7.

For the mean, add all 7 numbers and divide by 7 (the total number of scores): $\frac{(8 + 7 + 4 + 3 + 7 + 7 + 6)}{7}$. As CLEP questions are designed so that you do not need a calculator, you can add the numerator in steps: $\frac{(15 + 21 + 6)}{7} = \frac{42}{7} = 6$.

Add the median and the mean to get: $7 + 6 = 13$.

4. c. When you see the word *arrangements,* you should realize that order does matter and you are doing a permutation. Use $_nP_r$ where n is the total number of elements that can be selected and r is the number of elements that will actually be selected:

$$_nP_r = \frac{n!}{(n-r)!}$$

In this case, $n = 7$ and $r = 4$. The formula becomes:

$$_7P_4 = \frac{7!}{(7-4)!} = \frac{7!}{3!} = \frac{7 \times 6 \times 5 \times 4 \times 3 \times 2 \times 1}{3 \times 2 \times 1} =$$

$7 \times 6 \times 5 \times 4 = 42 \times 20 = 840$.

5. a. The range consists of all the y values that you get after putting an x value into a function. Here, the smallest y value will come from the smallest x value. The smallest x is 4, and $f(4) = 2$. The largest is $x = 20$ and $f(21) = 21$. Thus, the range is $2 \leq y \leq 21$, so choice **a** is correct. Choice **b** is incorrect because the $<$ is used instead of the $\leq$ symbol; y can equal 2 and 21. If you selected choice **c** or **d**, you confused the range with the domain; the domain consists of all the x values that you can put into a function. In this question, you are looking for the output.

6. c. The relationship between AB and $A'B'$ is such that $A'B'$ is $12.5 \div 5 = 2.5$ times the value of AB. Use this relationship to find the other two sides. Because this is an isosceles triangle, $B'C' = A'B' = 12.5$. Because $AC = 3$, $A'C'$ will equal $2.5 \times 3 = 7.5$. The sum of all sides for $A'B'C'$ is then $12.5 + 12.5 + 7.5 = 32.5$ units. Choice **a** is the perimeter of ABC, and is incorrect. Choice **b** is the sum of the two equal sides of $A'B'C'$ and does not include the third, so this is incorrect. Choice **d** is incorrect; it is the sum of $12.5 + 12.5 + 12.5$.

7. b. A' is the complement of A, so it consists of all the elements in the universe that are not in A. Set A would then be {101, 102, 103}. B' is the complement of B, and consists of all the elements in the universe that are not in B. Set B would then be {101, 102}. $B \cap A$ is the intersection of A and B, so we list what they have in common: {101, 102}. $B \cap A = C$, so $C = $ {101, 102}. Thus, B and C are identical and choice **b** is correct.

8. a. Given p represents "I am not hungry" and q represents "I have not eaten," the conditional statement "If I am not hungry, then I have not eaten" would be represented by choice **a**, $p \rightarrow q$. Choice **b** represents "If I am not hungry, then I have not not eaten," or "If I am not hungry, then I have eaten." Choice **c** represents "I am not hungry if and only if I have not eaten." Choice **d** represents "I am not not hungry if and only if I have not not eaten," which is the same as saying "I am hungry if and only if I have eaten."

9. c. This is a conditional probability question. The probability of A given B is written as $P(A|B)$. You are finding the probability of a queen, given that a king was drawn already and has not been put back. There were 52 cards to begin with, but after the first card was drawn, there are 51 cards, of which four cards are queens. $P(K|Q) = \frac{4}{51}$. Choice **c** is correct. Choice **a** is incorrect because it is the probability of drawing the first king. If you selected choice **b**, you may have forgotten to decrease the number of the cards in the deck by 1, and instead decreased the "favorable outcomes" by 1. Choice **d** is incorrect because it accounts for only three possible Q cards instead of four.

10. a. The nonzero integers v and z are both divisible by the whole number y. This means that y divided evenly into both v and z. To be an integer, the solution to the expression cannot be a fraction. The infinite set of integers is $\{\ldots, -3, -2, -1, 0, 1, 2, 3, \ldots\}$. Thus, look for the answer choice that shows either v and z being divided by y, since you know this operation must result in an integer value. Choice **a** shows $\frac{v}{y}$ and is correct. The other answer choices may or may not be integers, so only choice **a** is correct.

11. d. $(g \times h)x$ is equivalent to $g(x) \times h(x)$, so using the given functions, this becomes $(5x + 10) \times (\frac{1}{5})x$. This simplifies to $x^2 + 2x$, so choice **d** is correct. If you selected choice **a**, you calculated $h \circ g$ by mistake. If you selected choice **b**, you calculated $g \circ h$ by mistake. If you selected choice **c**, you may have made an error in your calculations.

12. d. Use $_nP_r$, where n is the total number of elements that can be selected and r is the number of elements that will actually be selected:

$$_nP_r = \frac{n!}{(n-r)!}$$

In this case, n and r are the same: There are five girls to be selected from, and we are lining up all five girls. The formula becomes:

$$_5P_5 = \frac{5!}{(0)!}$$

Recall that $0!$, by definition $= 1$. So the answer is $5! = 5 \times 4 \times 3 \times 2 \times 1 = 120$. There are 120 different possible arrangements, so choice **d** is correct.

13. c. $\frac{n}{2}$ is a whole number, so n must be even. $\frac{(b+1)}{n}$ is 2, so $b + 1$ is even, which means that choice **b** is incorrect. If $b + 1$ is even, b must be odd, and choice **c** is correct. Because $\frac{n}{2}$ is a whole number, 2 divides evenly into n, so n is even, making choice **a** incorrect. n is actually equal to $\frac{(b+1)}{2}$, so choice **d** is incorrect.

14. b. Recall that ∩ means intersection (find what the two sets have in common) and ∪ means union (combine the two sets). Do whatever is in the parentheses (or innermost set of parentheses) first. $(A \cap C)$ looks like this:

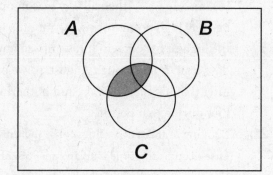

and $(B \cap C)$ looks like this:

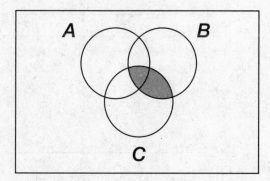

If you selected choice **c** or **d**, you incorrectly picked a partial answer. Next, take the union of these two to get

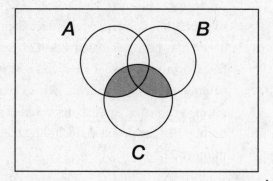

Choice **a** is $(A \cap C) \cap (B \cap C)$, where the intersection was taken at the last step instead of the union.

15. c. The existence of a planet with no moons would be a counterexample to the claim that "All planets have at least one moon" because it shows a case where a planet does not have at least one moon. All of the other statements do not counter the claim and are therefore incorrect.

16. b. $(h \circ g)x$ is the same as $h(g(x))$, so substituting in the given functions, you get:

$$\frac{(x+5)}{2} + 5 = \frac{x}{2} + \frac{5}{2} + 5 = \frac{x}{2} + 2\frac{1}{2} + 5 = \frac{x}{2} + 7\frac{1}{2},$$

so choice **b** is correct. If you selected choice **a**, you probably forgot to add in the $2\frac{1}{2}$. If you selected choice **c**, you probably forgot to keep x over 2. If you selected choice **d**, you probably calculated $(g \circ h)x$ by mistake.

17. b. Irrational numbers cannot be expressed in the form $\frac{a}{b}$, where a and b are both integers and b is not equal to zero. If you cannot think of a whole number that, when squared, will give you the number under the radical sign, then you are dealing with an irrational number. Because there is no number that when squared will equal 7, $\frac{\sqrt{7}}{1} = \sqrt{7}$ is the irrational number, and choice **b** is correct. Choice **a** is incorrect because imaginary numbers involve i, which is the square root of -1. Choice **c** is incorrect because rational numbers can be expressed as the ratio of two integers in the form $\frac{a}{b}$, which is not the case for $\sqrt{7}$; taking the square root of this number will result in a number with a nonterminating, nonrepeating decimal extension. A prime number is a positive integer that has only two distinct divisors, 1 and the number itself. $\sqrt{7}$ is neither an integer nor a prime number, so choice **d** is incorrect.

18. c. To get the i out of the denominator and yet still retain the same value, you can multiply by $\frac{i}{i}$, because any number divided by itself is 1, and any number times 1 is itself.

$$\frac{(1+i)}{i} \times \frac{i}{i} = \frac{i(1+i)}{i^2} = \frac{i(1+i)}{-1} = \frac{(i+i^2)}{-1} = \frac{(i-1)}{-1} = \frac{i}{-1} - \frac{1}{-1} = -i + 1$$

Choices **a**, **b**, and **d** represent computational errors and errors in sign. Be sure to use parentheses to keep track of your positives and negatives.

19. b. The range consists of the y values that are possible. Notice that the smallest point of the interval for y is –4, but y cannot equal –4. The largest y value is 4. Thus, the range is $-4 < y \leq 4$, so choice **b** is correct. Choice **a** is incorrect; it uses the highs and lows for the x values instead of the y values. Choice **c** is incorrect because the $\leq$ symbol is used instead of $<$. Choice **d** uses $\leq$ and $<$ in the wrong places.

20. a. First, note that m cannot be 14 or 20 because m is greater than 14 (not greater than or equal to 14) and m is less than 20 (not less than or equal to 20). The composite numbers that are within this range are 15, 16, and 18. 17 is prime, so choice **c** is incorrect. The smallest possible value of m would be 15, choice **a**.

21. c. The statements in both choice **a** and choice **b** can be inferred based on the highs and lows shown on the graph. November and December have the highest bars (most days missed); if Kevin's allergies are the cause of his missing work, then allergy season must be at its high point during the months with the highest bars. Kevin rarely missed any days from June through August, so we can infer that his allergies were not bothering him during that period.

22. b. Looking at the truth values for v, the only false occurs when r is true and s is false. Recall that this is exactly what happens for the conditional $r \rightarrow s$.

r	s	$r \rightarrow s$
T	T	T
T	F	F
F	T	T
F	F	T

Thus, choice **b** is the correct answer.

23. b. Because these groups have c elements in common, you cannot count these elements twice. The total would be *Math Students* + *Art History Students* – $c = 36 + 42 - 12 = 66$, so choice **b** is correct. If you selected choice **a**, you may have calculated $42 - 12$ by mistake. If you selected choice **c**, you may have counted the "both" students twice. If you selected choice **d**, you may have added all the numbers in the problem, including the bus number 22.

24. c. To solve, first rewrite the function in terms of x and y. To do this, replace $f(x)$ with y:

$$y = 4x - 1$$

Next, switch the x and y and solve for y:

$$x = 4y - 1$$

$$x + 1 = 4y$$

$$\frac{x+1}{4} = y$$

Finally, replace the y with $f^{-1}(x)$.

$$f^{-1}(x) = \frac{(x+1)}{4}$$

Thus, choice **c** is correct. Note that $1 - 4x$ is the additive inverse of $4x - 1$, which is not the inverse of the function, so choice **d** is incorrect. Choices **a** and **b** are distracters—though incorrect, they are tempting guesses because they use numbers from the problem.

25. d. Recall that the range is the difference between the highest number and lowest number of a set. Choice **d** is the correct answer because 98.0, the highest score, minus 91.3, the lowest score, is 6.7. Choice **a** is incorrect because range is the difference between the highest number and the lowest number, and this choice is the mean. Choice **b** is incorrect because it is the mode. Choice **c** is incorrect because it is the difference between the high-est number and the mode.

26. d. The problem states that $f(x)$ is linear, so you know that it must follow the formula $y = mx + b$. When $b = 0$, y is just a multiple of x. When $m = 1$, y is equal to x plus a constant. These two cases are pretty easy to spot, so it is worth looking to see if either of these cases applies. Because neither one does, you can use $\frac{(y_2 - y_1)}{(x_2 - x_1)}$ to find the slope. $\frac{(y_2 - y_1)}{(x_2 - x_1)} = \frac{(10 - 2)}{(4 - 0)} = \frac{8}{4} = 2$. The slope is 2. With a slope of 2, $y = mx + b$ becomes $y = 2x + b$, and when you substitute, you get $2 = 2(0) + b$, so $b = 2$. The equation is $y = 2x + 2$, so $f(20) = 2(20) + 2 = 42$. If you mistakenly selected choice **a**, you may have thought that because $f(0) = 2$ and 2 is 2 more than zero, 2 should be added to 20. This does not work with $f(4)$, so this is the incorrect rule. If you selected choice **b**, you may have mistakenly added 6 to 20, as $4 + 6 = 10$. Again, this rule does not work on $f(0)$ and is incorrect.

27. d. The statements in **a**, **b**, and **c** are all correct. Choice **d** is the false statement and is thus the correct answer. An even number multiplied by an odd number will yield an even number.

28. b. The inverse of a conditional statement negates both the antecedent and the consequent. This is represented in choice **b**, $\sim t \rightarrow \sim s$. Choice **a** switched the antecedent and the consequent, which is the converse, so this choice is incorrect. Choice **c** is a biconditional statement, and is incorrect. Choice **d** represents the contrapositive, and is incorrect.

29. a. A' is the complement of A and consists of all the elements in the universe that are not in A. Set A would then be $\{j, 1, n, p\}$. C' is the complement of C; it consists of all the elements in the universe that are not in C. Set C would then be $\{n, p\}$. $A \cap B$ is the intersection of A and B, so we list what they have in common: $\{n, p\}$. $A \cap B = D$, so $D = \{n, p\}$. Because C is also equal to $\{n, p\}$, sets C and D are equivalent and choice **a** is the correct answer.

30. c. To be an integer, the solution to the expression cannot be a fraction. The infinite set of integers is $\{\ldots, -3, -2, -1, 0, 1, 2, 3, \ldots\}$. Look for the answer choice that allows you to cancel out the denominator (the bottom of the fraction). In this case, choice **c** can be simplified to c^2 as follows:

$$\frac{(c \times d)^2}{d^2} = \frac{c^2 d^2}{d^2} = c^2$$

$c^2 a^2$ must be an integer. The other answer choices may or may not be integers, so only choice **c** is correct.

31. b. Recall that $f(x) + a$ slides $f(x)$ up a units. Thus, choice **b** is correct. $f(x) - a$ slides $f(x)$ down a units, so choice **a** is incorrect. In this case, you are applying the rule of the function (this gives you y) and then you are adding $\sqrt{2}$. This increases y by $\sqrt{2}$, which means the graph slides up.

32. a. To find the negation of $p \vee q$, remember that you are finding the negation of the disjunction itself, so put the disjunction in parentheses and then negate it to get $\sim(p \vee q)$, choice **a**. Choice **b** is not logically equivalent to negating the disjunction, but rather the disjunction of the negations of both p and q. Choice **c** is the negation of the negation of $(p \vee q)$, which would just be $(p \vee q)$. Choice **d** incorrectly takes the negation of p and then uses that value $(\sim p)$ in a disjunction, rather than taking the negation of the whole disjunction.

33. d. The counting principle states that if given event A can occur in a ways, event B can occur in b ways, and event C can occur in c ways, then the three events can occur together in $a \times b \times c$ ways. In this case, there are eight "ways" for color, three "ways" for opacity, and three "ways" for length. Solving, we get $8 \times 3 \times 3 = 72$ different choices. Choice **d** is correct. Choice **a** may have been chosen in error if you just multiplied 3×3 and forgot to include 8. Choice **b** may have been chosen in error if you added $8 + 3 + 3$ instead of multiplying. Choice **c** may have been chosen in error if you just multiplied 8×3 and forgot the other 3.

34. b. The composition $(g \circ f)x$ is equal to $10 - 25x^2$, which is the same as $10 + (5)^2 x^2$. Because $f(x) = 5x$, the composition $(g \circ f)x$ is equal to $10 - (f(x))^2$, so $g(x) = 10 - x^2$. Thus, choice **b** is correct. Choice **a** has the sign wrong. Choices **c** and **d** do not account for the 10, with choice **d** also using the incorrect sign.

35. a. x can equal 0 (because the circle is solid at 0), and is greater than 0, so you are looking for $0 \leq x$ on one end. x cannot equal b (because the circle is open), and it is less than b, so you are looking for $x < b$ on the other end. The correct answer is **a**, $0 \leq x < b$.

36. b. For set B to be a subset of A, every element in set B would also be found in A. Only set C fits these criteria. $C = \{8, 12, 16\}$, and all three of these elements can be found in A.

37. b. Let r represent the number of oranges and let $800 - r$ represent the number of apples. This works because a total of 800 pieces of fruit were harvested. You need to set up an equation for the amount of time taken. Each apple takes 10 seconds to harvest, each orange takes 15 seconds, and it took a total of 2.5 hours to harvest all the fruit. We need to work with the same units, so let's convert 2.5 hours into seconds:
2.5 hours $\times$ 60 min./hr $\times$ 60 sec./min. = 9,000 seconds

The formula is:

$10(800 - r) + 15r = 9,000$

$8,000 - 10r + 15r = 9,000$

$8,000 + 5r = 9,000$

$5r = 1,000$

$r = 200$

Thus, choice **b** is correct. Choices **a** and **c** are distracters—they are appealing guesses, because they look familiar based on the numbers in the question. Choice **d** is incorrect; it is the number of apples that were harvested.

38. c. First, solve all the absolute values:
$a = |{-17} + 5| = |{-12}| = 12$, $b = |{-3^2}| = |{-9}| = 9$, and $c = |\frac{1}{2} - 1| = |{-\frac{1}{2}}| = \frac{1}{2}$. We are given that $d = -3$. Next, put these in order: $-3, \frac{1}{2}, 9, 12$, which is the same as $d < c < b < a$, so choice **c** is correct.

39. d. To find the Cartesian product, $A \times B$, list all possible ordered pairs that would result by taking the first coordinate from set A and the second coordinate from set B. Solving, we get $\{(1, 2), (1, 4), (2, 2), (2, 4)\}$, or choice **d**. If you accidentally solved the intersection of A and B, you would get choice **a**. Choice **b** is an incomplete listing of ordered pairs. If you accidentally solved the union of A and B, you would get choice **c**.

40. c. The denominator of the fraction cannot equal zero, so x cannot equal 0. Every other real number value is fine. Note that when x is negative, $f(x)$ will be positive. When x is positive, $f(x)$ will also be positive. This makes choice **c** correct.

41. b. The square part of Adam's window will be $10'' \times 10'' = 100$ in.^{2}. On top of that is a semicircle with a radius of 5'' (the radius is $\frac{1}{2}$ the diameter). Because this is a semicircle (half of a circle), instead of using $A = \pi r^2$, use $A_{(top)} = \frac{1}{2}\pi r^2$. $A_{(top)} = \frac{(25\pi)}{2}$ in.^{2} = 12.5π in.^{2}. Adam's window has an area of $100 + 12.5\pi$ in.^{2} altogether. When we approximate π as 3, $100 + 12.5\pi$ in.^{2} amounts to approximately 137.5 in.^{2}. As for Brenda's triangle, use $A = \frac{1}{2}bh = \frac{1}{2}(6)(14) = 42$ in.^{2}. The difference in areas is 95.5 in.^{2}. If you selected choice **a**, you probably forgot to add the area of the semicircle. If you selected choice **c**, you probably forgot to use only $\frac{1}{2}$ the area of a circle. If you selected choice **d**, you probably accidentally mixed up the names.

42. c. Note that you do not have to figure out the rule of each function in order to solve the problem: You can simply read the values off of the tables. To find $g(f(12))$, first find $f(12)$. Reading the first chart, you get $f(12) = 11$. Next, find $g(11)$. Reading the second chart, you get $g(11) = 45$. Thus, choice **c** is correct. You may have chosen choice **a** if you calculated $f(12)$; however, this is incorrect. Choice **b** is $g(10)$ and is incorrect. If you selected choice **d**, 49, you probably calculated $g(12)$ by mistake.

43. d. To solve, use the rule $x^m \div x^n = x^{m-n}$ for each variable. The x term will then be $x^{2-(-2)} = x^4$. The y term will then be $y^{2-7} = y^{-5}$. The z term will then be $z^{-4-(-4)} = z^0 = 1$. Thus, we have $x^4 y^{-5}$, so choice **d** is correct.

44. b. The range is the highest value minus the lowest value. The highest temperature is $72°$ and the lowest is $32°$. Thus, the range is $72 - 32 = 40°$. Choice **b** is correct. Choice **a** is incorrect, and it is approximately the lowest temperature shown. Choice **d** is incorrect, and it is approximately the highest temperature shown.

45. d. Use $\log_b(m^n) = n \times \log_b(m)$ to change $\log_5(x^{25})$ into $25 \times \log_5 x$. This cannot be reduced any further, so choice **d** is the answer. If you selected choice **a**, you probably used the formula for $\log_b(\frac{m}{n})$ by mistake. If you selected choice **b**, you probably used the formula for $\log b(mn)$ by mistake. If you selected choice **c**, you may have seen the 25 and thought you could simplify the expression further by taking the square root; this is not correct.

46. c. When the equation for a line is written in the form $y = mx + b$, the slope is the value of m. Given $y = x - 6$, we know the slope is 1. The slope of a perpendicular line will have a negative reciprocal slope. This means we flip $\frac{1}{1}$ and change the sign of it, which is -1. Now look for the answer where $m = -1$. Choice **c** is correct, as $y = 5 - x$ is the same as $y = -1x + 5$. Choice **a** is incorrect, as $x = y - 6$ is the same as $y = x + 6$. This line is parallel to the given line. Choice **b** is incorrect, as $x = y + 4$ is the same as $y = x - 4$. This line is parallel to the given line. Looking at choice **d**, $y = 1 - 6x$ is the same as $y = -x + 1$. This line has a slope of -6, and choice **d** is incorrect.

47. d. Pythagorean triples are easy-to-remember triples that make the a-b-c right triangle. One example is the 3-4-5 right triangle. Another is the 5-12-13. Still another is the 6-8-10 right triangle. Multiples of the triples will also be triple and, thus, create similar triangles. This makes sense because you are actually multiplying the entire Pythagorean equation by a constant. The correct answer is choice **d**. $a^2 + b^2 = c^2$ will be equal to $5a^2 + 5b^2 = 5c^2$.

48. b. A and B have no elements in common and are therefore disjoint by definition, so choice **b** is correct. Because $A \cap B = \emptyset$, B cannot be a subset of A, so choice **a** is incorrect. Because $A \cap C = A$, these two sets do have elements in common (all of the elements in A). They are not disjoint, so choice **c** is not correct. C is not a subset of B, as C contains all the elements in A, and B contains no elements that are in A, so choice **d** is incorrect as well.

49. a. For a problem like this, it is easiest to list all possibilities and then see which fulfill the criteria. Because we are told that the pair 3, 4 is regarded to be the same as the pair 4, 3, we will not list duplicates:

3, 4	3, 5	3, 6	3, 7	3, 8
	4, 5	4, 6	4, 7	4, 8
		5, 6	5, 7	5, 8
			6, 7	6, 8
				7, 8

Next, decide which ones fulfill the criteria. Note that the sum has to be greater than 9. Do not pick pairs that add to 9.

3, 4	3, 5	3, 6	3, 7	3, 8
	4, 5	4, 6	4, 7	4, 8
		5, 6	5, 7	5, 8
			6, 7	6, 8
				7, 8

11 combinations will be greater than 9. Choice **a** is correct. Choice **b** is incorrect because it includes pairs that add to 9. Choice **c** is incorrect because it does not regard, for example, 3, 7 and 7, 3 as the same. Choice **d** is incorrect because it includes pairs that add to 9 and the doubles.

50. c. Because the question uses the term *estimate*, you can round 28% to 30%, or $\frac{1}{3}$. $\frac{1}{3}$ of 3,000 is 1,000. Thus, choice **c** is the correct choice. Choice **a** is incorrect because $30 is the best estimate for food. Choice **b** is incorrect because it would be the best estimate if the clothes were half of the budget. Choice **d** is incorrect because $2,800 is nearly all of the $3,000 total.

51. b. Solve all of the answer choices: Choice **a** is $|a + b| = |-7 + 9| = |2| = 2$, choice **b** is $|a - b| = |-7 - 9| = |-16| = 16$, choice **c** is $|b| + a = |9| + -7 = 9 + (-7) = 2$, and choice **d** is $|b + a| = |9 + (-7)| = |2| = 2$. Thus, choice **b** is the answer that has the greatest value.

52. c. There are four spots to fill for males and there are four male dancers. The multiplication principle for counting says there will be $4 \times 3 \times 2 \times 1 = 24$ ways these spots can be filled up. Similarly, there are four spots to fill for female dancers and there are four females, so there are 24 ways to fill these spots. Together the male-female-male-female-male-female-male-female ordering can occur in 24×24 different ways. The correct answer is choice **c**, 24^2.

53. d. First, set $x - 3$ equal to zero to get $x = 3$. The value of $f(x)$ at $x = 3$ will be the remainder when you divide $f(x)$ by $x - 3$. Using synthetic division is a quick way to find out the remainder.

The 3 outside of the L is the number you are dividing into the coefficients that you see in the equation. The top row inside the L lists all of the coefficients in the equation. Have all the powers of x descend and add in any necessary 0 coefficients for any powers not present: $3x^5 + 0x^4 + 0x^3 + 2x^2 + 5x + 1x^0$. Always bring down the leftmost coefficient in the L; in this case, we bring down a 3. The 3 outside of the L multiplies with this 3, and we fill in 9 in the next right column inside the L. Add down to get $0 + 9 = 9$ at the bottom. The 3 outside of the L multiplies with this 9, and we fill in 27 in the next right column inside the L. Add down to get $0 + 27 = 27$ at the bottom. The 3 outside of the L multiplies with this 27, and we fill in 81 in the next right column inside the L. Add down to get $2 + 81 = 83$. The 3 outside of the L multiplies with this 83, and we fill in 249 in the next right column inside the L. Add down to get $5 + 249 = 254$. The 3 outside of the L multiplies with this 254, and we fill in 762 in the next right column inside the L. Add down to get $1 + 762 = 763$.

3		3	0	0	2	5	1
			9	27	81	249	762
		3	9	27	83	254	763

When $3x^5 + 2x^2 + 5x + 1$ is divided by $x - 2$, the remainder is 763, so choice **d** is correct. If you selected choice **a**, you may have guessed that $x = 2$ would be a zero of $f(x)$; however, it is not. If you selected choice **b**, you forgot to make columns for two zeros: $0x^4$ and $0x^3$. If you selected choice **c**, then you forgot to make 1 of the two columns for 0 in your synthetic division L.

54. c. Of the three EMTs, one will go. There are three ways this can happen: EMT #1, EMT #2, and EMT #3. Next, there are two spots to fill and four other possible people (non-EMTs) who can fill these spots. Because order does not matter, use $_nC_r$, where $n = 4$ (selecting from 4) and $r = 2$ (choosing 2).

$$_nC_r = \frac{n!}{r!(n-r)!} = \frac{4!}{2!\,2!} = \frac{4 \times 3 \times 2 \times 1}{2 \times 1 \times 2 \times 1} = \frac{4 \times 3}{2 \times 1} = \frac{12}{2} = 6.$$

These two "events" can happen together in 3×6 ways = 18 different groups.

55. c. To calculate the mean, add all the numbers and divide by the total number of numbers. The interior angles of a circle add to 360, so $a + b + c + d = 360$, and this is the sum of all of the numbers as required by the mean formula. The total number of numbers is 4. Thus, the mean is $\frac{360}{4} = 90$.

56. d. The range consists of all possible y values. Here the smallest y value is -6 and the largest y value is 6, so the range is $-6 \le y \le 6$, and choice **d** is correct. Note you have to use the less than or equal to symbol because y can equal both -6 and 6. The -4 and the 4 represent the boundaries of the domain, and not the range, so choice **a** is incorrect. Choice **b** is incorrect because it uses the y-value of the endpoint, 1, instead of finding the full low to high range. Choice **c** is incorrect because it uses the less than symbol instead of the less than or equal to symbol.

57. a. A composite number is a positive integer that has a positive divisor other than 1 or itself. The smallest composite number is 3, so $\frac{2(3)}{2} = 3$, and choice **a** is correct. Choice **b** is incorrect because 2 was substituted for p in the expression $\frac{2p}{2}$, and 2 is prime, not composite. Choice **c** is incorrect because 1 was substituted for p in the expression $\frac{2p}{2}$, and 1 is neither prime nor composite.

58. d. Regard "If a word describes an action, then a word is an adverb" as the conditional statement $p \rightarrow q$, where p is "a word describes an action" and q is "a word is an adverb." To generate the contrapositive of a conditional statement, switch the antecedent and the consequent and negate them both. The contrapositive of $p \rightarrow q$ would be $\sim q \rightarrow \sim p$, or "If a word is not an adverb, then a word does not describe a verb." Thus, choice **d** is correct. Choice **a** is a biconditional statement and is incorrect. Choice **b** is the inverse and is incorrect. Choice **c** is the converse, so this choice is incorrect.

59. b. When two odd numbers are added together, the sum is an even number, so choice **b** is correct. An odd number plus an even number will result in an odd number, so choice **a** is incorrect. An odd number times an even number will yield an even number, so choice **c** is incorrect. An odd number minus an even number will be odd, so **d** is incorrect.

60. c. The median for a given set of values is found by ordering all of the values and either citing the middle number as the median for an odd number of values, or averaging the two middle numbers if there is an even number of values. The mean is the sum of all the values divided by the number of values. The variance, S^2, is the average squared deviation of values from the mean. The standard deviation is represented by S, and it is the square root of the variance. In this question, knowing the mean and the mode is not relevant. To solve, take the square root of the variance, so take the square root of n^4. $\sqrt{n^4} = n^2$; choice **c** is correct. Choice **a** is incorrect because it is the square root of the median, and this is not the standard deviation. Choice **b** is incorrect; it is the square root of the mean, and this is not equal to the standard deviation. Choice **d** is incorrect because it is the square root of the standard deviation, and this is not the standard deviation.

CLEP Natural Sciences
Practice Test 1

You are now familiar with the kinds of questions and answer formats you will see on the official CLEP Natural Sciences exam. Now take Practice Test 1 to identify any areas that you may need to review in more depth before the test day.

On this practice test, you will encounter 120 questions that are similar to the type you will find on the official CLEP Natural Sciences exam.

To simulate the test conditions, use the time constraints of the official CLEP Natural Sciences exam. Allow yourself 90 minutes to complete this practice test.

Remember, on the official CLEP, there is no penalty for incorrect answers, so always make a guess if you are unsure of an answer.

When you are finished, check the answer key on page 601 carefully to assess your results.

► **CLEP Natural Sciences Practice Test 1**

1. ⓐ ⓑ ⓒ ⓓ ⓔ	
2. ⓐ ⓑ ⓒ ⓓ ⓔ	
3. ⓐ ⓑ ⓒ ⓓ ⓔ	
4. ⓐ ⓑ ⓒ ⓓ ⓔ	
5. ⓐ ⓑ ⓒ ⓓ ⓔ	

1. ⓐ ⓑ ⓒ ⓓ ⓔ
2. ⓐ ⓑ ⓒ ⓓ ⓔ
3. ⓐ ⓑ ⓒ ⓓ ⓔ
4. ⓐ ⓑ ⓒ ⓓ ⓔ
5. ⓐ ⓑ ⓒ ⓓ ⓔ
6. ⓐ ⓑ ⓒ ⓓ ⓔ
7. ⓐ ⓑ ⓒ ⓓ ⓔ
8. ⓐ ⓑ ⓒ ⓓ ⓔ
9. ⓐ ⓑ ⓒ ⓓ ⓔ
10. ⓐ ⓑ ⓒ ⓓ ⓔ
11. ⓐ ⓑ ⓒ ⓓ ⓔ
12. ⓐ ⓑ ⓒ ⓓ ⓔ
13. ⓐ ⓑ ⓒ ⓓ ⓔ
14. ⓐ ⓑ ⓒ ⓓ ⓔ
15. ⓐ ⓑ ⓒ ⓓ ⓔ
16. ⓐ ⓑ ⓒ ⓓ ⓔ
17. ⓐ ⓑ ⓒ ⓓ ⓔ
18. ⓐ ⓑ ⓒ ⓓ ⓔ
19. ⓐ ⓑ ⓒ ⓓ ⓔ
20. ⓐ ⓑ ⓒ ⓓ ⓔ
21. ⓐ ⓑ ⓒ ⓓ ⓔ
22. ⓐ ⓑ ⓒ ⓓ ⓔ
23. ⓐ ⓑ ⓒ ⓓ ⓔ
24. ⓐ ⓑ ⓒ ⓓ ⓔ
25. ⓐ ⓑ ⓒ ⓓ ⓔ
26. ⓐ ⓑ ⓒ ⓓ ⓔ
27. ⓐ ⓑ ⓒ ⓓ ⓔ
28. ⓐ ⓑ ⓒ ⓓ ⓔ
29. ⓐ ⓑ ⓒ ⓓ ⓔ
30. ⓐ ⓑ ⓒ ⓓ ⓔ
31. ⓐ ⓑ ⓒ ⓓ ⓔ
32. ⓐ ⓑ ⓒ ⓓ ⓔ
33. ⓐ ⓑ ⓒ ⓓ ⓔ
34. ⓐ ⓑ ⓒ ⓓ ⓔ
35. ⓐ ⓑ ⓒ ⓓ ⓔ
36. ⓐ ⓑ ⓒ ⓓ ⓔ
37. ⓐ ⓑ ⓒ ⓓ ⓔ
38. ⓐ ⓑ ⓒ ⓓ ⓔ
39. ⓐ ⓑ ⓒ ⓓ ⓔ
40. ⓐ ⓑ ⓒ ⓓ ⓔ

41. ⓐ ⓑ ⓒ ⓓ ⓔ
42. ⓐ ⓑ ⓒ ⓓ ⓔ
43. ⓐ ⓑ ⓒ ⓓ ⓔ
44. ⓐ ⓑ ⓒ ⓓ ⓔ
45. ⓐ ⓑ ⓒ ⓓ ⓔ
46. ⓐ ⓑ ⓒ ⓓ ⓔ
47. ⓐ ⓑ ⓒ ⓓ ⓔ
48. ⓐ ⓑ ⓒ ⓓ ⓔ
49. ⓐ ⓑ ⓒ ⓓ ⓔ
50. ⓐ ⓑ ⓒ ⓓ ⓔ
51. ⓐ ⓑ ⓒ ⓓ ⓔ
52. ⓐ ⓑ ⓒ ⓓ ⓔ
53. ⓐ ⓑ ⓒ ⓓ ⓔ
54. ⓐ ⓑ ⓒ ⓓ ⓔ
55. ⓐ ⓑ ⓒ ⓓ ⓔ
56. ⓐ ⓑ ⓒ ⓓ ⓔ
57. ⓐ ⓑ ⓒ ⓓ ⓔ
58. ⓐ ⓑ ⓒ ⓓ ⓔ
59. ⓐ ⓑ ⓒ ⓓ ⓔ
60. ⓐ ⓑ ⓒ ⓓ ⓔ
61. ⓐ ⓑ ⓒ ⓓ ⓔ
62. ⓐ ⓑ ⓒ ⓓ ⓔ
63. ⓐ ⓑ ⓒ ⓓ ⓔ
64. ⓐ ⓑ ⓒ ⓓ ⓔ
65. ⓐ ⓑ ⓒ ⓓ ⓔ
66. ⓐ ⓑ ⓒ ⓓ ⓔ
67. ⓐ ⓑ ⓒ ⓓ ⓔ
68. ⓐ ⓑ ⓒ ⓓ ⓔ
69. ⓐ ⓑ ⓒ ⓓ ⓔ
70. ⓐ ⓑ ⓒ ⓓ ⓔ
71. ⓐ ⓑ ⓒ ⓓ ⓔ
72. ⓐ ⓑ ⓒ ⓓ ⓔ
73. ⓐ ⓑ ⓒ ⓓ ⓔ
74. ⓐ ⓑ ⓒ ⓓ ⓔ
75. ⓐ ⓑ ⓒ ⓓ ⓔ
76. ⓐ ⓑ ⓒ ⓓ ⓔ
77. ⓐ ⓑ ⓒ ⓓ ⓔ
78. ⓐ ⓑ ⓒ ⓓ ⓔ
79. ⓐ ⓑ ⓒ ⓓ ⓔ
80. ⓐ ⓑ ⓒ ⓓ ⓔ

81. ⓐ ⓑ ⓒ ⓓ ⓔ
82. ⓐ ⓑ ⓒ ⓓ ⓔ
83. ⓐ ⓑ ⓒ ⓓ ⓔ
84. ⓐ ⓑ ⓒ ⓓ ⓔ
85. ⓐ ⓑ ⓒ ⓓ ⓔ
86. ⓐ ⓑ ⓒ ⓓ ⓔ
87. ⓐ ⓑ ⓒ ⓓ ⓔ
88. ⓐ ⓑ ⓒ ⓓ ⓔ
89. ⓐ ⓑ ⓒ ⓓ ⓔ
90. ⓐ ⓑ ⓒ ⓓ ⓔ
91. ⓐ ⓑ ⓒ ⓓ ⓔ
92. ⓐ ⓑ ⓒ ⓓ ⓔ
93. ⓐ ⓑ ⓒ ⓓ ⓔ
94. ⓐ ⓑ ⓒ ⓓ ⓔ
95. ⓐ ⓑ ⓒ ⓓ ⓔ
96. ⓐ ⓑ ⓒ ⓓ ⓔ
97. ⓐ ⓑ ⓒ ⓓ ⓔ
98. ⓐ ⓑ ⓒ ⓓ ⓔ
99. ⓐ ⓑ ⓒ ⓓ ⓔ
100. ⓐ ⓑ ⓒ ⓓ ⓔ
101. ⓐ ⓑ ⓒ ⓓ ⓔ
102. ⓐ ⓑ ⓒ ⓓ ⓔ
103. ⓐ ⓑ ⓒ ⓓ ⓔ
104. ⓐ ⓑ ⓒ ⓓ ⓔ
105. ⓐ ⓑ ⓒ ⓓ ⓔ
106. ⓐ ⓑ ⓒ ⓓ ⓔ
107. ⓐ ⓑ ⓒ ⓓ ⓔ
108. ⓐ ⓑ ⓒ ⓓ ⓔ
109. ⓐ ⓑ ⓒ ⓓ ⓔ
110. ⓐ ⓑ ⓒ ⓓ ⓔ
111. ⓐ ⓑ ⓒ ⓓ ⓔ
112. ⓐ ⓑ ⓒ ⓓ ⓔ
113. ⓐ ⓑ ⓒ ⓓ ⓔ
114. ⓐ ⓑ ⓒ ⓓ ⓔ
115. ⓐ ⓑ ⓒ ⓓ ⓔ
116. ⓐ ⓑ ⓒ ⓓ ⓔ
117. ⓐ ⓑ ⓒ ⓓ ⓔ
118. ⓐ ⓑ ⓒ ⓓ ⓔ
119. ⓐ ⓑ ⓒ ⓓ ⓔ
120. ⓐ ⓑ ⓒ ⓓ ⓔ

► Practice Test Questions

Biological Sciences

1. Water molecules tend to stick together by cohesion. This may be attributed to
   a. covalent bonding.
   b. vaporization.
   c. hydrogen bonding.
   d. high viscosity.
   e. cold temperature.

2. The origin of life on Earth is estimated to have occurred
   a. 3.8 hundred years ago.
   b. 3.8 thousand years ago.
   c. 3.8 million years ago.
   d. 3.8 billion years ago.
   e. 3.8 trillion years ago.

3. Punctuated equilibrium refers to the
   a. idea that the number of species on an island reaches equilibrium when the immigration rate is equal to the extinction rate.
   b. process by which sodium ions enter a neuron while potassium ions exit.
   c. fact that the number of molecules on one side of a chemical equation must equal the number of molecules on the other side.
   d. evolutionary trend of long periods of stasis followed by abrupt periods of change.
   e. structures that are similar in two organisms as a result of a common ancestor.

4. Which of the following contributes to variation within a gene pool?
   a. mutation
   b. sexual recombination
   c. natural selection
   d. both a and b
   e. both b and c

5. Which of the following is NOT a feature of mammals?
   a. warm-blooded
   b. presence of hair or fur
   c. presence of an exoskeleton
   d. give birth to live young
   e. vertebrate

6. Binomial nomenclature is used to
   a. identify an organism by its genus and species.
   b. illustrate how mating can produce different genotypes.
   c. classify organisms into five kingdoms.
   d. analyze the frequency of an allele in a population.
   e. prevent pollution in urban areas.

7. The difference between aerobic respiration and fermentation is that
   a. aerobic respiration requires oxygen and fermentation does not.
   b. fermentation requires oxygen and aerobic respiration does not.
   c. aerobic respiration requires carbon dioxide and fermentation does not.
   d. fermentation requires carbon dioxide and aerobic respiration does not.
   e. none of the above

8. The process following mitosis whereby a cell fully divides into two cells is called
   a. prophase.
   b. metaphase.
   c. anaphase.
   d. interphase.
   e. cytokinesis.

9. In vascular plants, water is primarily transported through the
   a. phloem.
   b. xylem.
   c. leaves.
   d. pistil.
   e. stamen.

10. How many chambers are found in a human heart?
    a. zero
    b. one
    c. two
    d. three
    e. four

11. Which of the following hormones is involved in the "fight or flight" response?
    a. thyroid-stimulating hormone
    b. follicle-stimulating hormone
    c. insulin
    d. epinephrine
    e. glucagon

12. Traits that are controlled by more than one gene, such as height and skin color, are referred to as
    a. codominant.
    b. monogenic.
    c. polygenic.
    d. linked.
    e. mutations.

13. Which of the following statements about the human placenta is NOT true?
    a. The placenta provides the fetus with oxygen.
    b. The placenta allows for fetal blood to intermix with maternal blood.
    c. The placenta carries out fetal waste.
    d. The placenta provides the fetus with nutrients.
    e. The placenta provides the fetus with antibodies.

14. Which of the following is an example of a sex-linked trait?
    a. blue eye color
    b. Down syndrome
    c. red-green color blindness
    d. low intelligence
    e. all of the above

15. The layer in an embryo that will eventually become the inner lining of the digestive system is called the
    a. placenta.
    b. endoderm.
    c. mesoderm.
    d. ectoderm.
    e. hypoderm.

16. A plant growing toward a window where sunlight shines through is an example of
    a. thigmotropism.
    b. gravitotropism.
    c. phototropism.
    d. circadian rhythm.
    e. abscission.

17. A primary consumer retains about _____ of the energy harvested by a producer.
   a. 150%
   b. 100%
   c. 75%
   d. 50%
   e. 10%

18. _____ convert organic molecules to carbon dioxide.
   a. Producers
   b. Primary consumers
   c. Secondary consumers
   d. Tertiary consumers
   e. Decomposers

19. What effect does sexual recombination have on variation in a population?
   a. It increases variation.
   b. It decreases variation.
   c. It has no effect on variation.
   d. It increases variation in terrestrial ecosystems and decreases variation in aquatic ecosystems.
   e. It decreases variation in terrestrial ecosystems and increases variation in aquatic ecosystems.

20. A relationship between two organisms in which one party benefits and the other is unaffected is called
   a. commensalism.
   b. mutualism.
   c. parasitism.
   d. predation.
   e. competition.

21. The role that an organism plays in an ecosystem is called a(n)
   a. altruism.
   b. biome.
   c. niche.
   d. mimicry.
   e. edge.

22. The biome with the highest average rainfall per year is
   a. tundra.
   b. tropical forest.
   c. broadleaf forest.
   d. grassland.
   e. desert.

23. The most common cause of extinction in the world today is
   a. pollution.
   b. hunting.
   c. temperature change.
   d. habitat destruction.
   e. predation.

24. Which of the following is NOT a renewable energy source?
   a. coal
   b. wind
   c. solar
   d. tide
   e. hydroelectric

25. Islands A and B have the same size and the same rate of extinction, but Island A is closer to the mainland and therefore has a higher immigration rate. Which of the following statements is most likely to be true?

    a. Island A has a higher number of species than Island B.

    b. Island A has a lower number of species than Island B.

    c. Island A and Island B have the same number of species.

    d. Island A has less diversity than Island B.

    e. Island B has more terrestrial species than Island A.

Use the following figure to answer questions 26–28.

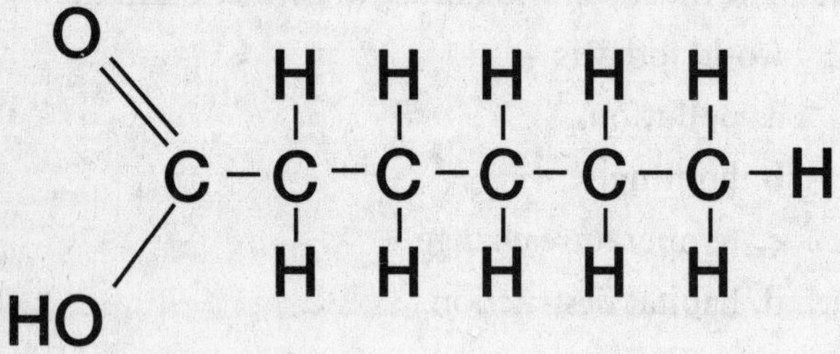

26. What type of molecule is shown in the figure?

    a. phospholipid

    b. amino acid

    c. fatty acid

    d. nucleic acid

    e. triglyceride

27. What is the chemical formula for the molecule shown in the figure?

    a. $C_6H_{12}O$

    b. $C_6H_{12}O_2$

    c. $C_6H_6O_2$

    d. $C_{12}H_6O_2$

    e. $C_6H_{12}O_6$

28. Which of the following statements about this molecule is correct?

    a. It is unsaturated.

    b. It contains an amino group.

    c. It contains a carboxyl group.

    d. It is nonpolar.

    e. It is inorganic.

Use the following table to answer questions 29–31.

	Second Letter				
First Letter	**U**	**C**	**A**	**G**	**Third Letter**
U	Phe	Ser	Tyr	Cys	U
	Phe	Ser	Tyr	Cys	C
	Leu	Ser	STOP	STOP	A
	Leu	Ser	STOP	Trp	G
C	Leu	Pro	His	Arg	U
	Leu	Pro	His	Arg	C
	Leu	Pro	Gln	Arg	A
	Leu	Pro	Gln	Arg	G
A	Ile	Thr	Asn	Ser	U
	Ile	Thr	Asn	Ser	C
	Ile	Thr	Lys	Arg	A
	Met	Thr	Lys	Arg	G
G	Val	Ala	Asp	Gly	U
	Val	Ala	Asp	Gly	C
	Val	Ala	Glu	Gly	A
	Val	Ala	Glu	Gly	G

29. What protein is formed by the RNA strand 5'-AUGCAUCUC-3'?

   a. Leu-His-Met

   b. Leu-Met-His

   c. His-Met-Leu

   d. Met-His-Leu

   e. Met-Leu-His

30. There is an RNA strand with the sequence 5'-AUGCAUCUC-3'. If a mutation causes an adenine nucleotide to be inserted after the guanine nucleotide in that RNA strand, which of the following amino acid sequences would result?

   a. Met-Leu-His

   b. Met-Thr-His

   c. Met-Thr-Ser

   d. Ser-Thr-Met

   e. His-Leu-Met

31. Which of the following mutations would probably be the most detrimental to the organism?

   a. the insertion of one nucleotide toward the start of the RNA sequence

   b. the insertion of one nucleotide toward the end of the RNA sequence

   c. the insertion of one codon toward the start of the RNA sequence

   d. the insertion of one codon toward the end of the RNA sequence

   e. the insertion of two codons in the middle of the RNA sequence

Use the following figure to answer questions 32–34.

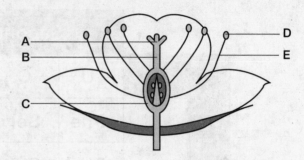

32. Which of the following constitutes the stamen?

   a. A, B, C

   b. D, E

   c. A, B

   d. B, C

   e. A, B, C, D, E

33. Which of the following constitutes the pistil?

   a. A, B, C

   b. D, E

   c. A, B

   d. B, C

   e. A, B, C, D, E

34. Which part of the flower becomes the fruit?

   a. A

   b. B

   c. C

   d. D

   e. E

Use the following figure to answer questions 35–37.

You have three slides of muscle cells taken from different parts of a mammal. When you put each slide under the microscope, you see the following images.

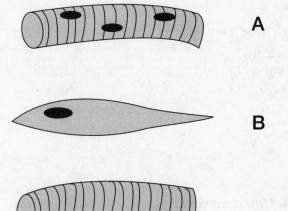

35. From what part of the animal might the cell marked A have been taken?
   a. heart
   b. upper arm
   c. small intestine
   d. cerebellum
   e. fingernail

36. From what part of the animal might the cell marked B have been taken?
   a. heart
   b. upper arm
   c. small intestine
   d. cerebellum
   e. fingernail

37. From what part of the animal might the cell marked C have been taken?
   a. heart
   b. upper arm
   c. small intestine
   d. cerebellum
   e. fingernail

38. Sea anemones sometimes attach themselves to the shell of a hermit crab. The sea anemone benefits because it receives food and transportation from the crab. The crab benefits because the sea anemone provides protection with its stinging tentacles. What type of relationship do hermit crabs and sea anemones exhibit?
   a. commensalism
   b. mutualism
   c. parasitism
   d. predation
   e. competition

39. A radioactive isotope has a half-life of 2 billion years. You find that a rock that originally contained 6 grams of the radioactive isotope now contains 1.5 grams. Approximately how many years old is the rock?
   a. 2 billion years
   b. 4 billion years
   c. 6 billion years
   d. 10 billion years
   e. 50 billion years

40. A radioactive isotope has a half-life of 3 billion years. A rock that was formed 6 billion years ago originally contained 10 grams of the radioactive isotope. Approximately how many grams of the isotope does the rock now contain?
   a. 10 grams
   b. 5 grams
   c. 2.5 grams
   d. 1 gram
   e. 0 grams

Use the following passage to answer questions 41–44.

Hardy-Weinberg equilibrium applies to populations that meet all of the following criteria:

1. a large breeding population
2. random mating
3. no change in allelic frequency due to mutation
4. no immigration or emigration
5. no natural selection

If all of these are true for a population, the Hardy-Weinberg equation can be used to estimate the frequency of alleles for a given trait within the population:

$p^2 + 2pq + q^2 = 1$ and $p + q = 1$

p = the frequency of the dominant allele
q = the frequency of the recessive allele
So:

p^2 = frequency of homozygous dominant individuals
$2pq$ = frequency of heterozygous individuals
q^2 = frequency of homozygous recessive individuals.

In a population of creatures that adheres to Hardy-Weinberg equilibrium, red body color is dominant over green body color. There are 16 creatures in the population, and 4 of them are green.

41. What is the frequency of the recessive allele?
   a. 16
   b. 4
   c. 0
   d. $\frac{1}{4}$
   e. $\frac{1}{2}$

42. What is the frequency of the dominant allele?
   a. 16
   b. 4
   c. 0
   d. $\frac{1}{4}$
   e. $\frac{1}{2}$

43. How many creatures in the population are heterozygous for the body color trait?
   a. 16
   b. 8
   c. 6
   d. 4
   e. 0

44. If you discovered that red creatures were more likely to survive through tornadoes (which are common in the creature's habitat), the population would no longer be in Hardy-Weinberg equilibrium because
   a. it would no longer be a large breeding population.
   b. there would no longer be random mating.
   c. there would be a change in allelic frequency due to mutation.
   d. there would now be immigration and/or emigration.
   e. there would now be natural selection.

Use the following figure to answer questions 45–48.

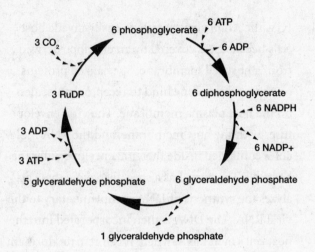

45. Which process is outlined in the figure?

   a. Krebs cycle

   b. Calvin cycle

   c. glycolysis

   d. electron chain reaction

   e. transcription

46. Where do the phosphate groups come from when 6 phosphoglycerate molecules are converted into six diphosphoglycerate molecules?

   a. ATP

   b. ADP

   c. NADPH

   d. NADP+

   e. CO_2

47. How many molecules of ADP are produced in one turn of the cycle?

   a. 3

   b. 6

   c. 9

   d. 12

   e. 18

48. How many molecules of NADP+ are produced in one turn of the cycle?

   a. 3

   b. 6

   c. 9

   d. 12

   e. 18

49. The codon for a specific amino acid is 5'-UAC-3'. What is the complementary DNA sequence for this codon?

   a. 5'-AUG-3'

   b. 3'-AUG-5'

   c. 5'-ATG-3'

   d. 3'-ATG-5'

   e. none of the above

50. How many nucleotides are needed for a protein with 600 amino acids?

   a. 200

   b. 300

   c. 600

   d. 1,200

   e. 1,800

Use the following information to answer questions 51–52.

In this figure, the enzyme E_1 catalyzes the conversion of molecule A into molecule B, E_2 catalyzes the conversion of molecule B into molecule C, and E_3 catalyzes the conversion of molecule C into molecule D.

51. If substance D inhibits E_1, which of the following best describes the course of the reaction?

  a. As the concentration of D increases, the reaction will slow down.

  b. As the concentration of D decreases, the reaction will slow down.

  c. As the concentration of D increases, the reaction will reverse.

  d. As the concentration of D increases, E_1 will convert to E_2.

  e. As the concentration of D increases, E_2 will convert to E_3.

52. You find that adding a large amount of substance A speeds up the reaction from A → B to a point, but then the rate drops off. What could you do to increase the rate of the reaction at this point?

  a. Lower the temperature slightly.

  b. Add more enzyme E_1.

  c. Add more enzyme E_2.

  d. Add more substance A.

  e. Add more substance D.

Use the following passage to answer questions 53–56.

HIV, the AIDS virus, is able to easily invade host cells because it is covered by an envelope derived from a host cell membrane. Specialized proteins on the viral envelope bind to receptor molecules on the host plasma membrane. The viral envelope fuses with the host membrane, and the RNA molecules contained inside the viral envelope enter the host cell. The virus has a special enzyme that catalyzes the synthesis of DNA complementary to the viral RNA. The DNA is then incorporated into the host cell's own DNA, where it can remain dormant for years. The viral genetic material is then converted to RNA, and the virus can burst forth from the cell through the plasma membrane.

53. What type of virus is HIV?

  a. protist

  b. prokaryote

  c. eukaryote

  d. retrovirus

  e. gametophyte

54. What is the process by which HIV RNA creates DNA?

  a. transcription

  b. reverse translation

  c. reverse transcription

  d. respiration

  e. mitosis

55. What type of life cycle does HIV undergo?

  a. lytic

  b. lysogenic

  c. homeostatic

  d. mutualistic

  e. meiotic

56. How does the virus acquire an envelope derived from the host membrane?

a. It uses the host DNA to build the membrane.

b. It contains genes that code for the same proteins found in the host membrane.

c. It transforms its own envelope into an envelope morphologically similar to the host membrane.

d. Its membrane is composed of RNA strands instead of phospholipids.

e. It takes part of the host membrane with it when it leaves the host cell.

Use the following figure to answer questions 57–60.

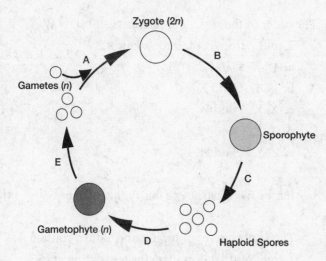

57. What process is illustrated in the figure?

a. photosynthesis

b. natural selection

c. alternation of generations

d. independent assortment

e. blastulation

58. Which of the following steps represents mitosis?

a. B, C, and E

b. B, C, and D

c. C and D

d. B, D, and E

e. C, D, and E

59. Which of the following is represented by step A?

a. meiosis

b. fertilization

c. oxidation

d. hydrolysis

e. crossing over

60. What type of organism would undergo the process shown?

a. mammal

b. reptile

c. virus

d. plant

e. all of the above

Physical Sciences

61. The correct order in which the phases of the moon occur is

a. full moon, waning moon, new moon, and waxing moon.

b. full moon, waning moon, waxing moon, and new moon.

c. full moon, waxing moon, new moon, and waning moon.

d. full moon, new moon, waning moon, and waxing moon.

e. full moon, new moon, waxing moon, and waning moon.

62. The sun's energy comes from
a. conduction.
b. convection.
c. nuclear fission.
d. nuclear fusion.
e. radiation.

63. The distances to nearby stars outside of the solar system are measured by
a. absorption spectra.
b. brightness.
c. color.
d. parallax.
e. temperature.

64. Each of the following is an "inner planet" EXCEPT
a. Earth.
b. Mars.
c. Mercury.
d. Phobos.
e. Venus.

65. The diagram shows how the brightness, color, size, and surface temperature of stars are related.

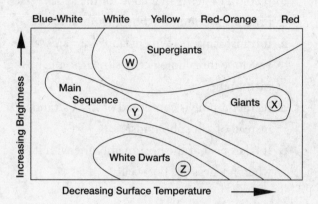

The order of the surface temperatures of stars *W*, *X*, *Y*, and *Z* from coolest to warmest is
a. *W*, *X*, *Y*, and *Z*.
b. *W*, *Y*, *Z*, and *X*.
c. *X*, *Y*, *Z*, and *W*.
d. *X*, *Z*, *Y*, and *W*.
e. *Z*, *Y*, *X*, and *W*.

Use the following passage to answer question 66.

"The atmospheres of Jupiter and Saturn contain gaseous jets that dominate the circulation at visible levels. The power source for these jets—solar radiation, internal heat, or both—and their vertical structure below the upper cloud are major open questions in the atmospheric circulation and meteorology of giant planets. Several observations found intense winds, which have been interpreted as supporting an internal heat source. This issue remains controversial. Here we report observations of two plumes in Jupiter's atmosphere that erupted at the same latitude as the strongest jet. The plumes reached a height of 30 km above the surrounding clouds, moved faster than any other feature, and left in their wake a turbulent planetary-scale disturbance containing red aerosols. On the basis of dynamical modeling, we conclude that the data are consistent only with a wind that extends well below the level where solar radiation is deposited."

66. What is the best title for this paragraph?
 a. "Jets versus Winds on Jupiter"
 b. "Discussion about an Observation of Gaseous Jets on Jupiter"
 c. "The Gaseous Jets of Jupiter and Saturn"
 d. "The Power Source of Gaseous Jets and Winds on Jupiter"
 e. "The Winds of Jupiter"

67. If the speed of light is approximately 3×10^8 meters per second, how long would it take a light signal to travel from Earth to a star four light years away and back?
 a. 1.5 years
 b. 3 years
 c. 4 years
 d. 8 years
 e. 12 years

68. The Doppler shift, z, in the wavelength of visible light from a galaxy that is moving in space is defined by the relationship $z = \frac{v}{c}$, where v is the object's velocity moving away from the observer, and c is the speed of light. Which of the following corresponds to a Doppler red shift, i.e., an object moving away from an observer on Earth? Assume that the frequency of the light source is constant.
 a. −0.1
 b. 0
 c. 0.2
 d. both **a** and **b**
 e. both **b** and **c**

69. The table gives some data about solar system asteroids.

Asteroid	Diameter (km)	Mass (10^{15} kg)	Rotation Period (hr.)	Orbital Period (yr.)
Ceres	~950	875,000	~9	~4.6
Pallas	~500	318,000	~8	~4.6
Juno	~250	20,000	~7	~4.4
Vesta	~550	300,000	~5	~3.6

Which asteroid has the shortest "day"?
 a. Ceres
 b. Ceres and Pallas
 c. Pallas
 d. Juno
 e. Vesta

70. The diagram shows the length of the semi-major axis of the elliptical orbits of the planets in a star system in the Milky Way galaxy plotted against the periods of the orbits. Note that the scale of the axes is in powers of ten.

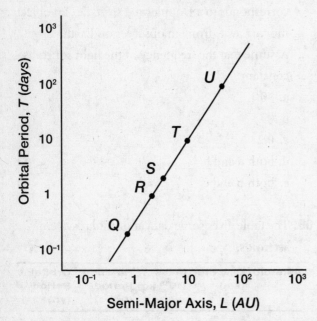

If L is the length of the semi-major axis and T is the period, which of the following gives the correct relationship between L and T?

a. $T \propto \frac{3}{2}L$
b. $2T \propto 3L$
c. $3T \propto 2L$
d. $T^2 \propto L^3$
e. $T^3 \propto L^2$

71. Which of the following is a chemical property of silver?

a. tarnish
b. melting point
c. malleability
d. magnetic properties
e. electrical conductivity

72. Which of the following is NOT an element?

a. aluminum
b. brass
c. copper
d. gold
e. lead

73. When you blow up a perfectly elastic but partially inflated balloon, it does not feel any warmer after you blow it up than it did before you blew it up more. This is an example of

a. Boyle's Law.
b. Charles's Law.
c. the combined gas law.
d. the pressure law.
e. the volume law.

74. Which of the following is a diatomic molecule?

a. Al_2O_3
b. CO_2
c. $CuSO_4 \cdot 5H_2O$
d. H_2O_2
e. O_2

75. The graph shows the change in solubility in water of three compounds *X, Y,* and *Z* as the temperature varies from 0° C to 30° C. The solubility is measured in grams per 100 cubic centimeters and at one atmosphere of pressure.

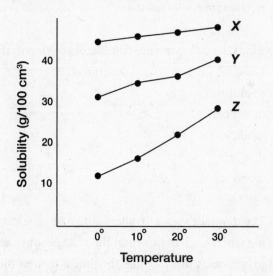

At what temperature is the solubility of compound *X* about double the solubility of compound *Z*?

a. about 7° C

b. about 12° C

c. about 23° C

d. about 25° C

e. about 30° C

Use the following passage to answer question 76.

The activity series works well as long as the predicted reactions occur at room temperature and in aqueous solution. However, there are reactions that are at odds with the metal and nonmetal activity series under other conditions. For example, copper can't displace hydrogen from acids, but it does react with acids like nitric and sulfuric because they can act as oxidizing agents.

76. A conclusion that can be made from this passage is that

a. the activity series of metals and metals provides a reliable guide for *all* reactions.

b. the activity series only applies to reactions that occur at room temperature and in aqueous solutions.

c. the activity series only applies to reactions that involve nitric and sulfuric acids.

d. the activity series predicts reactions with metals best.

e. the activity series predicts reactions at room temperature and in aqueous solutions best.

77. What numbers should replace the question marks in order to balance the following chemical equation?

$$\underline{?}\ NaNO_3 \rightarrow \underline{?}\ NaNO_2 + \underline{?}\ 3O_2 \uparrow$$

a. 1, 1, and 1

b. 1, 2, and 2

c. 2, 2, and 1

d. 2, 2, and 2

e. 3, 3, and 1

78. Which of the following balances the chemical reaction that results from heating $Al(OH)_3$?

a. $Al(OH)_3 \rightarrow Al_2O_3 + H_2O$

b. $Al(OH)_3 \rightarrow Al_2O_3 + 2H_2O$

c. $Al(OH)_3 \rightarrow Al_2O_3 + 3H_2O$

d. $2Al(OH)_3 \rightarrow Al_2O_3 + 3H_2O$

e. $2Al(OH)_3 \rightarrow 2Al_2O_3 + 3H_2O$

79. In the reaction $4NH_3 + 3O_2 \rightarrow 2N_2 + 6H_2O$, how many moles of nitrogen are produced if 192 grams of oxygen are produced and oxygen's average atomic weight is 16?

 a. 2
 b. 3
 c. 4
 d. 5
 e. 6

80. In the reaction rate equation $aA + bB \rightarrow cC + dD$, the concentration of A is 0.2 and the concentration of B is 0.2. Which result reflects a total reaction order equal to 3?

 a. $0.018k$
 b. $0.04k$
 c. $0.06k$
 d. $0.2k$
 e. $0.3k$

81. Power in a circuit is inversely proportional to which of the following?

 a. amperes
 b. kilowatts
 c. kilowatt-hours
 d. ohms
 e. volts

82. A cylindrical wire of radius r is carrying a current of I amperes with a voltage V at a temperature T. The magnetic field produced around the wire is a function of

 a. I.
 b. I and R.
 c. I and V.
 d. V.
 e. V and T.

83. Alternating current is to direct current as

 a. charge is to current.
 b. capacitance is to impedance.
 c. current is to voltage.
 d. ohms is to Farads.
 e. reactance is to resistance.

84. All of the following are conductors of electricity EXCEPT

 a. aluminum.
 b. copper.
 c. glass.
 d. iron.
 e. silver.

85. The diagram shows an alternating voltage changing with time. Assume that the voltage continues to behave as shown when the time is greater than the time at point T.

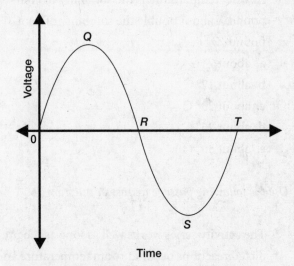

The *period* of the alternating voltage curve is

 a. the time at point O.
 b. the time at point R.
 c. the time at point T.
 d. the time between points O and R.
 e. the time between points R and T.

86. The diagram shows four voltage signals.

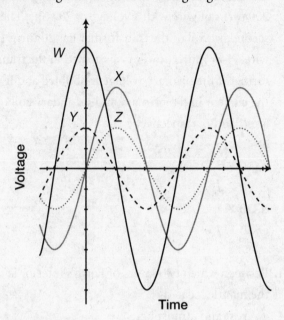

The following pairs of signals are out of phase EXCEPT

a. W and X.

b. W and Z.

c. X and Y.

d. Y and Z.

e. Y and W.

87. In the circuit shown, $R_1 = 1$ ohm, $R_2 = 2$ ohms, and $R_3 = 3$ ohms.

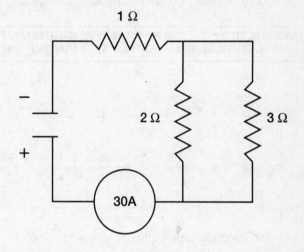

What is the source voltage?

a. $13\frac{7}{11}$ volts

b. $16\frac{4}{11}$ volts

c. 55 volts

d. 66 volts

e. 180 volts

88. The table shows the magnitude of a magnetic field, B, that is produced by a circular loop of wire of radius r with a current, I, passing through it.

MAGNETIC FIELD, B (TESLAS)	RADIUS, r (METERS)	CURRENT, I (AMPERES)
5×10^{-8}	1	1
1×10^{-7}	1	2
?	1	3
2.5×10^{-8}	2	1
5×10^{-8}	2	2

The magnetic field that goes with a radius of 3 meters and a current of 1 ampere is
a. 1.5×10^{-8} tesla.
b. 1.3×10^{-8} tesla.
c. 1×10^{-8} tesla.
d. 1.5×10^{-7} tesla.
e. 2×10^{-6} tesla.

89. What is the time constant of the current in *microseconds* in an *LR* circuit in which $L = 25$ mH and $R = 50\Omega$?
a. 5 μs
b. 20 μs
c. 50 μs
d. 200 μs
e. 500 μs

90. The primary coil of an iron-core transformer has 200 turns of wire with a voltage of 20 volts. The secondary coil of the transformer has 20 turns of wire. How much power is dissipated in the transformer if the primary voltage is doubled and if the current in the primary and secondary coils are I_p and I_s, respectively.
a. $4 \times I_p$
b. $10 \times I_s$
c. $20 \times I_p$
d. $20 \times I_s$
e. $40 \times I_p$

91. Between which two layers of Earth's interior is the mantle located?
a. crust and atmosphere
b. crust and lithosphere
c. inner core and outer core
d. lithosphere and outer core
e. outer core and Earth's center

92. During which Precambrian era are fossils least likely to be found?
a. early Archean
b. early Proterozoic
c. middle Archean
d. all of the above
e. both **a** and **c**

93. Which of the following pairs of rock types and subtypes are NOT sedimentary?
a. arkose and sandstone
b. carbonates and limestone
c. chert and flint
d. coal and peat
e. granite and rhyolite

94. A mineral's splitting along a particular direction when struck is called a

a. cleavage.

b. cut.

c. fracture.

d. hardness.

e. streak.

95. The diagram shows a seismogram.

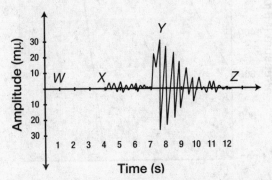

Which point(s) of the seismogram can be used to calculate the distance that the seismic event occurred from the seismograph?

a. *W*

b. *W* and *X*

c. *X* and *Y*

d. *Y*

e. *Z*

Use the following passage to answer question 96.

The oldest known rock formations on Earth date to about 4,000 million years ago, about the time that intense meteor bombardment abated. Glimpses of an even earlier time can be obtained from tiny grains of zircon—a mineral that is resistant to high pressures and temperatures and that could survive meteor bombardment unchanged. New isotopic analyses of zircons from the Narryer Gneiss Complex in Western Australia suggest that these samples are older than any

terrestrial grains previously identified, and are consistent with the presence of continental crust and liquid water on Earth's surface between 4,400 and 4,300 million years ago.

96. One logical conclusion that could be drawn from this paragraph is that

a. meteors produced zircon.

b. samples of zircon have been found that are more than 4,000 million years old.

c. the oldest zircon is no more than 4,000 million years old.

d. zircon samples came from outer space.

e. zircon is not resistant to high pressures and temperatures.

97. In this modified Le Maitre plot, the percentage composition of NaO_2, K_2O and SiO_2 is displayed for six minerals.

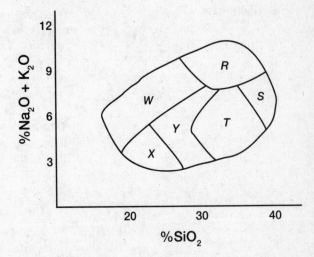

Which minerals contain more than 6% of NaO_2 + K_2O and fewer than 25% SiO_2?

a. *R*, *S*, and *T*

b. *R*, *S*, *T*, *W*, and *Y*

c. *R*, *S*, *T*, *W*, *X*, and *Y*

d. *W*, *X*, and *Y*

e. *W* and *Y*

98. The amplitude of seismic wave X is one-thousandth of the amplitude of Y. If the Richter scale reading for seismic wave Y is 2.5, what is the Richter scale reading for seismic wave X?

a. −0.0025

b. −0.5

c. 0.5

d. 2.499

e. 2,500

99. A study of the fault slip rates in the New Madrid (Missouri) seismic zone indicate a right lateral slip rate of about 2 mm per year. How long will take the rocks on either size of the fault zone to slip 3 meters?

a. 1.5 years

b. 6 years

c. 50 years

d. 150 years

e. 1,500 years

100. The diagram shows these different grades of metaphoric rock:

I—low; II—intermediate; III—high; IV—partial melt

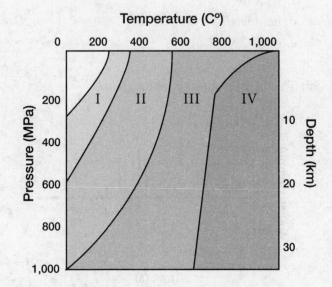

At what temperature(s) would the most different grades of rock be found?

a. 200° C

b. 500° C

c. 600° C

d. 800° C

e. 900° C

101. Sweating results in cooling after vigorous exercise because of

a. boiling.

b. condensation.

c. evaporation.

d. freezing.

e. sublimation.

102. The Third Law of Thermodynamics deals with

   a. energy, heat, and work.

   b. entropy.

   c. entropy and temperature.

   d. heat and work.

   e. temperature and thermodynamic equilibrium.

103. All of the following are endothermic processes EXCEPT

   a. condensation.

   b. evaporation.

   c. nuclear fission.

   d. photosynthesis.

   e. splitting a gas molecule apart.

104. Which of these statements is NOT an assumption about molecular behavior in an ideal gas?

   a. Molecules move randomly with an ever-changing distribution of speeds.

   b. Molecules obey Newton's laws of motion.

   c. Molecules undergo perfectly elastic collisions.

   d. The distances between molecules is very large in comparison to molecular size.

   e. The number of molecules is very large.

105. The diagram shows what happens to a substance as it is heated and as it changes from a solid to a gaseous state.

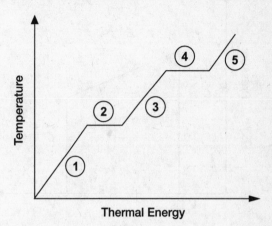

During which parts of the graph is the temperature of the substance rising?

   a. 1 only

   b. 1 and 3

   c. 1, 3, and 5

   d. 2 only

   e. 2 and 4

106. The diagram shows a system in which thermo-dynamic work has been done.

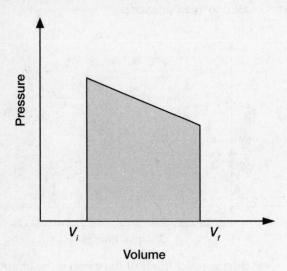

Which of the following represents the work done?
a. the area of the shaded region
b. the difference between the final and the initial volume
c. the pressure times the difference between the final and the initial volume
d. the pressure times the initial volume
e. the slope of the line between the final and the initial volume

107. The outside temperature reading is 10° C. What is the Fahrenheit temperature if the Celsius temperature reading doubles?
a. 5° F
b. 20° F
c. 41° F
d. 68° F
e. 100° F

108. The temperature of an object is 293° Kelvin. What is the object's temperature in Fahrenheit degrees?
a. −36° Fahrenheit
b. −4° Fahrenheit
c. 36° Fahrenheit
d. $43\frac{1}{5}$° Fahrenheit
e. 68° Fahrenheit

109. The diagram shows the work done during one cycle of a heat-engine.

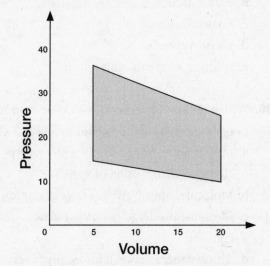

The work done during the heat-engine cycle is
a. 37.5 units.
b. 75 units.
c. 225 units.
d. 262.5 units.
e. 300 units.

110. The same amount of heat is applied to two substances *X* and *Y*. The mass of substance *X* is four times the mass of substance *Y*. The temperature of substance *Y* increases twice as much as the temperature of substance *X*. If the specific heat of substance *X* is 0.25 Joule per gram-Kelvin, what is the specific heat of substance *Y*?
  a. 0.125 Joule per gram-Kelvin
  b. 0.25 Joule per gram-Kelvin
  c. 0.5 Joule per gram-Kelvin
  d. 1 Joule per gram-Kelvin
  e. 2 Joules per gram-Kelvin

111. Which of the following have a positive atomic number?
I–alpha particle; II–beta particle; III–gamma ray; IV–neutron; V–proton
  a. I and II
  b. II and III
  c. III and IV
  d. IV and V
  e. V and I

112. The term that describes the difference between the mass of an atom and its parts is
  a. atomic mass.
  b. binding mass.
  c. critical mass.
  d. mass defect.
  e. nuclear mass.

113. In $^{88}_{36}$ Kr, what does the number 36 represent?
  a. the number of neutrons
  b. the number of protons
  c. the total number of electrons and neutrons
  d. the total number of electrons and protons
  e. the total number of neutrons and protons

114. Which of the following is a trans-uranium element?
  a. $^{92}_{42}$ Mo
  b. $^{237}_{93}$ Np
  c. $^{238}_{92}$ U
  d. $^{94}_{40}$ Zr
  e. both **b** and **c**

115. The diagram shows the number of neutrons and protons in an isotope, *I*. Other elements *G*, *H*, *K*, *L*, and *M* and their numbers of neutrons and protons are also shown.

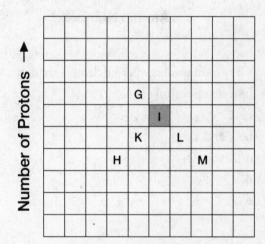

If isotope *I* decays by capturing a beta particle, which of the other elements would result?
  a. *G*
  b. *H*
  c. *H* or *M*
  d. *K*
  e. *K* or *L*

116. The diagram shows the binding energy of nucleons in elements.

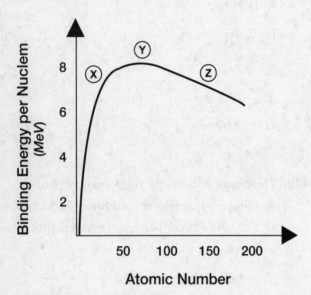

The binding energy per nucleon is changing the fastest at point(s)

a. *X*.

b. *X* and *Y*.

c. *X* and *Z*.

d. *Y*.

e. *Z*.

117. The relative abundance of the five most abundant isotopes of an element are shown in the table.

Atomic Weight	64	66	67	68	70
Abundance (%)	49	28	4	19	1

What is the chance that a random sample of the element will NOT contain isotopes with an atomic weight of 67 or 70?

a. 4%

b. 5%

c. 95%

d. 96%

e. 99%

118. The table shows how many milligrams of 100 milligrams of a radioactive isotope have decayed into other isotopes after 50 days.

DAYS (D)	AMOUNT OF 100 MG THAT HAVE DECAYED (MG)
0	0.000
10	50.000
20	75.000
30	87.500
40	93.750
50	96.875

After how many days has approximately one-fourth of the original mass of radioactive material decayed into other isotopes?

a. after 10 days

b. after 20 days

c. after 30 days

d. between 0 and 10 days

e. between 10 and 20 days

119. The table shows the mass, in atomic mass units, of a Helium 4 atom; the sum of the masses of its constituent electrons, neutrons, and protons; and the mass defect of the system.

PARTICLE	MASS (U)
Helium 4 atom	4.0026032
Particle mass	4.0329796
Mass Defect	0.0303764

If one atomic unit equals about 1.66054×10^{-27} kg, and the speed of light is about 3×10^8 meters per second, which expression represents the calculation of the nuclear binding energy of the Helium 4 system?

a. $(1.66054 \times 10^{-27}) \times (3 \times 10^8)$

b. $(1.66054 \times 10^{-27})^2 \times (3 \times 10^8)$

c. $(1.66054 \times 10^{-27}) \times (3 \times 10^8)^2$

d. $(1.66054 \times 10^{-27})^2 \times (3 \times 10^8)^2$

e. $[(1.66054 \times 10^{-27}) \times (3 \times 10^8)]^2$

120. How does the energy level of a photon with a wavelength of 300 nm compare to that of a photon with a wavelength of 100 nm?

a. nine times as large

b. one-ninth as large

c. one-third as large

d. 30,000 times as large

e. three times as large

▶ **Answers**

1. c. Hydrogen atoms are covalently bonded with oxygen atoms in each molecule of water, but each hydrogen atom is also attracted to the oxygen molecule of a neighboring molecule of water. Nearby molecules form hydrogen bonds through this attraction.

2. d. The first fossil microorganisms are estimated to be 3.8 billion years old. Before this time, it is believed that the earth was frequently struck with enormous asteroids and comets, making life impossible to sustain.

3. d. Punctuated equilibrium is the idea that evolution occurred in bursts of change separated by long intervals of constancy. Choice **a** defines the Equilibrium Theory of Island Biogeography. Choice **b** refers to an action potential in a neuron. Choice **c** refers to the Law of Conservation of Mass. Choice **e** refers to the concept of homology.

4. d. Mutation and sexual recombination produce the genetic variations that allow for evolution to occur. All new genes and alleles are produced by mutation, and sexual recombination allows for a myriad of alleles to be brought together to form new phenotypic combinations. Natural selection is the process through which evolution occurs, but does not actually contribute to variation in any way.

5. c. Mammals are categorically warm-blooded, viviparous (i.e., giving birth to live young) vertebrates with hair or fur. Exoskeletons are typical of some invertebrates such as arthropods and mollusks.

6. a. Binomal nomenclature was the classification system invented by Carolus Linneas that assigned each organism with a name composed of its genus and species.

7. a. Aerobic respiration requires oxygen in order to take place. Fermentation can occur with or without oxygen present. Carbon dioxide is not required for either reaction to occur, so choices **c** and **d** are incorrect.

8. e. In cytokinesis, the cytoplasm of the parent cell divides to form two identical daughter cells. Choices **a** through **d** describe the first four steps in mitosis.

9. b. Water is transported from the roots to other plant structures through the xylem tubes. Nutrients are primarily transported through the phloem. Pistil and stamen refer to female and male structures in angiosperms.

10. e. There are four chambers in the human heart: the right ventricle, left ventricle, right atrium, and left atrium. Other types of vertebrates have hearts that may have one or two atria and one or two ventricles.

11. d. The "fight or flight" response is the common term for the body's reaction to a stressful situation, mediated by the sympathetic division of the peripheral nervous system. Epinephrine is released by the adrenal medulla during a fight or flight response. The anterior pituitary releases thyroid-stimulating hormone and follicle-stimulating hormone to invoke the action of the thyroid gland and gonads, respectively. Insulin and glucagon are secreted by the pancreas to control blood glucose levels.

12. c. Polygenic traits are coded for by more than one gene. Complex features such as height and skin color are determined by a combination of different genetic factors; therefore, there are several genes that contribute to these phenotypes. Conversely, monogenic traits are coded by a single gene, so choice **b** is incorrect. Codominance refers to traits where more than one allele is dominant, so that both are expressed. Linked genes are genes that are located on the same chromosome. Mutations are any change in the DNA of a gene.

13. b. The placenta provides the fetus with oxygen, nutrients, and antibodies while filtering out fetal waste. However, fetal and maternal blood do not mix in the placenta, but rather nutrients are exchanged by diffusion across fetal and maternal capillary.

14. c. Red-green color blindness is common in males but very rare in females because it is caused by a recessive allele carried on the X chromosome. Because males only have one X chromosome, any males carrying the red-green color blindness allele will express this trait. Females have two X chromosomes, so heterozygous carriers of the allele will not express the red-green color blindness phenotype.

15. b. The endoderm layer of the embryo becomes the inner lining of the digestive system and of other organ systems in the body. The mesoderm eventually becomes major organ systems in the body, and the ectoderm becomes the skin and nervous system.

16. c. Phototropism is a growth response in a plant in response to light. Thigmotropism refers to a response to touch, and gravitotropism is a response to gravity. Circadian rhythm is a biological cycle that occurs with a frequency of about 24 hours. Abscission refers to the loss of leaves in deciduous trees.

17. e. A producer uses light energy from the sun to produce chemical energy, so it is the first, or base, level of the energy pyramid. Primary consumers are organisms that feed on producers directly. Moving up each level of the food pyramid, only about 10% of the previous level's energy is retained. Thus, primary consumers retain 10% of the energy harvested by a producer. A secondary consumer (an organism that feeds on primary consumers) would retain only 1% of the energy harvested by a producer.

18. e. Decomposers, including saprobic fungi and some prokaryotes, convert nonliving organic material and waste into inorganic forms. A producer is an organism that uses light energy from the sun to produce nutrients. Primary consumers are organisms that feed on producers directly. Secondary consumers feed on primary consumers, and tertiary consumers feed on secondary consumers.

19. a. Sexual recombination allows for a variety of alleles to be brought together in new phenotypic combinations. This is true for all organisms, regardless of habitat.

20. a. In commensalism, one organism benefits and the other is not affected. In a mutualistic relationship, each organism benefits by interacting with the other. In parasitism, one organism benefits and the other is harmed. Predation refers to one organism feeding on another. Competition refers to the struggle between organisms for any type of resource.

21. c. Organisms make use of the resources in a given region differently according to their different niches. This allows for a variety of organisms to coexist effectively. Altruism is a behavior that helps another member of a population at an individual's own expense. A biome is any of the world's major ecosystems, such as the rainforest or tundra. Mimicry refers to an organism adopting a trait or appearance that is similar to another organism, usually for adaptive advantage.

22. b. Tropical forests can get up to 200 cm of rain per year. This is the highest average among all of the biomes, and is a defining characteristic of the tropical forest biome.

23. d. Habitat destruction by humans is the single greatest threat to biodiversity throughout the globe.

24. a. Energy sources are currently dominated by nonrenewable resources such as coal, but renewable resources such as wind, solar, tide, and hydroelectric power are becoming increasingly used around the globe.

25. a. The equilibrium theory of island biogeography states that the number of species on an island reaches an equilibrium when the immigration rate and extinction rate are equal. All things being equal, the island with the higher immigration rate will probably have more species.

26. c. Fatty acids are carbon chain carboxylic acids, which means they contain the COOH group. Phospholipids contain two fatty acids and a phosphate group linked to a molecule of glycerol. Nucleic acids (DNA or RNA) are strings of nucleotides (five-carbon sugars bonded to a nitrogenous base and a phosphate group). Triglycerides, also called fats, are three fatty acids linked to a molecule of glycerol.

27. **b.** There are 6 carbons, 12 hydrogens, and 2 oxygens in this molecule, so the chemical formula is $C_6H_{12}O_2$.

28. **c.** The molecule contains a carboxyl group, which consists of a carbon atom bound to a hydroxyl (–OH) group and double-bound to an oxygen atom. Choice **a** is incorrect because the carbon atoms are bound by only single bonds. An unsaturated chain would contain carbon atoms bound by double or triple bonds. An amino group is a nitrogen atom bound to two hydrogen atoms, so choice **b** is incorrect. The oxygen atom of the carboxyl group possesses a partial negative charge, making the molecule polar, so choice **d** is incorrect. Any molecule containing covalent bonds between carbon and hydrogen is organic, so choice **e** is incorrect.

29. **d.** The amino acid coded by AUG is Met, CAU codes for His, and CUC codes for Leu. So, the protein formed is Met-His-Leu.

30. **c.** Insertion of a nucleotide into a base sequence will cause a frameshift mutation, meaning that the remaining length of the RNA strand will be grouped into different codons. The original grouping of the bases looks like this:
5'-AUG CAU CUC-3
After the inserting of an adenine, the bases will be grouped and translated like this:
5'-AUG ACA UCU C-3
So, the new protein will contain the amino acids coded by AUG, ACA, and UCU: Met-Thr-Ser.

31. **a.** If a single nucleotide is inserted at the beginning of an RNA sequence, all the subsequent codons will shift, and the entire chain will be translated incorrectly. If a codon is inserted, it will simply add an amino acid at this location, but all subsequent codons will be unaffected.

32. **b.** The stamen refers to the male structures of an angiosperm, the anther and the filament. Structure D represents the anther, and E is the filament. Structures A, B, and C represent the stigma, style, and ovary, respectively, which comprise the female structures of the flower, the pistil.

33. **a.** The pistil refers to the female structures of an angiosperm: the stigma, style, and ovary. Structure A is the stigma, B is the style, and C is the ovary. Structure D represents the anther, and E is the filament. Together these comprise the male unit of the angiosperm: the stamen.

34. **c.** The ovary of the flower becomes the fruit of the plant, and ovules become seeds. Structure C represents the ovary.

35. **b.** The muscle cell shown in figure A is a striated skeletal muscle. This type of muscle can be found in parts of the body that govern voluntary movements, such as the upper arm. Heart muscle is also striated, but these cells appear in bundles that are connected at both ends, as shown in figure C. Small intestine muscles and other involuntary muscles (excluding the heart) are smooth, like the cell shown in figure B. The cerebellum is a part of the brain, so this would not contain muscle cell, nor would fingernails.

36. c. Small intestine muscles and other involuntary muscles (excluding the heart) are smooth, like the cell shown in figure B. The muscle cell shown in figure A is a striated skeletal muscle. This type of muscle can be found in parts of the body that govern voluntary movements, such as the upper arm. Heart muscle is also striated, but these cells appear in bundles that are connected at both ends, as shown in figure C. The cerebellum is a part of the brain, so this would not contain muscle cell, nor would fingernails.

37. a. As shown in figure C, heart muscle is striated and the cells appear in bundles connected at both ends. Small intestine muscles and other involuntary muscles (excluding the heart) are smooth, like the cell shown in figure B. The muscle cell shown in figure A is a striated skeletal muscle. This type of muscle can be found in parts of the body that govern voluntary movements, such as the upper arm. The cerebellum is a part of the brain, so this would not contain muscle cell, nor would fingernails.

38. b. In a mutualistic relationship, each organism benefits by interacting with the other. Because the sea anemone receives food and transport and the crab receives protection, this is an example of mutualism. In commensalism, one organism benefits and the other is not affected. In parasitism, one organism benefits and the other is harmed. Predation refers to one organism feeding on another. Competition refers to the struggle between organisms for any type of resource.

39. b. The half-life of an isotope is the amount of time it takes for half of its mass to decay. If you originally had 6 grams and now have 1.5 grams, the mass was reduced by $\frac{1}{2}$ two times: from 6 grams to 3 grams, and from 3 grams to 1.5 grams. Thus, it would take 2×2 billion years, or 4 billion years, for this to occur.

40. c. In six billion years, the amount of the isotope would have been reduced by $\frac{1}{2}$ two times. After 3 billion years, there would be $\frac{10}{2}$ grams, or 5 grams. After another 3 billion years, there would be $\frac{5}{2}$ grams, or 2.5 grams.

41. e. If there are 16 creatures and 4 of them are green, that means that 4 individuals are homozygous recessive, so $q^2 = \frac{4}{16} = \frac{1}{4}$. To find q, take the square the root, which is $\frac{1}{2}$.

42. e. If there are 16 creatures and 4 of them are green, that means that 4 individuals are homozygous recessive, so $q^2 = \frac{4}{16} = \frac{1}{4}$. To find q, take the square the root, which is $\frac{1}{2}$ $p + q = 1$, so $p = \frac{1}{2}$ as well.

43. b. The values of p and q were determined in questions 40 and 41 to be the same value: $\frac{1}{2}$. The frequency of individuals in the population that are heterozygous is $2pq$, or $2(\frac{1}{2})(\frac{1}{2})$ $= \frac{1}{2} \cdot \frac{1}{2} \times 16$ creatures in total $= 8$.

44. e. If a trait is advantageous to survival, it increases the fitness of the organism, and the trait is more likely to be passed on to future generations. This is the basis of natural selection.

45. b. The Calvin cycle of photosynthesis is represented by the schematic shown in question 45. This reaction uses ATP and NADPH to convert carbon dioxide to sugar.

46. a. ATP (adenosine triphosphate) donates a phosphate group to 6 phosphoglycerate, which becomes 6 diphosphoglycerate. ATP is transformed into ADP (adenosine diphosphate).

47. **c.** ATP phosphorylates molecules at two steps in the cycle. First, 6 molecules of ATP are converted to ADP when 6 phosphoglycerate molecules are converted into 6 diphosphoglycerate molecules. Then, 3 more ADP are produced when 3 ATP molecules convert 5 glyceraldehyde phosphate molecules into 3 RuBP molecules. So, 9 molecules of ADP are produced in total.

48. **b.** 6 NADPH molecules are converted to 6 NADP+ molecules when 6 diphosphoglycerate becomes 6 glyceraldehyde phosphate.

49. **d.** The complementary DNA sequence will contain the complementary bases for U, A, and C: A, T, and G, respectively. Note that the orientation of the DNA strand will be the opposite of the amino acid code, as the RNA and DNA strands align in an inverse direction.

50. **e.** A codon is a sequence of 3 nucleotides that codes for a specific amino acid. For every amino acid in a protein, there must be 3 amino acids, so $600 \times 3 = 1,800$ amino acids.

51. **a.** If substance D inhibits E_1, then increasing amounts of substance D will cause the reaction from A → B to proceed at a decreased rate. This means that the subsequent steps in the reaction will also slow down. This process is often called negative feedback, or feedback inhibition.

52. **b.** Adding substance A will increase the rate of the reaction until there is not enough E_1 to associate with the amount of substance A. Thus, adding more E_1 will allow the reaction converting A → B to proceed rapidly.

53. **d.** A retrovirus is any virus that has RNA as its genetic material.

54. **c.** Reverse transcription is the process by which retroviruses code DNA from a complementary RNA strand, which is the opposite process that occurs in transcription.

55. **b.** Viruses that remain dormant within a host cell undergo the lysogenic cycle. After time, these viruses may eventually burst from the host cell and undergo the lytic cycle.

56. **e.** The virus forms its envelope as it crosses the host cell membrane, and it incorporates some of the constituents of the host membrane as it does so.

57. **c.** Organisms that undergo alternation of generations have a life cycle that includes both a multicellular haploid form (the gametophyte) and a multicellular diploid form (the sporophyte).

58. **d.** Mitosis is cellular division that creates a daughter cell with the same number of chromosomes as the parent cell. Haploid cells that undergo mitosis will produce haploid daughter cells, and diploid cells will produce diploid daughter cells. This occurs in steps B, D, and E.

59. **b.** Step A shows the joining of two haploid gametes to form the diploid zygote, which is the process of fertilization.

60. **d.** Only plants and some algae undergo alternation of generations during their life cycle.

61. **a.** Choice **b** is incorrect because the new moon occurs after the waning moon. Choices **c**, **d**, and **e** are incorrect because the waning moon follows the full moon.

62. **d.** Nuclear fusion is the source of the sun's energy. Choices **a**, **b**, and **e** are incorrect because they are energy transfer mechanisms, not energy sources. Choice **c** is incorrect because nuclear fission occurs with much heavier elements than those found in the sun's center.

63. d. Parallax is used to measure distances that are much larger than solar system distances. Choices **a**, **b**, **c**, and **e** are incorrect because none of those choices gives information about the distance to a nearby star outside of the solar system.

64. d. Phobos is one of the moons of Mars. Choices **a**, **b**, **c**, and **e** are incorrect because all are classified as "inner plants" in the solar system.

65. d. Temperature increases from right to left along the bottom horizontal scale. Choices **a** and **e** are incorrect because they are increasing order from bottom to top to bottom of the vertical scale (brightness). Choice **b** is incorrect because it gives the order in terms of decreasing temperature. Choice **c** is incorrect because the order of Y and Z are reversed.

66. b. This is the best (if general) description of the point of the paragraph. Choices **a** and **e** are incorrect because jets and winds are mentioned in the paragraph, but are not the main point of the paragraph, which is an observation about the behavior of a jet on Jupiter. Choice **c** is incorrect because only gaseous jets on Jupiter are discussed. Choice **d** is incorrect because the power sources of the jets on Jupiter are not the main point of the paragraph, which is an observation about the behavior of a jet on Jupiter.

67. d. A light year is the distance that light travels in a year; if it takes 4 years for the signal to get to the star, it will take 8 years for a round trip. Choice **a** is incorrect because the time is not found by dividing 3 by 4 and multiplying the result by 2. Choice **b** is incorrect because the time for the signal to travel to and from the star is eight years. Choice **c** is incorrect because 4 years is the time it would take the signal to travel to or from the star. Choice **e** is incorrect because the time is not found by multiplying 3 by 4.

68. c. The wavelength from a light source appears to be longer when the velocity is positive, i.e., moving away from the observer. Choice **a** is incorrect because if $z < 0$, the object is moving toward the observer and the light would be "blue shifted," which is not the case here. Choice **b** is incorrect because if $z = 0$, then $v = 0$, which is not the case for a moving object. Choice **d** is incorrect because the object cannot have both a zero and a negative non-zero velocity. Choice **e** is incorrect because the object cannot have both a zero and a positive non-zero velocity.

69. e. The rotation period is equivalent to a "day," and Vesta has the shortest "day." Choice **a** is incorrect because Ceres has the longest "day." Choice **b** is incorrect because Ceres and Pallas have the longest "year," not the shortest "day." Choices **c** and **d** are incorrect because their rotational periods are greater than that of Vesta.

70. d. Kepler's Third Law states that the square of the period is proportional to the cube of the semi-major axis of the orbit. Because these two variables are plotted on logarithmic scales, the slope of the line $(\frac{3}{2})$ means that $T \propto L^{\frac{3}{2}}$ or $T^2 \propto L^3$. Choices **a**, **b**, and **c** are incorrect because the relationship between L and T is not linear. Choice **e** is incorrect because the square of T is proportional to the cube of L, not vice versa.

71. a. Silver tarnishes in the presence of air. Choices **b** through **e** are physical properties of silver, not chemical properties.

72. b. Brass is an alloy of the elements copper and zinc. Choices **a**, **c**, **d**, and **e** are incorrect because aluminum, copper, gold, and lead are elements.

73. c. According to the combined gas law, $PV = nRT$, the pressure and volume increase as additional gas (n) is blown into the balloon, and they are proportional to the number of molecules of gas blown into the balloon. The temperature of the gas in the balloon remains constant in an ideal situation in which no energy goes into stretching the material out of which the balloon is made. Choices **a** and **b** do not by themselves explain why the temperature remains constant. Choices **d** and **e** are not the formal names of any of the gas laws.

74. e. Diatomic molecules are molecules with only two atoms. Choices **a**, **b**, and **d** are incorrect because even though they have only two elements, they consist of more than two atoms. Choice **c** is incorrect because the two compounds—copper (II) sulfate and the water molecules—contain more than two atoms.

75. c. The solubility of compound X is about $46 \frac{g}{cm^3}$ at about 23° C and the solubility of compound Z is about $23 \frac{g}{cm^3}$ at about 23° C. Choices **a** and **b** are incorrect because the solubility of compound X is more than double the solubility of compound Z at 7° C and 12° C. Choices **d** and **e** are incorrect because the solubility of compound X is less than double the solubility of compound Z at 25° C and 30° C.

76. e. This choice most accurately reflects the topic sentence of the paragraph. Choice **a** is incorrect because the activity series does not provide a reliable guide for all reactions, as the counterexample illustrates. Choice **b** is incorrect because the activity series to more types of reactions than those at room temperature and in aqueous solutions, as the counterexample illustrates. Choice **c** is incorrect because the activity series applies to reactions with other acids than nitric and sulfuric acids, as the last sentence states. Choice **d** is incorrect because the activity series applies to metals and nonmetals.

77. c. The same number of N, Na, and O atoms appear on each side of the equation. Choices **a**, **b**, **d**, and **e** are incorrect because different numbers of N, Na, and/or O atoms appear on each side of the equation.

78. d. The same number of Al, H, and O atoms appear on each side of the equation. Choices **a**, **b**, **c**, and **e** are incorrect because different numbers of Al, H, and/or O atoms appear on each side of the equation.

79. c. 192 grams corresponds to 12 times the gram atomic weight of oxygen; because there are six atoms of oxygen in the reaction, 12 corresponds to two moles (two times six), so the amount of nitrogen would be twice two moles or four moles. Choice **a** is incorrect because two moles, of nitrogen would correspond to three moles or 96 grams of oxygen. Choice **b** is incorrect because the number of moles of nitrogen is not equal to the number of moles of oxygen. Choice **d** is incorrect because the number of moles of nitrogen is not equal to the sum of the coefficients of nitrogen and oxygen in the reaction. Choice **e** is incorrect because the number of moles of oxygen is not equal to the product of the coefficients of nitrogen and oxygen in the reaction.

80. a. For $r = k \times [0.2]^1 \times [0.3]^2 = 0.018k$, $1 + 2 = 3$, which is the total reaction order for the reaction. Choice **b** is incorrect because for $r = k \times [0.2]^2 \times [0.3]^0 = 0.04k$, $2 + 0 = 2$. Choice **c** is incorrect because for $r = k \times [0.2]^1 \times [0.3]^1 = 0.06k$, $1 + 1 = 2$. Choice **d** is incorrect because for $r = k \times [0.2]^1 \times [0.3]^0 = 0.2k$, $1 + 0 = 1$. Choice **e** is incorrect because for $r = k \times [0.2]^0 \times [0.3]^1 = 0.3k$, $0 + 1 = 1$.

81. d. Power, P, can be defined by the formula $P = V \times I = \frac{V^2}{R}$, where I is the current in amperes, V is the voltage in volts, and R is the resistance in ohms in a circuit. Choices **a** and **e** are incorrect because power is directly proportional to the current, I, and to the voltage, V, in a circuit. Choice **b** and **c** are incorrect because they are measures of the rate of energy consumption (kilowatts) and the total energy in a circuit (kilowatt-hours).

82. b. The magnetic field is proportional to the current and inversely proportional to the radius of the wire. Choice **a** is incorrect because the magnetic field is proportional to the current and inversely proportional to the radius of the wire. Choices **c** and **d** are incorrect because the magnetic field is proportional to the current and inversely proportional to the radius of the wire, but is not related to the voltage. Choice **e** is incorrect because the magnetic field is proportional to the current and inversely proportional to the radius of the wire, but is not related to the voltage. Also, the magnetic field is not a function of the external temperature. However, the magnetic field is indirectly related to the temperature of the wire produced by the current flowing through it.

83. e. Reactance is a property of an alternating current circuit, whereas resistance is a property of a direct current circuit. Choice **a** is incorrect because current is a measure of the rate of charge flow past a point in any circuit. Choice **b** is incorrect because capacitance is a property of capacitors and impedance is a combined property of capacitance and resistance in a circuit. Choice **c** is incorrect because current and voltage are properties of both alternating and direct current circuits, but are not analogous properties of such circuits. Choice **d** is incorrect because ohms and Farads are units of resistance and capacitance, respectively, and are characteristics of both alternating and direct current circuits.

84. c. The resistivity of glass is anywhere from 15 to 25 orders of magnitude greater than that of the other four choices. Choices **a**, **b**, **d**, and **e** are all conductors of electricity.

85. **c.** It is the time at which the voltage begins a new cycle, according to the problem. Choice **a** is incorrect because the time at point O is zero. Choices **b**, **d**, and **e** are incorrect because they correspond to the time at which half of the cycle of the voltage is completed.

86. **e.** W and Y have maxima and minima at the same times, even though their amplitudes are different. Choices **a** through **d** are incorrect because each of the pairs of signals are out of phase, i.e., their corresponding maxima and minima do not coincide, regardless of their amplitudes.

87. **d.** The total resistance of the circuit is $\frac{11}{5}$ ohms. If the current is 30 Amperes and voltage is the product of the current and the resistance, the source voltage will be $30 \times \frac{11}{5}$, or 66 volts. Choices **a** and **b** are incorrect because the wrong formula relating current, resistance, and voltage was used. Choices **c** and **e** are incorrect because the resistance was calculated incorrectly.

88. **d.** B varies directly with I and inversely with r. Choice **a** is incorrect because the power of ten is incorrect. Choice **b** is incorrect because I and r are reversed from the pattern shown in the table. Choice **c** is incorrect because the answer is not a pattern, e.g., "5, 2.5, 1" times 10^{-8}. Choice **e** is incorrect because the answer is not a pattern that subtracts one from the power of ten as the current increases and that divides the preceding number by five.

89. **e.** The rise time is calculated according to the formula $\tau = \frac{L}{R}$. So, the time constant is 50 ohms divided by 25 millihenrys or 5×10^{-4}, or 500 μs. Choices **a** and **c** are incorrect because the calculations with exponents were done incorrectly. Choices **b** and **d** are incorrect because the formula used for the time constant is incorrect.

90. **e.** The doubled voltage (40 volts) times the primary current will give the power. Choice **a** is incorrect because the secondary voltage is multiplied by the primary current. Choice **b** is incorrect because the ratio of the primary and secondary turns times the secondary current does not give power. Choice **c** is incorrect because the primary voltage is doubled, not the same. Choice **d** is incorrect because the primary voltage is multiplied by the secondary current.

91. **d.** The mantle lies between Earth's lithosphere and outer core. Choice **a** is incorrect; the atmosphere is not one of the parts of Earth's interior. Choice **b** is incorrect because the crust surrounds the lithosphere, which surrounds the mantle. Choices **c** and **e** are incorrect because the mantle surrounds Earth's center and its inner and outer cores.

92. **d.** Few fossils have been traced to the Precambrian era. Choices **a**, **b**, **c**, and **e** are incorrect because they are not the only Precambrian era, which would be least likely to have fossils.

93. **e.** Granite and rhyolite are, respectively, intrusive and extrusive igneous rock types. Choices **a**, **b**, **c**, and **d** are sedimentary rock types and subtypes.

94. a. Cleavage is the tendency of a mineral to break along a preferred direction of its crystalline structure. Choice **b** is incorrect because it does not have a specific geologic denotation. Choice **c** is incorrect because fracture refers to the amount of force or pressure required to produce a break or cleavage in a mineral or rock. Choice **d** is incorrect because hardness refers to a mineral's ability to mark or be marked by another mineral, and is a property of the mineral's component elements and molecules, not a physical property like cleavage.

95. c. It is the time interval over which a *P* wave travels from the seismic event, and the distance can be calculated if the speed of the *P* wave is known (usually from another information source). Choice **a** is incorrect because point *W* is the beginning of the time interval over which the *P* wave travels, not the elapsed time. Choice **b** is incorrect because it is a time interval over which the *P* wave travels, but it is not known when the signal started travelling toward the seismograph. Choice **d** is incorrect because it is the time when the first *S* wave reaches the seismograph, and cannot be used to calculate how far away the seismic event occurred until the *P* wave's travel time is used to calculate the distance. Choice **e** is incorrect because point *Z* is the time at which the *S* wave disappears, and cannot be used to calculate how far away the seismic event occurred.

96. b. Choice **b** is the only conclusion of the ones listed that can be drawn from the paragraph. Choices **a** and **d** are incorrect because nothing is mentioned about how zircon is formed or where it comes from. Choice **c** is incorrect because the last sentence in the paragraph mentions zircon particles that are older than 4,000 million years of age. Choice **e** is incorrect because the paragraph states that zircon is resistant to high pressures and temperatures.

97. e. Parts of minerals *W* and *Y* contain more than 6% of $NaO_2 + K_2O$ and fewer than 25% SiO_2. Choices **a**, **b**, and **c** are incorrect because some of the minerals *R, S, T, W, X,* and *Y* contain fewer than 6% of $NaO_2 + K_2O$ and more than 25% SiO_2. Choice **d** is incorrect because mineral *X* contains fewer than 6% of $NaO_2 + K_2O$ and slightly more than 25% SiO_2.

98. b. An amplitude that is one thousandth of another amplitude corresponds to a Richter scale difference of −3; 2.5 − 3 = −0.5. Choice **a** is incorrect because the known Richter scale value is multiplied by 0.001 instead of being added to −3. Choice **c** is incorrect because 2.5 was subtracted from 3 instead of being added to −3. Choice **d** is incorrect because 0.001 was subtracted from 2.5, whereas 2.5 should have been added to −3. Choice **e** is incorrect because 2.5 is multiplied by 1,000, whereas 2.5 should have been added to −3.

99. e. $\frac{2\,mm}{year}$ converts to $\frac{1\,meter}{500\,years}$; a slip distance of 3 meters would take 3 times 500, or 1,500 years. Choice **a** is incorrect because the units have not been converted before dividing, i.e., 3 m divided by $\frac{2\,mm}{year}$. Choice **b** is incorrect because $\frac{2\,mm}{year}$ multiplied by 3 meters does not give a meaningful physical quantity, i.e., 6 meter millimeters per year. Choice **c** is incorrect because the metric conversion was done incorrectly (50 instead of 500) and the time span is for one year, not three. Choice **d** is incorrect because the metric conversion was done incorrectly (50 instead of 500).

100. a. A vertical line drawn from 200° C to the bottom of the diagram cuts across three different grades of rock (I, II, and III). Choices **b** and **c** are incorrect because at 500° C and 600° C, there is only one grade of rock (III). Choices **d** and **e** are incorrect because at 800° C and 900° C, there are only two grades of rock (III and IV) possible.

101. c. The evaporation of sweat from skin transfers thermal energy to the air. Choice **a** is incorrect because heat is being added to a substance to raise its temperature to the boiling point; sweat is not boiled off skin. Choice **b** is incorrect because condensation results when a substance changes phase from a gas to a liquid; sweat starts out in a liquid phase and evaporates. Choice **d** is incorrect because heat is being removed from a substance to change its state from a liquid to a solid phase; sweat evaporates from a liquid to a gaseous phase. Choice **e** is incorrect because sublimation results when a substance changes phase from a solid directly to a gas without passing through a liquid phase; sweat changes from a liquid to a gas.

102. c. The Third Law of Thermodynamics says that a substance has no entropy at absolute zero. Choice **a** is incorrect because it deals with the First Law of Thermodynamics. Choice **b** is incorrect because it deals with the Second Law of Thermodynamics. Choice **d** is incorrect because none of the laws of thermodynamics deal with only heat and work. Choice **e** is incorrect because it deals with the so-called "Zeroth" Law of Thermodynamics.

103. c. Nuclear fission releases energy, which is an *exothermic* process. Choices **a**, **b**, **d**, and **e** are *endothermic* processes, in which energy is absorbed.

104. a. The distribution of molecular speeds is unchanging at constant pressure, temperature, and volume conditions. Choices **b**, **c**, **d**, and **e** are incorrect because all are assumptions of the kinetic theory.

105. c. The temperature is rising on each of the parts 1, 3 and 5 as the thermal energy increases. Choices **a** and **b** are incorrect because the temperature is rising on all three parts 1, 3, and 5. Choices **d** and **e** are incorrect because the temperature is constant for parts 2 and 4.

106. a. $W = PV = nRT = nR$ times the natural logarithm of the quotient of the final and initial volumes, which is the area of the gray shaded region. Choice **b** is incorrect because work is not the difference between the final and the initial volume. Choice **c** is incorrect because work is not pressure times the difference of the initial and final volume. Choice **d** is incorrect because work is not the pressure times the initial volume, but pressure times the natural logarithm of the quotient of the final and initial volumes. Choice **e** is incorrect because the slope of the line between the final and initial volume would be in units of pressure per unit of volume, which is not the units in which work is measured.

107. d. The Fahrenheit temperature reading is found according to the formula
$F = (\frac{9}{5} \times C) + 32$.
If $C = 10$, then $F = (\frac{9}{5} \times 10) + 32$, or 50.
If $C = 20$, then $F = (\frac{9}{5} \times 20) + 32$, or 68. The outside temperature reading is 68° F.

108. e. 293° Kelvin is 20° Celsius, which is 68° Fahrenheit by the formula
$F = (\frac{9}{5} \times C) + 32$.
Choices **a**, **c**, and **d** are incorrect because the wrong formula was used to calculate Fahrenheit degrees. Choice **b** is incorrect because −20° Celsius was used in the formula, not +20° Celsius.

109. d. This result represents the difference between the area of the trapezoid formed by the pressure values that run from 25 to 35 and area of the trapezoid formed by the pressure values that run from 10 to 15, i.e.
$(\frac{1}{2})(15)(35 + 25) - (\frac{1}{2})(15)(10 + 15) = 262.5$
Choice **a** is incorrect because the work done is not the difference between the areas of the two triangular parts of the shaded region. Choice **b** is incorrect because the work done is not half of the difference of the pressure values times the difference of the volume values. Choice **c** is incorrect because the work done is not the sum of two rectangular regions formed by the pressure and volume values. Choice **e** is incorrect because the work done is not the difference of two rectangular regions formed by the pressure and volume values.

110. c. $Q_X = Q_Y$; $m \times 0.25 \times T = (\frac{1}{4} \times m) \times c_Y \times (2 \times T)$; $c_Y = 0.5$ Joule per gram-Kelvin. Choices **a**, **b**, **d**, and **e** are incorrect because the basic formula $Q = m \times c \times \Delta T$ and the problem relationship of $Q_X = Q_Y$ were misapplied, or the relationships between the masses and temperature were stated incorrectly in the calculations.

111. e. An alpha particle and a proton have positive atomic numbers, i.e., +2 and +1, respectively. Choice **a** is incorrect because a beta particle's atomic number is −1. Choice **b** is incorrect because a beta particle's atomic number is −1 and a gamma ray's atomic number is zero. Choice **c** is incorrect because both a gamma ray and a neutron have an atomic number of zero. Choice **d** is incorrect because a neutron's atomic number is zero.

112. d. Choice **d** is the accepted term to describe the difference between an atom's mass and the mass of its constituent neutrons and protons. Choice **a** is incorrect because atomic mass is the mass of an atom's constituent neutrons and protons. Choices **b** and **e** are incorrect because they are not synonyms for mass defect. Choice **c** is incorrect because critical mass is used in referring to a part of the process of nuclear fission, not to mass defect.

113. b. 36 is the atomic number, which is the number of protons (36). Choice **a** is the atomic weight (88) less the atomic number (36) or 52, choice **c** is the sum of the number of electrons (36) and the number of neutrons (52) or 88, choice **d** is the sum of the number of electrons and protons (72), and choice **e** is the sum of the number of neutrons (52) and the number of protons (36) or 88.

114. b. Neptunium's atomic number (93) is greater than that of uranium (92). Choices **a** and **d** are incorrect because their atomic numbers are less than that of uranium. Choice **c** is incorrect because uranium is not a trans-uranium element of itself. Choice **e** is incorrect because only neptunium is a trans-uranium element.

115. e. Elements K or L could result from decay by beta particle (a negative charge of one) capture, which would reduce the proton number of the decay products by one, regardless of how the neutron numbers change. Choice **a** is incorrect because the isotope loses a proton, and does not gain one. Choices **b** and **c** are incorrect because the isotope loses one proton, not two. Choice **d** is only partially correct, because element M could also result from beta capture.

116. a. The slope of a line through the point on the binding area curve is steepest at point X. Choice **b** is incorrect because the slope of a line through point Y is approximately zero, even though the binding energy per nucleon is greatest at point Y. Choices **c** and **e** are incorrect because the slope of a line through point X is greater in absolute terms than the slope of line through point Z. Choice **d** is incorrect because the slope of a line through point Y is approximately zero, even though the binding energy per nucleon is greatest at point Y.

117. c. The chance of a sample not containing isotopes with atomic weights of 67 or 70 is 100% less the sum of the percentage abundances—$100 - (1 + 4)$, or 95%. Choice **a** is incorrect because it is the abundance of the isotope with atomic weight 70 alone. Choice **b** is incorrect because it is sum of the abundance of the isotopes with atomic weights 67 *or* 70. Choice **d** and **e** are incorrect because they are, respectively, the chance that a random sample of the element will not contain an isotope with atomic number 67 or 70.

118. d. About one-fourth (25 milligrams) of the original amount has decayed into other isotopes at some time between 0 days when 100 milligrams remains and 10 days when half (50 milligrams) of the original amount remains. Choice **a** is incorrect because over half of the original mass has decayed into other isotopes after 10 days. Choice **b** is incorrect because over three-fourths of the original mass has decayed into other isotopes after 20 days. Choice **c** is incorrect because over seven-eighths of the original mass has decayed into other isotopes after 30 days. Choice **e** is incorrect because over half of the original mass has decayed into other isotopes between 10 and 20 days.

119. c. The nuclear binding energy is calculated by the celebrated formula $\Delta E = \Delta m \times c^2$, where Δm is the mass defect and c is the speed of light. Choices **a**, **b**, **d**, and **e** are incorrect because they are misstatements of the formula.

120. c. The photon's energy level is directly proportional to its frequency, which is inversely related to its wavelength. Choices **a** and **b** are incorrect because the photo's energy is directly or inversely related to the square of its frequency or wavelength. Choice **d** is incorrect because the photon's energy is not calculated by multiplying the two wavelengths. Choice **e** is incorrect because the photon's energy level is directly (not inversely) proportional to its frequency, which is inversely related to its wavelength.

CLEP Natural Sciences Practice Test 2

Now take CLEP Natural Sciences Practice Test 2 for additional CLEP practice. Similar to the official exam, you will answer 120 questions. Again, we suggest that you follow the time constraints of the official CLEP Natural Sciences exam (90 minutes).

Remember, on the official CLEP, there is no penalty for incorrect answers, so always make a guess if you are unsure of an answer.

When you are finished, check the answer key on page 645 carefully to assess your results.

▶ CLEP Natural Sciences Practice Test 2

1.	ⓐ ⓑ ⓒ ⓓ ⓔ		41.	ⓐ ⓑ ⓒ ⓓ ⓔ		81.	ⓐ ⓑ ⓒ ⓓ ⓔ
2.	ⓐ ⓑ ⓒ ⓓ ⓔ		42.	ⓐ ⓑ ⓒ ⓓ ⓔ		82.	ⓐ ⓑ ⓒ ⓓ ⓔ
3.	ⓐ ⓑ ⓒ ⓓ ⓔ		43.	ⓐ ⓑ ⓒ ⓓ ⓔ		83.	ⓐ ⓑ ⓒ ⓓ ⓔ
4.	ⓐ ⓑ ⓒ ⓓ ⓔ		44.	ⓐ ⓑ ⓒ ⓓ ⓔ		84.	ⓐ ⓑ ⓒ ⓓ ⓔ
5.	ⓐ ⓑ ⓒ ⓓ ⓔ		45.	ⓐ ⓑ ⓒ ⓓ ⓔ		85.	ⓐ ⓑ ⓒ ⓓ ⓔ
6.	ⓐ ⓑ ⓒ ⓓ ⓔ		46.	ⓐ ⓑ ⓒ ⓓ ⓔ		86.	ⓐ ⓑ ⓒ ⓓ ⓔ
7.	ⓐ ⓑ ⓒ ⓓ ⓔ		47.	ⓐ ⓑ ⓒ ⓓ ⓔ		87.	ⓐ ⓑ ⓒ ⓓ ⓔ
8.	ⓐ ⓑ ⓒ ⓓ ⓔ		48.	ⓐ ⓑ ⓒ ⓓ ⓔ		88.	ⓐ ⓑ ⓒ ⓓ ⓔ
9.	ⓐ ⓑ ⓒ ⓓ ⓔ		49.	ⓐ ⓑ ⓒ ⓓ ⓔ		89.	ⓐ ⓑ ⓒ ⓓ ⓔ
10.	ⓐ ⓑ ⓒ ⓓ ⓔ		50.	ⓐ ⓑ ⓒ ⓓ ⓔ		90.	ⓐ ⓑ ⓒ ⓓ ⓔ
11.	ⓐ ⓑ ⓒ ⓓ ⓔ		51.	ⓐ ⓑ ⓒ ⓓ ⓔ		91.	ⓐ ⓑ ⓒ ⓓ ⓔ
12.	ⓐ ⓑ ⓒ ⓓ ⓔ		52.	ⓐ ⓑ ⓒ ⓓ ⓔ		92.	ⓐ ⓑ ⓒ ⓓ ⓔ
13.	ⓐ ⓑ ⓒ ⓓ ⓔ		53.	ⓐ ⓑ ⓒ ⓓ ⓔ		93.	ⓐ ⓑ ⓒ ⓓ ⓔ
14.	ⓐ ⓑ ⓒ ⓓ ⓔ		54.	ⓐ ⓑ ⓒ ⓓ ⓔ		94.	ⓐ ⓑ ⓒ ⓓ ⓔ
15.	ⓐ ⓑ ⓒ ⓓ ⓔ		55.	ⓐ ⓑ ⓒ ⓓ ⓔ		95.	ⓐ ⓑ ⓒ ⓓ ⓔ
16.	ⓐ ⓑ ⓒ ⓓ ⓔ		56.	ⓐ ⓑ ⓒ ⓓ ⓔ		96.	ⓐ ⓑ ⓒ ⓓ ⓔ
17.	ⓐ ⓑ ⓒ ⓓ ⓔ		57.	ⓐ ⓑ ⓒ ⓓ ⓔ		97.	ⓐ ⓑ ⓒ ⓓ ⓔ
18.	ⓐ ⓑ ⓒ ⓓ ⓔ		58.	ⓐ ⓑ ⓒ ⓓ ⓔ		98.	ⓐ ⓑ ⓒ ⓓ ⓔ
19.	ⓐ ⓑ ⓒ ⓓ ⓔ		59.	ⓐ ⓑ ⓒ ⓓ ⓔ		99.	ⓐ ⓑ ⓒ ⓓ ⓔ
20.	ⓐ ⓑ ⓒ ⓓ ⓔ		60.	ⓐ ⓑ ⓒ ⓓ ⓔ		100.	ⓐ ⓑ ⓒ ⓓ ⓔ
21.	ⓐ ⓑ ⓒ ⓓ ⓔ		61.	ⓐ ⓑ ⓒ ⓓ ⓔ		101.	ⓐ ⓑ ⓒ ⓓ ⓔ
22.	ⓐ ⓑ ⓒ ⓓ ⓔ		62.	ⓐ ⓑ ⓒ ⓓ ⓔ		102.	ⓐ ⓑ ⓒ ⓓ ⓔ
23.	ⓐ ⓑ ⓒ ⓓ ⓔ		63.	ⓐ ⓑ ⓒ ⓓ ⓔ		103.	ⓐ ⓑ ⓒ ⓓ ⓔ
24.	ⓐ ⓑ ⓒ ⓓ ⓔ		64.	ⓐ ⓑ ⓒ ⓓ ⓔ		104.	ⓐ ⓑ ⓒ ⓓ ⓔ
25.	ⓐ ⓑ ⓒ ⓓ ⓔ		65.	ⓐ ⓑ ⓒ ⓓ ⓔ		105.	ⓐ ⓑ ⓒ ⓓ ⓔ
26.	ⓐ ⓑ ⓒ ⓓ ⓔ		66.	ⓐ ⓑ ⓒ ⓓ ⓔ		106.	ⓐ ⓑ ⓒ ⓓ ⓔ
27.	ⓐ ⓑ ⓒ ⓓ ⓔ		67.	ⓐ ⓑ ⓒ ⓓ ⓔ		107.	ⓐ ⓑ ⓒ ⓓ ⓔ
28.	ⓐ ⓑ ⓒ ⓓ ⓔ		68.	ⓐ ⓑ ⓒ ⓓ ⓔ		108.	ⓐ ⓑ ⓒ ⓓ ⓔ
29.	ⓐ ⓑ ⓒ ⓓ ⓔ		69.	ⓐ ⓑ ⓒ ⓓ ⓔ		109.	ⓐ ⓑ ⓒ ⓓ ⓔ
30.	ⓐ ⓑ ⓒ ⓓ ⓔ		70.	ⓐ ⓑ ⓒ ⓓ ⓔ		110.	ⓐ ⓑ ⓒ ⓓ ⓔ
31.	ⓐ ⓑ ⓒ ⓓ ⓔ		71.	ⓐ ⓑ ⓒ ⓓ ⓔ		111.	ⓐ ⓑ ⓒ ⓓ ⓔ
32.	ⓐ ⓑ ⓒ ⓓ ⓔ		72.	ⓐ ⓑ ⓒ ⓓ ⓔ		112.	ⓐ ⓑ ⓒ ⓓ ⓔ
33.	ⓐ ⓑ ⓒ ⓓ ⓔ		73.	ⓐ ⓑ ⓒ ⓓ ⓔ		113.	ⓐ ⓑ ⓒ ⓓ ⓔ
34.	ⓐ ⓑ ⓒ ⓓ ⓔ		74.	ⓐ ⓑ ⓒ ⓓ ⓔ		114.	ⓐ ⓑ ⓒ ⓓ ⓔ
35.	ⓐ ⓑ ⓒ ⓓ ⓔ		75.	ⓐ ⓑ ⓒ ⓓ ⓔ		115.	ⓐ ⓑ ⓒ ⓓ ⓔ
36.	ⓐ ⓑ ⓒ ⓓ ⓔ		76.	ⓐ ⓑ ⓒ ⓓ ⓔ		116.	ⓐ ⓑ ⓒ ⓓ ⓔ
37.	ⓐ ⓑ ⓒ ⓓ ⓔ		77.	ⓐ ⓑ ⓒ ⓓ ⓔ		117.	ⓐ ⓑ ⓒ ⓓ ⓔ
38.	ⓐ ⓑ ⓒ ⓓ ⓔ		78.	ⓐ ⓑ ⓒ ⓓ ⓔ		118.	ⓐ ⓑ ⓒ ⓓ ⓔ
39.	ⓐ ⓑ ⓒ ⓓ ⓔ		79.	ⓐ ⓑ ⓒ ⓓ ⓔ		119.	ⓐ ⓑ ⓒ ⓓ ⓔ
40.	ⓐ ⓑ ⓒ ⓓ ⓔ		80.	ⓐ ⓑ ⓒ ⓓ ⓔ		120.	ⓐ ⓑ ⓒ ⓓ ⓔ

▶ Practice Test Questions

Biological Sciences

Use the following figure to answer questions 1 and 2.

A.

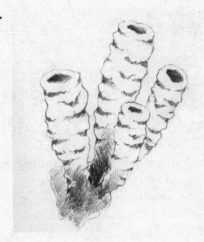

B.

C.

D.

E.

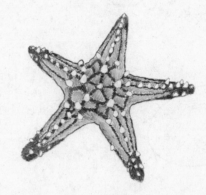

1. Which organism shown in the figure belongs to *Arthropoda*?
   a. A
   b. B
   c. C
   d. D
   e. E

2. Which organism shown in the figure belongs to *Porifera*?
   a. A
   b. B
   c. C
   d. D
   e. E

Use the following figure to answer questions 3–5.

A.

D.

B.

C.

3. Which of the structures shown is an example of a vestigial structure?

   a. A

   b. B

   c. C

   d. D

   e. none of the above

4. Which of the following choices is NOT an example of homologous structures?

   a. A and B

   b. B and C

   c. C and D

   d. B, C, and D

   e. B and D

5. Which of the following choices includes analogous structures?

   a. A and B

   b. B and C

   c. A and D

   d. B and D

   e. none of the above

Use the following figure to answer questions 6–8.

6. What type of molecule are the structures in the figure?

a. lipids
b. carbohydrates
c. polypeptides
d. amino acids
e. fatty acids

7. Which of the molecules in the figure has the strongest negative charge?

a. glycine
b. phenylalanine
c. serine
d. aspartate
e. lysine

8. If R represents the variable portion of each molecule, which of the following describes all of the molecules shown?

a. $H_3NCHRCOOH$
b. H_2NCH_2RCOOH
c. $HNCHRCOOH$
d. H_2NC_2RCOOH
e. $H_2NCHRCOOH$

Use the following figure to answer questions 9–10.

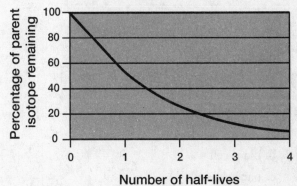

9. Based on the figure, what percentage of the parent isotope will exist after 5 half-lives?

a. 50%
b. 25%
c. 12.5%
d. 6.25%
e. 3.125%

10. If a rock contained 20 grams of the parent isotope originally, how many grams will remain after 3 half-lives?

a. 10 grams
b. 5 grams
c. 2.5 grams
d. 1.25 grams
e. 0.625 grams

Use the following figure to answer questions 11–14.

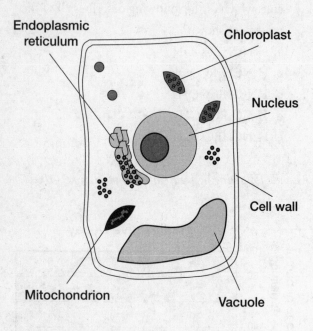

Endoplasmic reticulum

Chloroplast

Nucleus

Cell wall

Mitochondrion

Vacuole

11. What type of cell is shown here?

a. animal cell

b. plant cell

c. bacterial cell

d. virus

e. none of the above

12. Which structures may contain nucleic acids?

a. nucleus only

b. nucleus and mitochondrion only

c. nucleus and chloroplast only

d. nucleus, mitochondrion, and chloroplast only

e. mitochondrion and chloroplast only

13. This is a _____ cell because it contains a _____.

a. prokaryotic . . . mitochondrion

b. prokaryotic . . . chloroplast

c. prokaryotic . . . nucleus

d. eukaryotic . . . cell wall

e. eukaryotic . . . nucleus

14. Approximately how large is this type of cell in an actual organism?

a. between 10 and 100 meters

b. between 10 and 100 centimeters

c. between 10 and 100 millimeters

d. between 10 and 100 micrometers

e. between 10 and 100 nanometers

Use the following figure to answer questions 15–18.

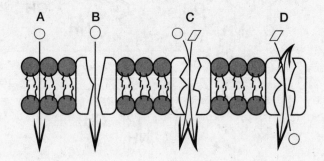

A   B   C   D

15. Molecule A is diffusing across the plasma membrane. Which of the following is most likely true about molecule A?

a. It has a positive charge.

b. It has a negative charge.

c. It is hydrophobic.

d. It is hydrophilic.

e. It is an amino acid.

16. What structure does molecule B move through?

a. first messenger

b. second messenger

c. phospholipid

d. fatty acid

e. transport protein

17. What type of transport is shown in C?

   a. symport

   b. antiport

   c. diffusion

   d. osmosis

   e. endocytosis

18. What type of transport is shown in D?

   a. symport

   b. antiport

   c. diffusion

   d. osmosis

   e. endocytosis

Use the following figure to answer questions 19–21.

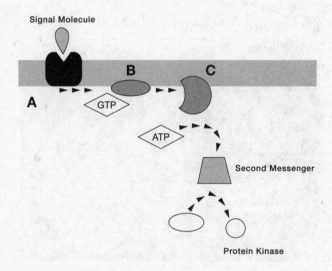

19. What type of molecule is the structure labeled A?

   a. receptor

   b. G-protein

   c. phospholipid

   d. fatty acid

   e. transport protein

20. What type of molecule is the structure labeled B?

   a. receptor

   b. G-protein

   c. phospholipid

   d. fatty acid

   e. transport protein

21. The process shown in the figure involves protein phosphorylation. From which molecule would you expect the phosphate groups to originate?

   a. ATP

   b. GTP

   c. signal molecule

   d. either **a** or **b**

   e. either **b** or **c**

Use the following Punnett square to answer questions 22 and 23.

F is a dominant allele for red petal color.
f is a recessive allele for white petal color.

	F	f
F	FF	Ff
f	Ff	ff

22. If the Punnett square is an example of incomplete dominance, what color petals do offspring with the Ff genotype have?

   a. red

   b. white

   c. pink

   d. blue

   e. These flowers do not have petals.

23. What is the ratio of red to pink to white phenotypes of the offspring in this cross?
   a. 4:0:0
   b. 3:0:1
   c. 2:0:2
   d. 1:2:1
   e. 1:0:3

Use the following figure to answer questions 24–27.

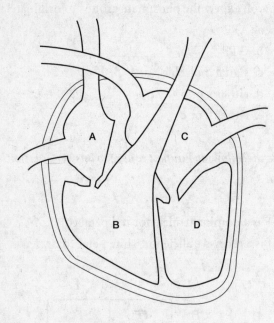

24. In the figure, which chamber of the heart is
labeled A?
   a. right atrium
   b. right ventricle
   c. left atrium
   d. left ventricle
   e. aorta

25. In the figure, which chamber of the heart is
labeled B?
   a. right atrium
   b. right ventricle
   c. left atrium
   d. left ventricle
   e. aorta

26. In the figure, which chamber of the heart is
labeled C?
   a. right atrium
   b. right ventricle
   c. left atrium
   d. left ventricle
   e. aorta

27. In the figure, which chamber of the heart is
labeled D?
   a. right atrium
   b. right ventricle
   c. left atrium
   d. left ventricle
   e. aorta

28. Identify the biome represented in the following
picture.

   a. tundra
   b. tropical forest
   c. broadleaf forest
   d. grassland
   e. desert

29. Identify the biome represented in the following picture.

   a. tundra

   b. tropical forest

   c. broadleaf forest

   d. grassland

   e. desert

Use the following passage to answer questions 30–32.

Multiple sclerosis (MS) is an autoimmune disease of the central nervous system. It is believed that the symptoms of MS are caused by the immune system attacking nerve cells in the brain and spinal cord, causing the breakdown of the myelin sheath. The symptoms of multiple sclerosis include blurry vision, numbness, fatigue, and dizziness. Areas of damage appear on an MRI as white plaques. Another diagnostic test for MS is called an evoked potential test. Electrodes are attached to various parts of the patient's body and an electrical signal is administered. The electrodes measure the length of time it takes for a signal to be transmitted from the body to the central nervous system.

30. Based on the passage, what results might you expect in an evoked potential test of a person with MS?

   a. Nerve impulses would be unusually strong.

   b. Nerve impulses would be unusually weak.

   c. Nerve impulses would be comparable to a healthy patient.

   d. Nerve impulses would be unusually fast.

   e. Nerve impulses would be unusually slow.

31. What would you expect to find on an MRI of an MS patient with blurry vision?

   a. abnormal nerve impulse speed

   b. a plaque on the optic nerve

   c. abnormal cerebellum structure

   d. a plaque on the spinal cord

   e. An MRI of an MS patient would not show any abnormality.

32. What is the role of myelin in the central nervous system?

   a. releasing neurotransmitters

   b. acting as a neurotransmitter receptor

   c. accelerating the action potential through the neuron

   d. sensing vision, balance, and touch

   e. control of involuntary functions

Use the following passage to answer questions 33–35.

Down syndrome is a genetic disorder that causes cognitive disabilities and abnormalities in physical appearance. Down syndrome is also called trisomy 21, as it is a result of having an extra chromosome 21.

33. Which of the following events might cause the development of Down syndrome?
   a. two homozygous recessive parents
   b. premature birth
   c. abnormal separation of chromosome 21 during meiosis
   d. incomplete dominance
   e. frameshift mutation

34. Down syndrome is an example of
   a. aneuploidy.
   b. polyploidy.
   c. linked genes.
   d. a silent mutation.
   e. a sex-linked trait.

35. Why might trisomy 21 be more common in the population than disorders caused by trisomy of other chromosomes?
   a. Chromosome 21 is more common.
   b. Chromosome 21 is a sex chromosome.
   c. Trisomy 21 is an advantageous trait.
   d. Trisomy of many other chromosomes is fatal to the fetus.
   e. Chromosome 21 is more susceptible to point mutations.

36. Identify the biome represented in the following picture.

   a. tundra
   b. tropical forest
   c. broadleaf forest
   d. grassland
   e. desert

37. Which of the following statements about natural selection is false?
   a. It requires a large population of individuals to occur.
   b. It involves adaptation to the environment that is acquired throughout life.
   c. It requires variation to exist among individuals in a population.
   d. It is a driving force in evolution.
   e. It is summarized by the phrase "survival of the fittest."

38. Which of the following observations would be most helpful in creating an accurate phylogeny?
a. Two organisms live in the same region.
b. Two organisms have similar mitochondrial DNA sequences.
c. Two organisms have similar life spans.
d. Two organisms have similar heights.
e. Two organisms both cannot fly.

39. Which of the following organelles is the site of protein synthesis?
a. chloroplast
b. plasma membrane
c. vacuole
d. ribosome
e. Golgi apparatus

40. If a plant cell is placed in a flask of pure water, it will
a. burst.
b. shrink.
c. increase in turgor pressure.
d. decompose.
e. undergo cell division.

41. Oxygen enters aveoli by
a. osmosis.
b. diffusion.
c. active transport.
d. transport proteins.
e. endocytosis.

42. A virus infects a cell, replicates DNA, undergoes a period of dormancy, then causes the cell to burst. What process has taken place?
a. lytic cycle
b. lysogenic cycle
c. phagocytosis
d. abscission
e. respiration

43. Non-coding portions of DNA molecules are called
a. exons.
b. introns.
c. stop codons.
d. operators.
e. amino acids.

44. Which organ is NOT part of the digestive system?
a. esophagus
b. stomach
c. small intestine
d. large intestine
e. heart

45. _____ are modified leaves that protect angiosperm buds before blooming.
a. Petals
b. Sepals
c. Stamens
d. Pistils
e. Stems

46. Sex-linked traits in a male are typically determined by genes passed on by
a. the mother.
b. the father.
c. either the mother or father.
d. both the mother or father.
e. neither the mother nor the father.

47. A man with type O blood and a woman with type A blood have a child. Which of the following statements is true?
a. The child cannot have type A blood.
b. The child cannot have type B blood.
c. The child will definitely have type A blood.
d. The child will definitely have type O blood.
e. The child may have type AB blood.

48. Eukaryotic autotrophs floating near the surface of water are called
a. consumers.
b. fungi.
c. phytoplankton.
d. angiosperms.
e. viruses.

49. Which cellular process produces energy by breaking down glucose?
a. photosynthesis
b. respiration
c. circulation
d. Calvin cycle
e. transcription

50. All of the following describe ways that foreign DNA maybe incorporated into a genome EXCEPT
a. specialized transduction.
b. generalized transduction.
c. transformation.
d. conjugation.
e. translation.

51. All the following are mammals EXCEPT
a. humans.
b. alligators.
c. whales.
d. tigers.
e. kangaroos.

52. Energy in an ecosystem begins primarily as solar energy and eventually ends up as
a. wind energy.
b. solar energy.
c. heat.
d. sound.
e. glucose.

53. Which trophic level has the greatest biomass?
a. producers
b. primary consumers
c. secondary consumers
d. tertiary consumers
e. omnivores

54. The phrase *you can't teach an old dog new tricks* has biological truth in instances of
a. natural selection.
b. imprinting.
c. adaptive radiation.
d. instinct.
e. genetic drift.

55. Increasing levels of carbon dioxide in the atmosphere contributes to
   a. punctuated equilibrium.
   b. migration.
   c. greenhouse effect.
   d. plate tectonics.
   e. Hardy-Weinberg equilibrium.

56. Chemical nutrients are recycled in ecosystems through
   a. pollution.
   b. sexual reproduction.
   c. biogeochemical cycles.
   d. active transport.
   e. circadian rhythms.

57. What is the coefficient of relatedness between a mother and her son?
   a. 1
   b. 0.75
   c. 0.5
   d. 0.25
   e. 0

58. The Earth is protected from UV radiation by
   a. the ozone layer.
   b. the sun.
   c. the oceans.
   d. continental drift.
   e. evolution.

59. Migration between two habitats may occur through a
   a. biome.
   b. ecosystem.
   c. movement corridor.
   d. biogeochemical cycle.
   e. niche.

60. A habitat is at equilibrium and supports its maximum population size when it reaches the
   a. geographic range.
   b. carrying capacity.
   c. reproductive isolation.
   d. half-life.
   e. biotic potential.

Physical Sciences

61. Which of the following is correct?
   a. Earth revolves around the moon once a month.
   b. Earth rotates on its axis once a month.
   c. The moon revolves around Earth once a year.
   d. The moon rotates on its axis once a day.
   e. The moon rotates on its axis once a month.

62. The table shows the temperatures of different parts of the sun.

Region	1	2	3	4
Temperature (° C)	1.5×10^7	2×10^6	6×10^3	7.5×10^3

Which parts of the sun correspond to the temperatures of the core and the photosphere?
   a. 1 and 4
   b. 3 and 4
   c. 2 and 4
   d. 1 and 3
   e. 2 and 3

63. If one star appears to be brighter than another when viewed from Earth, this is an example of

a. absolute brightness.

b. apparent brightness.

c. color.

d. luminosity.

e. temperature.

64. The asteroid belt lies between the planets

a. Earth and Mars.

b. Earth and Mercury.

c. Mars and Jupiter.

d. Mercury and Venus.

e. Venus and Mercury.

Use the following diagram to answer question 65.

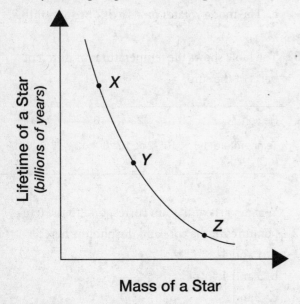

65. A star that is older and lighter than the star represented by point *Y* on the diagram could be located

a. at point *Y* on the curve.

b. between points *Y* and *Z* on the curve.

c. to the left of point *Y* on the curve.

d. to the right of point *Y* on the curve.

e. to the right of point *Z* on the curve.

66. The diagram shows the shadow thrown during a lunar eclipse.

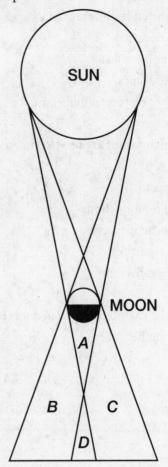

Which region(s) correspond to the antumbra?

a. *A*

b. *A* and *D*

c. *A*, *B*, and *C*

d. *B* and *C*

e. *D*

67. The table gives some data about the planets in a star system. The periods of revolution and rotation are in Earth days.

PLANET	DISTANCE TO THE STAR (10^8 KM)	PERIOD OF REVOLUTION (EARTH DAYS)	PERIOD OF ROTATION (EARTH DAYS)
W	500	100	5
X	800	275	15
Y	1,000	450	30
Z	1,500	700	50

Which of the following is NOT true, based on the data in the table?

a. Planet W is half as far from the star as Planet Y.

b. Planet W rotates on its axis one-sixth as fast as Planet Y.

c. The length of a "day" on Planet W is less than the length of a "day" on Planet Y.

d. The number of "days" in a "year" on Planet W is greater than the number of "days" in a "year" on Planets X, Y, and Z.

e. The speed of Planet W in its orbit is greater than the speed of Planet Z is in its orbit.

68. The diagram represents the sun's position relative to the center of the Milky Way, which is marked with the x.

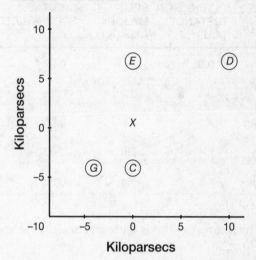

If signals are transmitted from Earth (E) to planets C, D, and G, what is the longest time that any signal would take to reach one of the planets? (*Hint:* 1 parsec ≈ 3×10^{16} meters.)

a. 5×10^8 seconds

b. 1×10^9 seconds

c. 1.25×10^9 seconds

d. 1.35×10^9 seconds

e. 1.6×10^9 seconds

69. The table shows some data about comets that travel through the solar system.

COMET	PERIHELION DISTANCE (A.U.)	SEMI-MAJOR AXIS (A.U.)	ORBITAL ECCENTRICITY (YR.)
Halley	~ 0.6	~ 18	~ 0.97
Encke	~ 0.3	~ 2.2	~ 0.85
Wirtanen	~ 1.1	~ 3.1	~ 0.65
Borrelly	~ 1.4	~ 3.6	~ 0.62
Kohoutek	~ 1.6	~ 3.4	~ 0.54

Which comet's orbit is the least circular in shape?

a. Borrelly

b. Encke

c. Halley

d. Kohoutek

e. Wirtanen

70. The table shows some data for the planet Mars.

Q. Mean Orbital Velocity (km/s)	24
R. Maximum Orbital Velocity (km/s)	26
S. Minimum Orbital Velocity (km/s)	22
T. Aphelion (10^6 km)	249
U. Perihelion (10^6 km)	207

Which velocity and distance measurements listed go together?

a. Q and T

b. Q and U

c. R and T

d. S and T

e. T and U

71. Which of the following is NOT a physical change in aluminum?

a. combining aluminum with oxygen to create aluminum oxide

b. making an alloy of aluminum and magnesium

c. polishing aluminum

d. rolling aluminum into sheets

e. solidifying molten (liquid) aluminum

72. A plastic water bottle "collapses" after it is taken off an airplane with a pressurized cabin and into the concourse via the jetway. What most likely changes when this happens?

a. pressure

b. pressure and temperature

c. pressure and volume

d. temperature

e. temperature and volume

73. Which of the following is NOT a molecule?

a. $Al(OH)_3$

b. Be

c. Cl_2

d. Fe_2O_3

e. H_4

74. If the temperature of 100 L of a gas in a container with a fixed volume is increased by 10° C, the pressure inside the container

a. decreases.

b. decreases ten times.

c. increases.

d. increases ten times.

e. stays the same.

75. The table shows the solubility of a gas in water in grams per hundred cubic centimeters.

PRESSURE (ATM)	0° C	10° C	20° C	30° C
1	89	70	56	44
2	175	140	110	90

Which of the following is NOT a conclusion that can be drawn from the table?

a. Pressure is directly related to solubility.

b. Pressure and temperature affect solubility.

c. Solubility doubles when the pressure is doubled.

d. Solubility is directly related to temperature.

e. Solubility is inversely related to temperature.

76. The table shows the charge of three negative and three positive ions.

Positive ions	Al^{3+}	Cu^{+}	Mg^{2+}
Negative ions	Cl^{-}	O^{2-}	PO_4^{3-}

Which of the following compounds could form from these ions?

a. $AlCl$

b. CuO_4

c. MgO

d. Cu_2PO_4

e. AlO_2

77. What numbers should replace the question marks in order to balance the equation that results from heating $Al_2(SO_4)_3$?

$$\underline{?}\ Al_2(SO_4)_3 \rightarrow \underline{?}\ Al_2O_3 + \underline{?}\ SO_3$$

a. 3, 3, and 3

b. 2, 3, and 3

c. 1, 3, and 3

d. 1, 2, and 3

e. 1, 1, and 3

78. Which of the following balances the equation that results from heating $MgCO_3$?

a. $MgCO_3 \rightarrow MgO + CO_2\uparrow$

b. $MgCO_3 \rightarrow MgO_2 + CO_2\uparrow$

c. $MgCO_3 \rightarrow 2MgO + CO_2\uparrow$

d. $MgCO_3 \rightarrow 2MgO_2 + 3CO_2\uparrow$

e. $MgCO_3 \rightarrow 3MgO + 2CO_2\uparrow$

79. In the reaction $N_2 + 3H_2 \rightarrow 2NH_3$, how much ammonia is produced if 28 grams of nitrogen react with hydrogen and if the gram atomic weights of hydrogen and oxygen are 14 and one, respectively?

a. 17 grams

b. 28 grams

c. 34 grams

d. 40 grams

e. 56 grams

80. The table shows the concentrations of soluble substance AB and its component ions A^+ and B^-, along with the equilibrium constant, K_{eq}, and the ion product, Q_i, for each pair of concentrations of A^+ and B^-.

A^+	B^-	AB	K_{eq}	Q_i
0.2	0.3	0.60	10.00	0.06
0.2	0.3	0.06	1.00	0.06
0.4	0.3	0.06	0.50	0.12
0.4	0.6	0.06	0.25	0.24
0.4	0.6	0.60	2.50	0.24

Which set of concentrations comes the closest to a solubility equilibrium?
a. 0.2, 0.3, and 0.6
b. 0.4, 0.6, and 0.6
c. 0.2, 0.3, and 0.06
d. 0.4, 0.3, and 0.06
e. 0.4, 0.6, and 0.06

81. The amount of charge flowing through a wire per second is a(n)
a. coulomb.
b. ampere.
c. ohm.
d. volt.
e. watt.

82. In the diagram, a magnetic field is produced by moving charges.

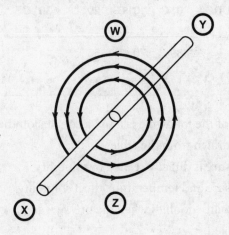

The conventional current flow is from
a. W to X.
b. X to Y.
c. X to Z.
d. Y to X.
e. Z to W.

83. Capacitance is
a. directly proportional to charge and inversely proportional to voltage.
b. directly proportional to voltage and inversely proportional to charge.
c. directly proportional to charge and voltage.
d. inversely proportional to charge and directly proportional to voltage.
e. inversely proportional to charge and voltage.

84. The resonance frequency in an alternating current circuit is related to

a. capacitance.

b. current.

c. inductance.

d. both **a** and **b**

e. both **a** and **c**

85. The diagram shows an alternating current or voltage.

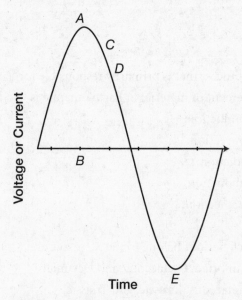

Which of the following corresponds to the *RMS* or effective value of the current or voltage?

a. the horizontal distance from *B* to *E*

b. the vertical distance from *A* to *B*

c. the vertical distance from *A* to *E*

d. the vertical distance from *C* to *B*

e. the vertical distance from *D* to *B*

86. The diagram shows the current decaying in a capacitor circuit.

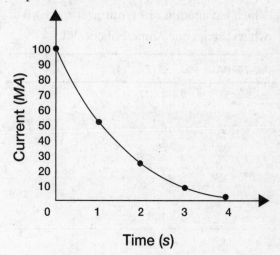

Over what time interval does the initial current (100 μA) fall from half to one-fourth value?

a. 0 to 1 second

b. 0 to 2 seconds

c. 1 to 2 seconds

d. 1 to 3 seconds

e. 2 to 4 seconds

87. The diagram shows a circuit with three capacitors in parallel.

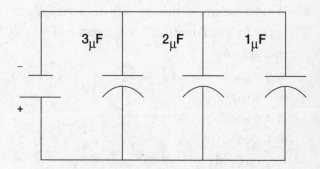

The total capacitance of the circuit is

a. $0 \, \mu F$.

b. $\frac{1}{6} \, \mu F$.

c. $\frac{5}{6} \, \mu F$.

d. $\frac{6}{5} \, \mu F$.

e. $6 \, \mu F$.

88. The table shows the magnetic field strength, B, of five wires made of different materials, each of which has a radius of 1 centimeter and each of which carries one Ampere of current.

MATERIAL	$B\ (T \times \frac{M}{A})$
R	1×10^{-3}
S	6×10^{-2}
T	1×10^{-1}
U	7
V	100

List the materials in order of how easily a magnetic field can be established in each one, starting with the material in which a magnetic field is most easily established.

a. R, S, T, U, V

b. T, S, R, V, U

c. U, S, V, T, R

d. V, U, S, R, T

e. V, U, T, S, R

89. What is the charge time for a circuit with a resistance of 1 mega ohms and a capacitance of 5 microfarad?

a. 0 seconds

b. 2 seconds

c. 4 seconds

d. 5 seconds

e. 20 seconds

90. A sound amplifier has an impedance of 24 ohms. What should be the turns ratio of the primary and secondary coils in a step-down audio transformer to match two 16-ohm speakers that are connected in parallel?

a. $\frac{1}{3}$

b. $\frac{\sqrt{3}}{3}$

c. $\sqrt{3}$

d. $3\sqrt{3}$

e. 3

91. The process that is primarily responsible for movement of material in Earth's mantle is

a. conduction.

b. convection.

c. radiation.

d. subduction.

e. submersion.

92. Which periods belong to the Mesozoic era?

a. Cambrian, Cretaceous, and Devonian

b. Cretaceous, Jurassic, and Triassic

c. Devonian, Silurian, and Triassic

d. Jurassic, Ordovician, and Triassic

e. Ordovician, Permian, and Silurian

93. The term that describes minerals with a simple cubic crystalline structure is

a. tetragonal.

b. monoclinic.

c. isometric.

d. hexagonal.

e. amorphous.

94. A geologic contour map is useful for all of the following EXCEPT
   a. calculating area.
   b. determining rock types.
   c. estimating slope.
   d. measuring distances.
   e. reading elevations.

95. In the diagram, the dotted and solid lines indicate the changes from one form of rock to another.

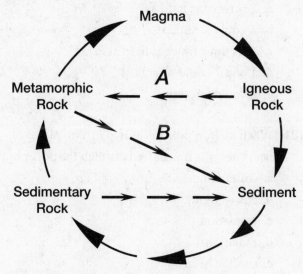

Which type of rock can change directly into sediment?
   a. igneous rock
   b. igneous, metamorphic, and sedimentary rock
   c. magma and metamorphic rock
   d. metamorphic and sedimentary rock
   e. sedimentary rock

96. The diagram shows *P* waves radiating through Earth from a seismic event.

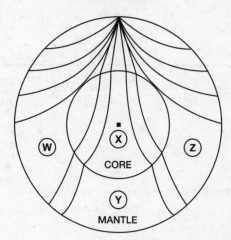

In which of the labeled regions are *P* waves NOT passing?
   a. *W*
   b. *W* and *X*
   c. *W* and *Y*
   d. *W* and *Z*
   e. *X* and *Y*

97. The table shows four types of volcanic rock and their percentage composition of silica.

ROCK TYPE	SILICA (%)
andesite	52–63
basalt	48–52
dacite	63–68
rhyolite	> 68

Which rock contains the greatest amount of material other than silica?
   a. andesite
   b. andesite and basalt
   c. basalt
   d. basalt and dacite
   e. rhyolite

98. The diagram shows a seismograph reading after a seismic event.

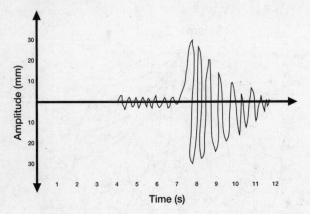

The time elapsed between the beginning of the seismic event and the arrival of the first *S* wave is

a. 3 seconds.

b. 4 seconds.

c. 5 seconds.

d. 7 seconds.

e. 12 seconds.

99. A geologist measures the overhang of a reverse fault after a seismic event as shown in the diagram.

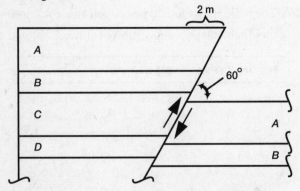

How far did the hanging wall block slip along the fault line?

a. 2 meters

b. about 3.5 meters

c. 4 meters

d. about 5.5 meters

e. 6 meters

100. The table shows the Mohs hardness of four minerals.

MINERAL	HARDNESS
W	7.5
X	6
Y	4.2
Z	3

Which of the following could be true?

a. *Z* is twice as hard as *X*.

b. *X* could scratch *W*.

c. *W* is three times as hard as *Z*.

d. *Y* and *Z* could scratch *W*.

e. *Z* could fracture *Y*.

101. When an iron poker is heated in a fireplace, heat energy is transferred through the poker by

a. conduction.

b. convection.

c. insulation.

d. radiation.

e. specific heat.

102. If the units of thermal conductivity are Watts per meter per Kelvin degree, what measurements are needed in order to calculate the thermal conductivity of a copper wire with a cross-section diameter of 1 millimeter and a length of 10 meters?

a. length

b. length and power

c. length and temperature

d. power and temperature

e. power, length, and temperature

103. Which of the following is NOT related to the quantity of heat in a system?
a. heat exchange
b. heat of fusion
c. heat of vaporization
d. molar heat
e. specific heat

104. The relationship $\Delta U = Q - W$ is the mathematical statement of
a. an adiabatic process.
b. molar heat capacity.
c. the First Law of Thermodynamics.
d. the law of heat conduction.
e. the Second Law of Thermodynamics.

105. The diagram shows three beakers of the same liquid:

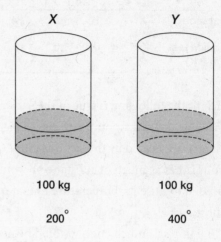

100 kg   100 kg

200°   400°

200 kg

400°

All of the following describe the average kinetic energy of the molecules in the beakers EXCEPT which choice?
a. The kinetic energy in beaker X is less than half of the kinetic energy in beaker Y.
b. The kinetic energy in beaker X is less than half of the kinetic energy in beaker Z.
c. The kinetic energy in beaker Y is double the kinetic energy in beaker X.
d. The kinetic energy in beaker Y is half of the kinetic energy in beaker Z.
e. The kinetic energy in beaker Z is more than double the kinetic energy in beaker X.

106. The table lists the specific heat constants for four substances.

Substance	X	Y	Z	W
Specific Heat (J/gm-° K)	0.9	0.4	0.1	2.5

Which of the following is true of the substances in the table if equal amounts (mass) of each substance are heated by the same amount (Q)?

a. Four times as much of substance Y would be needed to raise its temperature to that of substance Z.

b. Nine times as much energy would be needed to raise the temperature of substance X to the same temperature as substance Z.

c. The order of the temperatures, from lowest to highest, would be W, X, Y, and Z.

d. Twenty-five times as much mass of substance Z would be needed to raise its temperature by the same amount as substance W's.

e. Substance Y's temperature would be one fourth of substance Z's temperature.

107. The diagram shows four beakers filled with liquids W, X, Y, and Z that have different specific heats in Joules per kilogram-Kelvin.

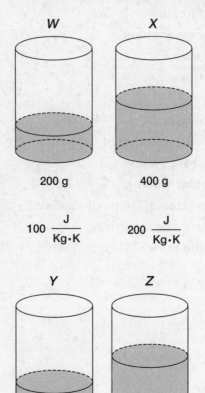

W X
200 g 400 g

$100 \dfrac{J}{Kg \cdot K}$ $200 \dfrac{J}{Kg \cdot K}$

Y Z
200 g 400 g

$150 \dfrac{J}{Kg \cdot K}$ $300 \dfrac{J}{Kg \cdot K}$

If an equal amount of heat was applied to each beaker, which choice gives the order, from hottest to coolest, of the liquids showing the greatest temperature increases?

a. W, X, Y, Z

b. W, X, Z, Y

c. W, Y, X, Z

d. X, Y, W, Z

e. Z, X, Y, W

108. A metal rod has a length of 10 meters, a temperature of 400° Kelvin, and a thermal expansion coefficient of 0.0000025 per degree Kelvin. What is the total length of the rod if the temperature increases to 500° Kelvin?

a. 0.0025 meter

b. 0.01 meter

c. 0.0125 meter

d. 10.0125 meters

e. 10.0025 meters

109. The table shows the relative diffusion rate, r, for molecules X, Y, and Z with different masses, m, at different temperatures, T. The constant k relates to the geometry of the container.

MOLECULE	r	m	T
X	$\frac{4}{5}k$	16	25
Y	$\frac{2}{3}k$	16	36
Z	$\frac{5}{7}k$	25	49

Which of the following shows the relationship of r to m and T?

a. $K \times \frac{m}{T}$

b. $K \times \frac{T}{m}$

c. $K \times (\frac{m}{T})^2$

d. $K \times \frac{\sqrt{m}}{T}$

e. $K \times \frac{\sqrt{T}}{m}$

110. The specific heat of an ideal monatomic gas at constant volume, c_v, is 12.5 Joules per mole degree Kelvin. The specific heat of an ideal monatomic gas at constant pressure, c_p, is 20.8 Joules per mole degree Kelvin. The universal gas constant, R, is about 8.3 Joules per mole degree Kelvin. Which of the following is NOT true of the relationship among these three values?

a. $c_p = c_v + R$

b. $c_p = \frac{5}{2}R$

c. $c_p + c_v = 4R$

d. $c_v = c_p + R$

e. $c_v = \frac{3}{2}R$

111. Radioactivity is characterized by

a. exponential decay.

b. exponential growth.

c. linear decay.

d. linear growth.

e. logarithmic decay.

112. The half-life of a radioactive element is

a. half of the atomic number of a radioactive element.

b. half of the original amount of a radioactive element.

c. the time after which half of all of the products of a radioactive element disappear from a living system.

d. the time required for half of the mass of the radioactive element to decay into other products.

e. the time required for the atomic number of a radioactive element to be cut in half.

113. The process of combining two nuclei to form a new heavier nucleus accompanied by a release of energy is called
   a. beta decay.
   b. radiation.
   c. fission.
   d. fusion.
   e. meltdown.

114. Which of the following isotopes have the same number of electrons?

   a. $^{106}_{48}$ Cd and $^{48}_{22}$ Ti

   b. $^{98}_{46}$ Pd and $^{102}_{46}$ Pd

   c. $^{102}_{46}$ Pd and $^{46}_{22}$ Ti

   d. $^{98}_{46}$ Pd and $^{46}_{22}$ Ti

   e. $^{98}_{46}$ Pd, $^{102}_{46}$ Pd, and $^{46}_{22}$ Ti

115. Uranium has an atomic number of 92. An alpha particle has an atomic number of 2 and an atomic weight of 4. Which of the following elements could be one of the products of bombarding a uranium 238 nucleus with an alpha particle?

   a. $^{241}_{93}$ U

   b. $^{241}_{93}$ Np

   c. $^{242}_{90}$ Th

   d. $^{234}_{92}$ U

   e. $^{234}_{92}$ Th

116. The diagram shows the energy level of an atom in an excited state before and after a reaction.

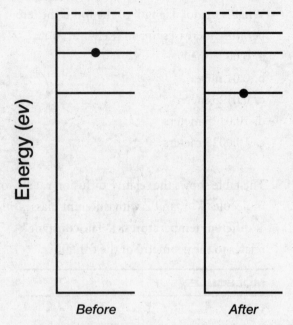

Before   *After*

What has happened to the atom in going from the "before" and "after" diagrams?
   a. The atom has absorbed energy.
   b. The atom has gained an electron.
   c. The atom has gone from an excited state to a ground state.
   d. The atom has ejected an electron.
   e. The atom has released energy.

117. The fission of one atom of ^{235}U releases about 3.2×10^{-11} watt-seconds of energy. The number of ^{235}U atoms that have to "split" to produce one watt of thermal energy per second is about
   a. 1×10^{11}.
   b. 3.1×10^{10}.
   c. 3.1×10^{11}.
   d. 3.2×10^{10}.
   e. 3.2×10^{11}.

118. The table shows average radiation dose amounts (rounded to the nearest multiple of ten) per year from a variety of sources.

SOURCE	DOSE (MILLIREMS)
rocks and soil	30
human body	40
radon	200
medical X-rays	40
consumer products	10

If a lethal dose of radiation is about 500,000 millirems delivered over a few minutes, which of the following is equivalent to a lethal dose of radiation over a year?

a. 100 doses from consumer products
b. 200 doses of radon
c. 2,000 doses from rocks and soil
d. 10,000 doses from medical X-rays
e. 1,000,000 doses from the human body

119. The average atomic weight of copper is 63.546. About how many atoms of copper are contained in 190 grams of copper?

a. 3×10^{21}
b. 9.5×10^{21}
c. 1.8×10^{24}
d. 1.9×10^{25}
e. 6.3546×10^{25}

120. The table shows the bond enthalpies (energy) of some chemical bonds, and some molecules made from these bonds.

Bond	C=O	C–H	O=O	O–H	C≡O
Enthalpy (kJ)	800	415	500	465	1,075

I–CH_4 II–CO_2 III–H_2O IV–O_2 V–CO

Which pair of molecules would require the most energy to break apart or form?

a. CH_4 and CO_2
b. CH_4 and H_2O
c. CO and CO_2
d. CO_2 and O_2
e. H_2O and O_2

▶ Answers

1. b. A grasshopper is an insect, and all insects belong to *Arthropoda*. Choice **a** is incorrect because a sponge belongs to the *Porifera* phylum. Choice **c** is incorrect because mollusks belong to the *Mollusca* phylum. Choice **d** is incorrect because roundworms belong to the *Nematoda* phylum. Choice **e** is incorrect because starfish belong to the *Echinodermata* phylum.

2. a. Sponges belong to the *Porifera* phylum, which includes filter-feeding animals that do not have true tissues. Choice **b** is incorrect because grasshoppers belong to the *Arthropoda* phylum. Choice **c** is incorrect because mollusks belong to the *Mollusca* phylum. Choice **d** is incorrect because roundworms belong to the *Nematoda* phylum. Choice **e** is incorrect because starfish belong to the *Echinodermata* phylum.

3. c. Flamingos are flightless birds, so these wings do not have any function. Flamingos probably evolved from flying birds, and the wings have persisted despite having lost their function through evolutionary time. This describes a vestigial structure. Choice **a** is incorrect because wings on bees are necessary for flight. Choice **b** is incorrect because wings on a hummingbird are necessary for flight. Choice **d** is incorrect; a human arm is used for sensory and motor function. Choice **e** is incorrect because choices **a**, **b**, and **d** describe structures that are all important functional structures for these organisms.

4. a. A bee's wings and a hummingbird's wings are similar but are not indicative of a common ancestor. These wings developed through separate evolutionary lines, so they are analogous, and not homologous.

5. a. A bee's wing and a hummingbird's wing are similar in function and design but are not a result of a common ancestor. This means they are analogous. Choice **b** is incorrect because a hummingbird's wing and a flamingo's wing are homologous structures. Choice **c** is incorrect because a bee's wing and a human's arm are not similar in function or morphology. Choice **d** is incorrect because a hummingbird's wing and a human's arm are homologous structures. Choice **e** is incorrect because choice **a** is an example of analogous structures.

6. d. The structures all contain an amino group and a carboxyl group, typical of an amino acid. Choice **a** is incorrect because lipids are all hydrophobic molecules, and several of the molecules shown are hydrophilic. Choice **b** is incorrect because carbohydrates are sugar monomers or polymers and do not contain the amino group. Choice **c** is incorrect because polypeptides contain more than one of these amino acids linked together. Choice **e** is incorrect because fatty acids do not contain an amino group.

7. d. Aspartate has a negatively charged acetic acid group. Choices **a**, **b**, and **c** are incorrect because glycine, phenylalanine, and serine do not have an electrically charged side group. Choice **e** is incorrect because lysine has a positively charged side group.

8. e. All the molecules shown have the amino group (H_2N), a carbon attached to one hydrogen and one side chain (CHR), and a carboxyl group (COOH). Choice **a** is incorrect because there are only two hydrogens attached to nitrogen in the amino group. Choice **b** is incorrect because there is only one hydrogen attached to the carbon that holds the side group. Choice **c** is incorrect because there are two hydrogens attached to nitrogen in the amino group. Choice **d** is incorrect because there are only two carbons in the core structure.

9. e. After each half-life, 50% of the isotope remains. So, after 2 half-lives, 50% of this 50%, or 25% of the parent isotope, will remain. After 3 half-lives, 12.5% of the parent isotope will remain. After 4 half-lives, 6.25% will remain. After 5 half-lives, 3.125% will remain. Choice **a** is incorrect because 50% of the parent isotope will remain after 1 half-life. Choice **b** is incorrect because 25% of the parent isotope will remain after 2 half-lives. Choice **c** is incorrect because 12.5% of the parent isotope will remain after 3 half-lives. Choice **d** is incorrect because 6.25% of the parent isotope will remain after 4 half-lives.

10. c. After three half-lives, 12.5% of the original parent isotope will remain. So, 20 grams $\times$ 0.125 = 2.5 grams will remain. Choice **a** is incorrect because 10 grams will remain after 1 half-life. Choice **b** is incorrect because 5 grams will remain after 2 half-lives. Choice **d** is incorrect because 1.25 grams will remain after 4 half-lives. Choice **e** is incorrect because 0.625 grams will remain after 5 half-lives.

11. b. The cell shown is a plant cell because it has a cell wall, chloroplasts, one large vacuole, and a true nucleus. These are defining features of a plant cell. Choice **a** is incorrect because animal cells do not have cell walls or chloroplasts. Choice **c** is incorrect because bacteria do not have a true nucleus. Choice **d** is incorrect because viruses are mainly genetic material surrounded by a protein envelope. Choice **e** is incorrect because the figure shown is a plant cell.

12. d. The nucleus contains the main DNA of the organism's genome. The mitochondrion and chloroplast also contain their own DNA, and are capable of synthesizing some of their own proteins. Choice **a** is incorrect because the mitochondrion and chloroplast also contain DNA. Choice **b** is incorrect because the chloroplast also contains DNA. Choice **c** is incorrect because the mitochondrion also contains DNA. Choice **e** is incorrect because the nucleus also contains DNA.

13. e. The cell shown must be eukaryotic because it contains a nucleus. Prokaryotic cells do not have true nuclei. Choices **a**, **b**, and **c** are incorrect because the cell has a nucleus and is therefore not a prokaryotic cell. Choice **d** is incorrect because prokaryotic cells may also have a cell wall.

14. d. A plant cell is typically between 10 and 100 micrometers. It is definitely smaller than 10–100 meters (choice **a**), 10–100 centimeters (choice **b**), and 10–100 millimeters (choice **c**). Choice **e** is incorrect because a plant cell is larger than 10–100 nanometers.

15. c. For a molecule to move freely across the plasma membrane, it must be hydrophobic. Hydrophobic molecules dissolve through the lipid bilayer with ease. Choices **a** and **b** are incorrect because charged molecules are impeded by the hydrophobic core of the membrane. Choice **d** is incorrect because hydrophilic molecules are impeded by the hydrophobic core of the membrane. Choice **e** is incorrect because there is not enough information given to determine the exact type of molecule.

16. e. A transport protein is a protein embedded in a membrane that allows molecules that cannot freely diffuse across the membrane to pass through. Choice **a** is incorrect because a first messenger is a substrate that causes a chain reaction within a cell. Choice **b** is incorrect because a second messenger is a molecule that is involved in a series of reactions within a cell. Choice **c** is incorrect because phospholipids compose each of the two layers of the membrane, and the molecule shown spans both layers. Choice **d** is incorrect because fatty acids line the inner portion of the plasma membrane, and the molecule shown spans the membrane bilayer.

17. a. Symport refers to the mutual passage of two substances across a membrane in the same direction. Choice **b** is incorrect because antiport refers to two substances moving in opposite directions across a membrane. Choice **c** is incorrect because the molecules are not diffusing across the membrane; they are helped across by a transport protein. Choice **d** is incorrect because osmosis refers to the diffusion of water across a membrane. Choice **e** is incorrect because endocytosis involves the engulfing of a particle by a portion of the plasma membrane to form a vesicle.

18. b. Antiport refers to two substances moving in opposite directions across a membrane. Choice **a** is incorrect because symport refers to the mutual passage of two substances across a membrane in the same direction. Choice **c** is incorrect because the molecules are not diffusing across the membrane; they are helped across by a transport protein. Choice **d** is incorrect because osmosis refers to the diffusion of water across a membrane. Choice **e** is incorrect because endocytosis involves the engulfing of a particle by a portion of the plasma membrane to form a vesicle.

19. a. A receptor molecule on the membrane binds with a signal molecule (or first messenger) in a second messenger cascade. Choice **b** is incorrect because a G-protein carries a GTP (or GDP). Choice **c** is incorrect because phospholipids in the membrane bilayer are not directly involved in signal transduction pathways. Choice **d** is incorrect because fatty acids in the membrane bilayer are not directly involved in signal transduction pathways. Choice **e** is incorrect because the protein in the figure is not transporting any molecule into or out of the cell.

20. b. G-proteins are sometimes associated with receptor proteins and use GTP to conduct a signal through the cell. Choice **a** is incorrect because the signal molecule binds directly to the receptor, not the G-protein. Phospholipids (choice **c**) and fatty acids (choice **d**) in the membrane bilayer are not directly involved in signal transduction pathways. Choice **e** is incorrect because the protein in the figure is not transporting any molecule into or out of the cell.

21. d. GTP and ATP donate a phosphate group to become GDP or ADP in many cellular reactions. Choice **a** is incorrect because GTP can also donate a phosphate group. Choice **b** is incorrect because ATP can also donate a phosphate group. Choice **c** is incorrect because the signal molecule is not within the cell and so could not phosphorylate a molecule within the cell. Choice **e** is incorrect because the signal molecule is not within the cell and so could not phosphorylate a molecule within the cell, and because ATP can also donate a phosphate group.

22. c. In incomplete dominance, heterozygotes will have a phenotype that is a blended version of both of the two homozygotic phenotypes. In this case, it will have petals that are a midway point between red and white, or pink petals. Choice **a** is incorrect because only the homozygous dominant flowers will have red petals. Choice **b** is incorrect because only the homozygous recessive flowers will have white petals. Choice **d** is incorrect because there is no combination that will produce blue flowers, as no blue or blue variant allele is mentioned in the cross. Choice **e** is incorrect because there is no indication that any flowers will not have petals.

23. d. The homozygous dominant (FF) flowers will be red, the heterozygous (Ff) flowers will be pink, and the homozygous recessive (ff) flowers will be white. As shown in the Punnett square, the ratios will be 1:2:1. Choices **a**, **b**, **c**, and **e** are incorrect because there are three different phenotypes possible.

24. a. The right atrium is located in the upper right quadrant of the heart. On paper, the right atrium is on the left. Choice **b** is incorrect because structure B represents the right ventricle. Choice **c** is incorrect because structure C represents the left atrium. Choice **d** is incorrect because structure D represents the left ventricle. Choice **e** is incorrect because the aorta is a major artery, not a chamber of the heart.

25. b. The right ventricle is located in the lower right quadrant of the heart. Choice **a** is incorrect because structure A represents the right atrium. Choice **c** is incorrect because structure C represents the left atrium. Choice **d** is incorrect because structure D represents the left ventricle. Choice **e** is incorrect because the aorta is a major artery, not a chamber of the heart.

26. c. The left atrium is located in the upper left quadrant of the heart. Choice **a** is incorrect because structure A represents the right atrium. Choice **b** is incorrect because structure B represents the right ventricle. Choice **d** is incorrect because structure D represents the left ventricle. Choice **e** is incorrect because the aorta is a major artery, not a chamber of the heart.

27. d. The left ventricle is located in the lower left quadrant of the heart. Choice **a** is incorrect because structure A represents the right atrium. Choice **b** is incorrect because structure B represents the right ventricle. Choice **c** is incorrect because structure C represents the left atrium. Choice **e** is incorrect because the aorta is a major artery, not a chamber of the heart.

28. e. The desert biome is characterized by very low precipitation and low, scattered vegetation. Choice **a** is incorrect because the tundra biome is characterized by a layer of frozen earth called permafrost. Choice **b** is incorrect because the tropical forest biome is characterized by thick forests of tall trees. Choice **c** is incorrect because a broadleaf forest is characterized by a highly diverse and layered forest. Choice **d** is incorrect because the grassland biome is characterized by mainly low-growing vegetation.

29. d. The grassland biome is characterized by mainly low-growing vegetation, as shown in the figure. Choice **a** is incorrect because the tundra biome is characterized by a layer of frozen earth called permafrost. Choice **b** is incorrect because the tropical forest biome is characterized by thick forests of tall trees. Choice **c** is incorrect because a broadleaf forest is characterized by a highly diverse and layered forest. Choice **e** is incorrect because the desert biome is characterized by very low precipitation and low, scattered vegetation, including cacti.

30. e. Myelin works to accelerate signals through neurons, so damage to the myelin will cause impulses to slow down.

31. b. The optic nerve carries nerve signals between the eye and the brain. A person with blurry vision would be expected to have a "short" in this circuit, so the correct answer is **b**. Choice **a** is incorrect because MRIs do not give information about nerve impulse speeds. Choice **c** is incorrect because visual stimuli are not transmitted to the cerebellum. Choice **d** is incorrect because the spinal cord is not involved in the visual pathway. Choice **e** is incorrect because plaques on an MRI are a classic manifestation of MS.

32. c. The myelin sheath surrounds the neuron and insulates the action potential as it moves along the length of the axon. Choice **a** is incorrect because neurotransmitters are released by the synaptic vesicles. Choice **b** is incorrect because receptors in the dendrites bind to neurotransmitters. Choice **d** is incorrect because myelin is not contained within a certain functional region of the nervous system. Choice **e** is incorrect because myelin is not contained within a certain functional region of the nervous system.

33. c. Nondisjunction is the term used for the phenomenon where chromosomes do not separate during meiosis, leading to trisomy. Choices **a** and **d** are incorrect because Down syndrome is not caused by an individual gene, but by the inclusion of an entire extra chromosome in the genome. Choice **b** is incorrect because there is no information in the passage to indicate that premature birth is related to Down syndrome. In fact, Down syndrome may be detected in certain prenatal tests. Choice **e** is incorrect because a frameshift mutation refers to the insertion or deletion of a nucleotide.

34. a. Aneuploidy refers to the condition of having one or more extra or deficient chromosomes in a genome. Choice **b** is incorrect because polyploidy refers to the condition of having more than two complete sets of chromosomes. Choice **c** is incorrect because linked genes refers to any genes that appear on the same chromosome. Choice **d** is incorrect because a silent mutation is one that has no apparent effect on an organism. Choice **e** is incorrect because a sex-linked trait is one that is coded by a gene on the X or Y chromosome.

35. d. The inclusion of an entire extra chromosome is a fairly serious mutation, and in most cases would be too severe for the fetus to survive. Choice **a** is incorrect because each chromosome is equally common, as the standard human genome has 46 chromosomes. Choice **b** is incorrect because chromosome 21 is not a sex chromosome, only the X and Y chromosomes are sex chromosomes. Choice **c** is incorrect because trisomy 21 causes cognitive difficulty and other unfavorable symptoms. Choice **e** is incorrect because there is no indication that chromosome 21 is more susceptible to point mutations, and because trisomy is not a point mutation.

36. b. The tropical forest biome is characterized by thick forests of tall trees and heavy rainfall. Choice **a** is incorrect because the tundra biome is characterized by a layer of frozen earth called permafrost. Choice **c** is incorrect because a broadleaf forest is characterized by a highly diverse and layered forest. Choice **d** is incorrect because the grassland biome is characterized by mainly low-growing vegetation. Choice **e** is incorrect because the desert biome is characterized by very low precipitation and low, scattered vegetation including cacti.

37. b. Natural selection involves inherited traits, not features that develop over the course of an organism's life. (The idea that natural selection involved acquired traits was theorized by Lamarck.) Choice **a** is incorrect because natural selection requires a large population so that substantial variation and competition can distinguish between advantageous and less favorable traits. Choice **c** is incorrect because certain traits cannot rise up above others unless there is variation among traits. Choice **d** is incorrect because evolution occurs as natural selection causes populations to preferentially retain favorable traits in successive generations. Choice **e** is incorrect because "survival of the fittest" is a common phrase used to summarize the concept of natural selection.

38. b. Mitochondrial DNA is especially useful in tracking evolutionary relatedness because it shows clear differences over short periods of evolutionary time.

39. d. Ribosomes are the site of translation and protein synthesis in the cell. Chloroplasts (choice **a**), the plasma membrane (choice **b**), the vacuole (choice **c**), and the Golgi apparatus (choice **d**) are not involved in protein synthesis.

40. c. A plant cell will absorb water and swell, increasing the turgor pressure inside the cell. Choice **a** is incorrect because the cell wall prevents a plant cell from bursting. Choice **b** is incorrect because water will be absorbed, so the cell will swell. Choice **d** is incorrect because water is beneficial, not toxic, to a plant cell. Choice **e** is incorrect because water would not affect cell division in any way.

41. b. Osmosis is the diffusion of water through a cell wall or membrane or any partially permeable barrier from a solution of low solute concentration to a solution with high solute concentration.

42. b. In the lysogenic cycle, viral DNA is incorporated into the host DNA, where it can remain dormant indefinitely. Under favorable conditions, the virus will then break out of the cell. Choice **a** is incorrect because there is no period of dormancy in the lytic cycle. Choice **c** is incorrect because phagocytosis is the uptake of a large substance by a cell. This is accomplished by the plasma membrane surrounding the substance and forming a vesicle around it. Choice **d** is incorrect because abscission refers to a plant process by which leaves or petals are shed. Choice **e** is incorrect because respiration can refer to either a cell's ATP-forming process (cellular respiration) or the physiological process of gas exchange.

43. b. Introns are spliced out of an mRNA molecule before translation. Choice **a** is incorrect because exons are the functional, coding regions of DNA. Choice **c** is incorrect because stop codons are codons that signal the end of translation. In the standard genetic code, there are three stop codons: UAG, UAA, and UGA. Choice **d** is incorrect because an operator is a section of DNA that regulatory proteins can bind to in order to mediate transcription. Choice **e** is incorrect because amino acids are not part of DNA.

44. e. The heart is the central part of the circulatory system. Choice **a** is incorrect because the esophagus moves food from the mouth to the stomach. Choice **b** is incorrect because the stomach churns food and moves it between the esophagus and small intestine. Choice **c** is incorrect because the small intestine processes food and absorbs nutrients. Choice **d** is incorrect because the large intestine further processes food and absorbs water.

45. b. Sepals are small leaf-like structures that enclose buds before blooming. Choice **a** is incorrect because petals are colorful structures usually designed to attract pollinators. Choice **c** is incorrect because stamens are the male reproductive structures of the plant. Choice **d** is incorrect because pistils are the female reproductive structures of the plant. Choice **e** is incorrect because the stem is the supporting structure of the plant containing vascular tubes for water and nutrient transport.

46. a. The mother passes along an X chromosome to her son, and the father passes along a Y chromosome. Because sex-linked traits are usually coded by genes on the X chromosome, these traits come from a maternal gene.

47. b. A man with type O blood has the genotype OO. A woman with type A blood can either have the genotype AO or AA. So there are two possible crosses:

	A	O
O	AO	OO
O	AO	OO

Or

	A	A
O	AO	AO
O	AO	AO

So, the possible genotypes of the child are AO or OO, which correspond to type A or type O blood. So, the only statement that is necessarily true is **b**.

48. c. Algae and other photosynthetic organisms that drift on the surface of water are called phytoplankton. Choice **a** is incorrect because consumers are heterotrophs. Choice **b** is incorrect because fungi are heterotrophs. Choice **d** is incorrect because angiosperms are flowering plants. Choice **e** is incorrect because viruses are not autotrophs.

49. b. Respiration is the process by which organic molecules and oxygen are used to produce energy in the form of ATP. Choice **a** is incorrect because photosynthesis is the process by which light energy is used to produce organic nutrients. Choice **c** is incorrect because circulation usually refers to the heart's pumping of blood through arteries and veins of the body. Choice **d** is incorrect because the Calvin cycle is a stage of photosynthesis. Choice **e** is incorrect because transcription is the cellular process that produces a complementary strand of mRNA from a strand of DNA.

50. e. Translation refers to the process by which polypeptide chains are created from RNA molecules. Choice **a** is incorrect because in specialized transduction, adjacent bacterial genes are transferred from one bacterial cell to another when a virus exits a host cell. Choice **b** is incorrect because in generalized transduction, bacterial genes are randomly transferred from one bacterial cell to another when a virus exits a host cell. Choice **c** is incorrect because in transformation, foreign DNA from the surrounding environment is incorporated into a bacterial genome. Choice **d** is incorrect because in conjugation, two adjoined bacterial cells swap genetic material directly between them.

51. b. Alligators are cold-blooded reptiles, not mammals. Humans (choice **a**) and tigers (choice **d**) give birth to live young and are warm-blooded vertebrates of the mammal class. Choice **c** is incorrect because whales are aquatic members of the mammal class. Choice **e** is incorrect because kangaroos are marsupials, which is a subset of animals in the mammal class.

52. c. Choices **a** and **d** are incorrect because energy is eventually dissipated into an ecosystem as heat. Choice **b** is incorrect because solar energy is where energy originates, but energy is eventually dissipated into an ecosystem as heat. Choice **e** is incorrect because glucose is the nutrient that is produced by autotrophs through solar energy.

53. a. Biomass is the fundamental amount of organic matter in an ecosystem. Because producers are the primary source of organic nutrients (as they create organic molecules from solar energy), these organisms have the highest biomass.

54. b. Imprinting refers to learned behaviors that are acquired during a limited "critical period" of an organism's life, after which the organism loses the ability to learn these behaviors. Choice **a** is incorrect because natural selection is the phenomenon where beneficial attributes are passed on to generations at a higher frequency than non-beneficial attributes. Choice **c** is incorrect because adaptive radiation refers to evolution that creates various species from a single ancestral species. Choice **d** is incorrect because instinct refers to inborn behaviors that organisms do not need to learn. Choice **e** is incorrect because genetic drift refers to variations in gene frequency between generations that is due to chance.

55. c. Carbon dioxide absorbs infrared radiation in the atmosphere, which contributes to the warming of Earth that is referred to as the greenhouse effect. Choice **a** is incorrect because punctuated equilibrium is an evolutionary trend in history, not a factor in global warming. Choice **b** is incorrect because migration generally has no effect on the atmosphere that would lead to a greenhouse effect. Choice **d** is incorrect because the movement of plates in the Earth does not affect the atmosphere or contribute to the greenhouse effect. Choice **e** is incorrect because the Hardy-Weinberg equilibrium is a method of calculating allele frequencies.

56. c. Biogeochemical cycles, such as the carbon cycle or nitrogen cycle, change chemical nutrients into different forms that are recycled in an ecosystem. Choice **a** is incorrect because pollution is a negative effect on the environment, whereas biogeochemical cycles are useful processes in ecosystems. Choice **b** is incorrect because sexual reproduction is a way of adding variation to a population, but does not directly cycle chemical nutrients. Choice **d** is incorrect because active transport refers to cellular processes that use ATP to move molecules against concentration gradients. Choice **e** is incorrect because circadian rhythms are 24-hour cycles in organisms.

57. c. A mother contributes half of her genetic material to a son, so their coefficient of relatedness is 0.5.

58. a. The ozone layer protects the Earth from UV radiation. Preserving the ozone layer is essential to keeping these harmful rays out. Choice **b** is incorrect because the sun is the source of various forms of radiation. Choice **c** is incorrect because the oceans do not protect the Earth from UV radiation. Choice **d** is incorrect because continental drift refers to the movement of land masses into the continents of the Earth today. Choice **e** is incorrect because evolution is the process by which a variety of species arise from ancestral species to adapt to a specific environment.

59. c. A movement corridor is a space between two regions through which organisms may migrate. Choice **a** is incorrect because a biome is a major ecosystem of the Earth. Choice **b** is incorrect because an ecosystem is the collection of the living and non-living factors that interact in a region. Choice **d** is incorrect because a biogeochemical cycle is a process through which chemical nutrients are recycled in an ecosystem. Choice **e** is incorrect because a niche is the specific role that an organism plays in an ecosystem.

60. b. The carrying capacity of a habitat is the point where populations are at their maximum and thus, tend to remain stable once reaching this level. Choice **a** is incorrect because this describes the actual area where a population exists. Choice **c** is incorrect because reproduction isolation refers to a method that distinguishes species and may lead to natural selection and evolution. Choice **d** is incorrect because a half-life is the amount of time it takes for an isotope to decay to half its mass. Choice **e** is incorrect because biotic potential is not used to describe the carrying capacity of a habitat.

61. e. The moon rotates once a month on its axis. Choice **a** is incorrect because Earth does not revolve around the moon. Choice **b** is incorrect because Earth rotates on its axis once a day. Choice **c** is incorrect because the moon revolves around Earth once a month. Choice **d** is incorrect because the moon rotates on its axis once a month.

62. d. The core and photosphere average temperatures correspond to the hottest and coolest temperatures listed, which are *1* and *3*. Choice **a** is incorrect because *1* is the hottest temperature listed, but *4* is not the coolest, which is the photosphere. Choice **b** is incorrect because 3 and 4 correspond to the chromosphere and the photosphere. Choice **c** is incorrect because *2* corresponds to the temperature of the corona, not the core, which is the hottest. Choice **e** corresponds to the temperatures of the corona and the photosphere, not the core and the photosphere.

63. b. The actual relative brightness of the two stars is only their apparent brightness when viewed from Earth. Choice **a** is incorrect because the absolute brightness can be determined only by looking at other physical data related to the star's features, e.g., age, distance, etc. Choices **c**, **d**, and **e** are incorrect, even though all three factors are used to determine a star's absolute brightness relative to another star.

64. c. The main asteroid belt lies between Mars and Jupiter.

65. c. A star on the curve to the left of point *Y* would be lighter and older. Choice **a** is incorrect because a star at point *Y* would not be heavier, lighter, older, or younger. Choices **b**, **d**, and **e** are incorrect because they represent points that correspond to stars that are heavier and younger.

66. e. The antumbra is the part of the moon's shadow that extends beyond the umbra. Choice **a** is incorrect because it is the umbra. Choice **b** is incorrect because the umbra and the antumbra are distinct regions. Choice **c** is incorrect because regions *A, B,* and *C* include the penumbra (*B* and *C*) and the umbra (*A*). Choice **d** is incorrect because regions *B* and *C* are the penumbra.

67. b. Planet *W* rotates six times faster than Planet *Y* on its axis. Planet *W* rotates six times on its axis in the time that it takes Planet *Y* to rotate once on its axis (30 Earth days). Choice **a** is incorrect based on the data in the table—$500 \times 2 = 1,000$. Choice **c** is incorrect because Planet *W* rotates six times on its axis in the time that it takes Planet *Y* to rotate once on its axis (30 Earth days). Choice **d** is incorrect because Planet *W* rotates faster on its axis than the other three planets. Choice **e** is incorrect because Planet *W* moves faster in its orbit than the other three planets—5×10^8 kilometers per revolutions versus 3×10^8 kilometers per revolutions, $\approx 2.2 \times 10^8$ kilometers per revolutions, and $\approx 2.1 \times 10^8$ kilometers per revolutions, respectively.

68. d. The distance from Earth to Planet *G*, about 1.35×10^{17} meters, is greater than the distance from Earth to Planet *C* (about 1.25×10^{17} meters) or Earth to Planet *D* (about 1×10^{17} meters). Because the speed of light is constant, the time required for it to travel between the two planets would be proportional to the distances between them. Choices **a** and **e** are incorrect because they do not include Earth. Choices **b** and **c** are incorrect because both are less than the distance from Earth to Planet *G*, and therefore, the time required for light to travel between them would be less than the time required for light to travel from Earth to Planet *G*.

69. d. The orbital eccentricity is a measure of how closely a comet's orbit approximate a circle, with a perfect circular shape having an orbital eccentricity of one. Choice **a** is incorrect because its orbit is the second most eccentric, not the most eccentric. Choice **b** is incorrect because its orbit is the second most circular of the eccentricities listed. Choice **c** is incorrect because its orbit is the most circular of the eccentricities listed. Choice **e** is incorrect because its orbital eccentricity is neither the most nor the least eccentric of those listed.

70. d. By Kepler's Law of Areas, the minimum orbital velocity occurs at aphelion. Choices **a** and **b** are incorrect because the mean orbital velocity is an average velocity for any orbital position. Choice **c** is incorrect because the maximum orbital velocity occurs at perihelion, not at aphelion. Choice **e** is incorrect because the aphelion and the perihelion are both distance measurements.

71. a. Aluminum combines with oxygen to produce a material with different chemical properties than its constituent materials. Choices **b**, **c**, **d**, and **e** are all physical changes—alloys, polishing, rolling, and changes of phase.

72. c. Choice **c** is the most likely answer because the water bottle's shape (volume) changes when it is taken off of the airplane and on to the concourse, assuming that the temperature stays about the same. Choice **a** is incorrect because it is only one of two factors that most likely change. Choice **b** is incorrect because pressure most likely changes, but not temperature in a jetway. Choice **d** is incorrect because temperature most likely stays roughly constant from the plane into the jetway and on to the concourse. Choice **e** is incorrect because the volume (shape) of the container changes, but most likely the temperature does not change in the given scenario.

73. b. Be is only one atom. Choices **a**, **c**, **d**, and **e** are incorrect because all are molecules.

74. c. The answer is based on the combined gas law. Choice **a** is incorrect because heating a fixed volume of gas would result in an increase in pressure, not a decrease. Choices **b** and **d** are incorrect because an increase (i.e., addition) or a decrease (i.e., subtraction) of 10° in temperature does not correspond to a corresponding tenfold increase or decrease in pressure according to the combined gas law. Choice **e** is incorrect because an increase in temperature of a gas at a constant volume will result in an increase in pressure according to the combined gas law.

75. d. Choice **d** is not supported by the table; pressure appears to be directly related to solubility. Choices **a**, **b**, **c**, and **e** are incorrect because they are supported by the table.

76. c. The positive and negative charges add up to zero. Choices **a**, **b**, **d**, and **e** are incorrect because the total positive charges and the total negative charges do not add up to zero.

77. e. This choice gives the same number of Al, O, and S atoms on each side of the equation. Choices **a**, **b**, **c**, and **d** are incorrect because they give different numbers of Al, O, and/or S atoms on each side of the equation.

78. a. The same number of Mg, C, and O atoms appear on each side of the equation. Choices **b**, **c**, **d**, and **e** are incorrect because different numbers of Mg, C, and/or O atoms appear on each side of the equation.

79. c. The gram atomic weight of ammonia is 14 plus three or 17; because 28 grams is twice the gram atomic weight of nitrogen, the mass of ammonia produced is two times 17 or 34 grams. Choice **a** is incorrect because 17 is the gram atomic weight of *one* mole of ammonia, not two. Choice **b** is incorrect because the mass of ammonia produced is not equal to twice the gram atomic weight of nitrogen. Choice **d** is incorrect because the mass of ammonia produced is not equal to sum of the gram atomic weights of hydrogen and nitrogen in the reaction. Choice **e** is incorrect because the amount of ammonia produced is not equal to twice the gram atomic weight of nitrogen.

80. e. The difference between K_{eq} and Q_i is the smallest (0.01) for all of the sets of concentrations. Choices **a**, **b**, **c**, and **d** are incorrect because in each case $Q_i < K_{eq}$, and the difference between K_{eq} and Q_i is greater than that for choice **e**.

81. b. An ampere is defined as one coulomb per second. Choice **a** is incorrect because a coulomb is the quantity of charge. Choice **c** is incorrect because the ohm is a unit of electrical resistance. Choice **d** is incorrect because a volt is a unit of electromotive force. Choice **e** is incorrect because the watt is a unit of power.

82. d. The conventional current flow is from Y to X in order to produced a magnetic field that is directed counterclockwise as shown. Choices **a**, **c**, and **e** are incorrect because the magnetic field lines do not extend to or from points W or Z. Choice **b** is incorrect because the electron flow is flow X to Y, not the conventional current flow.

83. a. $C = \frac{Q}{V}$, where C is capacitance, Q is charge, and V is voltage. Choices **b**, **c**, and **d** are incorrect because capacitance is not directly proportional to voltage. Choice **e** is incorrect because capacitance is not inversely proportional to charge.

84. e. An alternating current circuit's resonance frequency is inversely proportional to the square root of the product of the circuit's capacitance and inductance. Choices **a** and **c** are incorrect because both are a necessary but not a sufficient condition to determine the resonant frequency. Choice **b** and **e** are incorrect because current is not a factor in the resonant frequency of an LC circuit.

85. d. The *RMS* voltage is about 0.7 of the peak current or voltage. Choice **a** is incorrect because the horizontal distance *BE* corresponds to a net current or voltage of zero. Choice **b** is incorrect because *AB* corresponds to the peak positive current or voltage. Choice **c** is incorrect because it corresponds to the peak-to-peak current or voltage. Choice **e** corresponds to the average voltage, which is about 0.6 of the peak current or voltage.

86. c. The current falls to half of its initial value between 0 and 1 second, and to one-fourth of its initial value between 1 and 2 seconds. Choice **a** is incorrect because the current only falls to about a third of its initial value after 1 second. Choices **b**, **d**, and **e** are incorrect because the current falls from about a third of its initial value to smaller fractions of its initial value.

87. e. The total capacitance of capacitors in parallel is the sum of the capacitances of the individual capacitors. Choice **a** is incorrect because the total capacitance is not calculated by subtracting the capacitances of the individual capacitors. Choices **b**, **c**, and **d** are incorrect because they assume that the total capacitance is the reciprocal of the sum of the reciprocals of the capacitances of the individual capacitors; they also make errors in calculating the total capacitance under this assumption.

88. e. The ease with which a magnetic field can be established in the five materials is from the greatest magnetic field strength to the least. Choice **a** is incorrect because the order is from least to greatest. Choice **b** is incorrect because the materials with the greatest magnetic field strengths are listed after those with the least. Choices **c** and **d** are incorrect because the materials are ordered based on the magnitude of the significant digit in front of the power of ten.

89. d. The charge time is the product of the capacitance and the resistance; 1 mega ohm times 5 microfarads is 5 seconds, because the product of the "mega" (10^6) and the "micro" (10^{-6}) prefixes equals one. Choice **a** is incorrect because the product of the "mega" (10^6) and the "micro" (10^{-6}) prefixes does not equal zero. Choices **b** and **e** are incorrect because the time constant is not found by dividing the resistance by the capacitance. Choice **c** is incorrect because the time constant is not found by subtracting ohms from the capacitance.

90. b. The turns ratio is the square root of the ratio of the source impedance to the load impedance. The load impedance of both speakers is $\frac{(16 + 16)}{(16)(16)}$, or 8 ohms; so the turns ratio is the square root of $\frac{8}{24}$ or $\frac{1}{3}$, which reduces to $\frac{\sqrt{3}}{3}$. Choices **c**, **d**, and **e** are incorrect because a step-down transformer has a turns ratio that is less than one. Choice **a** is incorrect because the turns ratio is equal to the $\frac{\sqrt{3}}{3}$ not $\frac{1}{3}$.

91. b. Convection currents result from the transfer of heat from Earth's core to the mantle. Choices **a** and **c** are incorrect because they are not the cause of the movement of material in Earth's mantle, even though are means of heat transfer. Choices **d** and **e** are incorrect because they are not heat-transfer mechanisms in Earth's interior.

92. b. The Mesozoic era is made up of the Cretaceous, Jurassic, and Triassic periods. Choice **a** is incorrect; of the three periods listed, only the Cretaceous period belongs to the Mesozoic era. Choice **c** is incorrect; of the three periods listed, only the Triassic period belong to the Mesozoic era. Choice **d** is incorrect because the Ordovician period does not belong to the Mesozoic era. Choice **e** is incorrect because none of the three periods belong to the Mesozoic era.

93. c. An isometric crystalline structure is one with three congruent axes of symmetry that are orthogonal, which are characteristics of a cubic structure. Choice **a** is incorrect because a tetragonal system has one axis of symmetry that is not congruent with the other two. Choice **b** is incorrect because a monoclinic system has three axes of symmetry of unequal length. Choice **d** is incorrect because a hexagonal system has six axes of symmetry. Choice **e** is incorrect because an amorphous substance has no crystalline structure.

94. b. Geologic contour maps do not provide any information about surface or interior rock types of a particular locale. Choices **a, c, d,** and **e** are incorrect because all four types of information can be read or calculated from a geologic contour map.

95. b. The dotted and solid lines show igneous, metamorphic, and sedimentary rock changing into sediment. Choices **a** and **e** are incorrect because igneous and sedimentary rock are only two of three rocks that can change directly into sediment. Choice **c** is incorrect because magma does not change directly into sediment. Choice **d** is incorrect because metamorphic and sedimentary rock are only two of the three rocks that can change directly into sediment.

96. d. Those regions are "P wave shadow zones," because P waves are reflected off the core-mantle boundary at certain angles. Choice **a** is incorrect because W is only one of two regions through which P waves are not passing. Choices **b, c,** and **e** are incorrect because P waves pass through regions X and Y.

97. c. The lowest value of basalt's silica composition range is the lowest of the ranges of the four types of volcanic rock listed. Choices **a, b, d,** and **e** are incorrect because the lowest values of their silica composition ranges are greater than that of basalt.

98. a. The arrival of the S waves (larger amplitude) begins 7 minus 4 or 3 seconds after the first P wave arrives at 4 seconds. Choice **b** is incorrect because no seismic activity is recorded during the first 4 seconds. Choice **c** is incorrect because 5 seconds is the duration of the S wave recording, not a measure of when the event started. Choice **d** is incorrect because it is the sum of the time elapsed before the first P wave is recorded and the time when the first S wave is recorded. Choice **e** is incorrect because it is the sum of the time elapsed before the first P wave is recorded and the duration of the S wave recording, not a measure of when the event started.

99. c. The dip of the fault is 30° and the 2-meter overhang is opposite a 30° angle, which means the slip distance is twice 2 meters or 4 meters. Choice **a** is incorrect because the slip distance is not equal to the overhang. Choice **b** is incorrect because 3.5 meters is the vertical distance from the overhang to the fault interface. Choice **d** is incorrect because the slip distance is not the sum of the vertical distance from the overhang to the fault interface and the amount of overhang. Choice **e** is incorrect because the slip distance is not the sum of the overhang and the slip distance.

100. b. It is most likely to be true, given that harder minerals on the Mohs scale can scratch minerals with lower Mohs numbers. Choices **a**, **c**, and **d** are incorrect because the higher a mineral's Mohs number, the harder it is; harder minerals can scratch softer ones. Choice **e** is incorrect because a mineral with a higher Mohs number is not likely to fracture a mineral with a lower Mohs number. The correct answer is **b** because it matches the explanation described. Also, the statement "W is three times as hard as Z" in **c** is not true from the information given in the table.

101. a. Thermal energy is transferred from the fire to the iron in the solid poker. Choice **b** is incorrect because convection involves the flow of material, not the transfer of heat energy. Choice **c** is incorrect because insulation is the property of a substance that measures its inability to transfer energy. Choice **d** is incorrect because radiation is energy transfer through space, not through matter. Choice **e** is incorrect because specific heat is not an energy-transfer process.

102. d. By dimensional analysis, the measured power carried by the wire, its length, and its temperature are needed to calculate the thermal conductivity. Choice **a** is incorrect because length alone is insufficient information with which to calculate thermal conductivity. Choice **b** is incorrect because length and power are insufficient information with which to calculate thermal conductivity. Choice **c** is incorrect because length and temperature are insufficient information with which to calculate thermal conductivity. Choice **e** is incorrect because the length of the wire is stated as being 10 meters. Therefore, the missing parameters are power and temperature.

103. a. Heat exchange refers to the rate at which heat is transferred into or out of a system, not the quantity of heat in a system or per unit of mass or volume of a material. Choices **b**, **c**, **d**, and **e** all refer to the total quantity of heat or to the quantity of heat per unit mass or volume of a material under static conditions when no heat exchange is taking place.

104. c. The First Law of Thermodynamics states that the change in internal energy (ΔU) of a system is the difference between the heat added to a system and the work done by the system.

105. c. The average kinetic energy of beaker Y is four times that of beaker X; kinetic varies as the square of molecular velocity, of which temperature is the indicator here. Choices **a**, **b**, **d**, and **e** are incorrect because all are true of the average kinetic energy in the beakers in each case; kinetic energy varies linearly with the mass of the liquids and as the square of molecular velocity, of which temperature is the indicator here.

106. a. The specific heat is inversely related to its mass, i.e., Joules per gram-degree Kelvin. Choice **b** is incorrect because it's the reverse—nine times as much energy would be needed to raise the temperature of substance *Z* to the same temperature as substance *X*. Choice **c** is incorrect because it's the reverse order—*Z, Y, X,* and *W*. Choice **d** is incorrect because it's the reverse—25 times as much of substance *W* would be needed for it to achieve the same temperature increase as substance *Z*. Choice **e** is incorrect because substance *Y*'s temperature would be four times that of substance *Z*.

107. c. The liquids with the lowest specific heats would require less energy to raise their temperatures. The relationship between mass, specific heat, and temperature is given by dimensional analysis as

Mass (kg) $\times$ Specific Heat (J/kg–K°) $\times$ Temperature change (K°) = Energy (J).

Choice **a** is incorrect because liquid *Y* would show a greater temperature change than liquid *X*. Choice **b** is incorrect because *Y* has a higher temperature than *X* or *Z*. Choice **d** is incorrect because the temperature increase in *W* is greater than the temperature increase in *X* and *Y*. Choice **e** is incorrect because it lists the liquids in order from the smallest temperature increase to the greatest.

108. e. The total length of the rod is 10 meters plus the expansion, or 10 + (500 − 400) $\times$ 0.0000025 or 10.0025 meters. Choice **a** is incorrect because 0.0025 is the amount of the expansion only and not the total length. Choices **b** and **c** are incorrect because they result from using the temperature of 400 and 500° Kelvin, respectively, as the temperature difference to calculate the amount of the expansion; they also do not include the original length of the rod (10 meters) at 400° Kelvin. Choice **d** is incorrect because the length of the rod at 400° (10 meters) is added to the expansion that would result from a 500° increase in temperature (0.0125 meter), not the temperature difference between 400 and 500° Kelvin.

109. d. The square root of *m* divided by *T* times *k* gives each diffusion rate. Choices **a** and **b** are incorrect because neither *m* divided by *T* times *k* or *T* divided by *m* gives the diffusion rate. Choice **c** is incorrect because the square of the quotient of *m* and *T* does not give the diffusion rate. Choice **e** is incorrect because the square root of *T* divided by *m* does not give the diffusion rate.

110. d. It is not supported by the three values. Choices **a, b, c,** and **e** are all incorrect because they are each supported by the three values.

111. a. Radioactivity is characterized by exponential decay as radioactive nuclei transmute into other elements with an attendant release of energy and other particles. Choices **b, c, d,** and **e** are incorrect because radioactivity is characterized by exponential decay.

112. d. Half-life is the time after which half of the mass of a radioactive element decays into other products. Choice **a** is incorrect because the atomic number is not directly related to the half-life of a radioactive element. Choice **b** is incorrect because half-life is a time concept, not a mass concept. Choice **c** is incorrect because what is described is biological half-life of radioactive elements in a living system, not radioactive half-life. Choice **e** is incorrect because the atomic number of a radioactive element does not change as it decays.

113. d. Fusion is the formation of a new nucleus from the combination of two nuclei. Choice **a** is incorrect because beta decay is the ejection of an electron from a nucleus, which does not involve the creation of new nuclei. Choice **b** is incorrect because radiation is the transfer of energy via electromagnetic waves, not via particles, and does not involve the creation of new nuclei. Choice **c** is incorrect because fission is the splitting of a heavy nucleus into two or more lighter ones with an accompanying release of energy and/or particles. Choice **e** is incorrect because meltdown is a nuclear-energy engineering hazard, and is not the name of the process for nuclear fusion.

114. b. The atomic number (46) is the same for each isotope. Choices **a**, **c**, and **d** are incorrect because the atomic number (46 or 48) is the number of electrons or protons in an isotope, whereas the atomic weight (46 or 48) is the sum of the neutrons and protons, and is greater than the number of electrons in each isotope. Choice **e** is incorrect because the number of electrons in both isotopes of palladium (Pd) is the same, but different from the number of electrons in titanium (Ti).

115. b. Bombardment of a uranium 238 nucleus (atomic number 92) with an alpha particle ($_2^4$ He) could change the uranium to neptunium (atomic number 93) if a hydrogen atom ($_1^1$ H) was also produced in the process. Choice **a** is incorrect because bombardment of a uranium 238 nucleus (atomic number 92) with an alpha particle ($_2^4$ He) would change the uranium to another element with atomic number 93 (neptunium). Choice **c** is incorrect because bombardment of uranium (atomic number 92) with an alpha particle ($_2^4$ He) would increase the atomic number of the resulting product, not decrease it (thorium, atomic number 90). Choice **d** is incorrect because bombardment of uranium (atomic number 92) with an alpha particle ($_2^4$ He) would increase the atomic weight of the resulting product, not decrease it. Choice **e** is incorrect because bombardment of uranium (atomic number 92) with an alpha particle ($_2^4$ He) would increase the atomic number and the atomic weight. Also, the atomic number of thorium is 90, not 92.

116. e. The atom becomes energetic by releasing a photon (energy). Choice **a** is incorrect because the atom would be at a higher energy level if it had absorbed energy. Choices **b** and **d** are incorrect because the energy level diagram does not provide information about gaining or losing electrons. Choice **c** is incorrect because the atom would located on the bottom line of the diagram if it was in a ground state.

117. b. 3.1×10^{10} atoms $\times 3.2 \times 10^{-11}$ watt-seconds ≈ 1 watt-second, by dimensional analysis. One watt-second per second is one watt. Choices **a**, **c**, **d**, and **e** are incorrect because either the arithmetic calculations were done incorrectly or the dimensional analysis was not checked.

118. e. 10^6 doses of an average dose of 40 millirems from the human body would be 4×10^7, which is greater than 5×10^5 millirems. Choices **a–d** are incorrect because the product of the number of doses for each source and the average dose for each source are all less than 5×10^5 millirems.

119. c. 190 grams of copper is about 3 moles of copper. Because each mole contains 6.023×10^{23} atoms, 3 moles of copper would contain 3 times that amount, or about 1.8×10^{24} atoms. Choice **a** is incorrect because the number of atoms is not found by dividing Avogadro's number (6.023×10^{23}) by 190 grams. Choice **b** is incorrect because the number of atoms is not found by dividing Avogadro's number (6.023×10^{23}) by the atomic weight of copper. Choice **d** is incorrect because the number of atoms is not found by multiplying 10^{23} by 190 grams. Choice **e** is incorrect because the number of atoms is not found by multiplying 10^{23} by the atomic weight.

120. a. The total enthalpy of CH_4 is 4×415 or 1,660 kJ and of CO_2 is 2×800 or 1,600 kJ in the latter case. Choice **b** is incorrect because the total enthalpy of CH_4 is 4×415 or 1,660 kJ and of H_2O is 2×465 or 930 kJ. Choice **c** is incorrect because the enthalpy of the bond is greater than that of the other bonds, but not the total enthalpy of the molecules with the greatest enthalpies. Choice **d** is incorrect because the total enthalpy of CO_2 is 2×800 or 1,600 kJ, but the total enthalpy of O_2 is 2×500 or 1,000 kJ. Choice **e** is incorrect because the total enthalpy of H_2O is 2×465 or 930 kJ and that of O_2 is 2×500 or 1,000 kJ.

CLEP Humanities
Practice Test 1

You are now familiar with the kinds of questions and answer formats you will see on the official CLEP Humanities exam. Now take Practice Test 1 to identify any areas that you may need to review in more depth before the test day.

On this practice test, you will encounter 140 questions that are similar to the type you will find on the official CLEP Humanities exam. The questions cover two content areas:

- Literature
- Fine Arts

To simulate the test conditions, use the time constraints of the official CLEP Humanities exam. Allow yourself 90 minutes to complete this practice test.

Remember, on the official CLEP, there is no penalty for incorrect answers, so always make a guess if you are unsure of an answer.

When you are finished, check the answer key on page 695 carefully to assess your results.

▶ CLEP Humanities Practice Test 1

1. ⓐ ⓑ ⓒ ⓓ ⓔ	51. ⓐ ⓑ ⓒ ⓓ ⓔ	101. ⓐ ⓑ ⓒ ⓓ ⓔ
2. ⓐ ⓑ ⓒ ⓓ ⓔ	52. ⓐ ⓑ ⓒ ⓓ ⓔ	102. ⓐ ⓑ ⓒ ⓓ ⓔ
3. ⓐ ⓑ ⓒ ⓓ ⓔ	53. ⓐ ⓑ ⓒ ⓓ ⓔ	103. ⓐ ⓑ ⓒ ⓓ ⓔ
4. ⓐ ⓑ ⓒ ⓓ ⓔ	54. ⓐ ⓑ ⓒ ⓓ ⓔ	104. ⓐ ⓑ ⓒ ⓓ ⓔ
5. ⓐ ⓑ ⓒ ⓓ ⓔ	55. ⓐ ⓑ ⓒ ⓓ ⓔ	105. ⓐ ⓑ ⓒ ⓓ ⓔ
6. ⓐ ⓑ ⓒ ⓓ ⓔ	56. ⓐ ⓑ ⓒ ⓓ ⓔ	106. ⓐ ⓑ ⓒ ⓓ ⓔ
7. ⓐ ⓑ ⓒ ⓓ ⓔ	57. ⓐ ⓑ ⓒ ⓓ ⓔ	107. ⓐ ⓑ ⓒ ⓓ ⓔ
8. ⓐ ⓑ ⓒ ⓓ ⓔ	58. ⓐ ⓑ ⓒ ⓓ ⓔ	108. ⓐ ⓑ ⓒ ⓓ ⓔ
9. ⓐ ⓑ ⓒ ⓓ ⓔ	59. ⓐ ⓑ ⓒ ⓓ ⓔ	109. ⓐ ⓑ ⓒ ⓓ ⓔ
10. ⓐ ⓑ ⓒ ⓓ ⓔ	60. ⓐ ⓑ ⓒ ⓓ ⓔ	110. ⓐ ⓑ ⓒ ⓓ ⓔ
11. ⓐ ⓑ ⓒ ⓓ ⓔ	61. ⓐ ⓑ ⓒ ⓓ ⓔ	111. ⓐ ⓑ ⓒ ⓓ ⓔ
12. ⓐ ⓑ ⓒ ⓓ ⓔ	62. ⓐ ⓑ ⓒ ⓓ ⓔ	112. ⓐ ⓑ ⓒ ⓓ ⓔ
13. ⓐ ⓑ ⓒ ⓓ ⓔ	63. ⓐ ⓑ ⓒ ⓓ ⓔ	113. ⓐ ⓑ ⓒ ⓓ ⓔ
14. ⓐ ⓑ ⓒ ⓓ ⓔ	64. ⓐ ⓑ ⓒ ⓓ ⓔ	114. ⓐ ⓑ ⓒ ⓓ ⓔ
15. ⓐ ⓑ ⓒ ⓓ ⓔ	65. ⓐ ⓑ ⓒ ⓓ ⓔ	115. ⓐ ⓑ ⓒ ⓓ ⓔ
16. ⓐ ⓑ ⓒ ⓓ ⓔ	66. ⓐ ⓑ ⓒ ⓓ ⓔ	116. ⓐ ⓑ ⓒ ⓓ ⓔ
17. ⓐ ⓑ ⓒ ⓓ ⓔ	67. ⓐ ⓑ ⓒ ⓓ ⓔ	117. ⓐ ⓑ ⓒ ⓓ ⓔ
18. ⓐ ⓑ ⓒ ⓓ ⓔ	68. ⓐ ⓑ ⓒ ⓓ ⓔ	118. ⓐ ⓑ ⓒ ⓓ ⓔ
19. ⓐ ⓑ ⓒ ⓓ ⓔ	69. ⓐ ⓑ ⓒ ⓓ ⓔ	119. ⓐ ⓑ ⓒ ⓓ ⓔ
20. ⓐ ⓑ ⓒ ⓓ ⓔ	70. ⓐ ⓑ ⓒ ⓓ ⓔ	120. ⓐ ⓑ ⓒ ⓓ ⓔ
21. ⓐ ⓑ ⓒ ⓓ ⓔ	71. ⓐ ⓑ ⓒ ⓓ ⓔ	121. ⓐ ⓑ ⓒ ⓓ ⓔ
22. ⓐ ⓑ ⓒ ⓓ ⓔ	72. ⓐ ⓑ ⓒ ⓓ ⓔ	122. ⓐ ⓑ ⓒ ⓓ ⓔ
23. ⓐ ⓑ ⓒ ⓓ ⓔ	73. ⓐ ⓑ ⓒ ⓓ ⓔ	123. ⓐ ⓑ ⓒ ⓓ ⓔ
24. ⓐ ⓑ ⓒ ⓓ ⓔ	74. ⓐ ⓑ ⓒ ⓓ ⓔ	124. ⓐ ⓑ ⓒ ⓓ ⓔ
25. ⓐ ⓑ ⓒ ⓓ ⓔ	75. ⓐ ⓑ ⓒ ⓓ ⓔ	125. ⓐ ⓑ ⓒ ⓓ ⓔ
26. ⓐ ⓑ ⓒ ⓓ ⓔ	76. ⓐ ⓑ ⓒ ⓓ ⓔ	126. ⓐ ⓑ ⓒ ⓓ ⓔ
27. ⓐ ⓑ ⓒ ⓓ ⓔ	77. ⓐ ⓑ ⓒ ⓓ ⓔ	127. ⓐ ⓑ ⓒ ⓓ ⓔ
28. ⓐ ⓑ ⓒ ⓓ ⓔ	78. ⓐ ⓑ ⓒ ⓓ ⓔ	128. ⓐ ⓑ ⓒ ⓓ ⓔ
29. ⓐ ⓑ ⓒ ⓓ ⓔ	79. ⓐ ⓑ ⓒ ⓓ ⓔ	129. ⓐ ⓑ ⓒ ⓓ ⓔ
30. ⓐ ⓑ ⓒ ⓓ ⓔ	80. ⓐ ⓑ ⓒ ⓓ ⓔ	130. ⓐ ⓑ ⓒ ⓓ ⓔ
31. ⓐ ⓑ ⓒ ⓓ ⓔ	81. ⓐ ⓑ ⓒ ⓓ ⓔ	131. ⓐ ⓑ ⓒ ⓓ ⓔ
32. ⓐ ⓑ ⓒ ⓓ ⓔ	82. ⓐ ⓑ ⓒ ⓓ ⓔ	132. ⓐ ⓑ ⓒ ⓓ ⓔ
33. ⓐ ⓑ ⓒ ⓓ ⓔ	83. ⓐ ⓑ ⓒ ⓓ ⓔ	133. ⓐ ⓑ ⓒ ⓓ ⓔ
34. ⓐ ⓑ ⓒ ⓓ ⓔ	84. ⓐ ⓑ ⓒ ⓓ ⓔ	134. ⓐ ⓑ ⓒ ⓓ ⓔ
35. ⓐ ⓑ ⓒ ⓓ ⓔ	85. ⓐ ⓑ ⓒ ⓓ ⓔ	135. ⓐ ⓑ ⓒ ⓓ ⓔ
36. ⓐ ⓑ ⓒ ⓓ ⓔ	86. ⓐ ⓑ ⓒ ⓓ ⓔ	136. ⓐ ⓑ ⓒ ⓓ ⓔ
37. ⓐ ⓑ ⓒ ⓓ ⓔ	87. ⓐ ⓑ ⓒ ⓓ ⓔ	137. ⓐ ⓑ ⓒ ⓓ ⓔ
38. ⓐ ⓑ ⓒ ⓓ ⓔ	88. ⓐ ⓑ ⓒ ⓓ ⓔ	138. ⓐ ⓑ ⓒ ⓓ ⓔ
39. ⓐ ⓑ ⓒ ⓓ ⓔ	89. ⓐ ⓑ ⓒ ⓓ ⓔ	139. ⓐ ⓑ ⓒ ⓓ ⓔ
40. ⓐ ⓑ ⓒ ⓓ ⓔ	90. ⓐ ⓑ ⓒ ⓓ ⓔ	140. ⓐ ⓑ ⓒ ⓓ ⓔ
41. ⓐ ⓑ ⓒ ⓓ ⓔ	91. ⓐ ⓑ ⓒ ⓓ ⓔ	
42. ⓐ ⓑ ⓒ ⓓ ⓔ	92. ⓐ ⓑ ⓒ ⓓ ⓔ	
43. ⓐ ⓑ ⓒ ⓓ ⓔ	93. ⓐ ⓑ ⓒ ⓓ ⓔ	
44. ⓐ ⓑ ⓒ ⓓ ⓔ	94. ⓐ ⓑ ⓒ ⓓ ⓔ	
45. ⓐ ⓑ ⓒ ⓓ ⓔ	95. ⓐ ⓑ ⓒ ⓓ ⓔ	
46. ⓐ ⓑ ⓒ ⓓ ⓔ	96. ⓐ ⓑ ⓒ ⓓ ⓔ	
47. ⓐ ⓑ ⓒ ⓓ ⓔ	97. ⓐ ⓑ ⓒ ⓓ ⓔ	
48. ⓐ ⓑ ⓒ ⓓ ⓔ	98. ⓐ ⓑ ⓒ ⓓ ⓔ	
49. ⓐ ⓑ ⓒ ⓓ ⓔ	99. ⓐ ⓑ ⓒ ⓓ ⓔ	
50. ⓐ ⓑ ⓒ ⓓ ⓔ	100. ⓐ ⓑ ⓒ ⓓ ⓔ	

► Practice Test Questions

1. Concrete poetry can be traced back as early as the seventeenth century. Concrete poetry does NOT include
   a. visual words.
   b. cinquain.
   c. squiggly.
   d. shaping.
   e. acrostics.

2. She walks in beauty like the night
   Of cloudless climes and starry skies
   —*She Walks in Beauty*, Lord Byron

   These lines use what figurative technique?
   a. hyperbole
   b. simile
   c. metaphor
   d. personification
   e. onomatopoeia

Use the following passage to answer questions 3 and 4.

DEAR SON: I have ever had pleasure in obtaining any little anecdotes of my ancestors. You may remember the inquiries I made among the remains of my relations when you were with me in England, and the journey I undertook for that purpose. Imagining it may be equally agreeable to you to know the circumstances of my life, many of which you are yet unacquainted with, and expecting the enjoyment of a week's uninterrupted leisure in my present country retirement, I sit down to write them for you. To which I have besides some other inducements. Having emerged from the poverty and obscurity in which I was born and bred, to a state of affluence and some degree of reputation in the world, and having gone so far through life with a considerable share of felicity, the conducing means I made use of, which with the blessing of God so well succeeded, my posterity may like to know, as they may find some of them suitable to their own situations, and therefore fit to be imitated. That felicity, when I reflected on it, has induced me sometimes to say, that were it offered to my choice, I should have no objection to a repetition of the same life from its beginning, only asking the advantages authors have in a second edition to correct some faults of the first. So I might, besides correcting the faults, change some sinister accidents and events of it for others more favorable. But though this were denied, I should still accept the offer. Since such a repetition is not to be expected, the next thing most like living one's life over again seems to be a recollection of that life, and to make that recollection as durable as possible by putting it down in writing.

—*Autobiography of Benjamin Franklin*, Benjamin Franklin

3. In the excerpt, the most plausible writing to follow is a(n)
   a. autobiography.
   b. biography.
   c. letter.
   d. novel.
   e. story.

4. In the passage, the author infers that he
   a. had a perfect life.
   b. regrets a few incidents along the way.
   c. would like to change his life and start over.
   d. all of the above
   e. none of the above

5. What are you able to build with your blocks?
Castles and palaces, temples and docks.
Rain may keep raining, and others go roam,
But I can be happy and building at home.

　　　　　　　—from "Building Blocks" by
　　　　　　　　　Robert Louis Stevenson

This first stanza illustrates the use of
a. rhythm and rhyme.
b. rhyme and repetition.
c. repetition and alliteration.
d. rhythm and alliteration.
e. repetition and assonance.

6. Little brown baby wif spa'klin' eyes,
　　Come to yo' pappy an' set on his knee.
What you been doin,' suh—makin' san' pies?
　　Look at dat bib—you's es du'ty ez me.

　　　　　　　—from "Little Brown Baby"
　　　　　　　　　by Paul Laurence Dunbar

This poem is an example of
a. colloquialism.
b. dialect.
c. jargon.
d. simile.
e. paradox.

7. Once upon a midnight dreary, while I pondered,
　　weak and weary,
　Over many a quaint and curious volume of for-
　　gotten lore,
　While I nodded, nearly napping, suddenly there
　　came a tapping,
　As of some one gently rapping, rapping at my
　　chamber door.
　"'Tis some visitor," I muttered, "tapping at my
　　chamber door—
　Only this, and nothing more."
　　　　　—from "The Raven" by Edgar Allan Poe

Edgar Allan Poe's poem "The Raven" employs
several literary techniques. They include
a. alliteration, assonance, rhyme, and repetition.
b. alliteration, dissonance, rhythm, and
repetition.
c. rhyme, repetition, connotation, and
dissonance.
d. alliteration, consonance, assonance, and
resolution.
e. alliteration, assonance, resolution, and
dissonance.

8. The Romantic period of English literature began
in the
a. late fifteenth century.
b. late sixteenth century.
c. mid-seventeenth century.
d. late eighteenth century.
e. late nineteenth century.

9. Seen my lady home las' night,
   Jump back, honey, jump back.
Hel' huh han' an' sque'z it tight,
   Jump back, honey, jump back.
Hyeahd huh sigh a little sigh
Seen a light gleam f'om huh eye,
An' a smile go flittin' by—
   Jump back, honey, jump back.
                    —from "A Negro Love Song"
                      by Paul Laurence Dunbar

The two major literary techniques the author
uses are
a. alliteration and aphorism.
b. consonance and comedy.
c. personification and parody.
d. irony and personification.
e. rhyme and repetition.

10. Art is long and time is fleeting.
                    —from *A Psalm for Life* by Henry
                      Wordsworth Longfellow

This quotation is an example of
a. hyperbole.
b. metaphor.
c. personification.
d. simile.
e. paradox.

Use the following poem to answer questions 11 and 12.

If ever two were one, then surely we.
If ever man were loved by wife, then thee;
If ever wife was happy in a man,
Compare with me, ye women, if you can.
I prize thy love more than whole mines of gold
Or all the riches that the East doth hold.
My love is such that rivers cannot quench,
Nor ought but love from thee. Give recompense.
Thy love is such I can no way repay,
The heavens reward thee manifold, I pray.
Then while we live, in love let's so persevere
That while we live no more, we may live ever.
                    —"To My Dear and Loving Husband"
                      by Anne Bradstreet

11. The love expressed in this poem is
a. casual.
b. deep.
c. suppressed.
d. repressed.
e. shallow.

12. The word *quench* at the end of line 7 means
a. express.
b. ignite.
c. stimulate.
d. thirst.
e. suppress.

13. Which of the following is NOT an accurate statement about the *Egyptian Book of the Dead*?

  a. The climate in Egypt affected the fate of the *Egyptian Book of the Dead* manuscripts.

  b. The *Egyptian Book of the Dead* describes burial ceremonies.

  c. The *Egyptian Book of the Dead* contains funeral prayers.

  d. The *Egyptian Book of the Dead* explains significance of the pyramids.

  e. Eventually, even the common people had access to the *Egyptian Book of the Dead*.

14. Between the tenth and twelfth centuries in Europe, illuminated manuscripts were often used to

  a. point toward the religious significance of the text.

  b. further explain the meaning of the text.

  c. proclaim the munificence of the patron who funded the manuscript.

  d. emphasize the seriousness of the text's subject matter.

  e. infuse traditionally religious texts with fanciful subject matter.

15. Most illuminated manuscripts pertain to

  a. the passage from life to death.

  b. religion in some way.

  c. mythical and animal figures.

  d. an even mixture of the sacred and the secular.

  e. exotic subject matter.

16. It is reasonable to conclude that a person who studied history of the illuminated manuscript would also learn the most about which of the following?

  a. the history of the Vatican Library

  b. advancements in biology during the same time period

  c. advancements in art during the same time period

  d. the urbanization of Europe after the Middle Ages

  e. fictional accounts written before the invention of the printing press

17. It has been said that the printing press marked the beginning of the end for the illuminated manuscript because

  a. manuscripts could be produced more quickly and in greater numbers by machine than by hand.

  b. mass-produced manuscripts were less expensive than the old illuminated manuscripts.

  c. the less-educated citizenry preferred books that were machine-made.

  d. printed books were less fragile and more portable than illuminated manuscripts.

  e. the printing press for the most part eliminated illiteracy.

Use the following passage to answer questions 18–21.

(1) And the agreement of the law of nature in this our ground with the laws and constitutions of God and man already alleged will by two similitudes easily appear. The king towards his people is rightly com-
(5) pared to a father of children, and to a head of a body composed of diverse members. For as fathers the good princes and magistrates of the people of God acknowledged themselves to their subjects. And for all other well-ruled commonwealths, the
(10) style of Pater patriae (father of his country) was ever and is commonly used to kings. And the proper office of a king towards his subjects agrees very well with the office of the head towards the body and all members thereof. For from the head,
(15) being the seat of judgment, proceedeth the care and foresight of guiding and preventing all evil that may come to the body or any part thereof. The head cares for the body, so doth the king for his people. As the discourse and direction flows from
(20) the head, and the execution according thereunto belongs to the rest of the members, every one according to their office: so is it betwixt a wise prince and his people. As the judgment coming from the head may not only employ the members,
(25) every one in their own office, as long as they are able for it; but likewise, in case any of them affected with any infirmity must care and provide for their remedy, in case it be curable, and if otherwise gar cut them off for fear of infecting the rest: even so is
(30) it betwixt the prince and his people. And as there is ever hope of curing any diseased member by the direction of the head, as long as it is whole; but by the contrary, if it be troubled, all the members are partakers of that pain, so is it betwixt the prince
(35) and his people.

And now first of the father's part (whose natural love to his children I described in the first part of this my discourse, speaking of the duty that kings owe to their subjects), consider, I pray
(40) you, what duty his children owe to him, and whether upon any pretext whatever it will not be thought monstrous and unnatural for his sons to rise up against him, to control him at their appetite, and when they think good to slay him,
(45) or to cut him off, and adopt to themselves any other they please in his room. Or can any pretense of wickedness or rigor on his part be a just excuse for his children to put hand into him? And although we see by the course of nature that
(50) love useth to descend more than to ascend, in case it were true that the father hated and wronged the children never so much, will any man endued with the least sponk of reason think it lawful for them to meet him with the line? Yea,
(55) suppose the father were furiously following his sons with a drawn sword, is it lawful for them to turn and strike again, or make any resistance but by flight? I think surely if there were no more but the example of brute beasts and unreasonable
(60) creatures, it may serve well enough to qualify and prove this my argument. We read often the piety that the storks have to their old and decayed parents: and generally we know that there are many sorts of beasts and fowls that with violence and
(65) many bloody strokes will beat and banish their young ones from them, how soon they perceive them to be able to fend themselves; but we never read nor heard of any resistance on their part, except among the vipers; which proves such per-
(70) sons as ought to be reasonable creatures, and yet unnaturally follow this example, to be endued with their viperous nature.

And for the similitude of the head and the body, it may very well fall out that the head will
(75) be forced to gar cut off some rotten member (as I have already said) to keep the rest of the body in

integrity: but what state the body can be in, if the head for any infirmity that can fall to it be cut off, I leave it to the reader's judgment.

(80)   So as (to conclude this part) if the children may upon any pretext that can be imagined lawfully rise up against their father, cut him off, and choose any other whom they please in his room; and if the body for the weal of it may for an infir-

(85) mity that may be in the head strike it off, then I cannot deny that the people may rebel, control and displace, or cut off their king, at their own pleasure, and upon respects moving them.

　　　　　　　—from *The True Law of Free Monarchies*
　　　　　　　　　　　by King James I

18. In line 14, *members* refers to
   a. body parts.
   b. landowners.
   c. English citizens.
   d. government officials.
   e. members of nobility.

19. The main metaphor in paragraph 3 compares what two things?
   a. the head and the body
   b. the king's subjects and a body
   c. rebellion and disease
   d. the king and a body
   e. loyalty and death

20. In paragraph 2, the author refers to vipers
   a. to argue that a king must defend his beliefs.
   b. to demonstrate that nature supports his argument.
   c. as an example of how humans are superior to nature.
   d. as an example of how nature is superior to humans.
   e. to show exceptions to a behavioral pattern in nature.

21. The main metaphor in paragraph 2 compares what two things?
   a. disease and government
   b. readers and assassins
   c. peasants and beasts
   d. the king and a parent
   e. vipers and storks

22. In 1901, New York City's Broadway area earned the nickname
   a. the Big Apple.
   b. Cement City.
   c. the Strip.
   d. the Melting Pot.
   e. the Great White Way.

23. Which of the following statements about *The Great Train Robbery* is NOT true?
   a. It contains a scene where a cowboy shoots his pistol directly at the camera.
   b. The movie was directed and photographed by Thomas Edison.
   c. There are 14 scenes with parallel cross-cutting between simultaneous events.
   d. It was the first to use modern film techniques, such as using multiple camera positions, filming out of sequence, and later editing the scenes into their proper order.
   e. It was filmed in New Jersey, not in Hollywood.

24. The first feature-length film produced in Europe was
   a. *L'Age d'Or/Un Chien Andalou.*
   b. *A Nous la Liberte.*
   c. *L'Enfant Prodigue.*
   d. *L'Atalante.*
   e. *Ladri di Biciclette.*

Use the following passage to answer questions 25 and 26.

Meditation XVII

(1) Now this bell tolling softly for another, says to
me, Thou must die. Perchance he for whom this
bell tolls may be so ill as that he knows not it tolls
for him; and perchance I may think myself so
(5) much better than I am, as that they who are
about me and see my state may have caused it to
toll for me, and I know not that. The church is
catholic, universal, so are all her actions; all that
she does belongs to all. When she baptizes a
(10) child, that action concerns me; for that child is
thereby connected to that body which is my head
too, and ingrafted into that body whereof I am a
member. And when she buries a man, that action
concerns me: all mankind is of one author and is
(15) one volume; when one man dies, one chapter is
not torn out of the book, but translated into a
better language; and every chapter must be so
translated. God employs several translators;
some pieces are translated by age, some by sick-
(20) ness, some by war, some by justice; but God's
hand is in every translation, and his hand shall
bind up all our scattered leaves again for that
library where every book shall lie open to one
another. As therefore the bell that rings to a ser-
(25) mon calls not upon the preacher only, but upon
the congregation to come, so this bell calls us all;
but how much more me, who am brought so
near the door by this sickness . . . The bell doth
toll for him that thinks it doth; and though it
(30) intermit again, yet from that minute that the
occasion wrought upon him, he is united to God.
Who casts not up his eye to the sun when it rises?
but who takes off his eye from a comet when that
breaks out? Who bends not his ear to any bell
(35) which upon any occasion rings? but who can
remove it from that bell which is passing a piece
of himself out of this world?

No man is an island, entire of itself; every man
is a piece of continent, a part of the main. If a
(40) clod be washed away by the sea, Europe is the
less, as well as if a promontory were, as well as if
a manor of thy friend's or of thine own were. Any
man's death diminishes me because I am
involved in mankind, and therefore never send to
(45) know for whom the bell tolls, it tolls for thee.
Neither can we call this a begging of misery or a
borrowing of misery, as though we were not miserable enough of ourselves but must fetch in
more from the next house, in taking upon us the
(50) misery of our neighbors. Truly it were an excusa-
ble covetousness if we did; for affliction is a treasure, and scarce any man hath enough of it. No
man hath affliction enough that is not matured
and ripened by it and made fit for God by that
(55) affliction . . . Tribulation is treasure in the nature
of it, but it is not current money in the use of it,
except we get nearer and nearer our home,
heaven, by it. Another man may be sick too, and
sick to death, and this affliction may lie in his
(60) bowels as gold in a mine and be of no use to him;
but this bell that tells me of his affliction digs out
and applies that gold to me, if by his consideration of another's danger I take mine own into
contemplation and so secure myself by making
(65) my recourse to my God, who is our only security.

—John Donne

25. All of the following literary devices can be found
in this passage EXCEPT
a. repetition.
b. extended metaphor.
c. contrast.
d. personification.
e. formal diction.

26. John Donne's *Meditation XVII* inspired the novel *For Whom the Bell Tolls* by
   a. C. S. Lewis.
   b. Ernest Hemingway.
   c. Jorge Borges.
   d. Christopher Marlowe.
   e. John Steinbeck.

27. Who is the architect from the Italian Renaissance whose works include the following?
   ▪ dome of the Cathedral of Florence
   ▪ Basilica di San Lorenzo di Firenze
   ▪ lantern of the Florence Cathedral
   a. Donatello
   b. Michelangelo
   c. Lorenzo Ghiberti
   d. Paolo Uccello
   e. Filippo Brunelleschi.

Use the following picture to answer questions 28 and 29.

28. The structure pictured here was built to
   a. provide protection from military invaders to the north.
   b. provide protection from military invaders to the south.
   c. create a tourist attraction that would bring international travelers to China.
   d. protect Beijing from flooding rivers.
   e. create jobs for Chinese masons.

29. All of the following are true about this structure EXCEPT
   a. an estimated two to three million Chinese died as part of the centuries-long project of building it.
   b. it is visible from the moon by the human eye.
   c. signal towers were built upon hill tops or other high points along it.
   d. before the use of bricks, it was mainly built from earth, stones, and wood.
   e. it stretches to more than 6,700 kilometers.

30. According to Roman architect Vitruvius, author of *De architectura*, a good building should satisfy the three principles of *firmitatis, utilitatis,* and *venustatis,* which translates to utility, beauty, and what other principle?
   a. durability
   b. strength
   c. density
   d. power
   e. height

Use the following poem to answer questions 31–35.

The Garden
(1)　How vainly men themselves amaze,
　　To win the palm, the oak, or bays,
　　And their uncessant labors see
　　Crowned from some single herb or tree
(5)　Whose short and narrow-vergèd shade
　　Does prudently their toils upbraid,
　　While all the flowers and trees do close
　　To weave the garlands of repose!

　　Fair Quiet, have I found thee here,
(10)　And Innocence, thy sister dear?
　　Mistaken long, I sought you then
　　In busy companies of men.
　　Your sacred plants, if here below,

Only among the plants will grow;
(15) Society is all but rude
To this delicious solitude.

No white nor red was ever seen
So amorous as this lovely green.
Fond lovers, cruel as their flame,
(20) Cut in these trees their mistress' name.
Little, alas! they know or heed,
How far these beauties hers exceed!
Fair trees! wheres'e'r your barks I wound
No name shall but your own be found.

(25) When we have run our passion's heat,
Love hither makes his best retreat.
The gods, that mortal beauty chase,
Still in a tree did end their race;
Apollo hunted Daphne so,
(30) Only that she might laurel grow;
And Pan did after Syrinx speed,
Not as a nymph, but for a reed.

What wondrous life in this I lead!
Ripe apples drop about my head;
(35) The luscious clusters of the vine
Upon my mouth do crush their wine;
The nectarine, and curious peach,
Into my hands themselves do reach;
Stumbling on melons, as I pass,
(40) Ensnared with flowers, I fall on grass.

Meanwhile the mind, from pleasure less,
Withdraws into its happiness;—
The mind, that ocean where each kind
Does straight its own resemblance find;
(45) Yet it creates, transcending these,
Far other worlds, and other seas,
Annihilating all that's made
To a green thought in a green shade.

Here at the fountain's sliding foot,
(50) Or at some fruit-tree's mossy root,
Casting the body's vest aside,
My soul into the boughs does glide:
There, like a bird, it sits and sings,
Then whets and combs its silver wings,
(55) And, till prepared for longer flight,
Waves in its plumes the various light.

Such was that happy garden-state,
While man there walked without a mate
After a place so pure and sweet.
(60) What other help could yet be meet!
But 't was beyond a mortal's share
To wander solitary there:
Two paradises 't were in one,
To live in paradise alone.

(65) How well the skilful gardener drew
Of flowers, and herbs, this dial new;
Where, from above, the milder sun
Does through a fragrant zodiac run,
And, as it works, th' industrious bee
(70) Computes its time as well as we!
How could such sweet and wholesome hours
Be reckoned but with herbs and flowers?
　　　　　　　　　　　　—Andrew Marvell

31. The first stanza of the poem can be described as
　a. angry.
　b. light-hearted.
　c. apathetic.
　d. melancholy.
　e. resentful.

32. The word *rude* in line 15 suggests that individuals
   a. reject solitude.
   b. have no manners.
   c. are curt to one another.
   d. seek romantic partners and lovers.
   e. appreciate being alone.

33. In the poem, metaphoric significance is NOT given to which of the following?
   a. the ocean
   b. the oak
   c. the laurel
   d. a reed
   e. solitude

34. *Your sacred plants, if here below,*
   Only among the plants will grow

   These lines mean which of the following?
   a. The bond between people grows best in solitude.
   b. Nature is one of civilization's most precious gifts.
   c. The individual soul blossoms when among society's best.
   d. Innocence and quiet grow best amidst nature.
   e. Plants can only grow where other plants already exist.

35. In lines 43–47, the mind is compared to
   a. green shade.
   b. happiness.
   c. an ocean.
   d. apples.
   e. Apollo.

36. Which musician's legacy includes the legend that he met the devil at midnight at a crossroads and sold his soul so that he could play guitar?
   a. Jimi Hendrix
   b. Les Paul
   c. Muddy Waters
   d. Robert Johnson
   e. Ted Nugent

37. The blues is a neologism attributed to what American writer?
   a. Washington Irving
   b. Nathaniel Hawthorne
   c. Langston Hughes
   d. Edgar Allen Poe
   e. Jupiter Hammom

38. The main sentiment listeners should derive from the blues is
   a. melancholy.
   b. resentment.
   c. nostalgia.
   d. purification.
   e. mirth.

39. The blues evolved primarily from
   a. Greek tragedy.
   b. African ceremonies.
   c. urban music venues.
   d. African-American folk music.
   e. religious ceremonies.

40. Arts, religion, and public works in the Yuan Dynasty
   a. receded from their twelfth century levels to rise again only after the Mongol defeat.
   b. blossomed despite the repression of some Chinese cultural institutions.
   c. grew largely through European influence.
   d. continued to advance, despite the Mongol dynasty's apathy.
   e. were unknown to the world outside Asia until after the Mongols were defeated.

41. The first intentionally inclined building in the world is
   a. the Coliseum.
   b. Europe's Gate.
   c. the Leaning Tower of Pisa.
   d. the Capitol Building.
   e. Suurhusen Chapel.

42. The Bank of America Tower at One Bryant Park in New York City is a $1 billion skyscraper project currently undergoing construction. It includes all of the following environmentally friendly designs EXCEPT
   a. an automatic daylight dimming system.
   b. recycled and recyclable building materials.
   c. a 100% cement building mixture.
   d. a graywater system.
   e. floor-to-ceiling insulating glass.

43. The renowned political caricaturist Honore Daumier's chief medium was
   a. watercolor.
   b. mosaic.
   c. pop art.
   d. the lithograph.
   e. graphic novel.

44. Who of the following is NOT a member of the Impressionist movement?
   a. Claude Monet
   b. Camille Pissaro
   c. Auguste Renoir
   d. Edgar Degas
   e. Dante Gabriel Rossetti

45. In the ancient world, Egyptians, Sumerians, and Hebrews used all the following instruments EXCEPT
   a. harps.
   b. pianos.
   c. drums.
   d. flutes.
   e. trumpets.

46. In ancient Greece, Athenian drama was accompanied by what instrument that was used in the worship of Dionysus?
   a. cymbal
   b. drum
   c. stringed lyre
   d. violin
   e. aulos

47. The first polyphonic setting of a Catholic mass by a single composer was composed by what individual in the fourteenth century?
   a. Guillaume de Machaut
   b. Charles II of Navarre
   c. Jean de Berry
   d. King Charles V
   e. Pope Benedict XII

48. What is the name for a piece of orchestral music in one movement in which some extramusical program provides a musical picture or tells a story?
   a. art song
   b. piano concerto
   c. sonata
   d. symphonic song
   e. concerto

49. In ancient Greece, the dithyramb was a style of dance
   a. employing poetry and narrative.
   b. for athletic young men.
   c. used in fertility rituals.
   d. for the goddess Athena.
   e. used to display martial arts skills.

50. What instrument is believed to be an ancestor of the modern violin and is played by a musician drawing a bow across the strings?
   a. rabab
   b. piccolo
   c. timbala
   d. mellophone
   e. Wagner tuba

51. The Greek lyre was different from the rabab in all the following ways EXCEPT
   a. a musician played the instrument by plucking its strings.
   b. it had exactly three strings.
   c. it had a bowl-shaped body.
   d. it was not an early relative of the violin.
   e. each string was tuned to a particular pitch.

52. By about 1200, Europeans had combined the lyre and rabab into a new instrument called a
   a. bagpipe.
   b. bassanello.
   c. rebec.
   d. shawm.
   e. crumhorn.

53. "Camelot—Camelot," said I to myself. "I don't seem to remember hearing of it before. Name of the asylum, likely."

   It was a soft, reposeful summer landscape, as lovely as a dream, and as lonesome as Sunday. The air was full of the smell of flowers, and the buzzing of insects, and the twittering of birds, and there were no people, no wagons, there was no stir of life, nothing going on. The road was mainly a winding path with hoof-prints in it, and now and then a faint trace of wheels on either side in the grass—wheels that apparently had a tire as broad as one's hand.

   These are the first two paragraphs of what novel?
   a. Oscar Wilde's *Portrait of Dorian Gray*
   b. Thomas Mann's *Death in Venice*
   c. S.E. Hinton's *The Outsiders*
   d. Mark Twain's *A Connecticut Yankee in King Arthur's Court*
   e. Toni Morrison's *Jazz*

54. Charles Dickens's state-of-the-state novel that attempted to highlight the social and financial pressures some people were under is
   a. *Hard Times.*
   b. *Dickens's Dictionary of London.*
   c. *A Tale of Two Cities.*
   d. *Great Expectations.*
   e. *Oliver Twist.*

55. All of the following were associated with Renaissance Humanism EXCEPT

   a. Thomas More.

   b. Desiderius Erasmus.

   c. Petrarch.

   d. Niccolò Machiavelli.

   e. Upton Sinclair.

56. The "stream of consciousness" narrative method was developed by

   a. James Joyce.

   b. Virginia Woolf.

   c. Henrik Ibsen.

   d. Brett Easton Ellis.

   e. Tennessee Williams.

57. Which novel was a satire about feudalism and chivalry?

   a. *Valentine and Orson*

   b. *Romance of the Rose*

   c. *Don Quixote*

   d. *The Knight's Tale*

   e. *The Tempest*

58. "Mother died today . . . or maybe yesterday. I can't be sure."

This is the first line of

   a. *Finnegan's Wake.*

   b. *The Plague.*

   c. *Psycho.*

   d. *Candide.*

   e. *The Stranger.*

59. All the following were major works by Dostoyevsky EXCEPT

   a. *Crime and Punishment.*

   b. *Fathers and Sons.*

   c. *Poor Folk.*

   d. *The House of the Dead.*

   e. *Notes from Underground.*

60. Henry George's most famous book was

   a. *Pamela.*

   b. *Progress and Poverty.*

   c. *Vanity Fair.*

   d. *The Pickwick Papers.*

   e. *Dracula.*

61. All the following were utopian novels EXCEPT

   a. *Looking Backward.*

   b. *Herland.*

   c. *The Handmaid's Tale.*

   d. *City of the Sun.*

   e. *The New Atlantis.*

62. A piece of music designed to be played as an introduction is called

   a. mass.

   b. mento.

   c. melody.

   d. prelude.

   e. quartet.

63. Which of the following phrases contains an oxymoron?

    a. sorrowful indignation has depressed my spirits

    b. like the plants in too rich a soil, strength and usefulness are sacrificed to beauty

    c. one cause of this barren blooming is a false sense of security

    d. men attempt to make them alluring mistresses rather than loving wives and mothers

    e. reason raises men above the brute creation

64. A river that "drags itself sluggishly along" is an example of

    a. metaphor.

    b. personification.

    c. oxymoron.

    d. hyperbole.

    e. assonance.

65. Which of the following science fictions novels by H. G. Wells starts when a mysterious stranger arrives to stay at the local inn in an English village?

    a. *The War of the Worlds*

    b. *The Time Machine*

    c. *The Invisible Man*

    d. *The Island of Dr. Moreau*

    e. *The First Men in the Moon*

Use the following passage to answer questions 66–70.

She was not a good-looking woman, my sister; and I had a general impression that she must have made Joe Gargery marry her by hand. Joe was a fair man, with curls of flaxen hair on each side of his smooth face, and with eyes of such a very undecided blue that they seemed to have somehow got mixed with their own whites. He was a mild, good-natured, sweet-tempered, easy-going, foolish, dear fellow—a sort of Hercules in strength, and also in weakness.

My sister, Mrs. Joe, with black hair and eyes, had such a prevailing redness of skin that I sometimes used to wonder whether it was possible she washed herself with a nutmeg-grater instead of soap. She was tall and bony, and almost always wore a coarse apron, fastened over her figure behind with two loops, and having a square impregnable bib in front, that was stuck full of pins and needles. She made it a powerful merit in herself, and a strong reproach against Joe, that she wore this apron so much. Though I really see no reason why she should have worn it at all: or why, if she did wear it at all, she should not have taken it off, every day of her life.

Joe's forge adjoined our house, which was a wooden house, as many of the dwellings in our country were—most of them, at that time. When I ran home from the churchyard, the forge was shut up, and Joe was sitting alone in the kitchen. Joe and I being fellow-sufferers, and having confidences as such, Joe imparted a confidence to me, the moment I raised the latch of the door and peeped in at him opposite to it, sitting in the chimney corner.

"Mrs. Joe has been out a dozen times, looking for you, Pip. And she's out now, making it a baker's dozen."

"Is she?"

"Yes, Pip," said Joe; "and what's worse, she's got Tickler with her."

At this dismal intelligence, I twisted the only button on my waistcoat round and round, and looked in great depression at the fire. Tickler was a wax-ended piece of cane, worn smooth by collision with my tickled frame.

66. Based on the information in this excerpt, which of the following will most likely be Mrs. Joe's reaction when she finds the narrator?
  a. Mrs. Joe will welcome the narrator by tickling him.
  b. Mrs. Joe will complain about wearing an apron.
  c. Mrs. Joe will punish the narrator by hitting him.
  d. Mrs. Joe will ask the narrator to help her make pies.
  e. Mrs. Joe will say how worried she has been about him.

67. The main way Mrs. Joe's character is revealed in this excerpt is by
  a. showing what she thinks and feels.
  b. describing what she often wears.
  c. describing her husband.
  d. showing what other characters say about her.
  e. describing Pip's feelings for Mr. Joe.

68. The excerpt says that Joe Gargery was a sort of Hercules in strength, and also in weakness. The narrator means that Joe Gargery
  a. only had some strong muscles.
  b. would rather be weak than strong.
  c. was physically stronger than weak people.
  d. wanted to be a hero to everyone.
  e. was a strong man but also too kind.

69. What effect does the news about Mrs. Joe have on the narrator?
  a. The narrator is sad that Mrs. Joe is not there.
  b. The narrator is nervous and upset about what Mrs. Joe will do.
  c. The narrator is unaffected by the news about Mrs. Joe.
  d. The narrator wishes that he could disappear into the fire.
  e. The narrator is cold and wishes he had another coat.

70. Based on this excerpt, the relationship between the narrator and Mr. Joe Gargery can best be described as
  a. father and son.
  b. roommates.
  c. acquaintances.
  d. good friends.
  e. neighbors.

Use the following poem to answer questions 71–76.

Sundays too my father got up early
and put his clothes on in the blueblack cold,
then with cracked hands that ached
from labor in the weekday weather made
banked fires blaze. No one ever thanked him.
I'd wake and hear the cold splintering, breaking.
When the rooms were warm, he'd call,
and slowly I would rise and dress,
fearing the chronic angers of that house,
Speaking indifferently to him,
who had driven out the cold
and polished my good shoes as well.
What did I know, what did I know
of love's austere and lonely offices?
  —"Those Winter Sundays," copyright © 1966
    by Robert Hayden, from *Collected Poems of
    Robert Hayden* by Robert Hayden, edited by
    Frederick Glaysher. Used by permission of
    Liveright Publishing Corporation.

71. The speaker says that he would *hear the cold splintering, breaking*. What does the speaker mean by this?

  a. The speaker hears the wood floors creaking when his father walks.

  b. The speaker hears his father chopping wood outside.

  c. The speaker hears his father yelling at him to get up.

  d. The speaker hears the logs popping and crackling in the fire.

  e. The speaker hears frozen glass breaking from the cold weather.

72. Which of the following best describes the tone of the poem?

  a. angry

  b. remorseful

  c. indifferent

  d. grateful

  e. happy

73. Look at the dictionary definitions for the word *office*.

office n. 1. a room or set of rooms used for business 2. a position of duty, trust, or authority especially in the government or society 3. a service or task to be performed 4. the stables or barn of a farm 5. a business or professional organization

Which definition does the author most likely mean in the poem?

  a. definition 1

  b. definition 2

  c. definition 3

  d. definition 4

  e. definition 5

74. The speaker uses the word *blueblack* in order to show that

  a. it is very early in the morning.

  b. it is extremely cold outside.

  c. his father is badly bruised.

  d. his father wears dark clothing.

  e. his father dislikes getting up.

75. The reader can infer from the lines *then with cracked hands that ached / from labor in the week-day weather* . . . that the speaker's father

  a. does not have to work many hours during the week.

  b. works hard around the house every weekend.

  c. works on a computer many hours during a week.

  d. wishes that he did not have such a tough job.

  e. works many hours at a very physical job, probably outdoors.

76. Based on the poem, which of the following would the speaker most likely do if he saw his father again?

  a. The speaker would tell his father not to polish his shoes.

  b. The speaker would ask his father why he was so angry.

  c. The speaker would ask his father why he ran for office.

  d. The speaker would thank his father for all that he did.

  e. The speaker would speak indifferently to his father.

Use the following story to answer questions 77–82.

Kwan was anything but shy. She dropped her bag, fluttered her arms and bellowed, "Hall-oo! Hall-oo!" Still hooting and laughing, she jumped and squealed the way our new dog did whenever we let him out of the garage. This total stranger tumbled into Mom's arms, then Daddy Bob's. She grabbed Kevin and Tommy by the shoulders and shook them. When she saw me, she grew quiet, squatted on the lobby floor and held out her arms. I tugged on my mother's skirt. "Is that my big sister?"

Mom said, "See, she has your father's same thick, black hair."

I still have the picture Aunt Betty took: curly-haired Mom in a mohair suit, flashing a quirky smile; our Italo-American stepfather, Bob, appearing stunned; Kevin and Tommy mugging in cowboy hats; a grinning Kwan with her hand on my shoulder; and me in a frothy party dress, my finger stuck in my bawling mouth.

I was crying because just moments before the photo was taken, Kwan had given me a present. It was a small cage of woven straw, which she pulled out of the wide sleeve of her coat and handed to me proudly. When I held it up to my eyes and peered between the webbing, I saw a six-legged monster, fresh-grass green, with saw-blade jaws, bulging eyes, and whips for eyebrows. I screamed and flung the cage away.

At home, in the bedroom we shared from then on, Kwan hung the cage with the grasshopper, now missing one leg. As soon as night fell, the grasshopper began to chirp as loudly as a bicycle bell warning people to get out of the road.

After that day, my life was never the same. To Mom, Kwan was a handy baby-sitter, willing, able, and free. Before my mother took off for an afternoon at the beauty parlor or a shopping trip with her gal pals, she'd tell me to stick to Kwan. "Be a good little sister and explain to her anything she doesn't understand. Promise?" So every day after school, Kwan would latch on to me and tag along wherever I went. By the first grade, I became an expert on public humiliation and shame. Kwan asked so many dumb questions that

all the neighborhood kids thought she had come from Mars. She'd say: "What M&M?" "What ching gum?" "Who this Popeye Sailor Man?"

—*The Girl with Yin Eyes,* from *The Hundred Secret Senses* by Amy Tan, copyright © 1995 by Amy Tan. Used by permission of G.P. Putnam's Sons, a division of Penguin Group (USA) Inc.

77. Why does Kwan hold out her arms when she first meets the narrator?
   a. She wants the narrator to stay away from her.
   b. She wants to give the narrator a hug.
   c. She wants to stop herself from falling on the narrator.
   d. She wants to show that she has nothing in her hands.
   e. She wants the narrator to reach up her sleeve.

78. Based on this excerpt, what would the narrator's mother most likely do if she needed to pick up clothes at a dry cleaners?
   a. She would ask Kevin or Tommy to pick up the clothes.
   b. She would ask Kwan and the speaker to pick up the clothes.
   c. She would take Kwan with her when she picked up the clothes.
   d. She would have Kwan watch the speaker while she ran her errand.
   e. She would leave Kwan at home while she took the speaker.

79. Based on this excerpt, which of the following best characterizes Kwan?
    a. Kwan is a mean girl who tries to make others cry.
    b. Kwan is a slow girl who does not know very much.
    c. Kwan is a timid girl who rarely says anything.
    d. Kwan is a sad girl who does not make friends easily.
    e. Kwan is a friendly girl who wants to learn about the world.

80. The passage says that the neighborhood children thought that Kwan had come from Mars. Based on this information, how are kids at school most likely to treat Kwan if she sits at their lunch table?
    a. They will make fun of Kwan because she is different.
    b. They will ask Kwan questions about her homeland.
    c. They will be excited that Kwan has decided to sit with them.
    d. They will answer all of Kwan's questions to help her.
    e. They will take Kwan's lunch from her and make her cry.

81. Based on this excerpt, which of the following is most unlikely to occur?
    a. Kwan will be friendly to new people that she meets.
    b. The narrator will teach Kwan about life in America.
    c. Kwan will ask questions about things that confuse her.
    d. The narrator will get tired of spending time with Kwan.
    e. Kwan and the narrator will get another pet grasshopper.

82. The narrator compares the grasshopper to a bicycle bell in order to show that
    a. the grasshopper does not want anyone in its way.
    b. the grasshopper is sad about missing its leg.
    c. the grasshopper chirps very loudly.
    d. the grasshopper wants out of its cage.
    e. the grasshopper is afraid of the dark.

83. Under Roy Emerson Stryker, the Farm Security Administration (FSA) put together a photographic collection with contributions by all the following photographers EXCEPT
    a. Dorothea Lange.
    b. Ansel Adams.
    c. Arthur Rothstein.
    d. Walker Evans.
    e. Russell Lee.

84. What magazine did Alfred Stieglitz found in 1903?
    a. *Camera Work*
    b. *Photographers Weekly*
    c. *Photographic World*
    d. *The Camera Medium*
    e. *Picture Perfect*

85. The magazine in question 84's last issue was dedicated to the pictures of
    a. Jack Delano.
    b. John Vashon.
    c. Marion Post Wilcott.
    d. Paul Strand.
    e. Carl Mydans.

86. The Eight, a group of American realist artists who banded together against the National Academy of Design after some were not accepted into its 1907 spring show, consisted of all the following EXCEPT
a. Robert Henri.
b. Everett Shinn.
c. John Sloan.
d. George Luks.
e. E. E. Simmons.

87. Surrealism originated in
a. the United States.
b. England.
c. France.
d. Mexico.
e. Italy.

88. The style that developed in the early 1920s and was first named by painter Charles Sheeler is called
a. modernism.
b. surrealism.
c. regionalism.
d. precisionism.
e. impressionism.

89. This movement was influenced primarily by
a. photography.
b. watercolor.
c. charcoal.
d. montage.
e. pastel.

90. In 1902, Alfred Stieglitz left the New York Camera Club and founded
a. the American Camera Club.
b. the Photographers Association.
c. the Camera Club of America.
d. the Photographers Union.
e. Photo-Secession.

91. The group in question 90 included all the following members EXCEPT
a. Alfred Stieglitz.
b. Alvin Langdon Coburn.
c. Thomas Dewing.
d. Gertrude Kasebier.
e. Edward Steichen.

92. The type of art that attempts to reproduce the world around us accurately is called
a. neoclassicism.
b. realism.
c. abstract.
d. precisionism.
e. luminism.

93. The term for paintings that depict both actual and legendary figures of the past is
a. history painting.
b. genre painting.
c. folk art.
d. video art.
e. public art.

94. *The Land of the Lotus Eaters* was the work of what artist?
a. Charles Deas
b. George de Forest Brush
c. Jasper Francis Cropsey
d. Robert Duncanson
e. Walt Kuhn

95. *The Land of the Lotus Eaters* is partially based on a poem by
a. Alfred, Lord Tennyson.
b. Robert Frost.
c. Langston Hughes.
d. e.e. cummings.
e. Ralph Waldo Emerson.

96. Which photographer gained fame for his ardent environmentalism mostly on behalf of the Sierra Club?
  a. Kiki Smith
  b. Doris Ulmann
  c. Ansel Adams
  d. James VanDerZee
  e. Edward Weston

97. What early photographer attempted to create a visual record of the Civil War?
  a. Jack Delano
  b. Mathew Brady
  c. Roy Emerson Stryker
  d. Ann Hamilton
  e. Donald Judd

98. This photographer's work includes a portrait of which Civil War icon?
  a. Abraham Lincoln
  b. Ulysses S. Grant
  c. Jefferson Davis
  d. Robert E. Lee
  e. William Sherman

99. Which painter of found poetry stenciled the words "You Make Me" in black paint on a large sheet of white painted aluminum?
  a. Richard Avedon
  b. Andy Warhol
  c. Christopher Wool
  d. John Baldessari
  e. Tina Barney

100. The landmark exhibition of European and American art held in 1913 at the 69th Infantry Regiment Armory in New York City was officially titled
  a. New York Modern Art Exhibit.
  b. International Exhibition of Modern Art.
  c. New York Center for the Arts.
  d. Exhibition of American Artists.
  e. New York Artist Coalition.

101. The term used to described the process of positioning works in a gallery setting is
  a. showing.
  b. installation.
  c. exhibiting.
  d. assembling.
  e. displaying.

102. *Collage* comes from the French word *coller* meaning
  a. to stick.
  b. to place.
  c. to combine.
  d. to cool.
  e. to organize.

103. The artistic movement that first used collage as a serious artistic technique was
  a. surrealism.
  b. dadaism.
  c. cubism.
  d. realism.
  e. abstractism.

104. What type of art can be considered the visual equivalent of oral tradition?

   a. genre painting

   b. history painting

   c. collage

   d. pop art

   e. folk art

105. The name given to an international "anti-art" movement from 1915 to 1922 was

   a. pop art.

   b. surreal.

   c. bourgeoisie.

   d. dada.

   e. abstract.

Use the following passage to answer questions 106–108.

He was an old man who fished alone in a skiff in the Gulf Stream and he had gone eighty-four days now without taking a fish. In the first forty days a boy had been with him. But after forty days without a fish the boy's parents had told him that the old man was now definitely and finally *salao,* which is the worst form of unlucky, and the boy had gone at their orders in another boat which caught three good fish the first week. It made the boy sad to see the old man come in each day with his skiff empty and he always went down to help him carry either the coiled lines or the gaff and harpoon and the sail that was furled around the mast. The sail was patched with flour sacks and, furled, it looked like the flag of permanent defeat.

   The old man was thin and gaunt with deep wrinkles in the back of his neck. The brown blotches of the benevolent skin cancer the sun brings from its reflection on the tropic sea were on his cheeks. The blotches ran well down the sides of his face and his hands had the deep-created scars from handling heavy fish on the cords. But none of these scars were fresh. They were as old as erosions in a fishless desert.

   Everything about him was old except his eyes and they were the same color as the sea and were cheerful and undefeated.

   "Santiago," the boy said to him as they climbed the bank from where the skiff was hauled up. "I could go with you again. We've made some money."

   The old man had taught the boy to fish and the boy loved him.

   "No," the old man said. "You're with a lucky boat. Stay with them."

   "But remember how you went eighty-seven days without fish and then we caught big ones every day for three weeks."

   "I remember," the old man said. "I know you did not leave me because you doubted."

   "It was Papa made me leave. I am a boy and I must obey him."

   "I know," the old man said. "It is quite normal."

   "He hasn't much faith."

   "No," the old man said. "But we have. Haven't we?"

   —Excerpt from *The Old Man and the Sea* by Ernest Hemingway. Reproduced with the permission of Scribner, an imprint of Simon & Schuster Adult Publishing Group, from *The Old Man and the Sea* by Ernest Hemingway. Copyright 1952 by Ernest Hemingway. Copyright renewed © 1980 by Mary Hemingway.

106. Which word best describes the old man in the passage?

   a. tired

   b. weak

   c. overjoyed

   d. sad

   e. persistent

107. Based on the information in this excerpt, which of the following is most likely to occur if the old man catches some fish?

    a. The old man will want to continue to fish by himself.

    b. The boy will begin to fish with the old man again.

    c. The boy's parents will apologize for calling the man *salao.*

    d. The boy will stop carrying the old man's equipment.

    e. The old man will throw the fish back into the ocean.

108. What is most likely the boy's motivation in offering to go fishing with the man again?

    a. He thinks that he is a better fisherman than the old man.

    b. He prefers the equipment on the old man's boat.

    c. He thinks that he will bring some luck to the old man.

    d. He respects the old man and wants to help him.

    e. He thinks the other boat he has been fishing on is unlucky.

109. All of the following Martin Scorsese films received an Oscar EXCEPT

    a. *Raging Bull.*

    b. *Gangs of New York.*

    c. *The Departed.*

    d. *The Age of Innocence.*

    e. *Goodfellas.*

110. The only film that has garnered Scorsese a Best Director Academy Award is

    a. *Goodfellas.*

    b. *Casino.*

    c. *Raging Bull.*

    d. *The Last Temptation of Christ.*

    e. *The Departed.*

Use the following excerpt to answer questions 111–116.

LINDA: Did Mr. Oliver see you? . . . Well, you wait there then. And make a nice impression on him, darling. Just don't perspire too much before you see him. And have a nice time with Dad. He may have big news too! . . . That's right, a New York job. And be sweet to him tonight, dear. Be loving to him. Because he's only a little boat looking for a harbor. *(She is trembling with sorrow and joy.)* Oh, that's wonderful, Biff, you'll save his life. Thanks, darling. Just put your arm around him when he comes into the restaurant. Give him a smile. That's the boy . . . Good-by dear . . . You got your comb? . . . That's fine. Good-by, Biff dear.

(In the middle of her speech, Howard Wagner, thirty-six, wheels on a small typewriter table on which is a wire-recording machine and proceeds to plug it in. This is on the left forestage. Light slowly fades on Linda as it rises on Howard. Howard is intent on threading the machine and only glances over his shoulder as Willy appears.)

WILLY: Pst! Pst!

HOWARD: Hello, Willy, come in.

WILLY: Like to have a little talk with you, Howard.

HOWARD: Sorry to keep you waiting. I'll be with you in a minute.

WILLY: What's that, Howard?

HOWARD: Didn't you ever see one of these? Wire recorder.

WILLY: Oh. Can we talk a minute?

HOWARD: Records things. Just got delivery yesterday. Been driving me crazy, the most terrific machine I ever saw in my life. I was up all night with it.

WILLY: What do you do with it?

HOWARD: I bought it for dictation, but you can do anything with it. Listen to this. I had it home last night. Listen to what I picked up. The first one is my daughter. Get this. (*He flicks the switch and "Roll Out the Barrel" is heard being whistled.*) Listen to that kid whistle.

WILLY: That is lifelike, isn't it?

HOWARD: Seven years old. Get that tone.

WILLY: Ts, ts. Like to ask a little favor of you . . . (*The whistling breaks off, and the voice of Howard's daughter is heard.*)

HIS DAUGHTER: "Now you, Daddy."

HOWARD: She's crazy for me! (*Again the same song is whistled.*) That's me! Ha! (*He winks.*)

WILLY: You're very good! (*The whistling breaks off again. The machine runs silent for a moment.*)

HOWARD: Sh! Get this now, this is my son.

HIS SON: "The capital of Alabama is Montgomery; the capital of Arizona is Phoenix; the capital of Arkansas is Little Rock; the capital of California is Sacramento . . ." (*and on, and on*).

HOWARD (*holding up five fingers*): Five years old, Willy!

WILLY: He'll make an announcer some day!
　　　—Excerpt from *Death of a Salesman*
　　　　　　by Arthur Miller, © 1949,
　　　renewed © 1977 by Arthur Miller.
　　Used by permission of Viking Penguin,
　　a division of Penguin Group (USA) Inc.

111. What does Linda mean when she says *Because he's only a little boat looking for a harbor*?
　a. Willy is looking for a life where he can relax and belong.
　b. Willy would like to sail if he could find a place to do it.
　c. Willy is much smaller than other people and feels scared.
　d. Willy sometimes has difficulty with traveling and directions.
　e. Willy wishes that he could bring his boat home for everyone to see.

112. Based on the excerpt, which word best describes Willy?
　a. confused
　b. relaxed
　c. angry
　d. polite
　e. scared

113. Based on the excerpt, how would Willy most likely react if someone cut in front of him in a line at a grocery store?
- **a.** He would scream and yell at the person.
- **b.** He would allow the person to cut in front of him.
- **c.** He would tell the cashier that the person cut.
- **d.** He would cry and leave the store without groceries.
- **e.** He would call his wife Linda to ask for help.

114. Based on the excerpt, which is most likely something that Linda would do?
- **a.** Buy a boat so that she could travel around the world.
- **b.** Tell her son that first impressions are not important.
- **c.** Ignore her family because she is too busy.
- **d.** Try to help a friend who is having trouble.
- **e.** Go out of the house without worrying about how she looks.

115. Which word best describes how Howard feels about his children?
- **a.** indifferent
- **b.** annoyed
- **c.** proud
- **d.** cheerful
- **e.** remorseful

116. Based on the excerpt, what would Howard most likely do if a friend came to him with a problem?
- **a.** Talk about his own life.
- **b.** Tell his friend to go away.
- **c.** Listen intently to his friend.
- **d.** Take his friend out to lunch.
- **e.** Give his friend some money.

117. Why did the Farm Security Administration (FSA) hire photographers like Gordon Parks?
- **a.** to create advertisements that would recruit new farmers
- **b.** to produce photographs showing the conditions of life of American workers
- **c.** to take photographs that could be sold as souvenirs or mementos
- **d.** to make photojournalism more influential than print journalism
- **e.** to provide direct aid to struggling farmers and other workers

118. The first dance movement in the suites of Bach and his predecessors is called
- **a.** balata.
- **b.** allemande.
- **c.** gallop.
- **d.** jump blues.
- **e.** modal.

119. A triple-time dance, in most cases, that is accompanied by music with a low bass note on the first beat and two chords in the middle register for the following two beats is the
- **a.** swing.
- **b.** jive.
- **c.** waltz.
- **d.** meringue.
- **e.** foxtrot.

120. Original pieces of music performed by a small group of wind instruments from church steeples and towers were called
- **a.** church symphonies.
- **b.** tower sonatas.
- **c.** steeple symphonies.
- **d.** symphonic poems.
- **e.** symphonic sonatas.

121. When notes are played in succession, not simultaneously, this is called
   a. backbeat.
   b. cantata.
   c. basso continuo.
   d. coloration.
   e. arpeggio.

122. What is the word created around 1945 for a style of jazz that consists of improvised solo music performances with jarring and sophisticated patterns?
   a. jive
   b. swing
   c. scat
   d. bebop
   e. Latin jazz

123. What is another term for the harpsichords used in Italy?
   a. clavicembalo
   b. lyre
   c. swan's harp
   d. koto
   e. zither

124. A piece of music with no fixed form in which the composer decides the structure at his or her whim is called
   a. sonata.
   b. symphony.
   c. fantasia.
   d. opera.
   e. harmony.

125. The triple meter dance, performed during the last movement of a Baroque suite, is a
   a. gigue.
   b. Paso Doble.
   c. Lindy hop.
   d. gallop.
   e. waltz.

126. Music with one melodic line accompanied by chords or other minor material is called
   a. harmony.
   b. polyrhythm.
   c. homophony.
   d. rondo.
   e. polka.

127. Puerto Rican folk music, which reflects European rather than African influence, is named
   a. aquinaldo.
   b. punto.
   c. jiharo.
   d. bomba.
   e. salsa.

128. What is the name for the national dance of Poland, which is performed at an average speed in triple time and has distinct musical accents on either the second or third beat?
   a. mazurka
   b. polka
   c. barrynya
   d. troika
   e. sher

129. When a piece of music consists of a single theme, it is called
  a. harmonious.
  b. monophony.
  c. monothematic.
  d. polythematic.
  e. solothematic.

130. What is the term for a substantial musical work that deals with an extensive story and is executed in a concert hall or church without the use of scenery, costumes, or any physical action?
  a. oratorio
  b. madrigal
  c. opera
  d. chorale
  e. orchestra

131. A musical signal that violin strings should be plucked with the fingers, not bowed, is
  a. octaves.
  b. dissonance.
  c. staff.
  d. lavier.
  e. pizzicato.

132. A musical piece to be performed by exactly five instruments or voices is a
  a. pentant.
  b. pentata.
  c. quinata.
  d. quintet.
  e. quintenta.

133. The traditional jazz trio consisted of what three instruments?
  a. guitar, piano, double bass
  b. piano, double bass, drums
  c. piano, drums, guitar
  d. electric organ, electric guitar, drums
  e. piano, electric guitar, drums

134. The longest film ever made is
  a. *The Longest Most Meaningless Movie in the World.*
  b. *Titanic.*
  c. *Grandmother Martha.*
  d. *The Cure for Insomnia.*
  e. *The Burning of the Red Lotus Temple.*

135. The most expensive non-English film was
  a. *War and Peace.*
  b. *Apocoypto.*
  c. *Metropolis.*
  d. *Hero.*
  e. *Pan's Labyrinth.*

136. What is the informal term popularly used for the Mumbai-based Hindi-language film industry in India?
  a. Bombay
  b. Hinduema
  c. Bollywood
  d. Kapoor
  e. Raj Kumar

137. The blend of martial art, game, and dance that originated in Brazil is known as
  a. batuque.
  b. maculele.
  c. muay tai.
  d. tai chi.
  e. capoeira.

138. In the dance form in question 137, all the following instruments have typically been used to provide music EXCEPT
  a. tambourines.
  b. atabaque.
  c. berimbaus.
  d. rabab.
  e. bass.

139. The phrase *Existence precedes essence* was formulated in the twentieth century by
  a. Freud.
  b. Kierkegaard.
  c. Kafka.
  d. Camu.
  e. Sartre.

Use the following passage to answer question 140.

We hold these truths to be self-evident, that all men are created equal, that they are endowed by their Creator with certain unalienable Rights, that among these are Life, Liberty and the pursuit of Happiness.—That to secure these rights, Governments are instituted among Men, deriving their just powers from the consent of the governed,—That whenever any Form of Government becomes destructive of these ends, it is the Right of the People to alter or to abolish it, and to institute new Government, laying its foundation on such principles and organizing its powers in such form, as to them shall seem most likely to effect their Safety and Happiness . . . when a long train of abuses . . . evinces a design to reduce them under absolute Despotism, it is their right, it is their duty, to throw off such Government, and to provide new Guards for their future security.
                    —Excerpt from the Declaration of
                                        Independence.

140. Which of the following concepts is NOT included in this paragraph from the Declaration of Independence?
  a. The people sometimes have an obligation to overthrow the government.
  b. Governments are not necessary if the people are virtuous.
  c. Some statements are so obvious that they do not have to be proven.
  d. Governments draw their legitimate power from the support of the people.
  e. All men have natural rights that cannot be taken away without cause.

▶ Answers

1. b. Cinquain is a form of five-lined poetry containing 2, 4, 6, 8, 2 syllables, respectively. Choices **a**, **c**, **d**, and **e** are all forms of concrete poetry. Concrete poetry takes on visual shapes or patterns of the object it describes.

2. b. A simile is the comparison of two unlike objects using the words *like* or *as,* and is demonstrated in line 1.

3. a. In the *Autobiography of Benjamin Franklin,* Franklin introduces the book with a note to his son. An *autobiography* is the author's account of his or her life.

4. b. The author indicates he had a few faults, but generally, life was pretty good.

5. a. Rhythm is the order of free occurrences of sound. This stanza has a regular meter. The rhyme is the likeness or similarity of sounds in words. Rhyme occurs at the end of lines 1–2 and 3–4. Although there is rhyme in the poem, the writer is not repeating words (repetition), nor is he using alliteration or assonance.

6. b. Dialect is the local language of the people. This includes the accent, vocabulary, grammar, and idioms. Some might also describe this poem as African-American dialect or plantation dialect.

7. a. Alliteration is the repetition of initial sound of a word. Assonance is the repetition of vowel sounds. Rhyme is the likeness of sounds existing between two or more words. Repetition is repeating the same word or phrase. Dissonance indicates there are disagreeing sounds within the poem, which is not true. Connotation is the emotions and thoughts that a phrase or word can cause; it is not found in "The Raven." In addition, the poem does not have resolution—nothing is resolved.

8. d. Romanticism began in the second half of the eighteenth century. This period is often equated with poetry; however, novelist Sir Walter Scott also began writing during this period.

9. e. Rhyme is when words have similar word ending sounds, and repetition is repeating words and phrases in the body of the work.

10. b. A metaphor is a direct comparison of two objects without using any comparison words.

11. b. Anne Bradstreet's poem to her husband goes against the Puritan convention of expressing suppressed love to a spouse.

12. e. Nothing is going to suppress the speaker's love for her husband.

13. d. The *Egyptian Book of the Dead* does not contain any information about the pyramids.

14. b. Between the tenth and twelfth centuries, illuminated manuscripts became more interpretive, actually illustrating passages from the book.

15. b. Illuminated manuscripts mainly relate to churches, monasteries, and prayers and rites.

16. c. As the illuminated manuscript flourished, artists began to learn new skills, such as balance and perspective. The illustrations became more realistic and depicted more of the text. Therefore, a person who studied texts would see the advancements in art during the same time period.

17. a. The printing press made the mass production of manuscripts more efficient.

18. a. King James compares the king to *a head of a body* and members to the *body parts*.

19. b. In paragraph 3, the writer compares the king's subjects to the body. This metaphor was initially brought up in paragraph 1.

20. e. The passage is conveying that subjects should not resist their king, no matter how irrational his behavior may seem. It uses examples of animals whose young never resist their parents. The vipers are mentioned as an exception to this pattern.

21. d. In paragraph 2, the writer compares the king to a father *whose natural love to his children I described in the first part of this my discourse, speaking of the duty that kings owe to their subjects.*

22. e. With the arrival of electricity in 1901, Broadway had white lights stretching from 13th to 46th streets in New York City, inspiring the nickname "the Great White Way."

23. b. The movie was directed and photographed by Edwin S. Porter, a former Edison Studios cameraman. His work helped to shift film production toward narrative story telling.

24. c. This film, also called *The Prodigal Son,* was directed by Michel Carré and shot by a French film production company, the Gaumont Film Company.

25. d. There is no personification in this passage. The phrase *the bell tolls* is repeated throughout the passage (choice **a**); *affliction is a treasure* is a metaphor (choice **b**); and the statements in lines 32–34 demonstrate contrast (choice **c**). The diction in Donne's meditation shows that it was written in an earlier era, for a formal occasion, and for a specific audience (choice **e**).

26. b. Ernest Hemingway chose this line from Donne's work for the title of his novel. Like the titles of many books, it was carefully selected to hint at the theme of the book.

27. e. Filippo Brunelleschi (1377–1446) was one of the foremost architects of the Italian Renaissance. All his principal works are in Florence, Italy.

28. a. The most likely explanation for building the Great Wall was to provide protection. The photograph shows that the wall was tall and sturdy and would thus have presented a formidable obstacle to an invading army. Because the Great Wall is built along the northern portion of China (with the city of Beijing to the south of the wall), it is most likely that the wall was built to stop invaders from the north.

29. b. A cartoon from 1932 claimed that the wall was visible to the human eye from the moon; however, the Great Wall of China would not be visible to the unaided eye from the moon, and no lunar astronaut has ever claimed to have seen the Great Wall from the moon.

30. a. The third principle is durability—the building should stand up forcefully and remain in good condition.

31. b. The first stanza conveys light-heartedness with its playful flow of the single thoughts ending with the exclamation point at the end of the sentence.

32. a. In context, *rude* means that society spurn solitude in favor of companionship and group activity.

33. d. A reed has no metaphorical significance in this work. In context, it is Pan's pipe.

34. a. The word *Your* refers to sisters Fair Quiet and Innocence and *sacred plants* is a metaphor for the peaceful solitude found in nature.

35. c. The comparison is made by a dependent clause following the word *mind:* "that ocean where each kind / Does straight its own resemblance find . . ."

36. d. Johnson recorded only 29 songs before his death in 1938, purportedly at the hands of a jealous husband. He was only 27 years old, yet he left an indelible mark on the music world. Again and again, contemporary artists return to Johnson, whose songs capture the very essence of the blues, transforming our pain and suffering with the healing magic of his guitar.

37. a. This author of *The Legend of Sleepy Hollow* is credited with coining the term *the blues*, as it is now defined, in 1807.

38. d. A fundamental principle of the blues is that the music be cathartic. Listening to the blues will drive the blues away; it is music that has the power to overcome sadness. Thus, *the blues* is something of a misnomer, for the music is moving but not melancholy; it is, in fact, music born of hope, not despair.

39. d. The beginnings of the blues can be traced to songs sung in the fields and around slave quarters on southern plantations, songs of pain and suffering, of injustice, and of longing for a better life.

40. b. Taoism, a religion native to China, was repressed by the Mongols during the Yuan Dynasty; however, a cultural flowering still managed to take place during this period.

41. b. Europe's Gate are two twin office buildings in Madrid, designed by the American architects Philip Johnson and John Burgee. Each building has an inclination of 15°.

42. c. In fact, the mixture used in the tower is 55% cement and 45% slag—a byproduct of blast furnaces. Slag cement decreases the amount of cement needed for building, which in turn lowers the amount of carbon dioxide greenhouse gas produced through typical cement manufacturing.

43. d. Daumier's chief medium was the lithograph. His work paved the way for the stylistic and subject innovations of the Impressionists.

44. e. Dante Gabriel Rossetti belonged to the group known as the English pre-Raphaelites.

45. b. The invention of the piano is credited to Bartolomeo Cristofori around 1700. There are three surviving Cristofori pianos today that date from the 1720s.

46. e. Athenian drama was accompanied by the aulos, or double-piped oboe. The aulos was used for a variety of Greek activities— sacrifices, dramas, wrestling matches, the discus throw, and sailors' dances.

47. a. Machaut's cyclic *Messe de Nostre Dame* (*Mass of Our Lady*), composed for Reims Cathedral in the early 1360s, is the first by a single composer and conceived as a unit.

48. d. This is referred to as the symphonic poem, which can be traced to the overtures of Ludwig van Beethoven.

49. a. The dithyramb was performed by a Greek chorus of men or boys dancing in circular formation, probably accompanied by the aulos. The participants typically related an incident in the life of Dionysus.

50. a. The rabab is a pear-shaped piece of wood on which one, two, or three strings were stretched.

51. d. Like the rabab, the Greek lyre is an early relative of the violin.

52. c. Like the rabab, the rebec had a pear-shaped body and was bowed. Like the lyre, it had three strings that were tuned to specific tones. Some musicians still play the rebec at special concerts.

53. d. *A Connecticut Yankee in King Arthur's Court* is an 1889 novel and a very early example of time travel in literature.

54. a. In his novel *Hard Times,* Dickens showed an English community that was characterized by difficult personal, class, and environmental adjustments caused by the industrial order.

55. e. Upton Sinclair was a prolific twentieth century American author who wrote more than 90 books in many genres and was widely considered one of the best investigators advocating socialist views.

56. b. Many twentieth-century writers experimented with stream of consciousness; however, Woolf used the method almost exclusively.

57. c. Miguel Cervantes's *Don Quixote* tells of an aged Spanish knight whose semihumorous misadventures are parodies of medieval standards of chivalry. All the other choices are examples of romance novels as a narrative genre.

58. e. Albert Camus's *The Stranger* was the portrait of an alienated, emotionally uninvolved "hero." It is one of the most popular novels associated with existentialism.

59. b. *Fathers and Sons* is an 1862 novel by Ivan Turgenev. The title of this work in Russian literally translates to "Fathers and Children," but the work is often translated to Fathers and Sons in English.

60. b. *Progress and Poverty* was Henry George's most famous book.

61. c. This book by Margaret Atwood is a dystopia, which is an offshoot genre from the utopian novel. This genre usually takes elements of contemporary society and warns against some modern trend.

62. d. Preludes are also used for operatic overtures.

63. c. *Barren blooming* is an oxymoron combining the contradictory ideas of sterility and fertility.

64. b. This phrase attributes a human characteristic to an inanimate object (personification).

65. c. In this 1897 novel, the stranger arrives with his face hidden entirely by bandages, large goggles, and a wide-brimmed hat. He is reclusive and, thus, becomes the talk of the village.

66. c. Mr. Joe Gargery says that Mrs. Joe has been out looking for the narrator several times and that she has Tickler with her. Tickler is later revealed to be something used to hit the narrator. Choice **a** is incorrect because *Tickler* is an ironic term for something used to punish the narrator. It is not used for play. Mrs. Joe has Tickler with her, making choice **c** more likely than choice **b**. *Tickler* also makes choice **e** unlikely. Choice **d** is incorrect because Mr. Joe Gargery uses *a baker's dozen* to describe the number of times Mrs. Joe has gone out, not to indicate that she wants to bake.

67. d. The narrator describes himself and Mr. Joe Gargery as *fellow-sufferers* because they both live with Mrs. Joe. Mr. Joe reveals that Mrs. Joe brings Tickler with her when she goes to look for the narrator. Choice **a** is incorrect because Mrs. Joe is not actually present in the passage; she is only talked about by other characters. Choice **b** may give some insight into Mrs. Joe's character; however, the fact that she wears an apron does not capture her harsh nature as well as the other characters' comments. Choice **c** is incorrect because the description of Mr. Joe mostly tells the reader about his character, not Mrs. Joe's character. Choice **e** is incorrect because the description of Pip's feelings mostly tells about Pip's or Mr. Joe's character.

68. e. In the sentence with this comparison, the narrator says that Mr. Joe is good-natured and sweet-tempered but also foolish, indicating that his very strengths could also be his weaknesses. Choice **a** is incorrect because the sentence with the comparison does not talk about physical strength. Choice **b** is incorrect because the excerpt says that Mr. Joe is both weak and strong, not that he chooses one over the other. Choice **c** is incorrect because the narrator does not describe Mr. Joe's physical dominance over others in the sentence. Choice **d** is incorrect because the narrator describes Mr. Joe as easygoing and mild, not someone who strives to be a hero.

69. b. After the narrator hears the news, he twists the button on his waistcoat and looks sadly at the fire. He knows what Mrs. Joe will do with Tickler. Because of this physical change in behavior, choice **c** is incorrect. Choice **a** is incorrect because after the narrator hears the news, he is more focused on Tickler than the fact that Mrs. Joe is not there. Because the narrator focuses more on the Tickler than the fire, choice **d** is also incorrect. Choice **e** is incorrect; the narrator twists the coat button because he is nervous, not cold.

70. d. The narrator describes himself and Mr. Joe as having confidences. Mr. Joe warns the narrator about Mrs. Joe. These confidences that they share make choices **b** and **c** incorrect. The narrator and Mr. Joe know each other better than just acquaintances, and roommates do not necessarily share such confidences. Choice **a** is incorrect because a father would be more likely to punish a son for being out, not warn him that another adult is looking for him. Also, he is clearly the narrator's uncle because he is married to Pip's sister. Choice **e** is incorrect because the excerpt shows that Joe and Pip clearly live together. Joe's workplace—the forge—is attached to the house.

71. d. The speaker says that his father made fires in the first stanza. The speaker also talks about the rooms warming up in line 7. Choice **a** is incorrect because cold refers to the temperature of the room, not the floors. Choice **b** is incorrect because the rooms are warming up. The rooms would not warm up and the cold would not break just from chopping wood. Choice **c** is incorrect because even though the poem talks about chronic angers, the speaker says that his father would call, not yell, when the room was warm. Yelling would create a symbolic coldness, not break it. Choice **e** is incorrect because the poem says that the cold was breaking, not that that glass was breaking.

72. b. The repetition of *What did I know* shows that the speaker has come to some kind of realization. The reader also uses comments such as *No one ever thanked him* and the description of the father's actions to come to this conclusion. Choice **a** is incorrect because the speaker does talk angrily about his father; however, he says that he now understands *love's lonely offices.* Choice **c** is incorrect because the speaker says that he was indifferent when he was younger, but now he feels differently about his father. Choice **d** is incorrect because while the speaker now understands what his father did for him, the memories he recalls are how hard his father worked and how little appreciation the speaker showed him at the time. This creates a more remorseful tone than a grateful tone. Choice **e** is incorrect because the speaker is not happy about the way he treated his father when he was younger. He wishes he had thanked him.

73. c. The poem describes the tasks or services that the speaker's father did for him. This definition makes sense in the last line of the poem: the speaker did not understand at the time that the tasks his father did for him showed his father's love. Choices **a** and **d** are incorrect because the context clues in the last stanza do not show *office* to be an actual physical place. Choice **b** is incorrect because the father's service to his family, not his position of authority, is emphasized in the poem. In addition, definition 2 gives the connotation of a public position, not a family position. Choice **e** is incorrect because the poem does not talk about the father's business or professional organization.

74. a. *Blueblack* in line 2 is preceded by the idea that it is very early in the morning. During winter months, it is still very dark outside in the morning. Choice **b** is incorrect because *blueblack* appeals to the reader's sense of sight. It helps the reader see the speaker's father in the very early morning cold. Choices **c**, **d**, and **e** are incorrect because *blueblack* describes the type of cold (a very early morning cold), not the way the father looks or feels.

75. e. The poem describes injuries that occur from physical labor. In addition, the poem goes on to explain that these injuries resulted from labor in the weekday weather. This makes choice **c** incorrect. Readers cannot infer from these lines what the father does during the weekend. This makes choice **b** incorrect. The description of the cracked and aching hands leads the reader to believe the father works many hours, not just a few hours. This makes choice **a** incorrect. Choice **d** is incorrect because while the details show that the father's job is hard, the reader cannot determine how the father feels about his job.

76. d. The overall tone of the poem is remorseful, and the speaker makes the comment that no one thanked his father when he was younger. The end of the poem shows that the speaker now realizes all that his father actually did for him. Choice **a** is incorrect because the speaker does not suggest in the poem that he did not want his father to do things for him. Choice **b** is incorrect because the speaker's realization is not about how angry his father had been. The realization is that his father did a lot for him. Choice **c** is incorrect because the interpretation of the word office is incorrect. Office in this poem does not refer to a political position. Choice **e** is incorrect because the speaker's remorse would have him treat his father differently than he did when he was younger.

77. b. Kwan immediately says hello to the other family members by touching them. The reader uses prior knowledge and the text to come to this conclusion. Choice **a** is incorrect because she is trying to meet the family, not keep them away from her. Choice **c** is incorrect because the passage says that Kwan squats on the floor before holding out her hands. She is not described as falling. Choice **d** is incorrect because Kwan greets everyone in the first paragraph. She has no reason to show the narrator that she has nothing in her hands. Choice **e** is incorrect because the excerpt says that Kwan later reaches up her own sleeve to pull out a surprise for the narrator. She does not intend for the narrator to do it. Kwan more likely wants to say hello to the narrator.

78. d. The passage says that the narrator's mother used Kwan as a babysitter. The narrator's mother leaves the speaker with Kwan when she goes to the beauty parlor or goes shopping. This makes choice **e** incorrect. Choice **a** is incorrect because the passage does not give any clues that Kevin or Tommy run errands for the narrator's mother. Choice **b** is incorrect because the passage emphasizes that Kwan is a babysitter, not that Kwan runs errands for the narrator's mother. Choice **c** is incorrect because the narrator's mother does not take Kwan when she goes shopping or to the beauty parlor; she would probably not take her to pick up dry cleaning.

79. e. The narrator says that Kwan is outgoing, and she immediately greets the family with great enthusiasm. In addition, she often hangs out with the narrator and her friends and asks several questions about the world around her. This makes choice **c** incorrect. Choice **a** is incorrect because even though the narrator cries when Kwan brings out the grasshopper, Kwan does not mean to do it. She brings the grasshopper as a gift. Choice **b** is incorrect because Kwan is not dumb. She does not know about things like M&Ms and Popeye because she is from another country. Choice **d** is incorrect because none of the details in the excerpt show that Kwan is sad. She seems overjoyed to meet the narrator and the rest of the family.

80. a. The phrase *come from Mars* has a negative connotation. Children often point out the differences between themselves and others. The narrator also says that she feels public humiliation and shame from what Kwan says. Choice **b** is incorrect because the excerpt does not say that the kids seemed interested in Kwan. Choice **c** is incorrect because the children look at Kwan funny because she does not fit in. They would not be excited to have someone asking dumb questions at their table. Choice **d** is incorrect because the excerpt does not say that the children happily answer all of her questions; instead, they look at her like she is crazy. Choice **e** is incorrect because nothing in the excerpt suggests that the students would physically bully Kwan. They are more likely to make fun of her.

81. e. The narrator is afraid of the grasshopper at first and never says anything nice about it. In fact, she just says that it chirps very loudly, an annoying quality. Choice **a** is incorrect because the narrator says that Kwan is not shy. She is very outgoing when she first meets the family. Choices **b** and **c** are incorrect because Kwan and the narrator hang out a lot. Kwan asks a lot of questions, and the narrator is likely to answer them. Choice **d** is incorrect because the narrator already shows frustration with Kwan. She says that Kwan's questions humiliate her and that Kwan often tags along.

82. c. The narrator compares the sound of a bicycle bell to the sound of the grasshopper. This helps the reader to understand how loud the grasshopper sounds to her. Choice **a** is incorrect because the grasshopper is not going anywhere; it is stuck in its cage. The narrator says that the bicycle bell warns people, not the grasshopper, to get out of the road. Choice **b** is incorrect because the sentence about the missing leg is in a separate sentence from the comparison. The two ideas are not linked in this way. Choices **d** and **e** are incorrect because a grasshopper chirps at night even when it is not in captivity. The comparison does not explain the cause of the chirping.

83. b. Ansel Adams is best known for his black-and-white photographs of the West. All the other photographers mentioned contributed to the photographic collection of the FSA's historical section.

84. a. *Camera Work* went through 50 issues before it was discontinued in June 1917. It published the work of a broad range of significant photographers.

85. d. *Camera Work*, one of the most famous photographic magazines, dedicated its last issue to Strand's photos.

86. e. Simmons was a member of The Eight, a group of American painters formed in 1897 for the purpose of exhibiting independently of the Society of American Artists and the National Academy of Design

87. c. Surrealism originated in France in the 1920s. Surrealist pictures represented dreamlike or nightmarish images.

88. d. Precisionism was a style that took man-made forms as subject matter and represented these structures in high-contrast paintings that used large flat areas of color and straight lines.

89. a. The movement was influenced by photography, and many of its painters painted from photographs.

90. e. Stieglitz took the group's name from various secessionist movements occurring in European art at that time.

91. c. Thomas Dewing was a painter and a member of The Eight.

92. b. This term originated in the nineteenth century and was used to describe the work of a group of painters who rejected idealization and focused on everyday life.

93. a. History paintings were a popular medium for conveying historical themes to the public.

94. d. In this work, Duncanson explored the theme of cultural contrast, which may have originated from his feelings against rigid systems of social and economic power.

95. a. This painting was based on Alfred, Lord Tennyson's 1833 poem *The Lotus-Eaters*.

96. c. Adams was a well-known environmentalist who embarked on a project to photograph in all the U.S.'s national parks.

97. b. Brady put his money and reputation on the line to create a visual record of the Civil War. However, he hired experienced operators to do the work in the field.

98. b. In this portrait, Ulysses S. Grant poses at his Virginia headquarters next to a tree and in front of the campaign tent.

99. c. Wool was a painter of found poetry who incorporated words or nonverbal symbols on canvas. The phrase *You Make Me* could be a statement of love or an accusatory fragment, such as "You Make Me Angry."

100. b. This exhibition was organized by artists who came together to introduce American audiences to the latest trends in European and American art.

101. b. *Installation,* originally used to describe this process, has evolved to denote a distinct kind of art making.

102. a. *Collage* is a technique where pieces of paper, cloth, or other objects are pasted on to a flat surface.

103. c. The cubists were the first to use collage as a serious artistic technique, though it became an important technique in dadaism and surrealism.

104. e. Folk art is made by artists with no academic training, often using local materials to convey a set of beliefs that are unique to a culture or region. Methods may be handed down from generation to generation.

105. d. The name *dada* is deliberately meaningless, and the movement was a reaction to the elite traditional art establishment.

106. e. The excerpt describes the old man as still having undefeated eyes, even though he has gone 84 days without catching a fish. The old man comments that he still has faith. In addition, the boy recalls the last time the old man had difficulty catching fish. Eventually, he caught a lot of fish because he stayed with it. Choices **a** and **b** are incorrect because while the excerpt shows that the man is old, he still goes out fishing by himself. The description of the man does not emphasize a weakness or tiredness. Choice **c** is incorrect because even though the old man's eyes are cheerful, he is not joyful. He has not caught a fish in 84 days, and neither his dialogue nor his actions show that he is overly happy or joyous. The detail that his eyes are still cheerful makes choice **d** incorrect.

107. b. The boy used to fish with the old man when he was catching fish. The boy says that he wants to go back to fishing with the old man; however, the old man will not let the boy because he is not catching fish. If he did catch fish, he would likely welcome the boy. Choice **a** is incorrect because the story describes how the boy helps the old man even though he does not fish with him. The man would welcome help if he was catching fish. Choice **c** is incorrect because nothing in the excerpt describes the boy's parents as sympathetic or sorry. They want him to be where he can make money. Choice **d** is incorrect because the excerpt says that the boy loves the old man. He wants to help him whether he is catching fish or not. Choice **e** is incorrect because the old man is a fisherman. He needs to sell the fish in order to have food and money.

108. d. The excerpt says that the boy loves the old man. The old man taught the young boy to fish. In addition, the excerpt says that he already helps the old man by carrying his equipment. Choice **a** is incorrect because the excerpt does not show that the boy has excessive pride. He looks to the old man as a teacher. Choice **b** is incorrect because the old man's equipment is not nice. The sail is patched with flour sacks. Choice **c** is incorrect because the excerpt shows that the boy has faith. He shows this when he tells the story of when the old man went 87 days without catching fish. He does not think that the old man is unlucky; his parents do. Choice **e** is incorrect because the excerpt says that the other boat caught three good fish in the first week.

109. b. *Gangs of New York* was nominated for ten Academy Awards, including Best Picture and Best Director; however, it was largely overshadowed by *Chicago,* which took half of the awards for which *Gangs of New York* was nominated. The film failed to garner any Academy Awards at all.

110. e. In 2006, Scorsese won the Academy Award for Best Director, beating out the directors of *Babel, Letters from Iwo Jima, The Queen,* and *United 93.*

111. a. At the beginning of the excerpt, Linda says that Willy may be getting a new job. She also emphasizes to Biff that he needs to be sweet and smile at his father. These details all hint that Willy may be struggling with his current life. He is searching for happiness. Choices **b** and **e** are incorrect because they interpret the metaphor too literally. No details in the excerpt hint that Willy likes to sail or has a boat. Choice **c** is incorrect because it ignores the idea that Willy is searching for something. Little refers to Willy's vulnerability, not his actual size. Choice **d** is incorrect because the details surrounding the figurative language do not support the interpretation. No details actually refer to Willy traveling somewhere.

112. d. Most of the passage shows Willy listening to Howard's rambling, even though he needs to ask him something. He responds with *That is lifelike* and *He'll make an announcer some day* even after Howard ignores Willy's requests to talk. Choice **a** is incorrect because while Linda hints that Willy may be having a tough time, the majority of the excerpt shows Willy fully understanding Howard. Choice **b** is incorrect because Willy has something that he needs to ask Howard. Willy seems on edge when he gets into Howard's office. Choice **c** is incorrect because Willy does not show that he is angry that Howard will not listen to what he has to say. Instead, he participates in the conversation that Howard wants to have. Choice **e** is incorrect because none of the details in the excerpt support the idea that Willy is scared.

113. b. Willy does not demand to talk to Howard even after he is interrupted several times by him; instead, Willy acts passively and listens to all of Howard's stories. Willy would likely act passively in other instances. Choices **a, c,** and **d** are incorrect because Willy does not show that he is upset even after Howard keeps him waiting and then interrupts him. He waits patiently until Howard finishes his stories and does not seem overly concerned that he is not getting the respect he deserves. Choice **e** is incorrect because even though the excerpt shows that Linda cares for Willy and tries to help him, it does not show that Willy runs to Linda every time he has a problem.

114. d. Linda tells Biff to treat his father nicely because she wants her husband to be happy. She trembles partly because she is worried about her husband so much. This shows her caring side. Her concern for her family makes choice **c** incorrect. Choice **a** is incorrect because Linda uses a boat reference only to explain her husband's state of mind, not because she is interested in boats or traveling. Choices **b** and **e** are incorrect because Linda is worried about Biff's first impression on Mr. Oliver. She tells him not to sweat too much and makes sure he has his comb. It is unlikely that she would give such advice and then not worry about her own appearance.

115. c. Howard wants Willy to listen to his children on the recorder. He is thrilled that his daughter is crazy about him and impressed that his five-year-old can recite the capitals. Choice **a** is incorrect because Howard makes comments about how great his kids are and wants to listen to them on the recorder. Choice **b** is incorrect because Howard would not play the recording of his kids if he were annoyed by them. Choice **d** is incorrect because Howard feels more than cheerful about his kids. He brags to Willy about them and makes Willy listen to the recording. Choice **e** is incorrect because Howard does not feel sorry for anything that he has done concerning his kids.

116. a. Howard seems self-absorbed in the excerpt. He does not seem to care that Willy has something that he would like to discuss with Howard. He is more interested in talking about his children and the recorder. Choice **b** is incorrect because Howard tells Willy to come in. He does not tell Willy to go away because he is too busy. Choice **c** is incorrect because Howard does not listen to Willy at all. Willy tries a few times to talk to Howard about something, but each time Howard ignores him and keeps talking. Choice **d** is incorrect because Howard seems to care little about helping Willy. He does not recommend that he and Willy go some place to talk. Choice **e** is incorrect because none of the details in the excerpt suggests that Howard, who may very well have money, would give any to a friend. He would be more likely to spend money on something for himself or give it to his children

117. b. The FSA hired photographers to communicate "the plight of Americans" in difficulty, so choice **b** is the best option.

118. b. Allemande was the term and in the late eighteenth century the name was also used for quick waltzlike dances in three-four or three-eight time.

119. c. The dance's description indicates the waltz, which is considered both a ballroom and folk dance.

120. b. A sonata is a critical musical form that originated in the Baroque era and is still performed today. It usually consists of four independent movements, which each have distinct structures. When a sonata was played by woodwinds from church towers or steeples, they were called tower sonatas.

121. e. The Italian word *arpeggio* means "in the manner of the harp" and describes successive chord playing.

122. d. Bebop is an original form of jazz with accents on both the second and fourth beats. Sometimes, the music is accompanied by the singing of nonsense syllables.

123. a. Any harpsichord of Italian heritage is known as a clavicembalo.

124. c. Fantasia is a freestyle musical piece that is structured according to the composer's whim.

125. a. The gigue, or giga, is an energetic Baroque dance, usually performed in 6/8, 6/4, 9/8, or 12/16 meter.

126. c. Homophony is when two or more musical parts move in harmony, thus creating chords. This is different than polyphony, where parts move independently, and monophony, where parts move in parallel rhythm and pitch.

127. c. While many Puerto Rican music styles descended from African sounds, a few styles, like the jiharo, reflect a more European influence.

128. a. The mazurka is the national Polish dance. This folk dance became popular at ballroom dances in the rest of Europe during the nineteenth century.

129. c. A composition that is based upon a single theme is said to be monothematic.

130. a. An oratorio is a musical piece, partially modeled on the opera, with its use of a choir, soloists, an ensemble, various distinguishable characters, and arias. However, the oratorio is strictly a concert piece, and there is little or no interaction between the characters and no props or elaborate costumes. Also, the oratorio deals strictly with sacred subjects, making this form acceptable for church performances.

131. e. Pizzicato is a technique that involves plucking the strings of an instrument. It varies depending on the type of stringed instrument, but with a violin (or any bowed string instruments), this involves playing by plucking the strings with the fingers, rather than using the bow. The sound produced is short and percussive, rather than sustained.

132. d. A quintet is a musical composition of five instruments or voices.

133. b. The term *jazz trio* traditionally refers to a group comprising a pianist, a double bass player, and a drummer. In most cases, the pianist is considered the trio leader and groups are named after them.

134. d. *The Cure for Insomnia* is officially the world's longest movie, according to Guinness World Records. Running 87 hours, it has no plot, instead consisting of artist L. D. Groban reading his lengthy poem *A Cure for Insomnia* over the course of three and a half days.

135. a. The Soviet movie *War and Peace,* based on Leo Tolstoy's novel of the same name, took seven years to produce and cost over $100 million. With inflation, this amount equates to over $700 million today, making this the most expensive film ever made.

136. c. Bollywood is one of the largest film producers in the world. The name is a combination of Bombay (the former name for Mumbai) and Hollywood, the center of the American film industry.

137. e. Capoeira started up in Brazil during the sixteenth century, as a result of the slave trading that took place and the previously enslaved local natives.

138. d. All the other instruments are played in a row called the bateria during the capoeira dance. Other instruments typically include the medio, viola, reco-reco (rasp), and the agogo (double gong bell).

139. e. This philosophic concept, based on the idea of existence without essence, is a key foundational concept of existentialism. It was formulated by Jean-Paul Sartre in the twentieth century.

140. b. The Declaration of Independence states that governments are instituted among humans to secure inalienable rights. The last sentence makes it clear that even when a government is overthrown, a new one must be formed to provide new guards for their [the people's] future security.

CLEP Humanities
Practice Test 2

Now take CLEP Humanities Practice Test 2 for additional CLEP practice. Similar to the official exam, you will answer 140 questions. Again, we suggest that you follow the time constraints of the official CLEP Humanities exam (90 minutes).

Remember, on the official CLEP, there is no penalty for incorrect answers, so always make a guess if you are unsure of an answer.

When you are finished, check the answer key on page 747 carefully to assess your results.

▶ CLEP Humanities Practice Test 2

1.	ⓐ ⓑ ⓒ ⓓ ⓔ
2.	ⓐ ⓑ ⓒ ⓓ ⓔ
3.	ⓐ ⓑ ⓒ ⓓ ⓔ
4.	ⓐ ⓑ ⓒ ⓓ ⓔ
5.	ⓐ ⓑ ⓒ ⓓ ⓔ
6.	ⓐ ⓑ ⓒ ⓓ ⓔ
7.	ⓐ ⓑ ⓒ ⓓ ⓔ
8.	ⓐ ⓑ ⓒ ⓓ ⓔ
9.	ⓐ ⓑ ⓒ ⓓ ⓔ
10.	ⓐ ⓑ ⓒ ⓓ ⓔ
11.	ⓐ ⓑ ⓒ ⓓ ⓔ
12.	ⓐ ⓑ ⓒ ⓓ ⓔ
13.	ⓐ ⓑ ⓒ ⓓ ⓔ
14.	ⓐ ⓑ ⓒ ⓓ ⓔ
15.	ⓐ ⓑ ⓒ ⓓ ⓔ
16.	ⓐ ⓑ ⓒ ⓓ ⓔ
17.	ⓐ ⓑ ⓒ ⓓ ⓔ
18.	ⓐ ⓑ ⓒ ⓓ ⓔ
19.	ⓐ ⓑ ⓒ ⓓ ⓔ
20.	ⓐ ⓑ ⓒ ⓓ ⓔ
21.	ⓐ ⓑ ⓒ ⓓ ⓔ
22.	ⓐ ⓑ ⓒ ⓓ ⓔ
23.	ⓐ ⓑ ⓒ ⓓ ⓔ
24.	ⓐ ⓑ ⓒ ⓓ ⓔ
25.	ⓐ ⓑ ⓒ ⓓ ⓔ
26.	ⓐ ⓑ ⓒ ⓓ ⓔ
27.	ⓐ ⓑ ⓒ ⓓ ⓔ
28.	ⓐ ⓑ ⓒ ⓓ ⓔ
29.	ⓐ ⓑ ⓒ ⓓ ⓔ
30.	ⓐ ⓑ ⓒ ⓓ ⓔ
31.	ⓐ ⓑ ⓒ ⓓ ⓔ
32.	ⓐ ⓑ ⓒ ⓓ ⓔ
33.	ⓐ ⓑ ⓒ ⓓ ⓔ
34.	ⓐ ⓑ ⓒ ⓓ ⓔ
35.	ⓐ ⓑ ⓒ ⓓ ⓔ
36.	ⓐ ⓑ ⓒ ⓓ ⓔ
37.	ⓐ ⓑ ⓒ ⓓ ⓔ
38.	ⓐ ⓑ ⓒ ⓓ ⓔ
39.	ⓐ ⓑ ⓒ ⓓ ⓔ
40.	ⓐ ⓑ ⓒ ⓓ ⓔ
41.	ⓐ ⓑ ⓒ ⓓ ⓔ
42.	ⓐ ⓑ ⓒ ⓓ ⓔ
43.	ⓐ ⓑ ⓒ ⓓ ⓔ
44.	ⓐ ⓑ ⓒ ⓓ ⓔ
45.	ⓐ ⓑ ⓒ ⓓ ⓔ
46.	ⓐ ⓑ ⓒ ⓓ ⓔ
47.	ⓐ ⓑ ⓒ ⓓ ⓔ
48.	ⓐ ⓑ ⓒ ⓓ ⓔ
49.	ⓐ ⓑ ⓒ ⓓ ⓔ
50.	ⓐ ⓑ ⓒ ⓓ ⓔ

51.	ⓐ ⓑ ⓒ ⓓ ⓔ
52.	ⓐ ⓑ ⓒ ⓓ ⓔ
53.	ⓐ ⓑ ⓒ ⓓ ⓔ
54.	ⓐ ⓑ ⓒ ⓓ ⓔ
55.	ⓐ ⓑ ⓒ ⓓ ⓔ
56.	ⓐ ⓑ ⓒ ⓓ ⓔ
57.	ⓐ ⓑ ⓒ ⓓ ⓔ
58.	ⓐ ⓑ ⓒ ⓓ ⓔ
59.	ⓐ ⓑ ⓒ ⓓ ⓔ
60.	ⓐ ⓑ ⓒ ⓓ ⓔ
61.	ⓐ ⓑ ⓒ ⓓ ⓔ
62.	ⓐ ⓑ ⓒ ⓓ ⓔ
63.	ⓐ ⓑ ⓒ ⓓ ⓔ
64.	ⓐ ⓑ ⓒ ⓓ ⓔ
65.	ⓐ ⓑ ⓒ ⓓ ⓔ
66.	ⓐ ⓑ ⓒ ⓓ ⓔ
67.	ⓐ ⓑ ⓒ ⓓ ⓔ
68.	ⓐ ⓑ ⓒ ⓓ ⓔ
69.	ⓐ ⓑ ⓒ ⓓ ⓔ
70.	ⓐ ⓑ ⓒ ⓓ ⓔ
71.	ⓐ ⓑ ⓒ ⓓ ⓔ
72.	ⓐ ⓑ ⓒ ⓓ ⓔ
73.	ⓐ ⓑ ⓒ ⓓ ⓔ
74.	ⓐ ⓑ ⓒ ⓓ ⓔ
75.	ⓐ ⓑ ⓒ ⓓ ⓔ
76.	ⓐ ⓑ ⓒ ⓓ ⓔ
77.	ⓐ ⓑ ⓒ ⓓ ⓔ
78.	ⓐ ⓑ ⓒ ⓓ ⓔ
79.	ⓐ ⓑ ⓒ ⓓ ⓔ
80.	ⓐ ⓑ ⓒ ⓓ ⓔ
81.	ⓐ ⓑ ⓒ ⓓ ⓔ
82.	ⓐ ⓑ ⓒ ⓓ ⓔ
83.	ⓐ ⓑ ⓒ ⓓ ⓔ
84.	ⓐ ⓑ ⓒ ⓓ ⓔ
85.	ⓐ ⓑ ⓒ ⓓ ⓔ
86.	ⓐ ⓑ ⓒ ⓓ ⓔ
87.	ⓐ ⓑ ⓒ ⓓ ⓔ
88.	ⓐ ⓑ ⓒ ⓓ ⓔ
89.	ⓐ ⓑ ⓒ ⓓ ⓔ
90.	ⓐ ⓑ ⓒ ⓓ ⓔ
91.	ⓐ ⓑ ⓒ ⓓ ⓔ
92.	ⓐ ⓑ ⓒ ⓓ ⓔ
93.	ⓐ ⓑ ⓒ ⓓ ⓔ
94.	ⓐ ⓑ ⓒ ⓓ ⓔ
95.	ⓐ ⓑ ⓒ ⓓ ⓔ
96.	ⓐ ⓑ ⓒ ⓓ ⓔ
97.	ⓐ ⓑ ⓒ ⓓ ⓔ
98.	ⓐ ⓑ ⓒ ⓓ ⓔ
99.	ⓐ ⓑ ⓒ ⓓ ⓔ
100.	ⓐ ⓑ ⓒ ⓓ ⓔ

101.	ⓐ ⓑ ⓒ ⓓ ⓔ
102.	ⓐ ⓑ ⓒ ⓓ ⓔ
103.	ⓐ ⓑ ⓒ ⓓ ⓔ
104.	ⓐ ⓑ ⓒ ⓓ ⓔ
105.	ⓐ ⓑ ⓒ ⓓ ⓔ
106.	ⓐ ⓑ ⓒ ⓓ ⓔ
107.	ⓐ ⓑ ⓒ ⓓ ⓔ
108.	ⓐ ⓑ ⓒ ⓓ ⓔ
109.	ⓐ ⓑ ⓒ ⓓ ⓔ
110.	ⓐ ⓑ ⓒ ⓓ ⓔ
111.	ⓐ ⓑ ⓒ ⓓ ⓔ
112.	ⓐ ⓑ ⓒ ⓓ ⓔ
113.	ⓐ ⓑ ⓒ ⓓ ⓔ
114.	ⓐ ⓑ ⓒ ⓓ ⓔ
115.	ⓐ ⓑ ⓒ ⓓ ⓔ
116.	ⓐ ⓑ ⓒ ⓓ ⓔ
117.	ⓐ ⓑ ⓒ ⓓ ⓔ
118.	ⓐ ⓑ ⓒ ⓓ ⓔ
119.	ⓐ ⓑ ⓒ ⓓ ⓔ
120.	ⓐ ⓑ ⓒ ⓓ ⓔ
121.	ⓐ ⓑ ⓒ ⓓ ⓔ
122.	ⓐ ⓑ ⓒ ⓓ ⓔ
123.	ⓐ ⓑ ⓒ ⓓ ⓔ
124.	ⓐ ⓑ ⓒ ⓓ ⓔ
125.	ⓐ ⓑ ⓒ ⓓ ⓔ
126.	ⓐ ⓑ ⓒ ⓓ ⓔ
127.	ⓐ ⓑ ⓒ ⓓ ⓔ
128.	ⓐ ⓑ ⓒ ⓓ ⓔ
129.	ⓐ ⓑ ⓒ ⓓ ⓔ
130.	ⓐ ⓑ ⓒ ⓓ ⓔ
131.	ⓐ ⓑ ⓒ ⓓ ⓔ
132.	ⓐ ⓑ ⓒ ⓓ ⓔ
133.	ⓐ ⓑ ⓒ ⓓ ⓔ
134.	ⓐ ⓑ ⓒ ⓓ ⓔ
135.	ⓐ ⓑ ⓒ ⓓ ⓔ
136.	ⓐ ⓑ ⓒ ⓓ ⓔ
137.	ⓐ ⓑ ⓒ ⓓ ⓔ
138.	ⓐ ⓑ ⓒ ⓓ ⓔ
139.	ⓐ ⓑ ⓒ ⓓ ⓔ
140.	ⓐ ⓑ ⓒ ⓓ ⓔ

▶ Practice Test Questions

1. A song of serious artistic intent written by a trained composer is called a(n)

   a. art song.

   b. folk song.

   c. composition.

   d. aria.

   e. symphony.

2. Which writer of *Divine Comedy* spent most of his life in exile after being on the losing side in political struggles in Florence?

   a. Petrarch

   b. Boccaccio

   c. Dante

   d. Castiglione

   e. Chaucer

3. In *The Book of the Courtier,* all the following are deemed to be necessary qualities of a gentlemen EXCEPT

   a. an agreeable personal demeanor.

   b. an active life.

   c. knowledge of Latin and Greek.

   d. a cache of wealth.

   e. a non-contemplative life.

4. Medieval architecture includes all the following EXCEPT

   a. pointed arches.

   b. flying buttresses.

   c. symmetry.

   d. details filling every niche.

   e. sharply pointed spires.

Use the following passage to answer questions 5–8.

He was an old man who fished alone in a skiff in the Gulf Stream and he had gone eighty-four days now without taking a fish. In the first forty days a boy had been with him. But after forty days without a fish the boy's parents had told him that the old man was now definitely and finally *salao,* which is the worst form of unlucky, and the boy had gone at their orders in another boat which caught three good fish the first week. It made the boy sad to see the old man come in each day with his skiff empty and he always went down to help him carry either the coiled lines or the gaff and harpoon and the sail that was furled around the mast. The sail was patched with flour sacks and, furled, it looked like the flag of permanent defeat.

The old man was thin and gaunt with deep wrinkles in the back of his neck. The brown blotches of the benevolent skin cancer the sun brings from its reflection on the tropic sea were on his cheeks. The blotches ran well down the sides of his face and his hands had the deep-created scars from handling heavy fish on the cords. But none of these scars were fresh. They were as old as erosions in a fishless desert.

Everything about him was old except his eyes and they were the same color as the sea and were cheerful and undefeated.

"Santiago," the boy said to him as they climbed the bank from where the skiff was hauled up. "I could go with you again. We've made some money."

The old man had taught the boy to fish and the boy loved him.

"No," the old man said. "You're with a lucky boat. Stay with them."

"But remember how you went eighty-seven days without fish and then we caught big ones every day for three weeks."

"I remember," the old man said. "I know you did not leave me because you doubted."

"It was Papa made me leave. I am a boy and I must obey him."

"I know," the old man said. "It is quite normal."

"He hasn't much faith."

"No," the old main said. "But we have. Haven't we?"

—Excerpt from *The Old Man and the Sea* by Ernest Hemingway. Reproduced with the permission of Scribner, an imprint of Simon & Schuster Adult Publishing Group, from *The Old Man and the Sea* by Ernest Hemingway. Copyright 1952 by Ernest Hemingway. Copyright renewed © 1980 by Mary Hemingway.

5. The simile *as old as erosions in a fishless desert* helps emphasize

   a. the length of time the man has gone without a fish.

   b. how thin and gaunt the old man now looks.

   c. how few fish are in the ocean for the man to catch.

   d. how hot and sunny the weather has been lately.

   e. the way the old man aches after years of fishing.

6. Why do the boy's parents want the boy to fish with someone other than the old man?

   a. They think that the old man is a bad fisherman.

   b. They think that the boy spends too much time with the man.

   c. They are jealous of the boy's relationship with the man.

   d. They want the boy to get to know more people.

   e. They want the boy to make money for the family.

7. What does the description of the old man's fishing gear show about him?

   a. It shows that the old man does not take care of his equipment.

   b. It shows that the old man no longer wants to be a fisherman.

   c. It shows that the old man does not have much money.

   d. It shows that the old man has more supplies than other fishermen.

   e. It shows that the old man does not know as much as other fishermen.

8. Based on the information in this excerpt, if the boy's parents opened a business selling fruits and vegetables, how would they react if they didn't make a good profit after the first two months?

   a. They would try to sell something else that would make them more money.

   b. They would ask the old man to help them make their business more successful.

   c. They would hold out hope that business would pick up in the third month.

   d. They would try to do more advertising and give free samples to customers.

   e. They would sell some of their things in order to keep the business.

Use the following passage to answer questions 9 and 10.

Beginning in 1958 . . . local NAACP [National Association for the Advancement of Colored People] chapters organized sit-ins, where African Americans, many of whom were college students, took seats and demanded service at segregated all-white lunch counters. It was, however, the sit-in demonstrations at Woolworth's store in Greensboro, North Carolina, beginning on February 1, 1960, that caught national attention and sparked other sit-ins and demonstrations in the South. One of the four students in the first Greensboro sit-in, Joe McNeil, later recounted his experience: " . . . we sat at a lunch counter where blacks never sat before. And people started to look at us. The help, many of whom were black, looked at us in disbelief too. They were concerned about our safety. We asked for service, and we were denied, and we expected to be denied. We asked why we couldn't be served, and obviously we weren't given a reasonable answer and it was our intent to sit there until they decided to serve us."

Source: www.congresslink.org and Henry Hampton and Steve Fayer (eds.), *Voices of Freedom: An Oral History of the Civil Rights Movement from the 1950s through the 1980s*, Vintage Paperback, 1995.

9. The writer has not directly stated, but would support, which of the following statements?
   a. Without the sit-in in Greensboro, NC, the Civil Rights movement would never have started.
   b. Woolworth's served affordable lunches.
   c. Local NAACP chapters were causing trouble and upsetting citizens.
   d. Nobody was surprised when black college students took a seat at the all-white lunch counter.
   e. The college students showed courage when they participated in the Greensboro sit-in.

10. What is the author's purpose in including Joe McNeil's quotation?
    a. to show that young people are the most likely to push for societal change
    b. to demonstrate that everyone has a different point of view
    c. to give a firsthand account of what has become a historic event
    d. to discount the importance of the Civil Rights movement
    e. to show that the college students had not intended to create a stir

11. The line "Death is the end of every worldly pain" comes from which story in *The Canterbury Tales*?
    a. The Cook's Tale
    b. The Pardoner's Tale
    c. The Knight's Tale
    d. The Miller's Tale
    e. The Wife of Bath's Tale

12. Which John Steinbeck novel centers around two migrant workers in California during the Great Depression?
- **a.** *East of Eden*
- **b.** *The Grapes of Wrath*
- **c.** *Travels with Charley*
- **d.** *Of Mice and Men*
- **e.** *The Red Pony*

Use the following poem to answer questions 13–16.

War Is Kind

(1) Do not weep, maiden, for war is kind.
Because your lover threw wild hands toward the sky
And the affrighted steed ran on alone,
Do not weep.
(5) War is kind.
Hoarse, booming drums of the regiment
Little souls who thirst for fight,
These men were born to drill and die
The unexplained glory flies above them
(10) Great is the battle-god, great, and his kingdom—
A field where a thousand corpses lie.
Do not weep, babe, for war is kind.
Because your father tumbled in the yellow trenches,
Raged at his breast, gulped and died,
(15) Do not weep.
War is kind.
Swift, blazing flag of the regiment
Eagle with crest of red and gold,
These men were born to drill and die
(20) Point for them the virtue of slaughter
Make plain to them the excellence of killing
And a field where a thousand corpses lie.
Mother whose heart hung humble as a button
On the bright splendid shroud of your son,
(25) Do not weep. War is kind.

—Stephen Crane

13. Which of the following best conveys the theme of the poem?
- **a.** War is unkind, but necessary.
- **b.** There is no virtue in war.
- **c.** We should not weep for soldiers, because they died in glory.
- **d.** Everyone must sacrifice in a war.
- **e.** There are many ways to die in a war.

14. The speaker addresses three people in the poem: a maiden (line 1), a babe (a child, line 12), and a mother (line 23). What feeling in these listeners is the speaker addressing?
- **a.** their grief
- **b.** their pride
- **c.** their anger
- **d.** their joy
- **e.** their fear

15. From what you know about the speaker in the poem, what do you think he would do if his country went to war?
- **a.** Join the military right away.
- **b.** Travel around the country trying to rally support for the war.
- **c.** Protest against the war.
- **d.** Cover the war as a reporter.
- **e.** Hurt himself so he would not have to fight.

16. The speaker calls the *kingdom* of the *battle-god* (line 10) a *field where a thousand corpses lie* (line 11), and repeats line 11 again in line 22. What is the effect of this line and its repetition?

a. It demonstrates the might of the battle god.

b. It shows how many casualties you can expect in a war.

c. It reminds us to expect many deaths in a battle.

d. It makes us fear the anger of such a powerful god.

e. It shows us that the battle-god is a terrible god who should not be worshipped.

Use the following passage to answer questions 17–21.

[*Biff is talking with his brother, Happy. They are together with their parents in the home where they grew up.*]

BIFF: [*with rising agitation*] Hap, I've had twenty or thirty different kinds of jobs since I left home before the war, and it always turns out the same. I just realized it lately. In Nebraska, when I herded cattle, and the Dakotas, and Arizona, and now in Texas. It's why I came home now, I guess, because I realized it. This farm I work on, it's spring there now, see? And they've got about fifteen new colts. There's nothing more inspiring or—beautiful than the sight of a mare and a new colt. And it's cool there now, see? Texas is cool now, and it's spring. And whenever spring comes to where I am, I suddenly get the feeling, my God, I'm not gettin' anywhere! What the hell am I doing, playing around with horses, twenty-eight dollars a week! I'm thirty-four years old, I oughta be makin' my future. That's when I come running home. And now, I get here, and I don't know what to do with myself. [*After a pause.*] I've always made a point of not wasting my life, and

every time I come back here I know that all I've done is to waste my life.

HAPPY: You're a poet, you know that, Biff? You're a—you're an idealist!

BIFF: No, I'm mixed up very bad. Maybe I oughta get married. Maybe I oughta get stuck into something. Maybe that's my trouble. I'm like a boy. I'm not married, I'm not in business, I just—I'm like a boy. Are you content, Hap? You're a success, aren't you? Are you content?

HAPPY: Hell, no!

BIFF: Why? You're making money, aren't you?

HAPPY: [*moving about with energy, expressiveness*] All I can do now is wait for the merchandise manager to die. And suppose I get to be merchandise manager? He's a good friend of mine, and he just built a terrific estate on Long Island. And he lived there about two months and sold it, and now he's building another one. He can't enjoy it once it's finished. And I know that's just what I would do. I don't know what the hell I'm workin' for. Sometimes I sit in my apartment—all alone. And I think of the rent I'm paying. And it's crazy. But then, it's what I always wanted. My own apartment, a car, and plenty of women. And still, goddammit, I'm lonely.

—from *Death of a Salesman,*
by Arthur Miller

17. Biff has come home because

a. he needs a vacation.

b. he isn't earning enough money at his new job.

c. he feels like he isn't getting anywhere in life.

d. he likes to be home in springtime.

e. he misses his family.

18. Which of the following sentences best describes what's wrong with Happy?

   a. You can't run away from yourself.

   b. Money can't buy happiness.

   c. What goes around comes around.

   d. Good things come to those who wait.

   e. Money is the root of all evil.

19. Which of the following sentences best describes what's wrong with Biff?

   a. He needs to stop being selfish and find someone to love.

   b. He needs to grow up and stop acting like a baby.

   c. He needs to pick one career and work hard until he achieves success.

   d. He needs to stop moving around so much and just stay in one place.

   e. He needs to accept who he is and stop searching elsewhere for happiness.

20. Why isn't the merchandise manager happy?

   a. He doesn't have enough money.

   b. He knows Happy is after his job.

   c. The more he has, the more he wants.

   d. He is lonely.

   e. He didn't like the way his estate was built.

21. Based on this excerpt, which of the following can we conclude about Happy's name?

   a. It is ironic.

   b. It is appropriate.

   c. It is a nickname.

   d. It is not his real name.

   e. It is symbolic.

Use the following passage to answer questions 22–25.

The young officials laughed at and made fun of him, and told in his presence various stories concocted about him, and about his landlady, an old woman of seventy; declared that she beat him; asked when the wedding was to be; and strewed bits of paper over his head, calling them snow. But Akakiy Akakievitch answered not a word, any more than if there had been no one there besides himself. It even had no effect upon his work: amid all these annoyances he never made a single mistake in a letter. But if the joking became wholly unbearable, as when they jogged his hand and prevented his attending to his work, he would exclaim, "Leave me alone! Why do you insult me?" And there was something strange in the words and the voice in which they were uttered. There was in it something which moved to pity; so much that one young man, a newcomer, who, taking pattern by the others, had permitted himself to make sport of Akakiy, suddenly stopped short, as though all about him had undergone a transformation, and presented itself in a different aspect. Some unseen force repelled him from the comrades whose acquaintance he had made, on the supposition that they were well-bred and polite men. Long afterwards there recurred to his mind the little official with the bald forehead, with his heart-rending words, "Leave me alone! Why do you insult me?" In these moving words, other words resounded—"I am thy brother." And the young man covered his face with his hand; and many a time afterwards, in the course of his life, shuddered at seeing how much inhumanity there is in man. [. . .]

   It would be difficult to find another man who lived so entirely for his duties. It is not enough to say that Akakiy labored with zeal: no, he labored with love. In his copying, he found a varied and agreeable employment. Enjoyment was written on his face: some letters were even favorites with him; and when he encountered these, he smiled, winked, and worked with his lips, till it seemed as though each letter might be read in his face, as his pen traced it.

Moreover, it is impossible to say that no attention was paid to him. One director being a kindly man, and desirous of rewarding him for his long service, ordered him to be given something more important than mere copying. So he was ordered to make a report of an already concluded affair to another department: the duty consisting simply in changing the heading and altering a few words from the first to the third person. This caused him so much toil that he broke into a perspiration, rubbed his forehead, and finally said, "No, give me rather something to copy." After that they let him copy on forever.

—from *The Cloak*
by Nikolai Vasilievich Gogol

22. Most of the time, Akakiy's colleagues treat him with
   a. respect.
   b. admiration.
   c. contempt.
   d. pity.
   e. reverence.

23. What does the newcomer learn from his experience with Akakiy?
   a. Teasing is a form of cruelty.
   b. Some people cannot take a joke.
   c. The other officials are nice people.
   d. Akakiy and he are long-lost brothers.
   e. Akakiy deserves poor treatment.

24. Which best describes Akakiy's attitude toward his work?
   a. He resents being just a copier.
   b. He is a risk-taker.
   c. He starts trouble with other workers.
   d. He loves his work.
   e. He is bored with his work as a copier.

25. All of the following describe Akakiy EXCEPT
   a. patient.
   b. anxious.
   c. diligent.
   d. angry.
   e. shy.

Use the following passage to answer questions 26–28.

Young George Willard, who had nothing to do, was glad about the snow because he did not feel like working that day. The weekly paper had been printed and taken to the post office Wednesday evening and the snow began to fall on Thursday. At eight o'clock, after the morning train had passed, he went up to Waterworks Pond. There he built a fire against the side of a log and sat down at the end of the log to think.

The young reporter was thinking of Kate Swift, who had once been his school teacher. On the evening before he had gone to her house to get a book she wanted him to read and had been alone with her for an hour. For the fourth or fifth time the woman had talked to him with great earnestness and he could not make out what she meant by her talk. He began to believe she must be in love with him and the thought was both pleasing and annoying. Looking about to be sure he was alone he talked aloud, "Oh," he declared. "I am going to find out about you. You wait and see."

It was past ten o'clock when Kate Swift set out and the walk was unpremeditated. It was as though the boy, by thinking of her, had driven her forth into the wintry streets. Kate Swift's mind was ablaze with thoughts of George Willard. In something he had written as a school boy she thought she had recognized the spark of genius and wanted to blow on the spark. One day in the summer she had gone to the Eagle office and finding the boy unoccupied had taken him out Main Street to the Fair Ground, where the two sat on a grassy bank and talked. The school teacher tried to bring home to the mind of the boy some conception of the difficulties he would have to face as a writer. "You will have to know life," she declared, and her voice trembled with earnestness. She took hold of George Willard's shoulders and turned him about so that she could look into his eyes. A passerby might have thought them about to embrace. "If you are to become a writer you'll have to stop fooling with words," she explained. "It would be better to give up the notion of writing until you are better prepared. Now it's time to be living. I don't want to frighten you, but I would like to make you understand the import of what you think of attempting. You must not become a mere peddler of words. The thing to learn is to know what people are thinking about, not what they say."

—from *The Teacher* by Sherwood Anderson

26. Why does George suspect Kate loves him?
   a. She told him.
   b. She gave him good grades in school.
   c. She wrote him a letter.
   d. She embraced him once.
   e. She has spoken to him several times with great enthusiasm.

27. What is Kate's reason for pursuing George?
   a. She is, in fact, in love with him.
   b. She wants to encourage him in his writing.
   c. She wants him to teach her how to build a fire.
   d. She wants his advice about writing.
   e. She wants to frighten him.

28. Kate gives George the following advice: *It would be better to give up the notion of writing until you are better prepared. Now it's time to be living.* What does she mean by this?
   a. George will never be a good writer.
   b. George should forget about writing because he's going to die soon.
   c. George should have experiences in life before he starts writing.
   d. George should go to college go to learn how to write.
   e. George should make more time in his life for writing.

Use the following poem to answer questions 29–31.

If you can keep your head when all about you
Are losing theirs and blaming it on you;
If you can trust yourself when all men doubt you,
But make allowance for their doubting too:
If you can wait and not be tired by waiting,
Or, being lied about, don't deal in lies,
Or being hated don't give way to hating,
And yet don't look too good, nor talk too wise;

If you can dream—and not make dreams your master;
If you can think—and not make thoughts your aim,
If you can meet with Triumph and Disaster
And treat those two impostors just the same;
[. . .]

CLEP HUMANITIES PRACTICE TEST 2

If you can talk with crowds and keep your virtue,
Or walk with Kings—nor lose the common
   touch,
If neither foes nor loving friends can hurt you,
If all men count with you, but none too much;
[. . .]
Yours is the Earth and everything that's in it,
And—which is more—you'll be a Man, my son!
          —from "If" by Rudyard Kipling

29. The first stanza of this poem appears to give
advice about
  a. not allowing other people to influence you.
  b. following what other people do.
  c. how it's okay to lie if someone has lied to you.
  d. how you should only hate people who hate you.
  e. not waiting for good things to happen to you.

30. What is the best paraphrase of the following line:
If you can dream—and not make dreams your
master?
  a. Pursue your goals no matter what happens.
  b. Dreaming too much can ruin your life.
  c. Don't allow the pursuit of your dreams to take
over your life.
  d. Help others make their dreams come true.
  e. Mastering your dreams will make you
successful.

31. Which would make a good title for this passage?
  a. *Lying in Wait for Enemies*
  b. *Master your Dreams*
  c. *How to Be Rich and Famous*
  d. *Win Over Kings and Commoners*
  e. *Living Successfully*

Use the following passage to answer questions 32–34.

Being born female and black were two handicaps
Gwendolyn Brooks states that she faced from her

birth, in 1917, in Kansas. Brooks was determined
to succeed. Despite the lack of encouragement
she received from her teachers and others, she
was determined to write, and found the first
publisher for one of her poems when she was 11.

In 1945, she marketed and sold her first book;
national recognition ensued. She applied for and
received grants and fellowships from such organizations as the American Academy of Arts and
Letters and the Guggenheim Foundation. Later
she received the Pulitzer Prize for poetry; she was
the first black woman to receive such an honor.

Brooks was an integrationist in the 1940s and
an advocate of black consciousness in the 1960s.
Her writing styles show that she is not bound by
rules; her works are not devoid of the truth, even
about sensitive subjects like the black experience,
life in the ghetto, and city life.

Brooks's reaction to fame is atypical. She continues to work—and work hard. She writes, travels, and helps many who are interested in writing.
Especially important to her is increasing her
knowledge of her black heritage and encouraging
other people to do the same. She encourages
would-be writers to stay dedicated to their art.

32. Which of the following phrases best describes the
passage?
  a. a discussion of the importance of Gwendolyn
Brooks's writings
  b. an essay on the achievements of Gwendolyn
Brooks
  c. an essay on Gwendolyn Brooks as a black
female role model
  d. a biographical sketch on Gwendolyn Brooks
  e. a discussion of the handicaps faced by black
women writers

33. The passage implies that Brooks received less credit than she deserved primarily because of which of the following?

   a. She tried to publish too early in her career.

   b. She was aided by funds received through grants.

   c. She was a frequent victim of both racial and gender discrimination.

   d. Her work was too complex to be of widespread interest to others.

   e. She had no interest in the accolades of her colleagues.

34. According to the passage, Gwendolyn Brooks

   a. marketed her first book when she was 11 years old.

   b. achieved national recognition when she received the Pulitzer Prize.

   c. advocated black consciousness in the 1940s.

   d. received little encouragement from her teachers.

   e. avoided "black" topics in her writing.

Use the following passage to answer questions 35–38.

The little flat mail-pockets strapped under the rider's thighs would each hold about the bulk of a child's primer. They held many and many an important business chapter and newspaper letter, but these were written on paper as airy and thin as gold-leaf, nearly and thus bulk and weight were economized. The stagecoach traveled about a hundred to a hundred and twenty-five miles a day (twenty-four hours), the pony-rider about two hundred and fifty. There were about eighty pony-riders in the saddle all the time, night and day, stretching in a long, scattering procession from Missouri to California, forty flying eastward, and forty toward the west, and among

them making four hundred gallant horses earn a stirring livelihood and see a deal of scenery every single day in the year.

We had had a consuming desire, from the beginning, to see a pony-rider, but somehow or other all that passed us and all that met us managed to streak by in the night, and so we heard only a whiz and a hail, and the swift phantom of the desert was gone before we could get our heads out of the windows. But now we were expecting one along every moment, and would see him in broad daylight. Presently the driver exclaims:

"HERE HE COMES!—"

Every neck is stretched further, and every eye strained wider. Away across the endless dead level of the prairie a black speck appears against the sky, and it is plain that it moves. Well, I should think so! In a second or two it becomes a horse and rider, rising and falling, rising and falling, rising and falling—sweeping toward us nearer and nearer—growing more and more distinct, more and more sharply defined—nearer and still nearer, and the flutter of the hoofs comes faintly to the ear—another instant a whoop and a hurrah from our upper deck, a wave of the rider's hand, but no reply, and a man and a horse burst past our excited faces, and go swinging away like a belated fragment of a storm!

—from *Roughing It*, by Mark Twain

35. Based on the tone of the passage, which of the following words best describes the narrator's attitude toward the Pony Express rider?

   a. indifference

   b. fear

   c. bewilderment

   d. excitement

   e. resentment

36. The sighting of the pony rider is told from which viewpoint?
- **a.** a person sitting on a porch
- **b.** a passenger inside a stagecoach
- **c.** a passenger in a hot air balloon
- **d.** a person picnicking
- **e.** a pony rider

37. The reader can infer that the stagecoach in the passage did NOT
- **a.** carry mail.
- **b.** have windows.
- **c.** travel by night.
- **d.** travel a different route from that of the Pony Express.
- **e.** travel more miles daily than the pony rider.

38. Which of the following is NOT supported by the passage?
- **a.** The mail was strapped in a pouch under the rider's thighs.
- **b.** The rider rode great distances to deliver the mail.
- **c.** People did not care about the pony express rider.
- **d.** Usually 80 pony riders were in the saddle at any given time.
- **e.** The pony rider rode about 250 miles a day.

Use the following passage to answer questions 39–43.

Because I Could Not Stop for Death

Because I could not stop for Death,
He kindly stopped for me;
The carriage held but just ourselves
And Immortality.

We slowly drove, he knew no haste,
And I had put away
My labour, and my leisure too,
For his civility.

We passed the school where children played,
Their lessons scarcely done;
We passed the fields of gazing grain,
We passed the setting sun.

We paused before a house that seemed
A swelling of the ground;
The roof was scarcely visible,
The cornice but a mound.

Since then 'tis centuries; but each
Feels shorter than the day
I first surmised the horses' heads
Were toward eternity.

39. The image of Death presented in stanza 1 is that of
- **a.** an indifferent driver.
- **b.** a kindly gentleman.
- **c.** an immortal god disguised as a human.
- **d.** none of the above
- **e.** all of the above

40. The main idea of the poem is that
- **a.** death kidnaps its victims and drives away emotionlessly.
- **b.** death is dull; its chief torment is boredom.
- **c.** death is a gentle timeless journey, simply leaving life's cares behind.
- **d.** death is an eternity.
- **e.** death comes slowly calling on visitors.

41. In stanza 2, the word *haste* can be defined as
- **a.** sorrow.
- **b.** hurry.
- **c.** guilt.
- **d.** emotion.
- **e.** sloth.

42. The image described in stanza 4 most closely represents

a. a blurring of life and death.

b. an inability of the dead to focus on the world of the living.

c. a description of the grave.

d. a last image of security one sees before one dies.

e. a memory of a childhood home.

43. One can infer from the tone of the poem that the speaker

a. views Death as a pleasant companion.

b. views Death as an intruder.

c. views Death as a figure of authority.

d. views Death as an intimate friend.

e. views death as an unwanted visitor.

44. Seen my lady home las' night,
  Jump back, honey, jump back.
Hel' huh han' an' sque'z it tight,
  Jump back, honey, jump back.
Hyeahd huh sigh a little sigh
Seen a light gleam f'om huh eye,
An' a smile go flittin' by—
  Jump back, honey, jump back.
            —from "A Negro Love Song"
                by Paul Laurence Dunbar

This poem is an example of

a. colloquialism.

b. dialect.

c. jargon.

d. slang.

e. hyperbole.

45. Grendel is no braver, no stronger than I am! I could kill him with my sword; I shall not, easy as it would be. This fiend is a bold and famous fighter, but his claws and teeth . . . beating at my sword blade, would be helpless. I will meet him with my hands empty—unless his heart fails him, seeing a soldier waiting weaponless, unafraid. Let God in His wisdom extend His hand where He wills, reward whom he chooses!

Where are the above lines from?

a. *The Odyssey*

b. *Beowulf*

c. *The Kraken*

d. *The Iliad*

e. *The Faerie Queene*

46. What classical guitarist, who reportedly heard the blues for the first time in a Mississippi train station, was the first to compose and distribute "blues" music officially throughout the United States, although its popularity was chiefly among blacks in the South?

a. Bessie Smith

b. Willie Brown

c. Willie Dixon

d. Johnny Lee Hooker

e. W. C. Handy

Use the following passage to answer questions 47–49.

(1) Good things are commonly divided into three classes: (1) external goods, (2) goods of the soul, and (3) goods of the body. Of these, we call the goods pertaining to the soul goods in the highest

(5) and fullest sense. But in speaking of "soul," we refer to our soul's actions and activities. Thus, our definition [of good] tallies with this opinion, which has been current for a long time and to

which philosophers subscribe. We are also right
(10) in defining the end as consisting of actions and
activities; for in this way the end is included
among the goods of the soul and not among
external goods.

Also the view that a happy man lives well and
(15) fares well fits in with our definition: for we have
all but defined happiness as a kind of good life
and well-being. Moreover, the characteristics
which one looks for in happiness are all included
in our definition.

(20)   For some people think that happiness is a
virtue, others that it is practical wisdom, others
that it is some kind of theoretical wisdom; others
again believe it to be all or some of these accompanied by, or not devoid of, pleasure; and some
(25) people also include external prosperity in its
definition.

—from Book One of Aristotle's
Nicomachean Ethics

47. According to the passage, the greatest goods
  a. are theoretical.
  b. are spiritual.
  c. are intellectual.
  d. create happiness.
  e. create prosperity.

48. The author's definition of happiness in lines
15–19 is related to the definition of good in that
  a. living a good life will bring you happiness.
  b. happiness is the same as goodness.
  c. happiness is often sacrificed to attain the
good.
  d. all things that create happiness are good
things.
  e. happiness is a virtue.

49. The word *tallies* in line 7 means
  a. keeps count.
  b. records.
  c. labels.
  d. corresponds.
  e. scores.

50. Much of the Western world of the thirteenth and
fourteenth centuries knew about the Mongols
and Asia was the result of what famous travel
account written by Marco Polo?
  a. *Pausanias*
  b. *The Narrow Road to the Deep North and Other
Travel Sketches*
  c. *Pictures of Italy*
  d. *On a Chinese Screen*
  e. *Il Milione*

51. Whenever a violinist presses a finger of the left
hand onto a string, what happens?
  a. the possible melodies are limited
  b. a note is held
  c. the string is susceptible to breakage
  d. the length of the string is shortened
  e. the length of the string is extended

52. Denis Diderot's *Encyclopedia* primarily
pertained to
  a. religion.
  b. technology.
  c. nature.
  d. philosophy.
  e. romance.

53. "The person of the king is sacred, and to attack him in any way is an attack on religion itself. God has the kings anointed by his prophets . . . in the same way he has bishops and altars anointed . . . The respect given to a king is religious in nature. Serving God and respecting kings are bound together. . . ."

In this statement, Jacques Bossuet (1627–1704) is arguing for which of the following positions?
a. unlimited monarchy
b. the divine power of prophets
c. the importance of religious feeling
d. the Protestant attack on bishops and altars
e. the morality of deicide

Use the following quotes to answer question 54.

"You shall not deduct interest from loans to your countryman, whether in money or food or anything else that can be deducted as interest."
—Deuteronomy, 23:20

"That which you seek to increase by interest will not be blessed by God; but the alms you give for his sake shall be repaid to you many times over."
—Koran, 30:39

"If indeed someone has fallen into the error of presuming to stubbornly insist that the practice of interest is not sinful, we decree that he is to be punished as a heretic."
—Canon 29 of the Roman Catholic Council of Vienne (1311)

54. What is the best conclusion based on the three quotations?
a. Judeo-Christian law is the basis of modern economic theory.
b. Many religious precepts are at odds with banking.
c. Money lending was an honored position in medieval Europe.
d. It is simple to balance capitalist competition and spiritual brotherhood.
e. The Council of Vienne reversed the Catholic Church's long-standing ban on usury.

55. "Four score and seven years ago our fathers brought forth on this continent, a new nation, conceived in liberty, and dedicated to the proposition that all men are created equal."
—President Abraham Lincoln's *Gettysburg Address*

In this famous opening sentence from the *Gettysburg Address,* President Abraham Lincoln referred to what event in the past?
a. Columbus's arrival in the Americas
b. the landing of the Pilgrims on Plymouth Rock
c. the writing of the Declaration of Independence
d. the signing of the Constitution
e. the decisive Civil War battle at Gettysburg in 1863

Use the following excerpt to answer questions 56–61.

None of them knew the color of the sky. Their eyes glanced level, and were fastened upon the waves that swept toward them. These waves were of the hue of slate, save for the tops, which were foaming white, and all of the men knew the colors of the sea.

The cook squatted in the bottom as he bent to bail out the boat.

The oiler, steering with one of two oars in the boat, sometimes raised himself suddenly to keep clear of water that swirled in over the stern. It was a thin little oar and it seemed often ready to snap.

The correspondent, pulling at the other oar, watched the waves and wondered why he was there.

The injured captain, lying in the bow, was at this time buried in that profound dejection and indifference which comes, temporarily at least, to even the bravest and most enduring when, willy nilly, the firm fails, the army loses, the ship goes down.

As each slatey wall of water approached, it shut all else from the view of the men in the boat, and it was not difficult to imagine that this particular wave was the final outburst of the ocean. There was a terrible grace in the move of the waves, and they came in silence, save for the snarling of the crests.

In disjointed sentences the cook and the correspondent argued as to the difference between a life-saving station and a house of refuge. The cook had said: "There's a house of refuge just north of the Mosquito Inlet Light, and as soon as they see us, they'll come off in their boat and pick us up."

"As soon as who see us?" said the correspondent.

"The crew," said the cook.

"Houses of refuge don't have crews," said the correspondent. "As I understand them, they are only places where clothes and grub are stored for the benefit of shipwrecked people. They don't carry crews."

"Oh, yes, they do," said the cook.

"No, they don't," said the correspondent.

"Well, we're not there yet, anyhow," said the oiler, in the stern.

"Bully good thing it's an on-shore wind," said the cook. "If not, where would we be? Wouldn't have a show."

In the meantime the oiler and the correspondent sat together in the same seat, and each rowed an oar. Then the oiler took both oars; then the correspondent took both oars; then the oiler, then the correspondent.

The captain, rearing cautiously in the bow, after the dinghy soared on a great swell, said that he had seen the lighthouse at Mosquito Inlet.

"See it?" said the captain.

"No," said the correspondent slowly, "I didn't see anything."

"Look again," said the captain. He pointed. "It's exactly in that direction."

"Think we'll make it, captain?"

"If this wind holds and the boat don't swamp, we can't do much else," said the captain.

—from *The Open Boat* by Stephen Crane

56. Why did none of the four men know the color of the sky?
   a. They were keeping their eyes on the waves.
   b. They did not know what shade of gray the sky was.
   c. They were too tired to look at the sky.
   d. The sky was the same color as the water.
   e. The waves were too high to see the sky.

57. Why does the cook say . . . *good thing it's an on-shore wind. If not, where would we be?*
   a. An off-shore wind stirs up taller and more dangerous waves.
   b. An on-shore wind would blow them in toward land.
   c. He is trying to cheer up his companions by telling a lie.
   d. He doesn't know in which direction the land really is.
   e. He is echoing what the captain has said.

58. Why is the captain depressed and dejected?
   a. He is sad about losing his ship.
   b. He fears that a storm is coming.
   c. He is afraid that the waves will sink the dinghy.
   d. He knows that the wind is blowing the dinghy away from land.
   e. He is weak and tired from rowing.

59. Later in the story, the author writes:
   It would be difficult to describe the subtle brotherhood of men that was here established on the seas. . . . [T]here was this comradeship that the correspondent, for instance, who had been taught to be cynical of men, knew even at the time was the best experience of his life. But no one said that it was so. No one mentioned it.

   Which of the following is most likely the reason that the correspondent thought that this experience was the best of his life?
   a. He realized that the captain was the wisest man he had ever met.
   b. He discovered that working on a ship at sea was a wonderful life.
   c. He realized that the best things in life happen accidentally.
   d. He discovered the value of comradeship in the face of life-threatening danger.
   e. He realized that he and the other survivors would drown, no matter what they did.

60. Which of the following statements best compares the correspondent's and the cook's views about a house of refuge?
   a. Both men believe that crews from a house of refuge will rescue them.
   b. The correspondent says that a house of refuge has a crew, but the cook says it does not.
   c. Both men are sure that there are no houses of refuge along the coast.
   d. The cook says that a house of refuge has a crew, but the correspondent says it does not.
   e. Both men are doubtful that they will ever find a house of refuge.

61. How do you think the correspondent would react if the boat sprung a serious leak? He would probably
   a. become very frightened and upset the boat.
   b. ignore all orders from the captain.
   c. leap overboard and swim away.
   d. tell everyone to jump overboard.
   e. help the crew to bail out the water and keep the boat afloat.

62. Talking about his career choices, photographer Gordon Parks has said, "I picked up a camera because it was my choice of weapons against what I hated most about the universe: racism, intolerance, poverty." Why does Parks say that a camera is a *weapon*?
   a. It creates pictures that often get people fired.
   b. It is a tool an artist uses to capture beauty and light.
   c. It can capture and destroy the souls of people who are photographed.
   d. It is dangerous because it can be used to create propaganda.
   e. It can create photographs that lead to social and political change.

Use the following passage to answer questions 63–68.

It looked like a good thing: but wait till I tell you. We were down South, in Alabama—Bill Driscoll and myself—when this kidnapping idea struck us.

There was a town down there called Summit. Bill and me had a joint capital of about six hundred dollars, and we needed just two thousand dollars more to pull off a fraudulent town-lot scheme in Western Illinois.

We selected for our victim the only child of a prominent citizen named Ebenezer Dorset. The father was respectable and tight, a mortgage fancier [the narrator means "financier," someone who lends money to people who want to buy property]. The kid was a boy of ten. Bill and me figured that Ebenezer would melt down for a ransom of two thousand dollars to a cent.

About two miles from Summit was a little mountain. On the rear elevation of this mountain was a cave. There we stored provisions.

One evening after sundown, we drove in a buggy past old Dorset's house. The kid was in the street, throwing rocks at a kitten on the opposite fence.

"Hey, little boy!" says Bill, "would you like to have a bag of candy and a nice ride?"

The boy catches Bill neatly in the eye with a piece of brick.

"That will cost the old man an extra five hundred dollars," says Bill.

The boy put up a fight, but, at last, we got him down in the bottom of the buggy and drove away. We took him up to the cave. After dark I drove the buggy to the little village where we had hired it, and walked back to the mountain.

There was a fire burning behind the big rock at the entrance of the cave, and the boy was watching a pot of boiling coffee, with two buz-

zard tail-feathers stuck in his red hair. He points a stick at me when I come up, and says:

"Ha! Do you dare to enter the camp of Red Chief, the terror of the plains?"

"He's all right now," says Bill, rolling up his trousers and examining some bruises on his shins. "I'm Old Hank, the Trapper, Red Chief's captive, and I'm to be scalped at daybreak. By Geronimo! That kid can kick hard."

Yes, sir, that boy seemed to be having the time of his life. He immediately christened me Snake-eye, the Spy, and announced that I was to be broiled at the stake at the rising of the sun.

"Red Chief," says I to the kid, "would you like to go home?"

"Aw, what for?" says he. "I don't have any fun at home. I hate to go to school. I like to camp out. You won't take me back home again, Snake-eye, will you? I never had such fun in all my life."

We went to bed around eleven o'clock. I fell into a troubled sleep.

Just at daybreak, I was awakened by a series of awful screams from Bill. Red Chief was sitting on Bill's chest, with one hand twined in Bill's hair. In the other he had the sharp case-knife we used for slicing bacon; and he was trying to take Bill's scalp, according to the sentence that had been pronounced upon him the evening before.

I got the knife away from the kid and made him lie down again. But, from that moment, Bill's spirit was broken. He never closed an eye again in sleep as long as that boy was with us.

"Ain't it awful, Sam?" says Bill. "Do you think anybody will pay out money to get a little imp like that back home?"

—from *The Ransom of Red Chief* by O. Henry

63. Why do Sam and Bill want to kidnap the son of Ebenezer Dorset?

   a. They know that Ebenezer will pay them a ransom just to avoid publicity.

   b. They have failed to kidnap any other children from Summit.

   c. They need $100 and know that Ebenezer will pay that sum.

   d. Ebenezer's son is sickly and weak and will be easy to kidnap.

   e. They think that he is wealthy enough to pay a good deal of money to get his only son back.

64. Which of these lines of dialogue shows how the author uses nonstandard, informal grammar?

   a. "Do you dare to enter the camp of Red Chief?"

   b. "Red Chief, would you like to go home?"

   c. "I never had such fun in my life."

   d. "Oh, I got a kind of pain in my shoulder."

   e. "You was to be burned at sunrise."

65. How is Red Chief different from a typical kidnapping victim?

   a. Red Chief acts scared and pleads to go home.

   b. Red Chief scares and hurts his kidnappers.

   c. Red Chief doesn't like being kept hidden in a cave.

   d. Red Chief is afraid his father will not be able to meet the ransom.

   e. Red Chief is afraid he will be killed by his kidnappers.

66. Which words best describe the tone of the excerpt?

   a. dark and mysterious

   b. light-hearted and cheerful

   c. bitter and angry

   d. humorous and ironic

   e. objective and realistic

67. Later in the story, after another day spent with Red Chief, Sam and Bill write a ransom note to Ebenezer. They sign the note "Two Desperate Men." Based on this information and the excerpt, why do you think that the two men described themselves in this way?

   a. They cannot deal with Red Chief and are willing to do anything to get out of the situation.

   b. They want Ebenezer to understand that they will kill his son if they don't get the $2,000 ransom.

   c. They are wanted for crimes in other states.

   d. They are hungry and urgently need food.

   e. A storm is coming and they need more shelter than the cave can offer.

68. If Sam were to ask Bill to join him in another risky money-making scheme, how do you think Bill would respond? He would probably

   a. agree, because he owes Sam a lot of money.

   b. agree, because he enjoys doing risky things.

   c. refuse, because he doesn't trust Sam anymore.

   d. refuse, because he doesn't want to go to jail.

   e. be unable to decide, because he isn't used to doing anything on his own.

Use the following poem to answer questions 69–74.

He Had His Dream

(1) He had his dream, and all through life,
Worked up to it through toil and strife.
Afloat fore'er before his eyes,
It colored for him all his skies:
(5) The storm-cloud dark
Above his bark,
The calm and listless vault of blue
Took on its hopeful hue,
It tinctured every passing beam—
(10) He had his dream.
He labored hard and failed at last,
His sails too weak to bear the blast,
The raging tempests tore away
And sent his beating bark astray.
(15) But what cared he
For wind or sea!
He said, "The tempest will be short,
My bark will come to port."
He saw through every cloud a gleam—
(20) He had his dream.

            —Paul Laurence Dunbar

69. What is the meaning of the word *bark* in lines 6
and 14?
- **a.** heart
- **b.** storm
- **c.** ocean
- **d.** tree
- **e.** boat

70. Which of the following is true about the form of
the poem?
- **a.** Almost every pair of lines rhymes, and all
have the same rhythm pattern.
- **b.** The poem has two stanzas, and each follows
the same rhyme and rhythm pattern.
- **c.** The poem has no rhyming lines and no
regular rhythm pattern.
- **d.** Every other line of each stanza rhymes, and
has the same rhythm pattern.
- **e.** Every pair of lines rhymes, but there is no
regular rhythm pattern.

71. What is the main image presented by this poem?
- **a.** a hard-working man facing difficulties
- **b.** a ship being battered by a storm at sea
- **c.** a strong west wind
- **d.** a peaceful harbor
- **e.** a foolish man

72. Which word best describes the man who "had his
dream"?
- **a.** realistic
- **b.** optimistic
- **c.** sarcastic
- **d.** pessimistic
- **e.** analytic

73. Which of these sayings best expresses the message of this poem?
- **a.** A bird in the hand is worth two in the bush.
- **b.** A friend in need is a friend indeed.
- **c.** Necessity is the mother of invention.
- **d.** Keep your mind on your goal and never give
up.
- **e.** Wishing won't make it so.

74. In one of his most famous speeches, Dr. Martin Luther King, Jr., declared, "I have a dream." In the speech, Dr. King spoke of his hope to achieve a society in which people of all races are treated equally. How does the message of King's speech compare to the theme of Dunbar's poem?

a. Both writers emphasize the importance of pursuing a positive goal.

b. Both writers share their personal experiences about racial equality.

c. Neither writer actually believes that dreams can ever be truly fulfilled.

d. Neither writer accepts personal responsibility for taking steps to achieve a goal.

e. Both writers believe that dreams are important, but reality is unimportant.

Use the following passage to answer questions 75–80.

JULIET: Now, good sweet nurse,—O Lord, why look'st thou sad?
Though news be sad, yet tell them merrily;
If good, thou shamest the music of sweet news
By playing it to me with so sour a face.

NURSE: I am a-weary, give me leave awhile:
Fie, how my bones ache! what a jaunce [trip] I have had!

JULIET: I would thou hadst my bones, and I thy news.
Nay, come, I pray thee, speak; good, good nurse, speak.

NURSE: Can you not stay awhile?
Do you not see that I am out of breath?

JULIET: How are thou out of breath, when thou hast breath

To say to me that thou art out of breath?
The excuse that thou dost make in this delay
Is longer than the tale thou dost excuse.
Is thy news good, or bad? . . .
What says he of our marriage? what of that?

NURSE: Lord, how my head aches! what a head have I!
It beats as it would fall in twenty pieces. . . . Oh my back, my back! . . .

JULIET: I'faith, I am sorry that thou are not well.
Sweet, sweet, sweet nurse, tell me, what says my love? . . .

NURSE: Is this the poultice [medicated bandage] for my aching bones? . . .
Have you got leave to go to shrift [confession to a priest] to-day?

JULIET: I have.

NURSE: Then hie you hence to Friar Laurence's cell;
There stays a husband to make you a wife . . .
Hie you to church; I must another way,
To fetch a ladder, by the which your love
Must climb a bird's nest soon when it is dark . . .
Go; I'll to dinner; hie you to the cell.

JULIET: Hie to high fortune! Honest nurse, farewell.

—from *Romeo and Juliet*
by William Shakespeare

75. What is Juliet's response to the nurse when the nurse complains that she is out of breath?

   a. She says that if the nurse has breath enough to complain, she can't be out of breath.

   b. She says that the nurse is out of breath because she is ill.

   c. She is worried that the nurse will faint.

   d. She tells the nurse to rest and come back later.

   e. She says that if the nurse is out of breath, she should sit down and rest.

76. What is the real reason the nurse keeps complaining about her head and her back?

   a. She does not want to tell Juliet bad news.

   b. She was told by Romeo not to tell Juliet anything.

   c. She is afraid that Juliet will run away.

   d. She is teasing Juliet by withholding information about what Romeo has told her.

   e. The nurse is truly suffering aches and pains as a result of going to meet Romeo.

77. Why did Juliet send the nurse to meet Romeo?

   a. to find out whether anyone from her family has been spying on Romeo

   b. to find out whether Romeo is all right

   c. to find out when and where Romeo plans to marry her

   d. to tell him that she no longer wants to marry him

   e. to give the nurse something to do while Romeo is in the garden

78. Why does the nurse ask if Juliet has permission to go to confession?

   a. The nurse thinks Juliet should wait for Friar Laurence to come and visit her.

   b. The nurse wants to make sure that Juliet has an excuse to see Friar Laurence.

   c. The nurse is angry because Juliet has been disobedient.

   d. The nurse wants Juliet to stay with her until Romeo arrives.

   e. The nurse doesn't want Juliet to go to confession without her.

79. Which of the following events seems most likely, based on the information in this excerpt?

   a. Juliet's parents will prevent her from going to see Friar Laurence.

   b. Romeo will be killed before he and Juliet are married.

   c. Juliet will have an accident before she gets to see Friar Laurence.

   d. Friar Laurence will secretly marry Romeo and Juliet.

   e. Juliet will flee with Romeo to another country.

80. Earlier in the play, this conversation takes place between Romeo and the nurse.

ROMEO: Bid her devise
Some means to come to shrift this afternoon;
And there she shall at Friar Laurence' cell
Be . . . married.

NURSE: This afternoon, sir?
Well, she shall be there.

ROMEO: And stay, good, nurse, behind the
    abbey wall
Within this hour my man shall be with thee,
And bring thee cords made like a tackled stair. . . .

Based on this conversation and the excerpt,
which is the best conclusion?

a. The nurse is secretly spying on Romeo and
Juliet on orders from Juliet's parents.
b. The nurse will not provide the ladder Romeo
has asked for to climb to Juliet's chamber.
c. Romeo does not trust the nurse.
d. The nurse wants to help Juliet marry Romeo.
e. The nurse does not want Romeo to succeed in
marrying Juliet.

Use the following passage to answer questions 81–85.

(1) As Gregor Samsa awoke one morning from
uneasy dreams he found himself transformed in
his bed into a gigantic insect. He was lying on his
hard, as it were armor-plated, back and when he
(5) lifted his head a little he could see his domelike
brown belly divided into stiff arched segments
on top of which the bed quilt could hardly keep
in position and was about to slide off completely.
His numerous legs, which were pitifully thin
(10) compared to the rest of his bulk, waved helplessly
before his eyes.

What has happened to me? he thought. It was
no dream. His room, a regular human bedroom,
only rather too small, lay quiet between the four
(15) familiar walls. Above the table on which a collection of cloth samples was unpacked and spread
out—Samsa was a commercial traveler—hung
the picture which he had recently cut out of an
illustrated magazine and put into a pretty gilt
(20) frame. It showed a lady, with a fur cap on and a
fur stole, sitting upright and holding out to the
spectator a huge fur muff into which the whole
of her forearm had vanished!
. . . .
(25) He slid down again into his former position. This
getting up early, he thought, makes one quite stupid. A man needs his sleep. Other commercials
live like harem women. For instance, when I
come back to the hotel of a morning to write up
(30) the orders I've got, these others are only sitting
down to breakfast. Let me just try that with my
chief; I'd be sacked on the spot. Anyhow, that
might be quite a good thing for me, who can tell?
If I didn't have to hold my hand because of my
(35) parents I'd have given notice long ago, I'd have
gone to the chief and told him exactly what I
think of him. That would knock him endways
from his desk! It's a queer way of doing, too, this
sitting on high at a desk and talking down to
(40) employees, especially when they have to come
quite near because the chief is hard of hearing.
Well, there's still hope; once I've saved enough
money to pay back my parents' debts to him—
that should take another five or six years—I'll do
(45) it without fail. I'll cut myself completely loose
then. For the moment, though, I'd better get up,
since my train goes at five.

    —from *The Metamorphosis* by Franz Kafka

81. When Gregor Samsa wakes up, he realizes that he
  a. has been having a nightmare.
  b. is late for work.
  c. has turned into a giant bug.
  d. dislikes his job.
  e. needs to make a change in his life.

82. Which of the following best describes Gregor's job?
  a. magician
  b. traveling clothing salesman
  c. advertisement copywriter
  d. clothing designer
  e. magazine editor

83. Why must Gregor keep his current job for several more years?
  a. His parents owe his boss money.
  b. Gregor is an apprentice and must complete his program.
  c. Gregor wants to take over the chief's job.
  d. His parents own the company he works for.
  e. He needs to earn enough money to buy a bigger house for his family.

84. Based on the passage, which is the most logical conclusion to draw about Gregor's personality?
  a. Gregor is lazy and stupid.
  b. Gregor is a very successful salesman.
  c. Gregor resents being told what to do by people in authority.
  d. Gregor is hardworking and reliable.
  e. Gregor is very close to his family.

85. In lines 46–47, Gregor tells himself, *I'd better get up, since my train goes at five.* This suggests that
  a. Gregor has woken up as a bug before and is used to it.
  b. the other characters in the story are also bugs.
  c. Gregor is still dreaming.
  d. Gregor is going to be late.
  e. Gregor does not yet realize how serious his condition is.

Use the following passage to answer questions 86–90.

Alfonso

(1)　I am not the first poet born to my family.
　　We have painters and singers, actors and
　　　　carpenters.
　　I inherited my trade from my zio, Alfonso.
(5)　Zio maybe was the tallest man
　　in the village, he certainly was
　　the widest. He lost
　　his voice to cigarettes before I was born, but still
　　he roared
(10) with his hands, his eyes,
　　with his brow, and his deafening smile.
　　He worked the sea with my nonno
　　fishing in silence among the grottoes
　　so my father could learn to write and read
(15) and not speak like the guaglione,
　　filled with curses and empty pockets.
　　He would watch me write with wonder,
　　I could hear him on the couch, he looked at
　　the lines over my shoulder, tried to teach himself
(20)　to read
　　late in the soft Adriatic darkness.
　　Wine-stained pages gave him away.
　　But I learned to write from Zio—
　　He didn't need words, still he taught me the
(25)　language
　　of silence, the way
　　the sun can describe a shadow, a

gesture can paint a moment,
a scent could fill an entire village with words and
(30)   color and sound,
a perfect little grape tomato can be the most
    beautiful thing in the world,
seen through the right eyes.

—Marco A. Annunziata;
reprinted by permission of the author.

86. In line 3, the speaker says, "I inherited my trade from my zio, Alfonso." What trade did the speaker inherit?
a. painting
b. fishing
c. writing poetry
d. singing
e. carpentry

87. Which word best describes the speaker's feelings toward Alfonso?
a. shame
b. admiration
c. frustration
d. superiority
e. anger

88. Which of the following statements about Alfonso is true?
a. He was a writer.
b. He could not speak with his voice.
c. He could speak many languages.
d. He was a farmer.
e. He was a painter.

89. In lines 9–11, the speaker says that Alfonso *roared / with his hands, his eyes, / with his brow, and his deafening smile.* These lines suggest that Alfonso
a. was a very loud person.
b. was always angry.
c. was like a lion.
d. was always yelling.
e. was very expressive with his body.

90. Which of the following best sums up what the speaker has learned from Alfonso?
a. how to appreciate the beauty of the world
b. how to listen to others
c. how to appreciate his family
d. how to understand himself
e. how to read poetry

Use the following passage to answer questions 91–95.

[Helena is talking to Domain, the general manager of Rossum's Universal Robots factory.]

DOMAIN: Well, any one who's looked into anatomy will have seen at once that man is too complicated, and that a good engineer could make him more simply. So young Rossum began to overhaul anatomy and tried to see what could be left out or simplified. In short—but this isn't boring you, Miss Glory?

HELENA: No; on the contrary, it's awfully interesting.

DOMAIN: So young Rossum said to himself: A man is something that, for instance, feels happy, plays the fiddle, likes going for walks, and, in fact, wants to do a whole lot of things that are really unnecessary.

HELENA: Oh!

DOMAIN: Wait a bit. That are unnecessary when he's wanted, let us say, to weave or to count. Do you play the fiddle?

HELENA: No.

DOMAIN: That's a pity. But a working machine must not want to play the fiddle, must not feel happy, must not do a whole lot of other things. A petrol motor must not have tassels or ornaments, Miss Glory. And to manufacture artificial workers is the same thing as to manufacture motors. The process must be of the simplest, and the product of the best from a practical point of view. What sort of worker do you think is the best from a practical point of view?

HELENA: The best? Perhaps the one who is most honest and hard-working.

DOMAIN: No, the cheapest. The one whose needs are the smallest. Young Rossum invented a worker with the minimum amount of requirements. He had to simplify him. He rejected everything that did not contribute directly to the progress of work. In this way he rejected everything that made man more expensive. In fact, he rejected man and made the Robot. My dear Miss Glory, the Robots are not people. Mechanically they are more perfect than we are, they have an enormously developed intelligence, but they have no soul. Have you ever seen what a Robot looks like inside?

HELENA: Good gracious, no!

DOMAIN: Very neat, very simple. Really a beautiful piece of work. Not much in it, but everything in flawless order. The product of an engineer is technically at a higher pitch of perfection than a product of nature.

HELENA: Man is supposed to be the product of nature.

DOMAIN: So much the worse.

—from *R.U.R.* by Karel Čapek, translated by P. Selver

91. According to the passage, why are robots better workers than humans?
    a. Robots have a very simple anatomy.
    b. Robots are more intelligent.
    c. Robots are more honest and hardworking.
    d. Robots do not have a soul.
    e. Robots want things that are unnecessary.

92. Rossum created robots because
    a. humans are complicated and inefficient.
    b. humans are not honest enough.
    c. robots are always happy.
    d. he wanted to see if he could.
    e. there weren't enough people to do the work.

93. Which of the following best expresses Rossum's view of nature?
    a. Nature is beautiful.
    b. It is dangerous to try to improve upon nature.
    c. Nature is imperfect and unnecessarily complicated.
    d. Mother Nature is the greatest engineer of all.
    e. Machines are also a part of nature.

94. Based on the passage, Rossum is most likely
a. a robot.
b. a part-time inventor.
c. a retired doctor.
d. a foreman in the factory.
e. a very intelligent engineer.

95. Based on the passage, we can tell that Domain
a. admires Rossum's work.
b. fears Rossum will take over the world.
c. is romantically interested in Helena.
d. wants to replace the robots with human workers.
e. is jealous of Rossum.

Use the following passage to answer questions 96–99.

The President in Washington sends word that he wishes to buy our land. But how can you buy or sell the sky? The land? The idea is strange to us. If we do not own the freshness of the air and the sparkle of the water, how can you buy them?

Every part of this earth is sacred to my people. Every shining pine needle, every sandy shore, every mist in dark woods, every meadow, every humming insect. All are holy in the memory and experience of my people.

We know the sap which courses through the trees as we know the blood that courses through our veins. We are part of the earth and it is part of us. The perfumed flowers are our sisters. The bear, the deer, the great eagle, these are our brothers. The rocky crests, the juices in the meadow, the body heat of the pony, and man, all belong to the same family.

The shining water that moves in the streams and rivers is not just water, but the blood of our ancestors. If we sell you our land, you must remember that it is sacred. Each ghostly reflec-tion in the clear water of the lakes tells of events and memories in the life of my people. The water's murmur is the voice of my father's father.

The rivers are our brothers. They quench our thirst. They carry out canoes and feed our children. So you must give to the rivers the kindness you would give any brother.

If we sell you our land, remember that the air is precious to us, that the air shares its spirit with all the life it supports. The wind that gave our grandfather his first breath also receives his last sigh. The wind also gives our children the spirit of life. So, if we sell you our land, you must keep it apart and sacred, as a place where man can go to taste the wind that is sweetened by the meadow flowers.

Will you teach your children what we have taught our children? That the earth is our mother? What befalls the earth, befalls all sons of the earth.

This we know: The earth does not belong to man, man belongs to the earth. All things are connected like the blood which unites us all.

—from *This We Know* by Chief Seattle

96. According to the author, what sort of relationship do his people have with the land?
a. They own it and do whatever they want with it.
b. They respect it and do not understand how anyone can own it.
c. They are indifferent and can live anywhere.
d. They live there only because they have to and would be glad to sell it.
e. They believe it is haunted and full of spirits and ghosts.

97. The intended audience of this essay is most likely
   a. President George Washington only.
   b. Native Americans only.
   c. all new Americans.
   d. all Americans, Native and new.
   e. Chief Seattle himself.

98. What is the author's main goal in this essay?
   a. to convince the American government not to buy the land
   b. to convince Native Americans to fight the new Americans
   c. to persuade Americans that the land is not worth buying
   d. to convince the new Americans that the land is sacred
   e. to show how much power he has over his people

99. Former president Ronald Reagan is recorded as having said, "If you've seen one tree, you've seen them all." How does this idea compare with the ideas of Chief Seattle?
   a. They express essentially the same attitude toward the land.
   b. They express essentially opposite attitudes toward the land.
   c. Reagan seems to care more about the land than Chief Seattle.
   d. We cannot compare them, because Chief Seattle does not talk about trees.
   e. Chief Seattle would agree that trees are all alike, but he would not want them cut down.

Use the following passage to answer questions 100–104.

[Mrs. Mallard, having just learned of the death of her husband, has locked herself in a room.]

She sat with her head thrown back upon the cushion of the chair, quite motionless, except when a sob came up into her throat and shook her, as a child who has cried itself to sleep continues to sob in its dreams.

She was young, with a fair, calm face, whose lines bespoke repression and even a certain strength. But now there was a dull stare in her eyes, whose gaze was fixed away off yonder on one of those patches of blue sky. It was not a glance of reflection, but rather indicated a suspension of intelligent thought.

There was something coming to her and she was waiting for it, fearfully. What was it? She did not know; it was too subtle and elusive to name. But she felt it, creeping out of the sky, reaching toward her through the sounds, the scents, the color that filled the air.

Now her bosom rose and fell tumultuously. She was beginning to recognize this thing that was approaching to possess her, and she was striving to beat it back with her will—as powerless as her two white slender hands would have been.

When she abandoned herself a little whispered word escaped her slightly parted lips. She said it over and over under her breath: "free, free, free!" The vacant stare and the look of terror that had followed it went from her eyes. They stayed keen and bright. Her pulses beat fast, and the coursing blood warmed and relaxed every inch of her body.

She did not stop to ask if it were or were not a monstrous joy that held her. A clear and exalted perception enabled her to dismiss the suggestion as trivial.

She knew that she would weep again when she saw the kind, tender hands folded in death; the face that had never looked save with love upon her, fixed and gray and dead. But she saw beyond that bitter moment a long procession of years to come that would belong to her absolutely. And she opened and spread her arms out to them in welcome.

There would be no one to live for during those coming years; she would live for herself. There would be no powerful will bending hers in that blind persistence with which men and women believe they have a right to impose a private will upon a fellow-creature. A kind intention or a cruel intention made the act seem no less a crime as she looked upon it in that brief moment of illumination.

> —from *The Story of an Hour*
> by Kate Chopin

100. What is Mrs. Mallard doing at the beginning of the passage?
   a. comforting her child
   b. sleeping
   c. crying
   d. laughing
   e. feeling ill

101. Why does Mrs. Mallard stop crying and feel joy?
   a. She learns that her husband is not dead after all.
   b. She realizes that she will inherit a lot of money.
   c. She often has drastic mood swings.
   d. She that realizes she can now live for herself and do what she wants.
   e. She can marry someone else now.

102. Mrs. Mallard repeats the word *free* several times. What is it that she will be free from?
   a. debt
   b. fear
   c. criticism from others
   d. having to do what someone else wants
   e. problems with family members who meddle in her affairs

103. The last sentence of the passage states, *A kind intention or a cruel intention made the act seem no less a crime as she looked upon it in that brief moment of illumination.* What does Mrs. Mallard believe is a crime?
   a. imposing your will on someone else
   b. getting married
   c. being happy when someone you love has died
   d. selfishly wanting to do everything your way
   e. welcoming death

104. Given the evidence in the passage, which most accurately describes Mrs. Mallard's feelings toward her husband?
   a. bitter hatred
   b. unyielding contempt
   c. deep love
   d. gentle resignation
   e. aggressive rebelliousness

105. The ballerina whose name, along with that of Nijinsky, is synonymous with the art of ballet is
   a. Natalia Makarova.
   b. Fanny Cerrito.
   c. Marie Camargo.
   d. Anna Pavlovna Pavlova.
   e. Fanny Elssler.

106. This play by Sean O'Casey, set in the 1920s working-class tenements of Dublin, is the second of his well-known "Dublin Trilogy."
a. *Juno and the Paycock*
b. *The Shadow of a Gunman*
c. *Red Roses for Me*
d. *The Silver Tassie*
e. *The Plough and the Stars*

107. "Money can't buy what that piano costs. You can't sell your soul for money. It won't go to the buyer. It'll shrivel and shrink to know that you ain't taken on to it, but won't go with the buyer."

These lines are from *The Piano Lesson,* which garnered a Pulitzer Prize in 1990 for
a. Donald Margulies.
b. Lanford Wilson.
c. Stephen Sondheim.
d. Donald Coburn.
e. August Wilson.

108. One of the great innovators of the theater, he was the first to add a third actor. He also abolished the trilogic form.
a. Oedipus
b. Sophocles
c. Aeschylus
d. Euripides
e. Asclepius

109. *Graffiti* and *graffito* are from the Italian word *graffiato* meaning
a. written.
b. scratched.
c. sprayed.
d. painted.
e. colored.

110. Which of the following is NOT one of the four main elements of hip-hop culture?
a. graffiti
b. rapping
c. ebonics
d. DJing
e. breakdancing

111. A competition at which poets read or recite original work and have their performances judged on a numeric scale by previously selected members of the audience is known as
a. dub poetry.
b. performance poetry.
c. sound poetry.
d. poetry slam.
e. open mic night.

112. The improvisational comedy theater in Chelsea, New York, and Hollywood, California, which was founded by Matt Besser, Amy Poehler, Matt Walsh, and Ian Roberts, a group of comedians, is called
a. The Upright Citizens Brigade Theater.
b. The Groundlings.
c. The Compass Players.
d. The Second City.
e. Theatre Machine.

113. The first color film that did not need a special projector was
a. *Gone with the Wind.*
b. *The Toll of the Sea.*
c. *Cupid Angling.*
d. *The Gulf Between.*
e. *The Wizard of Oz.*

114. Which musician is often credited as "El Rey" of the timbales and "The King of Latin Music," and is best known for dance-oriented mambo and Latin jazz hits?
a. Marc Anthony
b. Tito Puente
c. Hector Lavoe
d. Eddie Palmieri
e. Carlos Santana

115. This literary work by Elie Wiesel was based on his experience of being sent with his family to the German concentration camps at Auschwitz and Buchenwald during World War II.
a. *Schindler's List*
b. *Sophie's Choice*
c. *Daybreak*
d. *Night*
e. *Dawn*

116. *A Clockwork Orange* was written by which of the following authors?
a. Carl Sandburg
b. John Milton
c. Anthony Burgess
d. Ambrose Bierce
e. John Crowe Ransom

117. *The English Constitution,* a book that argued that the British Cabinet system of government was superior to the American constitutional system, was written by
a. John Henry.
b. Alexis de Tocqueville.
c. John Adams.
d. Robert Peel.
e. Walter Bagehot.

118. One of Andy Warhol's infamous prints features four panels depicting a rock and roll legend as a gun-slinging cowboy. This musician was
a. Bob Dylan.
b. Elvis Presley.
c. Mick Jagger.
d. Jim Morrison.
e. John Lennon.

119. This artist used Benday dots, clichéd themes, and a figure from a DC Comic's romance cereal to create *Hopeless.*
a. Jasper Johns
b. Roy Lichtenstein
c. Robert Rauschenberg
d. Peter Halley
e. Al Hansen

120. In *Ken Moody and Robert Sherman,* which artist created a double portrait of a black man and a white man to demonstrate an appreciation for the beauty of skin?
a. Robert Mapplethorpe
b. Jean-Michel Basquiat
c. Raymond Pettibon
d. Charles Ray
e. Larry Rivers

121. The writers of the Declaration of Independence wanted the decent respect of the opinions of mankind. Their argument primarily rested on what foundation?
a. an appeal to reason
b. a plea for emotional connection
c. a request for partisan feeling
d. a demand for religious faith
e. a call for imprecise and illogical thought

Use the following passage to answer questions 122–126.

The Seven Ages of Man

(1) All the world's a stage,
     And all the men and women merely players;
     They have their exits and their entrances;
     And one man in his time plays many parts.

(5) His acts being seven ages. At first the infant,
     Mewling . . . in the nurse's arms.
     And then the whining schoolboy, with his
          satchel
     And shining morning face . . . And then the

(10)   lover,
     Sighing like a furnace . . . Then a soldier
     Full of strange oaths . . . Jealous of honor,
     Sudden and quick in quarrel . . . And then the
          justice . . .

(15) Full of wise saws and modern instances;
     And so he plays his part. The sixth age shifts
     Into the lean and slippered pantaloon.
     With spectacles on nose and pouch on side.
     . . . and his big manly voice, Turning again

(20)   toward
     Childish treble, pipes and whistles in his sound.
     Last scene of all,
     That ends this strange eventful history,
     Is second childishness, and mere oblivion,

(25) Sans teeth, sans eyes, sans taste, sans
          everything.
                              —William Shakespeare

122. What attitude does the speaker reveal by using
the word *merely* in the second line?
  a. sorrow
  b. anger
  c. amusement
  d. indifference
  e. mirth

123. What characterizes the period of life represented by the soldier?
  a. brash behavior
  b. his sense of honor
  c. his dedication to duty
  d. his fear of cowardice
  e. his love for his family

124. What is the main idea of this poem?
  a. Life is a misery that never gets any better at any time.
  b. Life is what each of us makes of it during our journey down the river of eternity.
  c. Life is a play and it follows a specific script, none of which should cause anguish or sorrow.
  d. Life is a comedy, and we are all buffoons in pantaloons no matter what we do.
  e. Life is unpredictable, so we never know what's in store at the end.

125. What is the theme of the poem?
  a. Death is to be feared.
  b. Life is a circle that brings us back to the beginning.
  c. The male of the species is the only true measure of the stages of life.
  d. The stages of life are unrelated and can be altered by each individual's free will.
  e. Life is fleeting, so it should be chased.

126. The poet uses the words *merely* (line 2) and *mere* (line 24)
  a. to soften the effect of the strong images he presents to us in those lines.
  b. to tie together his theme of the cycle of life.
  c. to convey his tone to the reader.
  d. all of the above
  e. none of the above

Use the following passage to answer questions 127–132.

The lives of the ancient Greeks revolved around *eris,* a concept by which they defined the universe. They believed that the world existed in a condition of opposites. If there was good, then there was evil; if there was love, then there was hatred; joy, then sorrow; war, then peace; and so on. The Greeks believed that "good" *eris* arose when one held a balanced outlook on life, and coped with problems as they came up. It was a kind of ease of living that came from trying to bring together the great opposing forces in nature. "Bad" *eris* was the violent conditions that ruled men's lives. Although these things were found in nature, and, sometimes could not be controlled, it was believed that "bad" *eris* occurred when one turned his back on his problem, letting it grow larger until it destroyed, not only that person, but his family as well. The ancient Greeks saw *eris* as a goddess: Eris, the Goddess of Discord, better known as Trouble.

One myth that expresses this concept of "bad" *eris* deals with the marriage of King Peleus and the river goddess Thetis. Zeus, the supreme ruler, learns that Thetis would bear a child strong enough to destroy its father. Not wanting to father his own ruin, Zeus convinces Thetis to marry a human, a mortal whose child could never challenge the gods. He promises her, among other things, the greatest wedding in all of Heaven and Earth and allows the couple to invite whomever they please. This is one of the first mixed marriages of Greek mythology, and the lesson learned from it still applies today. They do invite everyone ... except Trouble: Eris, the Goddess of Discord. In other words, instead of facing the problems brought on by a mixed marriage, they turn their backs on them. They refused to deal directly with their problems and the result is tragic. In her fury, Eris arrives, ruins the wedding, causes a jealous feud among the three major goddesses over a golden apple, and sets in place the conditions that lead to the Trojan War. The war will take place twenty years in the future, but it will result in the death of the only child of the bride and groom: Achilles. Eris will have destroyed the parents' hopes for their future, leaving the couple with no legitimate heirs to the throne.

Hence, when we are told, "If you don't invite trouble, trouble comes," it means that if we don't deal with our problems, our problems will deal with us ... with a vengeance! It is easy to see why the Greeks considered many of their myths "learning" myths, for this one teaches us the best way to defeat that which can destroy us.

127. According to the passage, the ancient Greeks believed that the concept of *eris* defined the universe as

a. a hostile, violent place.

b. a condition of opposites.

c. a series of problems.

d. a mixture of gods and man.

e. a peaceful utopia.

128. Most specifically, "bad" *eris* is defined in the passage as

a. the violent conditions of life.

b. the problems encountered by humans.

c. the evil goddess who has a golden apple.

d. the murderer of generations.

e. humans' thirst for vengeance.

129. It can be inferred that Zeus married Thetis off because

    a. he needed to "buy" the loyalty of a great king of mankind.

    b. he feared the gods would create "bad" *eris* by competing over her.

    c. he feared the Trojan war would be fought over her.

    d. he had tired of her faults.

    e. he feared having an affair with her and, subsequently, a child by her.

130. It can also be inferred that Zeus did not fear a child sired by King Peleus because he knew that

    a. the child could not climb Mt. Olympus.

    b. the child would be killed in the Trojan war.

    c. no matter how strong a mortal child was, he couldn't overthrow an immortal god.

    d. Thetis would always love him above everyone else.

    e. the child would not survive into adulthood.

131. According to the passage, Achilles

    a. defeated Zeus during the Trojan War.

    b. died during the Trojan War.

    c. was born 20 years after the war because of the disruption Eris caused at the wedding.

    d. was the illegitimate son of Peleus.

    e. died in battle with Zeus.

132. Which of the following statements is the message offered in the myth?

    a. Do not consider a mixed marriage.

    b. Do not anger the gods.

    c. Do not ignore the problems that arise in life.

    d. Do not take myths seriously.

    e. Do not attempt to alter your destiny.

Use the following passage to answer questions 133–138.

She was one of those pretty, charming women who are born, as if by an error of Fate, into a petty official's family. She had no dowry, hopes, nor the slightest chance of being loved and married by a rich man—so she slipped into marriage with a minor civil servant.

Unable to afford jewels, she dressed simply: but she was wretched, for women have neither caste nor breeding—in them beauty, grace, and charm replace pride of birth. Innate refinement, instinctive elegance, and wit give them their place on the only scale that counts, and these make humble girls the peers of the grandest ladies.

She suffered, feeling that every luxury should rightly have been hers. The poverty of her rooms—the shabby walls, the worn furniture, the ugly upholstery caused her pain. All these things that another woman of her class would not even have noticed, made her angry. The very sight of the little Breton girl who cleaned for her awoke rueful thoughts and the wildest dreams in her mind. She dreamt of rooms with Oriental hangings, lighted by tall, bronze torches, and with two huge footmen in knee breeches made drowsy by the heat from the stove, asleep in the wide armchairs. She dreamt of great drawing rooms upholstered in old silks, with fragile little tables holding priceless knickknacks, and of enchanting little sitting rooms designed for tea-time chats with famous, sought-after men whose attentions all women longed for.

She sat down to dinner at her round table with its three-day-old cloth, and watched her husband lift the lid of the soup tureen and delightedly exclaim, "Ah, a good homemade beef stew! There's nothing better!" She visualized elegant dinners with gleaming silver and gorgeous china. She yearned for wall hangings peopled with knights and ladies and exotic birds in a fairy forest. She dreamt of eating the pink flesh of trout or the wings of grouse. She had no proper wardrobe, no jewels, nothing. And those were the only things that she loved—she felt she was made for them. She would have so loved to charm, to be envied, to be admired and sought after.

—from *The Necklace*
by Guy de Maupassant

133. Which word best describes the actual living conditions of the couple in the selection?
a. destitute
b. poor
c. comfortable
d. wealthy
e. royal

134. Which line best demonstrates the couple's true economic standing?
a. "She had no dowry, no hopes, not the slightest chance of being married by a rich and distinguished man . . ."
b. "The poverty of her rooms—the shabby walls, the worn furniture, the ugly upholstery caused her pain . . ."
c. "She sat down to dinner at her round table with its three-day-old cloth, and watched her husband lift the lid of the soup tureen . . ."
d. "The very sight of the little Breton girl who cleaned for her awoke rueful thoughts and the wildest dreams in her mind . . ."
e. "She yearned for wall hangings peopled with knights and ladies and exotic birds in a fairy forest."

135. According to the selection, what can be stated about the marriage of this woman?
a. She married but was ashamed of the insignificant position her husband held.
b. She married on the rebound after a wealthy suitor had abandoned her.
c. She married for love without realizing the consequences to her social standing.
d. She never loved her husband.
e. She was fooled into thinking her husband had an inheritance.

136. What can be inferred about the values of both the husband and the wife in this passage?
a. They share the same values.
b. The husband values family and simple comforts of home, whereas his wife views these comforts as cause for her anguish.
c. The husband has ceased to enjoy the simple things and strives only to quench his wife's insatiable desire for luxury.
d. The husband believes that a wholesome meal can solve all problems, while his wife believes it is the presentation of the meal that counts.
e. The wife is willing to make sacrifices because of her love for her husband, whereas her husband will not be happy unless they possess the finest things.

137. The purpose of the passage is

    a. to have the reader feel great sympathy for the wife.

    b. to have the reader feel great sympathy for the husband.

    c. to show the class distinctions that were so obvious during the setting of the story.

    d. to show the reader how selfish and self centered the wife is.

    e. to show the reader a marriage built on lies will never work.

138. What part of speech does de Maupassant employ to weave the rich images he presents through the wife's descriptions?

    a. adjectives

    b. adverbs

    c. nouns

    d. verbs

    e. prepositions

139. Two of Johnny Cash's most successful albums were recorded

    a. in Memphis, Tennessee.

    b. in New York's Greenwich Village.

    c. in his home recording studio.

    d. in Hollywood.

    e. live in prisons.

140. Johnny Cash's hit song "A Boy Named Sue" was based on a novelty song by which children's author?

    a. Dr. Seuss

    b. Maurice Sendak

    c. Shel Silverstein

    d. Madeleine L'Engle

    e. J. R. R. Tolkien

▶ Answers

1. a. Most art songs are settings of lyric poetry, not part of a staged work (such as an opera), and intended for performance as part of a recital or other relatively formal social occasion.

2. c. Dante's pinnacle work of medieval poetry, *Divine Comedy,* describes a journey through hell, purgatory, and heaven. It conveys that reason can take one only so far; then, God's revelations come into play.

3. d. In Castiglione's work, all the other choices depict qualities necessary of a gentleman. The book was translated into many languages and greatly influenced Western ideas about the correct education and behavior.

4. c. Medieval architecture is characterized by the absence of symmetry, not its presence.

5. a. The simile comes after the idea that none of the scars on the old man's hands are fresh. This emphasizes the time the man has gone without a fish. The words erosion and fishless desert also illustrate this fisherman's slump by comparing it to a drought.

6. e. The boy's parents force the boy to go with a boat that will catch more fish. Later the boy says that he might be able to return to the old man's boat because he has made some money.

7. c. The description says that the sail is patched with flour sacks. It probably needs to be replaced because it looks like the flag of permanent defeat. However, the man does not have enough money to replace it because he has not caught any fish.

8. a. The boy's parents force the boy to stop fishing with the old man after 40 fishless days. This shows that the parents are not afraid to make a change in order to make money for the family.

9. e. Although the author does not state that the college students were brave, the firsthand account notes that the African-American Woolworth's employees "were concerned" about the students' safety. This implies that the students could not be sure of what consequences they would face.

10. c. The author uses Joe McNeil's account to give a firsthand description of what it was like to be a part of a significant event in the Civil Rights movement.

11. c. This famous line is from *The Canterbury Tales*'s first story, The Knight's Tale. In this tale, two imprisoned knights fall in love with the same woman. Geoffrey Chaucer based his tale on the much longer epic *Teseida delle nozze di Emilia* by Giovanni Boccaccio.

12. d. John Steinbeck's *Of Mice and Men* tells the story of two migrant ranch workers—the quick-witted dreamer George Milton and Lennie Small, who is mentally challenged but physically very strong.

13. b. The tone of the poem makes it clear that war is not kind and that there is no virtue in slaughter or excellence in killing. There is no suggestion in the poem that war is necessary, so choice **a** is incorrect. The poem shows that the soldiers did not die in glory (indeed, the glory is "unexplained"), so choice **c** is incorrect. Each of the people the speaker addresses has sacrificed, but the theme of the poem is that such sacrifice is unnecessary and wrong, so choice **d** is incorrect. The poem describes a few ways to die in a war (choice **e**), but this is not a central idea of the poem.

14. a. The speaker is telling the maiden, child, and mother not to weep, and they have all lost a loved one, so he is addressing their grief. They may also be proud (choice **b**), angry (choice **c**), or afraid (choice **e**), but their main emotion concerning the death of their loved one is grief. They are not weeping with joy, so choice **d** is also incorrect.

15. c. The speaker does not approve of war and would most likely protest against it. Because he does not believe war is kind and he does not see any virtue in slaughter, he would not join the military (choice **a**). The speaker is clearly anti-war, so he would definitely not travel the country rallying support for the war (choice **b**). He probably would not want to fight, but there is no evidence that he would attempt to hurt himself so he would not have to fight (choice **e**). Rather, his aim seems to be to help prevent war, making choice **c** the most logical answer. There is no evidence to suggest that he would cover the war as a reporter (choice **d**).

16. e. If the kingdom of a god is only corpses, he must be a powerful god (he can create such death and destruction), but he is also a terrible god who lacks love and compassion. In addition, if his kingdom is only corpses, then he has no living worshippers to follow him, so his power is paradoxical and, essentially, useless. These lines do show that the battle-god is mighty (choice **a**), but the theme of the poem is the terrible nature of war, so **e** is a better choice. There are indeed many casualties in a war (choice **b**) and many deaths in a battle (choice **c**), but these ideas do not convey an attitude toward war, and repetition is usually used to help convey theme. The poem does not try to make us afraid of war; rather, it wants us to see the terrible nature of war, so choice **d** is incorrect.

17. c. Biff tells Happy, "And whenever spring comes to where I am, I suddenly get the feeling, my God, I'm not gettin' anywhere! [. . . .] I oughta be makin' my future. That's when I come running home." The answer is clearly stated in this passage, so choices **a**, **b**, **d**, and **e** are incorrect.

18. b. Happy seems to think that money can buy him happiness (Biff seems to think this, too). Happy tells the story of his manager, who built himself a wonderful house and can't enjoy it—and he says he'd do the same thing. He tells Biff: "I think of the rent I'm paying. And it's crazy. But then, it's what I always wanted. My own apartment, a car, and plenty of women. And still, goddammit, I'm lonely." Happy believed that these material things would bring him happiness. He doesn't try to run away from himself (that's what Biff does), so choice **a** is incorrect. There's no evidence that he's getting what's coming to him, or that he's done something that he will be retaliated for, so choice **c** is incorrect. The passage suggests that he doesn't have a lot of patience, so choice **d** is incorrect. Although money isn't making Happy happy, it has not made him evil, just lonely; choice **e** is therefore incorrect.

19. e. Biff seems to keep moving around as if he is trying to get away from something (himself, his past) and searching for something else (happiness). But as he tells Happy, every spring, wherever he is, he realizes he is still not happy and he doesn't know what he's doing with his life. There is no evidence that he is selfish, so choice **a** is incorrect. He does not appear to be very mature, but he does not act like a baby (he is independent enough to travel around and support himself through work), so choice **b** is incorrect. Settling on one career won't necessarily bring him happiness, and he can't pick the right career until he accepts who he is and what sort of work is best suited for him, so choice **c** is not correct. Moving around (choice **d**) and switching careers are further part of the root problem, which is Biff's attempt to run away from himself and his past.

20. c. Happy explains that the manager built a "terrific estate" but only lived there for two months because "He can't enjoy it once it's finished" (line 41). Happy says he would do the same thing, and Happy is also a character who always wants more. The manager clearly has a lot of money, so choice **a** is incorrect. There is no evidence that he knows Happy is after his job, so choice **b** is incorrect. Happy tells us that he is lonely, but we do not know if the manager is also lonely, so choice **d** is incorrect. Happy says that the estate was "terrific," and there is no evidence that the manager didn't like the way it was built, so choice **e** is incorrect.

21. a. Happy is clearly not happy. As he tells Biff, he is very lonely. Thus, his name contradicts his state of being. Choice **b** is therefore incorrect. We do not know if Happy is a nickname or not his real name, so choices **c** and **d** are incorrect. Because *happy* is an adjective, not a thing, it is difficult for it to be symbolic and represent something else, so choice **e** is incorrect.

22. c. The opening lines of this passage show Akakiy's colleagues making jokes about him, throwing paper over his head, and disrupting his work. These are all signs of contempt. Nowhere is there evidence of his colleagues having respect (choice **a**), admiration (choice **b**), or reverence (choice **e**) for Akakiy. Although one colleague feels sorry after making fun of Akakiy, this is only one man, not most of his colleagues, most of the time, which is why choice **d** is incorrect.

23. a. The newcomer at first joins the other officials in teasing Akakiy, but when Akakiy finally objects, the newcomer realizes that people can be very cruel to one another. This lesson actually remains with him throughout his life, Although the officials are joking with Akakiy (choice **b**), the jokes are clearly at his expense, and in fact, he does ignore the jokes until they interfere with his work, so this choice is incorrect. Choice **c** is clearly not true as the other officials are portrayed as fairly mean. The passage states that Akakiy's hidden meaning in his objection to the teasing is, "I am thy brother." This is not meant to be taken literally but to remind the newcomer (and the reader) that we are all human and deserve a certain amount of respect; therefore choice **d** is incorrect. There is nothing to indicate that Akakiy deserves this poor treatment (choice **e**).

24. d. The passage states, "It is not enough to say that Akakiy labored with zeal: no, he labored with love." He does not resent being a copier (choice **a**), and actually becomes nervous when given a more responsible duty (choice **b**). He insists on going back to copying and remains doing that "forever," so it can be assumed that he is not bored with it (choice **e**). The other workers do tease Akakiy, but he himself does not start the trouble (choice **c**).

25. d. Despite all the teasing, there is no indication that Akakiy ever becomes angry. When he objects, the text states, *And there was something strange in the words and the voice in which they were uttered. There was in it something which moved to pity.* All the other choices accurately describe Akakiy. He is patient in his work and with his colleagues (choice **a**); he becomes anxious when given additional responsibility (choice **b**); he is a hard worker (choice **c**); and he presents as rather shy (choice **e**).

26. e. The passage states, *For the fourth or fifth time the woman had talked to him with great earnestness and he could not make out what she meant by her talk. He began to believe she must be in love with him and the thought was both pleasing and annoying.* Choice **a** is incorrect because Kate has not told George that she loves him; that is why he is confused about it. Choice **b** is incorrect because there is no indication that Kate gave him good grades; he was apparently intelligent and earned good grades. The passage makes no reference to Kate writing a letter (choice **c**). Although the passage states that a passerby might have thought they were about to embrace, Kate and George do not embrace in this passage.

27. b. The passage states, *In something he had written as a school boy she thought she had recognized the spark of genius and wanted to blow on the spark,* and then continues to show Kate discussing writing with George. There is no indication that Kate is in love with George (choice **a**). The reference to a *spark* is symbolic and has nothing to do with a real fire (choice **c**). Kate gives George advice about writing, rather than George giving Kate advice (choice **d**). Kate explains that she is not trying to frighten George (choice **e**).

28. c. Apparently Kate believes that good writers draw from life experiences. Choice **a** is incorrect because Kate clearly sees George's writing talent. Choice **b** is incorrect because there is no indication that George is going to die. Choice **d** is incorrect because Kate mentions nothing about college. Choice **e** is incorrect because Kate actually encourages him to spend less time writing.

29. a. The first stanza states several examples of what not to do, even though others are doing that very thing: losing their heads, hating, and lying. The first stanza essentially states not to do what others are doing, so choice **b** is incorrect. The poem mentions lying, hating, and waiting, but not in the contexts of choices **c**, **d**, and **e**.

30. c. This line advises that a person should have dreams but not allow the pursuit of them to take over (master) his or her life. Choice **a** states the complete opposite of he speaker's intention. Choice **b** is incorrect because the speaker encourages the person to dream. The speaker does not mention anything about helping others (choice **d**). Although choice **e** may be true, it is not what the speaker is stating in this line.

31. e. The poem offers advice to a young person about how to obtain true success in life. The speaker implies that true maturity and success have nothing to do with power and riches, but rather, are measured by integrity. Although choices **a**, **b**, **c**, and **d** are all items mentioned in the poem, they do not reflect the theme of the poem.

32. d. The passage includes a discussion of the importance of Brooks's writing (choice **a**), mentioning the awards she's won and her use of black topics; provides a list of her achievements (choice **b**); discusses her importance as a role model (choice **c**), referring to her helping young writers and encouraging blacks to learn about their heritage; and addresses the handicaps of being black and female (choice **e**). All of these phrases, however, are too specific to describe the passage well, because the passage encompasses all of these themes. The best phrase to describe the passage is choice **d**, a biographical sketch on Gwendolyn Brooks.

33. c. Brooks was a published writer by eleven; choice **a** is incorrect. Grants did not lessen, but heighten, her prestige, so choice **b** is incorrect. Choice **c** is the correct answer. After her first book was sold, she received nationwide recognition; choice **d** is wrong. Brooks takes an interest in others; choice **e** is incorrect.

34. d. All of the statements are false except choice **d.** It was Brooks's first poem that was published when she was eleven; her first book was not marketed until 1945. Choice **a** is false. Brooks received national recognition after her first book was published, before she won the Pulitzer Prize; choice **b** is false. Brooks was an integrationist in the 1940s and advocated black consciousness in the 1960s; choice **c** is false. Brooks did write about the black experience, so choice **e** is false. Brooks did receive little encouragement from her teachers (choice **d**), and succeeded despite this lack.

35. d. The tone of the passage is one of anticipation and excitement.

36. b. A stagecoach rider is narrating the story.

37. b. All of the statements can be supported in the passage except this choice.

38. c. The passage reflects all of the choices except this one.

39. b. Line 2 of stanza 1 states that Death *kindly stopped* for the speaker. Therefore, Death is presented as a kindly gentleman.

40. c. This choice fits the kindness of Death, as stated by the speaker, as well as the fact that Death *knew no haste.* It also includes the idea that the speaker *put away . . . labour and leisure, too, for his civility.* This supports the image of Death as gentle and timeless, and of the *leaving of life's cares behind.*

41. b. The meaning of the word can be derived from the context of the line. Since he is driving slowly, *Death knows no haste.* This is a matter of opposites. None of the other choices are the opposite of *slowly.*

42. c. The *swelling of the ground . . . the roof scarcely visible . . . [the cornice] but a mound.* All of these are descriptive of a grave with its gravestone.

43. a. Death is a pleasant companion; the speaker describes it only in positive, gentle terms.

44. b. *Dialect* is the local language of the people. This includes the accent, vocabulary, grammar, and idioms. Some might also describe this poem as black dialect or plantation dialect.

45. b. These are lines 677 through 687 of *Beowulf,* an epic poem of unknown authorship. Grendel is one of the violent enemies that the poem's hero, Beowulf, must battle.

46. e. The blues began to take shape as a musical movement in the years after emancipation, around the turn of the century when blacks were technically free but still suffered from social and economic discrimination. Its poetic and musical forms were popularized by W. C. Handy just after the turn of the century.

47. b. The passage states that the goods pertaining to the soul are called goods in the highest and fullest sense.

48. a. In the second paragraph, Aristotle states that we have all but defined happiness as a kind of good life and well-being. Thus, the definitions of happiness and goodness are intertwined; living a good life will bring happiness.

49. d. Although modern usage of the word *tallies* means counts or keeps track of, in this context, it means *corresponds* or goes along with.

50. e. The account of his travels, *Il Milione* (or, *The Million,* known in English as the *Travels of Marco Polo*), appeared about the year 1299 and astounded the people of Europe, who knew little of the highly developed culture of East Asia.

51. d. This action changes the length of the vibration and produces different notes, making it possible to play any melody.

52. b. Technological advances were emphasized in this illustrated work.

53. a. Although the word *monarchy* never appears in the quotation, Bossuet is stating the theory of the divine right of kings. By linking them with God, Bossuet believes a king's power is unlimited.

54. b. All three quotations condemn the practice of charging interest, which is at the heart of modern banking and economics. Thus, choice **a** is not the best conclusion. All three religions, based on these written texts, were initially hesitant to support capitalism (invalidating choice **d**). Choice **c** is incorrect because, as the Council of Vienne makes clear, money lending was a despised position in medieval Europe. Usury is the lending of money at excessive interest; choice **e** certainly supports a ban on usury.

55. c. Lincoln delivered the *Gettysburg Address* in 1863. Four score (4 × 20) and seven equals 87. If you subtract 87 from 1863, you get 1776. More importantly, Lincoln's entire speech is based on the idea that the foundation document of the United States was not the Constitution (choice **d**), which allowed slavery, but the Declaration, dedicated to the proposition that all men are created equal. Choice **e** is incorrect because although this is the *Gettysburg Address*, the town or battle is not mentioned in the first sentence. Choices **a** and **b** have no relevance whatsoever.

56. a. The first paragraph implies that the reason the men did not know the color of the sky was because they were too busy watching the waves. This was the only way to avoid being hit by a wave that would capsize their frail lifeboat (choice **a**). Choices **b**, **c**, **d**, and **e** might seem to be plausible answers, but they are not supported in the passage.

57. b. An on-shore wind blows from the ocean toward the land. Choice **a** is incorrect because an off-shore wind comes from land and would blow the boat further out to sea. There is no evidence in the text to support choices **c**, **d**, or **e**. All the sailors know the direction in which the land lies, and a little bit later, the captain does see signs of land.

58. a. The text makes it clear that the captain is dejected because his ship has sunk. Choice **b** is not true because nothing in the text suggests that a storm is coming. Choice **c** is false because no one, least of all the captain, has given up hope of surviving the waves. Choice **d** is incorrect because the wind is blowing toward shore, not away from it. Choice **e** is not correct since the correspondent and the oiler, not the captain, are rowing. The captain is in charge of the dinghy and its small crew.

59. d. The author clearly states that the comradeship of men struggling together to save their lives is the best experience of his life. None of the other choices is supported by the excerpt. The correspondent never speaks of the captain as a wise man (choice **a**). There is no reference in the excerpt to life on the ship before the sinking (choice **b**), or to accidental occurrences (choice **c**). And no one in the boat ever voices the fear that they will all drown (choice **e**).

60. d. In the conversation between the correspondent and the cook, it is the cook who says that a house of refuge has a crew. The correspondent says it doesn't.

61. e. There is no evidence that the correspondent would do anything but help the others to keep the boat afloat (choice **e**). He has been calm throughout the ordeal, and it is unlikely that he would suddenly do anything to upset the boat (choice **a**). He has always followed the captain's orders, so it is unlikely that the correspondent would ignore the captain if there were a leak (choice **b**). He would not abandon the boat to save himself (choice **c**), nor would he try to take command and give an order to jump overboard (choice **d**).

62. e. Parks calls a camera a weapon because it can create influential images like *American Gothic.* It is a weapon that contributes directly to social and political change.

63. e. The text clearly states that Ebenezer Dorset is a prominent citizen who lends money to people needing mortgages. He is therefore a fairly well-to-do person.

64. e. The line *You was to be burned at sunrise* contains an error in subject-verb agreement. The sentence should be "You were to be burned at sunrise."

65. b. The irony in this passage is that Red Chief does not act like the usual kidnapping victim. Rather than being frightened and mistreated, he scares his captors and inflicts pain on Bill repeatedly.

66. d. The tone of the excerpt is clearly humorous and ironic. The basic irony (the opposite of what was expected) in the situation is that the roles of kidnappers and victim are reversed. The kidnappers suffer at the hands of their victim, and they want out of their scheme at any price. Their victim is enjoying camping out and playing, but Bill and Sam are miserable.

67. a. Choice **b** is incorrect because the two never threaten to kill Red Chief. Choices **c, d**, and **e** are not supported by evidence in the text.

68. c. In this excerpt, Bill willingly does everything that Sam asks him to do to keep Red Chief happy, but suffers greatly in the process. Bill's experience with the attempted kidnapping would lead him to refuse because he has learned to mistrust Sam's scheming as a way to make money. Choice **a** is incorrect because there is no evidence that Bill owes anyone money. Choice **b** may be true, but there is no evidence in the excerpt that Bill enjoys taking risks. Choice **d** is incorrect because Bill shows no sign of being worried about going to jail for his illegal acts. Choice **e** might be true, but there is no evidence that Bill is not capable of doing anything for himself.

69. e. The context of the poem makes it clear that *bark* here means boat or ship. The images of the first and second stanza depict a boat that is tossed and battered by a storm.

70. b. The poem is divided into two stanzas that follow the same pattern. Pairs of lines rhyme, but the rhythms vary from couplet to couplet. Although the rhythms vary from couplet to couplet, each stanza follows the same rhythmic pattern.

71. b. Although the poem is about a man motivated by a goal or dream, the image presented to the reader is that of a ship at sea struggling to survive battering winds and water. The other options are either literal interpretations, or name small parts of the whole.

72. b. The man's dream allows him to remain optimistic (choice **b**) despite the difficulties of his life, as symbolized by the metaphor of the storms at sea. Because he "labored hard and failed at last," the dreamer cannot be called realistic (choice **a**). Nothing about the dreamer and his dream is sarcastic (choice **c**), and his hopefulness against all odds makes him the opposite of pessimistic (choice **d**). Last, he is not particularly analytic (choice **e**); if he were, he might realize the impossibility of his dream.

73. d. The poem describes how having a dream helped a man maintain optimism in the face of challenges. The saying that best expresses this idea is choice **d**. Choice **e** is precisely the opposite of this idea. Choice **a** means that one should be satisfied with what one can attain, which also goes against the theme of striving against all odds. Choices **b** and **c** have nothing to do with the content of the poem.

74. a. Dunbar is not relating a personal experience, so choice **b** cannot be correct. Dunbar's protagonist and King himself certainly do believe that dreams can be fulfilled, which makes choice **c** an incorrect answer. Personal responsibility in the form of hard work is key to Dunbar's protagonist, and personal responsibility in the form of working toward social change is important to King, so choice **d** does not fit, either. The contrast between reality and dreams (choice **e**) is important to both writers. Dunbar's poem shows how pursuing a goal can make a life rewarding and joyful; King's speech showed how pursuing a dream can lead to social and political change.

75. a. Juliet tells the nurse that she can't be so out of breath if she has breath enough to tell Juliet that she is out of breath. The text does not support any of the other options.

76. d. It is clear from the dialogue between Juliet and her nurse that the nurse purposely delays telling Juliet what Romeo has said. Juliet asks *What says he of our marriage?* and *what says my love?* but gets no direct answer. The nurse wants to tease Juliet a bit before telling her the news.

77. c. The dialogue in the excerpt makes it clear that Juliet has sent the nurse to find out from Romeo when and where he plans to marry her. She clearly wants to marry him, so choice **d** is incorrect. Romeo is not in the garden, and sending the nurse was not simply a way to get rid of her, so choice **e** is not correct. Juliet may or may not suspect that her family is spying or that Romeo may not be all right, but there is no evidence in the text for either of these choices. So choices **a** and **b** are incorrect.

78. b. Before telling Juliet to go and see Friar Laurence, the nurse first asks whether Juliet has permission to go to shrift (confession). She wants to make sure that Juliet has an excuse for going to the friar's cell where the secret wedding is to take place. So choice **b** is the correct answer. Choices **a**, **c**, **d**, and **e** are not supported by evidence from the excerpt.

79. d. There is nothing in the excerpt to suggest that Juliet's parents will learn about or prevent Juliet's plans to marry Romeo, so choice **a** is not correct. There is nothing in the excerpt to suggest that anything will happen to Juliet, that Romeo will be killed, or that Juliet and Romeo have plans to escape to another place. Choices **b**, **c**, and **e** are not correct.

80. d. Information from these two excerpts makes it clear that the nurse is doing whatever she can to further the marriage plans of Romeo and Juliet. So choice **d** is the correct answer. The nurse says that she is to provide a ladder, as Romeo had asked, so choice **b** is incorrect. Romeo certainly trusts the nurse; otherwise, he would not confide in her, making choice **c** incorrect. Nothing in either passage suggests that the nurse is spying on the couple for Juliet's parents, or that the nurse does not want Juliet to marry Romeo. Choices **a** and **e** are incorrect.

81. c. The first sentence states that when Gregor awoke, *he found himself transformed in his bed into a gigantic insect.* The sentence clearly states that he *awoke,* so he is not dreaming, and choice **a** is incorrect. The last sentence reveals that he has to catch a train at five, and he plans on getting up to catch that train, so he is not late, and choice **b** is incorrect. There is no evidence in the passage that Gregor dislikes his job (choice **d**). He does wish he could get more sleep and tell his boss what he thinks of him, but there's no evidence in the passage that Gregor realizes he needs to make a change in his life (choice **e**).

82. b. We learn that on Gregor's table, *a collection of cloth samples was unpacked and spread out* and that Gregor *was a commercial traveler.* Thus, we can conclude that he is a traveling clothing salesman. There is no evidence that he is a magician (choice **a**), and though he has an advertisement hanging on his wall, it is just a decoration, not something from his work (choice **c**). Because the passage specifically states he is a commercial traveler, we can also eliminate choices **d** and **e**.

83. a. In lines 42–45, Gregor reveals that he must keep his job because his parents are indebted to his boss: *once I've saved enough money to pay back my parents' debts to him.* There is no evidence that he is an apprentice (choice **b**); in fact, an apprentice is not likely to be traveling about on his own. He wants to tell his boss what he thinks of him and quit, not take his boss's job, so choice **c** is incorrect. The quote from lines 42–45 rules out his parents owning the company (choice **d**), and there is no evidence that he needs the money to buy a bigger house (choice **e**). The passage does mention that his room is small, but the only reason given for Gregor keeping his job is to pay off those debts.

84. d. Gregor clearly works hard—he comes to breakfast only after he's already gotten some orders (lines 28–31), and he gets up early to travel to his destinations. He is also reliable; he plans on getting up and catching the train even though he is an insect. This evidence rules out choice **a**; he is not lazy. While we learn that Gregor does get orders, we do not know the level of his success as a salesman, so choice **b** is incorrect. Gregor does resent his boss (see lines 35–37), but that could very well be personal, not a matter of general resentment of authority, so choice **c** is not the best answer. We do know that Gregor is working to pay off his parents' debts, but there is no indication in the passage of how close Gregor is to his family, so choice **e** is incorrect.

85. e. Gregor is so preoccupied with work and his routine that he seems to think he can just get up and go to work, even if he appears to be a bug. The tone and word choice in the opening sentence of the passage (which is also the opening sentence of this short story) suggest that this is the first time this happened to Gregor. He also asks, *What has happened to me?* If this had happened before, he would not likely ask that question, and his internal dialogue would be quite different. Thus, choice **a** is incorrect. There is no evidence in the story that the other characters are also bugs. The woman in the picture, at any rate, is a real woman, not a bug. Choice **b** is therefore incorrect. The first sentence clearly states that he awoke, so choice **c** is incorrect. Gregor says *I'd better get up, since my train goes at five,* suggesting that he still has time to catch that 5:00 train. Choice **d** is therefore incorrect.

86. c. Line 1 states, *I am not the first poet born to my family,* and line 23 states, *But I learned to write from Zio.* Thus, he learned to write poetry from Zio. There is no evidence that either of them paints, except through words and gestures (see lines 24–33), so choice **a** is incorrect. Zio's trade was fishing, but the speaker is not a fisherman, so **b** is incorrect. There is no evidence that he is a singer or carpenter, so choices **d** and **e** are incorrect.

87. b. The speaker clearly admires Alfonso's way of seeing beauty in simple things, and is impressed by how Alfonso can communicate without a voice. The speaker is not ashamed of Alfonso (choice **a**) even though Alfonso cannot read or write. The speaker seems to be able to understand Alfonso very well, so he is not frustrated with Alfonso's inability to speak with his voice (choice **c**). The speaker makes much of how he learned to write and see beauty from Alfonso. The speaker does not feel superior to Alfonso; rather he feels indebted to Alfonso (choice **d**). Finally, there is no evidence in the poem to suggest the speaker was ever angry with Alfonso (choice **e**).

88. b. The speaker states that Alfonso *lost his voice to cigarettes before [the speaker] was born.* Therefore, Alfonso cannot speak with his voice, although he does communicate well with gestures and expressions. The speaker states that Alfonso watched him *write with wonder* and that Alfonso tried to teach himself to read, so clearly Alfonso could not write (choice **a**). Obviously choice **c** is incorrect since Alfonso could not speak at all. Choices **d** and **e** are incorrect because the speaker states Alfonso fished for a living. The reference to painting is symbolic, not literal.

89. e. Alfonso could not speak, so he could not be loud (choice **a**) or always yelling (choice **d**). There is no evidence that he was always angry (choice **b**) or that he was like a lion (choice **c**). Rather, the poem suggests that he was fun-loving and kind.

90. a. Lines 24–34 show that the speaker has learned how to appreciate and express the beauty of the world. Alfonso does not talk, so he does not teach the speaker how to listen (choice **b**). There is no evidence that the speaker learns how to appreciate his family or understand himself (choices **c** and **d**). Line 20 reveals that Alfonso couldn't read, so choice **e** is incorrect.

91. d. Domain states that the best workers are those who are *the cheapest* and *whose needs are the smallest*. To create a creature with minimal needs, Rossum created machines with no soul, because the soul "did not contribute directly to the progress of work"—it made people want to play the fiddle, for example. Robots do have a more simple anatomy (choice **a**), but anatomy does not have to do with the needs that might distract a robot from work. Robots are more intelligent (choice **b**), but Domain clearly states that price, not intelligence, is the key factor. Helena suggests that honesty and work ethic are most important, but Domain's statement contradicts this, so choice **c** is incorrect. Robots were designed so that they did not want anything that was not necessary, so choice **e** is also incorrect.

92. a. Domain tells us that Rossum *began to overhaul anatomy and tried to see what could be left out or simplified* because he thought *man is too complicated*. He also states that the things humans like to do (e.g., play the fiddle) are *unnecessary*, and *that a working machine must not want to play the fiddle if it is to be* efficient. He does not question the honesty of humans (choice **b**) or mention anything about the robot's level of happiness (choice **c**); in fact, the passage suggests that the robots aren't able to feel any emotions at all. Choice **d** is incorrect because Rossum had a specific reason for creating the robots. There is no evidence that there weren't enough people to do the work (nor is there any indication of what sort of work it is), so choice **e** is incorrect.

93. c. Rossum wanted to simplify nature, and Domain states that *the product of an engineer is technically at a higher pitch of perfection than a product of nature*, showing that Rossum felt nature was imperfect and unnecessarily complicated. Rossum seems to think that machines are more beautiful (more perfect) than nature, so choice **a** is incorrect. Rossum clearly tries to improve upon nature and seems to think he's a better engineer, so choices **b** and **d** can be ruled out. There is a clear distinction in the passage between products of humans (engineers) and products of nature, so choice **e** is incorrect.

94. e. Domain tells Helena that *any one who's looked into anatomy will have seen at once that man is too complicated, and that a good engineer could make him more simply. So young Rossum began to overhaul anatomy.* This makes **e** clearly the best choice. Rossum created robots, so choice **a** is incorrect. Rossum was clearly an inventor (choice **b**), but the emphasis in the passage is on his engineering skills. Domain mentions engineers again: *The product of an engineer is technically at a higher pitch of perfection than a product of nature.* There is no evidence that Rossum was a doctor (choice **c**) or that he was a foreman in the factory (choice **d**).

95. a. Clearly Domain admires Rossum as Domain calls Rossum a *good engineer* and describes the robots as *beautiful pieces of work* and *flawless.* There is no evidence that Domain fears Rossum in any way (choice **b**). Domain gives no indication of a romantic interest in Helena (choice **c**); he is simply explaining the robots to her. Domain repeatedly indicates that he feels robots are superior workers to humans, so choice **d** is incorrect. Finally, Domain's continued praise of Rossum and his work indicates admiration, not jealousy (choice **e**).

96. b. Throughout the essay, the author expresses his people's respect for the land. *Every part of the earth is sacred to my people,* he states, for example, and *The earth does not belong to man, man belongs to the earth.* They clearly do not think they own the land (choice **a**); the author states, *how can you buy or sell the sky? The land? The idea is strange to us. If we do not own the freshness of the air. . . .* Their reverence for the land contradicts choices **c** and **d**. There is no evidence that they believe the land is haunted (choice **e**).

97. c. The author is addressing all new Americans—the people to whom he would be selling the land. There is a clear distinction between the *you* of the new Americans and the *we* of the Native Americans, so choices **b**, **d**, and **e** are incorrect. Choice **a** is incorrect because he speaks of President Washington in the third person.

98. d. The questions the author asks and the statements he makes are aimed at convincing the new Americans to treat the land with respect: *you must give to the rivers the kindness you would give any brother; if we sell you our land, you must keep it apart and sacred.* He does not offer any reasons for the new Americans not to buy the land, so choice **a** is incorrect. He does not address the Native Americans nor suggest that they fight, so choice **b** is incorrect. He does not state any reasons not to buy the land, and he praises the land rather than pointing out any flaws, so choice **c** is incorrect. There is no evidence of the power he has over his people, so choice **e** is also incorrect.

99. b. For Chief Seattle, every part of nature was sacred. *We know the sap which courses through the trees as we know the blood that courses through our veins,* he writes suggesting that each tree is important and valuable. This directly contrasts the indifference of Reagan's statement, so choice **a** is incorrect, and so is choice **e.** Reagan does not seem to care about the land, so choice **c** is also incorrect. Chief Seattle does talk about trees, as previously noted, so choice **d** is incorrect.

100. c. The introduction to the passage states that Mrs. Mallard has just learned of her husband's death; this alone would indicate that she is crying, but the text makes reference to *sobs* and compares Mrs. Mallard to a *child who has cried itself to sleep.* The text mentions a child, but it is for comparison purposes; there is no literal child in the text (choice **a**). Again, the text refers to a sleeping child, but this is a comparison, so choice **b** is incorrect. Choice **d** has no textual support at all, and it would be highly unlikely that Mrs. Mallard would be laughing at such a time. Later in the passage, the author states that Mrs. Mallard feels joy, but there is no indication that she is laughing. Choice **e** also has no textual support. Although she is motionless and has a *dull stare,* it is due to her emotional state, not illness.

101. d. Mrs. Mallard *saw beyond that bitter moment*—her husband's funeral—*a long procession of years to come that would belong to her absolutely. There would be no one to live for during those coming years; she would live for herself* reveals the root of her joy. There is no suggestion in the story that she learned her husband was not dead, so choice **a** is incorrect. There is no evidence that she realizes she will inherit a lot of money—in fact, there is no mention of money at all in the passage— so choice **b** is incorrect. We do not know if she has drastic mood swings—there is no evidence of it in the passage—so choice **c** is incorrect. She does not mention any desire to marry someone else, so choice **e** is also incorrect.

102. d. The freedom, again, will be from *a powerful will bending hers in that blind persistence with which men and women believe they have a right to impose a private will upon a fellow-creature.* There is no evidence that she lives in debt (choice **a**) or fear (choice **b**) or that she is often criticized by others (choice **c**). We do not know anything about any other family members, so choice **e** is also incorrect.

103. a. The freedom she embraces is the freedom from another's will. In her mind, it is criminal to try to bend someone's will. The sacredness of the individual—the freedom to do as one pleases—is the ultimate right of a person, and to violate that is a crime. There is no evidence that she thinks getting married is in and of itself a crime (choice **b**). She *did not stop to ask if it were or were not a monstrous joy that held her,* so she does not consider her joy a crime (choice **c**), nor does she seem to consider wanting to do things your way a crime (choice **d**); rather, she thinks having someone try to make you do it any other way is a crime. She does not welcome death, and that is not the focus of her joy, so choice **e** is also incorrect.

104. d. The passage makes it clear that although Mrs. Mallard's husband was kind and loved her, Mrs. Mallard feels a great sense of freedom at his death. There is no indication that their marriage was stormy or violent, but rather that Mrs. Mallard submitted to her husband's will quietly even though she did not like doing it. Choice **a** is incorrect because Mrs. Mallard does feel sadness at her husband's death; there is no indication that she hates him. Although Mrs. Mallard appears to have resented the fact that her husband imposed his will upon her, she does not appear to feel superior to him in any way (choice **b**). Choice **c** is incorrect because although the passage states that Mr. Mallard *never looked save with love upon her,* there is no indication that Mrs. Mallard deeply loved her husband. She appreciated his kindness and love, but does not seem to have fully reciprocated it. Choice **e** is incorrect because there is no evidence that Mrs. Mallard ever rebelled against her husband; in fact, part of why she feels such freedom is because she has always acquiesced to his will.

105. d. Anna Pavlovna Pavlova was a famous Russian ballerina of the late nineteenth and early twentieth century who traveled around the world and brought ballet to people who had never seen it. She is remembered for her famous dance *The Dying Swan.*

106. a. *Juno and the Paycock* is one of the most performed plays in Ireland. It was first staged at the Abbey Theatre in Dublin in 1924.

107. e. August Wilson's "Pittsburgh Cycle," also often referred to as his "Century Cycle," consists of ten plays—the fourth of which is *The Piano Lesson.* The plays are each set in a different decade to sketch the African-American experience in the twentieth century. (*The Piano Lesson* takes place in the 1930s.)

108. b. Aeschylus is credited with introducing a second actor; Sophocles with a third. Sophocles also chose to make each tragedy a complete entity in itself.

109. b. The Italian word *graffiato* means "scratched," and the name *graffiti* is applied to works of art made by scratching a design into a surface. In ancient times, graffiti was carved on walls with a sharp object, chalk, or coal.

110. c. Hip hop is a cultural movement, developed in New York City in the 1970s, which has four historic "elements": MCing (rapping), DJing, urban inspired art/tagging (graffiti), and b-boying (breakdancing).

111. d. At a poetry slam, poets perform and then members of the audience are chosen to act as judges for the event. Most slams last multiple rounds, and many involve the elimination of lower-scoring poets in successive rounds. Most slams enforce a time limit.

112. a. The Upright Citizens Brigade Theater features a variety of comedy-related acts, including one-person shows, stand up, and sketch comedy acts, but the theater is best known for its long-form improvisation shows.

113. b. *The Toll of the Sea,* released in 1922, was also the seventh color feature and the second technicolor feature.

114. b. Tito Puente is internationally recognized for his significant contributions to Latin music as a bandleader, composer, arranger, and percussionist. In his career, he recorded more than 100 albums, published more than 400 compositions, and won five Grammy awards.

115. d. *Night* is the first book in a trilogy—*Night, Dawn,* and *Day.* The titles signifies the author's journey from darkness to light.

116. c. *A Clockwork Orange,* a speculative fiction novel by Anthony Burgess, was published in 1962. In 1971, it was adapted into a film by Stanley Kubrick.

117. e. Walter Bagehot was a British essayist and journalist who wrote extensively about government affairs.

118. b. The source of the image is a still from one of Elvis's films, *Flaming Star* (1960).

119. b. Lichtenstein had once hoped to make "a painting so despicable no one would buy it," but his combination of "low culture" and handmade "high" art made him a pop art pioneer.

120. a. Mapplethorpe used an all-encompassing studio light to give these subjects' flesh the solid appearance of a marble sculpture.

121. a. The Declaration of Independence reads like a logical treatise.

122. d. The poet uses *merely* to simply make a statement with no emotion attached to it. Therefore the other answers are all incorrect as anger, amusement, and sorrow are emotions.

123. a. The soldier's behavior is aggressive: cursing, jealous of others who receive honor, and quick to fight. The lines do not reveal a sense of honor, but rather the soldier's dishonorable behavior. There is no mention of dedication, nor anything to suggest a fear of cowardice.

124. c. The poem begins by stating *the world is a stage* and that we are *merely players.* There is no emotion attached to the exits and entrances of man in the poet's tone, thus there is no need for anguish or sorrow.

125. b. This is supported by the *Last scene of all,* in which Shakespeare suggests that old age is a second childhood that will lead to oblivion without control of the senses, like the infant in the first act. The infant has come full circle back to his beginning.

126. d. The poet accomplishes all three. It softens the effect of both suggestions that we are only actors on the world's stage, and that the seventh age of man results in oblivion. It ties his theme together by carrying us from the first stage to the last and then back again. And, the words convey his tone of indifference as previously discussed.

127. b. This is stated explicitly in sentence 2 of the passage.

128. a. This is a definition explicitly stated in sentence 6.

129. e. This is stated in sentence 3 of paragraph 2. Zeus did not want to sire (father) a child who could eventually overthrow him. According to the passage, he felt it was safer to arrange for the child's father to be a mortal. There is no support in the passage for any of the other choices.

130. c. This answer follows the logic of the previous answer. A mortal *child could never challenge the gods* implies that Zeus feared that if the child were immortal, it would overthrow him. The other choices mention individual words that appear in the passage but have no support.

131. b. The second to the last line in paragraph 2 tells us that Achilles was the son of Thetis and Peleus and that the war would result in his death.

132. c. This lesson is discussed explicitly in paragraph 3. All other choices are irrelevant.

133. c. The husband had a civil servant's job and received a steady salary; the wife had a servant who cleaned for her. The couple lived in a dwelling that had several rooms. This implies that they lived comfortably.

134. d. This question relates to the previous one. This choice presents the fact that the wife had a maid.

135. a. It is obvious from the description of the wife's thoughts in paragraph 1 that she wished she had married a rich man. Instead, she *slipped into marriage with a minor civil servant.* The woman is ashamed of her marriage and of her husband's occupation to the point of making it sound like an accident, as one may slip on a wet floor.

136. b. The husband's delight with the homemade stew only seems to send his wife into another bout of daydreams to escape her middle class prison.

137. d. This is reinforced by the last two sentences of the passage. The wife admits she loves only rich things, believes she was made for them, and focuses all her desires on being *admired and sought after,* thinking only of herself at all times.

138. a. Adjectives are the words that describe nouns. These are the words that truly add dimension to the descriptions of the home and the day-dreams of the wife. *Innate, instinctive, grandest, gorgeous, gleaming,* and *pink* are some of the adjectives that enrich the nouns of the wife's dreams. *Shabby, worn, ugly,* and *homemade* are adjectives that add to the undesirable view she has of her present situation. None of the other choices add such richness to the passage.

139. e. Johnny Cash began performing concerts at various prisons starting in the late 1950s. These performances led to a pair of live albums—*Johnny Cash at Folsom Prison* (1968) and *Johnny Cash at San Quentin* (1969).

140. c. Cash's hit single "A Boy Named Sue" was based on a Shel Silverstein-penned novelty song. This song reached No. 1 on the country charts and No. 2 on the U.S. Top Ten pop charts, making it a crossover hit.

NOTES

NOTES

NOTES

NOTES

NOTES

NOTES

NOTES

NOTES

NOTES

NOTES

NOTES

NOTES

NOTES

NOTES

NOTES

NOTES

NOTES

NOTES

NOTES